Keynes and The General Theory Revisited

Every time the economy goes through a period of crisis, Keynes' name is called upon by economists and politicians from diverse backgrounds. However, 80 years after the publication of *The General Theory of Employment, Interest and Money*, specialists are still far – maybe everyday further – from reaching agreement about the genuine contents of Keynes's most important work. This controversy has been marked by a paradoxical turn: it is above all the literature about Keynes which, in the last decades, has imposed the terms of the debate, while *The General Theory* lacks readers. Accused by both its detractors and admirers of being a confusing book that is inconsistent and even plagued with logical errors, the most important contribution of the most influential economist of the twentieth century has been condemned to be forgotten or, at best, to live uncomfortably in the voices of those who have spoken on his behalf.

This book is the result of rigorous critical research which reconstructs the spectrum of discussion surrounding Keynes's main work. The book begins by describing the historical background and the state of the pre-Keynesian economic theory, subsequently immersing the reader in a concise but detailed – as well as innovative – interpretation of the original text. The revision of some of the main interpretative currents prepares the field for the book's ultimate contribution: the identification of the fundamentals that sustain the analytical structure of *The General Theory*. At the same time, this exploration of the theoretical fundamentals of *The General Theory* makes this book an original intervention on the genesis and relevance of the divide between micro and macroeconomics – a division that has been fully accepted by contemporary macro theorists.

Axel Kicillof (Buenos Aires, 1971) has a PhD in Economics from University of Buenos Aires. He has been a researcher at CONICET (Argentina's National Scientific and Technical Research Council) and at the Economic Research Institute (UBA), as well as Professor at several universities in Argentina. He is a specialist in History of Economic Thought and Macroeconomics. He is the author of "Fundamentos de la Teoría General", "Economía sin Corbata" y "De Smith a Keynes" ("Fundamentals of the General Theory", "Economy without a Tie" and "From Smith to Keynes"). He has held the office of Minister of Economy of the Argentine Republic. He is currently a member of Argentina's national parliament, representing the City of Buenos Aires in the Chamber of Deputies.

Routledge Advances in Heterodox Economics

Edited by Mark Setterfield
The New School for Social Research, USA
and
Peter Kriesler
University of New South Wales

For a full list of titles in this series, please visit www.routledge.com/series/RAHE

Over the past two decades, the intellectual agendas of heterodox economists have taken a decidedly pluralist turn. Leading thinkers have begun to move beyond the established paradigms of Austrian, feminist, Institutional-evolutionary, Marxian, Post Keynesian, radical, social, and Sraffian economics – opening up new lines of analysis, criticism, and dialogue among dissenting schools of thought. This cross-fertilization of ideas is creating a new generation of scholarship in which novel combinations of heterodox ideas are being brought to bear on important contemporary and historical problems.

Routledge Advances in Heterodox Economics aims to promote this new scholarship by publishing innovative books in heterodox economic theory, policy, philosophy, intellectual history, institutional history, and pedagogy. Syntheses or critical engagement of two or more heterodox traditions are especially encouraged.

Keynes and The General Theory Revisited

Axel Kicillof
Translated by Elena Odriozola

LONDON AND NEW YORK

First published 2018 by Routledge

2 Park Square, Milton Park, Abingdon, Oxfordshire OX14 4RN

52 Vanderbilt Avenue, New York, NY 10017

Routledge is an imprint of the Taylor & Francis Group, an informa business

First issued in paperback 2019

British Library Cataloguing-in-Publication Data
A catalogue record for this book is available from the British
Library

Library of Congress Cataloging-in-Publication Data
A catalog record for this book has been requested

ISBN: 978-1-138-09601-1 (hbk)
ISBN: 978-0-367-88461-1 (pbk)

Typeset in Times New Roman
by Apex CoVantage, LLC

Contents

Foreword

This book is the result of a research effort I undertook, albeit intermittently, between late 1998 and early 2005, with the aim of obtaining a doctoral degree in Economics at the University of Buenos Aires. However, the questions that gave rise to this undertaking, whose answers I believe to have approached through this study, were born and nurtured in a much earlier period, which I now situate at the very inception of my education as an economist.

By the time when I was conducting my undergraduate studies, I was forced to lead a double intellectual life, so to speak. On one hand, my regular university courses forced me to struggle with the more common textbooks, and a myriad papers, most of which were based on the vernacular version of the *neoclassical synthesis*, a synthesis that, in turn, was then undergoing an international crisis. But on the other hand, all my "extracurricular" activity, stimulated by a few teachers and by my own theoretical and practical concerns, was geared towards the classical texts. Smith, Ricardo, and particularly, Marx, authors that were almost completely non-existent in the canon of the mainstream were the ones that most attracted me. Although I found these readings absorbing and helpful, as they provided me myriad clues to understand the current economic conditions, the regular bibliography seemed to me, instead, almost always dull and, although purporting to be more concrete, paradoxically, completely cut off from reality and intensely conditioned by its ideological prejudices. By the time when I started to devote myself to research, I had not yet resolved this conflict – what is more, I had not even addressed it. But then, the courses leading to my doctoral degree in Economics directed me, once again, to the authors of the mainstream economics.

Discovering that in his *General Theory*, Keynes establishes an open conversation with the concerns of the classical authors was a liberating finding for me. Contrary to the version metabolized by the *synthesis*, the most fundamental economist of the twentieth century offers his own view of the foundations of economics: the theory of capital, the theory of money, and the theory of commodities. A forgotten truth was thus revealed before me: behind the enormous amount of fragmentary "models" populating the study programs of traditional economics, hidden in an as yet unexplored under-world lay their own ultimate explanations regarding the origin of value and surplus.

There is, therefore, another economics behind economics. During its own development, this study became, thus, what it is today: a settling of scores with the education that the mainstream economics offered me. An almost inexhaustible research plan is therefore outlined – the task of linking the huge volume of material offered by the official economics with the more important and long-lasting theoretical traditions. This effort will not always lead to major contributions to the foundations of the theory, but will no doubt be rewarded by the new appearance and the new conceptual order that such volume of material will begin to take on. The apparently peaceful, or rather, indifferent coexistence of the different "models" thus gives way to the major controversies of economic theory.

I am not aware whether this search now articulates a need that is more general than my own. I am, instead, well aware that if such pursuit is to realize all its critical potential it will have to be carried out as a collective undertaking.

Prologue to the English edition

In the Preface to the *General Theory*, Keynes declares that the main purpose of the book is "to deal with difficult questions of theory, and only in the second place with the applications of this theory to practice." However, despite this revelatory clarification, the book did not only become one of the most influential theoretical texts of the twentieth century: its influence has been perhaps even greater and more decisive in the realm of political economy, or rather, the realm of "practical applications." In effect, nobody disputes the importance that Keynes's vision achieved in political economy: first, in escaping the Great Depression in the 1930s, and later and more generally, in the formation of what has come to be known as the postwar "Keynesian Welfare State."

So it shouldn't surprise us that Keynes's intellectual legacy has gained a new relevance, in both academic discussion and in the general interest press, with the onset of the international financial crisis of 2008. Keynes's portrait began to occupy the covers of the most important international newspapers. Some analysts compared the current crisis, for its intensity and duration, to the 1930s crisis. Inevitably, Keynes' name came up. Some of his works were reprinted and some old debates about his points of view reopened. In the opinion of many, Keynes had to come, seventy years after his death, to the rescue of a world economy in crisis.

This book is the product of a research undertaken long before the onset of the current global crisis, and its original publication in Spanish coincides – fortuitously – with the beginning of that crisis. Eight years have already passed since then; however, far from having been definitively concluded, the crisis continues its dramatic development. To contrast it with the Great Depression, the label of the Great Recession has come to characterize this long cycle of tenuous growth without signs of a robust recovery. Does Keynes have anything to tell us about this current crisis?

Let's return to some images from the beginning of the crisis in September of 2008. After the spectacular collapse of the housing bubble and sub-prime mortgages, events accelerated: the collapse of Lehman Brothers; the near bankruptcy of AIG, the largest insurance firm in the world; and later the bankruptcy of General Motors, the largest automaker on the planet. It's a true oddity to remember that in those first months a good number of the analysts believed that it was only a financial crisis, and that its reach would not pass beyond the borders of the United States. The term "decoupling" was used to describe how the crisis wouldn't "spread" to the sphere of production or to the rest of the world. However, by December of 2008, the United States and Europe had both fallen into a recession, doubling their rates of unemployment, which reached their highest in recent history, with a 10 percent unemployment rate in the EEC, or more than 35 million people.

From then on, a period of notable economic instability ensued, and even today the rate of product growth and global business has still not returned to pre-crisis levels. It's as if this crisis, instead of ending, spread like an oil stain, moving and mutating from one region to another with different features in each place. After going from the United States to Europe, the crisis arrived in the developing world. At the end of 2014, with a Europe still far from recovery, the fall of commodity prices and the financial turbulence fully impacted countries that until that point had remained relatively safe from the international turbulence.

Like Keynes' *General Theory*, this book doesn't describe the present economic situation nor does it evaluate the different tools that political economy has to confront it. However, the reading of the *General Theory* that this book proposes can surely contribute to the consideration of its true causes and its possible remedies.

In the last pages of the *General Theory*, there is an unsettling sentence: "Practical men, who believe themselves to be quite exempt from any intellectual influence, are usually the slaves of some defunct economist." Today Keynes is one of these defunct economists. What influence did Keynes have in the responses that governments tried out during the 2008 crisis? It's worth it to return briefly to some aspects of this story. When the housing bubble popped, and the stock market fell, George W. Bush, was the president of the United States. Confronted with this somber panorama, on October 3, 2008, he got congressional approval for the largest bailout package in world history: 700 billion dollars that later reached 4 trillion. In a disturbing speech before the United States Congress, he maintained: "I'm a strong believer in free enterprise, so my natural instinct is to oppose government intervention. I believe companies that make bad decisions should be allowed to go out of business. Under normal circumstances, I would have followed this course. But these are not normal circumstances. The market is not functioning properly. There has been a widespread loss of confidence, and major sectors of America's financial system are at risk of shutting down. The government's top economic experts warn that, without immediate action by Congress,

America could slip into a financial panic and a distressing scenario would unfold."

It was, by all appearances, a "Keynesian" response to the crisis, one based on state intervention. However, the program known as Quantitative Easing, and the one that the Central European Bank tried out later were both based on a very different doctrine: one defended by one of the most renowned anti-Keynesians, the Nobel-Prize-winning founder of monetarism, Milton Friedman.

In his *A Monetary History of the United States, 1867–1960*, published in 1965, Friedman maintained that the real cause of the Great Depression was to be found in the faulty monetary policy deployed by the government through the Federal Reserve. When the speculative real estate bubble popped in October of 1929, many investors had trouble paying their banking debts, which produced a wave of bankruptcies and the collapse of the financial system. The figures are staggering: out of the 25,000 banks that operated in 1929, only 12,000 of those still survived by the beginning of 1933. In his book, Friedman affirms that the Federal Reserve's monetary policy was responsible for the crisis because it didn't know how to halt the sharp contraction of monetary supply, and instead of providing liquidity to the system, it let the banks fall.

Friedman maintains:

> The System could have provided a far better solution by engaging in large-scale open market purchases of government bonds. That would have provided Banks with additional cash to meet the demands of their depositors. That would have ended – or at least sharply reduced – the stream of bank failures and have prevented the public's attempted conversion of deposits into currency from reducing the quantity of money. Unfortunately, the Fed's actions were hesitant and small. In the main, it stood idly by and let the crisis take its course – a pattern of behavior that was to be repeated again and again during the next two years.
>
> (Free to Choose, p. 83)

To summarize: the Federal Reserve should have saved the banks, and, because it didn't, the economy fell into a profound depression.

This strictly monetary explanation of the crisis would be only anecdotal were it not for the fact that, in a speech given in honor of Friedman in November of 2002, Ben Bernanke, the Chairman of the Federal Reserve when the crisis broke out in 2008, affirmed: "Let me end my talk by abusing slightly my status as an official representative of the Federal Reserve. I would like to say to Milton and Anna: regarding the Great Depression. You're right, we did it. We're very sorry. But thanks to you, we won't do it again."[1] It was Bernanke who was in charge of the program of massive buyouts by the Federal Reserve of the "toxic assets" that were in the portfolios of the banks at the beginning of the current crisis.

Essentially, it could be said that the first – and most persistent – response to the crisis of 2008 was associated, precisely, with the policy of the state buying assets to "clean" the banks' balance sheets. This response to the crisis was clearly inspired by "monetarist," not Keynesian, ideas. The monetarist diagnosis sustains the idea that the crisis is a consequence of monetary disturbances, and that, therefore, its remedies should also be monetary. It's because of this that the entire artillery was directed towards saving the financial sector by absorbing the uncollectable assets and increasing the system's liquidity.

But the expected result of these polices was, additionally, the reduction of the interest rate on loans. In fact, the Federal Reserve lowered the interest rate to a negligible 1.5 percent, and other central banks soon followed suit. It was expected that the lowering of the interest rate would contribute to recovery, because the discounted credit would be able to foster investment and, consequently, stimulate economic activity.

During the Great Depression of 1930, there existed the general opinion – which Keynes labeled "orthodox" – that the economic system had automatic, internal mechanisms that drove the economy towards full employment. One of these was the lowering of the interest rate. Keynes questioned the existence of such economic laws; that is to say, he believed that the interest rate doesn't "naturally" lower when there is a recessionary situation. Furthermore, he maintained that the lowering of the interest rate didn't necessarily lead to a recovery: "I am now somewhat skeptical of the success of a merely monetary policy directed towards influencing the rate of interest" (p. 143). It's because of this that his position is generally identified with the expansion of public spending. This element can also be seen in the current crisis.

Having recently assumed the presidency, Barack Obama got Congress to approve the American Recovery and Reinvestment Act (known as the ARRA) on February 19, 2009. It was a "fiscal stimulus" package of some 800 billion dollars made up of various measures, among which figured public investment, certain supports to balance the federal and local government budgets, as well as tax cuts and direct aid to individuals.[2] Announcing it, Obama said:

> I urge them to pass at least a down-payment on a rescue plan that will create jobs, relieve the squeeze on families, and help get the economy growing again [. . .]. If Congress does not pass an immediate plan that gives the economy the boost it needs, I will make it my first order of business as President. [. . .] And that starts with the kinds of long-term investments that we've neglected for too long. That means putting

two million Americans to work rebuilding our crumbling roads, bridges, and schools. It means investing 150 billion dollars to build an American green energy economy that will create five million new jobs, while freeing our nation from the tyranny of foreign oil, and saving our planet for our children. It means making health care affordable for anyone who has it, accessible for anyone who wants it, and reducing costs for small businesses. [] If this financial crisis has taught us anything, it's that we cannot have a thriving Wall Street while Main Street suffers.[3]

Because it was a policy that necessitated the expansion of public spending, Obama's plan was immediately labeled "Keynesian." The criticisms of the plan were based on the fact that it would increase the budget deficit and that public investment would only "displace" private investment, without raising demand (the so-called "crowding out").

Meanwhile, the European Central Bank reacted to the crisis with its own bond and asset buyout plan, injecting liquidity and substantially lowering the interest rate with the aim of counteracting the recession. A notable aspect of the European case is that the aid and emergency credit which went to the countries that had difficulties paying their debts was conditional on the implementation of large and ever-intensifying policies of austerity. It was demanded that these countries achieve fiscal balance through a reduction in spending and so-called "structural reforms." It was thus that countries like Portugal, Ireland, Greece and Spain, with elevated levels of debt and deep recessions, had to implement policies that cut spending to refinance their debt. This harkens back to the debates that emerged during the Great Depression, in which the "orthodoxy" also demanded that the state implement policies of austerity. Keynes, obviously, did not agree with such a solution.

As we've seen, a good number of current economic debates mimic the polemics from Keynes's times. Meanwhile, the crisis, as previously stated, still has not been overcome, which makes it impossible to make any final conclusions as to the efficacy of the solutions that have been tried out so far, although their limitations in producing a sustained recovery are plain to see. Moreover, the ultimate consequences of each decision the governments made continue to be debated. For some, Obama's fiscal stimulus plan was excessive and also failed; while for others, the results were minimal because so too was the quantity invested; and for another group, the fiscal stimulus was the key piece which mitigated the effects of depression in the United States, limiting its intensity and reducing its duration. The same occurs with the austerity plans applied in a good number of the European countries, although it's already being insinuated that developing countries with large external debts will also be subjected to these policies. There has also been a heated debate about the results of the bank bailout, about the lowering of the interest rate, and about the high liquidity supplied by the central banks.

The present discussions and dilemmas are extremely similar to those that developed during – and after – the Great Depression.

From this perspective, the relevance that *The General Theory* holds today is hard to exaggerate. Keynes traverses each and every one of these discussions. In fact, it was precisely these debates that in his own time brought him to publish his book that saw light almost six years after the start of the 1930 crisis and as a response to the inability of conventional economic theory to find effective solutions.

However, Keynes believed that the problems of conventional theory couldn't be resolved simply by debating the "model" of determination of level of employment and, on this basis, the most effective policies to achieve recovery. The problem was much deeper and required a total theoretical reformulation, which, as we will attempt to show, separates *The General Theory* even from the numerous "Keynesian" models that emerged later. According to Keynes, not even the most superficial of the controversies of "practical application" could be solved without having a profound discussion about the "fundamental concepts" and "premises" of economic theory. It is this profound theoretical discussion to which this book is dedicated.

Notes

1 Bernanke, B. S., "On Milton Friedman's Ninetieth Birthday", November 2002 (www.federalreserve.gov/boarddocs/Speeches/2002/20021108/default.htm).
2 Council of Economic Advisers, Executive Office of The President, "The economic impact of the American Recovery and Reinvestment Act. Five years later. Final report to congress", February 2014.
3 Obama, B., "Second President-Elect Weekly Transition Address" (www.americanrhetoric.com/speeches/barackobama/barackobamaweeklytransition2.htm)

Previous publications

This book was originally published as *Fundamentos de la Teoría General – Las consecuencias teóricas de Lord Keynes* (translates to: *Fundamentals of the General Theory – The theoretical consequences of Lord Keynes)* in Buenos Aires by EUDEBA, the University of Buenos Aires Press in 2007, and then as *Volver a Keynes* (translates to: Back to Keynes) in Spain jointly by Clave Intelectual and EUDEBA, publishing editor Daniel Vila Garda, in 2012. The English translation for this Routledge edition was by Elena Odriozola.

Introduction

In 2011, the 75th anniversary of the publication of the *The General Theory of Employment, Interest and Money* (*The General Theory* from now on) was commemorated; this work made John Maynard Keynes the most influential economist of the twentieth century. The name of Keynes is still closely linked to expansive economic policies and, from a broader perspective, to any advance of state intervention in economic affairs.

The road that led Keynes to fame follows, however, an odd path: while his personality conquered an indisputable leading role in economics, politics, and the public debate, his most important work sank into oblivion. It is true that all epochal books in the field of economics – and also in every other science – have been generally subjected to an unending process of discussion and reinterpretation; however, most of them still have some direct participation – not mediated by proxies – in current theoretical debates. Therefore, what seems strange in this case is not that *The General Theory* may have given rise to diverse and even rival interpretations, but the fact that, soon after being published, the book was no longer read. And most remarkably, it was Keynes's followers themselves (the highly mixed group of "Keynesians") who, from the very beginning and up to the present reached a surprising agreement: *The General Theory* – they almost unanimously argue – is not only badly written and confusing, but considered as a whole, the book's argument is inconsistent. Keynesians acknowledge Keynes's genius and originality, but, strangely enough, they admit that the different explanations and theories posited by *The General Theory* are irreconcilable, and that many of the arguments contained therein are plainly ill conceived. Keynes's leadership over his own school thus becomes strange: his self-proclaimed disciples seem to be well above their master, feeling empowered to report the numerous and obvious mistakes that allegedly plague the book. As will be seen, however, such flaws supposedly contained in *The General Theory* were not proved through a rigorous analysis. To the contrary, Keynes's alleged mistakes are generally posited without any discussion.[1]

Now, what were the consequences of this general accusation of inconsistency? First, it may be surmised that this is probably one of the aspects explaining the wide diversity of "schools" and orientations that may be observed in Keynesianism. The hypothesis that the whole argument of *The General Theory* lacks a coherent and consistent internal link allowed each of the authors to go far beyond a mere interpretation. A critic who argues that the book is flawed believes to have legitimate reasons to discard whole portions of the argument, distinguishing, according to his exclusive judgment, the "correct" fragments that are worth rescuing from those that should be plainly discarded. But he also authorizes the different interpreters to reject the explicit arguments of the book to undertake the search of the "hidden spirit" of the volume, so as to detect the implicit "intuitions", and use them as a substitute for what the text effectively says. And so it happened: some of Keynes's ideas were incorporated by economic theory, but others, on the other hand, were thrown away without being even subjected to a critique. It will be shown here that this process of selective appropriation did not follow each author's whim but rather a remarkably precise pattern – the theories condemned to oblivion were in all cases the same.

Seen in this light, the accusation of inconsistency served the purpose of first justifying the arbitrary conservation of the "correct" portions of the book, and then the almost complete neglect of the volume. The mystery is solved when it is taken into account that the incorporation of Keynes's contributions was mainly carried out by his adversaries, that is, the economists that belonged to the theoretical school he criticized and sought to displace.

This is one of the key aspects that, as will be seen, sheds light on the history of twentieth-century mainstream economic thought, wherein interpretations of Keynes's work played a leading role that was usurped from *The General Theory* itself.

Keynes, history, and the prison of macroeconomics

To study the so-called Keynesian revolution, it is necessary to consider some of the historical events that marked its origin and developmental stage. Although, with the purpose of focusing the attention on the ideas and not on his character, no reference will be made to Keynes's personality in the following pages, it should be remembered that the theories to which Keynes gave precise shape were already captivating most contemporary economists, and what is even more decisive, that many of the practical recommendations associated with those doctrines had already been "spontaneously" implemented by several governments. The kind of public policies that Keynes promoted was, therefore, commonplace in the 1930s, and even supported by some of the most renowned "orthodox" economists.[2] No doubt, a book published in 1936 can hardly be considered to be the source of inspiration for the "Keynesian" policies that had been implemented for some years. This sequence – practices and even general ideas preceding their precise formulation – does not reduce Keynes's merit but rather enhances his attributes. He was a theoretician capable of capturing some outstanding aspects of the metamorphosis undergone by capitalism and, particularly, by the capitalist state[3] and not, as some would contend, an economist that put forward "what everybody wanted to hear".

Keynes's theories constitute, as will be shown, a deliberate effort to depict the deep changes that, during the early twentieth century, radically modified the shape of the capitalist system. In other words, beyond the influence that Keynes's personal qualities may have exerted on his work, *The General Theory* is a book that articulates a broader need: that of breaking with the hegemony of orthodox economics.

Such need transcended his own motivations, and was imposed by reality itself, by the climate prevailing in the period; it was fueled by a large group of mainstream economists who found the inherited theory unsatisfactory, and its recipes futile. *The General Theory* is, thus, the expression of a crisis of the orthodox economic theory, framed in the larger crisis of the capitalist system.

Keynes was, no doubt, as well predisposed as he was equipped to bring about that rupture, on account of both the position he held in academic and political circles, and the character and scope of his earlier theoretical concerns. First, Keynes had been one of Alfred Marshall's direct and favorite disciples; he was also heir to one of Marshall's chairs in Cambridge. Marshall, in turn, was probably one of the most recognized economists of the period, even after his recent death, and the most qualified representative of mainstream economics. In short, with Keynes, criticism of the orthodox theory came from the pen of a *believer*, who in the Preface to *The General Theory* confessed: "I myself held with conviction for many years the theories which I now attack, and I am not, I think, ignorant of their strong points" (Keynes 1939 [1936]: 17). Second, Keynes had arrived at some conclusions that came to have, later on, a privileged place in his *General Theory*: on one hand, in different writings and public presentations he argued that with the turn of the century, the world had undergone a decisive transformation, and that, on account of those changes, the capitalist nations of the West ran the risk of being buried by the course of history. His perception of this impending danger became one of the subjective drives of his theoretical production. On the other hand, Keynes was persuaded that, even though the historical situation was sensitive, some very effective remedies were beginning to emerge on the horizon; he always believed that the possibility of finding the right prescription was in the hands of intellectuals and thinkers. Therefore, innovative ideas and theories should play a decisive role in the outcome of the period. His main criticism regarding the orthodox economic theory (which he called "*classical theory*") runs along these lines: that doctrine had been devised for a historical stage that had concluded, "with the result that its teaching is misleading and disastrous if we attempt to apply it to the facts of experience", says Keynes.

Keynes's diagnosis of the prevailing economic situation took shape along a period plagued with historical events that were as gruesome as they were novel. The sequence opens with the outbreak of First World War and the Russian Revolution. It continues with acute monetary disturbances and the unprecedented international labor conflicts of the 1920s, to end with the social catastrophe triggered by the Great Depression, in the 1930s. Keynes took a public stand in connection with each of these events, trying to show that all of them were, actually, different manifestations of the underlying economic changes that the system was experiencing.

Infused by the spirit of his age, in almost all his articles and public statements he referred to the impending danger of a terminal collapse, a *memento mori* that could put an end to capitalism in the West. In 1919, in *The Economic Consequences of the Peace*, he argued that

> the labouring classes may be no longer willing to forgo so largely, and the capitalist classes, no longer confident of the future, may seek to enjoy more fully their liberties of consumption so long as they last, and thus precipitate the hour of their confiscation.

When in 1923 he wrote on the causes of the inflation and deflation that ravaged the main European countries, he advocated a scientific management of currency, arguing that

> we must free ourselves from the deep distrust which exists against allowing the regulation of the standard of value to be the subject of deliberate decision. We can no longer afford to leave it in the category of which the distinguishing characteristics are possessed in different degrees by the weather, the birth-rate, and the Constitution, – matters which are settled by natural causes, or are the resultant of the separate action of many individuals acting independently, or require a Revolution to change them.

In 1930, in an article on the causes of the Great Depression, he stated that

> it must be doubtful whether the necessary adjustments could be made in time to prevent a series of bankruptcies, defaults, and repudiations which would shake the capitalist order to its foundations. Here would be a fertile soil for agitation, seditions, and revolution. It is so already in many quarters of the world.

Last, in *The General Theory*, Keynes argues along exactly the same lines: "It is certain that the world will not much longer tolerate the unemployment which, apart from brief intervals of excitement, is associated – and, in my opinion, inevitably associated – with present-day capitalistic individualism".

These excerpts illustrate Keynes's diagnosis concerning the difficult situation that capitalist countries were facing, which inspired all his views and theoretical developments. However, it should not be inferred that Keynes conceived the ultimate collapse of the system as its inevitable denouement. Much to the contrary, it could even be said that he held an optimistic stance, as he was persuaded that based on an accurate perception of what was actually happening, certain policies could be devised and implemented that, although excessively drastic and painful for some parties, were crucial to protect and even reform the capitalist system. In turn, this perception of an imminent danger played, undoubtedly, a decisive role in his decision to definitively sever his ties with the inherited theory. The fact is that, according to Keynes, orthodoxy did nothing but stubbornly defend a theory that was adequate for the past, but not for the present, and still less for the future.

In fact, when the time came for the "*classical theory*" to face the novel economic phenomena of the early twentieth century, such as unchecked inflation, violent deflation, and chronic unemployment, the conclusions drawn on the basis of its conceptual framework were disappointing. Its anachronistic set of theoretical tools inevitably led to attribute all catastrophes to the operation of two "forces" that acted to prevent the full (and virtuous) working of the automatic market laws – those two forces were the state and organized labor. Thus, when the time came to deal with postwar inflation or when, soon afterwards, the depression arrived, economic orthodoxy advocated for and tried to implement – and succeeded in doing so in many cases – the traditional contractive policies, aimed at cutting public spending, limiting credit and liquidity, and exerting pressure to achieve a generalized wage reduction.

Both in a context of inflation and high unemployment, contraction is the economic orthodoxy's panacea, premised on the notion that a freely-acting market is infallible, so that the answer is avoiding any interference with its workings.

Keynes, instead, believed that all those orthodox efforts were basically aimed at reinstating the economic conditions of the past, ignoring recent transformations:

> the Treasury and the Bank of England are pursuing an orthodox nineteenth-century policy based on the assumption that economic adjustments can and ought to be brought about by the free play of the forces of supply and demand. The Treasury and the Bank of England still believe that the things, which would follow on the assumption of free competition

and the mobility of capital and labor, actually occur in the economic life of today.

The same could be said regarding his explanation of recession and unemployment: "[t]he orthodox answer is to blame it on the working men for working too little and getting too much", and based on that assumption, the prescription is "to apply economic pressure and intensify unemployment by credit restriction, until wages are forced down. This is a hateful and disastrous way."

In Keynes's view, instead, the renewed ability of the state to intervene in the economy should not be understood as a malformation nor as a misfortune, but as one of the genuine and irreversible outcomes of the ongoing economic transformation process. There was no point in complaining or trying to rebel against its effects and manifestations. The instruments and the power now acquired by the state were, according to Keynes, part of the cure, not the cause of the disease. Fighting inevitable changes as the economic orthodoxy sought to do was not only useless or, even worse, a dangerous sign of conservatism, but it also prevented finding solutions that were more suitable to the new times.

On the basis of all these elements, it is possible to outline the intellectual project that Keynes sought to develop from the 1920s onwards through his critique of orthodoxy: the leading role of capitalist reform would be played by the state:

> Socialism offers no middle course, because it also is sprung from the presuppositions of the era of abundance, just as much as laissez-faire individualism and the free play of economic forces, before which latter [. . .] the City editors, all bloody and blindfolded, still piteously bow down.

Economic and social transformations should follow its swift course, and even though these will be radical changes, they do not need to assume the form of a revolutionary process. After visiting Bolshevik Russia, he stated that

> [a]t least theoretically, I do not believe that there is any economic improvement for which Revolution is a necessary instrument. On the other hand, we have everything to lose by methods of violent change. In Western industrial conditions, the tactics of Red Revolution would throw the whole population into a pit of poverty and death.

In short, his explicit aim was contributing to the construction of a capitalism that, through the novel and powerful forms of state intervention, would succeed in overcoming the nasty secondary effects of the past:

I think that capitalism, wisely managed, can probably be made more efficient for attaining economic ends than any alternative system yet in sight, but that in itself it is in many ways extremely objectionable. Our problem is to work out a social organization which shall be as efficient as possible without offending our notions of a satisfactory way of life.

And then he adds, "The next step forward must come, not from political agitation or premature experiments, but from thought".[4]

Both his diagnosis and his stated aims drove Keynes to develop a critique aimed at subverting the theoretical foundations of the mainstream in his day – what he himself called *classical theory*.

In this connection, the first aim of our book is to demonstrate that the fundamental contribution of *The General Theory* is not limited to the original "model" it proposes for establishing the level of employment. This is not the essential contribution it makes, an assertion that may be proved by the fact that the same model (called *economic system* by Keynes), keeping many of its most distinctive features, may be easily adapted and reframed to turn it into a discrete part that may even be "added" to the corpus of the previous classical economics without it being essentially transformed.[5]

Keynes's major contribution is not to be found there, but lies instead in two other aspects, also present in the pages of *The General Theory*: on one hand, his highly acute critique of the *classical economics*, and on the other, his search of *theoretical foundations* other than those provided by orthodoxy.

It will be shown here that *The General Theory* – the book – actually consists of three different expository segments: a critique of the orthodoxy, the development of an *economic system* (today, a *model* of income determination), and last, the search for new theoretical foundations to conceptually support such a *system* (we will later specify what is understood here by *foundations*).

In previous pages, it was pointed out that both Keynesians and anti-Keynesians discarded some portions of *The General Theory*, these portions being in all cases the same. Well, two of the three components of *The General Theory* were customarily discarded without subjecting them to any discussion – the critical portion and the theoretical foundations. Not surprisingly, as it was precisely the criticized orthodoxy that undertook the task of "selecting" the "digestible" parts of Keynes's whole argument, they maintained the model, but got rid of the critique and the foundations, which were irreconcilable with the core of the mainstream theory. However, this study will seek to show that when closely analyzed, these three components are found to be intimately linked, and that, therefore, by retaining only the employment determination model, bereft of its theoretical foundations, tacitly conceived of as compatible with the rest of the orthodox theory, a mutilation of Keynes's original argument (compounded in many cases by a misrepresentation) is performed. Such mutilation involves no less than the portions of the argument that, according to what is stated in *The General Theory*, constitute its most relevant contribution to economic thought. It will be also shown that, contrary to what most interpretations point out, in this selective incorporation maneuver lies the key to understanding the current split of the corpus of economic theory into two different branches: microeconomics and macroeconomics.

And there is even more to it: in this way, through a division of its core, the orthodox theory managed to overcome most of the attacks it received, particularly since the 1930s crisis, and to survive to our days; it also managed to remain impervious, dodging – by silencing it – the hard blow stricken by Keynes's critique.

To be successful, it had to disguise and misrepresent Keynes's contribution in a specific fashion: it created a tailor-made prison, so to speak, where it remained locked up, as if with nothing to say regarding the theoretical foundations of economic orthodoxy. That cell is called macroeconomics.

Keynes's critique: the origin of the neoclassical failure

The General Theory offers, therefore, apart from a "model", a pungent critique of the orthodoxy, and a proposal for a new set of theoretical foundations; all three elements are closely linked together. *The General Theory* should be thus considered as the expression of an unsolved theoretical crisis that violently manifested during the first third of the twentieth century, when the *classical theory* turned out to be completely unsuitable for understanding, even less for reflecting upon, and still less for addressing the capitalist system's transformations, and clung, instead, to the old orthodox dogma. However, all the elements in Keynes's contribution aimed at the theoretical core of the mainstream were hastily left out of the debate. The only component retained within the framework of the official theory was his "model", which provided a conceptual framework suitable for discussing state's intervention forms and effects, an ability almost completely lacking in the old *classical theory*.

When Keynes's contribution is analyzed from this point of view, the historical and theoretical origin of the current division of mainstream economic theory into two different unconnected realms – macroeconomics and microeconomics – is revealed. This divide seems to be a taboo topic among economists. On one hand, it is accepted that this clear-cut division is intimately connected to Keynes's contribution – the connection is undeniable from a chronological point of view. But it is also argued that the split of the theory into two branches is, actually, the *natural* way of studying economic processes, separating the study of social and individual phenomena.

However, this divide is not based on strong conceptual grounds: it is nothing but the scar that Keynes's critique left on the body of the official economic theory.

With the publication of *The General Theory*, the economic orthodoxy was faced with a difficult problem. On one side, a part of Keynes's argument allowed some evident gaps in the field of economic policy discussion to be filled; Keynes's "model" provided the necessary grounds to discuss the consequences of the use of the new economic instruments that were now in the hands of the state after the war and the abandonment of the gold standard: the issuance of non-convertible currencies, and a much larger budget allowing large-scale government spending. Needless to say that this did not mean that the *classical theory* was willing to acknowledge the advantage of implementing at all times (or even in some cases) expansionary monetary and fiscal policies, but rather that it was forced to accept that those tools – which the traditional theory had never explored – existed in practice, and that something should be done with them. However, on the other hand, it was soon evident that the orthodoxy was not willing to concede even a word of Keynes's critique to its old devices and, even less, to its distinctive theoretical roots.

This double move of "selective" acceptance and rejection gives largely account of the protracted and turbulent history of the incorporation of Keynes's contributions by the mainstream, and helps understand the motivation and the purposes of many of the attacks on *The General Theory*. As has been mentioned, it was criticized, on one hand, as unconnected and contradictory. Those challenges were accepted almost unanimously, without discussing each topic in a rigorous fashion. But nevertheless such accusations provided each follower and interpreter, and even each rival of Keynes's, an excuse to feel empowered – and even forced by the alleged inconsistencies – to choose, according to his particular judgment, the portions of the argument he considered worthy of keeping, discarding forthwith the rest of the book. Additionally, the belief that Keynes – one of Marshall's most recognized disciples – had been unable to thoroughly grasp the actual content of the traditional theory became widespread. Sometimes he was branded as ignorant, and some other times, it was assumed that he had deliberately falsified arguments. Whatever might be the reasons that led him to do so, it was said, the theories held by his opponents had been misrepresented, all the more reason to argue that the criticisms leveled at the orthodoxy were not valid – they were aimed, actually, at a theory fabricated by him, therefore non-existent and with no actual supporters.

Against these highly widespread views, this book seeks to prove that it is possible to establish – as his author intended to – a unity across the different components of *The General Theory*. By proving this contention, the accusation of inconsistency is invalidated. *The General Theory* does not contain only a "model" to determine the level of employment; its pages, rather, articulate a critique of the foundations of marginalism, and expound other different foundations. There is no part that can be simply cut off from the rest and discarded. Either the whole structure is supported, or it collapses to the ground as a whole, in one piece. The second accusation that Keynes did not criticize the traditional theory but an imaginary one will also be rebutted. It will be shown that the depiction of the orthodoxy outlined in *The General Theory* is not mistaken; much to the contrary, those theories dominated economic thought in those days. Moreover, the orthodoxy criticized by Keynes in *The General Theory* may be easily recognized by anyone who is familiar with present-day economics, since, in the field of microeconomics, the old certainties of the *classical theory* have been preserved, almost unchanged, till today.

However, the selective, limited incorporation of Keynes's contribution was not free for the economic orthodoxy, which had to bear a high cost. Once the critical portion and the foundations propounded in *The General Theory* had been discarded, the mainstream had to sacrifice its own unity with the purpose of adding, at least, the employment volume determination "model": it had to tear its own body to split into two branches, microeconomics and macroeconomics. This divide, now considered to be natural, is not only alien to the thought of Smith and Ricardo, but also to that of the founders of marginalism; it only came to be after Keynes's charge.

In the realm of microeconomics, the mainstream treasured its old orthodox doctrine, and sent the new discussion on the determination of employment to the new field, that of macroeconomics, where the modes and the effects of state intervention in economic policy began to be debated. This is the typical anatomy of the so-called "neoclassical synthesis" that began to take shape soon after 1936. This is the reason why *The General Theory* holds the keys to explain the, so to speak, mainstream's *original sin:* resorting to such resources the economic orthodoxy managed to hide and defer, at least in part, its own theoretical crisis, without solving it; however, the price paid for this deferral was high. In fact, it did nothing but sow in its own bosom the seed of a new crisis that, after brewing for some time, eventually broke out, resulting in the current fragmentation of the official economic theory. Synthesis economists themselves began to challenge this artificial divide.

From neoclassical dualism to the current theoretical crisis

It is generally accepted that *The General Theory* was the starting point of a theoretical *revolution* within the marginalist school. In light of its outcomes, however, it is difficult to pinpoint its revolutionary character. First, when the revolution is studied from the official story's point of view, it is not easy to identify the authors and the theories against which Keynes rebelled. It would seem to be a strange case of theoretical revolution, as, although victorious, it left no defeated enemy in its wake. It is a revolution without any clear adversaries. The depiction of Keynes's contribution to the economic theory that has become commonplace has made current a tale in which Keynes's self-proclaimed heirs wage hard struggles to defend the doctrine, while Keynes himself appears as making, instead, only a "positive" contribution. Thus, the Keynesian revolution would consist, more strictly, in the invention, founding or discovery of a new field of development for economic theory, that of macroeconomics, not a fight between different strands of thought for supremacy. Chapter 2 will seek to prove that this depiction is completely distorted, and that the so-called "neoclassical synthesis", the origin of which may be found in J. R. Hicks's interpretation of Keynes's thought, is at the origin of such distortion. Second, neither does it seem to be true, as the usual story states, that the Keynesian revolution triumphed. In fact, as opposed to the "marginalist revolution" of the late nineteenth century, which ousted its declared rival, Ricardian political economy, from orthodoxy, thereby managing to impose a new corpus of doctrine, the Keynesian revolution, on the other hand, did not lead to the replacement of a theoretical system with a different, novel one, but was settled, rather, through a "synthesis". As has been previously said, it was a highly particular synthesis that did not lead to a new unified doctrine, but to a breakup within the prevailing theory: the original *marginalist* components were confined to the realm of microeconomics, while Keynes's alleged contributions, chosen and "interpreted" by the orthodoxy itself, ended up in the area of macroeconomics.

Now, this way of resolving, through a deferral, its own theoretical problems did nothing but give rise to new conflicts or, rather, duplicate them. The synthesis's microeconomics and macroeconomics are completely disconnected, and, worse, their explanations are contradictory in many fields. They not only differ as to their theoretical foundations, but they also provide different explanations for most economic phenomena.

Although concealed in the official economic teaching, basic microeconomics and macroeconomics have different theories to explain the determinants of the level of employment, of interest rates, of prices, of investment and savings, and so on. This dualism may be illustrated with two simple examples, familiar even to a beginner.

All microeconomics textbooks devote one special chapter to the "labor market". After obtaining the labor supply curve for an individual and the labor demand curve for a firm, the demand and supply curves for the economy as a whole are traced out by simple aggregation. The labor market equilibrium is located at the point where the supply curve and the demand curve intersect. The message inferred from this mechanism is that, given the problem parameters, there are economic forces derived from the free decisions of individual agents capable of pushing both the level of employment and the real wage towards that equilibrium point. If the labor market is equilibrated, real wage is compatible with full employment; all the individuals willing to work may do so, because supply equals demand. When the explanation of the same phenomenon is looked up, this time, in the corresponding chapter of the book on standard macroeconomics of the *neoclassical synthesis*, the result is surprising. The level of income (and employment) of the economy is determined at the point where aggregate demand and aggregate supply are equal, which implies, in turn, that savings and investment are also equal. An equilibrium position is also involved here, but such equilibrium occurs in the *aggregate* market of goods and services. In this case, however, no automatic tendency to full employment is observed; the output level may perfectly be equilibrated at levels that are below that of full employment. In the next paragraph, the explanation of the expenditure multiplier begins; relevant variables are now the propensity to consume, government expenditures, aggregate investment, *et hoc genus omne*. A simple comparison of the theories of employment in the realms of microeconomics and macroeconomics shows the presence of a theoretical dualism: the determined variables are the same, but the explanations provided are different.

Something similar occurs regarding the theories of the origin and determination of the rate of interest. The microeconomics handbook argues that the interest rate is the price that balances capital (or loans) supply and demand. At an equilibrium state, the amount of capital sold and bought is located at the point where the interest rate equals capital productivity and the "rate of impatience". In turn, the macroeconomics textbook asserts that the interest rate is set on the money market, and that the point of equilibrium is reached when the money supply set by the monetary authority equals "liquidity preference", or more plainly said, money demand. The rate of interest appears now as an essentially monetary phenomenon, which is not "real", that is, linked to capital. Again, both explanations are completely different.

There is nothing new in the incompatibility that has just been pointed out regarding the explanations offered by conventional microeconomics and those provided by macroeconomics. Today, most theoretical economists accept the discomfort provoked by this inconsistency, even though it tends to be minimized in undergraduate education.

Even more, this inconsistency is generally considered to be the main "theoretical" cause of the disruption of the consensus that prevailed among synthesis economists until the 1970s. The mainstream admits, additionally, that the breakup of such consensus sank macroeconomics into "a period of confusion, division, and excitement that still continues" (Mankiw 1990: 6). In fact, with the theoretical crisis of the 1970s the era of broad and general agreements came to an end for the *neoclassical synthesis*; its ranks broke into a myriad sub-groupings that have not been able to reach a new consensus up to now: among those groups, the "real" Keynesians, the post-Keynesians, the new Keynesians, the advocates of disequilibrium, the monetarists, the new classicists, and so on, may all be found.

While the scope of this study is restricted to discussing mainly the background and the contents of *The General Theory*, we believe that the findings put forth here help understand the causes of the state of confusion (to use Mankiw's words) that currently prevails. The answer may not be found in the recent history of conventional economic theory, or in the detailed study of the differences opposing the various factions into which the mainstream is now divided. The key here contributed is a different one: to understand the current fragmentation, it is necessary to go back to the origin of the problem itself, in 1936. As has already been mentioned, the conventional theory reacted to the Keynesian revolution splitting its theories into two discrete branches, microeconomics and macroeconomics. This split was accepted without any complaint during the twenty or thirty years when the so-called consensus prevailed, but then that agreement was disrupted, and from then on, a new reconciliation began to be sought after, reconciliation that many consider to consist simply in restoring the older theory, erasing all trace of Keynes's contribution and its sequels.

The successive crises, however, deferred the discussion of the foundations of the orthodox economic theory. With *The General Theory*, Keynes attempted to place this controversy at the heart of the debate. His attempt failed. The challenge now is, precisely, to revive that discussion, and the need to go back to its origin arises from the current lack of fertile ground where that debate may yield fruit, be it in microeconomics or in macroeconomics: none of them provides room for questioning the theoretical foundations.

According to Mankiw, in fact, the collapse of the consensus was brought about by a lack of "microfoundations", but also as a result of its empirical flaws, specifically, the fact that it was unable to explain the causes of the so-called "stagflation". Still, in 1990, he admitted the disappointing state of the official theory after the abandonment of the standard model: the last twenty years of research in macroeconomics, says Mankiw, have not borne practical fruit.

Keynes's contribution and its limits

In the following chapters, it will be shown that Keynes's criticism was leveled at the central ideas of the mainstream of his day, ideas that were essentially identical to those which microeconomic theory holds today. But what is the relation among the different elements that constitute *The General Theory?* After challenging the traditional explanations, Keynes put forth his own particular theories aimed at understanding the same phenomena. Both aspects, the critical and the positive, are necessary for the other. These new theories sought to express the causal relations connecting the different economic phenomena; it is a "model" designed to determine the value of certain variables. However, this being done, Keynes decided to move further into the theoretical sphere. After identifying the factors that affect the determination of the interest rate, the real wage, the employment volume, consumption, investment etc., he sought to contribute some insights to the *theoretical foundations* underlying this model. The term "foundations" (which should not be mistaken for "micro-foundations") refers to the study of the nature of economic categories itself. An example will illustrate the meaning of this word. Keynes's model argues that the interest rate *depends on* money supply and demand. This implies that interest *should be considered* a reward for relinquishing money, and not, as the *classical theory* had asserted, a compensation for deferring consumption. From there, new questions are raised concerning the *foundations* of the theory: What is money? What differentiates it from products in general and from durable commodities in particular? Why is money capable of yielding an interest rate? Could there be an economy where no money existed? What is the relationship between money and commodities' value? And the same happens as regards capital and its return: What is the nature of capital? Why are capital owners entitled to profit? What is the relationship between interest rate and rate of profit?

The most outstanding balance of the so-called neoclassical synthesis is that neither of its compartments, either microeconomics or macroeconomics, provided room for the discussion of the *theoretical foundations*. Thus, the mainstream stopped discussing openly, either within itself or with other schools, the nature of money and capital, the origin of interest and profit, the theory of value and capitalism historical determinations. Such debates were replaced with an odd competition among different fragmentary models.

It will be seen, therefore, that the foundations, actually, both predate and contain the so-called "micro-foundations". In fact, it is only when money, capital, and goods have been analyzed, when the nature of these economic forms has been theoretically researched that the way in which individuals behave when facing such forms, and the representation they have of their own actions can be studied. As will be later seen, according to Marshall's conception, what individuals do when faced with capital is different from their behavior regarding capital as explained by Keynes. To different foundations correspond different individual behaviors.

To avoid misunderstandings, it should be noted that economic theory should be capable of explaining both "social" economic processes and the representations individuals and classes have of such processes, since their actions are informed by these perceptions. The current dichotomy, instead, extrinsically divides the object of study into two discrete spheres; given that each of these is supported by different foundations, social and individual behavior cannot be reconciled, and neither can, at a deeper level, the objective and subjective aspects of economic laws.

However, an unbiased enquiry into *The General Theory* will stumble upon Keynes's contributions to the economic theory's fundamental categories. Such enquiry arises from a conceptual need, for the relations among the variables put forth by the "model" are irreconcilable with the foundations supporting the *classical theory*. In the chapters devoted to the theory of capital, the theory of money, and the theory of value, Keynes moves clearly away from the orthodoxy. In this book, the conclusions drawn by *The General Theory* will not be defended, but it will be posited, instead, that it is necessary to once more discuss the foundations of economic theory themselves, and that Keynes has a contribution to make to that debate.

From this point of view, and beyond the limitations of his research that will be pointed out in due time, Keynes is undoubtedly above his mainstream opponents and his followers. On one hand, he takes into account the deep transformations capitalism underwent, and tries to explain their relationship with economic doctrines. On the other, he voices his disagreement with the foundations of the *classical theory*, promoting a new debate on the nature of value and surplus. This may well be the more compelling explanation of the unanimous rejection that turned *The General Theory* into a book which seems almost cursed, to which little credit is given, and whose reading is very seldom recommended.

A tour of this book

The starting point for the entire conceptual development of *The General Theory* is a critique of the prevailing orthodox theory. In spite of the alleged victory of the Keynesian revolution, such critique was completely ignored and remained unanswered, so that all the elements challenged by Keynes still survive in the current mainstream.

As has been said, it is not the aim of this study to discuss in depth the diverse interpretations of *The General Theory*. However, it should be pointed out that our approach differs from that adopted by most of the authors who attempted to "rescue" the original elements of Keynes's thought, attempts that reached their peak after the theoretical crisis of the 1970s. All such authors implemented a similar strategy: they identified as the most fundamental contribution of *The General Theory*'s argument some "hidden" aspect that had been presumably neglected or forgotten, partly because Keynes's exposition lacked clarity or else the required emphasis to attract attention on that essential component of the theory.

Along these lines, apparently crucial but generally neglected different elements were identified.[6] The hypothesis of this book is diametrically opposite: the most fundamental contribution of *The General Theory* is neither hidden in some obscure corner of the book nor was overlooked on account of it being originally framed somehow timidly or lacking in clarity or vigor. Neither was it discarded, either deliberately or unintentionally, owing to a flawed, obscure or contradictory exposition. Here, much to the contrary, we will give Keynes credit. We will explore the hypothesis that the most relevant aspects of *The General Theory* are, precisely, those explicitly stressed by the author when expounding his project, that is, the ambitious attempt to unify the theory of value and the theory of money, an attempt that leads to a particular reframing of the theory of capital, of profit, of interest etc., i.e. a new corpus of foundations for the economic theory. The purpose of our work does not consist in *interpreting* some selected excerpts from *The General Theory* seeking to find a hidden, mysterious key, translating what Keynes really *meant* but never said. Our aim is, rather, to once again explore *The General Theory* as a whole, stressing the internal unit of the different elements of the argument: the critique, the system, and its foundations. These aims dictate the structure of the book.

Chapter 1 and Chapter 2 are devoted to the background of *The General Theory*. Only two very specific aspects will be addressed, aspects that tend to be overlooked even though they are important: the ideas endorsed by Keynes concerning capitalism's historical stages and the state of the official economic theory in the period.

When reviewing Keynes's earlier work, it may be seen that, even long before writing his most influential book, he had begun to develop his own "theory of history". Like the majority of the early twentieth century's most insightful observers of the economy, he was convinced that the world was experiencing a period of deep transformation. He argued, more precisely, that the First World War signaled the end of one stage or phase of capitalism, and the beginning of a new, different one, the particular traits of which had to be identified, since they substantially affected and changed all economic mechanisms as they were known.

In Chapter 1 I will discuss these background economic changes and stress their more relevant characteristics.

There are three main aspects repeatedly mentioned by Keynes when referring to those mutations: the aspects observed in the structure of the capitalist class, those in the features of the working class, and the changes in the monetary sphere. This characterization is also present in *The General Theory*. From this point of view, Keynes's criticism of the conventional theory becomes historical: he argues that, beyond its many logical flaws, orthodox economics insists in describing a reality that simply does not exist any longer. This is the reason why it is argued in many passages that the conventional theory is, first and foremost, anachronistic. Few interpreters have paid attention to this argument that explains, however, most of the claims made by Keynes to his predecessors. Remarkably, this inclination to study economic processes from a point of view that is completely devoid of historical content is especially widespread among the authors of present-day macroeconomics, who insist on comparing different theories without any reference to the period and the circumstances in which they were devised.

Across his intellectual trajectory, Keynes struggled to understand and frame his arguments and theories within a larger picture that would take long-term economic transformations into account. Thus, he gradually developed his own particular depiction of the major stages traversed by human society during its historical development. In this endeavor, a particular trait of Keynes's thought stands out: he is an author who not only acknowledges the importance of major economic transformations, but who is also concerned with matching changes in economic processes, with modifications in the doctrines and theories prevailing in each historical period. He argues that theories achieve a high degree of political influence when their conclusions address the problems typical of the era, but that to reach intellectual predominance, they must enlist the support of hegemonic forces and interests. This is the reason why, no sooner a society leaves the last station of an era to cross into the threshold of the next, there occurs an inevitable discrepancy between orthodox theories and a transformed reality, the understanding of which eludes them.

At the beginning of the twentieth century, Europe was in full metamorphosis, going through a sensitive transition stage; it was immersed in a process signaled by deep economic transformations that, not having reached maturity, had not found adequate theoretical formulation still. The circumstances and the spirit typical of the nineteenth century – that is, *individualist capitalism*, in the economic realm, and *laissez-faire*, in the political – inspired *classical theory*. This stage, however, had come to an end; the war and the prevailing crisis should not be considered lasting disasters but rather labor pains typical of the birth of a future that, not without difficulties, made its way in history. The modern world would have to face unprecedented problems, but those very same difficulties made it possible, through analysis, to find suitable instruments to devise novel solutions. No doubt, to decipher new enigmas it was crucial to get to know first the deep nature of such changes, to understand that previous economic conditions had already collapsed, to learn how to use the new available tools, and above all, get rid of the ideological prejudices of the past. Meanwhile, the attempts carried out by the orthodoxy and conservatism, persisting in prescribing the old remedies to cure new diseases, could only result in unfortunate consequences.

In the field of the economy, the recommendations based on the anachronistic assumptions and tenets of the *classical theory* proved disastrous in its effects, as they failed to grasp the hidden root of modern world disturbances.

On the other hand, casting a historical glance, we will attempt to relate *The General Theory* not only to the previous economic theory works by Keynes, as is usually done – particularly *A Tract on Monetary Reform* (1923) and *A Treatise on Money* (1930) – but also to other writings considered minor or, better, unclassifiable, due to their apparently eminently "political" character and their lack of useful economic content, as *The Economic Consequences of the Peace* (1919) and the numerous articles written and lectures delivered during the gestation period of *The General Theory*, 1919–36, among others: "Am I a Liberal?" (1925); "The Economic Consequences of Mr. Churchill" (1925); "Alfred Marshall" (1926); "The End of Laissez-Faire" (1926); "Economic Possibilities for our Grandchildren" (1930); "The Means to Prosperity" (1933). It is thus sought to challenge the widespread view that Keynes led a split intellectual life: that of a politician and that of a theoretician. The overlapping dates seem to suggest that all the writings share a single general conception.

To research the background of *The General Theory*, it is also necessary to attempt a reconstruction of the economic doctrine at which Keynes leveled his criticism. Chapter 2 explores this area, which poses some difficulties that have largely been either completely neglected or unsatisfactorily or not thoroughly addressed. This may be due to the fact that theoreticians working in the official macroeconomics tend to show scant interest in – when not explicit contempt for – the history of economic thought.

However, to understand *The General Theory*, it is crucial to clearly identify the precise target of Keynes's criticism. Even though the answer seems obvious, doubt began to grow after the publication of his book.

In *Mr. Keynes and the Classics* (1937), the article that gave origin to the construction of the neoclassical synthesis, Hicks states that the characterization of the orthodoxy of his time offered by Keynes is completely mistaken. With time, the suspicion that Keynes either ignored or, as some would argue, deliberately misrepresented the actual content of the official theory became widespread. It is for this reason that it is advisable to briefly specify what were the most relevant elements of the orthodox theory prevailing during the early twentieth century. The aim of Chapter 2 is to show that Keynes did not incur in error when he sketched that outline, on the contrary, that his criticism was well oriented. Even more, as will be seen, the theory being challenged is, basically, identical to the one now prevailing in the field of microeconomics.

An attempt will be made to cast light on the particular label chosen by Keynes to name his opponents. When he refers to the official economics, he uses the curious term "classical theory". Today, the term *classical theory* is linked to the pioneer ideas of Adam Smith, David Ricardo, his contemporaries and successors. Keynes, instead, calls Ricardo and John Stuart Mill "classicists", as well as some contemporary prominent authors such as Marshall and Pigou, economists who, according to the current conventions, belong to the *neoclassical* or *marginalist* school. Why would Keynes gather this particular group of Ricardians and marginalists under the label *classical theory*? Who was he really challenging? A close inspection of the problem reveals that such gathering of Ricardians and marginalists was not the result of some whim of Keynes's, but rather that he drew on the ideas of his teacher, Alfred Marshall, who as opposed to Walras and Jevons, made an effort to trace a line of continuity (not of breakup) unifying English economic thought throughout time.

Surprisingly, Marshall – one of the most prominent neoclassical theoreticians – considered himself an heir to Ricardo, main proponent of classical political economy. Even though it might seem to be a subtlety, reviewing economic doctrines is crucial when trying to appraise Keynes's originality and theoretical affiliation.

Once the question regarding who the *classicists* were in Keynes's view is answered, the more relevant elements of that doctrine will be summarized: the labor market, the capital market, the theory of money, and the role played by the so-called Say's law, considered a device apt to link the different components of the system. Three outstanding aspects of his criticism of *classical theory* will be stressed: his explanation of the normal price as determined by production costs and not by the simple balancing of the *already produced* supply of an item and its demand on the market; the artificial and inconsistent separation of the theory of value and the theory of money; and, last, the assumption of the full employment of resources in the different versions of Say's law.

With these historical and theoretical references, the most relevant background, in our view, will have been provided to approach the study of *The General Theory*. What Keynes calls the "economic system" will then be expounded. The *system* is a set of causal sequences linking different economic phenomena, expressed by means of several variables.

Keynes's system will be explained considering its two main components separately: critique and positive contribution. Chapter 3 will discuss *The General Theory's* criticism of the *classical theory*. Even though generally overlooked, this is one of the most enlightening and original segments of Keynes's exposition. The labor market, the capital market, and the theory of money in the *classics* are subjected to a close scrutiny that leads to the need of replacing these theories. In spite of Keynes's insightful objections, current microeconomics still preserves these very same elements. This chapter traces the unconventional scientific path that Keynes ventured to tread to develop his critique. It is not just a rejection of the *classical theory* grounded on the fact that its predictions do not match facts. Keynes did not limit himself to an "empirical test" of *classical theory* by observing merely the quantitative values of the previous model variables to check whether its predictions were verified or not. He did not criticize the assumptions and recommendations of the orthodoxy from an eminently ideological point of view. The critical device adopted by Keynes is in a certain way original, at least within the framework of the mainstream. His investigation focused on the historical roots explaining the failure of the *classical theory*. With this purpose, he built a characterization of the deeper transformations that took place in society, transformations that underlay their apparent manifestations.

This approach led him to a conclusion – the *classical theory* was to be abandoned, first and foremost, not exclusively on account of it being "incorrect" – that is, incapable of explaining an unchanging reality – but because it was anachronistic. While the orthodoxy tends to minimize all the transformations experienced by the capitalist society, Keynes bases his rejection of the prevailing economic "thought" on the opposite belief.

The objective, ever present in his works, of figuring out the historical character of economic doctrines is what makes Keynes's general approach distinctive. Keynes believes, therefore, that there is a transformation dynamic regarding social forms, and he adopts this as his object of study. Although scarcely explored, this aspect of his contribution is crucial, because once history enters the realm of economic categories, rigidly established discipline borders dissolve, and novel questions about the origin, the nature, and the future of current society are raised. It is neither fair nor accurate to affirm that economic theory – even the official one – completely ignores the existence of a historical era previous to the emergence of modern society; on the contrary, it is a generally acknowledged fact. In its explanations, economic theory usually resorts, since Smith's days, to a mythical "rude and primitive state of society". Equally, "historic" material is used to apply modern theory to earlier periods, such as the Middle Ages and Antiquity. But such references to the past – as the resort to an isolated man, a "Robinson" – are generally intended to show that the social forms that are typical of capitalism – commodities, money, capital – were present from the beginning of time, albeit dressed in primitive garments. On the other hand, although the existence of a previous history is admitted, it is usual to consider that with the advent of the capitalist society, the essential course of history came to a stop. Regarding this stance, Marx argues in *The Capital*:

> Economists have a singular method of procedure. There are only two kinds of institutions for them, artificial and natural. The institutions of feudalism are artificial institutions, those of the bourgeoisie are natural institutions. In this, they resemble the theologians, who likewise establish two kinds of religion. Every religion which is not theirs is an

invention of men, while their own is an emanation from God. *Thus,
there has been history, but there is no longer any*".

(Marx, 1986 [1871]; emphasis added)

Contemporary economics tends to ignore these embarrassing issues that, on
the other hand, are not quite relevant from the point of view of the fundamentally practical ends of the discipline.[7]

Chapter 4 explores the new proposals regarding causal relationships
among economic phenomena, expressed through mathematical functions,
that is, the system to determine the level of employment put forth by *The
General Theory*. The *classical system* has, tacitly, effective mechanisms
that react to any disturbance, restoring full employment equilibrium. It is
also furnished with devices that enable it to expand its productive capacity
until the complete depletion of usable resources. This is why it assumes
equilibrium to be synonym of full employment. The fact is that until the
beginning of the twentieth century, generalized chronic unemployment – a
historical novelty – had not been considered a real practical problem requir-
ing a close analysis. The task carried out by Keynes is threefold: he exposes
those hidden mechanisms on which classical economists had placed their
trust; dismantles them through his critique; and finally, on the ruins of the
classical system, he erects his own *economic system*. Before the publication of *The General Theory*, only outlines of a theory of employment as a
whole had been put forward. For this reason, the effort aimed at collecting
disperse material and leveling a powerful criticism at the orthodoxy's premises, method, and conclusions is to be considered one of the substantive
contributions of Keynes's.

A second factor of originality is to be found in the *economic system*
itself. Apart from raising new questions, Keynes's system has to offer an
alternative method to that of the *classical theory*, which through analogy
or aggregation, intended to explain the behavior of the whole as a mere
amplified projection of the deliberate, voluntary behavior of the parties, or
as a mechanical addition of undetermined individual actions. By taking as
a *point of departure* the laws ruling the movement of the system as such,
the restrictions imposed by such workings to individuals' "free" decisions
appear one by one.

A further characteristic of Keynes's *system* lies in that it distinguishes,
classifies, and, finally, hierarchically orders the relevant phenomena in a
completely original way. A "causal sequence" is thus offered linking the
different variables; certain circumstances are taken to be invariant, *given*;
the rest of the relevant elements become the endogenous or exogenous variables of the system, linked through causal relationships. Keynes prefers this
sequential over a simultaneous exposition, which obscures and hides the
main cause-effect relationships. He finds virtue in this way of presenting his

system, not so much because of the "apparatus mechanical precision" as in the fact that it furnishes the economist with a thinking method that enables him to weigh the importance of the different elements intervening in a complex reality, to study later the deviations of each particular case.

Last, *The General Theory* brings monetary elements to bear on the determination of employment and prices through their influence on aggregate demand. Value and money are thus reconciled, according to Keynes. The book becomes "a study of the forces that determine changes in the scale of output and employment as a whole". By introducing the possibility that insufficient aggregate demand may cause the underutilization of the capacity of the industrial sector, Keynes's system means the emancipation of the mainstream theory from the oppression of Say's law.

A victory may be scored in this regard for Keynes: he managed to attract economists' attention to his *system* and to his main pursuit (*quaesitum*). Immediately after the publication of *The General Theory*, controversy broke out regarding this new approach. But Keynes's victory may also be appreciated by considering the aforementioned schismatic effects that this work provoked within the orthodox theory. The theory of value and distribution (the First Treatise of classical economy), which until then had been practically the entire corpus of economics, became a particular branch of economics: microeconomics, humbler in its claims than it had primitively been. Most – if not all of it, as some scattered comments and only one of the six books could be excluded – of Marshall's *Principles of Economics*, that had been considered so far the economics treatise par excellence, what used to be the entire economic theory, now would fall within the realm of microeconomics. The same happened with the rest of the works of the most prominent pre-Keynesian marginalists.

Before Keynes, economics was one, claiming to explain economic phenomena with a unitary approach; after Keynes, it was split into two different "departments". Practically all the insights of the *classical theory*, as was known up to then, were locked up in a compartment created ad hoc, microeconomics. A science that, according to Ricardo, Mill, but also Marshall, Walras, Jevons, Menger etc., aspired to explain the general economic laws of society's movement began to be treated as a particular branch of economics, restricted exclusively to depicting the behavior of individual agents. All the elements pertaining to society as a whole were transferred to the new field of macroeconomics. But if the *classical theory* was corseted, so was *The General Theory*, its executioner. It was locked up, together with the debates it raised, in the other watertight compartment into which the discipline was split. Thus, Keynes's achievement regarding the way his novel system was dealt with was, at most partial: owing to the new fragmentation of the economic theory, some of the contributions contained in *The General Theory* were left without the soil they needed to bear fruit.

It is not the aim of this book to discuss the different economists' reactions, favorable or hostile to Keynes's claims. As soon as his *system* entered the fray, it was locked up in the field of macroeconomics. A discussion of each of the hypothesis supporting it began at this time. Now, what was – and is currently – the topic of debate? What is the customary form of settling disagreements? Even today, the innumerable disputes will revolve around the selection of independent and dependent variables, function form, causal relationships direction and, even, the most convenient method to represent links between phenomena. Once the legitimacy of the new field as a research area was acknowledged, all such elements were discussed. One of the main objectives of Keynes's opponents focused on a detailed work aimed at restoring the old mechanisms leading to full employment or, in some cases, devising new ones. Factions are divided among those who believe that unemployment is a possible equilibrium, those who think that it is possible, but not as equilibrium, and, last, those who understand it to be impossible (whether in the short or the long run) in equilibrium conditions.

These debates are premised on the general acceptance of the main question raised by *The General Theory*, and also of the elements of its explanation. The objections considered to be valid may be based on results obtained in empirical research, but also involve challenges of the assumptions regarding the behavior of the agents, including government. The history of macroeconomics is nothing but a tight succession of skirmishes of this kind, over all the strategic points of Keynes's system. The debate, on the other hand, is by no means abstract: each new solution attempts also to make sense of past events (crises, inflation, unemployment), distinguishing failures from successes and identifying their causes. Moreover, each contribution is intended to yield a set of recommendations and proposals concerning state action. Macroeconomics has thus seized much of the "political" potential of economic theory. Keynes bitterly regretted the fact that *classical theory* had lost its "practical influence". No doubt, the emergence of macroeconomics regained it. For this reason, it is not surprising that most economists' energies and passions have been focused on this sensitive field.

This book, however, intends to emphasize two debates mainly, which have different origins. Although both are present in *The General Theory*, where they play a leading role, they have been discarded or even completely ignored.

The division between micro and macroeconomics that prevails in current mainstream economic thought deprived a fundamental component of economic theory of the field required for its development. In fact, Keynes sternly criticized the split of the *classical theory* into two Treatises, one devoted to value, the other to money; he would point out that they involved contradictory explanations of the same phenomena. A paradoxical consequence of the publication of *The General Theory* is that the current structure of theoretical economics – resulting from Keynes's criticisms – reproduces that old separation, with the only difference that the current border cuts the object of study, so to speak, longitudinally. In the present division, the laws that rule individuals' behavior are different from those concerning society as a whole, and should be studied separately. There is no bridge connecting both margins.[8]

Such fracture of the theoretical corpus is, besides, the clearest signal of the total abandonment of the two contributions that, as was argued, are central to *The General Theory*. The first of these is Keynes's criticism of the *classical theory* but, particularly, of Marshall's marginalism. In fact, in Keynes's book the introduction of the new *system* is preceded by a rigorous enumeration of the theoretical and logical inconsistencies that diminish the *classical theory*. Some of these criticisms are equally leveled at the two strands that conform to it: the adherence to Say's law, the flawed conception of money, and the supposedly full employment are elements that characterize both the *Ricardian* and the *marginalist* theory. The same may be said concerning the classical quantitative theory of the Second Treatise. But when Keynes challenges the construct of the labor market and the capital market, his objections are specifically aimed at the *marginalist* theory, which, particularly through Marshall, had intended to replace the *Ricardian theory of distribution* with these new developments. Keynes thus rejects the *classical theory* of distribution providing new *general* explanations of the determination of wage, profit, and interest. Contrary to the explanations of the orthodoxy, Keynes's may be applied to unemployment situations.

Keynes's criticism of the First Treatise, instead, was summarily discarded – there was no room for it in macroeconomics or in microeconomics. Thus, at least one third of *The General Theory* was lost, a third that includes, besides, his deepest insights, as well as the most transcendental theoretical contribution of Keynes's *General Theory*, as will be shown in Chapter 5. This is also a portion of Keynes's argument that has been definitively silenced in the cloisters of orthodoxy.

To end, Chapter 5 deals with the "theoretical foundations" of Keynes's system, that is, his theory of money and his theory of capital. The term "theory" is used here with a very specific connotation: these theories are explanations of the nature of money and capital themselves. They represent an attempt to discuss what is it that is particular to money, and what differentiates it from capital and the rest of commodities, to move then from there to reveal the origin of interest and profit. This discussion leads Keynes to raise questions of enormous conceptual relevance: What are the essential traits of capitalist societies? Can an economy exist without money, without capital, or without both? What are the cellular economic forms of present day society? What are the limits that an attempt to reshape capitalism encounters? The notion that Keynes has nothing to say regarding such "fundamental" questions is thus rejected. The deep social transformations suggested in the last chapters of *The General Theory* are not disparate ideas but, as will be shown, are logically derived from the concepts of money and capital framed by Keynes.

Chapter 5 puts forward the most controversial ideas of our work; therefore, a particular effort will be exerted to persuade the reader of the relevance of this debate, highlighting three consequences stemming from it. First, even though not currently flaunting them, the *(neo)classical theory* has its own, well-determined theoretical foundations, which set it apart from the rest of the schools of economic thought. Second, those foundations are, from their very root, irreconcilable with the "economic system" that Keynes put forward. It will be shown thus that all *systems* or models are inseparable from their foundations; it will also be shown that reconciling the *classical theory* – microeconomics – and Keynes's system – ill-summarized by macroeconomics – is inherently impossible, as their respective foundations are essentially different.

Apart from reviewing Keynes's ideas and displaying their necessary internal connection, in this last chapter it is necessary that a general assessment of the results obtained by his contribution be made. To begin with, it is difficult to exaggerate the relevance and the reach of the objective set by Keynes, as he seeks to modify the premises on which the orthodox theory rests. His critique of the classics deserves the credit of unveiling a set of conceptual problems that plagued *marginalism* from its origins. However, some manifest weak points can also be identified in the findings concerning capital and money expounded in *The General Theory*. While the debate among Keynes's self-proclaimed heirs seldom focused on these crucial issues linked to the theory of money and capital, the purpose of this book is to draw economists' attention to those topics, which will inevitably lead us to the controversies over the tenets of the economic theory, controversies that oppose classical, neoclassical, and Marxist economists. We will then be in a position to put forth some hypotheses regarding Keynes's affinities in this terrain, since otherwise his contributions would appear to be disparate elements that could be annexed by any school of thought.

Last, it should be pointed out that the numerous interpretations of *The General Theory* that appeared in the wake of its publication will not be systematically studied here. Nor will a "positive" exposition of the fundamental categories of economics be offered here; we will instead restrict ourselves to providing elements for a critique of the account of such categories put forward by the *classical theory* and Keynes. As has been mentioned, the main objective of this work is to cast light over the so-called Keynesian revolution and its consequences, particularly as regards the mainstream's current form. As far as possible, it is also my intent to persuade my colleagues of the convenience of abandoning for a moment "mathematical models" lacking explicit foundations, no matter how "explicative" and "applicable" they might be and to devote at least part of their energies to reflect upon the inner nature of the elemental economic forms implicit in those models. Without this necessary enquiry, models multiply and become a polyphonic choir offering plentiful options, but no progress is made in understanding present-day society and the current historical stage. That is, I believe, the most crucial lesson offered by the study of *The General Theory*.

Notes

1 A small collection of testimonies reveals the degree of acceptance reached by this view among specialists in the field. Axel Leijonhufvud asserts that "as theoretical economist, Keynes was not free from mistakes or logic inconsistencies, and, apart from defects, he had certain annoying habits regarding analysis and presentation, which have not been at all helpful for the students that came after him. These facts cannot be denied" (1976a: 12). For John Kenneth Galbraith, *The General Theory* "[i]s a deeply obscure, badly written, prematurely published book [. . .]. Part of its influence originated in the fact that it was mostly unintelligible" (1983 [1975]: 257). According to Athanasios Asimakopulos, "[t]he *General Theory* is not an easy book to read, in part because the inherently difficult nature of its material does not allow for a simple treatment, and in part because Keynes did not spend (or have) the time necessary to work everything out in a consistent manner" (1991: xv-xvi). Oliver Blanchard, in turn, argues in his popular textbook that "when Keynes's *General Theory* was published, in 1936, nearly everybody agreed that it was a fundamental but, at the same time, undecipherable book," and Blanchard adds between brackets,"(perhaps, the reader may wish to give it a glimpse to see for himself)" (1997: 97). Mark Blaug is even more categorical: "*The General Theory* is simply an unclear, badly written book" (1985 [1962]: 807, 797). Seymour Harris, in the introduction to the renowned *Guide* by Hansen, wrote that "[t]he exposition was difficult because many ideas had not been clearly thought; there were some misunderstandings and even mistakes; the relationship between *The General Theory* and the established doctrine was not very clear, and Keynes, as many other innovators, particularly those that are not well-acquainted with the matter, chose to exaggerate the novelty of his approach and his development" (1966 [1953]: 9).
2 Furthermore, in the 1930s, there was a strong and widespread belief that the mainstream theory was inadequate. Minsky says: "Regardless of whether economists identified themselves as conservative, liberal, or radical, it seems that during the 30s all of them reached the same disconsolate conclusion: with capitalism, depressions would occur and follow their course" (1987 [1975]: 18).
3 Hicks points out that Great Britain's economic policy since 1931, Germany's in 1932 and 1933, and the United States' since 1933 – specifically, the New Deal – may be framed in what today is known as expansive Keynesian policies; they were, in fact, largely an inevitable outcome of the economic situation: "Britain left the gold standard in 1937 because she had no alternative; interest rates were brought down to lighten the budget; the rather wild collection of measures introduced by the Roosevelt administration in April 1933, when it came into office, were obviously uninspired by any consistent doctrine. All these events, of course, preceded *The General Theory*" (Hicks, 1974: 2). If this is so, then Keynes should

not be considered the Father of the Keynesian State but, rather, the relation is, precisely, the opposite – a nascent Keynesian state largely boosted and "produced" Keynes ideas. Blaug argues that "the Keynesian revolution triumphed because Keynes draw the economic policy conclusions that most economists anyway wished to support [. . .] " (1985: 807). Keynes's contribution, thus, seems to be reduced to the sorry role of providing an allegedly scientific mere justification for the ideological need of economists and statesmen. Klein posits, instead, that the road that led Keynes to his conclusions went from actual practice to theory: "it was not his theory that led Keynes to practical policies, but practical policies aimed at curing economic diseases that eventually led him to his theory" (1961:31). Keynes's ideas did not bring about changes in economic conditions, but succeeded in articulating them from a theoretical perspective.

4 The excitement with which Ricardians and Marxists of the 1950s onwards (particularly the Americans led by Paul Sweezy) welcomed Keynes's contribution is hard to explain if their political positions are taken into account. Keynes confessed in an address to a group of young liberals that, although sympathizing with some of their proposals, he had not joined the Labor Party because "[t]o begin with, and the class is not my class. If I am going to pursue sectional interests at all, I shall pursue my own. When it comes to the class struggle as such, my local and personal patriotisms, like those of every one else, except certain unpleasant zealous ones, are attached to my own surroundings. I can be influenced by what seems to me to be Justice and good sense; but the *Class* war will find me on the side of the educated *bourgeoisie*" (Keynes 1997b [1925]: 300).

5 This is what happened with the well-known IS-LM model.

6 We will mention only some of these: variable rigidity (Modigliani, 1944; Akerlof and Yellen, 1985; Mankiw, 1990); the presence of non-competitive markets (Sawyer, 1985); an approach based on disequilibrium (Patinkin, 1959 [1956]; Malinvaud, 1977), caused by the inherently imperfect character of agent's information or coordination (Clower, 1965; Leijonhufvud, 1976a); finance instability (Minsky, 1987 [1975]). In this list, authors are mentioned only as examples with the sole purpose of illustrating the diversity of existing positions, not to characterize each approach in all its complexity.

7 There are, no doubt, honorable exceptions, among them, e.g. Hicks, who in *A Theory of Economic History* states, "We are to classify states of society, economic states of society; we are to look for intelligible reasons for which one such state should give way to another. It will be a sequence not unlike the 'Feudalism, Capitalism, Socialism' of Marx" (Hicks, 1984 [1969]: 7).

8 In the last section of this book, it will be shown that the division between micro and macroeconomics, apart from being result of Keynes's criticism, is based on a proposal explicitly put forward in *The General Theory*. Probably, Keynes imagined what the economic theory would look like after (poorly) digesting his contributions.

1   Keynes and his understanding of early 20th century capitalism

Keynes and the historical moment

In 1914, John Maynard Keynes celebrated his 32nd birthday. On September 28, the assassination of Archduke Franz Ferdinand of Austria in Sarajevo became the pretext for the outbreak of First World War. Thus, what E. Hobsbawm called the twentieth-century's *Age of Catastrophe* began, an age that would last for more than thirty years, until Keynes was more than 60 years old. The Great War put an end to an era of prosperity, ending an approximately century-long period when relative peace prevailed among the great European powers. Such peace was interrupted solely by isolated two-power confrontations, such as the Crimean War and the Russian-Japanese dispute, or by internal conflicts, such as the United States Civil War. According to Hobsbawm, the First World War

> marked the breakdown of the (Western) civilization of the 19th century. This civilization was capitalist in its economy; liberal in its legal and constitutional structure; bourgeois in the image of its characteristic hegemonic class; glorying in the advance of science, knowledge and education, material and moral progress.
>
> (Hobsbawm, 1998 [1987])

Keynes witnessed the end of nineteenth-century civilization. His place of observation was nothing less than London, the hub of world trade, finance, and industry. It could be said that the Great Depression of the 1930s broke out in England, ahead of time though less violently than elsewhere, by the end of First World War, in anticipation of what would become an unprecedented economic convulsion at a global level. While the 1920s brought remarkable prosperity – the so-called "Roaring Twenties – to the United States, in England production collapsed during the first postwar period, and remained halted for approximately two decades. It did not recover to its pre-1919 level until 1935. A long stretch of the most intellectually productive phase of Keynes's life – from his thirties to his mid-forties –[1]elapsed during a period that for England was marked by chronic economic stagnation. In the period 1921–38, the unemployment rate neared, in average, 14 percent (Temin, 1990). The decrease in output that begins in 1919 seems to reverse in 1922, but the expansive cycle appears to be feeble. This cycle is briefly interrupted by a light slump in 1926 – associated with the return to the pre-war pound parity – and is finally reverted when the world collapse of the 1930s sweeps British economy. The real recovery of industrial production will begin together with Second World War.

In England, Keynes played a leading political role in economic events since his youth. When he was 35 years old, he publicly resigned his post in the British delegation gathered in Versailles to negotiate a Peace Treaty in the wake of the Armistice. At that moment, he published *The Economic Consequences of the Peace,* a work that denounced the unfair conditions that the victorious powers, mainly England and France, wanted to impose on a defeated Germany. The book would earn him fame throughout Europe and the United States. In the first chapters of *The Economic Consequences*, before devoting himself to a detailed discussion of the Treaty, Keynes warns his readers:

> The power to become habituated to his surroundings is a marked characteristic of mankind. Very few of us realize with conviction the intensely unusual, unstable, complicated, unreliable, temporary nature of the economic organization by which Western Europe has lived for the last half century.
>
> (Keynes, 1919: 5)

Even though the book delves into the personalities of the great men who played a leading role in the Conference and offers a detailed literarily masterful depiction of them, the spirit of the text points to something else. It seeks to show that, behind their incidental appearance, social processes hide the slow but inescapable motion of deep economic processes. It is those deep movements that Keynes seeks to unveil.

> The great events of history are often due to secular changes in the growth of population and *other fundamental economic causes*, which, escaping by their gradual character the notice of contemporary observers, are attributed to the follies of statesmen or the fanaticism of the atheists.
>
> (Keynes, 1919: 10, emphasis added)

It is necessary, therefore, to probe below the surface and to consider the situation in a broader framework. Keynes's hypothesis, crucial to understanding the historical process that was then developing, is that one of the great stages of the history of capitalism came to its end in 1914.

> After 1870, there was developed on a large scale an unprecedented situation, and the economic condition of Europe became during the next fifty years unstable and peculiar [. . .] What an extraordinary episode in the economic progress of man that age was which came to an end in August 1914!
>
> (Keynes, 1919: 8)

Remarkably, this very same characterization of a transition to a new economic stage in the history of humankind persists and is even reinforced over time; it is part of the hidden backdrop against which *The General Theory*, which will be published twenty years later, is written.

It is for this reason that the hypothesis that a "new economic period or age" was commencing is crucial to understanding the theoretical and practical stances Keynes will adopt from then on. Even more, these deep economic transformations are also key to understand the evolution of scientific theories: in Keynes's view, history plays a central role in the explanation of scientific revolutions and the victory of orthodoxies. Indeed, it is also the historical factor that gives account of why certain ideas, although involving scientific truths, fail to succeed and are, instead, rejected by public opinion, statesmen, and scholars. Society's evolving needs explain the success and failure of the economic ideas prevailing in each period. According to Keynes, his own teachers had become prominent, first and foremost, because their work reflected "the environment" where it was developed. For example, on Marshall's *Industry and Trade* he said,

> Thus such unity as the book possesses derives from its being an account of the forms of *individualistic capitalism* as this had established itself in Western Europe at about the year 1900, of how they came to pass, and of how far they served the public interest.
>
> (Keynes, 1924: 37; emphasis added)

There is a direct relationship between each historical period and the prevailing economic theory: *individualistic capitalism* is the term Keynes chooses to refer to the stage whose fundamental traits Marshall's doctrine articulates. The same kind of link is stressed in *The General Theory* to account for the success of Ricardo's ideas:

> The completeness of the Ricardian victory is something of a curiosity and a mystery. It must have been due to a complex of suitabilities in the doctrine to the environment into which it was projected [. . .] That it

afforded a measure of justification to the free activities of the individual capitalist, attracted to it the support of the dominant social force behind authority.

(Keynes, 1939 [1936]: 32–33); I.3.III)

Something similar occurs regarding the causes that, according to Keynes, limited the acceptance gained by his pre-1931 works. In the preface to his book *Essays in Persuasion*, a collection of articles written since 1919, he states that

> The volume might have been entitled "Essays in Prophesy and Persuasion", for the Prophesy, unfortunately, has been more successful than the Persuasion. But it was in a spirit of persuasion that most of these essays were written, in an attempt to influence opinion. They were regarded at the time, many of them, as extreme and reckless utterances. But I think that the reader, looking through them today, will admit that this was because they often ran directly counter to the *overwhelming weight of contemporary sentiment and opinion, and not because of their character themselves.*
>
> (Keynes, 1931: 1; emphasis added)

In short, for Keynes, nineteenth-century *individualistic capitalism* was already exhausted by the 1920s. More than a decade and a half would still have to pass until the publication of *The General Theory;* however, the work plan to which Keynes would devote his research efforts was already outlined. Economic theory must always be an accurate reflection of the social processes of its time. If a stage of capitalism had come to its end, economic theory had to be worked out anew, adapting it to the new era. In a lecture delivered in 1925, collected in *Essays in Persuasion*, Keynes publicly challenged mainstream thinking,

> Half the copybook wisdom of our statesmen is based on assumptions which were at one time true, or partly true, but are now less and less true day by day. We have to invent new wisdom for a new age. And in the meantime we must, if we are to do any good, appear unorthodox, troublesome, dangerous, disobedient to them that begat us.
>
> (Keynes, 1925: 338)

Keynes's diagnosis runs along these same lines of reasoning: the orthodox theory had turned the traits that characterized nineteenth-century society into its own doctrinary assumptions, its premises. Among the properties of the economic system that had become undisputed axioms, there is one that bears terrible consequences.

The assumption that the economy will always be moving towards a position of full employment may have been suitable to describe a social form that, according to Keynes, ceased to exist by the end of the nineteenth century. It is evident that the endemic stagnation of world economy cannot be understood from the point of view of a doctrine that categorically denies the possibility that resources may remain unemployed.

> All our ideas about economics, instilled into us by education and atmosphere and tradition are, whether we are conscious of it or not, soaked with theoretical pre-suppositions which are only *applicable to a society that is in equilibrium, with all its productive resources already employed*. Many people are trying to solve the problem of unemployment with a theory which is based on the assumption that there is no unemployment.
>
> (Keynes, 1933)

A theoretical project begins to take definite shape: whereas the *classical theory* believed that full employment was the only equilibrium possible, Keynes will seek to show that the system can also be in equilibrium when there is unemployment. Neither could the monetary or global exchange forms that had plainly disappeared be taken for granted, as the orthodoxy did. The postulates of the gold standard and of free universal trade did not correspond to this new reality as"

> The various currencies, which were all maintained on a stable basis in relation to gold and to one another, facilitated the easy flow of capital and of trade to an extent the full value of which we only realize now, when we are deprived of its advantages.
>
> (Keynes, 1919: 10)

The evidence put forward is enough to show that Keynes did believe to be witnessing the end of a phase of capitalism but also, more importantly, the chaotic beginning of a new one. Such transformation of society is what, in his view, makes a reframing of economic theory imperative. So what are the more relevant characteristics of this new stage of capitalism?

At the dawn of the twentieth century, there were many thinkers who, with different and sometimes even opposite approaches, announced that a deep economic change was imminent. Authors such as J.A. Hobson (1902), R. Hilferdin (1985 [1910]) or V.I. Lenin in his well-known *Imperialism: the Highest Stage of Capitalism* (1917), but also, among others, J.A. Schumpeter (1939) support the thesis of the beginning of a new historical stage.

The following paragraphs, however, do not intend to review, compare or critically assess the different theories purporting to explain such global transformations that are contained in this voluminous literature. It will neither be discussed whether a transformation of such magnitude and relevance as to be considered a hinge in world history was, in fact, emerging then. What in our view is relevant here is that Keynes held the hypothesis that a change of proportion was underway; reflecting such change in the economic theory was his aim.

This book will try to show that *The General Theory* is a genuine product of such need. What is relevant here is not to identify the nature of this process in itself but of *Keynes's perception of it*, finding the references to that historical change in *The General Theory* and Keynes's previous works. Some authors pertaining to the schools known as regulationist, institutionalist, post-Keynesian, and Marxist have researched, albeit from different perspectives, links between economic changes and Keynes's theories.[2] How can it be shown that the transformations of differing importance and nature highlighted by Keynes are *effectively reflected* by the innovative theoretical system he will later build and make public in 1936? With the purpose of confirming such correspondence we will adopt a strict criterion. The theoretical system, inasmuch as it can be mathematically represented, has, simply put, two elements, each of a different nature. Some variables are considered to be *endogenous* because their determination may be expressed by means of a cause-effect relationship or a mechanism of economic nature. Other variables, instead, are treated as *exogenous* or *given*, since their explanation falls outside the economic system.

We will therefore collect references to the transformations of capitalism by differentiating those variables that, according to Keynes, are determined by economic processes apt to be represented by means of laws (endogenous) from those that are, instead, the exogenous variables of the system. If we are right, both sets of variables will differ from the ones derived from the *classical system* constructed in the nineteenth century. It will then remain to be discussed what the laws determining these endogenous variables are, that is, both the variables that were already considered to be such and the newly-listed ones. We will devote Chapter 3 of this study to that task – expounding Keynes's system. By the time we reach that point, we will have already made some progress, since the aspects of economic reality whose changes the new economic theory has to reflect will have already been identified. In this sense, Keynes's idea of economic transformations is part of the relevant background of *The General Theory*.

In the following section, we will summarize the general characteristics of the new stage of capitalism that began during the first decades of the twentieth century, as described in some writings before 1936. Then, in subsequent sections, three crucial aspects that concentrated the most important changes will be discussed: the fragmentation of the capitalist class, the organization of labor, and the transformations that took place in the monetary regime and the banking system.

II The stages of capitalism

Three stages of capitalism – scarcity, abundance and stabilization

At first sight, Keynes's views on world history seem to be loaded with pessimism, the same pessimism attributed to Malthus. Humankind was crossing the threshold of an era burdened with tensions, and even though state intervention might to some extent relieve the situation, the tragic core of the "economic problem"[3] would remain untouched. The years during which Keynes developed and introduced his theories to the academy and the public seemed to nurture this bleak view of the future. Moreover, the 1930 crisis could have worked as irrefutable evidence of his most pessimistic premonitions. However, Keynes predicted a future of redoubled prosperity for humankind. Hence, his attitude of concern towards the present mixed with optimism regarding future possibilities.

Next, we will summarize a glossed selection of Keynes's historical arguments that will allow us to support our contention regarding their relevance to his entire argumentation. Even though we agree with the procedure applied by Keynes, we do not consider his periodization of the "economic" history of man adequate, as we will explicitly state later. However, we believe that the approach he chose – linking theory and history – is correct, and sets him apart from most of his followers.

In August 1925, Keynes delivered an address to the Liberal Summer School at Cambridge, which would later be published, with slight changes, as an article titled "Am I a Liberal?" In this text, he makes the conclusions of a work by Professor Commons his own; according to Keynes, Commons "has been one of the first to recognize the nature of the economic transition amidst the early stages of which we are now living, distinguishes three epochs, three economic orders, upon the third of which we are entering" (Keynes, 1925: 335).

The first stage, which Commons – and Keynes accordingly – calls the "Era of Scarcity", runs from the emergence of man until the fifteenth or sixteenth century, that is, the long period that preceded the rise of capitalism. Throughout that stretch, humankind suffered all kinds of material deprivation. From the political point of view, individuals were subjected to extreme governmental control and enjoyed minimum liberties. The seventeenth century marked the beginning of the second stage, the "Era of Abundance". Through technical innovations, humankind made extraordinary progress multiplying the productive capacity of labor. During the eighteenth century, this process gained momentum, but development would not reach its peak until a century later.

This is a stage marked by economic opulence, greater individual freedom, and minimum governmental control. The ideology of *laissez-faire*, uncompromising liberalism, is identified with the heyday of the era of abundance.

However, in the early twentieth century, the Era of Abundance meets its own limits. A third stage thus begins; Keynes (as always, following Commons) calls this period the "Era of Stabilization". It is the beginning of a new economic order where individual liberty, characteristic of the previous period, is gradually restricted as a result of the emergence of

> governmental sanctions, but mainly by economic sanctions through concerted action, whether secret, semi-open, open, or arbitrational, of associations, corporations, unions, and other collective movements of manufacturers, merchants, labourers, farmers, and bankers.
>
> (Keynes, 1925: 336)

Keynes argues that the world is transversing an unstable phase, characteristic of a transition period between an era of abundance and an era of stability. As happens whenever an accelerated transformation takes place, new political forms appear in a spontaneous, disorderly fashion, forms that gradually begin to match the economic changes underway. Thus, individualistic capitalism and *laissez-faire*, typical of the now past "Era of Abundance", must undergo a crisis, as sooner or later they will be only history. This is the panorama he has in mind when he claims that the proposals of Conservatives, of the men in the City and in Parliament are disgraceful and ineffective: they are the consequences of insistently and rigidly clinging to the economic and moral principles of an age that has already finished:

> [t]here is now no place [. . .] for those whose hearts are set on old-fashioned individualism and *laissez-faire* in all their rigour – greatly though these contributed to the success of the nineteenth century. I say this, not because I think that these doctrines were wrong in the conditions which gave birth to them [. . .] but because they have ceased to be applicable to modern conditions.
>
> (Keynes, 1925: 330)

The world is now entering a stage where the state will have a greater degree of intervention and, above all, a qualitatively different kind of intervention. The twentieth century had already yielded two new political systems: Socialism and Fascism. However, Keynes describes both as aberrations or, more precisely, as an inadequate overreaction in the face of the instability that ensued in the wake of the end of the Era of Abundance. Their main shared flaw is comparable to that of the conservatives, as it is founded on "the presuppositions of the [already finished] Era of Abundance". In the political realm, Keynes claims, the end of the abundance demands the search for a new balance between individual liberty and state intervention, hence the name "Era of Stabilization". It is not a question of individual's complete freedom or full governmental control; rather, the historical evolution will lead to a middle point between both extremes.

> The transition from economic anarchy to a régime which deliberately aims at controlling and directing economic forces in the interests of social justice and social stability, will present enormous difficulties both technical and political.
>
> (Keynes, 1925: 336)

This periodization of human history is taken from Commons, but the basic idea that the "Era of Abundance" was coming to an end is present in Keynes's first writings, even though it was not yet totally systematically framed. In *The Economic Consequences of the Peace* (1919), Keynes tries to analyze the war based on the major economic changes, which act implacably, but in a way that is hidden from the notice of the superficial observer, who tends to attribute responsibility for the great events of history "to the follies of statesmen or the fanaticism of atheists". In his hypothesis regarding the causes of war, some of the trends that he will then seek to represent using theoretical instruments are already outlined.

What are the hidden economic causes of the First World War? Here is the key to understanding the final stretches of the Era of Abundance, the causes of its crisis, but also of its achievements. Europe was self-sufficient until 1870, but from then on the population increase forced the Old World to resort to foreign production to meet its food needs. The population grew steadily and, for the moment, it was not difficult to provide it with sustenance: labor productivity was also increasing, and the growth of the work force was rewarded by an ever-increasing amount of product per inhabitant. However, by the early twentieth century, this virtuous relationship came to an end. Even so, for a while, the discovery and incorporation of renewed sources of natural resources – the growth of trade with tropical Africa and the exchange of oilseed crops – made it possible to defer the emergence of the latent conflict between the decreasing yield of production and the accelerated increase in population, with its ensuing growing needs; such a particular combination enabled the deferral but not the eradication of the conflict. The Era of Abundance flourished until it reached its peak. Finally, the mismatch between increasing needs and decreasing productivity broke out in plain sight of everyone in the First World War. Keynes points out that the symptoms of this latent conflict had become more or less visible a long time before.

There is no need to guess at the Malthusian origin of Keynes's reasoning, as he himself admits he draws on that author:

> Before the 18th century, mankind entertained no false hopes. To lay the illusions which grew popular at that age's latter end, Malthus disclosed a devil. For half a century, all serious economic writings held that devil in clear prospect. For the next half century he was chained up and out of sight. Now perhaps we have loosed him again.
>
> (Keynes, 1919: 8)

Keynes seeks to show how these two opposing trends began to appear even during the years before the First World War. The "economic problem" became deeper: the number of arms and mouths to feed began to grow at an ever-increasing rate. The European population – particularly, that of Central Europe and Russia – grew at an unprecedented rate from 1870 to 1914. Germany's accelerated economic development provided material support for this demographic growth. Following its unification, Germany left its earlier agriculture-based economy definitively behind to become a powerful industrial hub that was capable of sustaining the new workers that the European continent generated, providing prosperity and a strong economic organization. In these conditions, it was able to expand its productive capacity, and to obtain, in exchange for surplus, means of subsistence that came from abroad and were distributed through free world trade. German industry organized goods and capital, and offered a market that could absorb the output of the rest of Europe. But apart from this factor, Keynes mentions two other aspects that were crucial to the reproduction of pre-war European economy. To sustain the rate of growth, capitalists had to accumulate wealth and invest it productively. This savings capacity was supported, in turn, by a deep inequality in the distribution of wealth. Income differences could be tolerated inasmuch as capitalists assigned their surplus to accumulation and not to enjoyment. And this was precisely the case,

> The immense accumulations of fixed capital which, to the great benefit of mankind, were built up during the half century before the war, could never have come about in a society where wealth was divided equitably [. . .] Thus this remarkable system depended for its growth on a double bluff or deception. On the one hand the labouring classes accepted from ignorance or powerlessness, or were compelled, persuaded, or cajoled by custom, convention, authority, and the well-established order of society into accepting, a situation in which they could call their own very little of the cake [. . .] And on the other hand the capitalist classes

were allowed to call the best part of the cake theirs and were theoretically free to consume it, on the tacit underlying condition that they
consumed very little of it in practice.

(Keynes, 1919:12)

This high rate of savings was not the result of some whim, fashion trend,
or kind of Franciscan ethics, but of the economic conditions of the period:
"The cake was really very small in proportion to the appetites of consumption, and no one, if it were shared all round, would be much the better off
by the cutting of it". The surplus capital that Europe produced and placed
throughout the world was, besides, a condition to support its own economic
equilibrium, since the potential of growth rested on the acquisition of foodstuffs coming, mainly, from America. Thus, surplus adopted the form of
available capital to be invested abroad, but also became processed products
to be exchanged for raw materials. Money interests accrued on such investment returned to Europe as foodstuffs. Such was the delicate scheme that
began to crack *even before 1914*.

> Even before the war, however, the equilibrium thus established between
> old civilisations and new resources was being threatened. The prosper-
> ity of Europe was based on the facts that, owing to the large exportable
> surplus of foodstuffs in America, she was able to purchase food at a
> cheap rate measured in terms of the labour required to produce her own
> exports, and that, as a result of her previous investments of capital, she
> was entitled to a substantial amount annually without any payment in
> return at all.
>
> (Keynes, 1919: 13)

The trigger would be the level of development reached by the countries
incorporated to the system in the last wave: the overseas nations were also
growing at an accelerated rate, so that they needed an ever-increasing proportion of the produce of their lands for their own sustenance. The export-
able surplus of the periphery was also becoming depleted. With time,
America would also suffer the "economic problem": the inevitable conflict between population growth and increasing foodstuff costs in terms of
labor. The terms of trade, previously favorable to Europe, would change
their sign.

> Europe's claim on the resources of the New World was becoming pre-
> carious; the law of diminishing returns was at last reasserting itself,
> and was making it necessary year by year for Europe to offer a greater
> quantity of other commodities to obtain the same amount of bread.
>
> (Keynes, 1919: 14)

War did nothing but dramatically bring to light the concurring action of these factors that slowly performed their invisible task. When the trend became firm and, finally, the population surpassed the capacity to produce cheap foodstuffs, the old Era of Abundance came to its end.

The "economic problem" seems to have no solution. In fact, the three major stages into which Keynes divides human history have so far been introduced. During the first third of the twentieth century, the world was moving towards the third stage. But was this the *last* stage of capitalism? At first sight, the Era of Abundance would seem to have come extinct by late nineteenth century, and from then on, the needs of a multiplied mass of population could only be expected to inevitably collide with the barrier imposed by diminishing labor productivity. According to Keynes, however, humankind has the resources required to enter a stage not of scarcity or abundance, but of stability (epoch of stabilization). In other article, "Economic Possibilities for our Grandchildren" (1930), written halfway through the crisis, the panorama we have so far depicted is completed:

> We are suffering just now from a bad attack of economic pessimism. It is common to hear people say that the epoch of enormous economic progress which characterised the nineteenth century is over; that the rapid improvement in the standard of life is now going to slow down – at any rate in Great Britain; that a decline in prosperity is more likely than an improvement in the decade which lies ahead of us. I believe that this is a wildly mistaken interpretation of what is happening to us.
>
> (Keynes, 1963 [1930]: 358)

Crisis and stagnation are only temporary phenomena, and the calamities ensuing thereof might be alleviated provided that the disease be accurately diagnosed and then treated with the adequate remedies. Nothing will be achieved if the old prescriptions are implemented, prescriptions that may have been effective in the previous stage, but are powerless and damaging in the face of the evolution of the new developments. To perceive this promising future, it is necessary to look beyond appearance.

> The prevailing world depression, the enormous anomaly of unemployment in a world full of wants, the disastrous mistakes we have made, blind us to what is going on under the surface – to the true interpretation of the trend of things.
>
> (Keynes, 1963 [1930]: 358)

In *The Economic Consequences of the Peace*, war was presented as the inevitable consequence of a disproportionate increase in population relative to agricultural labor productivity. This perverse mismatch between needs and means, however, would only be transitory. Keynes argued that the accelerated progress of science under the capitalist regime would succeed in overcoming the last hindrance that subjected mankind to the *economic problem*, and that if that had not yet been achieved it was only because the new production methods had not yet pervaded the entire productive fabric. Behind the prevailing crisis, a new panorama began to take shape, a panorama that Keynes perceived when closely observing the recent economic changes. He pointed out, specifically, that technical progress was beginning to enter food production industries.

When this happens, the tourniquet will be released. On the one hand, the rapid increase in labor productive capacity will reach agriculture, and on the other, birth rate increase will slow down. In short, even though Keynes's explanation might seem to draw on Malthus, it is also true that, again, an attempt is made to treat this doctrine taking into account the prevailing circumstances of the period.

Keynes's optimism regarding the near future is based on this relationship between technical development and population increase. Once a new equilibrium is reached, a new stability stage will begin, to which a different form of state intervention, but also a different economic theory corresponds. The crisis of the early twentieth century may thus be placed in its rightful place: this troubled transition may be attributed to "the painfulness of readjustment between one economic period and another". The catastrophes experienced by the world are a consequence of that turbulent period of readjustment.

The scarcity of means of livelihood brought about war; however, the effects of the new techniques were not pleasant either. When the labor productive capacity finally succeeded in making progress, the old institutions typical of the Era of Abundance were not flexible enough to adapt to the new economic conditions, and the theoretical economists lacked the acuteness required to perceive that transformation.

> The increase of technical efficiency has been taking place faster than we can deal with the problem of labour absorption; the improvement in the standard of life has been a little too quick; *the banking and monetary system of the world has been preventing the rate of interest from falling as fast as equilibrium requires*.
>
> (Keynes, 1963 [1930]: 358; emphasis added)

This means that neither institutions nor ideas had succeeded in adapting to the new economic conditions. In the remaining pages of Chapter 1, we will discuss the more relevant economic aspects that were affected, according to Keynes, by such transformations. Among the difficulties experienced, a central role is played by the high level of interest rates resulting from the typical dealings of an archaic monetary and banking system (the changes that took place in the monetary sphere will be discussed later).

But these transformations have an additional fundamental consequence. Keynes believed he was observing an incongruity similar to that of the "economic problem", but in the opposite direction: during the first decade of the twentieth century, the means of livelihood were insufficient for a population that was growing, and that was the hidden cause that triggered the war. However, once the new technical improvements revolutionized food production methods and became widespread throughout industry, a large portion of the population lost their jobs.

> For the moment the very rapidity of these changes is hurting us and bringing difficult problems to solve [. . .] We are being afflicted with a new disease of which some readers may not yet have heard the name, but of which they will hear a great deal in the years to come – namely, *technological unemployment*. This means unemployment due to our discovery of means of economising the use of labour outrunning the pace at which we can find new uses for labour.
>
> (Keynes, 1963 [1930]: 360; Keynes's emphasis)

If there was an excess of population and a lack of food before, now production required less labor, leading to a novel kind of unemployment – technological unemployment. Both factors, the anachronistic character of the monetary system, resulting in an excessively high rate of interest, and high unemployment are separately mentioned. There is no theoretical system yet – as that which will be expounded in *The General Theory* – linking both symptoms.

Once the process of transformation is over, and a new equilibrium reached, Keynes claims, some of the past's most disgraceful social problems, particularly poverty and inequality, will disappear. He imagines that humankind will then have to change some of the fundamental traits of its previous value system: "When the accumulation of wealth is no longer of high social importance, there will be great changes in the code of morals". As concerns economic doctrines, the old *laissez-faire* principle will no longer have its *raison d'être*. Keynes predicts a future where capitalism will be free from the evils that beset it in the present.

This same notion will play an important role in *The General Theory*. Regarding the values that will prevail in that future world, Keynes has more than a few illusions:

> We shall be able to afford to dare to assess the money-motive at its true value. The love of money as a possession – as distinguished from the love of money as a means to the enjoyments and realities of life – will

be recognised for what it is, a somewhat disgusting morbidity, one of those semi-criminal, semi-pathological propensities which one hands over with a shudder to the specialists in mental disease. All kinds of social customs and economic practices, affecting the distribution of wealth and of economic rewards and penalties, which we now maintain at all costs, however distasteful and unjust they may be in themselves, because they are tremendously useful in promoting the accumulation of capital, we shall then be free, at last, to discard.

(Keynes, 1963 [1930]: 363)

When facing these new challenges, society should stay away from applying outdated doctrines that do nothing but delay its progress to the promise of fulfillment that the nascent stage holds. Keynes's theoretical project is thus outlined, as are the reasons why he rejects the inherited theory. The doctrine of *laissez-faire*, no matter how mistaken in its beginning, was adequate in the context of the economic conditions pertaining to the already concluded Era of Abundance.

Rise and fall of the laissez-faire doctrine

The Era of Abundance began in the seventeenth century but reached its peak during late nineteenth century. This is also the heyday, according to Keynes, of *individualistic capitalism* and the *laissez-faire* doctrine. In his essay "The End of Laissez-faire" (1926), Keynes explores the field of political theory and philosophy, with the purpose of unveiling the origins of nineteenth-century liberal thinking. In the late eighteenth century, Locke and Hume sought to provide a rationale for property rights and individual freedom. Later, Paley, Rousseau, and Bentham extended the scope of these ideas stressing the equality precept; they intended to show that the pursuit of self-interest leads to public welfare. It was these three strands that made up the doctrine that took definitive shape with the so-called "principle of *laissez-faire*".

[The principle of *laissez-faire* supposes] that by the working of natural laws individuals pursuing their own interests with enlightenment in condition of freedom always tend to promote the general interest at the same time [. . .]. To the philosophical doctrine that the government has no right to interfere, and the divine that it has no need to interfere, there is added a scientific proof that its interference is inexpedient [. . .]. The political philosopher could retire in favour of the business man – for the latter could attain the philosopher's *summumbonum* by just pursuing his own private profit.

(Keynes, 1926: 3)

For Keynes, thus, neither the scientific or philosophical virtues that characterize this reasoning, nor its power to persuade was what secured its enormous doctrinary influence. Quite the contrary, the ultimate reason for the dominance of the principle of *laissez-faire* is to be found in the particular historical situation in which it was put forth, that is, the height of the Era of Abundance. These ideas were perfectly suited to the needs of the times, for one simple reason: their prescriptions openly favored the interests of the dominant social force: "individualism and *laissez-faire* could not [. . .] have secured their lasting hold over the conduct of public affairs, if it had not been for their conformity with the needs and wishes of the business world of the day". In this, as in other passages, the strong causal link that Keynes finds between economic processes, politically dominant sectors, and the most influential currents of scientific, moral, and practical thinking is evidently manifest.

> [M]aterial progress between 1750 and 1850 came from individual initiative, and owed almost nothing to the directive influence of organised society as a whole. Thus practical experience reinforced *a priori* reasonings. The philosophers and the economists told us that for sundry deep reasons unfettered private enterprise would promote the greatest good of the whole. What could suit the business man better? [. . .] Thus the ground was fertile for a doctrine that, whether on divine, natural, or scientific grounds, state action should be narrowly confined and economic life left, unregulated so far as may be, to the skill and good sense of individual citizens actuated by the admirable motive of trying to get on in the world.
>
> (Keynes, 1926: 3)

If the principle of *laissez-faire* succeeded in prevailing in spite of its meager scientific content, the transition to a different economic stage unveiled the distance between doctrine and reality. In fact, the incongruity between the premises of *laissez-faire* and the economic reality of the twentieth century became evident in ways that were as noticeable as they were diverse. First, the changes in economic organization that the First World War forced the belligerent nations to implement showed that there was a viable alternative to *laissez-faire* individualistic capitalism.

> War experience in the organisation of socialised production has left some near observers optimistically anxious to repeat it in peace conditions. War socialism unquestionably achieved a production of wealth on a scale far greater than we ever knew in peace [. . .]. Nevertheless, the dissipation of effort was also prodigious.
>
> (Keynes, 1926: 13)

The "socialization" of production is, in Keynes's view, an "automatic" outcome, a required change in the new era into which capitalism was entering. It should not be inferred that this economic process leads Keynes to endorse the traditional Socialist ideas; much to the contrary, he also rejects "State Socialism", since both doctrines originate in the same mistaken diagnosis. According to Keynes, State Socialism

> is [. . .] little better than a dusty survival of a plan to meet the problems of fifty years ago, based on a misunderstanding of what someone said a hundred years ago [. . .] is a clearer, in some respects a more muddled version of just the same philosophy as underlies nineteenth-century individualism. Both equally laid all their stress on freedom, the one negatively to avoid limitations on existing freedom, the other positively to destroy natural or acquired monopolies. They are different reactions to the same intellectual atmosphere.
>
> (Keynes, 1926: 14)

To the "Socialism of the war", which involved the transfer of a previously inconceivable proportion of the economic process organization to the hands of the state, the evolution of private production should be added. According to observers of the period, the increase in capital concentration that took place during the first years of the twentieth century brought about a change in the capitalist society. This too was a spontaneous – and irreversible – "socialization" of the production, although it was undoubtedly different from the Soviet "State Socialism".

> One of the most interesting and unnoticed developments of recent decades has been the tendency of big enterprise to socialise itself. A point arrives in the growth of a big institution – particularly a big railway or big public utility enterprise, but also a big bank or a big insurance company – at which the owners of the capital, i.e. its shareholders, are almost entirely dissociated from the management [. . .]. [Big enterprises] are, as time goes on, socialising themselves [. . .]. In fact, we already have in these cases many of the faults as well as the advantages of State Socialism. Nevertheless, we see here, I think, *a natural line of evolution. The battle of Socialism against unlimited private profit is being won in detail hour by hour.*
>
> (Keynes, 1926: 13; emphasis added)

The spontaneous development of the economy had led to the creation of gigantic enterprises that reached unprecedented dimensions and "half-monopolistic" positions in their respective markets. The consequences of this process were fantastical. Firm management no longer answered, nor could it owing to its formidable size, to the direct interests of individual shareholders, exclusively obsessed with increasing their immediate profits. Such changes meant the end of the individual capitalist, unchallenged protagonist of the nineteenth century. Capital concentration and the emergence of large monopolies bring about a clear-cut division between ownership and business management. Thus, the prioritarian aims of these corporations are modified (we will return to this later). For the time being, an evident assertion in Keynes's view should be repeated: nineteenth-century ideology cannot address the challenges of the new era. Old doctrines have been superseded by the natural evolutionary process of society in spite of the fact that those responsible for the official doctrine and economic policy may not have realized it.

> [T]he Treasury and the Bank of England are pursuing an orthodox nineteenth-century policy based on the assumption that economic adjustments can and ought to be brought about by the free play of the forces of supply and demand. The Treasury and the Bank of England still believe [. . .] that the things, which would follow on the assumption of free competition and the mobility of capital and labour, actually occur in the economic life of to-day.
>
> (Keynes, 1925: 337)

The "socialization" of production put an end to the *individualistic capitalism* of the Era of Abundance and, therefore, to the premises of the economic theory associated to it, of which free competition and the mobility of capital and labor are here mentioned.

Keynes's diagnosis is thus expounded: the victory of *laissez-faire* is explained in the same way as its failure – both stem from the relationship between theory, ideology, and historical period. Some of Keynes's first "proposals" regarding the reforms to be implemented to adjust to these novel circumstances should be mentioned here. In 1926, he concludes his essay on "The End of Laissez-Faire" stating his aims regarding the renovation of the theory and the practice in the field of economics.

> These reflections have been directed towards possible improvements in the technique of modern capitalism by the agency of collective action [. . .]. For my part I think that capitalism, wisely managed, can probably be made more efficient for attaining economic ends than any alternative system yet in sight, but that in itself it is in many ways extremely objectionable. Our problem is to work out a social organisation which shall be as efficient as possible without offending our notions of a satisfactory way of life.

The next step forward must come, not from political agitation or premature experiments, but from thought.

(Keynes, 1926: 15)

The task is, therefore, to develop an economic theory for the new era, capable of guiding public policies. It could be said that it is this project precisely which ten years later was implemented in the pages of *The General Theory*. It is also thus proved that the main drive behind Keynes's incursion into the field of theory originates in an unsuspected source: his conception of historical change. In the following section, it will be seen that during those ten years, his fundamental diagnosis remained unchanged, at least in its essential aspects.

A preview: the end of laissez-faire in the general theory

Our main purpose in studying Keynes's works prior to 1936, particularly those of a supposedly "non-economic" nature, is to show that the ideas regarding economic transformations laid out there are the same as those which will be expounded later in his subsequent theoretical proposals. More precisely, it may be shown that the choice of his system's given, endogenous, and exogenous variables is influenced by those ideas. Now, before exploring the different specific areas, one more question needs to be answered.

From his early writings, Keynes's conception of the major stages undergone by human economy remains basically unchanged. In many of his essays, such characterization serves as a general far-reaching historical framework, extending from the remote past to a distant future; in this framework, he sets an assessment of current events that therefore achieves deepness and perspective. It might be argued that the Keynes to which we have referred and whose ideas have been displayed hereof is not the same Keynes that would later initiate a scientific revolution with *The General Theory*. It could be thought that his most "prophetic" phase gave way afterwards to a purely scientific production. It could be held, finally, that *The General Theory* is not imbued by this conception of history, but that it is a purely theoretical text, uncontaminated by other "disciplines".

Instead of seeing Keynes as a single author, this interpretation splits him into at least two different experts. Such a maneuver is not original. On the contrary, this *splitting* operation is frequent among the more widespread interpretations of some of the most influential theoreticians' contributions. It is habitual, for example, to split the stages of youth and maturity; also, works or passages of certain works that seem to fit into the different disciplinary fields into which the horizon of the social sciences is fragmented today are considered separately – thus, "Keynes, the economist" becomes, through this operation, a particular author that should be studied independently from "Keynes, the historian", the philosopher, the social reformer, or the mathematician. Or else, in an extreme case, there appears a clear-cut division between a scientific Keynes – serious and moderate – and a political Keynes, persuasive but somehow extravagant and exaggerated.[4] However, far from the insurmountable gaps that his interpreters think they find among writings of different periods, the study of Keynes's entire production as a single whole makes such interpretation difficult to support. No doubt, stressing lines of continuity does not mean asserting that he never changed his opinion on certain topics during his whole life, as a result of the evolution of his thinking. However, in those cases, Keynes was typically honest to admit such changes, making an effort to state their nature and scope. A case in point is the differences of opinion that distinguish the *Treatise on Money* and *The General Theory*. In the Preface to the First Edition, he points out:

> The relation between this book and my *Treatise on Money* [*JMK* vols. v and vi], which I published five years ago, is probably clearer to myself than it will be to others; and what in my own mind is a natural evolution in a line of thought which I have been pursuing for several years, may sometimes strike the reader as a confusing change of view.
>
> (Keynes, 1939 [1936]: vii; Preface)

However, the view we challenge is the one that prevails in the different readings, interpretations, debates, and vulgates yielded by post-Keynes economic literature. It could be argued that such a generalization is unfair, as many interpreters have not passed judgment on this issue. However, indifference towards everything but "pure economics" is the most extreme form in which the hypothesis of the splitting may be supported.

Along these lines ran, almost in its entirety, the discussion in the field of economic theory, where the protracted debate "*Mr. Keynes and the classics*" is to be included. The operation was taken to extremes: the background of *The General Theory* was blatantly ignored, discarding also an important proportion of its content to exclude any consideration regarding the historical evolution of capitalism. It would seem, therefore, that the historical aspects may be eliminated without any loss.

It remains to be shown that to reject these impoverishing readings there is no need to search Keynes's first works to find a theory on the stages of history – much to the contrary, the material for such refutation is contained in his most relevant work. In fact, *The General Theory* openly endorses the account he developed during the fifteen previous years.[5] Only an exercise of deliberate selective blindness allows one to ignore the numerous direct references and to destroy all the links between "pure theory" and history. Otherwise, it is possible to find in *The General Theory* all the categories applied in earlier works, which have now become deeply meaningful: once again, Keynes refers to the *individualistic capitalism* and the principle of *laissez-faire*. No doubt, *The General Theory* is framed in the same conception regarding the stages of capitalism.

The usual elimination of *The General Theory's* historical references does not affect exclusively the possible interpretations. It also sets Keynes's approach fundamentally apart from that of most of the so-called Keynesians; in fact, Keynes tries to link the particular phenomena he discusses with economic transformations, but above all, he also acknowledges the historical character of the different theories. Along the centuries, capitalism features did not remain static and unchanging. To the contrary, society went through different stages during its development. There is a history of capitalism that is worth studying and conceptualizing; the same happens regarding the economic categories used to describe that changing reality.

Both the failure and the success of social theories are conditioned by two circumstances: their relationship with economic phenomena and with the interests of the dominant forces. If this is the case, any attempt to contrast different theories corresponding to different historical stages that does not take into account the social transformations entailed, limiting itself to merely contrasting them on the basis of their logical consistence, their descriptive power, or any other purely internal aspect relative to its formulation will be inherently useless.

To summarize, in Keynes's works published during the period 1919–36, an account of the successive economic stages of the history of mankind may be found. The era of scarcity was followed by the era of abundance, whose end gives way to a conflictive transition stage. However, according to Keynes, the near future held the promise of a new era of stability. This time, output will largely exceed the needs of the population, whose growth will slow down. Businesses, in turn, will have increased their size to such an extent that capital will move to its "socialization" following its own drive. Firms' dimensions will exceed the individual capitalists' capacity of management and supervision, while investment sizes will surpass their accumulation capacity. Direct owners of public companies, the shareholders, will become mere owners with no active role, while the real management of the firms will be in the hands of professional managers. From this new arrangement, it follows that state action will have to tread a different path, irreconcilable with the nineteenth-century doctrine of *laissez-faire*.

Until the transformation is completely developed, society will be condemned to go through a stage of chronic technological unemployment. However, neither the economic theory developed in the nineteenth century, that is, when the previous and already finished period reached its peak, nor, therefore, the recommendations and prescriptions derived from it will be able to provide an effective answer to these transitory ailments.

It will be now seen that this view is also present in Keynes's "economic" work, particularly, in *The General Theory*, but also in the *Tract* and the *Treatise*. In Chapter 2, the outstanding traits of the *classical theory* criticized by Keynes will be systematically (though briefly) presented.

First and foremost, it is evident that the *classical* assumption of full employment of the available resources cannot be part of the theoretical system in the new historical situation: "Many people are trying to address the problem of unemployment with a theory based on the assumption that there is no unemployment". Therefore, the task does not lie in finding an explanation for the acute unemployment associated to the crises or to the business cycle's troughs, but rather the economic theory must be able to give account of unemployment in a new stage characterized by the pervading presence of unused capacity in the capital equipment and by the involuntary unemployment of an important proportion of the active worker population. This diagnosis is identical to that of *The General Theory*,

> [I]t is an outstanding characteristic of the economic system in which we live that, whilst it is subject to severe fluctuations in respect of output and employment, it is not violently unstable. Indeed it seems capable of remaining in a *chronic condition of sub-normal activity* for a considerable period without any marked tendency either toward recovery of towards complete collapse. Moreover, the evidence indicates that full, or even approximately full employment, is of rare and short-lived occurrence.
> (Keynes, 1939 [1936]: 249; IV.18.III; stress added)

It should be noted that it is this characteristic of the new economic stage that prevents the economic theory to axiomatically discard the *possibility* of unemployment, even though it would also not be correct to consider it a *necessity*. Keynes gives the name of *The General Theory of Employment* to an explanation capable of casting light on the causes that lead an economy to operate *at an equilibrium with unused capacity and unemployed labour*, while no forces push it to recovery but neither to collapse. It is a "general" theory because it can explain, with the same instruments, the full employment case. It should also be taken into account that *chronic* unemployment cannot be represented as a state of disequilibrium, as in that case there would be a "marked tendency" for the system to abandon that position. Without this crucial update, the *classical theory* will be condemned to offer prescriptions that are powerless to address chronic unemployment. In *The General Theory*, Keynes reiterates his idea that the spontaneous "socialization" of investments that signals the era of stabilization should be accelerated,

> In conditions of *laissez-faire* the avoidance of wide fluctuations in employment may, therefore, prove impossible without a far-reaching change in the psychology of investment markets such as there is no

reason to expect. I conclude that the duty of ordering the current volume of investment cannot safely be left in private hands.

(Keynes, 1939 [1936]: 320; VI.22.II)

The state must be directly involved in managing concentrated capital, and hasten its rate of growth in a deliberate and coordinated manner. The *classical* assumption of full employment is the more despotic restriction from which the economic theory must free itself first. The real situation of the economy is far from that ideal world: the under-utilization of equipment and unemployment has turned into a nearly permanent situation; no automatic trends towards either recovery or collapse may be observed. Unemployment must then be represented in the theory as a characteristic situation in stable equilibrium, not as a transitory situation at a disequilibrium position. However, the new stage of capitalism demands that other aspects of social change be taken into account; although such aspects may be deduced from Keynes's earlier works, their inclusion in a broader conceptual framework is only to be found in *The General Theory*. More precisely, each of these changes will be reflected in the theoretical system through the modification of the variables representing the phenomenon. In the remaining pages of this Chapter 1, we will discuss each of these changes in detail.

We will present the fundamental traits of the period of transition separately, in three sections. First, we will discuss the effects of "capital concentration" on enterprises' size and structure, and therefore, on the features of the capitalist class. Next, we will analyze the changes brought about by this new configuration of the capital regarding the way in which the working class is organized, and therefore, the way in which the nominal wage is set. Finally, we will explore the new monetary forms corresponding to these transformations. Particularly, we will deal with the consequences of the definitive abandonment of the gold standard identified by Keynes. The monetary sphere will be addressed last because, as Keynes had specialized in the field of monetary problems – he was a "monetary economist", the issue demands a more detailed and thorough treatment: it involves his two theoretical works previous to *The General Theory, A Tract on Monetary Reform* (1923, *Tract* from now on) and *A Treatise on Money* (1930, *Treatise* from now on).

III Transformations in the capitalist class investment decisions

The owners' class splits into businessmen and investors

The last stage of capitalism, the beginning of which Keynes traces to the early twentieth century or, more precisely, to the outbreak of the First World

War, is characterized by the emergence of big "semi-monopolic" firms. Briefly put, according to Keynes, the novelty lies in the fact that these big firms tend to spontaneously become "socialized" in three aspects. The magnitude of the capital investments required to set these gigantic undertakings into motion surpasses the possibilities of savings and credit of any individual capitalist. A second distinctive feature follows from here: the goals of these firms are different in nature from the ones pursued by the businesses of the previous period and their owners, i.e. their goals go necessarily beyond the maximization of profit. Last, and by the same token, this change in scale has direct bearing over the way in which these firms are managed and controlled: "A point arrives [. . .] at which the owners of the capital, *i.e.* the shareholders, are almost entirely dissociated from the management". On one hand, the individual capitalist cannot continue to be the sole owner of the firm but, on the other, the increased size of the firm surpasses his personal capacity of management and control. Thus, capital concentration changes the features of the capitalist class, which no longer fits the usual description of the *classical theory*.

For a lengthy and detailed treatment of this question, we must turn to one of Keynes's first works during the period preceding *The General Theory: A Tract on Monetary Reform*, 1923. In the *Tract*, Keynes argues in favor of a broad reform of the monetary system but also, consistent with his usual presentation style, frames this strictly monetary analysis within a series of reflections regarding the past historical development, and the future trends of the economic process.

The publication date explains, in part, Keynes's concerns: postwar hyperinflation episodes had disbalanced the main European economies, and to make things worse, no theoretical or practical answer could be found in the *classical theory*. His ultimate goal is to devise a currency management system that may help ensure the stability of money's purchasing power.

The need to study the distributive consequences of money phenomena leads Keynes to further his analysis of the different groups into which society is divided. Resorting to the concept of social class, he distances himself from the marginalist thinking of his time, which had rejected the class approach to undertake the study of society from an exclusively individual perspective. In line with the Ricardian economists, he argues that class distinctions are relevant, independently of whether an individual may simultaneously play more than one role, because "in the current organization of society such division corresponds to a social distribution and to an effective divergence of interests". As has already been pointed out, what Keynes calls *classical theory* is, in fact, a combination of what is generally known as the Ricardian school and the English marginalist school. When Keynes wants to make a strict reference to the Ricardian school, he uses the term "pre-classicists", as he cannot use the term "classicists". The division of society into classes, however, had long been accepted by economists, up to the moment when the marginalist school – in line with Say – dropped this concept to replace it with factors of production offering productive services. These "factors" are not only men, but also natural objects such as "land", and produced objects, "capital". The owners, instead, are always individuals who receive the fruit of the productive activity performed by the factors they own, even when such factors are not any capacity of the owners' body.

To paint in broad strokes, according to Keynes's typification, there are two social classes: the salaried class and the owners' class. But the difference vis-à-vis the Ricardians is that the latter is in turn divided into two sub-groups with differing specific interests. This division becomes particularly relevant in his explanation, inasmuch as the effects of money value changes will be different for each sub-group within the owners' class. During the nineteenth century, different arrangements began to be implemented to separate the effective ownership of the capital from its management. There were three typical methods. The common stock of a public company allows its holders to retain ownership of the capital while relinquishing, instead, the effective control of the firm. Under the system of leasing – the second method – the owner temporarily cedes ownership in exchange for an amount of money. Upon completion of the agreed term, he recovers full control. The third method is implemented through mortgages, bonds, liabilities, and preferred stock. In this case, there is an assignment of ownership in exchange for a fixed perpetual annuity or else a temporary assignment with repayment of the principal at the end of the term. These methods did not emerge during the era of abundance, but at its peak, they became increasingly important, giving rise to a differentiation of the capitalist class.

> [D]uring the 19th century they developed a new and increased importance and had, by the beginning of the 20th, divided the propertied classes into two groups – the "business men" and the "investors" [. . .]. By this system, the active business class could to the aid of their enterprises not only their own wealth but the savings of the whole community, and the professional and propertied classes, on the other hand, could find an employment for their resources, which involved them in little trouble, no responsibility and (it was believed) small risk.
>
> (Keynes, 1923:6)

During the early twentieth century, the divide between the two fractions of the owners' class deepens: one takes on the direct management of the business; the other simply contributes capital to business ventures that are actually out of its control. Thus, the barrier that the individual capitalist sets to the accumulation capacity is therefore deposed.

Small investments are aggregated to create gigantic businesses. However, between the individual capitalist who was an owner and also directed his own firm, and the simple "investor" who merely contributes his capital, there are crucial differences regarding the dynamics of the accumulation. For a while, these new modalities gave new impetus to capitalist development.

> For a hundred years the system worked, throughout Europe, with an extraordinary success and facilitated the growth of wealth on an unprecedented scale. To save and to invest became at once the duty and the delight of a large class. The savings were seldom drawn on, and, accumulating at compound interest, made possible the material triumphs which we now all take for granted. The morals, the politics, the literature, and the religion of the age joined in a grand conspiracy for the promotion of saving. God and Mammon were reconciled. Peace on earth to men of good means. A rich man could, after all, enter into the Kingdom of Heaven – if only he saved. A new harmony sounded from the celestial spheres.
>
> (Keynes, 1923: 7)

It will be seen that, given the division of the capitalist class into businessmen and investors, it becomes necessary to revisit some economic phenomena taking into account the differences between both sub-groups. In the *Tract*, Keynes focuses exclusively on the effects of the devaluation of money and the fall of prices on the capitalist class, a class now split into owners and managers. The weakness of the new system became apparent in the violent changes in currency value that came about after the First World War, the characteristics of which we will discuss later.

Meanwhile, in a context of absolute trust in *laissez-faire*, an ideology perpetuating the way in which capitalism had worked in the era of abundance had emerged. The profit obtained by the business class in inflation periods comes from two sources: on one hand, from the wealth lost by investors and creditors, as the purchasing power of their income disappears. If price increase is particularly high, debtors may even enjoy a negative rate of interest in real terms.

But the rise in prices is also advantageous for all the parties that obtain their earnings from production and trade. Inflation fills their pockets with windfall profit, originating in the artificial difference between the price paid for inputs and the higher price at which the product is finally sold. Profit grows effortlessly, on account of the mere passage of time. These are times of easy money but, in Keynes's view, precisely because this inflationary prosperity rests on "fictitious" earnings, it damages the social image of the businessman. The capitalist obtains an illegitimate benefit that bears no connection with his skills and effort. Return grows exclusively on account of monetary imbalances, and, always according to Keynes, businessmen lose their prestige, while capitalism is deprived of one of its most powerful ideological justifications. It becomes obvious that profit is not the result of the capitalist's effort or of his privation and sacrifice. A general increase in prices, although advantageous in the short run for some classes, should be avoided at all costs.

> To convert the businessman into the profiteer is to strike a blow at capitalism, because it destroys the psychological equilibrium which permits the perpetuance of unequal rewards. The economic doctrine of normal profits, vaguely apprehended by every one, is a necessary condition for the justification of capitalism. The businessman is only tolerable so long as his gains can be held to bear some relation to what, roughly and in some sense, his activities have contributed to society.
>
> (Keynes, 1923: 25–26)

Monetary imbalances thus provoke marked redistributive effects. The split into an investor class and a businessman class leaves the former in a situation of helplessness in the face of the loss of money's purchasing power: "We conclude that inflation redistributes wealth in a manner very injurious to the investor, very beneficial to the business man". As may be seen, if the capitalist class is approached as an undivided block, the true effects of inflation, that affects the different groups differently, cannot be seen.

While in the *Tract* Keynes studies the effects of changes in money purchasing power on the income of the different fractions of the capitalist class, in *The General Theory* he explores the consequences of this new arrangement on investment. We have seen that there is a particular sub-group within the capitalist class that risks their money but largely ignores the real business operation, in which they are not actively involved. So how are investment decisions taken when such split has finally been consummated?

The consequences of capital concentration

The discussion of the results of the structural modifications to the capitalist class takes on a more definite shape in *The General Theory*. In the *Tract*, the differential effect of changes in prices is analyzed, but now the focus is on a more central issue: the way in which the volume of investment is defined. In Chapter 12, a clear distinction is established between the old form of business organization and its new modalities; the general idea coincides with what had been put forward more than ten years before. The "old" way of investment decision-making rested on the identity of the active businessman and the capital owner. Both functions were combined in one individual who invested his own capital in a more or less impulsive fashion and, being in charge of the business, enjoyed the immediate benefits, as well as the prestige afforded by his success. The businessman lacked, in general, the means required to make a rational, moderately accurate calculation of his business economic prospects; however, he compensated for such lack with his individual fearlessness and his entrepreneurial spirit.

> Businessmen play a mixed game of skill and chance, the average results of which to the players are not known by those who take a hand. If human nature felt no temptation to take a chance, no satisfaction (profit apart) in constructing a factory, a railway, a mine or a farm, there might not be much investment merely as a result of cold calculation.
> (Keynes, 1939 [1936]: 150; IV.12.III)

The characterization remains unchanged, as the split of the capitalist class is described in the same terms as in the 1923 *Tract*. Only the names of the sub-groups are slightly modified: in other passages of *The General Theory*, the capitalists who receive a fixed income on their investments are called "rentier class", and those who effectively manage businesses are referred to as "business class". This divide is used to assess the consequences of different economic phenomena on classes. In Chapter 8, the redistributive results triggered by a change in nominal wages is discussed; Chapter 19 furthers the same discussion; in Chapter 20, when the classical quantitative theory of money is criticized, the conclusions contained in the *Tract* regarding the redistributive effects of price fluctuations are reiterated, thus exhibiting a clear consistence with regard to the previous views.

> Since that part of his profit which the entrepreneur has to hand on to the rentier is fixed in terms of money, rising prices, even though unaccompanied by any change in output, will redistribute incomes to the advantage of the entrepreneur and to the disadvantage of the rentier.
> (Keynes, 1939 [1936]: 290; V.20.III)

But it is in Chapter 12 where this divide becomes more relevant. This chapter studies in detail the changes stemming from the new configuration of businesses and the capitalist class regarding investment determination. Usually, Chapter 12 of *The General Theory* is considered to be a component totally unconnected to Keynes's argument and his explanations of the determination of the economic variables.

It is deemed to be a sort of eminently descriptive *excursus*. Such readings restrict themselves to emphasizing the unstable character of the system, tracing such instability to the nature of its financial institutions. In fact, Chapter 12 tends to be favored by those followers of Keynes's who show an "institutionalist" bias. However, such interpretation seems to be misguided. What Keynes intends to show in these passages is how the transformations that affected the features of the capitalist class resulting from capital concentration also modified how investment decisions are made in this new phase of capitalism characterized by a strong increase in the size of capital enterprises and, as a consequence, by the separation of ownership and management. It is not a question of a detour in the exposition; rather, on one hand, it should be taken as a further development of his earlier ideas on the deeper economic transformations and, on the other, the conclusions reached there appear strictly reflected in the construction of his "system". This is why it is inaccurate to argue that there is a lack of consistency between Chapter 11 of *The General Theory*, where how the investment volume is established is explained, and Chapter 12, where what has just been asserted would be qualified by the abrupt emergence of "financial" instability. It will be later seen that the ideas put forward in both chapters are consistent. This is a description of the specific historical basis supporting the particular way in which the investment volume is determined. Also, the mechanism involved is completely different from the one posited by the *classical theory*, bogged down in its attempts to continue backing up an outdated theory, associated with "private business of the old-fashioned type", not with twentieth-century capitalism.

> Decisions to invest in private business of the old-fashioned type were, however, decisions largely irrevocable, not only for the community as a whole, but also for the individual. With the separation between ownership and management which prevails to-day and with the development of organised investment markets, a new factor of great importance has entered in, which sometimes facilitates investment but sometimes adds greatly to the instability of the system. In the absence of security markets, there is no object in frequently attempting to revalue an investment to which we are committed. But the Stock Exchange revalues many investments every day and the revaluations give a frequent opportunity to the individual (though not to the community as a whole) to revise his commitments.
>
> (Keynes, 1939 [1936]: 150; IV.12.III)

Therefore, in this new stage, it is the investor class, and not the business class, who decides the investment volume. In the *Tract*, Keynes had already pointed out that the separation of ownership and management resulted in the emergence of several instruments that allowed one to delegate the effective control of the business without resigning ownership or to cede it for definite periods of time: common stock, preferred stock, bonds, mortgages, and obligations. The mechanism of old-time investment was, so to say, direct – the owner of the firm added new capital to the company he directed, and his contribution entailed an "irrevocable" commitment. In the last stage of capitalism – beginning in the twentieth century – decision-making concerning when, how much, and how a new investment is made is substantially modified. The different securities entitling their holder to receive a fixed or variable earning from an enterprise are bought and sold in the "organized investment markets". On this basis, the value of each business is redefined daily, and each investment is valued hourly, according to the price of the shares, the negotiable obligations etc. The first effect of such a transformation is that the investor may opt to buy a portion of an ongoing business, a perfectly viable operation that may be easily conducted on the stock exchange, instead of venturing to start up a new firm.[6] This is what Keynes is talking about when he says that investments are no longer "irrevocable" and "fixed". Through the purchase and sale of these instruments, all investments, even if involving the acquisition of machinery and fixed assets, are, for the investor, "liquid".

> But the daily revaluations of the Stock Exchange, though they are primarily made to facilitate transfers of old investments between one individual and another, inevitably exert a decisive influence on the rate of current investment. For there is no sense in building up a new enterprise at a cost greater than that at which a similar existing enterprise can be purchased; whilst there is an inducement to spend on a new project what may seem an extravagant sum, if it can be floated off on the Stock Exchange at an immediate profit. Thus certain classes of investment are governed by the average expectation of those who deal on the Stock Exchange as revealed in the price of shares, rather than by the genuine expectations of the professional entrepreneur.
>
> (Keynes, 1939 [1936]: 150; IV.12.III)

Next, Keynes remarks and discusses in detail the high level of volatility of stock prices when they are ruled by factors other than the genuine return on investments. The point is that the price of the papers openly and massively traded on the stock exchange cannot reflect but the state of the expectations regarding profits that are not based on the performance of the business itself but on the fluctuations of the stock prices. Before studying the predominantly speculative aspect that imbues the process of investing in this new stage of capitalism, we wish to point out the most relevant change in regards to how investment decisions are taken. The theory must necessarily reflect this new modality through its analytical constructs, and not reflect that of the old-fashioned type businesses, where the individual capitalist managed his firm, was its owner and made the decisions concerning the widening of his capital. The existence of an investor class that does not assume an irrevocable commitment to an enterprise, coupled with the permanent revaluation of businesses on the stock exchange allow the capitalists to get involved and withdraw from firms. Investments in fixed capital become, as we pointed out, "liquid" as investors can buy and sell their participation at any moment. Thus, the investments that are "fixed" for the community become "liquid" for the individual.

The *classical theory*, particularly its marginalist strand, has always considered that the ability to represent, albeit in a simplified way, the behavior of individuals represents one of its major theoretical strong points and one of its distinctive traits. This is what today is called "micro-foundations", i.e. explaining all sorts of phenomena in terms of rational individual behavior.

But, according to Keynes, the agent who makes investment decisions is not the one who the *classical theory* claims she or he is, and, even worse, the individual who actually invests pursues other goals than those identified.

In the (Neo)classical capital market, the investment demand curve corresponding to firms shows a negative slope relative to capital return, represented by interest rates. This inverse relationship between the incentive to invest and the capital reward stems, in turn, from the maximization of benefits: for each factor of production, the optimal volume to hire is that for which the reward equals its marginal product. According to this explanation, the agent who decides upon and performs the investment act is the business, embodied in the individual entrepreneur, its owner. But this is, precisely, what Keynes challenges with his criticism: the *classical theory* does not depict the actual investment process as it occurs in the new stage of capitalism. Beyond the mismatch between the account offered by the *classical theory* and the facts, Keynes develops a critique of the classical theory of the rate of interest, of investment, and of capital that will be expounded in Chapter 3. We will not discuss now the account offered by Keynes in replacement for the one provided by the classical authors; for the time being, we will focus on how is the investment volume decided upon when the capitalist class is divided into two sub-groups. Investors are not active businessmen but owners of certain mass of money in exchange for which they wish to obtain a future return.

With that aim, they go to the organized investment market and calculate the probable yield of a particular investment, equivalent to the relationship between the price paid for the stock and the discounted expected future income; this calculation has all the limitations we have already pointed out. To decide if buying an "investment", represented by the offered stock, is convenient or not, the investor compares its future yield with the current monetary interest rate. He may then buy the title to an ongoing business entity, contribute capital for a new business, or else buy bonds or make a bank deposit. He may also choose to save otherwise and retain his money until he finds the rate of interest or the return on investments attractive. But as regards the decision to invest, if the rate of interest surpasses the rate of expected return, the investment will not be made. When the split of the capitalist class into investors and businessmen is taken into account, all these options become available.

> So long as it is open to the individual to employ his wealth in hoarding or lending *money*, the alternative of purchasing actual capital assets cannot be rendered sufficiently attractive (especially to the man who does not manage the capital assets and knows very little about them), except by organising markets wherein these assets can be easily realised for money.
>
> (Keynes, 1939 [1936]: 160–161; IV.12.VI)

When representing the "market of capital purchase and sale", the *classical theory* does not display the set of options actually available to the investor. The fact is that if it did, it should accept that the decision to invest does not stem from the maximization of benefits of the individual capitalist, nor of the comparison between the physical marginal productivity of capital as a *productive* factor – determined by the function of production with diminishing returns – and its reward. For the classicists, there is only one way of investing: that of the businessman hiring the services of new capital equipment. But, even worse, *since the emergence of the rentier, it may neither be asserted that every act of saving will bring about, in turn, an equivalent act of investment: now, the "agents" who make investment decisions are not the ones who "save"*. Savings and investment become equal, but it is not the push of savings that causes an equivalent increase in investment. The rentier has several options to maintain his wealth, so that he is not forced to buy new equipment of productive capital. The *classical theory* cannot reflect the conditions prevailing in the twentieth century. Keynes, in turn, after identifying these changes, sets out to build a theory that is appropriate for the new situation.

Besides, this novel investment mechanics deepens the uncertainty surrounding decisions to purchase new capital equipment, i.e. the "actual" act of investing. The level of volatility is heightened due to the extreme liquidity of the titles traded on the stock exchange. The investor does not manage his own business, but rather buys ownership titles. Stock prices and not the originally invested amount come to be the indicators used to estimate the expected return.

And there still remain to be studied the numerous instability factors that affect business stock prices and, through them, return calculations and, therefore, investment volumes. This chain of uncertainty particularly affects investments in large businesses with long maturity periods. Movements in expected return play a crucial role across the entire economic system, as they are involved in the decisions to risk capital taken by the investor class.

As may be seen, when looking closely at the actual process involved in making new investments, the dramatic consequences of the capitalist class split become evident. The investor, apart from investing in a new business, may buy the titles to an ongoing firm. Stock prices are set daily on the market. Keynes wonders what the principles ruling the price of ongoing businesses' shares as determined on the stock exchange are. The price of a business should reflect its potential to generate future benefits. However, he concludes that it is in fact impossible to mathematically calculate, on objective bases, the profit that a business will really yield. Naturally, the uncertainty regarding the future is heightened by the term involved in the calculation. This is an insurmountable obstacle in the system, as there is not, nor will there ever be, certain knowledge concerning the future, and the future is involved in every decision to invest.

> The outstanding fact is the extreme precariousness of the basis of knowledge on which our estimates of prospective yield have to be made. Our knowledge of the factors which will govern the yield of an investment some years hence is usually very slight and often negligible. If we speak frankly, we have to admit that our basis of knowledge for estimating the yield ten years hence of a railway, a copper mine, a textile factory, the goodwill of a patent medicine, an Atlantic liner, a building in the City of London amounts to little and sometimes to nothing; or even five years hence. In fact, those who seriously attempt to make any such estimate are often so much in the minority that their behaviour does not govern the market.
>
> (Keynes, 1939 [1936]: 149–150; IV.12.III)

The problem of the lack of definitive knowledge on the future is, in fact, inevitable, and becomes a factor of error and also of instability regarding the demand of capital assets. Investment decisions will always involve a proportion of irrationality. What happens in this new stage of capitalism is that the share of uncertainty is heightened because investment liquidity is far greater.

> We are merely reminding ourselves that human decisions affecting the future, whether personal or political or economic, cannot depend on strict mathematical expectation, since the basis for making such calculations does not exist.
>
> (Keynes, 1939 [1936]: 162–163; IV.12.VII)

Therefore, the expansion of the organized markets where "investments" are traded ends up strengthening instability, as those who try to make a careful estimation of future returns based on the available information are a very small proportion of all the investors, so that their opinions are not what rules stock prices. The vast majority of participants in the investments market are almost completely ignorant of the nature and prospects of the actual businesses, so that instead of depending on expectations based on facts and calculations regarding the evolution of enterprises' earnings, the value of the firms ends up relying on mere convention. Therefore, the total volume of investment fluctuates but it is also negatively affected, since it is not possible to estimate the actual benefits, and given the conditions of this new capitalist stage, there are many who do not even attempt to invest.

> For if there exist organised investment markets and if we can rely on the maintenance of the convention, an investor can legitimately encourage himself with the idea that the only risk he runs is that of a genuine change in the news *over the near future*, as to the likelihood of which he can attempt to form his own judgment, and which is unlikely to be very large [. . .] It has been, I am sure, on the basis of some such procedure as this that our leading investment markets have been developed. But it is not surprising that a convention, in an absolute view of things so arbitrary, should have its weak points. It is its precariousness which creates no small part of our contemporary problem of securing sufficient investment.
>
> (Keynes, 1939 [1936]: 153; IV.12.IV)

As a result of these circumstances, the value of companies' stocks becomes independent of their actual condition and prospects, and turns into a mainly conventional, therefore arbitrary, value. Detachment from the actual yield of the business is compounded by a series of factors, all of them associated with the expansion of the organized markets of investment. This is a process that feeds back on itself: large corporations concentrate the savings of broad sectors of society so that investors are increasingly distanced from the knowledge of how is productive activity determined.

> As a result of the gradual increase in the proportion of the equity in the community's aggregate capital investment which is owned by persons who do not manage and have no special knowledge of the circumstances, either actual or prospective, of the business in question, the element of real knowledge in the valuation of investments by whose who own them or contemplate purchasing them has seriously declined.
>
> (Keynes, 1939 [1936]: 153; IV.12.V)

Gradually, the determination of the market price of corporations is dominated by a mass of investors ignorant of the mechanisms that drive businesses and incapable of predicting their actual performance. From this situation stem the marked fluctuations originated by trivial events. Therefore, certain conventions divorced from reality, which investors believe to be valid, end up prevailing. And no matter how capricious such perceptions may be, their outcome is validated in practice, as long as these perceptions are maintained over time they work as self-fulfilling prophesies. But the framework on which businesses rest is exceptionally fragile.

> A conventional valuation which is established as the outcome of the mass psychology of a large number of ignorant individuals is liable to change violently as the result of a sudden fluctuation of opinion due to factors which do not really make much difference to the prospective yield; since there will be no strong roots of conviction to hold it steady.
>
> (Keynes, 1939 [1936]: 154; IV.12.V)

It is true that most investors are ignorant of the real situation of the businesses. It could be thought, however, that a certain degree of rationality might be contributed by professional investors who, in spite of being few, could exert some influence that would be heightened by their prestige and recognition. If this were the case, the system would be guarded from the mood swings that are as unfounded as they are sudden. Keynes considers, however, that the very same dynamics of the way in which investments and business value are determined drives the experts to act in a peculiar and no less detrimental manner.

> It might have been supposed that competition between expert professionals, possessing judgment and knowledge beyond that of the average private investor, would correct the vagaries of the ignorant individual left to himself. It happens, however, that the energies and skill of the professional investor and speculator are mainly occupied otherwise. For most of these persons are, in fact, largely concerned, not with making superior long-term forecasts of the probable yield of an investment over its whole life, but with foreseeing changes in the conventional basis of valuation a short time ahead of the general public.
>
> (Keynes, 1939 [1936]: 154; IV.12.V)

Instead of correcting, smoothing and contributing rationality to the private market of investments, experts' behavior compounds instability. Professional investors focus on anticipating the capricious movement of securities, which in turn are determined by the malleable and unfounded psychology of the masses: they seek to obtain large gains by accurately predicting short-term fluctuations; they are concerned with moving ahead of the opinions of the masses that rule the value of investments (to "beat the gun", "guess better than the crowd how the crowd will behave"). Even when they do not try to predict the movement of the prices ruled by the majority of uninformed investors, professional investors may compete among themselves: some of them will obtain benefits while others will lose their fortune (Keynes illustrates this behavior with his well-known examples of the musical chairs game and the newspaper beauty contest).

> The social object of skilled investment should be to defeat the dark forces of time and ignorance which envelop our future. The actual, private object of the most skilled investment to-day is 'to beat the gun', as the Americans so well express it, to outwit the crowd, and to pass the bad, or depreciating, half-crown to the other fellow.
>
> (Keynes, 1939 [1936]: 155; IV.12.V)

In sum, on account of all the aforementioned factors, this new stage of capitalism is characterized by high volatility in the value of investments, represented by the different kinds of negotiable securities in organized markets. These securities are bought by a large mass of investors who know nothing about the actual condition and prospects of the businesses involved – securities' prices do not reflect returns. Professional investors, in turn, who are qualified to analyze the actual situation and viability of the different investments, devote themselves to *speculation* rather than to *entrepreneurial* activity. Securities' value bears direct influence on investment decisions and return estimates, but their determination is dominated by speculation. This is a product of historical change, particularly, of the increasing concentration of capital.

> If I may be allowed to appropriate the term *speculation* for the activity of forecasting the psychology of the market, and the term *enterprise* for the activity of forecasting the prospective yield of assets over their whole life, it is by no means always the case that speculation predominates over enterprise. As the organisation of investment markets improves, the risk of the predominance of speculation does, however, increase. [. . .] Speculators may do no harm as bubbles on a steady stream of enterprise. But the position is serious when enterprise becomes the bubble on a whirlpool of speculation.
>
> (Keynes, 1939 [1936]: 158–159; IV.12.VI)

As has already been mentioned, in Keynes's view, however, this is merely a transitory stage. To conclude this section, we still have to review his opinions regarding the future evolution of investment markets. What by now is quite evident is that Keynes makes the recommendations associated with the ideology of *laissez-faire* somehow responsible for the tolerance of speculation and, therefore, of investment volatility, whose result may well be private profit but never ensuring social welfare (similar arguments were put forward in "The end of *laissez-faire*", 1926).

> When the capital development of a country becomes a by-product of the activities of a casino, the job is likely to be ill-done. The measure of success attained by Wall Street, regarded as an institution of which the proper social purpose is to direct new investment into the most profitable channels in terms of future yield, cannot be claimed as one of the outstanding triumphs of *laissez-faire* capitalism, which is not surprising, if I am right in thinking that the best brains of Wall Street have been in fact directed towards a different object.
>
> (Keynes, 1939 [1936]: 159; IV.12.VI)

What has been stated so far suffices to show in what aspects, resulting from the mentioned historical transformation, the *classical theory* fails when attempting to model investment decisions. Those aspects require a theoretical reframing that will need to be reflected in the system built by Keynes. But the stage of capitalism that Keynes attempts to portray is, in his view, as has already been mentioned, a stage that is also transitory. In "Economic Possibilities for our Grandchildren", he argued that the concentration of capital, the multiplication of monopolies, was equivalent to a spontaneous "socialization" of businesses. In *The General Theory*, after describing the uncertainty surrounding long-term investment decisions, he mentions "certain important factors which somewhat mitigate in practice the effects of our ignorance of the future". Such factors foster long-term investment, which otherwise fluctuates and wanes, subjected to the whims of the private speculative markets. They are:

1   In large real estate investment undertakings, the risk is transferred to or shared between the investor and the occupier by means of long-term contracts.
2   In the case of public utilities, monopoly privileges and the right to charge rates that will ensure the obtainment of certain minimum level of benefits guarantee a proportion of the prospective yield.
3   The state takes directly on a significant proportion of large investments "which are frankly influenced in making the investment by a general presumption of there being prospective social advantages from the investment, whatever its commercial yield may prove to be within a wide range, and without seeking to be satisfied that the mathematical expectation of the yield is at least equal to the current rate of interest" (Keynes, 1939 [1936]: 163; IV.12.VIII).

These are "natural trends" resulting from this new phase. A greater state involvement in investment, as is pointed out in 2 and 3, is supported by its larger protagonism in society's savings. The socialization of investment puts the state center stage, both as an investment guarantor and as a savings vehicle.

> Apart from the savings accumulated by individuals, there is also the large amount of income, varying perhaps from one-third to two-thirds of the total accumulation in a modern industrial community such as Great Britain or the United States, which is withheld by central and local government, by institutions and by business corporations.
>
> (Keynes, 1939 [1936]: 108; III.9.I)

In brief, Keynes maintained his previous beliefs, shaping them more accurately in *The General Theory*, where they translate into an explanation of how comes the amount of aggregate saving and investment to be determined in this new stage. These decisions do not originate in the psychology of the individual saver that demands a reward for his wait, or in the convenience of the individual business taking into account the additional earnings produced by capital's physical productivity. Rather, the determination of investment now involves phenomena linked to the "mass psychology" of the investors, whose perceptions are reflected by the organized investment markets.

The new system, in turn, is strongly marked by speculation whose powerlessness to spontaneously support significant long-term investments, independently of their actual prospects and social convenience, assigns a key role to the state – in its hands is placed a large proportion of social savings and the capacity to promote major undertakings. The principle of *laissez-faire* and its optimistic predictions based on the virtues of the pursuit of individual benefit fail in a context that has experienced a radical transformation.

IV Working class transformations: collective bargaining

Keynes and the modern history of the labor movement

In 1923's *Tract on Monetary Reform*, Keynes argued that there are two main classes to be considered when studying society: the owners' class and the salaried class. In the *Tract*, he remarks,

> The organisation of certain classes of labour – railwaymen, miners, dockers, and others – for the purpose of securing wage increases is better than it was.
>
> (Keynes, 1923: 27)

The *classical theory* and the ideology of *laissez-faire* share a blind trust in the free operation of markets, which acts as a mechanism that guarantees an adjustment towards full employment. As early as 1925, Keynes makes his first observations regarding the consequences of global changes over workers' lifestyles and organization. Since the early twentieth century, the labor class resolutely advanced towards the consolidation of their own trade unions and national policies. Trade unions took charge of wage negotiations, a highly significant change, as negotiating wage levels became a collective not individual affair for workers. The struggle over workers' labor conditions thus became a national issue.

> The idea of the old-world party, that you can, for example, alter the value of money and then leave the consequential adjustments to be brought about by the forces of supply and demand, belongs to the days of fifty or a hundred years ago when Trade Unions were powerless, and when the economic Juggernaut was allowed to crash along the highway of Progress without obstruction and even with applause.
>
> (Keynes, 1925: 337)

In post-war England – which was then undergoing a protracted period of economic stagnation – the renewed and unprecedented power of the workers assembled in their own organizations allowed trade unions to have an impact on national politics. During the first years after the war, there were successive strikes and a few uprisings. Later on, however, the Labor Party, which had initially been supported by trade unions, grew rapidly and it soon found itself in a previously unimaginable situation: it came to power, thus succeeding in overcoming the historical alternation between Liberals and Conservatives. Undoubtedly, no observer of this period could fail to notice such a development: things had radically changed since the times of Smith and Ricardo, when workers had practically no institutions of their own; most of the time such institutions were banned, and the efforts aimed at creating them were persecuted by law enforcement. This is not the place to delve into the history of the British working class; suffice to say that between 1890 and 1927, trade unions developed into actors with direct involvement in wage negotiations. This mutation is precisely what Keynes noticed as, according to his view, the unprecedented progress in the organization of the labor movement and the emergence of new roles for its organizations are also typical traits of this new economic stage.

> [N]ot only the facts, but public opinion also, have moved a long distance away in the direction of Professor Commons's epoch of Stabilisation. The Trade Unions are strong enough to interfere with the free play

of the forces of supply and demand, and Public Opinion, albeit with a grumble and with more than a suspicion that the Trade Unions are growing dangerous, supports the Trade Unions in their main contention.

(Keynes, 1925: 336; emphasis added)

The economic theory inherited by Keynes could not represent this new situation. The *classical theory* posits that nominal (and real) wages are set in the labor market as a result of the reciprocal action of supply and demand. Supply and demand reflect the optimal decisions of both individual workers and firms. In the early 1920s, Keynes begins to point out that by massively joining trade unions, onto which they delegate wage bargaining, workers can hinder this mechanism. When supply is not balanced by demand, it is expected that in any market the automatic economic forces meant to restore equilibrium will be triggered. From this point of view, every time trade unions manage to raise wages to a level surpassing that where supply becomes equal to demand, the ensuing situation would be considered an instance of disequilibrium. Implicit in this representation is the belief that, in practice, certain automatic tendencies should push back wages down towards their resting position, and that these actual and effective forces will not be at rest until they have reduced real wage. In fact, this is the only way of including trade unions in the marginalist economic theory – as a distortion that causes market disequilibrium.

Classical theory, unionization and Keynesian theory

In the explanation provided by the *classical theory*, wages fall as a result of the decisions of individual workers who will be willing to offer more hours of work as long as the marginal "disutility" of labor is less than wage utility.[7] If the wage more than compensates for the sacrifice of working, *individual workers will be willing to reduce their wages and work longer.* This is why, according to the *classical theory*, employment is increased by reducing wages, thus "solving" unemployment, that is, the excess of labor supply offered. Therefore, the adjustment occurs only and exclusively because individual employed and unemployed workers accept to work at a wage that is lower than the current one. In Keynes's words, this time taken from *The General Theory*:

> The postulate that there is a tendency for the real wage to come to equality with the marginal disutility of labour clearly presumes that labour itself is in a position to decide the real wage for which it works, though not the quantity of employment forthcoming at this wage.
>
> (Keynes, 1939 [1936]: 10; I.2.II)

For the classical labor market to act as the "locus" where the determination of wages and employment is decided upon, the behavior attributed to the individual worker must be generalized to the working class as a whole. The individual worker must have the intention and, also, the possibility to reduce his wage every time he is unemployed (or underemployed). The wage being cut should not be taken to be exclusively his individual wage, but the wage current in the economy as a whole, that is:

> The classical conclusions are intended, it must be remembered, to apply to the whole body of labour and do not mean merely that a single individual can get employment by accepting a cut in money-wages which his fellows refuse.
>
> (Keynes, 1939 [1936]: 11; I.2.II)

The gist of the argument lies, once again, in the *classical theory's* unmediated transition from the representation of individual will and behavior to the representation of collective behavior. It has already been mentioned that the *classical theory* explains investment based on the identification of individual businessman and investor, and inferring therefrom the determination of investment as a whole. In the case of wage and employment determination, the direct aggregation of individual behaviors assumed by the *classical theory* may be supported in two different ways.

One possibility is to think that each worker behaves as he does individually, without any interference or interaction with the rest of the workers, in an atomistic competitive market. If this is the case, the behavior of the whole is identical to the simple aggregation of individual behaviors. The other option is replacing the labor class with a "representative worker" displaying the same behavior as an individual laborer. But, whatever the option chosen, *classical theory* excludes the possibility that the workers will usually act in conjunction. This would imply that the situation of the rest of the workers became a parameter in the function of individual utility or even that the wage should be taken into account in the same function, leading to unsolvable formal problems: the functions of individual utility cannot include either somebody else's utility or any price. For in that case, the behavior of the working class regarding wage determination, dropping out of work and willingness to work could not be deduced, by analogy, from the behavior of the individual worker. But the actual behavior of workers in the new economic stage prevents the identification of an isolated laborer and the labor class as if they were one and the same subject. Specifically, the *classical theory* does not take into account labor class solidarity as displayed in their organizations, solidarity that *bears no resemblance whatsoever to strictly individual behavior*. Moreover, when mentioned, workers' solidarity and their collective action are compared to a "monopsony", ignoring its specificities. It would thus seem that the power of trade unions would not derive from the changes underwent by the economic organization, but that it was nothing but an expedient alliance of interests among the sellers of the same merchandise. In any case, it is not a question of ethics but of reflecting the new reality of labor.

If, as Keynes argues, trade unions can effectively and permanently interfere in the workings of the market, the adjustment of the classical labor market will never occur: it is no use forecasting it, criticizing workers for unionizing or, even, waiting for such an adjustment to simply take place. The fact is that workers no longer make individual decisions, observing the utility function that best reflects their tastes to determine whether they accept a wage cut. The "normal operation" of the economy is another, and very different. It is furthermore not a situation of transitory disequilibrium, where the same known laws are operating, albeit hindered or retarded by a circumstantial hindrance. The solution is drastic – discarding the market as the "analytic locus" where wages and level of employment are determined to replace it with other account suitable to the new historical situation. This will be one of the main targets of *The General Theory*.

As may be seen, Keynes offers again the same diagnosis: the problem does not lie in that the *classical theory* is abstractly mistaken, but that it has become inadequate in the face of historical development. In the nineteenth century, there prevailed a situation that "is rightly described as due to a balance of forces in an age when individual groups of employers were strong enough to prevent the wage unit form rising much faster than the efficiency of production". This description is at odds, however, with the conditions of the new stage where the labor class has become organized at national level and defines its wages collectively. Now the value of the nominal wage is set by "*the bargains reached between employers and employed*", while the real wage is determined by "other forces" of the economic system unrelated to the disutility perceived by the individual worker when devoting his time to work instead of leisure.

> There may exist no expedient by which labour as a whole can reduce its real wage to a *given figure by making revised money bargains with the entrepreneurs*. This will be our contention. We shall endeavour to show that primarily it is certain other forces which determine the general level of real wages. The attempt to elucidate this problem will be one of our main themes. We shall argue that there has been a fundamental misunderstanding of how in this respect the economy in which we live actually works.
>
> (Keynes, 1939 [1936]: 13; I.2.II; emphasis added)

The *classical theory* assumed that the aggregation of the optimal decisions of individual workers inevitably pushed the nominal wage towards
a position of equilibrium. At the same time, as money's purchasing power
is assumed to be, primarily, constant, this same mechanism was used to
describe movements in real wages. From there stemmed the *classical theory's* prescriptions to address unemployment. Reality, however, rebuts these
accounts, one after the other. In the light of the 1930s, the *classical theory*
casts ridicule upon itself when it tries to give account of unemployment.

> [T]he contention that the unemployment which characterises a depres-
> sion is due to a refusal by labour to accept a reduction of money-wages
> is not clearly supported by the facts. It is not very plausible to assert
> that unemployment in the United States in 1932 was due either to
> labour obstinately refusing to accept a reduction of money-wages or
> to its obstinately demanding a real wage beyond what the productivity
> of the economic machine was capable of furnishing. Wide variations
> are experienced in the volume of employment without any apparent
> change either in the minimum real demands of labour or in its pro-
> ductivity. Labour is not more truculent in the depression than in the
> boom – far from it. Nor is its physical productivity less. These facts
> from experience are a prima facie ground for questioning the adequacy
> of the classical analysis.
>
> (Keynes, 1939 [1936]: 9; I.2.II)

As opposed to the *classical theory, Keynes's system* must be capable of
reflecting the following circumstances:

1   The current nominal wage is set by means of the negotiations between
    trade unions and entrepreneurs; it is not a result of individual will (of
    labor disutility).
2   The real wage cannot be set by a contract.

V Transformations in the monetary system: the incongruity between classical monetary theory and reality

Tract on monetary reform

Before publishing *The General Theory*, Keynes was already recognized as
an expert in a particular branch of economic analysis – monetary theory.
In his previous theoretical works, 1923's *Tract on Monetary Reform* and
1930's *Treatise on Money*, he had studied the "monetary issues" that during
the first years of the twentieth century were in an unusual state of turmoil.

In this field, as in his observations on the situation of the labor class and the capitalist class, he sought to show that the economic reality had experienced a definitive transformation, while the theory had remained, instead, frozen, portraying the features of an age that had already ended. Keynes's procedure is therefore different from the frequent "transhistorical" comparison of several theories.

To understand a particular current of thought in depth, it is crucial to characterize, first, the evolutionary stages which the society is undergoing, rather than analyzing it on its own terms testing its consistency to compare it later with "competing" contemporary or subsequent theories.[8] In this way, each theory becomes linked to a specific economic period. The first question that should be addressed when approaching a theory is establishing, first and foremost, whether the explanations it offers are anachronistic, that is, whether its premises conform to the essential features of the economic process it intends to describe. Keynes tests the *classical theory* in this way, and the results he obtains suggest that, relative to the society of his time, the orthodoxy does not meet the aforementioned requirement in various respects. That is also the case regarding the classical school's monetary theory.

Next, we will explore the two works on monetary theory published by Keynes before *The General Theory*, to trace his gradual distancing from the *classical theory* resulting from the incongruity between this theory and the new economic stage.

The first of these is the *Tract on Monetary Reform*, written during the first post-war period and published in 1923, a time when European economies experienced strong inflationary processes. National currencies suffered an extraordinary sudden loss in their capacity to represent value. Yet, that was not all: some European countries overcame the marked inflation only to fall into a deep deflationary abyss. In such a context of unprecedented monetary episodes, it is obvious that a theory, such as the classical, that assumes the "value" of money to be constant, is not able to make substantial contributions to address the practical and conceptual problems of its times.

The argument put forward by Keynes in the *Tract* displays his first attempts to reflect the deep economic changes that were affecting the monetary sphere by means of a theory, which is still essentially classical, yet modified to some extent. It is the mismatch between the premises of the traditional theory and the most salient features of the new historical stage that provides the initial impetus to cut adrift from the classical explanations. Yet, as will be seen, it's one thing to pinpoint an incongruity and even denounce it; it's a very different and more sensitive one to articulate a new and complete theoretical explanation. To do so, it is crucial to trace all the consequences of such changes, both the obvious and the hidden, exploring all the corners of the economic theory and providing a whole new set of interconnected explanations. Furthermore, a question is, besides, raised: is it enough to replace a segment of the theory or should the review reach to its very foundations? Keynes drifted gradually away from the *classical theory*. Monetary theory is the field where this gradual distancing may be more easily detected, step by step, as the sequence constituted by the three works regularly published every seven years, approximately – *Tract, Treatise, General Theory* – left written evidence of Keynes's intellectual trajectory.

Even Keynes himself contributed to the portrayal of this evolution; aware of and satisfied with his own progress, he makes explicit reference to his new ideas in each book, pointing out what has already been achieved and what remains to be done. It would seem that during the gestation period, different elements were being collected until finally, in *The General Theory*, the resolute and defiant emancipation from the orthodoxy is carried out.

The imperfect correspondence between reality and theory is plainly reported at the very beginning of the *Tract*. It is there argued that the novel forms that the monetary phenomena have adopted are historically unprecedented. This accelerated rate of transformation manifests itself in the incongruity between actual phenomena and the premises and tenets of the monetary theory: "Events in the world of money move fast, but it does not follow that principles shift as quickly" (Keynes, 1923).

Thus, the same point made regarding investment and wages is now repeated in the sphere of money: the world has changed, but theory has not been able to keep up with it. To what changes is Keynes now referring? The historical break is located once again in 1914. Until then, the value standard had been relatively stable, albeit with interruptions. Since the outbreak of the First World War, the path followed by money's purchasing power in different countries began to enter into a period with strong turbulence.

> The fluctuations in the value of money since 1914 have been on a scale so great as to constitute, with all that they involve, one of the most significant events in the economic history of the modern world. The fluctuation of the standard, whether gold, silver, or paper, has not only been of unprecedented violence, but has been visited on a society of which the economic organisation is more dependent than that of any earlier epoch on the assumption that the standard of value would be moderately stable.
>
> (Keynes, 1923: 2)

Not only had the economic organization grown accustomed to trusting in the stability of currency value, but also the theory became a mirror image of the firmness of the general pattern of prices.[9] It could be said that the relative stability of the general level of prices – the opposite of money's purchasing power – had made the assumption *reasonable* until then, but the events of the early twentieth century shattered that image. It is true that the *classical theory* intended to unravel the causes and consequences of price fluctuations, in works specifically devoted to the subject of money. Yet, those explanations were provided in a book that was independent of the main body of theory, *precisely* because strong devaluations and revaluations were taken to be exceptional sporadic events. The monetary history of post-war Europe turned these violent exceptional fluctuations into the rule.

The extreme case is the German post-war hyperinflation, but even excluding that exception, fluctuations were violent in all countries. What might be the cause of this novel price behavior? Responsibility seemed to lie, first, in the monetary regime itself. In fact, the global collapse of the gold standard was believed to have triggered the inflationary episodes. With the outbreak of First World War, countries were forced to abandon the convertibility of their national currencies into gold, leaving their rates of exchange to float. No doubt, the *classical theory* had been built for a world operating under the gold standard. If convertibility was suspended during a certain period, this was considered to be an exceptional, anomalous situation that should be urgently corrected.

> Most academic treatises on monetary theory have been based, until lately, on so firm a presumption of a gold standard regime that they need to be adapted to the existing regime of mutually inconvertible paper standards.
>
> (Keynes, 1923: 71)

This was not the first time that in England – the global financial center – the British pound's convertibility was being interrupted. However, the heated debate over the advantages and disadvantages of the gold standard was abruptly finished when, in 1931, the world crisis forced the government to devaluate the pound once again, abandoning the official parity.[10] And this was the last time it had to – England would never again return to the convertibility of the pound into gold. Beyond passionate stances, the gold standard had naturally died.

Gold and the value of money

In its First Treatise on value and distribution (Chapter 2 will discuss its content), the *classical theory* posited the assumption that money's purchasing power is constant. Keynes admits that this assumption was, to a certain extent, accurate, as it was supported by the reality of its times. However, the same assumption could not be held in the *Tract*, a work meant, precisely, to explain the causes and consequences of the marked fluctuations of money's purchasing power. In 1923, Keynes attempted not only to reflect a new reality but also to identify what economic circumstances had changed leading to deep fluctuations in the value of currency that had never been seen until then.

The innovations as compared to the *classical theory* put forward in the *Tract* – which are several – may be considered attempts to reframe the monetary theory, dispensing with the gold standard or rather considering the case of the gold standard as a mere instance in the context of a more *general* explanation of monetary phenomena.

However, the break with orthodoxy is still far from complete. At every step, as much in the way the author expresses himself as in the nature of the explanations offered, a classical inspiration of which he had not completely freed himself may still be perceived. The *Tract* will also be his first attempt to break the dualism displayed by the theories of money of the First and the Second treatises, that is, of *leaving* the Ricardian marginalist *nest* of the *classical theory*.

During the almost entire century, from 1826 until the outbreak of the war, there had been observed a relative stability in money's purchasing power. Prices showed variations no greater than 30 percent. On this basis, commodity money, that is, gold – or the gold convertible paper money replacing it in its circulation functions – achieved a "good reputation". In the long period of "monetary peace", gold circulated physically or replaced by notes, and the prices were relatively stable, which resulted in the natural incorporation of commodity money and the assumption of price stability to theoretical explanations. It seemed that the gold standard should not be considered one of the possible monetary systems, an option among others – convertibility was the rule, and its abandonment a mere accident. The *classical theory of money* thus transformed the direct circulation of gold or of freely convertible notes in the *general* case, but history would show that it was actually a *particular case*, a mere "possibility" conditioned by certain circumstances that should be identified.

> The metal *gold* might not possess all the theoretical advantages of an artificially regulated standard, but it could not be tampered with and had proved reliable in practice.
>
> (Keynes, 1923: 12)

This practical trust became fossilized in science, and came to be an assumption of the theory. The *classical theory* was then divided into two separate bodies or Treatises: one studied value and distribution; the other, money. In the First Treatise of the *classical theory*, the role of money was always represented by a commodity, generally gold.[11] Through its embodiment in gold, money had a utility derived from its physical traits at the inception of the analysis. The money typical of the First Treatise circulated having its own "intrinsic value", based on its own normal price determined by its production cost.

A contradiction thus emerged: money as such did not seem to have any other utility than that derived from its purchasing power; however, gold, which served as money, had utility in itself as well as "intrinsic value". Therefore, money only worked as a *value standard*, but it was not required for any other use, not even as *means of circulation*. The First Treatise overlooked this contradiction, which was "solved" when in the Second Treatise on money – not before, the *classical theory* took an interest in the determination of the volume of money in actual circulation. It would stumble then with the problem of the "double utility" of gold-money because, on one hand, it was demanded as gold to be directly used in production and consumption, being a precious metal, but on the other, it was specifically required in its role as money, as a medium of exchange to conduct all transactions. In brief, the commodity money or gold-money involved major problems that the theory would ignore or turn into contradictions between the First Treatise on value and the Second Treatise on money.

In the *Tract*, Keynes points out that the (definitive, in his view) fall of convertibility would allow the theory to free itself from the uncomfortable burden of the double utility of commodity money. The new historical situation enabled the monetary theory rid itself of this contradiction that troubled the *classical theory* and was a possible cause of its explanations being included in two separate treatises. A new monetary theory would be freed from the usual difficulty involved in establishing commodity money as a starting point for the analysis, to show subsequently that gold could be "substituted" in circulation by valueless notes, and to consider, finally, the possibility that paper money might not need the tutelage of gold to circulate. In the *Tract*, Keynes does not yet mention the contradictions incurred in by his predecessors but simply refers to the complications faced by the classical monetary theory until that point.

In contrast to the usual expositions, Keynes's does not take as its starting point commodity-money, i.e. gold, but being more general, it seeks to consider gold circulation as a particular case of circulation in general.[12] This is a completely new approach; let's see its results.

First, the demand of money comes to play a dominant role in determining bills' purchasing power. Paper money now has only *indirect utility*, no "intrinsic value" but just "purchasing power". Its demand originates, then, exclusively from the need to conduct purchase and sale transactions, not in the use of this commodity-money in production or consumption. How is the supply of currency in circulation determined and what relationship does it have with the "value" of money?

In its Second Treatise, the *classical theory* linked the amount of money in circulation to its purchasing power through the quantitative theory. In the

Tract, Keynes still endorses this theory, though introducing, as will be seen, certain nuances into the explanation to make it suitable for the new facts. The Cambridge version of the quantitative theory – developed by Marshall and afterwards disseminated by Pigou – assumed that the level of output was a given and argued that the habits of the people regarding the use of money also defined a fixed proportion between real income and that which was to be kept in cash. Thus, once the *classical theory* approached the actual circulating forms, abandoning the idyllic world of the First Treatise where the theory of value was expounded without considering any genuine currency, it was forced to replace gold with non-convertible bills. The quantitative theory would thus become the instrument used to explain changes in the general level of prices (and in money's purchasing power). In its simpler version, this theory argues that if the amount of currency is duplicated, the purchasing power of each piece will be halved, whereas its total purchasing power will remain constant. Therefore, thanks to the two supplementary assumptions (full employment – or the constant level of output in real terms, which is equivalent for that matter – and invariant circulatory habits) the level of prices is, inevitably, proportional to the volume of currency. In the *Tract*, the quantitative theory is still a valid reference for Keynes.

By excluding gold from the explanation, Keynes turns the quantity theory into the only determinant of money prices, thus eliminating the previous inconsistency or rather cutting adrift from the First Treatise's currency with intrinsic value. Also, by articulating the explanation in "real" terms, the theory becomes simpler. As the real value of wealth – the amount of transactions that the people make calculated in real terms – is fixed, the "real" value of paper money does not change either, as long as the proportion of wealth that is kept as cash on hand is not changed. Based on the quantitative theory mechanics, it should be expected that whenever the number of bills increases, the real unit value of each bill will fall, therefore, the money price of a unit of product will increase; the proportion in real terms remains constant. This is the last word of the *classical theory* in its Second Treatise regarding the determinations of the purchasing power of money with no intrinsic value, that is, non-convertible paper money. The Keynes of the *Tract* still endorses this theory, although he promises to *qualify* and *explain* it.

From the quantity theory in its simpler version, it is inferred that if, for example, the government decided to double the amount of bills in circulation, prices would simply double. The government, in turn, would thus manage to appropriate a portion of income through the emission of money, levying the so-called "inflation tax". It would seem that this form of tax collection has no limits, since by merely putting bills into circulation, the authorities seize a portion of the country's resources, even though, according to this theory, each bill has afterwards a lesser value in real terms.[13]

In the *Tract*, Keynes rejected the premises that support the quantity theory in its simple classical version.

The *classical theory* assumed that the elasticity of money demand was equal to one. Asserting this is equivalent to affirming that any amount of money put into circulation, no matter how large, would be unable to affect the will or the habits of the public regarding the possession of cash on hand. But this assumption is at odds with reality, as the public reacts to changes in the amount of money in a highly precise way: modifying the proportion of real income that they wish to keep in cash. Keynes is not the first economist to consider the possibility that such a proportion might change. However, what other economists had timidly accepted will now have to be fully developed in the field of theory to account for changes in the monetary sphere.

Keynes began thus his gradual distancing from the *classical theory of money*. Under the classical assumptions, the demand for money was always considered to be a fixed proportion of real income – unitary elasticity of demand of purchasing power relative to buying power. Keynes still endorses the quantity theory and does not have any new instruments to replace it. Yet, he modifies the assumptions regarding the behavior of the intervening variables, thus transforming the theory into a tool capable of giving account of the new monetary phenomena.

The traditional quantity theory was not suitable to explain real and effective variations in money's purchasing power and prices. In fact, there were sufficient elements to reject the classical assumptions: in practice, it could be observed that when the amount of currency emitted by the government changed, the level of prices did not experience a *proportional* modification. The effects of changes on prices were not absolute. As may be seen, Keynes did not completely break with the theory but rather, as he announced, limited himself to qualifying the quantitative equation. His innovation is not in the equation itself, but in the cause-effect relationships he established, which distances him from classical monetary theory. Yet, the apparently minor effects of such modifications are amplified when seen from a broader perspective, in the context of the subsequent evolution of his thinking. This, for the time being, minor reframing opened up a novel theoretical path that Keynes would tread throughout the following decade.

In contrast to the more common version of the quantity theory, in this account, when the amount of currency changes, prices do not react directly and proportionately; rather, it is necessary to analyze the different elements intervening in the demand of money, as well as their respective changes, to subsequently assess price behavior.

Even though absent in his short-term analysis, Keynes's subjection to the quantity theory is still marked when he studies a longer analytical period. Probably, once a transition period had passed, the values of the variables may return to their usual levels as dictated by habit. This is what most certainly will occur in "the long term". But even if it were so, for Keynes this would not be relevant, as in the meantime, prices will have risen in a certain proportion. If the aim of the theory is to explain inflation and deflation, the effects of the changes in the amount of money that are relevant are the ones that take place in the "short term".

> Now, in the "long run" this [what the traditional quantity theory asserts, AK] is probably true [. . .]. But this "long run" is a misleading guide to current affairs. *In the long run* we are all dead. Economists set themselves too easy, too useless a task if in tempestuous seasons they can only tell us that when the storm is long past the ocean is flat again.
>
> (Keynes, 1923: 80)

This well-known passage deserves a brief commentary, as from now on Keynes will focus most of his studies on short-term phenomena and mechanisms. Marshall's "analytical" long term was, in fact, devised as a tool to "abstractly" assess a future stage that, as he himself admits, will never come to be. In the context of this theory of prices – where this distinction was originally introduced – the current moment, with its *accidental market* price may be distinguished from the "normal" or trend price. In practice, the only truly observable price is market price, but, precisely for this reason, it is the least relevant from a theoretical point of view. Normal price, instead, introduces elements that cannot be directly observed to give account of the trend movement of the visible phenomenon. If Keynes focuses on the short-term analysis it is not because he believes that the theory should exclusively devote itself to describing accidental "market" factors, but rather because he assumes that there are two "analytical moments", the long and the short term. Adjustments in both are of different nature, and it is necessary to understand their differences. In this case, the wish to keep cash becomes a variable factor and, therefore, a factor that may be explained by the economic theory to give account of the causes that affect a phenomenon (price variation), while the action of banking, monetary, payment etc. "habits" become fixed factors "in the long term".

The changes introduced deserve an in-depth discussion. In its original sense, Keynes's well-known phrase should not be read as if it exclusively meant that "we should hasten and act today because otherwise we will not see the effects of what is done". Its meaning is "theoretical": immediate events cannot be explained, nor can the causal chain of the elements be involved in determining a phenomenon if certain phenomena that are highly sensitive in the short run are considered fixed, that is, if certain variables are turned into constant values. In the long term, there may exist a more or less stable proportion between income and required cash, but, in fact, changes in prices should be explained bearing in mind that the amount of cash that the public wishes to keep at any moment depends on variations in the amount of money. How are the effective variations in prices to be accounted for if one of the dependent variables is taken as given and fixed? As may be seen, it is not just a distinction in terms of the time the system takes to "make adjustments". If it is assumed that certain variable is fixed and nothing else is stated in this connection, then all the changes that occur, independently of their persistence, will be considered to be phenomena typical of disequilibrium or, rather, as stations in a process of "adjustment" towards equilibrium.

"In the long run we are all dead" means, then, that the theory is, indeed, inadequate if it is incapable of explaining the reality of things asserting, axiomatically, that the values of variables should be considered intermediate instances within a never explained trajectory towards long-term equilibrium, equilibrium that, on the other hand, is never reached because before reaching the last station, a new disturbance always emerges. When the theory is static, the path leading from one equilibrium to the next tends to remain hidden. Theory is dead if it only describes that hypothetical long-term equilibrium. And here end the advances expounded in 1923's *Tract* where directions that will guide future research are laid out, although not fully developed.

To summarize, this new version of the quantity theory or, more precisely, this novel causal interpretation contains a series of innovations, which are once again listed below, but this time ordered by the variable involved. If the quantity theory is broken down as if it were a description of money supply and money demand, both factors determining the level of prices are modified in Keynes's version.

Money supply is transformed due to the fact that, with the collapse of the gold standard, it comes to be determined by monetary authorities, thus becoming a truly "exogenous" supply of currency. It does not depend on the influx of gold from abroad, on the trade balance, on mine productivity etc., aspects that had been considered crucial – and rightly so, during the global reign of gold – by the *classical theory*.

Money demand is also modified. It is no longer a curve with constant elasticity, but it now depends on a variety of short-term decisions made first by the public when they decide to increase or decrease the real amount of money they wish to keep in cash and the amount they wish to deposit in banks.

According to Keynes, this more sophisticated instrument can help to make the main modern monetary events comprehensible. But also, as will be seen, being *more general*, this modified version of the quantity theory makes it possible to contrast the previous gold standard system and the new monetary regime constituted by non-convertible national currencies. This is the kind of answer Keynes provides to address the anachronism of the *classical theory:* he seeks to replace the theory with an explanation encompassing the previous historical situation as well as also the current one.

From these advances, some practical recommendations may also be inferred. In fact, the policy aimed at stabilizing the currency value on the basis of the "modified" quantity theory takes on very definite novel traits.

According to the *Tract*, on account of several powerful reasons, one of the main goals of a government is guaranteeing the stability of money's purchasing power. Under the nineteenth-century gold standard regime, attempting to reach price stability through state action was not completely feasible. Paradoxically, it begins to become feasible at the standard's collapse. Therefore, the end of the gold standard could be, according to Keynes, the beginning of a period of greater stability in currency value. As he had already hinted at in connection with other spheres, this requires a more resolute action on the part of the authorities. A central bank under state control will allow a convenient regulation of the reserve level.[14]

Keynes transmitted optimism, although ineptitude had so far provoked marked fluctuations. When operating a non-convertible regime, the state can, by regulating cash reserve ratios and the volume of currency, compensate for the non-controllable modifications of the demand of cash on hand and deposits that depend on the public's wishes. The principle of *laissez-faire* censored state action, assuming that the blind forces of individual initiative would lead the economy to its optimal equilibrium. However, the fall of the gold standard *forces* the state to decide upon the volume of the monetary supply. In Keynes's view, far from being a disaster, this furnishes an opportunity to "scientifically" regulate monetary variables that were previously in the hands of capricious economic processes. Well-employed, these instruments – which came to land in the hands of the state as a result of an irreversible historical process – could improve monetary management and help stabilize the price pattern.

Before going back to the discussion of the relevant historical events, which in the light of these theoretical innovations are seen from a new perspective, an implicit aspect of this approach should be stressed. Keynes not only remains captive to quantity theory – albeit a modified version – but he has not been able to free himself either of the assumption of the given level of output (which implies, in the extreme case, assuming full employment as a permanent state of the economy). As in the case of the *classical theory*, neither the increases in output and employment, nor their determinants are considered to be short-term phenomena.

In view of the direction that Keynes's ideas would later take, as expounded more than a decade later in *The General Theory*, it could be said that the *Tract* foreshadowed at least two of his more important contributions but left one aside. First, the volume of currency in circulation – non-convertible paper money – depends only on the will of the entity that issues it, not on the influx and efflux of metal as a result of foreign trade. In other words, the amount of currency is not a given but rather a variable though an exogenous variable that depends on factors considered alien to the economic explanation. Second, the abandonment of the classical version of quantity theory implies, as has already been seen, upholding that the demand of currency may change when the amount of money changes. This means, implicitly (and only implicitly) accepting that money has an additional function other than serving as means of circulation. In fact, Keynes argues that the public is in a position to decide whether keeping more or less money in cash on hand, according to the volume of currency in circulation emitted by the monetary authority. For the time being, such changes are "instinctual" and an attempt to protect against money devaluation through faster circulation.

This, however, implies that the public can "hoard" any amount of money for "speculative" reasons, that is, to avoid (or obtain) short-term earnings. The *Tract* thus frees itself from the assumption of the fixed speed of circulation of money that, although considered adequate in the "long term", is completely useless for studying the abrupt movements of the price index, which have to be explained in the "short term".

As regards the classical bonds from which Keynes has not yet freed himself, the assumption of a fixed level of income and a fixed level of employment should obviously be mentioned. It is not that Keynes (or the classicists) posits that the level of output cannot effectively change, but clearly such variations used to be included within the set of problems to be considered in the long term.

Everybody knows that the level of employment, output, and income is the main unknown quantity in *The General Theory*, where it is treated as a short-term issue, that is, as an endogenous variable in the system, liable to be studied until its determinations are unveiled.

So far, that is, in the 1923 *Tract*, it is a given, a fact, that experiences no variation. The level of employment still remains, thus, to be turned into an endogenous variable, as was done with the demand of money, which changes in the short term. This is an outstanding task. For, as Keynes asserts, "in the long run we are all dead".

After the gold standard

In the context of his "novel" monetary theory, Keynes still has one more thing left to explain: what is the cause of the collapse of the gold standard, so full of consequences for the theory, which opened up new possibilities of money (and price) management for the state? But before turning to that question, other aspect that Keynes did not ignore should be considered:

the determination of the exchange among currencies, once freed from their bonds to gold, and the relationship between rates of exchange and trade.

> When the currencies of the world were nearly all on a gold basis, their relative value (i.e. the exchanges) depended on the actual amount of gold metal in a unit of each, with minor adjustments for the cost of transferring the metal from place to place.

This is the state of affairs that the *classical theory* described when asserting that the global distribution of gold was also ruled by the quantity theory, according to a price-specie flow mechanism.[15] According to the well-known formulation of Hume's, the quantity of money acted "directly" on its purchasing power, thereby influencing exports' and imports' relative prices, thus balancing the trade balance and redistributing gold globally. Under the gold standard, there was a system of fixed rates of exchange that were pegged to the metal. When for any reason the quantity of gold in the country changed, internal prices adjusted to the new circumstances, and foreign trade would guarantee the return of the gold stock to its equilibrium level. Under this system, exchange was stable, but prices fluctuated according to gold flows. The self-regulation of the currency exchange system had as its downside the instability of internal prices.

> In pre-war days, when almost the whole world was on a gold standard, we had all plumped for stability of exchange as against stability of prices, and we were ready to submit to the social consequences of a change of price level for causes quite outside our control, connected, for example, with the discovery of new gold mines in foreign countries or a change of banking policy abroad. But we submitted, partly because we did not dare trust ourselves to a less automatic (though more reasoned) policy, and partly because the price fluctuations experienced were in fact moderate.
>
> (Keynes, 1923: 155)

But it was not, mainly, the fear associated with a greater governmental intervention what extended the presence of the gold standard for so long. According to Keynes, if the system prevailed during such a protracted period, it was because prices were also stable. As we've mentioned, during the nineteenth century price fluctuations were not significant. Keynes is once again interested in revealing the deep economic causes underlying changes in the policies implemented by governments, since, as in other opportunities, he refuses to blame changes in the monetary system on statesmen's whims, on actual power pressures, or on inexplicable changes in habits. He had said earlier that the gold standard meant stable rates of exchange and unstable prices. How could it be, however, that prices did not fluctuate markedly?

> Nevertheless, even so, the convenience of traders and the primitive passion for solid metal might not, I think, have been adequate to preserve the dynasty of gold, if it had not been for another, half accidental, circumstance; namely, that for many years past gold had afforded not only a stable exchange but, on the whole, a stable price level also. In fact, the choice between stable exchanges and stable prices had not presented itself as an acute dilemma.
>
> (Keynes, 1923: 158)

A rather appreciable number of fortuitous events ensured, during a protracted period, the stability of the price levels under the gold standard.

> The considerable success with which gold maintained its stability of value in the changing world of the 19th century was certainly remarkable [. . .]. After the discoveries of Australia and California it began to depreciate dangerously, and before the exploitation of South Africa it began to appreciate dangerously. Yet in each case it righted itself and retained its reputation.
>
> (Keynes, 1923: 164–165)

Prices remained stable during the nineteenth century owing to a series of fortuitous events that helped maintain a particular correspondence for a long time: the increase of the global amount of gold roughly kept pace with the growth of the economy as a whole. This virtuous relationship could remain through time, in turn, on account of the peculiar form that capitalist development had assumed in that stage: "the progress of that period, since it was characterized by the gradual opening up and exploitation of the world's surface, not unnaturally brought to light *paripassu* the remoter deposits of gold". The expansion of capitalist production during this period coincided with a territorial expansion that gradually incorporated new regions of the world into the system until well into the nineteenth century. Therefore, world production grew, and in its wake, new veins to extract precious metals were discovered.

However, by the end of the nineteenth century, the world had been almost completely explored and, therefore, according to Keynes, "this stage of history is now almost at an end. A quarter of a century has passed by since the discovery of an important deposit". The accidental harmonious symmetry between economic growth and the progressive discovery of gold came to an end. Thus finished that age when the rhythm of capital accumulation coincided with the geographical expansion of capitalism and, therefore, with the increase in the supply of available metal for circulation.

A new era then opened when the velocity of gold extraction and, thus, the increase in the supply of money was no longer supported by the discovery of new mines in unexplored regions rich in precious metals. According to Keynes, the increase in the supply of gold – like economic growth – came to depend now exclusively on the chaotic and unpredictable rhythm of technical progress.[16] The previous regularity gave way to the sudden leaps that are typical of the rhythm of scientific discoveries. Keynes even indulges in taking this argument to extremes.

> Material progress is more dependent now on the growth of scientific and technical knowledge, of which the application to gold-mining may be intermittent. Years may elapse without great improvement in the methods of extracting gold; and then the genius of a chemist may realise past dreams and forgotten hoaxes, transmuting base into precious like subtle, or extracting gold from sea-water as in the Bubble. Gold is liable to be too dear or too cheap. In either case, it is too much to expect that a succession of accidents will keep the metal steady.
>
> (Keynes, 1923: 166)

There are, also, other historical circumstances that contributed to definitively modifying the previously fortuitous conditions under which gold offered a stable pattern of prices and exchange. While the quantity of gold was exclusively determined by the discoveries of new mines, gold extraction, as the production of any other commodity, was subject to the law of production costs; its value was essentially independent from the action of governments, banking etc. Intense competition in the sector devoted to mining exploitation prevented producers from arbitrarily setting prices, eluding the strong determinations of the law of value. This is the reason why in the First Treatise of the *classical theory*, money could be considered, without many obstacles, as just another commodity with "intrinsic value"; in the nineteenth century, its value was determined as that of the rest of the regular commodities whose value it expressed. But after the First World War, everything changes.

> The value of gold has not depended [until 1919, AK] on the policy or the decisions of a single body of men [. . .].This is what is meant by saying that gold has "intrinsic value".
>
> (Keynes, 1923: 166)

But with war, apart from an end to that age when discovering deposits of precious metals was frequent, came another unprecedented change in the distribution of the gold already in circulation. When the war broke out, most of the countries were forced to abandon the gold standard, but the United

States did not. To prevent their own standard from depreciating, the United States gradually enlarged their reserves, but they did not put into circulation more than a small portion of their available gold. Thus, the gold standard, ceased to be what it had been.

> It [the United States] has been driven, therefore, to the costly policy of burying in the vaults of Washington what the miners of the Rand have laboriously brought to the surface. Consequently gold now stands at an "artificial" value, the future course of which almost entirely depends on the policy of the Federal Reserve Board of the United States. The value of gold is no longer the resultant of the chance gifts of Nature and the judgment of numerous authorities and individuals acting independently.
>
> (Keynes, 1923: 167)

Since the moment when gold came to be largely hoarded in the reserves of a single country, the volume of metal in circulation came to be subjected, in practice, to the same set of determinations ruling the quantity of non-convertible money paper. Therefore, to the chagrin of those who argued for the gold standard because under such arrangement the quantity in circulation could not be manipulated, the determination of the supply of currency available, even if restoring the gold standard, would fall "unintentionally" and on account of the historical evolution, in the hands of a few governments: "convertibility into gold will not alter the fact that the value of gold itself depends on the policy of the Central Banks". For that reason, Keynes believed to have reduced to the absurd the claims and illusions of gold's supporters: even if the old metal standard was restored, the quantity of gold in circulation would be arbitrarily managed, so arbitrarily as in the case of a non-convertible paper money.[17] The *classical theory* explained the behavior of a country's reserves in terms of the traditional needs of the treasury, that is, the willingness to maintain a fix and reasonable ratio between the bank's liabilities and assets (deposits and liabilities of any kind), guaranteeing the soundness of the financial system. The upper limit to the hoarding of reserves stemmed from the cost of immobilizing gold. But none of the assumptions supporting the old explanation seem to hold. The hoarding of gold in the vaults of a few banks that took place after the war would inevitably modify the laws that, according to the theory, set the value of the metal and determine the behavior of central banks.

> It differs significantly from the doctrine of gold reserves which we learnt and taught before the war. We used to assume that no Central Bank would be so extravagant as to keep more gold than it required or so imprudent as to keep less. From time to time gold would flow out into the circulation or for export abroad; experience showed that the

quantity required on these occasions bore some rough proportion to the Central Bank's liabilities [. . .]. Already before the war, the system was becoming precarious by reason of its artificiality. The "proportion" was by the lapse of time losing its relation to the facts and had become largely conventional. Some other figure, greater or less, would have done just as well. The War broke down the convention; for the withdrawal of gold from actual circulation destroyed one of the elements of reality lying behind the convention and the suspension of convertibility destroyed the other.

(Keynes, 1923: 171–172)

There is still an additional monetary transformation to be added, leaving the old system out. As we have already seen, during the nineteenth century the need for gold was determined by the output volume, which grew at the same rate than world dominance. Therefore, it was the rate of discovery of new deposits that ensured a more or less regular and parallel increase of new gold supply, and contributed to preventing marked fluctuations in its value. But the expansive – colonial? – stage of capitalism was, according to Keynes, exhausted: the exploration of the planet in search of gold had come to its end, and, besides, a significant portion of the existing metal had gone out of circulation as it was kept in the vaults of a few central banks, which were from this point on capable of regulating supply. Thus, Keynes rose above the ongoing discussion about the advantages of adopting one system or other: he claimed that the end of the gold standard was, in fact, an irreversible fact, not only because *it was not convenient to adopt it* but also because the prevailing conditions had radically changed; global economic transformations had led to the gold standard no longer being able to automatically guarantee price stability.

If, indeed, a providence watched over gold, or if Nature had provided us with a stable standard ready-made, I would not, in an attempt after some slight improvement, hand over the management to the possible weakness or ignorance of Boards and Governments. But this is not the situation. We have no ready-made standard. Experience has shown that in emergencies Ministers of Finance cannot be strapped down. And – most important of all- *in the modern world of paper currency and bank credit* there is no escape from a "managed" currency, whether we wish it or not; – convertibility into gold will not alter the fact that the value of gold itself depends on the policy of the Central Banks.

(Keynes, 1923: 170; emphasis added)

In short, under the new circumstances, gold, the commodity-money par excellence, no longer had the valuable attributes it used to. It no longer had an "intrinsic" value like other commodities since its bid price did not depend now on production costs. The quantity of gold could be manipulated by the countries that had hoarded the metal in circulation during the war. In theoretical terms, the classical dualism between commodity-money, whose value depends on production costs – First Treatise – and symbol-money, whose value is determined exclusively by the quantity in circulation, according to the quantity theory, was no longer applicable; such dichotomy was solved, at least as regards gold. Its volume had come to be as "regulatable" as that of paper money.

Keynes's work offers a warning about the risks of returning to gold and also attempts to understand long-term economic changes, the new laws ruling monetary phenomena. His argument is forceful: whether the supporters of the old gold standard like it or not, valueless money will be, from then on, the new rule. The world marched unaided and due to the will of world events dynamics towards "regulated" money. No matter the desire of authorities and academics, the government has and will have a new duty: that of administrating the quantity of non-convertible money put into circulation. Governments may do so arbitrarily or act in agreement with theoretically founded rules.

Keynes, aware of this change, attempts to show the laws concerning money circulation and its relationship with prices, to elaborate, based on such laws, a plan that may allow for the "scientific management" of currency. Such regulation does not exclusively concern emission. The death of the gold standard also brings under the remit of the government the modification of the rate of exchange and the rate of interest. Both variables were previously ruled by more or less automatic mechanisms. But since First World War, the transition to regulated money is no longer an option and becomes a compulsory outcome of the "automatic" course of history.

> The non-metallic standards, of which we have experience, have been anything rather than scientific experiments coolly carried out. They have been a last resort, involuntarily adopted, as a result of war or inflationary taxation, when the State finances were already broken or the situation out of hand. Naturally in these circumstances such practices have been the accompaniment and the prelude of disaster. But we cannot argue from this to what can be achieved in normal times.
>
> (Keynes, 1923: 170)

The gold standard died a natural death: from then on, the duty of managing the quantity of money becomes inescapable. Until then, every time the emission of notes surpassed the level of reserves, the situation was considered an anomaly provoked by some desperate circumstance: "anything rather than scientific experiments". Keynes's predicted that regulated supply currency would be the new rule, and that the door to the scientific regulation of emission had been opened. As regards this prediction, at least, he was not mistaken. England returned to the gold standard in 1925, in spite of Keynes's warnings, but soon had to abandon it amidst a new storm, which this time would be the last. It would be necessary to wait until the crisis of the 1970s to see the United States definitively bury the system based on convertibility into gold.

During the times of the free convertibility of pounds to gold at a fixed pre-established rate, that is, under the system of fixed gold parity rates, the *classical* mechanism represented by the quantity theory seemed to work adequately.

This simple mechanism worked as follows: when there was an – exogenous – increase in the quantity of gold surpassing circulation needs, the "excess" gold was added to the central reserves. This abundance triggered, in turn, an easing of credit conditions, and a change in the bank's discount policies (a period of *easy money* began). Credit availability, in turn, stimulated the demand of goods whose purchase depends on bank financing which, in turn, triggered an increase in prices. Such increase in prices spread throughout the economy.[18] "Internal inflation" then emerged, with each piece of gold standing for a lower purchasing power in terms of goods. The mechanism stressed the balancing effect of this movement in internal prices regarding global prices. The price of the commodities produced in the country experienced a relative rise; the volume of imports grew, and exports decreased. The inflow of commodities was balanced by the outflow of metal. Gold flew abroad bringing credit terms back to normality. The long-term final outcome was that surplus gold escaped from the circulation sphere, credit cooled down, and prices returned to their normal level. Equilibrium was restored, and the initial (exogenous) increase in the quantity of currency reverted without visible consequences.

It is clear, then, that the credit system thus became the mechanism that connected the increase in the quantity of gold to the rise in prices. In fact, classical quantity theory, which linked gold movement to price variations, made the rate of interest its main transmission belt.

For this reason, during the period of the gold standard, the rediscount policy of the central bank was considered to be "automatic": the Bank of England raised and lowered the rate almost reflexively. The recipe was simple: when gold flowed into the Bank's vaults, the authorities had to do nothing but ease credit conditions, so that prices would do the rest. Keynes argues that, in the age of the gold standard, this attitude could bring about certain "imperfections" in the operation of the mechanism. Fluctuations in the rate of interest attracted or expelled capitals, balancing the quantity of gold in the country *before* the mechanism of adjustment of the trade balance, which became active when internal prices changed, had completed its work. The "signals" that ensured that the adjustment would be made, were not always sufficiently clear. The Central Bank would lower the interest rate upon finding that the reserves had increased too much, waiting for the credit to ease, the prices to increase, and imports to evacuate the surplus gold.

When the reserves fell, the rate of interest was raised again. However, by reducing the rate of interest, the gold flowed out, not to settle commodity purchases abroad, but in the form of capital pursuing a higher return. The Bank raised the interest rate again in the belief that the adjustment had operated successfully, through the trade balance, when in fact it had not.

> [T]he movement of the rate of interest up or down sometimes had more effect in attracting foreign capital or encouraging investment abroad than in influencing home prices. [. . .] [T]he adjustment even before the war might be imperfect; for the stimulus to foreign loans, whilst restoring the balance for the time being, might obscure the real seriousness of the situation, and enable a country to live beyond its resources for a considerable time at the risk of ultimate default.
>
> (Keynes, 1923: 160)

Conversely, the Bank reacted by "automatically" raising the rate of interest in the face of a shortage of gold reflected in the loss of reserves. Credit constraint should then act through a reduction in prices. The fall of the prices should, in turn, increase net exports, feeding reserves once again and restoring prices to their previous level. However, the high rate of interest could attract capitals in search of short-term financial gains. Reserves would thus also increase, but here as a symptom of the movement of the capital account, not of the commodity account, without exerting any pressure on prices to increase. Again, an influx of additional financing could deceive the Bank, leaving the "real" imbalance unsolved.

During the age of the gold standard, therefore, the central banks managed interest rates with the sole purpose of maintaining metallic reserves at a "suitable" level – a determined relationship, based on practical experience, between the amount of gold kept in their vaults and their total amount of liabilities. Credit creation obeyed merely the goal of respecting that "healthy proportion"; the real "adjustment" would come as a consequence, but it was not an immediate objective of banking policy. The war, however, shattered that scenario: gold became concentrated in some countries, and was withdrawn from circulation – trade, on the other hand, was strongly restricted – and currency convertibility collapsed. Keynes points out that under such circumstances the old canon could no longer rule rates of interest's movements since, in practice, it no longer worked as a passive instrument in the service of the objective of maintaining certain volume of gold reserves.

> It would have been absurd to regulate the bank-rate by reference to a "proportion" which had lost all its significance; and in the course

of the past ten years a new policy has been evolved. *The bank-rate is now employed, however incompletely and experimentally, to regulate the expansion and deflation of credit in the interests of business stability and the steadiness of prices.* In so far as it is employed to procure stability of the dollar exchange, where this is inconsistent with stability of internal prices, we have a relic of pre-war policy and a compromise between discrepant aims.

(Keynes, 1923: 171; emphasis added)

Keynes points out that, if until then the interest rate had played an "automatic" role in maintaining gold parity, that role had also "automatically" ceased to be. His observation could not be more insightful, although it is currently considered an obvious fact when in reality it was the result of a remarkable economic transformation: the rate of interest turned into an instrument capable of regulating prices and employment movements in national economies. Faced with this new scenario, it is pointless to subordinate it, tightly tying it to the reserves' movements, when the circulating currency is unconvertible.

This method belongs indeed to a period when the preservation of convertibility was all that any one thought about (all indeed that there was to think about so long as we were confined to an unregulated gold standard), and before the idea of utilising bank-rate as a means of *keeping prices and employment steady* had become practical politics.

(Keynes, 1923: 194; emphasis added)

In spite of his split with classical thinking and his capacity to identify the new possibilities of monetary policy, an evident tension between Keynes's new views and the elements of the traditional theory that persist in his discourse may be observed. The *classical theory*, from which he had still not freed himself, assumes that the level of employment is given and equal to full employment. Keynes's main concern in the *Tract* is the steadiness of the level of prices – assuming employment to be a constant, but timidly, the goal of regulating the rate of interest to promote the creation of new jobs, to stabilize output rather than prices, begins to take shape. Seen in this light, an incipient contradiction may be perceived: the quantity theory, the only available tool to explain the consequences of monetary changes, assumes a fixed level of employment; however, Keynes states that the management of the rate of interest and, therefore, of the quantity of money, has a new aim: it does not only seek to balance prices but also the level of employment. The contradiction lies in that the quantity theory posits that the changes in the quantity of money or in the interest rate affect prices, but never the volume of transactions. The theoretical instrument is not adequate because the rate of interest spontaneously begins to be used to regulate the activity cycle, not the reserves.

The dynamic of the interest rate becomes more complex, as do its management and their varied and changing effects. This new line of argument will finally see the light of day, accompanied by acute theoretical consequences, a decade later in *The General Theory*. In the *Tract*, Keynes also discusses another novel economic policy instrument that falls into the hands of governments after the collapse of the gold standard: the rate of exchange, turned into an instrument of economic policy free from the bonds of convertibility. Strange though it may seem, until then, the theory had only imperfectly examined the results of deliberate intervention in the exchange market.

Faced with price changes in the rest of the world, if the stability of the rate of exchange is to be ensured, the stability of internal prices has to be sacrificed, and vice versa. These dilemmas have not always existed in connection with the economic policy; they are the result of the troubled transition to what Keynes called the "Era of Stabilization". *Laissez-faire* was simply no longer an option, as the intervention of the state in the monetary sphere is no longer a possibility that may be deliberately chosen or discarded but rather a need after the collapse of the gold standard. Some criteria have to be adopted when the old patterns are no longer applicable.

Some advances in the Tract's conclusions

Thus, the premises of the gold standard disappeared: the determination of the quantity of currency and the interest rate fell into the remit of the monetary authority. And thereby, an unprecedented power over prices and the rate of exchange was granted to the state. The government received these instruments unaware of the rules under which the new system operated. According to Keynes, in their desperation at the changes that had taken place, conservatives preferred to return to an already extinguished past rather than modify the theory and use the new instruments deliberately and purposefully.

However, the course of history could not be reverted and, from then on, governments would necessarily *have to* decide over these variables: rate of interest, quantity of money, prices, and rate of exchange. It was crucial, then, to reframe the laws explaining these processes to be in a position to "scientifically regulate" the monetary aggregates under the control of the authority. In answer to the conservatives, Keynes would argue that a return to the old world was not feasible.

> Advocates of the ancient standard do not observe how remote it now is from the spirit and the requirements of the age. A regulated non-metallic standard has slipped in unnoticed. *It exists*. Whilst the economists dozed, the academic dream of a hundred years, doffing its cap

and gown, clad in paper rags, has crept into the real world by means of the bad fairies – always so much more potent than the good – the wicked ministers of finance.

(Keynes, 1923: 173)

It is not just a question of comparing the value of the old theories, but of accepting facts: the non-metallic regulated standard, as Keynes says, *exists*, without asking for permission.

Besides, it is not difficult to appreciate the virtues that characterize the new system, as long as it is well managed. It is possible to decisively influence prices by controlling the situation of credit. In the past, the rate of interest moved passively to maintain an adequate level of reserves and preserve, by that means, convertibility, but now it has become a weapon wielded by the Treasury and the Bank of England. Keynes asks: "How far can these two authorities control their own actions and how far must they remain passive agents? In my opinion, the control, if they choose to exercise it, is mainly in their hands". Therefore, the *Tract* concludes with a passionate plea for the abandonment of the old prejudices prescribing government passivity, typical of the gold standard, which thus assumed full deliberate control over monetary variables.

> we must free ourselves from the deep distrust which exists against allowing the regulation of the standard of value to be the subject of *deliberate decision*. We can no longer afford to leave it in the category of which the distinguishing characteristics are possessed in different degrees by the weather, the birth-rate, and the Constitution, – matters which are settled by natural causes, or are the resultant of the separate action of many individuals acting independently, or require a Revolution to change them.
>
> (Keynes, 1923: 40)

In the quoted passages, a new objective for the government's monetary policy is – although somehow hesitantly still – set: to support the level of business and employment. Besides, in this way, such objectives turn into a *short-term* issue. More precisely, it is the collapse of the gold standard which brings about the possibility of – and the need for – making and implementing a deliberate monetary policy whose purposes exceed the exclusive aim it had in the previous stage: to support a fixed rate of exchange, the parity of the national currency to gold. In practice, the regulation of the monetary variables was already in the authority's hands; it only had to take resolute command of it.

To end, it is possible to point out a decisive difference between the claims made at the beginning of the *Tract* and the new theoretical and practical

dimensions that begin to take shape as the discoveries regarding the transformations of the monetary system, and the new tenets ruling its novel configuration begin to emerge. The book begins with a discussion of the effects
that the general level of prices' fluctuations have on income distribution and
production itself. At the beginning of the text, price stability seems to be
the priority objective of the state. At the end of the *Tract*, other means and
other ends are identified. With the gold standard collapsed, the monetary
authority can arbitrarily determine the volume of currency and the rate of
interest, thus influencing the credit situation. Credit, in its turn, stimulates
or discourages, speeds up or delays the increase in output and the creation
of jobs. When treading these paths, it becomes obvious that monetary variables can no longer be studied independently from real variables. Until the
war, monetary policy was exclusively concerned with preserving convertibility. But now, a new purpose emerges.

When the *Tract* is seen against the subsequent path followed by Keynes's
thinking, it may be considered as a first step in a protracted effort to integrate the real sphere of the economy – the volume of employment and output, and income distribution – with the monetary sphere, constituting thus a
single *system*. In other words, the purpose is joining the theory of value and
the theory of money, which in the *classical theory* were separated.

However, by clinging to the quantity theory as the only tool in his explanation, Keynes remains prisoner to the assumption of constant output and income.

Thus, references to output, savings, investment, consumption can only be
indirect. Seen in this light, they are epiphenomena, dependent on changes
in credit conditions, but have not become yet "target variables". A contradiction, therefore, persists: on one hand, income is assumed to be fixed,
but on the other, credit changes are supposed to modify employment and
production.

From the Tract to the Treatise on Money: continuity
in Keynes's breakup with the classicists

A Treatise on Money was published in 1930. In a preface characterized by a
remarkable frankness and humbleness – an attitude largely opposite to the
one Keynes will adopt in the preface to *The General Theory* – the author
gives two warnings concerning the contents of the book that are worth
stressing. First, once again, he relates the theory to its historical origins,
when stating that although monetary problems had largely caught the attention of economists since the beginnings of this science, an accurate formulation of monetary laws, as they operated at that moment, had not yet been
achieved. Such a gap originated in the fact that the principles had to be modified as a consequence of the then recent global economic transformations.

However, in spite of the fact that the book stems from the need to systematize the available knowledge on the novel traits of the then current world, the *Treatise*, Keynes admits, is not a compilation of clear ideas, but a moment of transition in his own intellectual trajectory. It is – avowedly – a work of transition. In light of the subsequent events, it could be said that the publishing of *The General Theory* would have to be waited for to get to know the theoretical system in its definitive shape.

> [A] good deal in this book represents the process of getting rid of the ideas which I used to have and of finding my way to those which I now have [. . .]. I feel like someone who has been forcing his way through a confused jungle. Now that I have emerged from it, I see that I might have taken a more direct route and that many problems and perplexities which beset me during the journey had not precisely the significance which I supposed at the time.
>
> (Keynes, 1935 [1930]: vi)

The honesty with which Keynes recognizes, from the very preface, the unfinished character of his work is, in itself, peculiar. According to Keynes, the objective pursued but not fully attained in the *Treatise* is to offer a systematic treatment of "the theory and the facts of token money", which he considered to be a novel historical phenomena. After analyzing the advances made in the *Tract*, this aim should not surprise us in the very least. In the *Tract*, Keynes had traversed only the first stretch of the way to his emancipation from the old *classical theory:* he was still tied to the quantity theory, exclusive and excluding heritage of the *classical theory* of money.

Now, in spite of the acknowledged limitations of the book, the *Treatise* seems to offer some contributions to the understanding of the nature and the behavior of the Representative Money mentioned in the Preface. What does Keynes refer to when using this category, whose particular laws must be unraveled? The *Treatise* puts forward a complex taxonomy classifying the different modalities that money may adopt. Representative Money is defined in contrast to Commodity Money, whose nature had already been extensively discussed in the *Tract*.

> The true link between Commodity Money and Representative Money is to be found, perhaps, in Commodity Money, the supply of which is limited by absolute scarcity rather than by cost of production, and the demand for which is wholly dependent upon the fact that it has been selected by law or convention as the material of money and not upon its intrinsic value in other uses.
>
> (Keynes, 1935 [1930]: 14)

Representative money (or token) is characterized, therefore, by its "intrinsic value" being divorced from its "monetary value". Its supply is fixed, and its demand stems from law or convention. There are, in turn, two "forms" of representative money: fiat money and managed money.

Both are issued by the state, but the former is non-convertible. Apart from these two forms of state-emitted money, Keynes mentions bank money, private debt securities that may be used to conduct transactions.

The emergence of the first known forms of money may be traced to the sixth century BC, but representative money is, instead, a modern device that becomes definitively established as a consequence of the French Revolution. However, according to Keynes, it was necessary to wait until well advanced the nineteenth century to see the first attempts at establishing certain scientific principles that would provide the elements to adequately manage the emission of representative money. Such principles were aimed at subjecting this money to a standard to turn it into managed money. *The British Bank Charter Act*, 1844, embodies the outcome of these debates; tightly restricting the emission of money, it thus becomes the first attempt at systematizing the management of representative money. Keynes's discussion of the *Bank Act* of 1844, additionally, displays the theoretical advances that distinguish the *Tract* from the *Treatise*.

In Keynes's words, the Bank Act "was compounded of one sound principle and one serious confusion". The "sound principle" imposed a limit to the amount of representative money that the Bank had to issue; its purpose was keeping the standard fixed. The confusion lay in the fact that its definition of the quantity of money in circulation completely ignored the existence of bank money. The ultimate objective of the norm was to have representative money mimic the behavior of gold's, the commodity money, movements, but by ignoring the existence of bank money, that objective became unattainable. Now, according to Keynes, the system did not collapse in spite of this confusion because a second principle was deeply ingrained in the behavior of banking policy-makers, a principle that although not expressly included in the Bank Act, worked in practice as a clause guaranteeing its effectiveness: Keynes calls it "the principle of the Bank-Rate". In practice, banks set the level of bank interest rate applying a single criterion: maintaining the standard. This principle dominated banking policy during the seventy years that followed the passing of the Bank Act, working as a spell that – underhandedly – accompanied the explosive growth of the British monetary system, and supported its development.

> [T]he practical efficacy of Bank-rate became not merely familiar but an article of faith and dogma, its precise *modus operandi* and the varying results to be expected from its application in varying conditions were

not clearly understood – and have not been clearly understood, in my opinion, down to this day.

(Keynes, 1935 [1930]: 17)

In other words: when national currencies were convertible into gold at a fixed parity, the movement of the bank-rate was subjected to certain automatic rules that had been forged by practice and not by theory. According to Keynes, this is the reason why the principles regulating the system were then unknown and remained hidden even in 1930. It was therefore necessary to discover what the effects were that brought about the changes in the interest rate that had surreptitiously supported the gold standard. The *Treatise* will seek to unveil the workings of those laws.

It could be said that what is sought is a general explanation comprising both the gold standard (Commodity Money) and the non-convertible money (Representative Money). Therefore, major economic changes become fundamental when reframing the theory. In the *Treatise*, the First World War appears again as a definitive historical breaking point. Shortly before its outbreak, the United States, based on the British experience regarding inconvertibility, adopted the most sophisticated system of managed money ever known through the creation of the Federal Reserve. In England, after the war, the Currency Act of 1925 puts a definitive end to the pre-war age of commodity money, and moves, as well, towards a regulated system.

In the *Treatise*, the reasons behind the abandonment of the gold standard are reviewed again, in line with the analysis conducted seven years earlier in the *Tract*. The original argument was only slightly modified, attributing now the stability of commodity money's value to the particular way in which it was managed rather to the particular rate at which gold surfaced.

The explanation put forward in the *Tract* is repeated, but now qualified by a reference to a period of coexistence of Commodity Money and Representative Money, a stage when the system was mixed, so to speak. During the first half of the gold standard period, many gold deposits were, in fact, discovered, and an increasing number of countries joined in the system. But during the last fifty years, it was the methods implemented to economize the use of gold that increased its supply much more effectively than deposit extraction; actually, demand decreased.

In the *Treatise*, it is argued that the gold standard coexisted during a long time with what by then was, strictly speaking, a form of representative money. Paradoxically, the protracted survival of commodity money must be attributed to the increasing, albeit hidden, predominance of representative money, as it was the latter which ensured an adequate level of currency in circulation, even though gold ore extraction was insufficient. For this reason, "gold has depended, and will continue to depend, for its stability of

value, not so much on the conditions of its supply, as on deliberate regulation of the demand".

Six years after the end of the First World War, in spite of the opposition
of numerous experts – Keynes, among them – England returned to the gold
standard restoring the pre-war parity. The debate over the convenience of
this painful return, which implied an overvaluation of the currency, still
emerges in the pages of the *Treatise*. To show that the old regime was
inadequate, Keynes risks an educated guess. If the annual rate of growth of
the global economy was set at 3 percent, the supply of gold would not be
enough – under the practices prevailing in the period – to maintain the level
of prices, therefore, a decreasing trend in prices reaching an annual cumulative percentage of 1 percent would have been recorded. The causes that
would provoke deflation are similar to those mentioned in the *Tract*. When
England returned to the pre-war parity, the distribution of gold among
nations was not remotely proportional – as it was assumed in the nineteenth
century – to the corresponding level of economic activity. Under these circumstances, it was impossible to reinstate the practices accompanying the
old system. Instead of "free competition" in the production of metal, more
than 90 percent of gold was in the vaults of central banks and governments:
more than half was under the control of the United States and France. The
First War signaled, therefore, the end of an era: "the long age of Commodity Money has at last passed away before the age of Representative
Money".

From this perspective, the *Treatise* may be interpreted as a step forward
in the realization of the program outlined seven years earlier in the *Tract;*
now, the theoretical undertaking practically fills the stage through the definition of the adequate categories: a system of representative money and,
more specifically, as will be seen, a managed system replaces the classical
gold pattern. Now, it is necessary to establish the principles that will enable
a scientific management of money. The interest rate will no longer be subjected to gold's movements, so that, naturally, no similar effects could be
expected from its variations: the causes and consequences of the rate of
interest's fluctuations should be researched once again. The same may be
said regarding the determination of the quantity of money and the general
level of prices. In the new historical framework, it became evident that the
rate of interest and the volume of currency not only influenced prices, but
were also involved in the determination of capital stock and output variations. Thus, with the overbearingness of the fait accompli, investment and
employment barge into monetary theory. Seen in this light, the *Treatise* is
an additional step in the pursuit of unity between the theory of value and the
theory of money, between real variables and monetary variables, between
what Keynes calls First Treatise and Second Treatise of *classical theory*.

The abandonment of the quantitative theory

Along the development of the *Tract*, Keynes discovered – and revealed – that, after the fall of the gold standard, certain variables that used to be considered to be exclusively monetary were in fact linked to a group of modern real-world economic phenomena in a completely novel fashion. However, this intuition was not enough to free Keynes in the *Tract* from the theories of the classical school: he worked with a somehow more complex and versatile version of the old quantity theory.

That old instrument was the only one that the *classical theory* could contribute to enquire into the relationship between money and prices. However, it became gradually evident that the monetary theory's trains of causation could not be treated as completely independent from the phenomena involved in the theory of value and distribution. In the *Tract*, progress in this direction was still fragmentary and partial.

No doubt, the *Treatise* constitutes a step forward in the road to Keynes's intellectual emancipation; there, he begins to break his ties with the *classical monetary theory*. However, for the time being, it is nothing more than a preliminary reconnaissance – as the Prologue warns the reader. The new scope, the new relationships, the renewed power that the variables that once were restrictively "monetary" achieve in this new post-war historical stage can only be appraised but indirectly. The *Treatise's* most original contribution lies in a single but decisive move: to mirror those unprecedented connections, Keynes was forced to definitively drop the quantitative theory.

The only purely monetary instrument that the *classical theory* provided was, in the new context, insufficient and rudimentary. But Keynes still had strong ties to the monetary theory. His concerns focused mainly in price level variations. However, along the level of prices, new characters began to march, characters until now absent in any treatise on money: the amount of savings, investment, and consumption of the economy as a whole. These variables become part of the equations with which the laws of the system are described.

What Keynes calls "Fundamental Equations" take the place of the quantitative theory. The old classical variables – quantity of money and income velocity of money – cede their place to a motley group of economic phenomena that had not been previously explicitly connected to the general level of prices. However, the result of this merger is still an unclear sketch, a rehearsal that is more remarkable for its ambition than for its consistency. Whatever the case may be, the blocks with which the "economic system" of *The General Theory* will be built have already been made, although they still coexist in a sterile disorder.

The reasons Keynes puts forward to discard the old quantitative theory, cornerstone of the whole classical monetary theory, unveil the core of his new concerns, related to the workings of the "modern economic system".

> The Fundamental Problem of Monetary Theory is not merely to establish identities or statistical equations relating (e.g.) the turnover of monetary instruments to the turnover of things traded for money. The real task of such a Theory is to treat the problem dynamically, analysing the different elements involved, in such a manner as to exhibit the causal process by which the price level is determined, and the method of transition from one position of equilibrium to another.
>
> (Keynes, 1935 [1930]; 133)

The quantitative theory, as has already been stated, is inadequate because although it leaves out certain factors and includes others, it is unable to show how the adjustment mechanism proceeds (the *Tract's* proverb "in the long run . . ." resonates here). Before reviewing those mechanisms and their reach, it is worth quoting a passage from the Prologue to *The General Theory* that points out the limitations that still weighed down on the *Treatise*.

> When I began to write my *Treatise on Money* I was still moving along the traditional lines of regarding the influence of money as something so to speak separate from the general theory of supply and demand. When I finished it, I had made some progress towards pushing monetary theory back to becoming a theory of output as a whole. But my lack of emancipation from preconceived ideas showed itself in what now seems to me to be the outstanding fault of the theoretical parts of that work (namely, Books III and IV), that I failed to deal thoroughly with the effects of *changes* in the level of output. My so-called 'fundamental equations' were an instantaneous picture *taken on the assumption of a given output*. They attempted to show how, assuming the given output, forces could develop which involved a profit-disequilibrium, and thus required a change in the level of output. But the dynamic development, as distinct from the instantaneous picture, was left incomplete and extremely confused.
>
> (Keynes, 1939 [1936]: vi; Preface; emphasis added)

The *Treatise's* acknowledged flaws can be summarized in a sentence: the development stops halfway through it. Actually, the result obtained is contradictory, as will be later shown, in line with Keynes's own admission. Monetary theory is linked, albeit imperfectly, to output theory. We should not lose sight of the flaw pointed out by Keynes, as it is the main one. In fact, the contradiction we identified in the *Tract* is displayed again in the *Treatise* taking on, if possible, an acuter form. According to Keynes, the fundamental equations assume that the level of output is given while explaining that the adjustment takes place, precisely, through changes in the level of income. Besides, the different levels of employment seem to be assimilable only to the disequilibrium positions of the system, not to stable situations.

Keynes's split with the classicists stemmed from the impossibility of quantitative theory to highlight causal relationships or describe the process through which price levels change. Keynes means to put his own Fundamental Equations on the pedestal left by the quantitative theory, but finds that to explain price variation mechanisms, it is crucial to include a wide range of elements that increasingly distance his concerns from the habitual interests of a treatise on monetary theory. Thus, in the Fundamental Equations of the Value of Money, it is clear that "real" factors interfere. The *Treatise on Money* is not, indeed, a treatise on money – it is more than that; however, neither is it a general theory of employment.

The sequence of this breakup may be split into two stages. The first step in breaking with the quantitative theory consists in disassociating the public's income from their spending decisions, and, at the same time, breaking down such decisions according to the kind of expense involved.

The monetary problem is no longer the object of study; to gain access to the secrets of price levels, it is necessary to identify the equilibrium conditions of the economic system as a whole.

> I propose, therefore, to break away from the traditional method of setting out from the total quantity of money irrespective of the purposes on which it is employed, and to start, instead – for reasons which will become clear as we proceed – with the flow of the community's earnings or money-income, and with its twofold division (1) into the parts which have been *earned* by the production of consumption-goods and of investment-goods respectively, and (2) into the parts which are *expended* on consumption-goods and on savings respectively.
>
> (Keynes, 1935 [1930]: 134)

One of the most striking ambiguities of classical quantitative theory lay in that aggregate real income (the real volume of transactions) was considered to be an unspecified whole. The simultaneous twofold division of the components of the product into income and expense, on one hand, and consumption and savings and investment, on the other, that Keynes proposes in the *Treatise* leads to surprising analytical results. Always mainly focused on the changes in prices, Keynes puts forward an explanation that, in contrast to the traditional quantity theory, draws a distinction between the level of prices of consumption goods and the level of prices of investment goods.

Two disparate sets of decisions are now at play: consumption decisions and investment decisions. This apparently harmless reframing of the quantitative theory will open, in fact, a real Pandora's box.

As he will later do in *The General Theory*, Keynes relies on Marshall's theory of value: equilibrium is reached in a market when a price reaches its normal price, that is, when it equals production costs. For equilibrium to be reached, total supply has to be divided so that the proportion of goods destined for consumption and those devoted to investment is exactly equivalent to the proportion of income destined to "purchase" goods of each type. The division of material output into consumption and investment goods has to be equivalent to the division of expenditure into consumption and savings. When the proportion is identical, supply and demand are even in both "markets"; the prices of both groups are equal to the corresponding production costs. This is the conceptual core of the fundamental equations, since if such equivalence is not reached, there is disequilibrium, which triggers an adjustment process that will modify prices.

The approach is completely novel. In the classical quantitative theory, price determination rested on purely monetary phenomena. It is true that the real total income (equal to total output) level, considered to be one of the factors affecting the amount of money demanded to conduct transactions during certain period, had a bearing on the issue. However, it was assumed that any change in the real level of holdings was due to a variation in the income velocity of money, not in income or output, as these were considered given factors. And, in any case, equilibrium was restored through the adjustment of prices, not of the produced quantities. In the *Tract*, the possibility that the public's and the banks' monetary habits might change was considered, but the analysis was still enclosed in the purely monetary sphere. In the *Treatise*, the theory takes a decisive turn: prices have to meet the equilibrium conditions specified by the theory of value (First Treatise), that is, in normal conditions, prices must equal production costs. What's more: at a closer look, this is an equilibrium scheme where two different markets are considered: that of consumption goods, and that of investment goods. How far the adjustment towards equilibrium may be carried out through price changes, and when the possibility of modifying quantities emerges will next be seen.

Price adjustment dynamic is simple. When prices are over (or below) costs, an extraordinary – that is of a larger (or smaller) amount than the level considered normal – profit (or loss) is obtained.[19] Businessmen's profits or losses act as a force driving changes in the system. In fact, they do not determine those changes, but work as a mechanism transmitting price imbalances, stemming from the differences between prices and costs: "Profits (or losses) [. . .] are the mainspring of change in the existing economic system".

The level of prices is established as follows: The First Fundamental Equation sets the "equilibrium" relationship between consumption goods prices and production costs. Algebraically, and taking into account that income and expenditure are divided between the goods of both kinds, Keynes shows that prices rise above costs (mainly remuneration costs) when the cost of production of investments exceeds the total amount of global savings. Thus, when investments surpass savings, consumption goods producers make extraordinary profits. In this way, the relationship between savings and investment becomes crucial to explaining prices.

According to the *Treatise*, the fundamental cause of disequilibrium lies in the fact that investment and consumption decisions (and, by subtraction, the amount of savings) are made by different groups of individuals acting in isolation. Thus, equilibrium is never ensured, but stems, rather, from the reciprocal reactions triggered when both sets of variables become "disproportionate".

> For workers are paid just as much when they are producing for investment as when they are producing for consumption; but having earned their wages, it is they who please themselves whether they spend or refrain from spending them on consumption. Meanwhile, the entrepreneurs have been deciding quite independently in what proportions they shall produce the two categories of output.
>
> (Keynes, 1935 [1930]: 136)

The factors of production – receptors of national income, excluding extraordinary profits, which, by definition, are not a component of income – decide the amount of their consumption. The difference between the community's total income and consumption determines the amount of savings. However, the non-consumed portion of income does not necessarily coincide with the investment goods produced volume. To complete the system, it is necessary to account for how the amount of investment is determined, and to additionally study different modalities that savings may adopt.

> When a man is deciding what proportion of his money-income to save, he is choosing between present consumption and the ownership of wealth. In so far as he decides in favour of consumption, he must necessarily purchase goods – for he cannot consume money. But in so far as he decides in favour of saving, there still remains a further decision for him to make. For he can own wealth by holding it either in the form of money (or the liquid equivalent of money) or in other forms of loan or real capital. This second decision might be conveniently described as the choice between "hoarding" and "investing", or, alternatively, as the choice between "bank-deposits" and "securities".
>
> (Keynes, 1935 [1930]: 140–141)

This explanation challenges the automatic identity of savings and invest-ments, an established dogma for the classicists. A portion of savings becomes hoarding, that is, money or bank deposits. The other is devoted to investment, through the purchase of shares – the distinction between active business-men and investors already mentioned in this section is repeated here. Seen in perspective, this division of the decisions and of the forms that savings may adopt anticipates a substantial argumentation that will only come to be com-plete in *The General Theory*. The decision concerning the portion of wealth that adopts the form of hoarding and that which becomes investment depends on the comparison of the return yielded by each. The yield of bank deposits is a function of the interest rate; the return on investments, in turn, involves the prices of shares and the expectations regarding their future movement.[20]

In spite of the inclusion of novel elements, the "monetary" spirit of the *Treatise* influences the whole explanation: Keynes is more concerned with the price of investments than with their volume. The general level of prices is formed, as a whole, by the price of consumption goods and the price of investment goods, and the expectations of the public affect, through this via, the price of investments (this is the Second Fundamental Equation).[21]

Besides, there is room here for "intervening" in the private economy: if the price of securities fell because the public was unwilling to purchase them, the banking system might buy them to back new deposits. It is for this reason that "the actual price-level of investments is the resultant of the sen-timent of the public and the behaviour of the banking system". Specifically, investment price is set at the point where the public's desire to hold savings in the form of bank deposits balances the volume of deposits effectively created by the banks. In this specific way, the banking system intervenes in price determination. It is no longer considered to display the "automatic" behavior of the gold standard period; now, its capacity to devise its own credit policies is acknowledged.

The *Tract* forwards a complete theory of prices. The price of consumption goods is equal to the addition of the production cost of a unit and the excess savings (per unit) over the cost of the investment (extraordinary profits). The price of investment goods will depend on the relationship between sav-ings and investment.

> The price-level of consumption-goods, relatively to the cost of produc-tion, depends *solely* on the resultant of the decisions of the public as to the proportion of their incomes which they save and the decisions of the entrepreneurs as to the proportion of their production which they devote to the output of investment-goods – though both of these deci-sions, and particularly the latter, may be partly influenced by the price-level of investment goods.
>
> (Keynes, 1935 [1930]: 143)

It should be noted that, in the system dynamic, the focus is on the determination of prices in general. Four factors are fundamental determinants: the rate of savings, the cost of new investments, the propensity of the public to hold bank deposits instead of securities (*bearishness*), and the volume of deposits created by banks. Changes in prices are triggered when there is an excess of savings over investment costs and when the public's desire to keep their wealth (hoard) surpasses the will and the capacity to create deposits in the banking system.

It is not our concern here to study the complex relationships between the different sets of prices; however, as may be seen, when the public desires to increase their savings, the price of consumption goods tends to fall. In turn, if the public decides to increase their *hoarding* in banks, the price of securities diminishes. Prices, in general, depend not only on the relationship between savings and investment, but also, and particularly, on the effect that the form of saving (investing or hoarding) exerts on the value of investments. Both movements interact and reciprocally condition each other.

> [A] change in the disposition of the public towards securities other than savings-deposits, uncompensated by action on the part of the banking system, will be a most potent factor affecting the rate of investment relatively to saving and a cause of disturbance, therefore, to the purchasing power of money.
>
> (Keynes, 1935 [1930]: 144)

This brief exposition of the *Treatise's* content shows that the *Treatise* is quite far from the *classical theory of prices*, which essentially was not much more than the quantity theory of money. When going through the pages of the *Tract*, we witnessed Keynes's first steps away from the classical quantitative theory; as has been mentioned, however, Keynes was still locked in a world of exclusively "monetary" variables. The novel elements introduced in the explanation offered in the *Treatise* allow variations in prices to be now understood as the result of causes altogether different: the decisions of the public concerning the amount of consumption, of savings and how they will keep their wealth and entrepreneurs' decisions the regarding investment, and banks' decisions regarding deposits.

In the *Tract*, the results of the quantity theory were qualified, giving it new meanings. Now, the theory is completely abandoned. With the modifications that Keynes introduces, the old results of the quantitative theory may, however, be reproduced using new instruments, but resorting to a number of totally arbitrary assumptions. In this sense, the final proof that a purely monetary explanation of prices has been abandoned lies in the fact that the Fundamental Equations may yield variations in price level and in money purchasing power even when assuming that the amount of money and the "velocity of circulation" remain constant.

This proof is, in fact, equivalent to a refutation of the classical quantitative theory, a refutation that, on the other hand, had already been rehearsed using the modified quantity theory of the *Tract*. The outcome is conclusive, for the proportionality between the variables involved in the equation, depicted by the quantitative theory, bears no relationship whatsoever to the real causal sequences.

> [T]he degrees of change in the quantity of money, the velocities of circulation, and the volume of output will not be related in any definite or predictable ratio to the degrees of change in the fundamental price-levels.
>
> (Keynes, 1935 [1930]: 147)

The *Treatise* signals the end of Keynes's subjection to the classical quantitative theory. He abandons the instrument, but does not drift definitively away from the traditional questions of orthodox theory.

In spite of the abandonment of the classical quantitative theory, the new elements that Keynes introduces are not enough yet to escape the strictly monetary framework: in fact, his main concern is still linked to changes in price level. However, during his explanation, some novel analytic features are displayed. In fact, the inquiry into equilibrium conditions in order to establish money's purchasing power on the basis of the Fundamental Equations offers, albeit as a by-product, a "theory" of the changes in the level of output and employment. Although a long tradition of reciprocal isolation is thus interrupted, the monetary and real aspects are, for the time being, linked only rudimentarily. After completing his main explanation, Keynes lists the effects of changes in prices on employment volume.

When extraordinary profits – considered as the difference between sale price and cost price, that is, the demand price and the supply price, in Marshall's sense – are not zero, entrepreneurs will have an incentive to expand or reduce the volume of output and employment. The banking system, in turn, is in a situation to regulate loans so that investment exceeds savings, which will provide entrepreneurs a mass of profits that will encourage them, in a context of credit abundance, to increase the value of remunerations, creating employment. Monetary disequilibrium is redressed through its effects on "real" variables. What Keynes will later call a "monetary explanation of employment" begins thus to take shape, albeit embryonically. Two aspects stand out. First, these are "short term" mechanisms, for independent of adjustment velocity; they do not involve an increase in population or capital stock. In the second term, the state (or the banking system) may help generate employment.

Therefore, the *Treatise* describes some state intervention mechanisms that are implicit in the system of Fundamental Equations and assesses its consequences. As has already been mentioned, banks have a crucial tool that allows them to exert influence on the amount of investment. If the theory is in a position to assert that this tool is always available to the banks, it is precisely because the manifestations of the recent historical changes have been taken into account – this option is available only in a system operating with *Representative Money*. The influence of banks on investment is a historical novelty with a two-fold base: on one hand, they acquire the power to manage credit policy without being subject to gold's moves, and this liberty stems from the non-convertibility of national currencies.

> By the scale and the terms on which it is prepared to grant loans, the banking system is in a position, under a regime of Representative Money, to determine – broadly speaking – the rate of investment by the business world.
>
> (Keynes, 1935 [1930]: 153)

Also, this explanation is capable of representing in the theory the emergence of a broad "investor class", different from the entrepreneurial class, whose link to the businesses is limited to the purchase and sale of ownership interests in new and old investments in an "organized market". The act of investing is synonymous with buying stock.

Thus, in the contemporary world, where *representative money* prevails, the banking system has a renewed capacity to influence the state of credit. The state of credit, in turn, influences the bank rate level, which defines, finally, the rate of interest. Hence it follows the movement of the level of prices (and of the product, an issue that for Keynes is, by now, secondary). Actually, the mechanism by which the banking system acts on investment was not unknown to the classicists, but the quantity theory established that relationship exclusively in supplementary explanations.

> We have, therefore, something with which the ordinary Quantity Equation does not furnish us, namely, a simple and direct explanation why a rise in the Bank-rate tends, in so far as it modifies the effective rates of interest, to depress price-levels.
>
> (Keynes, 1935 [1930]: 155)

The rate of interest becomes, thus, a transmission belt between monetary and real variables. The workings of this mechanism are described here with a much higher level of detail and complexity than in the sketches forwarded in the *Tract*. When the banking system raises the rate of interest, the future return on investments is reduced, and with it, the price of capital goods and the volume of investment itself.

But on the other hand, a higher rate of interest works as an incentive for saving. Thus, increases in the rate of interest tend to increase the saved amount over the value of investments.[22] According to the Fundamental Equations, this brings about a reduction in price level. As a result of its effect on entrepreneurs' decisions, an adjustment is triggered: the impossibility of selling commodities at a price equal to the cost of production brings about losses that will drive them to decrease output and wages. Costs finally fall as a result of remuneration reduction, and equilibrium is restored. The rate of interest is, first, linked to the investment and savings volume. The difference between savings and investment affects prices. When prices are over or below costs, extraordinary profits or losses occur. Keynes considers himself an innovator for having put forward a complete causal chain among these phenomena, which used to be scattered across disparate folds of the *classical theory*.

> No systematic treatment of the subject exists in the English language, so far as I am aware. You will search in vain the works of Marshall, Pigou, Taussig or Irving Fisher. Even Professor Cassel's treatment, which is somewhat fuller, does not examine the train of causation in any detail.
>
> (Keynes, 1935 [1930]: 186)

The depicted mechanism operates mainly on prices, but the adjustment triggered in the presence of profits or losses also provokes the increase or decrease of the volume of output and, therefore, of employment. The *classical theory* had never undertaken a complete treatment of the rate of interest movements and their effects on price levels. As may be to certain extent surmised, Keynes does not assign the responsibility either for this absence or his own findings to the others' or his own mediocrity or talent, but rather to the historical context in which the theories were developed. If the effects of the rate of interest on prices were not subject to a close analysis it was simply because it was not feasible yet – and, in fact, it was not until the collapse of the gold standard, when the rate of interest freed itself from its eminently exchange purposes – to outline or support a real "policy" concerning bank rate of interest management.

> "Bank-rate Policy", in the modern sense, was originated in the discussions which followed the monetary crisis of 1836–7 and preceded the Bank Act of 1844. Before 1837, such ideas did not exist – in the work of Ricardo, for example, nothing of the sort is to be found; and the explanation is not far to seek. For throughout the life of Ricardo, and

up to the repeal of the Usury Laws in 1837, the rate of interest was subject to a legal maximum of 5 per cent. For seventy-six years – from 1st
May 1746 to 20th June 1822, the Bank-rate stood unchanged at 5 per
cent. From 1822 to 1839 there were small fluctuations between 4 and
5 per cent. The rate of 5 ½ per cent established on 20th June 1839 (and
raised six weeks later to 6 per cent) was the first occasion on which the
official rate of the Bank of England had ever exceeded 5 per cent.

(Keynes, 1935 [1930]: 187)

How could a theory aimed at systematizing the effects of, and prescribing
practical policies associated to, the movements of the bank rate possibly
be developed when such a rate was fixed? From then on, the rate of interest started being manipulated, but only to transform it into an instrument
exclusively devoted to regulating the level of gold reserves, as has already
been discussed. It is true that certain authors such as Cassel or Wicksell
began to study its effect on prices. But it is Keynes who, in addition to
researching how changes in the interest rate affect the price level, highlights the fact that the adjustment of the system involves changes in the
level of employment. However, until now, employment variation is shown
exclusively as a problem inherent to disequilibrium and to the movement
towards equilibrium. Even so, it is not conceived of as a long-term issue,
because the system would be in a short-term disequilibrium until the product is adjusted.

On the other hand, Keynes states that an inadequate policy may seriously interfere in the creation of employment through a fall of prices. By
acknowledging that monetary and banking policies can bring about unemployment, he paves the way for formulating and answering separately a
question related to the opposite effect: may an adequate monetary policy
help create new jobs?

The *Treatise*'s argument regarding monetary intervention may be summarized by means of a simple sequence: the banking system primarily
manages the rate of interest, the rate of interest affects investment, and
investment affects prices. The missing link in the chain is evident: what
effects does the deliberate management of the rate of investment have on
employment? Not only is a greater resolve to focus efforts on an explanation of unemployment rather than prices missing, but also the economic
policy of the state is conceived of as exclusively restricted to the monetary
sphere. Even so, investment becomes a factor of crucial importance in the
system, a point of view that will also be present, on stronger grounds, in *The
General Theory*

it is broadly true to say that the governor of the whole system is the rate
of discount [. . .]. This means, in substance, that the control of prices

is exercised in the contemporary world *through the control of the rate of investment.*

(Keynes, 1935 [1930]: 22; II)

A rehearsal of an explanation of unemployment causes emerges for the first time in the framework of the monetary theory. When developing his theory of prices, Keynes comes across aggregate consumption, savings, and rate of investment. Perhaps on account of an excessive subjection to the traditional subjects and competences of the monetary theory, he does not overtly undertake the study of the differences between his theory and the usual explanations. But the restrictions that bore upon him are even stronger: he does not wonder if these new laws affect in any way the elemental categories of the classical school: money, capital, and commodity. These questions are not addressed, but the purpose of articulating a complete theory makes it necessary to find the answers.

On the road to *The General Theory*: advances in the *Treatise*

In the *Tract*, and as a result of his attempt to offer an explanation of the marked changes experienced in the general level of prices, Keynes had begun to free himself from the *classical monetary theory*.

It could be said that in the *Treatise* Keynes fully devotes himself to finishing the task he had undertaken almost ten years earlier. In a sense, the nature of the problems he addresses seems to be more tied to the *classical theory* than to his explanations, since the main purpose of governmental intervention is to guarantee the stability of the price pattern. However, an original "monetary" theory of employment is beginning to take shape, and to show itself, behind the discussions on the level of prices.

The *Treatise* turns investment into one of the main determinants of the price level and, therefore, of profits. Investment, in turn, may be managed – to certain extent – through the control that the banking system exerts over the rate of interest. The adjustment of the system proceeds first through prices, second by means of variations in the volume of employment, and finally through changes in the earnings of the factors of production.

> When there is a disequilibrium between savings and investment, this is much more often due to fluctuations in the rate of investment than to sudden changes in the rate of savings, which is, in normal circumstances, of a fairly steady character.
>
> (Keynes, 1935 [1930]: 95; II)

If the *Tract* had as its objective studying anew the monetary theory to adapt it to a world that had changed, the research dynamic itself forced Keynes to discard the quantitative equation and to involve "real" phenomena in price determination. The most volatile factor of the system is investment and this, in turn, depends on the rate of interest. As the monetary economist that he still was, Keynes feels uncomfortable, and even apologizes for the intromission of this "variable" in his work, as it is an essentially real factor. But in practice, and without making any declaration of principles, he refuses to endorse the *classical* division between the First and the Second Treatises, whose reconciliation will be one of *The General Theory*'s fundamental objectives.

At this point of his intellectual development, it may be said that only a single step distances Keynes from his final objective: building a "system" capable of determining the level of output and employment, incorporating the monetary variables into his explanation. He has already done away with the quantitative theory. But he still has to move forward so as to transform what was a mere process of adjustment towards equilibrium, that is, the fluctuations of investment seen as a reaction to disequilibrium, into an explanation of unemployment as a situation of equilibrium. He will devote the six years that run from the *Treatise* to *The General Theory* to finding this solution.

Chapter 1 began by positing Keynes's awareness of the relationship between historical transformations and the diverse theoretical accounts that try to depict a changing reality. That connection is the real source of inspiration for first the *Tract* and later for the *Treatise*. The last section shows that Keynes's perception of global monetary changes remains intact when writing *The General Theory*. The point is that his early conception of long-term economic transformations is one of the main inputs of the book that revolutionized twentieth-century economic theory, in spite of the indifference it generated among his followers and interpreters. It is not a detail – just another "antecedent" element, among others – but rather one of the fundamental bases to understand the scope – and the limitations – of his contribution.

After completing the *Treatise*, Keynes will still have to take one crucial final step to develop a real theory of equilibrium employment in a monetary economy. To succeed in his endeavor, he has to discard the key assumption that the economy is always at a point of full employment. But he will also have to change the axis around which the whole explanation revolves: instead of taking the level of prices as the main unknown quantity, he will have to keep that post for the volume of output. In fact, he had already covered a large stretch of that road in 1930. As he will say in the preface to *The General Theory* when referring to the Fundamental Equations of the *Treatise:* "They attempted to show how, [. . .] forces could develop which involved a profit-disequilibrium, and thus required a change in the level of output". Changes in output appear still as a secondary issue, a by-product of adjustment, which in addition led employment to its initial point. In *The General Theory*, Keynes will capitalize on his earlier findings.

This is precisely why where the reader may detect a break, he finds instead evidence of the continuity of his line of enquiry: his initial questions gradually find adequate answers.

> The relation between this book and my *Treatise on Money*, which I published five years ago, is probably clearer to myself than it will be to others; and what in my own mind is a natural evolution in a line of thought which I have been pursuing for several years, may sometimes strike the reader as a confusing change of view.
>
> (Keynes, 1939 [1936]: vii; Preface)

From the point of view of Keynes's forays in the field of economic policy, an evolution may also be observed, more marked by the problems of each historical moment than by a lack of continuity in his own ideas. In 1923, he advocated for the definitive abandonment of the gold standard. In 1930, he resignedly accepted England's return to the old parity and predicted that, as it was a relic of the past, time would do away with it. In 1936, it was already evident that the road back to convertibility into gold was definitively closed. One of the major consequences of the changes that took place in the monetary system was that the government was finally freed from limits to its interventions, formerly tightly restricted by the imperative to keep a fixed parity.

In hindsight, looking at what was now a past event, Keynes asserted in *The General Theory* that, under the rule of the *laissez-faire* and the gold standard regime of the nineteenth century, the only possible measure available to governments, if they were willing to contribute to the national economic expansion, was to actively participate in the search of new foreign markets. Colonialist greed, Keynes said, could be replaced with a profitable management of Representative Money (and then by the state direct investment).

> [U]nder the system of domestic *laissez-faire* and an international gold standard such as was orthodox in the latter half of the nineteenth century, there was no means open to a government whereby to mitigate economic distress at home except through the competitive struggle for markets. For all measures helpful to a state of chronic or intermittent under-employment were ruled out, except measures to improve the balance of trade on income account.
>
> (Keynes, 1939 [1936]: 382; VI.24.IV)

However, for the reasons already pointed out, the world economy had undergone a deep metamorphosis. In the new context, the government was in a position to fix the quantity of currency and to thereby ease credit, that is, to control, at least to certain extent, the rate of interest and through it to exert influence over the volume of investment and employment. It is not that the *classical theory* had overlooked this evident fact but rather, simply, that those instruments were unavailable in the era of generalized currency convertibility. As is stated in the *Treatise*, returning to the gold standard meant depriving society of the tools to deliberately contribute to its own progress.

> Thus the gold standard is, as I have said above, part of the apparatus of Conservatism. For Conservatism is always more concerned to prevent backsliding from the degree of progress which human institutions have already attained, than to promote progress in those quarters which are ready for progress, at the risk of 'upsetting the ideas' of the weaker brethren and bringing into question precarious and hard-won conventions which have the merit that they do at least preserve a certain modicum of decent behavior.
>
> (Keynes, 1935 [1930]: 300; II)

To conclude, while present-day macroeconomics imagines a timeless struggle between ideas and theories, Keynes is aware of the impact of history over economic thought. The needs of each period even prevail, frequently, over the criteria of scientific validity. In Keynes's view, the mere possibility of implementing a policy such as the contemporary economic policy is the result of society's evolution. Hence, when *The General Theory* is studied without such background, it also loses part of its merit and becomes an insipid, non-historical, and therefore abstract, "model".

Notes

1 "Keynes's involvement in the purely scientific aspects of the Keynesian revolution came to an end with a heart attack suffered in early 1937, soon after the publication of *The General Theory*" (Minsky, 1987 [1975]).
2 See, among others, Boyer (1985), Minsky (1982), De Brunhoff (1985), Clarke (1988), De Angelis (1997), Holloway (1996), Negri (1988 [1967]), and from an essentially empirical perspective, Klein (1954). Authors such as Bleaney (1985), instead, explicitly deny the relationship between *The General Theory* and historical transformations. Within macroeconomics, most debates deny the existence of this link *in practice*; in fact, it is not even discussed, making an intentional selection of Keynes's ideas.
3 In other works, he refers to this lack of synchrony between the increasing needs of a growing mass of population and its productive capacity subjected to the law of diminishing returns in the long term as the "economic problem of humankind".
4 In a previous work (Kicillof, 2000) we refuted this splitting of an author's thinking into many unconnected personalities; on that occasion, we referred

to a widespread approach among both the followers and the critics of Marx's work. In fact, it is not that Keynes or Marx suffers a sort of "schizophrenia" but, on the contrary, it is this gaze that feels compelled to split, divide, and classify that stems from the current confinement of the knowledge on society in the airtight compartments corresponding to the concerns of each academic and professional discipline. But there is no doubt that using this method to discuss the work of a major author is also appealing because it allows the contemporary reader to save energy. Instead of struggling to find coherence across the different aspects of the complete works of an author, a fragmentary reading is enabled that allows the reader to arbitrarily isolate different elements of the whole. It has also been shown that such procedure may easily ignore all the efforts the author may originally have made to emphasize continuity and avoid the fragmentation of his ideas.

5 And, conversely, it may be shown that during the first half of 1930, Keynes had already developed – and put forward in the courses he taught – most of the new theoretical ideas that he would make public in 1936. After studying the six sets of students' notes of Keynes's lectures delivered in the fall of 1933 in Cambridge, Skidelsky concludes that "If they had been published as soon as he delivered them, the world would have had quite an accurate idea of what was later received as *The General Theory of Employment, Interest, and Money*. What was missing was some tidying up – a mere question of formalization and filling gaps in the exposition" (Skidelsky, 1994).

6 Minsky considers this representation of investment decisions as one of Keynes's fundamental contributions that sets him apart from the orthodox theory: "In *The General Theory,* the speculative nature of asset holding and financing choices dominates production-function characteristics in determining investment output" (Minsky, 1983 [1975]). However, Minsky values this contribution because it is a more realistic description of the investment process. He does not manage, instead, to establish a connection between this description and a broader conception of the historical forms of capitalist development.

7 The expression "wage utility" refers to real wages because the satisfaction obtained from receiving a money payment depends, obviously, on its purchasing power, save that variations in the nominal wage amount be capable of deceiving the worker, that is, that he is assumed to be victim of the "monetary illusion".

8 This kind of analysis should not be mistaken for the epistemological currents inspired in Kuhn or Lakatos. For them, "scientific revolutions", "paradigm changes" or "research programs" are not shaped by social changes but by relationships and agreements within the scientific community, which seems to be isolated and impervious to social transformations.

9 The *classical theory* and its main proponent, Marshall, considered the stability of money's purchasing power as a theoretical premise, as is the case in the *Principles of Economy*.

10 Keynes ardently opposed the return to the gold standard, as he emphatically states in *The Economic Consequences of Mr. Churchill*, 1925. There he claims that such a revaluation, the government-proposed increase of 10 percent on the value of the pound, would place the hardship of the adjustment on the workers: "The orthodox answer is to blame it on the worker for working too little and getting too much".

11 The predominance of this approach in Marshall's *Principles of Economics,* Ricardo's *Principles of Political Economy and Taxation,* and Walras's *Élements* will be discussed later.

12 Keynes, who only intended to re-write the Second Treatise on money in this first work, did not contemplate here the reciprocal problem caused by this "money with no value or utility" in the First Treatise on the theory of value. In fact, the resource of commodity-money plays a crucial role that shapes the whole exposition of the theory of value, either in the Marshallian or in the Walrasian accounts. It is not so easy, instead, to include money paper from the beginning. Only when writing *The General Theory* will Keynes explore its consequences for the theory of value and distribution and try to expound the whole system without resorting to gold.

13 Keynes considers the levying of the inflation tax, in fact, as one of the main causes of excessive emission: "by the process of printing the additional notes the government has transferred to itself an amount [. . .] just as successfully as if it had raised this through taxation".

14 It should be remembered that the Bank of England was not strictly a government central bank; it was created as a joint-stock company, in spite of having the monopoly over the emission of pounds and acting as "lender of last resort", particularly for the government itself.

15 The influential Cunliffe Report, sternly criticized by Keynes after the war, recommends a return to the gold standard in order to once again implement the automatic regulation of money, free from government intervention: "There was therefore an automatic machinery by which the volume of purchasing power in this country was continuously adjusted to world prices of commodities in general. Domestic prices were automatically regulated so as to prevent excessive imports; and the creation of banking credit was so controlled that banking could be safely permitted a freedom from state interference which would not have been possible under a less rigid currency system" (Cunliffe Report). The report submitted to Parliament suggested that the best course of action for England was to return to monetary *laissez-faire,* the gold standard, since this system exempted the state of its duty to control foreign trade to avert high deficit and the banks of the need to take precautions to avoid lending in excess.

16 This explanation may easily be included into Keynes's idea of economic changes, and his division of the history of capitalism into different "ages". A clear parallel can be perceived regarding the deep causes of historical events. In fact, the problem of food availability in Europe stemmed from a limitation comparable to the one which is now considered to have a bearing on the quantity of gold.

17 In the *Tract,* Keynes warned the British advocates for the return to the gold standard about the dangers such a decision would entail for England. In practice, the new global distribution of gold forced England into subjection to and direct dependence on the policy of the US Federal Reserve, capable of modifying the quantity of gold in circulation and, therefore, of influencing the price pattern of the rest of the countries, independently of the situation of their trade balances.

18 This argument rests (tacitly) on the classical assumption of a fixed level of employment. Thus, the incentive of credit and demand will have as its exclusive outcome an increase in prices, without any variation regarding the level of activity.

19 It has to be borne in mind that Keynes separates (extraordinary) profits from ordinary income throughout the development. In several passages, he states that it is convenient to isolate profits precisely on account of their special character as regards the movement of the system. The dividing line between entrepreneur's

normal income and his extraordinary profits is somehow blurred, at least in practice. It is necessary to establish an entrepreneur's average or normal rate of "remuneration" above (or below) which his income is considered to be an extraordinary profit (or loss). In other words, cost is calculated including entrepreneurs' average, normal or "equilibrium" profit.

20 Similarly, in *The General Theory,* the investment equilibrium amount is reached when the expected return on investments is equal to the current rate of interest. This explanation will be studied later.

21 Keynes here divides investors into two groups: the group of the "bulls", who believe that prices will rise, and the group of "bears", who fear a fall in securities prices. They negotiate the market price. In *The General Theory,* bulls and bears determine interest rates, based on the amount of cash on hand available for speculation, once the amount needed for transactions has been established. This mechanism will be discussed in detail in the following section.

22 A connection of this kind between rate of interest and savings is plainly rejected in *The General Theory*.

2 What did Keynes call classical theory?

My readers will sometimes wonder what I am talking about when I speak, with what some of my English critics consider a misuse of language, of the 'classical' school of thought and 'classical' economists.
                    —*Preface to the first French edition of The General Theory*

Introduction

The issue we will try to settle in the following pages is the following: what is the content of the *classical theory*, target of *The General Theory's* criticism? Is it an adequate description of pre-Keynesian orthodoxy, or, on the contrary, is it a "straw man" set up by Keynes to challenge and defeat? And, lastly, does that *classical theory* coincide with the current orthodoxy? According to Hicks and many others, the *classical theory* is a freak, an artifact of Keynes's but not a mirror reflection of the early twentieth-century orthodoxy.

Before undertaking this enquiry, two questions should be clarified. First, although the reconstruction of the *classical theory* seems to be a problem exclusively pertaining to the history of economic doctrines, this task becomes crucial when attempting to assess Keynes's contributions. The debate known as "Keynes vs. the *classicists*" generally focused on discussing, interpreting, and weighing Keynes's contributions but neglected discussing the contents of the other "corner of the ring", where the classicists were. The idea therefore prevailed that Keynes had – deliberately or not – misrepresented the ideas of his rivals and teachers.

As mentioned, however, it is not possible to draw any definite conclusion regarding Keynes's contributions without reaching, first, an agreement concerning the essential traits of the pre-Keynesian orthodox theory, which following Keynes we will call *classical theory*. Paradoxically, the main beneficiaries of this misunderstanding were the followers of that orthodoxy that Keynes attacked, that is, the heirs and successors of the classicists. The absence of clear ideas on the precise content of the classical economics paved the way for an ambiguity that was used to restore – sometimes surreptitiously – the old tradition. In practice, defying the classicists' depiction that Keynes offered made it possible to accept some of his ideas without the need to discard the old beliefs en masse. As will be seen, this is one of the effects – and perhaps also one of the hidden causes – of the split of economics into two separate fields: microeconomics and macroeconomics. The hypothesis we will try to support by means of this reconstruction is that the *classical theory* that Keynes sought to rebut with his critique managed to survive, impervious to those challenges, by seeking refuge in the realm of economic theory that has since then been known as microeconomics, and that it is an adequate characterization of the *classical theory* of his times. Hereby, the *classical theory* did not even bother to respond or reject Keynes's criticism claiming that it was leveled at a theory that nobody endorsed.[1]

Second, the inevitable difficulties inherent in a task such as that which Keynes undertook should be taken into account. It is not easy – it is never easy – to depict the state of the art, the content of the "dominant theory" in a discipline in a rigorous and undisputable way. As could not be otherwise, *The General Theory*, apart from the examples it includes, did not aspire to criticize a particular text, certain author, or even a group of authors, but rather, it sought to challenge the *theoretical corpus* of a whole school of thought that, on top of everything, was its contemporary. Even assuming the best of intentions, and even admitting that in each period and place, for each generation, such generally accepted corpus of ideas has a practical actual existence, any attempt at identifying and specifying its main statements will always be subjected to an equal amount of challenges. There is an unfavorable asymmetry between the orthodoxy's criticism and defense: the former is demanded an almost impossible-to-attain rigor, while the latter can afford to be fragmentary and not thorough.

Keynes, however, was undoubtedly in a privileged position to face this challenge. His authority was undisputed and undisputable. In fact, as he himself admits, in criticizing the orthodoxy he became a convert, as up to then he was one of the most renowned proponents of that *classical, orthodox or traditional theory* that he now attacked.

> For a hundred years or longer, English Political Economy has been dominated by an orthodoxy. That is not to say that an unchanging doctrine has prevailed. On the contrary. There has been a progressive evolution of the doctrine. But its presuppositions, its atmosphere, its method have remained surprisingly the same, and a remarkable continuity has been observable through all the changes. In that orthodoxy, in that continuous transition, I was brought up. I learnt it, I taught it,

I wrote it. To those looking from outside I probably still belong to it. Subsequent historians of doctrine will regard this book as in essentially the same tradition. But I myself in writing it, and in other recent work which has led up to it, have felt myself to be breaking away from this orthodoxy, to be in strong reaction against it, to be escaping from something, to be gaining an emancipation.

(Keynes, 1973 [1936])

To the usual difficulties involved in reconstructing a contemporary theory, a matter of dates has to be added. In the early twentieth century, marginalism had just become the new orthodoxy, replacing earlier schools; it had just carried out a theoretical revolution of its own. The main advocates of this young current of thinking were far from sharing a perfectly homogeneous view of the doctrinary content of the new current. In Cambridge, one of the main hubs of scientific production, most of what would later be the official theory was not yet ready to be published, but was rather going through a dynamic process of consolidation.

The famous "oral tradition of Cambridge" is largely responsible for the difficulties faced when attempting to specify the exact content of the orthodox system, since nobody could obtain a comprehensive and clear idea of the system as a whole even when resorting to the most widely read texts of the period. However, Keynes, heir to Marshall's chair, can hardly be considered to be ignorant of or alien to the emergence of the new theories.

Now then, this limitation can hardly be taken as a pretext to challenge Keynes's reconstruction, while attempting, at the same time, to replace it with another that is, finally, recognized to be a legitimate depiction of the orthodoxy (this is what Hicks, for example, does). In any case, this argument nulls the possibility of identifying the standard theoretical corpus, and turns it invulnerable to any criticism in the process. The ultimate outcome of this kind of questioning is thus revealed – undermining or avoiding any attempt at controversy.

In the following pages, therefore, we will try to reconstruct the main aspects of the *classical theory* criticized by Keynes. To do so, we will resort to fragments scattered across *The General Theory* and to some of the works of the major proponents of the *classical theory*, particularly Alfred Marshall, the undisputed master for Keynes's generation.[2]

Chapter 2 is organized in the following way: First, a mystery is unveiled. Keynes places under the label *classical theory* the ideas of a motley group of economists, where *marginalists* such as A. Marshall and *classicists* such as D. Ricardo are included.

This term does not correspond to the label that is most frequently used at present, so that it is necessary to enquire the reasons that led him to gather apparently heterogeneous or even opposite ideas into such group. Once this issue is solved, two aspects of the *classical theory* criticized by Keynes will be described: the theory of money and the assumption of full employment. The reader used to the current framing of the orthodox theory will find those theories familiar.

Next, we will explore the *classical theory of money*. The classicists split the theoretical corpus of economics into two major branches or segments. On one hand, they expounded the theory of value and the theory of distribution. The former explained the determination of the price of goods; the latter established the amount of retribution earned by the factors of production, labor, and capital. Along the exposition, it was assumed (for the sake of simplicity) that there was no money or, rather, that the money was a fixed value commodity. The discussion of "money value" determinants was the subject of another book.[3] Keynes calls the study of value and distribution "First Treatise", and the classical theory of money "Second Treatise".

According to Keynes, both theories are different and contradictory, and imply different conceptions of the rate of interest and prices. A review of the First and Second Treatises of the *classical theory* will show the accuracy of such characterization. Besides, if there is one area where all the authors Keynes classifies as "classicists" (and even pure *marginalists*, such as Walras) concur, it is their conceptions regarding the monetary theory.

Finally, we will discuss the so-called "Say's Law". Keynes posits that the classicists (all of them) endorsed this principle that "supply creates its own demand". This assertion requires to be specifically studied, because although Ricardo and John Stuart Mill explicitly include this law into their system, the *marginalists*, such as Marshall or Pigou, never mention it. A historical review of the original doctrines will therefore be conducted, showing that Say's Law was used to deal with long-term issues. This study will culminate in a visit to the "mature" classicists, in whose ideas the same notions associated with Say's Law may be traced, but in connection with short-term problems.

I From Ricardo to Keynes through Marshall

The classical theory: a merging of Ricardians and marginalists

Beyond the (generally ungrounded) objections that may be raised against the portrait of the *classical theory* offered by Keynes, and discarding the hypothesis that the theory was deliberately misrepresented, it has to be accepted that this was Keynes's idea of the orthodoxy. Even more, it is the doctrine he endorsed before moving away from the *classical theory*: "I myself held with conviction for many years the theories which I now attack, and I am not, I think, ignorant of their strong points" (Keynes, 1939 [1936]: Preface).

The first enigma we will try to uncover has to do with the name Keynes uses to refer to the prevailing tradition of the period, the orthodoxy, which he calls *classical theory*. The choice of that name in itself is worth some research, as the label *"classicists"* is currently universally used – as in Keynes's times – to refer to the school of thought headed by Adam Smith and David Ricardo, the classical political economics. Keynes openly admits that he is suggesting the modification of the use of the term.

> 'The classical economists' was a name invented by Marx to cover Ricardo and James Mill and their *predecessors*, that is to say for the founders of the theory which culminated in the Ricardian economics. I have become accustomed, perhaps perpetrating a solecism, to include in 'the classical school' the *followers* of Ricardo, those, that is to say, who adopted and perfected the theory of the Ricardian economics, including (for example) J. S. Mill, Marshall, Edgeworth and Prof. Pigou.
>
> (Keynes, 1939 [1936]: 3; I.1.I)

Is this change in names due to Keynes's eccentricity or mischievousness? May it be assigned a purely persuasive role, thus becoming a further display of his renowned rhetorical skills? Or rather, do the group and its name carry a meaningful clue regarding the content of the orthodox theory that Keynes sought to criticize and replace?

Certain malicious intent could even be suspected: the presumed exaggeration implied in classifying some of his contemporaries as "classicists" would be but an elegant trick to get rid of his rivals – if anything may be surmised regarding "classical" authors it is that, beyond their prestigious trajectories or everlasting validity, their thought is lacking in topicality. Seen from this angle, "classical" is the opposite of "contemporary", "topical" "modern". This kind of interpretation, quite usual on the other hand, fantasizes and exaggerates Keynes's argumentative skills, to the point of seeing a real conspiracy at every turn of the language. When such interpretations are turned into hypotheses aimed at understanding his ideas, they become, instead, completely useless. Therefore, we will presume here that there is a relevant *conceptual* reason that led Keynes to choose that name to refer to his rivals.

The most shocking trait in this grouping is that some of the authors that are currently classified as classicists or, more precisely, Ricardians, as Ricardo and John Stuart Mill, coexist side to side with other famous marginalists, such as Marshall, Edgeworth, and Pigou.[4] The mysterious marriage of Ricardians and marginalists is also intriguing on account of some absences: none of the marginalism's "founding fathers", K. Menger, L. Walras, and, especially not, W. S. Jevons, the English member of this trio, is part of the group. What should be investigated is why Keynes decided to refer to two variously oriented schools, the Ricardians and some marginalists, when talking about the orthodoxy of his times.

Two different questions are raised in this connection: what is the common factor, on one hand, and what are the differences between the included *marginalists* and those excluded from this list? Even though it may not seem so, none of these questions involve a mere terminological subtlety or a simple detail relative to the history of doctrines; the answers, rather, are relevant to understanding crucial, though neglected, aspects of *The General Theory*.

A good start in trying to unveil these enigmas may be found in a telling passage of the Preface to the first German edition of *The General Theory*, quoted below.

> Alfred Marshall, on whose *Principles of Economics* all contemporary English economists have been brought up, was at particular pains to emphasise *the continuity of his thought with Ricardo's*. [. . .] In my own thought and development, therefore, this book represents a reaction, a transition away from the English classical (or orthodox) tradition. My emphasis upon this in the following pages and upon the points of my divergence from received doctrine has been regarded in some quarters in England as unduly controversial. But how can one brought up a Catholic in English economics, indeed a priest of that faith, avoid some controversial emphasis, when he first becomes a Protestant?
>
> (Keynes, 1973 [1936]; emphasis added)

The first clue is revealed in this passage: including David Ricardo and Alfred Marshall in the same tradition is not an idea of Keynes's but rather a reflection of Marshall's stance. It is through Marshall's economics that a line of continuity – not of breakup – with the Ricardian theory may be established. This clue leads us to the times when *marginalism* emerged, and to the differences between Marshall's and the founding trio's views.

The first marginalists: two opposite stances concerning Ricardo

In the early 1870s, when the contributions of the three founders of the marginalist tradition were almost simultaneously published, Ricardo's, and particularly, John Stuart Mill's (his avowed disciple) influence was strong. In that context, the marginalist revolution was such, if at all, precisely on account of its bitter opposition to the prevailing Ricardian doctrines. Today, it is agreed that the revolutionary aspects of the new school were: in the field of the theory of value,[5] the principle of marginal utility relates the value of commodities with the "intensity of the last want satisfied" (Walras's *rareté*), the "final degree of utility" (Jevons), or the "recognized utility" (Menger's *Grenznutzen*); in the field of the theory of distribution, the principle of marginal productivity relates the reward of the productive *factors* with their physical contribution to output, so that wages are equal to labor productivity, and rates of interest to capital productivity.

The first marginalists rebelled, therefore, against Ricardian orthodoxy. Beginning in the second half of the nineteenth century, Mill's *Principles of Political Economy* (1848) had become the most common account of the economic theory, that is, the official interpretation of Ricardo's theories. In fact, through a synthesis, Mill undertook to settle the existing disagreements, which had provoked vocal controversies between Ricardians and anti-Ricardians. The argument focused, mainly, on the theory of value. Mill posited that, excluding the goods whose quantity is fixed and cannot be multiplied, the value of commodities is proportional to production costs, if average or normal profits are considered.

Ricardo's theory of value stated, instead, that

> [t]he value of a commodity, or the quantity of any other commodity for which it will exchange, depends on the relative quantity of labour which is necessary for its production, and not on the greater or less compensation which is paid for that labour.
>
> (Ricardo, 1821 [1817])

Most of his explanatory efforts were directed at rejecting the theory of production costs (in the above quotation, for example, he stresses that wages, as a component of costs, do not determine value, but rather that only the amount of work has an impact on value). However, the difficulties encountered by his argument, which Ricardo was unable to solve, led him to later admit that the principle should be modified considering "the employment of machinery and other fixed and durable capital". The undisputed ambiguity of this theory of value triggered heated disputes with his critics (such as Malthus, Say, or Senior) but also provoked deep disagreements among his followers (such as James Mill, McCulloch, Ramsey, De Quincey, or Torrens). In its purest version, the only source of value is labor, but in the account of some of his disciples, capital use and time of production have a bearing on price determination.

Thus, Mill attributes Ricardo a theory of value based on production costs, also known as "additive theory of value", since according to this explanation, value tends to equal the addition of the costs involved in the production of each commodity. Besides, Mill challenges and displaces the prevailing interpretation concerning the position held by Ricardo in this respect, that commodity value only reflected the quantity of labor used to produce it:

> It will have been observed that Ricardo expresses himself as if the *quantity* of labour which it costs to produce a commodity and bring it to market, were the only thing on which its value depended. [. . .] we found that there is another necessary element in it besides labour. There is also capital; and this being the result of abstinence, the produce, or its value, must be sufficient to remunerate, not only all the labour required, but the abstinence of all the persons by whom the remuneration of the different classes of labourers was advanced. The return for abstinence is profit.
>
> (Mill, 1909 [1848]; III.IV.5)

Even though this is a modified version of Ricardo's theory, with time, it became the canonical interpretation of his explanation of value and, therefore, of the entire Ricardian theoretical edifice. By the time the marginalist school began its revolt, this was the prevailing orthodoxy regarding the theory of value.

Jevons, Walras, and Menger all, but particularly the first two, level their criticisms at Ricardo and Mill, his self-proclaimed heir. The first and main target of their attack is, precisely, the theory of value based on production costs. It is worthwhile quoting some of the heated passages of Jevons's *The Theory of Political Economy* (1871) and of Walras's *Elements of Pure Economics* (1874) to appreciate the tone of the conflict.

> When at length a true system of Economics comes to be established, it will be seen that that able but wrong-headed man, David Ricardo, shunted the car of Economic science on to a wrong line, a line, however, on which it was further urged towards confusion by his equally able and wrong-headed admirer, John Stuart Mill. There were Economists, such as Malthus and Senior, who had a far better comprehension of the true doctrines (though not free from the Ricardian errors), but they were driven out of the field by the unity and influence of the Ricardo-Mill school. It will be a work of labour to pick up the fragments of a shattered science and to start anew, but it is a work from which they must not shrink who wish to see any advance of Economic Science.
>
> (Jevons, 1888 [1871]: PS.45)

Jevons aims to debunk Ricardian economics. The theory of value based on costs should be replaced with a new one. In the Preface to the fourth edition of his *Elements*, Walras claims shared rights over the principle of value as determined by the marginal utility, while stating that the whole marginalist system rests on this pillar.

> Everyone competent in the field knows that the theory of exchange based on the proportionality of prices to intensities of the last wants satisfied (i.e. to Final Degrees of Utility of Grenznutzen), which was evolved almost simultaneously by Jevons, Menger and myself, and which constitutes the very foundation of the whole edifice of economics, has become an integral part of the science in England, Austria, the United States, and wherever pure economics is developed and taught.
>
> (Walras, 2003 [1874]: 44)

It is now suitable to briefly expose the core of the argument put forth by the *marginalists*, in its more sophisticated and complete version, that is, Walras's. His and Jevons's explanations share their point of departure: it is assumed that the quantities of each of the available goods are given, and that the same occurs in connection with the original distribution of those goods among individuals. The determination of value is thus reduced to how *exchange relationships* among different commodities are established, relationships based on the voluntary interaction of their holders, who go to the market to trade them for profit.

In fact, Ricardo, first, and then Mill, had analyzed a similar case, that of non-reproducible goods, and had arrived at the conclusion that, only in such a case, the price did not depend on the quantity of labor or on production costs, but was exclusively determined by the utility and scarcity of the commodity in question. They held, however, that most commodities were not subjected to that exchange law, since the quantity of each could be increased "whimsically" by means of production, and in fact it so would, every time the market price surpassed the corresponding cost of production.

Therefore, the movement of capital between the different spheres of production would result in an increase of the supply of those commodities that were transitorily "scarce". As production and supply grew relative to demand, prices would fall until reaching their *natural* level. As Mill states, the natural price or value is the core around which the market prices of all reproducible commodities revolve; only the market price depends on utility and scarcity, except in the case when the quantity of a good cannot be raised by means of production.

Menger, Jevons, and Walras's value theory turns this last case into the general case since, in principle, initial stocks cannot be modified.

The analytical exercise that the *marginalists* laid out deliberately isolates the moment of exchange by assuming that all commodities are, in principle, non-reproducible. Thus, an "economy of pure exchange" is built. From then on, the owners of the goods will set the value in exchange. Each individual has a pre-established quantity of goods (his initial stock) and goes to the market where he will attain maximum satisfaction or utility if, when trading, his behavior follows a simple rule: he will hand over the units of a commodity in exchange for other units provided the (marginal) utility of his commodities is less than the (marginal) utility of the units he receives.

It is also assumed that the utility afforded by each additional unit of a good is less than that furnished by the preceding unit (principle of the finally diminishing marginal utility). Marginalism does not recognize any value other than that which reflects the will of individuals at the moment of the exchange: it therefore rejects the distinction between market price and natural price, on one hand, and between reproducible and non-reproducible commodities on the other. Value is not an attribute of the object stemming from its production costs but, rather, something purely relative and circumstantial.

> Let us turn to Mill's definition of Exchange Value, and we see at once the misleading power of the term. He tells us – "Value is a relative term. The value of a thing means the quantity of some other thing, or of things in general, which it exchanges for." Now, if there is any fact certain about exchange value, it is, that it means not an object at all, but a circumstance of an object. Value implies, in fact, a relation; but if so, it cannot possibly be *some other thing*.
>
> (Jevons, 1888 [1871]: IV.4; emphasis added)

Although *Elements* is practically published simultaneously with Jevons's book, unaware of his colleague's work, Walras seems to be solving each of the difficulties that Jevons left unsolved. First, from the explanation provided, the relationship between prices should be obtained, but Jevons's exercise departs from these to give account of the optimal individual behavior. Second, the equilibrium attained on the market should include all the individuals and all the commodities of the economy, but Jevons only explains individual behavior assuming the existence of two goods.

The solution to both problems is the "theory of exchange of several commodities or the theorem of the general equilibrium". The approach is, basically, the same, but Walras's incorporates an additional assumption that makes it possible to solve the outstanding difficulties: it is assumed that the price of all commodities tends to its level of equilibrium, understood as a resting point that is reached only when the quantity offered equals the quantity demanded. This "law" according to which price is modified until the equality of supply and demand is secured was well known to all earlier theoretical economists; it had even been discovered in the prehistory of the economic theory.[6]

The novelty in Walras's account lies in the notion of "supply" in a context of pure exchange. For the marginalists, the exchanged goods have not been produced – they "appear" in the hands of individuals, so that the quantity of each commodity available for exchange is not the result of businessmen's decisions but of the holders of those goods who have received them for free and who act, in fact, as consumers. They offer that which they do not wish to consume because the exchange provides them with more desirable items.

As may be seen, the difference in approach as compared to Ricardian economics is remarkable: the quantity of each good cannot be increased simply because it is given, and no new item can be produced. In this context, offer decisions do not stem from entrepreneurs' behavior as based on return, but rather the law determining offered quantities is the exact opposite of the law determining demanded quantities: each individual offers or demands seeking maximum satisfaction, which he attains when "the ratio of the intensities of the last wants satisfied, or the ratio of *raretés*, is equal to price" (Walras, 2003 [1874]: 125)

To sum up, Jevons's exercise begins with a given price relationship and shows that an individual will exhaust his desire to trade when an equality between the relationships of utility and those of price is reached. Walras's exercise, instead, departs from a general equality between the quantities offered and demanded in all markets, which implies, *ex definitione*, that the law of Jevons is verified in all of them. By showing that there is a set of prices that meets this condition of equality, he arrives at the conclusion that those are, in fact, the relative prices of all commodities.

Walras's explanation goes on: he assumes now that those are the equilibrium prices and quantities of all commodities, and wonders what the equilibrium retribution of the factors of production (land, labor, and capital) will be. The factor endowment is also given beforehand. By means of an analytical exercise similar to the previous one and introducing the condition that the previously determined selling price for each commodity be equal to the unit cost of the services employed in its production, the equilibrium retribution of the production factors is determined. Thus, a simultaneous equilibrium of exchange and production is reached.

> Our solution of the problem of exchange led to a scientific formulation of the law of offer and demand. Our solution of the problem of production brings us to a scientific formulation of the law of the cost of production or of cost price [loi des frais de production ou du prix de revient]. Though, in the end, I shall do no more than rediscover two well-known fundamental laws of economics, I shall do so with this difference, that instead of presenting them as conflicting and mutually contradictory in the determination of prices, I shall assign to each its proper role by showing how the determination of the price of products

is founded on the first of these laws, while the determination of the price of productive services is founded on the second. It is a truth long acknowledged by economists – and I hope I may be believed when I say that this point has not completely escaped me – that under certain normal and ideal conditions, the selling prices of commodities are equal to their costs of production.

(Walras, 2003 [1874]: 211)

What is of interest here is showing that the first *marginalists* did not reject the classical formula according to which prices equaled production costs, but rather they believed they had reframed it by inverting the order in which phenomena are determined: prices are not determined by costs but rather by utilities, and these, in turn, determine the retribution of the factors of production and, therefore, costs. So, in its inception, *marginalism* introduces itself as the anti-Ricardian doctrine: for Ricardians, cost is the cause, and price the effect; for *marginalists*, the correct formula is exactly the opposite.

The conclusions yielded by such inversion of causality are remarkable: in the first place, the rewards of land, labor, and capital become an indirect reflection of the utility of the goods produced using those factors.[7]

Thus, the first marginalists introduce a contrast between two theories of value: the theory of the costs of production and that of utility, which in turn imply two theories of distribution. As will be shown, it is surprising that Marshall, Keynes's teacher, should choose the Ricardian theory over the marginalist.

Marshall's theory of value: four analytical moments

Much has been said about the differences between Marshall's and Walras's (and the rest of the founders of *marginalism*) conceptions. A well-known discrepancy concerns their partial and general approach to equilibrium. But the distance widens when it is assumed that another element distinguishing Marshall from Walras is that, while the former posits that market equilibrium is realized through changes in quantities, the latter considers that the adjustment is conducted by means of price movements (later we will discuss in detail this alleged difference). This enables the discussion of a further hypothesis – the discrepancy between both approaches is deeper. What distances both authors is the very theory of value, that is, the ultimate explanation of price determination. This claim may be surprising when compared to the usual interpretations; however, it is based on the assertions of Marshall, who, in his most significant work, *Principles of Economics* (1890), explicitly rejects the theory of value posited by Jevons, Walras, and Menger and emphatically advises returning to the Ricardo and Mill's old explanation.

Twenty years after publishing its seminal works, the marginalist school came to be enormously influential thanks to Marshall. In the course of the 1890s, the *Principles* gradually but resolutely overthrew – particularly in England – John Stuart Mill's treatise. Its predominance would last four decades.[8]

To a certain extent, Marshall's word became the word of the official economics.

The first marginalists particularly wanted to highlight their breakup with earlier economic thinking, stressing a discontinuity with Ricardian ideas. However, their eagerness to emphasize their distance from the old tradition began to weaken – naturally, it might be said – as they increasingly conquered academic circles and gradually became the new orthodoxy.

Marshall planned to turn economics into a mature science, thereby free of domestic quibbles among its practitioners. It was therefore crucial to smooth things over and dilute disputes that conspired against the unity and the seriousness that the new discipline needed to show. The Latin maxim *natura non facit saltum* quoted on the first page of the *Principles* was a true *motto* for Marshall, who, as a fervent follower of Darwin's theory, believed it to be valid both for the evolution of the species and historical phenomena, but also for the progress of science: "Economic evolution is gradual. Its progress is sometimes arrested or reversed by political catastrophes" (Marshall, 1920 [1890]; Preface to the eighth edition). His theoretical program therefore consisted in giving shape to a synthesis reestablishing the lost unity in the field of economic doctrines, which meant, in the late nineteenth century, consummating what was really a forced marriage between Ricardian theory and the new ideas, instruments, and peculiar language of *marginalism* – bringing together irreconcilable enemies.[9]

How to achieve that synthesis between marginalism and Ricardian theory? The road that Marshall finds does not entail ignoring marginalism's innovations, but rather placing them where they should be, next to the also correct Ricardian ideas. He identifies the principle of diminishing marginal utility as marginalism's distinguishing contribution, but he rejects the "semi-mathematical" method used to express this relation; in his *Principles*, formal demonstrations and graphs are usually consigned to footnotes and appendices.

> A great change in the manner of economic thought has been brought about during the present generation by the general adoption of semi-mathematical language for expressing the relation between small increments of a commodity on the one hand, and on the other hand small increments in the aggregate price that will be paid for it: and by formally describing these small increments of price as measuring corresponding small increments of pleasure [. . .] developed and published

almost simultaneously by Jevons and by Carl Menger in 1871, and by Walras a little later. Jevons almost at once arrested public attention by his brilliant lucidity and interesting style. He applied the new name final utility so ingeniously as to enable people who knew nothing of mathematical science to get clear ideas of the general relations between the small increments of two things that are gradually changing in causal connection with one another.

(Marshall, 1920 [1890]: 68n; III.III.2)

The second marginalist contribution concerned, according to Marshall, the theory of distribution. The retribution of the factors of production is equated to its additional contribution to output; thus, wage is equated to the marginal product of labor, and interest to the marginal product of capital, the productivities of which are also considered to be diminishing. Acknowledging these achievements does not imply, however, endorsing marginalists' claims.

In fact, Marshall considers the marginalists' reproaches to Ricardo exaggerated, if not absolutely unwarranted. Regarding Jevons, for example, he states:

His success was aided even by his faults. For under the honest belief that Ricardo and his followers had rendered their account of the causes that determine value hopelessly wrong by omitting to lay stress on the law of satiable wants, he led many to think he was correcting great errors; whereas he was really only adding very important explanations. He did excellent work in insisting on a fact which is none the less important, because his predecessors, and even Cournot, thought it too obvious to be explicitly mentioned, viz. that the diminution in the amount of a thing demanded in a market indicates a diminution in the intensity of the desire for it on the part of individual consumers, whose wants are becoming satiated.

(Marshall, 1920 [1890]: 68n; III.III.12)

As could not be otherwise, the integration between the Ricardian and marginalist thinking that Marshall intends to achieve has at its core the theory of value. From his point of view, both the principle of utility and that of the costs of production are part of the complete explanation of the phenomenon. While one is the foundation of demand, the other is that of supply. Broadly speaking, it could be said that supply and demand have, in relation to prices, a symmetrical effect.

The "cost of production principle" and the "final utility" principle are undoubtedly component parts of the one all-ruling law of supply and demand; each may be compared to one blade of a pair of scissors.

When one blade is held still, and the cutting is effected by moving the other, we may say with careless brevity that the cutting is done by the second; but the statement is not one to be made formally, and defended deliberately.

(Marshall, 1920 [1890]: App. I.21)

Marshall therefore accuses both schools of being somehow unilateral although, as will be later shown, he believes that the truth is on Ricardo's side. The battle cry of *marginalism*, its furious disdain of the theory of production costs, led it to posit, according to Marshall, that only demand determines value. But demand is just one of the forces acting in that field; utility affects demand and, through it, price, so that asserting that utility is the only cause of price, as marginalism does in its three original versions, is making a severe mistake.

We must not indeed forget that, at the time at which he wrote, the demand side of the theory of value had been much neglected; and that he did excellent service by calling attention to it and developing it. There are few thinkers whose claims on our gratitude are as high and as various as those of Jevons: but that must not lead us to accept hastily his criticisms on his great predecessors.

(Marshall, 1920 [1890]: 820; App. I.22)

Ricardo too receives a reprimand from Marshall, not on account of the content of his ideas (as instead happens in the case of *marginalism*), which Marshall deems basically correct, but mainly because of his harsh, excessively synthetic and abstract style, which was responsible for successive and recurring interpretation mistakes.[10] Furthermore, Marshall intends to "rehabilitate" Ricardo's theory of value, challenged by the *marginalists*, testing three hypothesis: i) Ricardo knew the principle of marginal utility as a foundation of demand; ii) In fact, he did not endorse the labor theory of value but rather the cost of production theory (a point of view that, in any case, had become established by Mill); and finally, iii) capital is, at par with labor, an original source of value.

No doubt, a considerable effort should be made to find such theoretical positions where most authors had read exactly the opposite. Marshall even argues that

[t]hroughout the whole discussion [about the difference between 'Value and Wealth'] he is trying to say, though (being ignorant of the terse language of the differential calculus) he did not get hold of the right words in which to say it neatly, that marginal utility is raised and total utility is lessened by any check to supply.

(Marshall, 1920 [1890]: App. I.4)

The idea that for Ricardo only labor creates value is strongly supported by his texts, which is not unknown to Marshall, who acknowledges that "[i]t is not disputed that this interpretation has been accepted by many able writers: otherwise there would have been little need for rehabilitating, i.e. clothing more fully his somewhat too naked doctrines" (Marshall, 1920 [1890]).[11] Therefore, such rehabilitation has to make explicit the alleged "hidden assumptions" of Ricardo's theory.

Broadly speaking, Marshall's theory of value posits a symmetry between supply and demand, although, at a closer look, it is an "uneven" symmetry, because to make both principles compatible, he is forced to once again split the analysis of value that the *marginalists* had tried to unify through a single category: the relationship of exchange. Ricardians had split the phenomenon of price into two: the value market, circumstantial and determined by utility and scarcity, on one hand, and the natural value or price, a basically cost price towards which the market price necessarily moved. Marshall's rehabilitation of Ricardo, based on which he hopes to achieve a reconciliation with the *marginalists*, recovers that old distinction, incorporating an analytical division of the problem into different "terms":

> The carelessness of Ricardo with regard to the element of Time has been imitated by his critics, and has thus been a source of twofold misunderstanding. For they [the first *marginalists*] attempt to disprove doctrines as to the ultimate tendencies, the causes of causes, the *causæ causantes*, of the relations between cost of production and value, by means of arguments based on the causes of temporary changes, and short-period fluctuations of value. Doubtless nearly everything they say when expressing their own opinions is true in the sense in which they mean it; some of it is new and much of it is improved in form. But they do not appear to make any progress towards establishing their claim to have discovered a new doctrine of value which is in sharp contrast to the old; or which calls for any considerable demolition, as distinguished from development and extension, of the old doctrine.
>
> (Marshall, 1920 [1890]: App. I.24)

From this viewpoint, Ricardo developed, without knowing or admitting it, a theory of value in the "long term", as determined by production costs. *Marginalists*, instead, focused exclusively on the transitory modifications of prices, which Marshall associates with the "short term". Thus, as may be seen, supply and demand determine, in fact, price, but in different (analytical) moments. Therefore, for Marshall, Ricardians were not completely mistaken but, at the same time, the *marginalists* were not completely original.

None of them managed to establish the conciliatory distinction between the short and the long term, which should be credited to Marshall.

> Thus we may conclude that, *as a general rule*, the shorter the period which we are considering, the greater must be the share of our attention which is given to the influence of demand on value; and the longer the period, the more important will be the influence of cost of production on value.
>
> (Marshall, 1920 [1890]: V.III.31)

Initially, it would seem that "there exists" a long-term value, ruled by supply conditions, and a short-term value, governed by demand; however, the radical difference between this approach and that of the first marginalists cannot be hidden, as production costs have returned. A closer look at the explanation reveals an even more evident distance.

Notwithstanding the subtleties that it introduces, Marshall's theory of value is, at all rates and at its roots, a theory of production costs faithful to the Ricardian tradition. The first and more relevant analytical division separates "market price" from what Marshall calls "*normal* price". The first is (similarly to the *market* price in Smith's *Wealth of Nations*, Chapter 7; in Ricardo's *Principles*, Chapter 4; and in Mill's Book III, Chapter 4) a price reflecting an equilibrium that is transitory and circumstantial, because it assumes that the available quantities of each of the goods cannot be multiplied. In this case, the amount offered is just the part of the already produced stock that entrepreneurs are willing to sell under certain conditions. The quantity demanded is regulated by the principle of marginal utility. The equilibrium reached is merely transitory.

A more detailed analysis begins when the possibility of increasing the produced volume is taken into account. The entrepreneurs take this market price as a reference to decide whether to modify the quantity produced. "Normal price" is an updated term for the "natural price" of the Ricardians. Normal equilibrium takes into account potential changes in output: manufacturers compare the price that the demanders are willing to pay for each volume of product (demand price) with the price at which it is profitable for them to produce different quantities of commodities (supply price). The adjustment now involves changes in the amounts produced, because if the demand price exceeds the supply price, entrepreneurs will obtain an additional profit that will encourage them to increase scale, while in the opposite case, there will be a tendency to decrease the amount produced. The only resting point where the amount produced does not show any tendency towards increase or decrease is that where demand price equals supply price, that is, when the normal equilibrium price is equal to the cost of production.

The *market price* assumes, therefore, a given stock of commodities. The *normal price*, instead, considers a potential increase or decrease in output. Normal (or cost, *Ricardian*) price is the center of gravity around which the market (or of pure exchange, *marginalist*) price fluctuates, thus reduced to a mere transitory, contingent level. At the same time, Marshall also analytically distinguishes between a short-term, a long-term, and a longer-term normal price; all of these are "normal" because they involve changes in output and, therefore, refer to supply conditions. In the short term, the stock of "plant", both "personal" as "impersonal", remains unchanged (during a number of months or a year). In the long term (a few years), that plant may be modified, in one branch or individual firm. The very long term (from one generation to the other) takes into account the long-term increase of knowledge, population, and capital. These are analytical moments, relevant to the analysis of the phenomenon of current prices: in each particular situation, the observable price is the market price, but "there is" a *normal* price corresponding to costs under the hypothesis of a short, a long, and a longer term. Or, so to speak, in each situation, from the point of view of the theoretical explanation of the phenomenon, each commodity has these four different equilibrium prices that are mutually related:

> As there is no sharp line of division between conduct which is normal, and that which has to be provisionally neglected as abnormal, so there is no between normal values and 'current' or 'market' or 'occasional' values. The latter are those values in which the accidents of the moment exert a preponderating influence; while normal values are those which would be ultimately attained, if the economic conditions under view had time to work out undisturbed their full effect. But there is not impassable gulf between these two; they shad into one another by continuous graduations.
>
> (Marshall, 1920 [1890]: P.5)

Like the Ricardians, Marshall analyzes the visible phenomenon through its hidden determinations, which implies splitting the category value or price. Now, as any theory of value based on production costs, this should also answer the question concerning the ultimate determination of prices (which Jevons had scornfully disregarded because it was an intrinsic value).

In fact, if the normal price is governed by costs, what determines, in turn, input costs? Marshall, obviously, furnishes an answer. As a last resort, if enough headway is made, the original costs involved in the production of each commodity – called "real costs" – may be found. Real costs represent "the efforts and sacrifices which have been directly and indirectly devoted to its production" (Marshall, 1920 [1890]: V.III.23).

In Marshall's words: *real cost* represents, therefore, the effort and sacrifice associated with labor and the effort or sacrifice associated with waiting.[12]

We will later discuss this explanation in detail, although, for the time being, it is evident that Marshall's theory of value distances itself substantially from the marginalist one; it is, instead, closely related to the Ricardian tradition, particularly to Mill's account. The waiting is the same sacrifice that Mill (and others) called "abstinence", a sacrifice that had to be suffered by the owner of wealth when devoting it to savings. However, Marshall credits Ricardo for the discovery of that theory of value, and it is the explanation he endorses and takes as a departure point for his entire conceptual development.

> Ricardo's theory of cost of production in relation to value occupies so important a place in the history of economics that any misunderstanding as to its real character must necessarily be very mischievous; and unfortunately it is so expressed as almost to invite misunderstanding. In consequence there is a widely spread belief that it has needed to be reconstructed by the present generation of economists. [. . .] [Ricardo] knew that demand played an essential part in governing value, but that he regarded its action as less obscure than that of cost of production, and therefore passed it lightly over in the notes which he made for the use of his friends, and himself; for he never essayed to write a formal treatise: also that he regarded cost of production as dependent – not as Marx asserted him to have done on the mere quantity of labour used up in production, but – on the quality as well as quantity of that labour; together with the amount of stored up capital needed to aid labour, and the length of time during which such aid was invoked.
>
> (Marshall, 1920 [1890]: V.XV.22)

The classical theory of value according to Keynes

This detour in our exposition leads us again to the work of Keynes, who had in mind this amalgam of Ricardians and marginalists, not any other doctrine, when talking about the *classical theory of value*. His support of the thorny endeavor of unifying English economics in its traditional and modern versions went so far as to mention it among Marshall's main contributions in the obituary he wrote immediately after his teacher's death, while "rehabilitating" Ricardo and reconciling him with the first marginalists.[13]

> The unnecessary controversy, caused by the obscurity of Ricardo and the rebound of Jevons, about the respective parts played by Demand

and by Cost of Production in the determination of Value was finally cleared up. After Marshall's analysis there was nothing more to be said.

(Keynes, 1924; 349–350)

After revisiting the controversy over the theory of price, it may be safely said that when Keynes talks about the equilibrium price or value of a commodity, he means, in fact, its normal price, as determined by production costs, not its market price, governed by marginal utility.

It follows that there are three aspects where fundamental differences between the Marshallian and the purely marginalist approaches may be found: the adjustment process; the "partial" or "general" character of equilibrium; and, more importantly, the *fundamental theory of value* endorsed by each school.

It has been frequently said that the fundamental difference between Walras's perspective (the most complete among the *marginalists'*) and Marshall's lies in that while in the former adjustment is realized through prices, in the latter adjustment is achieved by means of quantity changes. Thus framed, however, this distinction is inaccurate, which becomes obvious when a rigorous analysis is conducted. In both cases, when modifying any of the parameters, for example, the "structure of preferences", both the equilibrium price and the equilibrium quantity are modified until a new equilibrium point is reached: the adjustment involves prices and quantities in both perspectives. The actual difference, as regards the meaning of "equilibrium", lies in that Marshall studies how the *market price* is established just as much as he studies how the *normal price* is determined: there are forces driving the market (circumstantial) price towards the *normal price* level, the one pertaining to a steady equilibrium. This means that, for Marshall, adjustment towards a new *normal* equilibrium when there is some disturbance requires a change in production scale; in Walras's explanation, quantities also change, but here the change concerns traded quantities, that is, the quantity of existing stock of commodities that change hands. In Walras, supply is supply of stock goods, while the *normal supply*, in Marshall, refers to production scale. In the first case, it is a supply of available goods, goods that are held by consumers; in the second, it is a supply of produced goods, originating in a manufacturing process controlled by firms.

For Marshall, then, even when there is market equilibrium, the demand price may exceed the normal cost price. In that case, there is an increase in benefits, which encourages entrepreneurs to enlarge the normal amount produced of that item. What happens then with prices? It is an error to think that only quantities are adjusted, as prices may also vary, and generally, that is the case. While the produced quantity grows, the normal price or cost price will increase or decrease according to the return yielded: with increasing returns, costs fall; with diminishing returns, costs rise.[14]

Second, as to the discrepancies between Marshall and the first *marginalists*, it is necessary to remark on a little known aspect of the controversy between the partial equilibrium and the general equilibrium approaches, as revealed by the theoretical exchanges conducted by Walras and Marshall after the latter's publication of his *Principles of Economics*. It was stated here that Marshall was more interested in accounting for the determination of normal price than of market price, which he considered transitory and mainly governed by demand. For this reason, he studied the adjustment process in one particular market in detail, an adjustment that tends to set the price at the level determined by costs, and implies changes in the quantities normally produced and taken to the market. This analytical resource of isolating a particular market, however, deserved an explicit reproach from Walras. In an appendix to the third edition of the *Elements*, dated 1894, Walras objected to the Marshallian curves of supply and demand "which a number of English economists, following the lead of Mr. Marshall of Cambridge, are wont to employ".

As to the demand curve, he states:

> The *demand curve*, i.e. the *curve representing the quantity sold* as a function of the *selling price*, cannot be regarded as a rigorously exact curve. The quantity sold of any product is a function not only of its own selling price, but also of the selling prices of all other products and the prices of all productive services. [. . .][It is assumed] that the selling prices of other products and the prices of all productive services can be held constant, while the selling price of the product under consideration varies. Theoretically, they have no right to do this.
>
> (Walras, 2003 [1874]: 484)

Walras prioritizes his own discovery, the general equilibrium, which takes into thorough account the interaction between demands and endowments of *all* goods simultaneously. His objection to the supply curve is also significant, and points in the same direction. Walras argues that the supply curve reflects the changes in the production costs of a commodity that are brought about every time the offered quantity increases or decreases. However, he objects to the accuracy of the curve's representativeness, since if the supply price varies, it is because the prices of the productive services have changed, and therefore the price of all the commodities that employ these factors will also change, so that, in his words, "the entire economic equilibrium will be disturbed" (Walras, 2003 [1874]: 486). Indeed, he asserts, the supply (cost) curve of an isolated product cannot be traced, as this implies assuming that the rest of the prices and the quantities of the rest of the goods remain unchanged. In other words, the point where supply intersects demand is not a genuine equilibrium point only because each move will necessarily affect the rest of the markets, impacting, in turn, the original market, whose curves should reflect the new conditions. In brief, Walras argues, Marshall's study does not result in a "rigorous and complete" (Walras, 2003 [1874]: 487) theory of price determination.

This accusation is unfair but also mistaken. First, Marshall did not disregard the interaction among the prices of different commodities as concerns *market equilibrium*, and he neither ignored the impact triggered by changes in factors' retribution. However, in Marshall's system, this impact becomes essential only when studying the problem of market prices, for which this mutual influence is crucial, being as they are eminently subjected to demand conditions. The problem of the interaction among the prices of different commodities becomes decisive when studying pure exchange, without production, which is the starting point of Walras's analysis, but not of Marshall's.

However, it seems appropriate to assume that the prices of the other commodities remain fixed if the objective is to study the relationship between two prices of the same commodity, analytically separated: the market price and the cost normal price. The main factor to be taken into account then (as occurs in Keynes's system) is profit: discrepancies between demand price and supply price yield profits or cause losses which, in turn, trigger changes in the production level. The general equilibrium of normal prices is reached when all the commodities are sold at the price corresponding to their production cost, and such prices coincide with demand prices, and not merely when all the commodities in stock that their holder wishes to place – the amount of which is contingent – are sold. Marshallian normal general equilibrium implies and contains, so to speak, Walrasian general equilibrium. The importance of this difference to the conception of equilibrium and of the "adjustment process" cannot be overstated.

Finally, a conceptual difference that rises like a wall between both approaches should be mentioned. As has been said, marginalism undertakes the debunking of the Ricardian theory of value, based on production costs. Particularly, it declares war on Ricardo's own account, which sustains that ultimately value represents the amount of labor incorporated in commodities.[15] In its place, it proposes a theory of value based on marginal utility (a reflection of utility and scarcity). As an elated Jevons states, "[t]he Theory of Exchange, as explained above, rests entirely on the consideration of quantities of utility, and no reference to labour or cost of production has been made" (Jevons, 1888 [1871]). The prices of goods show, thus, consumers' preferences; the prices of the factors of production, wage and interest, in turn, also become a reflection, albeit indirectly, of the satisfaction offered by produced final goods when using them. Marshall categorically rejects such change of front, consigning the prevalence of utility to the limited area of the circumstantial market price, and returns, in his own way, to a

Ricardian explanation. Prices represent, in the last analysis, the difficulties, efforts or sacrifices involved in the productive process. These sacrifices are, according to Marshall, two: labor and waiting. That is the hard, irreducible core of this theory of prices.

More synthetically, the main difference between the first marginalists and Marshall does not lie in the fact that the adjustment be realized in terms of prices or quantities, nor in the partial or general nature of equilibrium, but should be found, instead, in the sphere of the fundamental theory of value. In one case, the (marginal) utility is the origin and cause of price determination, and production costs are an effect of that *causa causantes*; in the other, the ultimate explanation of value resides in the "real" costs of labor and waiting, and the observable price is a consequence of such deep determination.

So far, the differences between the *marginalism*, on one hand, and the synthesis between the new ideas and Ricardian interpretations that Marshall tries to develop, on the other, have been pointed out; now we have to briefly mention some of the most important similarities between both. We will not expound here, however, a critique of those doctrines.

It could be said that both value theories restrict themselves, fundamentally, to the market, albeit observing it from different angles; one because it exclusively focuses on the exchange of non-produced goods, setting completely aside the study of the conditions of production; the other because it explains prices resting on costs, which are, actually, other prices. Both fundamental explanations of value are based, in turn, on individuals' "sentiments", be they pleasurable or painful. One observes the upside of production, placing the source of value in the pleasure that its outcomes provoke; the other focuses on its painful side, by placing the source of value in the effort made and the deprivation suffered by individuals to obtain the products they need. For the pure marginalist explanation, prices are proportional to the welfare brought about by consumption; for the Marshallian account, prices are proportional to the "sacrifice" that has to be made to obtain goods, whether it be working or abstaining from consuming wealth awaiting for a result. In this sense, Keynes is not mistaken when considering both theories as part of the *classical theory*. Viewed from this perspective, both explanations are the opposite of the original genuine *Ricardian* conception – which is, on the other hand, as Marshall acknowledges, the more widespread interpretation of his theories – which posits that value represents the time of labor required to produce each good; and are even more opposed to the Marxist theory of value, where value is nothing but the material representation of a social substance, representation that confers upon the products the capacity of exchange, when labor is conducted privately. Therefore, the *classical theory* to which Keynes refers, and at which he levels his criticism, departs from a conception that, even acknowledging marked differences, displays a common conceptual core.

Both theories of value also lead to a conception of commodity that does not admit specific historical determinations. In fact, in every social form men "appreciated" the goods they consumed, and these were scarce relative to needs; and, in every society, too, men had to work and use some of the produce of their labor not for consumption but as means of production involved in the manufacturing of other items. It can therefrom be inferred that in every historical past period, but also in every social form that may be conceived of, men have to produce goods with value, that is, commodities. This is why both marginalist and Ricardian economics usually resort to metaphors that are completely alien to the history of human society – such as a "primitive rude state", the "society of the savage" or Robinson Crusoe's "individual society" – to illustrate the workings of economic laws.[16] In brief, both the theory of marginal utility and the theory of marginal cost consider that commodities have always existed and will always do, which is untenable from a historical point of view.

The classical theory of distribution according to Keynes

After discussing price determination, the *classical theory* of wages and of interest rates should be examined. The *classical* (Marshallian) *theory* of value equates normal price with production cost. The production cost of an item, in turn, is composed of all the inputs required to manufacture it. Its normal or cost price is, therefore, equal to the addition of the normal prices or supply prices of those inputs, which include raw materials as well as wage costs and rates of interest. Once the direct costs are figured out, a further step may be taken to consider the costs of such costs etc. By grouping inputs adequately, Marshall finds the so-called factors of production.

To determine the cost price, it is also possible to move in the opposite direction: ultimately, "real" costs are set by labor and abstinence, the two original sacrifices of any production, associated with "human nature".[17] Now, in practice, these "real" costs achieve concrete expression through their monetary form: wages and rates of interest. The conclusion is thus reached that the monetary prices of the factors of production (labor and capital) are the main production costs of any commodity, as their prices cannot be reduced to further costs. The rate of interest represents the retribution for the sacrifice of waiting.

> [H]uman nature being what it is, we are justified in speaking of the interest on capital as the reward of the sacrifice involved in the waiting for the enjoyment of material resources, because few people would save much without reward; just as we speak of wages as the reward of labour, because few people would work hard without reward.
>
> (Marshall, 1920 [1890]: IV.VII.30)

Thus, the *classical theory* of value is closely linked to the *classical theory* of distribution. It could even be said that they both constitute one block, as normal wages and the normal rate of interest compose the normal cost, and that is the level around which the market price oscillates, and towards which it tends. How are the wage and the rate of interest levels determined in the *classical theory?* First, we have already seen that both "represent" as money the cost of a "sacrifice". In other words, she or he who contributes his labor (working) and who furthers capital ("waiting") experiences suffering that has to be rewarded. However, this does not mean that the wage and the rate of interest obey exclusively the law of utility or rather, as Marshall states, the magnitude of his or her suffering, that is, the law of labor and waiting "disutility". To the contrary, in connection to distribution, the symmetrical relationship that the market establishes between supply and demand is also involved:"[T]he general theory of the equilibrium of demand and supply is a Fundamental Idea running through the frames of all the various parts of the central problem of Distribution and Exchange" (Marshall, 1920 [1890]: P.7).

The supply of labor and the supply of capital are regulated by the maximization of utility: working and waiting bring about suffering, but the wage and the interest obtained as rewards are sources of enjoyment. The worker and the owner of the capital contrast the compensation promised against the suffering originated by the last traded unit. The higher the salary or the rate of interest, the higher the quantity the laborers and the owners of capital will be willing to offer.

In this connection, Marshall moves decidedly away from the Ricardian theory of wages and rates of interest to endorse the *marginalist* explanations. He even argues that the Ricardians were already aiming at the solution:

> [t]he modern doctrine of the relations between labour and capital is the outcome to which all the earlier doctrines on the subject were working their way; and differs only in its greater exactness, completeness and homogeneity, from that given by Mill in the third chapter of his fourth book; the only place in which he collects together all the various elements of the problem.
>
> (Marshall, 1920 [1890]: VI.II.41)

The modern doctrine moves away from the old theories of subsistence wage, of wage fund, and of the natural rate of profit to restrict the determination of labor and capital retribution to the forces operating in the corresponding markets. The "disutility" sets the supply conditions that may be represented by means of a table (positively) relating supply prices with different quantities. To this, the other arm of the market is added: an explanation of demand grounded in the production process. For the entrepreneur, the hiring of labor and capital is subjected to the relationship between the retribution they demand and their marginal product.

Both the employment of labor and the use of capital are subjected to the law of diminishing returns. Thus, entrepreneurs define their demand of factors weighing the retribution of each factor against its physical return. When wages or rates of interest increase, if there is no accompanying productivity change, firms' demand will decrease. When hiring (marginally) more labor or capital, the additional product diminishes, so that the hired volume grows only when the retribution decreases. By applying this method, a table may be thus built (negatively) relating the prices of factors' demand with the different volumes that may be hired.

In brief, the determination of the normal price of labor and capital takes place in two different markets operating in the same way. The curve of labor supply represents the points at which the marginal disutility of labor equals wage utility. As marginal disutility increases (conversely to the law of diminishing marginal utility), an increased salary will induce a greater willingness to work, which is reflected by the positive slope of the curve. Entrepreneurs, in turn, will hire a unit more of labor only when the marginal product obtained exceeds the real salary: the demand curve contains all the points at which the marginal product equals the real wage. On account of diminishing productivity, the demand curve is negatively sloped.

> The tendencies of diminishing utility and of diminishing return have their roots, the one in qualities of human nature, the other in the technical conditions of industry. But the distributions of resources, to which they point, are governed by exactly similar laws. In mathematical phrase, the problems in maxima and minima to which they give rise are expressed by the same general equations.
>
> (Marshall, 1920 [1890]: 27n; IV.III)

Keynes calls this explanation "*classical theory* of distribution", i.e. of wages and rates of interest. It is fair to call them, similarly and by the same token, *classical theory* of employment and *classical theory* of investment. In fact, it is only a question of verifying that in both markets, the forces driving those "prices" to the equilibrium level are present. It may then be said that the real wage is (or tends to be, since if it were not, then the inequality would automatically be corrected) at the same time, equal to labor marginal disutility and to labor marginal product. Equally, the rate of interest is at a level where the marginal product of capital is equal to the marginal disutility of waiting, because elsewhere there are tendencies that will not be at rest until the "price" reaches that resting point. But the adjustment process at the respective markets sets not only the price but also the equilibrium quantity. The quantity that balances the labor market is none other than the equilibrium level of employment. The classical labor market constitutes in itself a theory of employment and a theory of wages. The same happens regarding the capital market, as the equilibrium quantity equals the level of new employed capital, and the equilibrium investment volume. The classical capital market provides a theory of investment, in addition to a theory of the rate of interest. On the capital market, two endogenous variables of the classical system are established: the equilibrium values of the rate of interest and of saving (investment). The salary and the equilibrium level of employment are set on the labor market.

Keynes will base his critique of the laws put forth by the classicists to determine wage, employment, interest, and investment on these explanations.

So far, we have offered a brief depiction of what in Keynes's view constitutes the *classical theory* of value and distribution, which is no other than the Marshallian account of the economic theory, the most widespread in his times, particularly in England.

This section is devoted to examining two implicit aspects of this system: the tacit axiom of full employment and the static method. The interest in this study comes from two sources. First, it is important to elucidate what is exactly meant when talking about fixed output and static analysis, as these are two terms that may be very differently employed, giving rise to numerous misunderstandings, misinterpretations, and false controversies. Second, because these are for Keynes two characteristic aspects of the classical system, aspects that he intends to supersede with his own contribution.

Concerning the static state, he argues that "[T]he fact that the assumptions of the static state often underlie present-day economic theory imports into it a large element of unreality" (Keynes, 1939 [1936]: 146; IV.11.V). Regarding the given level of resources and the given level of output, in the preface to the first English edition, he states,

> Most treatises on the theory of value and production are primarily concerned with the distribution of a *given* volume of employed resources between different uses and with the conditions which, assuming the employment of this quantity of resources, determine their relative rewards and the relative values of their products.
>
> (Keynes, 1939 [1936]: 4; I.2)

And he asserts once again in the preface to the first German edition,

> [Marshall's] theory of output and consumption as a whole, as distinct from his theory of the production and distribution of a *given* output, was never separately expounded. Whether he himself felt the need of such a theory, I am not sure. But his immediate successors and followers have certainly dispensed with it and have not, apparently, felt the lack of it.
>
> (Keynes, 1939 [1936])

Now, what is the exact meaning of an allegedly *given* volume of output and resources on which the *classical theory* rests? The issue may be easily understood if the case of the marginalist (Walrasian) theory of pure exchange is first discussed. The general equilibrium of exchange studies the way in which the existing output – the volume of which is *given* – is distributed among the different individuals, according to their preferences. More specifically, it shows how the system of prices provides for the allocation of those goods so that individual welfare is optimal. When equilibrium is reached, no individual will have a desire to conduct any other transaction or, in other words, supply will equal demand in all markets. The difference between the beginning and the end of the period may be perceived in the endowments held by each individual, which are modified as a result of exchange, but not in the total volume of commodities of each kind nor, therefore, in the total amount of commodities taken as a non-differentiated whole. If instead of the equilibrium of exchange what Walras calls *production equilibrium* is studied, it is possible to see that both the starting situation and the results are analogue. It is also assumed that the total amount of available labor and capital are given quantities. Each individual may sell the services of labor and capital or keep them. The set of equilibrium prices ensures that all those holders wishing to sell them may do so in the quantity that maximizes their utility. The salary and the rate of interest are at the point where supply equals demand. This does not mean, obviously, that all the available labor and the available capital will be employed, but it does mean that all that holders desire to sell may be placed on the market. Nobody, in this situation, intends to work more or save or invest more, since if that were the case, then, by definition, there would be no equilibrium. In this case, Keynes's description can be recognized beyond any doubt: resources and output are given.

In the (Marshallian) *classical theory*, the problem is slightly different. In contrast to the pure marginalist theory, Marshall intends to study changes in output, which leads him to distinguish between market circumstantial prices and normal prices in his theory of value. However, the result is ultimately the same. When he studies the short-term normal price, which is the relevant one in this connection, the volume and the quality of the "personal and impersonal" stock of plant, i.e. facilities and labor, are given. From there, he sets out to study how resources are allocated among the different branches of production. Contrary to the previous case, where a given quantity of commodities is taken as a departing point, to analyze then how they are exchanged and then produced, the opposite direction is followed. This theory posits that all prices tend to move towards their normal equilibrium level, equivalent to their relevant production costs, that is, "the volume of production adjusting itself to the conditions of the market, and the normal price being thus determined at the position of stable equilibrium of normal demand and normal supply" (see Marshall, 1920 [1890]: IV.III.3). This means that resources may go to one industry or another until profits become stabilized at their normal level across all branches.[18]

> When therefore the amount produced (in a unit of time) is such that the demand price is greater than the supply price, then sellers receive more than is sufficient to make it worth their while to bring goods to market to that amount; and there is at work an active force tending to increase the amount brought forward for sale. On the other hand, when the amount produced is such that the demand price is less than the supply price, sellers receive less than is sufficient to make it worth their while to bring goods to market on that scale; so that those who were just on the margin of doubt as to whether to go on producing are decided not to do so, and there is an active force at work tending to diminish the amount brought forward for sale. When the demand price is equal to the supply price, the amount produced has no tendency either to be increased or to be diminished; it is in equilibrium.
>
> (Marshall, 1920 [1890]: V.III.18)

Output increases and decreases in a particular branch as long as that variation is compensated in one or more branches while capital and labor flow from one branch to the other. By this means the relative value of the different products is set, but the total volume is *given*. The same happens in connection with the available resources on hand. When the labor market and the capital market are balanced, the retribution of the factors equals its marginal product and its "marginal disutility" respectively. This last condition implies that, with given available resources, the system sets the balance rewards that enable the production of an also given amount.

Except in the cases when classical economics dealt with the very long term, which would currently be a chapter of the *classical theory* of growth, the determinants of changes in the aggregate volume of production, conditioned by growth in population, equipment, and technical developments, were not discussed.

As regards method, the static character of the pure marginalist theory is not worth discussing. Walras, for example, states almost at the end of his *Elements:* "the problems of exchange, production and capital formation already treated without abandoning the static point of view" (Walras, 2003 [1874]). This is also the case in the *classical theory*, although, as usual, Marshall tends, here too, to embellish and qualify definitions.

> [T]his volume is concerned mainly with normal conditions; and these are sometimes described as Statical. But in the opinion of the present writer the problem of normal value belongs to economic Dynamics: partly

because Statics is really but a branch of Dynamics, and partly because all suggestions as to economic rest, of which the hypothesis of a Stationary state is the chief, are merely provisional, used only to illustrate particular steps in the argument, and to be thrown aside when that is done.

(Marshall, 1920 [1890]: 36n; V.V)

However, more may be said concerning the static-dynamic contradiction.

Contrary to Walras's instantaneous *tâtonnement* (groping), Marshall's system intends to depict an adjustment process unfolding over time through changes in output level, not through the redistribution of the initial and final endowments of each good held by each individual. However, the aim is to show that the system tends to its normal equilibrium position, an equilibrium that, notwithstanding what Marshall states in the above quoted paragraph regarding its "uses", is ultimately a static condition.

An additional remark concerning the difference between statics and dynamics should still be made.

When Keynes uses the term "dynamics", he is not referring to the (disequilibrium) trajectory between one equilibrium position and other such position. As has already been mentioned and will be later shown, Keynes's system does not intend to portray disequilibrium situations nor transitions from one equilibrium to the next, but rather states of normal equilibrium with unemployment. It does not refer either to conditions enabling the study of the equilibrium trajectories of variables. As will be seen, it specifically displays a system where individuals take the future into account when they make their current decisions. Through their causal relationships, static systems represent the present, as if it were the last or the only "day", so to speak. A dynamic system, as that of Keynes's, includes also individuals' perceptions of their future. However, this change of front entails a deeper conceptual modification.

In Keynes's system, such "expectations" are "embodied" in their singular representation, money and capital. This discussion, however, will have to be postponed until we address Keynes's system.

II The classical theory of money

First and Second Treatises of the classical theory

By the time Keynes was developing his new ideas and preparing his revolt against orthodoxy along with the *classical theory* of value and of distribution, a specific field of study had emerged to which economists (Keynes among them) devoted their efforts: the theory of money. The *classical theory*, in fact, was composed of these two major specialized branches: the theory of value and the theory of money.

This divide of the conceptual corpus, which separated the theory of value and the theory of money, became one of Keynes's major theoretical concerns. In the preface to *The General Theory* he admits, for example, that he had previously accepted such a divide as natural and unchangeable: "When I began to write my *Treatise on Money* I was still moving along the traditional lines of regarding the influence of money as something so to speak separate from the general theory of supply and demand" (Keynes, 1939 [1936]: vi; Preface).However, in *The General Theory*, that split of the economic theory into two watertight compartments is emphatically rejected: "The division of Economics between the Theory of Value and Distribution on the one hand and the Theory of Money on the other hand is, I think, a false division [. . .]. (Keynes, 1939 [1936]: 293; V.21.I).

The separation of the economic theory into a "real" and a "monetary" – to use the usual terms – realms was so extreme that Marshall himself, the most renowned *classical* economist, had devoted a special treatise to each of these subjects: his famous *Principles of Economics* (1920 [1890]), and the late *Money, Credit and Commerce* (1923), published one year before his death, treat each subject separately.

Marshall is not the only *classical* economist who chose this course of action: although Ricardo did not write two different books like Marshall, he dealt with the monetary theory proper in the last chapters of his *Principles of Political Economy and Taxation* (chapters XXVII and XVIII) after completing the discussion of all the issues pertaining to value and distribution. Walras, to take a *pure marginalist* as an example, also dealt with the question of money separately, in the section VI of his *Elements of Pure Economics*, after resolving the main questions of his theory of exchange (commodities' price) and his theory of production (factors of production's price). That is, in their conception of money – even more so than in their theory of value – the economists that make up the *classical theory* become partners: the Ricardians, the English marginalists headed by Marshall, and the founders of marginalism, conveniently represented by Walras.

On account of reasons that will be discussed, Marshall, but also Ricardo and Walras, prefer to develop their theory of value and distribution, that is, their explanation of prices in general and of "factors" retribution disregarding almost completely money. All of them state that such omission has as its sole purpose simplifying the exposition.

The idea that the fundamental principles are not affected when a detailed discussion of money is introduced is implicit (and sometimes explicit). For this reason, it is deemed convenient to postpone the study of money's nature, particular traits, and effects on the rest of the economic variables. The Second Treatise (or the final chapters of the First) is almost exclusively devoted, instead, to disentangling the nature of money. However, approaching money *separately* brings about certain highly relevant theoretical difficulties. In fact, when money proper appears on the theoretical stage, many of the economic laws that had been posited, discussed, and taken to be valid in the First Treatise are modified or, equally, new fundamental determinations are now put forth to explain some of the more relevant economic phenomena, such as the rate of interest or the general level of prices. Thus, some "subjects" that had allegedly been clarified in the First Treatise turn up again in the Second, with new aspects. Such intertwining challenges, at the very least, the relevance of the split. Moreover, what constitutes a real weakness of the *classical theory* then emerges: the independent approach to money seems to in fact hide that the system offers two incompatible explanations for the same economic processes, one when an economy without money is considered, the other when a monetary complete economy is studied. Such an approach hides, then, an inconsistency lodged within the core of the *classical theory*.

On the other hand, it would seem that the difference between the First and the Second Treatise of the *classical theory* does not lie in the fact that in the first the nonexistence of money is "assumed" – with a simplifying purpose – and in the second money is "added on" to the same system in order to assess its effects, but in the fact that the notion of money itself is modified. Therefore, the problem is one of a theoretical nature, which concerns content, and not a merely expository choice of formal character.

The complexity of the problem in question demands a reasoned exposition, although for the sake of brevity, we will resort to the relevant passages only occasionally.

The "Non-Monetary Money" of the First Treatise

As was mentioned before, *classical (marginalist and Ricardian)* economists try to completely ignore money when putting forth their theories of value and distribution. Apparently, depicting a moneyless economy, or an economy where money plays very limited roles, does not entail any loss in conceptual terms, but does involve, instead, tangible benefits from the point of view of the propaedeutics. This is one of the numerous "simplifications" to which the *classical theory* resorts, thus managing to have money disappear or at least lose its connection to the rest of the economic phenomena.

In the First Treatise, it is assumed that only gold (or silver) works as money; that is, money is, first and foremost, a commodity that, in itself, has no more traits than those stemming from the fact that it has been arbitrarily chosen as money by the author. The choice of a precious metal as money, without even discussing the question of coinage, seems to rest on a simple immediate observation: civilized countries "generally" adopt precious metals as currency. This is, therefore, the first assumption about money that permeates the whole exposition: resorting to it, all other "materials" that could play the same role are set aside: bank deposits, debt securities of all kinds, checks and documents, convertible or non-convertible paper money, certain types of "liquid" durable assets, and so on. By considering that money is a mere commodity, it is possible to dispense with a deeper and more accurate definition of money, and, further, with a serious discussion of the nature of money. Specifically, this choice, apparently based on practice and common sense, implies considering money equivalent to commodities in general and thinking that the laws that determine the value of money are exactly the same as those that govern the value of other commodities. In terms of classical economics, this commodity money would also have a market price fundamentally ruled by demand, assuming a fixed stock, and a normal or cost price to which the circumstantial price would tend to adjust. In principle, the conditions of supply and demand would not have any distinctive traits, and the value of the metal would change on account of the same reasons and in the same way as any other commodity. On the other hand, regarding its demand, it would seem that, as happens with the rest of the goods, there is a desire to own gold on account of its utility as commodity, that is, of its different uses, both in the realm of consumption and of production. Supply, on the other hand, also seems to be controlled by capitalist firms that behave according to the general laws. As is the case with all commodities, changes in production costs (or in demand) affect the "price of money". The only differences seem to lie in the obvious fact that the price of a monetary commodity cannot be expressed in money, and, on the other hand, in that a change in the "intrinsic value" of money owing to changes in its production conditions has a bearing on the price of all the rest of the commodities that is, by definition, its exchange relationship with money expressed in "units of money". For this reason, the phrase "price of the money" is awkward and frequently replaced by "money's purchasing power", although it always refers to the quantities of all the other goods that can be bought with a unit of money, which in turn is the inverse of the general level of prices.

Basically, commodity money thus conceived plays only one role: expressing value or, in other words, being a *general measure of value* for the other commodities: "the price of anything will be taken as representative of its exchange value relatively to things in general, or in other words as representative of its general purchasing power" (Marshall, 1920 [1890]: II.II.28)1920 [1890]. The *classical school* also calls this function "price pattern or standard" indistinctly. So far, it suffices to call "price" the value relationship of any commodity with the commodity that acts as money; however, this value measure does not seem to be fully accurate as money has no distinctive feature and, precisely for that reason, as will be seen, its own value undergoes changes, which turns it into a highly imperfect unit of measurement, a material unfit for measuring value. As Adam Smith himself asserted before everyone else (and after him, all the economists that tried to use a commodity as a measure of value for all the rest):

> Gold and silver, however, like every other commodity, vary in their value, are sometimes cheaper and sometimes dearer, sometimes of easier and sometimes of more difficult purchase. [] But as a measure of quantity, such as the natural foot, fathom, or handful, which is continually varying in its own quantity, can never be an accurate measure of the quantity of other things; so a commodity which is itself continually varying in its own value, can never be an accurate measure of the value of other commodities.
>
> (Smith, 1904 [1776]; I.V.7)

Marshall's theory of value asserts that every commodity has its "intrinsic", so to speak, natural price, conditioned by its costs of production, and tries to express it in terms of money, using with this purpose a commodity chosen to that effect. However, the value of a commodity can never be accurately manifested by means of its relationship with another commodity whose own value also undergoes changes, because a change in price would not actually express a change in the value of the first commodity – it would rather be an ambiguous indicator, as the variation in price could convey a change in the value of money or in both values at the same time. The normal price that Marshall purports to set and measure with money demands an absolute, not purely relative, expression. However, being a commodity like the rest, the value of money is also subject to fluctuation: can this issue be in any way solved?

The solution arrives hand in hand with a new assumption. To the first assumption (which enables the avoidance or deferral of all discussions on the nature of money) a second supplementary assumption is thus added: in the First Treatise, a certain commodity plays the role of money, but once chosen for that role, it is no longer subjected to the laws determining the value of the rest of the commodities, as it is axiomatically established that the value of the monetary commodity is fixed. Money works as an invariable measure of value because it is decreed, by means of an assumption, that its own value is fixed:

> Throughout the present volume we are supposing, in the absence of any special statement to the contrary, that all values are expressed in terms of money of fixed purchasing power, just as astronomers have taught us to determine the beginning or the ending of the day with reference not to the actual sun but to a mean sun which is supposed to move uniformly through the heavens.
>
> (Marshall, 1920 [1890]: VI.VI.31; emphasis in the original)

Thus, with a new assumption, a fundamental problem that is not expository but theoretical is solved: having its own value fixed, gold, the commodity money, becomes the invariable measure of value for all the other commodities. The cost paid for this maneuver lies in that all general determinations of value are suppressed in connection with money, although initially being treated like any other commodity. That is, on the basis of "empirical" observation, it is assumed that money is an ordinary commodity, in order to later assume, now claiming an "analytical" need that money is anything but an ordinary commodity, since its value is exempt from change. Beyond the astronomical metaphor, which is not very actually compelling, an investigation is needed with respect to how the artifice of the assumption that money has a fixed purchasing power contributes to the construction of the First Treatise of the *classical theory*, apart from serving the need to properly and unambiguously express the value of the rest of the commodities.

Marshall's theory of value, which Keynes integrates into the *classical theory of value*, intends to study the value or price of each commodity considering it in isolation. A closer look at the problem reveals – from the point of view of the author of this book – that the money with fixed purchasing power is not a mere didactic or expository simplification but actually a device of crucial theoretical significance: it becomes the cornerstone of the "partial equilibrium" approach. Three are its main theoretical consequences. First, asserting that the price of money does not change means saying that its purchasing power is not modified, which in turn implies that the general level of prices does not change, so that it is the same as assuming that the value of all the rest of the commodities is fixed. Only on the basis of this assumption can it be asserted, in a theory of value such as the classical one, based on costs and preferences, that the value of commodities depends exclusively on their own demand and their own supply: through the fixed price of money, it is implicitly established that the rest of the prices (of supplementary or substitute products, and of the factors of production) will also remain fixed. Second, the assumption of a fixed purchasing power for money is the condition that ensures, no more and no less, that all the demand curves "behave", that is, that all of them are negatively sloped. It has been empirically shown that there are certain goods whose demand rises when income decreases (the so-called inferior goods). If this is true, then the positively sloped demand curve could undermine the determination of market prices. Marshall himself admits the existence of such anomalies:

> as Sir R. Giffen has pointed out, a rise in the price of bread makes so large a drain on the resources of the poorer labouring families and raises so much the marginal utility of money to them, that they are forced to curtail their consumption of meat and the more expensive

farinaceous foods: and, bread being still the cheapest food which they can get and will take, they consume more, and not less of it.

(Marshall, 1920 [1890]: III.VI.17)

However, the problem is more general, as any increase in the consumption or the price of a good entails a decrease in the wealth of the individuals that consume it, which implies an increase in their personal appreciation of the "value" of money:

> In other words, the richer a man becomes the less is the marginal utility of money to him; every increase in his resources increases the price which he is willing to pay for any given benefit. And in the same way every diminution of his resources increases the marginal utility of money to him, and diminishes the price that he is willing to pay for any benefit.

(Marshall, 1920 [1890]: III.III.12)

However, as it has been assumed that money always has a constant purchasing power, it should also have a constant marginal utility, both at general and individual level. As a result, when discussing demand, Marshall is allowed to neglect the so-called "income effect" as a determinant of the relationships between the values of all commodities.[19] And the last of the consequences that this new assumption has for the analysis, which we will of course discuss, is no doubt the more theoretically relevant.

Money with constant purchasing power represents a constant marginal utility (and regarding its normal price, a constant marginal cost, too) for individuals; this characteristic is essential in Marshall's account, as it makes money itself disappear, turning it into a mere vehicle linking the price market of the commodity that is being studied in isolation with the prices of the rest of the commodities:

> we have as yet taken no account of changes in the marginal utility of money, or general purchasing power. At one and the same time, a person's material resources being unchanged, the marginal utility of money to him is a fixed quantity, so that the prices he is just willing to pay for two commodities are to one another in the same ratio as the utility of those two commodities.

(Marshall, 1920 [1980]; III.III.10)

That is, if the utility of money is considered constant, then relative prices in money become an equivalent of the relationship between their marginal utilities. Even more, nothing prevents us from stating that the price of a commodity (its exchange relationship to the constant marginal utility money) is a reflection of the marginal utility of the good itself. Money is turned into an invariable perfect measure of value, which means, in terms of market equilibrium, that the price of each commodity in money reflects its utility at the margin, and in the case of the normal equilibrium, that each normal price in money reflects the production costs at the margin.[20] Equally, through money, it can be said that the wage is equivalent to labor marginal disutility, and the rate of interest, to the marginal disutility of the waiting, which are the two pillars of the Marshallian theory of real cost.

Even so, Marshall states that it is advisable to postpone a more detailed study of the nature of money, as well as of its effects on the other economic phenomena in order to examine them independently in a special Treatise (that Keynes calls Second Treatise); he adds that such a split does not entail any analytical problem. He makes this comment when studying prices: "The theory of buying and selling becomes therefore much more complex when we take account of the dependence of marginal utility on amount in the case of money as well as of the commodity itself" (Marshall, 1920 [1890]: V.II.13); when examining the determination of the rate of interest:

> the rate of interest which the borrower is willing to pay measures the benefits that he expects to derive from the use of the capital only on the assumption that the money has the same purchasing power when it is borrowed and when it is returned.
>
> (Marshall, 1920 [1890]: VI.VI.31)

When discussing wages:

> In endeavouring to ascertain the real wages of an occupation at any place or time, the first step is to allow for variations in the purchasing power of the money in which nominal wages are returned. This point cannot be thoroughly dealt with till we come to treat of the theory of money as a whole.
>
> (Marshall, 1920 [1890]: VI.III.16)

Prices, rate of interest, wages – all of them will have to wait to be thoroughly studied until a theory of money, which has been postponed on behalf of simplicity, is put forth. However, the analysis of the assumptions introducing money in the First Treatise shows that not only simplicity and expository order are to be made responsible for the characteristics attributed to money.

Much to the contrary, the constant purchasing power of money is at the very core of the classical theory of value. And the accusations could even be more serious: it could happen that by introducing a notion of money, both more complex and more similar to actual money, the laws put forth in the First Treatise to explain prices, the rate of interest and wages might be affected or even replaced with other, different laws; as a result, the *classical theory* would be necessarily fractured.

With the aim of showing that this conception of money does not stem from a mistake, an eccentricity, or some whim of Marshall's but rather from an analytical need derived from the classical approach, it will suffice to briefly examine the First Treatise's concept of money associated to the theory of value in Ricardo's *Principles of Political Economy*, and in Walras's *Elements*. It will be thus seen that this monetary conception in inherent to the *classical theory* of value.

In Chapter 1 of his most significant book, Ricardo lays out a theory of value that, beyond the unsolved issues it involves, he summarizes better than anyone else in the first paragraph of his text: "The value of a commodity [. . .] depends on the relative quantity of labour which is necessary for its production" (Ricardo, 1821 [1817]). Later, Ricardo discusses the issue openly, instead of introducing money (like Marshall) assuming both that it is a commodity and that its value is constant, thereby rendering it an invariable measure of value.

Immediately after admitting that the search for an invariable measure of value is an inherently fruitless task, as his own theory of value assumes that the changing conditions of production of all commodities affect their value, that is, after acknowledging the inexistence of such a fixed "anchor" in the system, Ricardo puts forward an argument similar to Marshall's to justify the expository convenience of this mechanism:

> To facilitate, then, the object of this enquiry, although I fully allow that money made of gold is subject to most of the variations of other things, I shall suppose it to be invariable, and therefore all alterations in price to be occasioned by some alteration in the value of the commodity of which I may be speaking.
>
> (Ricardo, 1821 [1817]; 1.78)

This analytical contraption is only abandoned later, practically at the end of the book, in the chapters devoted to studying the "real" effects of money. In the First Treatise, Ricardo uses the same mechanism as Marshall.

Walras's general equilibrium cannot do without a currency with fixed and arbitrary value either, without its own invariable measure of value. The departing point for the exposition of the theory of value (as in the case of Jevons) is the analysis of a "model" where only two commodities exist. From the exercise consisting of the "pure" exchange of a fixed given amount of two commodities, arbitrarily distributed among individuals, Walras derives the conclusion that the *rareté* (the intensity of the last want satisfied or, modernly, the marginal utility) is the "cause of the value in exchange", as the equilibrium prices are equal to the quotient of the *raretés*

(Walras, 2003 [1874]). Here the problem of money is not even raised as, for the hypothetical case of two commodities, there is only one relative price. Exchange is synonymous with barter.

In the following section, Walras examines the problem of the exchange of several commodities, showing that the same criteria applied to pairs of commodities applies here, which is the same as stating the conditions of general equilibrium, since from indirect exchanges arbitrage gains may be obtained:

> if one wished to leave arbitrage operations aside and at the same time to generalize the equilibrium established for pairs of commodities in the market, it would be necessary to introduce the condition that the price of either one of any two commodities [. . .] expressed in terms of the other be equal to the ratio of the prices of each of these two commodities in terms of any third commodity [. . .].The commodity in terms of which the prices of all the others are expressed is the "numéraire".
>
> (Walras, 2003 [1874]: 161)

Through the introduction of the *numéraire*, a first theoretical problem is solved: all commodities will now have only one price in terms of the *numéraire*, which prevents any arbitrage operation, that is, obtaining gains by intermediating exchange. As may be seen, the laws determining "value", that is, the exchange relationship of the commodity chosen as *numéraire* to the rest is the same general law, that is, the *numéraire* is an ordinary commodity whose only difference with the rest is the fact that it has been chosen to express the prices of all other commodities.

Yet, there still remains a problem to solve: the presence of the *numéraire* ensures compatibility across all the relative prices (i.e. exchanging A for B, and then for D would not be different from exchanging A for C and then for D), that is, the law of the "single price" (also called Jevons's or Gresham's law) is ensured. In other words, the general equilibrium furnishes a system of relative prices that is undetermined in terms of magnitude. This indeterminacy is corrected by fixing the value of the *numéraire*, whose price is conventionally equated to one unit: "the situation of a market in a state of general equilibrium can be completely defined by relating the values of all the commodities to the value of any particular one of them. That particular commodity is called the *numéraire* and a unit quantity of this commodity is called a standard" (ibid.). The relative value of money is set by the conditions of general equilibrium, but by giving it a determinate absolute price equal to one, the rest of the commodities get to have their own price too, equivalent to the amount of units of commodity money obtained in exchange for a unit of that commodity.

Immediately after having introduced, in practice and to meet an essentially analytical need, a money with constant purchasing power, that is, a unit price *numéraire*, Walras acknowledges that the *numéraire* is, actually, different from real money owing to two circumstances: first, "generally, the same commodity that serves as *numéraire* serves also as *money* and plays the role of medium of exchange", apart from being a value measure. Once this happens, "[e]very trader keeps available a stock of money for eventual exchange; and, this being the case, the use of a commodity as money does affect its value in ways that we shall study later on" (Walras, 2003 [1874]: 190). That is, the discussion of all the questions related to the value of money is postponed in order to be *separately* undertaken in the Second Treatise.

All told, the money of the First Treatise is, in all these cases (Marshall, Ricardo, and Walras), embodied in any commodity turned into invariable measure of value by means of an analytical assumption: its value remains constant, canceling the influence of the general laws of value on the commodity. Money is considered a commodity, at the cost of no longer being so, since if it was an ordinary commodity, its price would depend on its utility or cost. Money, in any case, has an intrinsic value, to the extent that it is impossible to change. Beyond the needs that brought it into being, nothing is yet known about money's nature. Why is there money in the economy? How is its value determined, when are these assumptions disregarded? How do its changes influence prices in general, rates of interest and wages? Are the explanations contained in the First Treatise modified?

The money of the Second Treatise

Until now, money was any commodity – gold, for example – to which a fixed value was imposed, turning it into a measure of value while depriving it, by decree, of the attributes that characterize any other commodity. If it is true that the money of the First Treatise is not a commodity proper, it is also true, paradoxically, that it is not money proper either. It is not money because, in spite of acting as general measure of value, in practice, it is not used actually as money, at least in its usual sense; and this is so because the money of the First Treatise does not play the role of general means of exchange. The system has been conceived analogously to a barter economy; although all the values are expressed in a common unit, exchange works as a direct exchange (a commodity is traded for other) with no mediation of money, as there is no law establishing that an amount of it is enough to trade in commodities. Any theory of money, no matter how rudimentary, should take into account this evident truth: on the market, goods are always exchanged for money. The *classical theory*, however, could not reflect upon the consequences of this function of money until its Second Treatise. Next, we will briefly review how Marshall grapples with the questions raised by an economy where money effectively works as a medium of exchange, problems whose discussion the classical theory of value had postponed instead of addressing or solving them. The First Treatise lacks a "fundamental" theory of money. Nothing is said there about its nature or its origins. Furthermore, its relationship to the rest of the commodities and to value in itself is totally external, since as soon as it is turned into an ordinary commodity, it is deprived of that character by fixing its value. If a different, deeper treatment of the subject is expected in the Second Treatise, specifically devoted to the discussion of money, the reading of the text will be disappointing. Instead of founding the emergence of money on the results obtained in the First Treatise, two alternative, disparate accounts are offered: a historical one – the description of the evolution of the different monetary forms – and a functional one – a listing of the different purposes for which money is effectively used once it appears on stage. The functional, apparently theoretical, explanation is exclusively limited to describing what money is for, leaving aside, once again, a logically precedent question: what is money?

> [T]he chief functions of money fall under two heads. Money is, firstly, a *medium of exchange* for bargains that are completed almost as soon as they are begun; it is a 'currency'; it is a material thing carried in purses, and 'current' from hand to hand, because its value can be read at a glance. This first function of money is admirably discharged by gold and silver and paper based on them [. . .]. The second function of money is to act as *standard of value*, or *standard for deferred payments* – that is, to indicate the amount of general purchasing power, the payment of which is sufficient to discharge a contract, or other commercial obligation, that extends over a considerable period of time: and for this purpose stability of value is the one essential condition.
>
> (Marshall, 1923: 16; I.I.3)

Marshall's enumeration raises two comments: on one hand, it is immediately recognized that the first role of money is precisely that which the money of the First Treatise was unable to play; on the other hand, the second role, that of acting as a standard of value, is premised on an attribute of money which was previously granted by means of an assumption: its value has to be stable. For the first time, the determinants of the value of money have to be directly discussed. This more detailed study would not be traumatic for the *classical theory* were it not for the fact that, as will be shown, by playing this first and novel role (medium of exchange), certain particular traits are introduced in the determination of its value that threaten its capacity as an appropriate measure or standard of value, a role that although being now presented as its second function, was the only one played by money in the First Treatise. Things, therefore, are far from simple.

How is the value of money established? If deemed to be a commodity, money has an "intrinsic" value determined by demand and supply;

according to this view, money seems to enter into circulation to act as a medium of exchange endowed with its own value. This is, more or less, what Marshall posits, although he immediately stumbles upon a problem. The value of money does not refer exclusively to itself, but rather at the same time expresses its purchasing power with respect to other goods. It is as though its value doubled, since in this case value does not seem to come from money itself but rather from the rest of the commodities, giving it the appearance of pure fiction: money has no value in itself, but an external factor grants value upon it or recognizes value in it. Therefore, money would have an attributed value, which is not inherent to its own conditions of production and its own demand. Initially, Marshall rejects this impression, and tries to subject money to the general laws of value.

> In early times it was commonly said that the values of gold and silver are 'artificial'. But in fact they are governed on the side of supply by cost of attainment, and on the side of demand by the needs of people for ready purchasing power based on gold and silver, together with the demand for these metals for the purposes of industry and display.
>
> (Marshall, 1923: 40; I.IV.2)

Even though money still appears as an ordinary commodity, by acknowledging its role as a medium of exchange, the reasons for demanding money multiply. The demand of the commodity "money" in its capacity as commodity has nothing particular, as it depends, ultimately, on consumers' preferences and needs based on its utility. But it is also demanded as a medium of exchange, and for this reason its value seems to be artificial, as the utility of money is not its own, but the reflection of the utility of the rest of the commodities that may be purchased with money. This line of reasoning is disappointing: the market price of any commodity must reflect its utility, but the price of money when considered as medium of exchange must reflect the utility of all the rest of the commodities. Moreover, if money is used to conduct all purchases, the quantity of money demanded depends, more specifically, on the addition of the prices of the commodities that will enter into circulation. But if the prices of the commodities depend on the relationship between its value and the value of money, then the value of money depends (through demand) on the values of the other commodities that, in turn, depend on the value of money. If, conversely, it is held that the utility of money stems from its purchasing power, then the utility of money's source is its own price, which leads us to a new circular reasoning: money's utility is proportional to its value, but its value is, at the same time, proportional to its utility.

This gobbledygook can be easily resolved assuming, as the First Treatise does, that money has a fixed value. However, the *classical theory* promised to properly solve the issue of the value of money, without appealing to this assumption, in the Second Treatise.

The difficulties derived from the analysis of money demand, however, do not end here. In contrast to the other commodities, whose marginal utility diminishes as the purchased volume increases, money does not seem to be subject to any satiety principle – the thirst for money does not have any apparent limit, unless money has other attributes, apart from acting as a medium of exchange, that set a limit to the demanded quantity. Marshall confesses then that money *functions* as capital. More precisely, apart from the fact that the capacity of acting as medium of exchange is now added, it turns out to be in itself capital or, at least, to share with capital one of its main attributes: yielding interests.

> [C]urrency held in the hand yields no income: therefore everyone balances (more or less automatically and instinctively) the benefits, which he would get by enlarging his stock of currency in the hand, against those which he would get by investing some of it either in a commodity – say a coat or a piano- from which he would derive a direct benefit; in some business plant or stock exchange security, which would yield him a money income.
>
> (Marshall, 1923: 40; I.IV.2)

The demand of commodity money exhibits certain peculiarities: it stems from its character of commodity – on account of its utility – but also from its role as medium of exchange. The latter is conditioned by an alternative use of money: buying an investment that yields benefits. Money, considered as wealth, becomes a medium for saving and, therefore – and apparently, automatically – for investment. However, the idea of money as capital raises a new problem, since the rate of interest is, on one hand, a parameter of money demand, but in its capacity as capital, money must be part of the supply of savings and, therefore, must also affect the determination of the rate of interest. On the other hand, when the value of money changes, prices also change, and with them, interest in real terms. It is obvious that none of this was part of the theory of interest in the First Treatise. Most embarrassing is the fact that money, initially an ordinary commodity, became, when analyzing demand, capital, with no explanation other than phenomenal observation.

In contrast to the difficulties entailed by the study of demand, the examination of money supply seems to provide, in principle, a fixed reference to determine the value of money. The reason is that the supply price of precious metals is ruled, ultimately, by its costs of production. This being so, apart from the multiple sources of variation introduced by demand, the value of money will adjust, in the end, to its normal or cost price: "the value of a gold coin, freely minted, will tend to be held rather close to the cost of attainment of the gold which it contains" (Marshall, 1923: 39; I.IV.1).

The so-called quantitative equation of money, which expresses the necessary equality during a period between the total amount of transactions and the total amount of currency times its velocity of money, when the value of money is determined by cost, simply states that the amount of money adjusts itself to demand and that, if the amount if fixed, the velocity of circulation should be modified.

Until there, it would seem that the First Treatise's assumption that turns money value into something fixed is, anyway, harmless, with all the caveats concerning the specificity of money demand. For if, as Marshall states, the amount of commodity money would be increased "by decree of nature", its price and quantity would be modified only for some time, since as soon as metal leaves circulation, the variables return to their resting point. However, in the Second Treatise, the *classical theory* is forced to analyze the laws that govern the behavior of prices when metal is substituted by paper money (convertible or non-convertible).

Sadly, the emergence of non-convertible currency was mostly considered an anomaly, so that the laws governing local prices, the rate of exchange, and the amount of money when what circulates is paper money, although included in the exposition, are treated as the exception and not the rule. And little or no effort is made to make these laws compatible with the general theory of value, and even less to offer a new fundamental theory of money compatible with the prevailing non-convertible money. The theoretical difficulties entailed in unifying the theory of value and the theory of money (when it is non-convertible) are obvious. First, as they are useless for any other purpose, notes have no other utility than exchange value, and their demand is purely monetary. On the other hand, its quantity may not be adjusted as a result of money escaping from internal circulation to the world market, since its value is only recognized in the issuing country. But notes have no considerable production cost either that may rule its normal price. That is, neither demand nor supply grants it intrinsic value. This host of differences does not simply modify the laws that govern the price and the quantity of money, but plainly turns them upside down. When commodity money is replaced with non-convertible notes, given the demand of money, instead of it being price what governs quantity, it is now the arbitrary quantity put into circulation that governs the value of money. The quantitative equation remains valid, but the endogenous and exogenous variables have changed. Renewed increases in the amount of money put into circulation can only reduce the unit real value of each note and, if the public manages to protect themselves modifying the velocity of money, this decrease in money's purchasing power will be more than proportional.

On what does the value of non-convertible money then depend? The economic automatic mechanisms that ensured that the value of money would be equal to its production cost vanish when currency is produced at practically no cost, while paper money is only recognized in its emitting country and serves no purpose other than that of circulation, so that it has no escape when its quantity is excessive. Thus, the alleged connection with the First Treatise's theory of value is broken. The value of money depends now, basically, on the trust of the public, on its prestige, on custom, and on the authority.

> For immediate (current) business money needs only to be a clearly defined, easily handled, and generally acceptable medium of exchange. These conditions can be satisfied by anything which has obtained adequate prestige from customs, of from the edict of a public authority, even though is not capable of performing any other direct service, and would be valueless but for this prestige. The credit derived from prestige is sometimes rather frail: partly because it is liable to be undermined by an undue increase in its quantity.
>
> (Marshall, 1923: 16–17; I.I.3)

Money entered into circulation with a certain value and, seemingly, for that very reason it served as a measure of value and as a medium of exchange. The roles it played depended upon money's intrinsic qualities. Now, instead, it seems to owe its value to its very function. Anything can be money, and its price is not ruled by economic laws but by a quantity that the monetary authority arbitrarily defines and a trust that also depends largely on quantity. Instead of struggling to explain the economic laws that govern the value of money, Marshall feels now forced to suggest the authority to act wisely and to strive to keep the value of money steady for the benefit of the public: "if an inconvertible currency is controlled by a strong Government, its amount can be so regulated that the value of a unit of it is maintained at a fixed level" (Marshall, 1923: 49–50; I.IV.3).

It should not be overlooked that this explanation of the value of money that makes it depend on quantity (known as quantitative theory of money) implies accepting a new explanation of the determination of the general level of prices, which is nothing but a different name for money's purchasing power. It could be thus said that the *classical theory* provides two different theories of prices as a whole: one appears in the First Treatise, and a different (opposite) one in the Second.

The same happens in connection with the explanations of the rate of interest. In the context of the theory of value, that is, in the *Principles of Economics*, the rate of interest was the price that balanced the supply of capital, savings, and the demand of capital, investment. In an equilibrium situation, the rate of interest had to be identical to waiting disutility and capital productivity. In the Second Treatise, *Money, Credit & Commerce*, the determination of the rate of interest slips towards the market of loans or loanable funds.

The rate of interest is no longer the reward of the factor of production called capital, reward stemming from the sacrifice of postponing consumption, but a payment to a lender who relinquishes the control over his money for a period. The loan market is a new scenario where the rate of interest is set, initially independently from its determination in the "free" capital market of the First Treatise. It would thus seem that there is not a single rate of interest but rather two: one corresponding to loans; the other, to capital. Marshall finds, besides, that the rate of interest may be modified as a result of changes in prices. When money value falls, the rate of interest will tend to grow, but this happens only when price modification is anticipated by suppliers and demanders; otherwise, the real rate of interest will be changed, at least transitorily, since, in the end, it will have to adopt the level corresponding to capital productivity and time preference. However, at least in the short term, changes in the quantity of money manage to modify the rate of interest. This leads, inevitably, to a reformulation of the quantitative theory. In fact, the rate of interest starts intervening as a transmission belt driving prices when the quantity of money changes.

Without strong theoretical support, in passing, Marshall intends, besides, to draw the differences between capital and money, and money and commodity, since he becomes aware that money has now irreparably meddled in the theory of the rate of interest, when the explanation of the First Treatise ignored it completely.

> [T]he influx of a good deal of bullion into the city is likely to lower the rate of interest. This does not increase the amount of capital, in the strictest sense of the work; it does not increase the amount of building materials, machinery, etc. but it does increase the amount of command over capital which is in the hands of those whose business it is to lend to speculative enterprise. Having this extra supply, lenders lower still more the rate, which they charge for loans; and they keep on lowering it till a point is reached at which the demand will carry off the larger supply. When this has been done, there is more capital in the hands of speculative investors, who come on the markets for goods as buyers, and so raise the prices.
>
> (Marshall, 1923: 256)

This passage helps show that the *classical theory* only managed to partially include in its explanation what the financer, the banker, and, of course, the minister of the economy know perfectly well: through the quantity of money, credit and, therefore, the rate of interest can be controlled. However, the *classical theory* can only examine these relations imperfectly, since when it discusses the rate of interest in the First Treatise, money is absent. And when it appears in the Second Treatise, the *classical theory* has to improvise a weak connection between its theory of interest and the effects of changes on the monetary and credit markets.[21]

Even so, the general level of prices is the main variable subject to scrutiny throughout the whole development. In fact, both the simple quantitative theory and its more sophisticated version, which contemplates variations in the rate of interest, admit changes in the aggregate monetary income, although they always assume that the level of output is constant, and that income increases and decreases exclusively through price variations. This means that, as Keynes asserts, the classical theory as a whole considers that the levels of output and employment are given. As has been shown, Keynes is not mistaken either when he argues that the conceptual corpus of the *classical theory* is divided into two different and contradictory Treatises, since each of them gives a different explanation for the same phenomena. The same features of Marshall's exposition are essentially present in the monetary theory of Ricardo's and Walras's, who only in the final chapters of their books admit the role of money as a medium of exchange. Both have to abandon then the idea of a fixed-value money and soon afterwards give up the representation of money as an ordinary commodity, subject to the same laws as the rest. Last, when discussing the movement of inconvertible paper money, Walras and Ricardo endorse the quantitative theory of prices, which leads Walras to hold that:

> a rise of fall in prices [is] proportional to a given increase or decrease in the quantity of money [. . .]. We shall see, in our study of applied economics, how far-reaching are the consequences of this law which places the whole equilibrium of the market at the mercy of mine operators, issuers of bank notes and drawers of cheques.
>
> (Walras, 2003 [1874]: 366)

Ricardo, in turn, asserts that:

> Experience, however, shows that neither a State nor a Bank ever have had the unrestricted power of issuing paper money, without abusing that power: in all States, therefore, the issue of paper money ought to be under some check and control.
>
> (Ricardo, 1821 [1817]: XXVII.16)[22]

In his *Principles*, Ricardo, like Marshall, admits that changes in the monetary conditions affect the rate of interest, and he tries unsuccessfully (although more elegantly) to integrate this explanation with that of the First Treatise (see Ricardo, 1821 [1817]: XXI).

A general panorama

As regards the fundamental theory of money, the classical theory does not manage to reach an agreement. The First Treatise reduces money to the rank of commodity, and even further as its value is considered to be fixed. Its only function lies in being, thanks to the decree establishing its fixed value, the (invariable) measure of value for the rest of the commodities. In the Second Treatise, money loses its fixed value but, by eliminating this assumption, it has ultimately no value at all. It becomes a mere medium, a vehicle that enables the exchange of one commodity for other. In other words, money does not make any difference, as it does not affect relative prices or the rewards of labor and capital in real terms. *En passant*, however, an alternative use is recognized to it: when money is lent, it yields a rate of interest. Its qualities, therefore, seem to be similar to those of capital, which is considered, following Marshall, productive and prospective. However, in a best case scenario, changes in the rate of interest due to the effects of money will only be deemed transitory, as the rate of interest depends, ultimately, on the productivity of capital and time preferences.

These confusing ideas about money have serious consequences. In the next chapter, we will see that when the money is only considered as a *medium*, and the economy is analogous to a moneyless economy, the so-called Say's Law is necessarily fulfilled. Why? Because although individuals' and even the community's income may be in the form of money, if money is only a vehicle, it should be assumed that this money is always spent, that is, it is used to purchase a product.

It would seem that this assertion cannot be justified, because it would have to be admitted that an individual, and a society for that matter, may, if he or she so wishes, decide not to spend all his income or, at least, not to devote it entirely to consumption. The portion of income not devoted to consumption is called saving. In a non-monetary economy, the only way of saving is buying commodities, but not immediate-consumption commodities. For that reason, this conception of money assumes that all new output will always meet with demand, as there is nothing else income may be used for: either demanding consumer goods or saving goods, which are, in turn, investment goods. Say's Law holds this synthetically – supply *creates* demand.

III Say's law in the classical system

Old (Explicit) version and contemporary (Implicit) version of say's law

In the preceding section, what in Keynes's times was the core of the monetary theory was presented and then linked, as far as possible, to the *classical theory* of value. A strong contact point between the *classical theory* of value and the *classical theory* of money lies in an assumption or, better still, an axiom that hovers over the whole theoretical edifice, becoming an unnoticed source of inspiration for many of the most dubious results of the classical doctrine: the assumption of full employment of all the available resources. This subject is as significant as it is sensitive, so that it requires a specific, detailed discussion. Keynes must be credited with its "discovery", since it is he who calls this debate "Say's Law" and identifies the essential role it plays in the *classical theory* story.

> I believe that economics everywhere up to recent times has been dominated, much more than has been understood, by the doctrines associated with the name of J.-B. Say. It is true that his 'law of markets' has been long abandoned by most economists; but they have not extricated themselves from his basic assumptions and particularly from his fallacy that demand is created by supply. Say was implicitly assuming that the economic system was always operating up to its full capacity, so that a new activity was always in substitution for, and never in addition to, some other activity. Nearly all subsequent economic theory has depended on, in the sense that it has required, this same assumption. Yet a theory so based is clearly incompetent to tackle the problems of unemployment and of the trade cycle.
>
> (Keynes, 1939)

In this fragment of the preface to the first edition in French of *The General Theory*, Keynes highlights the originality and the eminently controversial nature of his discovery; he argues that, in spite of being crucially important to the *classical theory*, Say's Law had been kept till then as a "tacit assumption", as something always unsaid, as an article of faith, but that its spirit was, in fact, the hidden culprit of many of the most gross limitations of the orthodox theory. From then on, the so-called Say's Law started to be talked about again by economists, to occupy an outstanding place in economic theory; however, as will be shown, it has been treated less seriously than it deserves to be. Even today, after Keynes's denunciation, it is generally considered to be a banal assertion, evidently false, hastily discarded after barely being mentioned; however, an aspect that Keynes clearly highlighted is no longer enquired into: even though Say's Law is present in the *classical theory*, its influence is only implicit, so that to reject Say's Law, an additional work is required – the surreptitious, hidden mechanisms through which it operates should be exposed. For this reason, Say's Law is different from the other fundamental elements of the *classical theory* pointed out so far; here, Keynes is forced to make a theoretical reconstruction. While Say,

Ricardo, or Mill openly announced their endorsement of Say's principle, Keynes admits that

> it would not be easy to quote comparable passages from Marshall's later work or from Edgeworth or Professor Pigou. The doctrine is never stated to-day in this crude form. Nevertheless it still underlies the whole classical theory, which would collapse without it.
>
> (Keynes, 1939 [1936]: 19-20; I.2.VI)

For this reason, the hypothesis that Say's Law is at the forefront of the *classical* system requires a special test. The ground for this discussion has already been prepared, since contrary to the founders of the classical economics, such as Ricardo and Mill, who explicitly put forth some version of the characteristic dictum ("supply creates its own demand") in the works of the *marginalist* classical economists, Say's Law is fundamentally present in their conception of money, to whose discussion the previous section has been devoted:

> The conviction, which runs, for example, through almost all Professor Pigou's work, that money makes no real difference except frictionally and that the theory of production and employment can be worked out (like Mill's) as being based on 'real' exchanges with money introduced perfunctorily in a later chapter, is the modern version of the classical tradition. Contemporary thought is still deeply steeped in the notion that if people do not spend their money in one way they will spend it in another.
>
> (Keynes, 1939 [1936])

If Keynes was right, the notion of money as a mere "medium" to conduct transactions is in itself an indication of the veiled presence of Say's Law. Moreover, if that was the case, the split into First and Second Treatises is another clue that leads to Say's Law.

A brief historical review will allow us to discern the genealogy of the modern version of Say's Law and check its continued gravitation in the universe of the *classical theory*. Specifically, there are three aspects that have to be analyzed: i) the *classical theory's* assumption that all available resources are employed implicitly rests on the mechanics of Say's Law; ii) holding that supply creates its own demand means believing that money does not make any real differences; and iii) Keynes reintroduces Say's Law in the classical system by challenging the actual mechanisms that go from output to expense. To that end, the contributions of Say, Ricardo, Mill, and Marshall himself in this area will be first briefly discussed. Each of them resorted to Say's Law to solve a different problem, but the tacit assumptions underlying its *modus operandi* remained intact.

Say's Principle – as Say himself called it – played a decisive role in the defense of *laissez-faire* from early nineteenth century onwards. However, it was never strictly used for the theoretical purposes Keynes assigns to it in *The General Theory*, hence the difficulty of analyzing it. In the *Traité d'Economie Politique*, 1803, Say wields for the first time this argument to reject the usual explanations put forth by long-distance merchants whenever trade between the metropolis and the colonies collapsed. In fact, periods of blossoming and prosperity in businesses were periodically followed by acute trade crises where the trading companies of the imperial powers came across serious difficulties in placing their products on foreign markets. Suddenly and with no apparent explanation, markets were saturated with goods, prices then plummeted, and bankruptcies vertiginously followed, one after the other, ruining many traders. Merchants' common sense tended to mistake the causes of this phenomenon with its immediate manifestations: the reason why products did not find a "solvent market" – they argued – was the weakness of demand, which, in turn, was due to a lack of money, of currency in circulation. Appealing to this argument, merchants demanded the aid of the state, which through its intervention had to promote demand by injecting liquidity into colonial markets.

Displaying extraordinary rhetoric skills, Say mocks the argument put forth by capitalists – if the actual problem was demand's depression, then the question should be raised, in turn, about the real source of the exhaustion of demand. He thus arrives at a simple conclusion. Although it may be dressed up in monetary clothes, the body of the demand is made of products. Values are bought with other values, he asserts; and thus he reaches a conclusion that "may at first sight appear paradoxical, namely, that it is production which opens a demand for products" (Say, 1855 [1803]: I.XV.3). Demand, ultimately, is nothing but production. Merchants might answer that what they pursue when selling their articles is money, but Say preempts them and asks: "For what, in point of fact, do you want the money? Is it not for the purchase of raw materials or stock for your trade, or victuals for your support? [. . .] For, after all, money is but the agent of the transfer of values" (Say, 1855 [1803]: I.XV.4). Thus, Say's main thesis is formulated; from it, several theoretical and practical corollaries are inferred: products are bought with products and, therefore, money is just a vehicle, a medium, a wrapper for commodities, with no laws or movements of its own – "Money performs but a momentary function in this double exchange; and when the transaction is finally closed, it will always be found, that one kind of commodity has been exchanged for another" (*ibid.*).

Such a refutation lets us understand that the key to promoting trade does not lie in breathing life into demand when it is exhausted or in injecting increasing quantities of money, but in stimulating production. Money will automatically distribute itself according to what is required by the level of activity. This being so, to uphold the purchasing power of the colonies it is crucial, in any case, to promote their industries and to let free trade follow its natural course.

In brief, goods are bought with goods, so purchasing power can only be increased by strengthening production. Say explicitly asserts that every increase in production is, in turn, accompanied by a purchasing power that is equal to the new product: value production "produces" solvent demand.

Say thus purported to have rebutted the explanation of the crisis furnished by merchants; however, his persuasive effort was not nearly enough to eliminate the crises themselves. It should be asked, then, what alternative theory did he put forward to account for the difficulties regularly experienced in connection with trade. Another element, also highlighted by Keynes, is then introduced, which plays a fundamental role in supporting Say's Law: when certain commodities cannot be placed, when they do not find a market, it is simply because output has been excessive in *that particular branch* of industry. Following Say, it is assumed that production has fallen short in another branch. Actually, according to Say's principle, there is no other option: all output "generates" an equivalent purchasing power, so that, in aggregate terms, there could never be a general absence of demand. What could happen, instead, is that the *composition* of the output is not adequate to meet the demand as distributed across different items, according to the preferences and needs of buyers. If there is a glut, a saturation of a certain market, this should not be misinterpreted, as glut is never general but only partial, affecting only one or some markets and should also be compensated by an equivalent shortage in one or some other markets.

If this is so, then the disturbance contains in itself the required means to solve it autonomously, as the prices of the "scarce" commodities will rise, thus stimulating its production, while the prices of the superabundant goods will decrease on account of an excess supply, pushing producers away from these branches.

> I answer that the glut of a particular commodity arises from its having outrun the total demand for it in one or two ways; either because it has been produced in excessive abundance, or because the production of other commodities has fallen short. It is because the production of some commodities has declined, that other commodities are superabundant. [. . .] It is observable, moreover, that precisely at the same time that one commodity makes a loss, another commodity is making excessive profit. And, since such profits must operate as a powerful stimulus to the cultivation of that particular kind of products.
>
> (Say, 1855 [1803]: I.XV.10–11)

Even though this exposition was originally intended to explain the causes of the difficulties experienced by colonial trade, the same analysis provides arguments that may be used to shed light on the most disparate problems. According to Say, only production stimulates commerce and, therefore, only it, and not demand or a lack of liquidity, may bring its growth to a halt. Money is exclusively a vehicle of value, a medium; it is only required and demanded to purchase products, and not for any other purpose. From this conception or principle, many conclusions follow. First, there are no reasons for demand to lose strength as a result of its own lack of push, since behind demand there is always production and, therefore, insufficient demand is but an indication of insufficient production. If the colonies cannot buy manufactured products, then every possible effort must be made to have their industry grow. Difficulties in trade stem from supply, not from demand.

Regarding increases in production, it may be said – according to this principle – that every increase in production value entails an equivalent increase in its producers' purchasing power, which Say identifies with the creation of demand or market for that very same production. At worst, it may happen that production is not adequately distributed according to the needs of the producers. There will then be a *partial* glut in those markets where production was excessive, but only on condition that there is an unmet demand in other markets. This is a symptom of an inadequate management or distribution of production, but prices will react to market stimuli, so there will be profits and losses that, on their own merit, will act as signals to move production from one branch to other. In brief, Say seems to understand that the difficulties of commerce always originate in production conditions, which may cause a problem: when the production of value grows at a quicker pace in the imperial metropolis than in the colonies, there is a partial saturation that may be compounded by the fact that the new production is devoted to the inappropriate branches. Capital movements will tend to solve the problem by relocating production.

In Ricardo's *Principles*, the law of Say's is also used for controversial purposes. Here, the problem studied is not the expansion of commerce; what the author tries to elucidate is an unmistakably *Ricardian* question concerning the possibility of stagnation – can capital accumulation ever find an absolute limit? This analysis concerns the long term (or, in more modern terms, the conditions for economic growth). Ricardo seeks to distance himself from a widespread view supported by the authority of Adam Smith. In the *Wealth of Nations*, it is stated that a particular country, but also the system as a whole, will stumble upon a barrier to the increase of output, and this is due to the fact that when output steadily grows, sooner or later, it will end up saturating the market. In other words, demand in general tends to exhaust, so that prices and, with them, profits, fall. It is for this reason that Smith argues that, paradoxically, capital return always tends to be more attractive in a nation whose wealth is declining than in another experiencing a "progressive" phase, rapidly increasing, because the opportunities for profitable investments are diminishing. To rebut this theory of stagnation owing to demand and profitable businesses exhaustion, Ricardo resorts to Say's explanation.

In Ricardo's view, a falling production motivated by a lack of demand as posited by Smith is analytical nonsense. Say's arguments are literally repeated, but with the elegance, the parsimony, and the analytical accuracy that are characteristic of Ricardo. In his argumentation, the connection between Say's Law and the conception of money may be observed: an increase in produced value is reflected by an equivalent demand; money "leads" demand from one commodity to another. This theory contemplates the possibility of insufficient demand, but only on condition that it is partial, limited to a particular market, and compensated by an excess demand in other market, and therefore incapable of turning into a general crisis of realization.[23]

Ricardo resorted to Say's Law to show that capital increase cannot be stopped by a lack of demand. Again, it is accepted that, under certain circumstances, the production of a given commodity may surpass the existing demand of that item. But this implies that on the other side of the system, the opposite is true. How may this belief be explained? When a certain amount of goods is produced, a mass of value is generated that necessarily translates into purchasing power or demand. Output total value is equal to demand total value. If in any branch the produced value exceeds the value that is necessarily demanded in other branch, the opposite situation occurs. The representation is accurate and inevitable in a hypothetical money-less economy, where all output is exclusively devoted to consumption (individual or productive).

John Stuart Mill also enters the same discussion as Ricardo, but he brings some highly original elements with him. Some economists (such as Chalmers, Malthus, or Sismondi) held that the accumulation of capital will always meet an internal limit due to the endemic exhaustion of demand, whose cause might be found in the unequal distribution of income across classes, compounded by their peculiar biases towards consumption. They argued, synthetically, that while workers continually wish to widen consumption, they lack the means to do so; capitalists, in turn, have enough resources to broaden their demand, but have a psychological tendency to saving and frugality. The contradiction between a social class that can but does not want to consume and another that wants but cannot, makes the accumulation of wealth at the capitalists' extreme and the accumulation of poverty at the workers' extreme an obstacle for the widened reproduction of the economy, since, at some point in time, consumption will come to a halt.

In the long term, only stagnation may be foreseen, since, once a certain scale is reached, new output will not be sold on the market. This diagnosis allowed for the ingenious "theory" put forward by Malthus to justify the convenience of supporting the "leisure" classes, since being groups (such as nobility and the Curia) characterized, precisely, by consuming without producing anything at all, they should not be persecuted but, rather, cherished, as they fed the flame of demand, thus safeguarding the process of accumulation.

The riddle Mill intends to solve is similar to Ricardo's, save that Mill does not approach it from the perspective of isolated markets for different commodities, but rather groups production according to its use, i.e. according to who demands it. With the purpose of rejecting the argument of stagnation brought about by under consumption by means of a *reductio ad absurdum*, he evaluates a hypothetical case where, suddenly, the consumption of the higher classes is substantially reduced: will demand therefore become exhausted thus reducing the volume of output? In such a situation, Mill holds, output will be greater than demand on the market of luxury goods consumed by the higher classes, so that there will be a surplus of products and wealth. Capitalists will be forced to use their excess resources to broaden production, employing a higher number of workers. Two possibilities now open. If there are available hands for work in the country, employment will rise; if, instead, there is no idle labor, workers' wages will tend to increase. In the first case, production composition will have to change: the production of luxury goods will decrease, and the production of wage goods will increase. In the second case, the wages of workers will rise, which will enable them to access a level of consumption surpassing their immediate needs, thus allowing them to buy luxury goods. There will not be, therefore, a lack of "market" to place production, but rather, as Say and Ricardo held, output composition will have to change. This very same argument may be used to reject all the family of theories positing that demand poses a limitation to the increase in production.

When demand is reduced in one place, it will always increase somewhere else; and if production increases, it will always find an equivalent purchasing power. Again, the only limit to production is production itself.

> Thus the limit of wealth is never deficiency of consumers, but of producers and productive power. Every addition to capital gives to labour either additional employment, or additional remuneration; enriches either the country, or the labouring class. If it finds additional hands to set to work, it increases the aggregate produce: if only the same hands, it gives them a larger share of it; and perhaps even in this case, by stimulating them to greater exertion, augments the produce itself.
>
> (Mill, 1909 [1848]: I.5.8)

Say and Ricardo held that, in general terms, if production exceeded the volume of demand in one branch, then production would necessarily fall short in other branch: they were therefore thinking in terms of isolated individual commodities. With Mill's intervention, the debate comes closer to its modern version.

In his argument, production is split into two major groups: luxury goods and wage goods; the former represent pure consumption, the latter are part of productive capital, since they are the condition to hire more hands. Money is, again, absent in the causation chain or, at least, its presence does not seem to introduce any difference in the analysis. However, the explanation reveals another foothold that remarkably simplifies it and will shape the modern debate: for Mill, capitalists' "investment" takes the form of a "wage fund", that is, if the capitalist class as a whole wants to broaden production, it has to produce more means of subsistence to support a larger mass of labor. Mill thus touches the heart of the controversy: if capitalists reduce consumption, the portion of income not devoted to consumption, i.e. savings, increases, at least in the short run. It would thus seem that savings is a reduction of consumption and the reduction of consumption, an obstacle for production.

But it is not so, at least in Mill's view (and according to his conceptual foundations):

> For, what do these persons do with their savings? They invest them productively that is, expend them in employing labour. In other words, having a purchasing power belonging to them, more than they know what to do with, they make over the surplus of it for the general benefit of the labouring class.
>
> (Mill, 1909 [1848]: III.14.9)

As Keynes claims, the classical notion of money plays a key role in this debate from here onwards. If money did not exist, output as a whole would consist of goods that are exchanged for other goods. There is no possible exit, the system always conserves the same "energy", i.e. value, and in any case, it adjusts by changing its composition by switching between goods, that is, consumer goods are replaced by investment goods. Actually, in a moneyless economy, if an individual or group of individuals would decide to save instead of consume, it would have to demand goods anyway. Under such circumstances, saving is, in practice, synonymous with investment:

> In opposition to these palpable absurdities, it was triumphantly established by political economists, that consumption never needs encouragement. All which is produced is already consumed, either for the purpose of reproduction or of enjoyment. The person who saves his

income is no less a consumer than he who spends it: he consumes it in a different way; it supplies food and clothing to be consumed, tools and materials to be used, by productive labourers.

(Mill, 1874 [1844]; II.4)

This is the whole secret of Say's Law, as it was applied by then, since all new production is destined for consumption or, when not consumed, becomes savings, and savings is, in itself, equivalent to an increase in capital, that is, investment as, by definition, the goods in which non-consumption, i.e. saving, may be embodied are capital goods – investment. Say, Ricardo, and Mill arrive at the conclusion that, in an economy that they easily equate to a barter system, any sale is at the same time a purchase; however, from this belief they infer something completely different and mistaken: that all production translates into or, rather, is at the same time, new demand, whether it be of consumer goods or investment goods. This is the same as positing, as they actually tend to do, that every act of saving is equivalent to an act of investing. The belief that saving is synonymous with investment was inherited by the mature *classical* economy, whose main representative is Marshall.

> Marshall, for example, surely believed, although he did not expressly say so, that aggregate saving and aggregate investment are necessarily equal. Indeed, most members of the classical school carried this belief much too far; since they held that every act of increased saving by an individual necessarily brings into existence a corresponding act of increased investment.
>
> (Keynes, 1939 [1936]: 177; IV.14.I)

In fact, to end this brief historical review that sheds light on the genetic makeup of Say's Law, a passage of Marshall's *Principles* that is, in fact, a true profession of faith, is quoted here:

> Mill well observed that 'What constitutes the means of payment for commodities is simply commodities'. Each person's means of paying for the productions of other people consist of those which he himself possesses. All sellers are inevitably, and by the meaning of the word, buyers. Could we suddenly double the productive powers of the country, we should double the supply of commodities in every market; but we should, by the same stroke, double the purchasing power. Everybody would bring a double demand as well as supply; everybody would be able to buy twice as much, because everyone would have twice as much to offer in exchange.
>
> (Marshall, 1920 [1890]: VI.XIII.50)

This conception of demand as unlimited and capable of absorbing any volume of production is, logically, accompanied by the *classical* notion of money as a mere *medium*, as has already been seen. The moneyless production of commodities and an economy with money are perfectly compatible, if money has the characteristics as have been pointed out. And from this notion of money, stems, in turn, the contemporary version of Say's Law, which Marshall explicitly endorses.

No doubt, one of the *classical theory's* assumptions is the action of Say's Law, whether it be explicitly mentioned or tacitly accepted through the notion of money and saving in commodities as equivalent to investment. However, Keynes should be credited for situating this problem in the sphere of the short term. Or rather, he should be credited for attracting attention to and showing that the classical system tacitly rests on the workings of the mechanisms associated with Say's Law also in its conception of the short term.

It should not be understood, however, that "short term" is synonymous with an ephemeral, circumstantial or transitory analysis. For the *classical* theory, drawing on Marshall, "short term" simply means that changes over the course of centuries in the stock of capital, technologies, qualification, or number of workers will not be taken into account, that is to say, briefly, that the total available resources in the economy remain fixed. It is for this reason that, in fact, studying unemployment as a short-term phenomenon implies, no more and no less, undertaking to analyze reality: in practice, the economic system may be (and in fact, frequently is) in a position where, even though the volume and the quality of the "equipment "of facilities and men may remain unchanged, it is unemployed, and such a situation may persist during a long period. As has been said, for Marshall, "short term" is not an elegant or sophisticated term to refer to the period of adjustment towards the long term: it is not a "moment" in a longer process, a still of a film or a "transitory" instant, but rather denotes a particular problem. This is the reason why a "short-term" situation (such as unemployment) may last for decades. In the short term, simply, resources are considered to be a given, and what should be studied is whether there is a tendency to employ such resources fully. The classical system assumes that the available resources are always fully used and studies the prices of the products and the factors associated with the only possible equilibrium of which it conceives, that of full employment. This approach to the economic system is secretly premised on Say's Law.

Say's Law and its working in the short term: equilibrium without unemployment

How can the fact that Keynes considers Say's Law as a key component of the classical doctrine – both in its early as its "mature" versions – be interpreted, when neither Marshall, Walras, Edgeworth, nor Pigou mention it explicitly, and none of them directly endorses this old tenet? The theoretical problem that Keynes faces is, in few words, the following: capitalist economies had shown (particularly during the first decades of the twentieth century) that employment could remain at levels that were below full employment of the available resources, both technical as human, during long periods. In a Marshallian framework, this is clearly a *short term* issue, as it is not a problem that requires analyzing the effects of plant enlargement, but focuses, instead, on the causes that determine the different degrees of employment of the existing capacity; also, it is clearly an issue that has to be considered in the light of *equilibrium*, since the system does not react with a spontaneous move tending to recover full employment. Both quantity and prices are at rest. In other words, it has to be shown that, in the short term, the system may be at a rest position that includes unemployment. And the classical system did not, does not, and will never admit unemployment as short-term equilibrium on account of its premises.

And herein lies the problem, since when the *classical theory* studies the short-term equilibrium conditions, as in Marshall's *Principles*, but also in Walras's *Elements*, it never contemplates a continuing level of employment below the full utilization of resources. In fact, it has never come across the specific question. Specifically, explaining unemployment means translating into theoretical terms – to discover its causes – a situation in which, although there is available and willing labor, capitalists decide not to hire: for some reason that has to be figured out, entrepreneurs prefer to maintain a lower level of production than they could potentially reach. For some reason, they decide to restrict production, and nothing drives them to increase it. After going through the previous section, it may be seen that this situation is precisely what any theory imbued in the beliefs derived from Say's Law would consider utterly impossible; the *classical* authors had examined and rejected this state of affairs in a long-term context by asserting that whenever the available productive capacity exceeds the employed capacity, there will exist the necessary stimulus to raise production or, to the same effect, they argued that there may never exist a long-term equilibrium situation where production is in any way hampered by the absence of demand. This was the view these authors endorsed concerning long-term issues, but it is not unfair or illegitimate to think that they must have believed exactly the same, and all the more so, concerning short term equilibrium, since, even though they did not mention it, they must have believed that obstacles to attain full employment may arise when the available resources have not even been enlarged, that is, in the short term. In their system, they go beyond mere belief, because they replace the detailed discussion of this situation with an axiom: when they study the short term, they simply *assume* that the level of production is given, and that this level coincides with full employment. This *substitution of an explanation for an assumption* is, precisely, what Keynes discovers and manages to expose, when he states that the classical theories of value and distribution depart from a *given* level of production, and that they restrict themselves to wondering how the prices of products and the rewards of factors are established but never afford to study the aggregate changes in the volume of production.

The relationship between equilibrium and the different "terms" may now be further clarified. For Marshall, in the short term, the normal price prevails, that is, capital moves across the different branches until extraordinary profits are evacuated. At that point, the labor market and the capital market are also depleted. This explanation assumes full employment, as no situation is examined where available labor at the current wage (excluding frictional unemployment) exists in the economy as a whole. In the long term, Say's Law is also valid: any volume of new capital and new population find productive employment, and this result may not be conditioned by the absence of demand.

Keynes is the one who demonstrates this, and nobody before him had exposed the significance of this assumption or of its consequences. No doubt, he is right. In the Walrasian system, supply *instantaneously* equals demand in all markets, including the markets of factors. Equilibrium is synonymous with full employment, since on all markets, the goods offered for sale find, by definition, their buyer.

The very system of equations representing the general equilibrium looks for the prices at which offer equals demand on all markets and does not even admit a single transaction if the whole economy does not comply with the condition of equilibrium (the "auctioneer" guarantees the absence of transactions at fake prices).

This is valid for all products (or rather, for all the available goods in pure exchange) but also for labor and capital: all the workers that desire to work at the going wage may do so. By definition, there is no unemployment as supply reflects exactly the desire to work and equals demand, representing the will to hire. The same happens in Marshall's account, though with slight differences. Marshall analyzes, on one hand, the balance of demand and supply of an *available stock*, which he terms "market equilibrium", and on the other, the normal equilibrium which ensues when profits are equal across branches – all producers obtain the normal profit – and prices cover exactly production costs, with no excess or defect, which is the same. Unemployment is not possible in this world, either. The precise distinction between Say's Law and the so-called Walras's law has brought about some controversy among economists. According to the analysis offered here, which applies Marshall's categories, Walras's law explains the determination of the equilibrium *market price* (assuming fixed stocks of commodities), while Say's Law discusses the possibility of production increasing until the *normal* equilibrium prices are reached. From this perspective, the only way that the possibility of anything less than full employment may even be admitted is to consider unemployment as a *disequilibrium* situation. However, this apparent solution is of no use for Keynes or, rather, it is a fake solution that not only remains locked within the enclosure of the inherited theory, but is also misleading. In fact, the classical theory has no objection to considering unemployment a state of equilibrium; such conception does not demand a critique or a reframing of the conventional theory. Indeed, disequilibrium emerges when the quantity offered is different from the demanded quantity. That is, some suppliers want to sell but cannot find any buyer (or else, the opposite is the case). If this mismatch occurs in the labor market, there is, by definition, unemployment, only that unemployment becomes another name for an excess supply of labor. This understanding of unemployment is equivalent to holding that when there is unemployment in the system, as happens in all cases of disequilibrium, the automatic drives aimed at overcoming this difficulty will be triggered. In other words, sooner or later, the system attains equilibrium and unemployment disappears, so that, from the classical point of view, unemployment can only persist for one of two reasons: because the adjustment is slow or because some hindrance, external to the system (non-economic) prevents the variables from moving to the appropriate position, corresponding to equilibrium. The explanations of unemployment based on the belief that certain variables are "rigid" and not "flexible" or that there is any other cause that prevents adjustment, whether it be lack of coordination, of information, or any other reason, but that do not eliminate the idea that in a situation of equilibrium there is always full employment persist, deliberately or not, in the classical conception that Keynes sought to overcome.

Keynes's work in this field is strenuous. In *The General Theory*, the argument reconstructed herein is not presented in a compact fashion.

What follows is a reconstruction of Keynes's hypotheses regarding the working of Say's Law in the short term, hypotheses that are scattered across different chapters of his book. Excerpts from *The General Theory* will be regularly quoted to support the legitimacy of our reconstruction. Keynes discovers that the *classical theory* introduces its argument for full employment *by decree*, that is to say, it includes it surreptitiously among its premises when assuming that the only possible equilibrium is that which is synonymous with full employment, thus transforming full employment in the *normal* state of the economic system in the short term, in the only stable equilibrium or resting point. In Keynes's words,

> [T]he classical school ignored the problem [of unemployment, AK], as a consequence of introducing into their premises conditions which involved its non-existence; with the result of creating a cleavage between

the conclusions of economic theory and those of common sense. The extraordinary achievement of the classical theory was to overcome the beliefs of the 'natural man' and, at the same time, to be wrong.

(Keynes, 1939 [1936]: 350; VI.23.IV)

The point of departure for this research should be the system built by Marshall, who assumes that the markets of all commodities, taken individually, move towards normal equilibrium, so that in the aggregate market of goods, as in the aggregate market of labor and the aggregate market of "free" capital, supply equals always and necessarily demand. For the system to be at rest, all resources must be employed. It could be said that Keynes meticulously tests the implicit argument on which this statement rests: what is the list of additional beliefs linked to this axiom? As will be seen, Say's Law for the short term is the theoretical drive behind the multiple mechanisms guaranteeing this result. Next, we will give an account of each of these devices, following their development and exposing the necessary connection between what takes place in each of the markets into which Marshall divides his explanation: labor market, goods market, and "free" capital market.

From the perspective of the *classical* system, unemployment can only be understood as an excess of labor supply. Its cause must be sought, first and foremost, in the labor market, and, therefore, there should also be found the elements required to overcome the situation. In fact, the labor market, like any other market, "tends" to equilibrium. When a state of equilibrium is reached, real wage is, by definition, simultaneously equal to labor marginal productivity (demand curve) and to labor marginal disutility (supply curve). Seen in this way, there is nothing special (or bad) about unemployment, since it is a necessary stage for the price to reach its resting position, given that an excess of supply is reversed through a fall in nominal (and real, as in Marshall's account money's purchasing power is considered to be constant) wage. For the *classical theory*, unemployment represents disequilibrium in the labor market.

> Thus writers in the classical tradition, overlooking the special assumption underlying their theory, have been driven inevitably to the conclusion, perfectly logical on their assumption, that apparent unemployment (apart from the admitted exceptions) must be due at bottom to a refusal by the unemployed factors to accept a reward which corresponds to their marginal productivity.
>
> (Keynes, 1939 [1936]: 16; I.2.IV)

If the state of disequilibrium and unemployment persists in time it is because something prevents the adjustment from happening. Therefore, the only form of prolonged unemployment of which the *classical theory* conceives stems from the refusal of workers (whatever their motive) to accept the reduction of their wages: "the *Classical Theory* has been accustomed to rest the supposedly self-adjustment character of the economic system on an assumed fluidity of money-wages; and, when there is rigidity, to lay on this rigidity the blame of maladjustment(Keynes, 1939 [1936]: 257; V.19.I).[24] This is the first segment of the argument where Say's Law makes its appearance, as examining exclusively the labor market, the *classical theory* seems to have shown that, should there not exist a whimsical and anti-economic hindrance posed by labor, the system would march towards equilibrium in the labor market, and that equilibrium means full employment (i.e. everyone desiring to work at the going wage may do so).

Let's assume that the labor market automatically develops, sooner or later, a solution to this problem: wages eventually decrease and employment grows until it reconciles supply and demand. Is this a complete solution? Is the state of unemployment, without further analysis thus extinguished? The answer is evidently negative. Following the line of argument implicit in the *classical* system, a new problem arises, albeit situated in a different scenario: once the adjustment is complete, wages will be lower, and there will be more employment, but production will have to have grown. Although in Marshall's account the way out of unemployment inevitably implies an increase in production, the classical economists never examined an obvious question – how will this increase in production be absorbed, if at all? This question was exactly the same as the one that was raised in connection with the long term, but now situated in a short-term scenario: either because the system is "growing" or because it is "automatically" escaping an unemployment situation, production will only increase when the entrepreneurs are willing to hire more workers, but they will be ready to increase production only if the new supply guarantees *always and in all cases* an equivalent increase in demand. Say's Law now moves to a new station, as the analysis of unemployment that began in the labor market now has to consider what happens in the market of goods in order to find out if there is "market" for the additional production or if, on the contrary, demand may turn out to be insufficient.

What happens in the market of goods when, as unemployment begins to cease, production begins to increase? A new dilemmas is added to the old one of the long-term Say's Law; in the short-term analysis, an aggravating circumstance emerges, since the adjustment in the labor market implies a fall in wages, which means that workers will now have a lower consumption power. As *the classical theory assumed* that there would always be full employment, such a circumstance did not merit any direct comment. However, it is necessary to reconstruct the tacit mechanisms guaranteeing that in the face of an increase in production, even with falling wages, demand will grow proportionally. The transmission belt linking the adjustment in the labor market to the situation in the market of goods lies in the *classical theory* of value, which states that the normal price of commodities is, in the short term, equal to their cost of production. And wages are a key component of such costs:

> [T]he classical theory, [. . .] has taught us to believe that prices are governed by marginal prime cost in terms of money and that money-wages largely govern marginal prime cost. Thus if money-wages change, one would have expected the classical school to argue that prices would change in almost the same proportion [. . .]. They seem, however, to have been diverted from this line of thought, partly [. . .] by preoccupation with the idea that prices depend on the quantity of money.
>
> (Keynes, 1939 [1936]: 12; I.2.II)

Keynes put forth a hypothesis concerning what the classical economists must have thought regarding the issue of absorption of this new supply.

The simplest explanation seems to be the following: the fall in wages reduces the prices of goods in general and thus stimulates demand in the aggregate market of goods. Through this reduction in prices, supply "creates" demand. The reasoning is as simple as it is rudimentary. But, initially, an analysis of aggregate demand is introduced that does not take into account the simultaneous fall of workers' income. Now then, without an explicit admission, the *classical theory* trusted that, even though the purchasing power of labor as a whole was reduced, that fall in prices would raise the income of the rest of the factors in real terms, compensating for the reduction of workers' consumption. Therefore, this loss of consumption capacity would be compensated by an increase in the demand of the other social classes, particularly of the entrepreneurs, as their profits would rise as a consequence of the fall in wages and of the other "factors" receiving a fixed revenue. Last, it might also be assumed that wages decrease in a lesser proportion than the increase in employment volume, which means that the wage mass would not fall. Trusting, as the classicists do, in Say's Law, requires endorsing one of these hypotheses, which lead to claim that any increase of employment in the labor market entails an increase of the demand in the market of goods. But the tentacles of Say's Law are even longer. To this optimistic panorama, new components may be added.

Let's now assume that these mechanisms fail. That is, production rises as wage falls, and prices fall too; let's then assume that the aggregate demand of goods does not increase in proportion to the increase in output. Again, a new question is raised in connection with Say's Law, but it leads us to a new station: the classical market of capital. For if production outgrows consumption (the aggregate demand of goods), saving will forcibly need to increase. Saving is none other than what the *classical theory* (in Marshall's *Principles*, for example) calls "capital supply". The classical market of capital tends, in turn, to equilibrium. This means that an increase in saving as a result of a decrease in consumption (the aggregate demand of goods cannot absorb the new output) should trigger a fall in the rate of interest, which in turn leads to an increase in the volume of investment. And the *classical theory* blindly believes that this is precisely what happens. The rate of interest of the First Treatise of the classical theory is the price that matches capital supply and demand.

> Certainly the ordinary man – banker, civil servant or politician – brought up on the traditional theory, and the trained economist also, has carried away with him the idea that whenever an individual performs an act of saving he has done something which automatically brings down the rate of interest, that this automatically stimulates the output of capital, and that the fall in the rate of interest is just so much as is necessary to stimulate the output of capital to an extent which is equal to the increment of saving; and, further, that this is a self-regulatory process of adjustment which takes place without the necessity for any special intervention or grandmotherly care on the part of the monetary authority.
>
> (Keynes, 1939 [1936]: 177; IV.14.I)

The *classical theory's* implicit endorsement of Say's Law in the short term is thus reinforced. According to this mechanism, any increase in output triggers an equivalent increase in aggregate demand. If consumption does not grow sufficiently, the level of savings will rise, thus diminishing the rate of interest and stimulating investment. The classical dogma equates an increase in saving to an increase in investment, a characteristic belief subordinated to Say's Law: "Indeed, most members of the classical school carried this belief much too far; since they held that every act of increased saving by an individual necessarily brings into existence a corresponding act of increased investment" (Keynes 1936: 177; IV.14.I). The complexity of the argument relevant to saving is slightly deepened because the *classical theory*, as has been mentioned, has two different theories concerning the determination of the interest rate, one corresponding to the First Treatise, a different one corresponding to the Second Treatise.

When explaining their theory of money, the classicists tended to think that the rate of interest was regulated by the quantity of money in circulation, as liquidity influenced the state of credit. However, even if the rate of interest was subject to the influence of money and not of "real" saving, the *classical theory* includes a device that guarantees the increase in investment. The fall in prices increases the quantity of money measured in real terms, so that, according to the classicists, the rate of interest should fall stimulating investment, thus strengthening faith in Say's Law.

> It is, therefore, on the effect of a falling wage- and price-level on the demand for money that those who believe in the self-adjusting quality of the economic system must rest the weight of their argument; though I am not aware that they have done so. If the quantity of money is itself a function of the wage- and price-level, there is indeed, nothing to hope in this direction. But if the quantity of money is virtually fixed, it is evident that its quantity in terms of wage-units can be indefinitely increased by a sufficient reduction in money-wages.
>
> (Keynes, 1939 [1936]: 266; V.19.II)

To summarize, when the *classical theory* assumes that the system always returns, by its own merits and without difficulty, to the rest position with full employment, it is actually secretly trusting in some or all of these mechanisms associated to Say's Law. Because it is these mechanisms that lead to the belief that whenever production grows because new employment is created, and in spite of wage fall, demand expands in exactly the same proportion, thus unconditionally absorbing the new commodities produced. Keynes simply compiles all the arguments supporting the notion of permanent full employment that are tacitly contained in the *classical theory*. If, as the *classical theory* asserts, the only steady equilibrium is that corresponding to full employment, any increase in output should always trigger, some way or other, an increase in purchases. The devices implicit in this conception of equilibrium are, schematically, the following:

When employment grows, there is an increase in demand based on:

1   An increase in the aggregate indiscriminate demand of goods. Cause: the fall in wages brings about a reduction in costs and therefore in the prices of all commodities, which stimulates aggregate demand.
2   An increase in consumption demand. Cause 1: Even though wages are reduced, the wage volume increases because labor demand elasticity is higher than 1. Cause 2: The fall in prices is reflected in an increase in real income of fixed income earners, which compensates for the reduction in workers' consumption. Cause 3: Profits rise as a result of wage reduction, and therefore capitalists' consumption increases.
3   An increase in investment demand. Cause 1: Aggregate consumption decreases, which displaces the saving curve in the capital market, reducing the rate of interest, and stimulating investment (First Treatise). Cause 2: Price fall triggers an increase in money supply in real terms, reducing the rate of interest, and stimulating investment (Second Treatise). In short, it may be said that underlying the assumption of

equilibrium with full employment are these mechanisms whose result coincides with that of Say's Law – increases in production are always accompanied by increases in demand. This leads to the assertion that the system relentlessly moves towards full employment in the short term, as Keynes claims, since if idle resources exist, the entrepreneurs will always be in a position to raise production and employment: "the forces of competition between entrepreneurs may be expected to push it to this maximum value. Only at this point, on the classical theory, can there be stable equilibrium" (Keynes, 1936). When reviewing the historical roots of Say's Law and its first manifestations in the classical arrangement, it may be clearly perceived that behind this explanation a particular conception of money is also hidden; when money is considered to be exclusively a "medium" to exchange commodities, with no other role to play, the economy works exactly like a non-monetary economy, even when money may be formally included in the explanation. If money is not spent in one way (consumption), it will be spend in some other (savings equivalent to investment): there is no way out, therefore – supply creates its own demand.

The mechanisms of Say's Law in the short term have therefore been exposed.[25] Keynes, in turn, intends to dismantle this network of devices guaranteeing the existence of full employment. As opposed to the *classical theory*, his original theoretical construction will have to consider the possibility that unemployment be conceived as a situation of steady equilibrium.

Equilibrium unemployment will be a situation wherein the whole output is demanded, since according to the definition of equilibrium, aggregate supply should equal aggregate demand; however, this is not the same as asserting that a higher level of production might also be placed on the market. In other words, the fact that aggregate supply should equal aggregate demand does not mean positing that any increase in offer will always result in a commensurate increase in aggregate demand, through equivalent increases in consumption or investment. Say's Law states that any additional output generates a commensurate additional expense.

> From the time of Say and Ricardo the classical economists have taught that supply creates its own demand; -meaning by this in some significant, but not clearly defined, sense that the whole of the costs of production *must necessarily be spent* in the aggregate, directly or indirectly, on purchasing the product.
>
> (Keynes, 1939 [1936]: 18; I.2.VI; emphasis added)

In Keynes's case, disassembling all the mechanisms of Say's Law means, specifically, analyzing and challenging all and every field where those mechanisms act: the classical market of labor, the classical market of goods, and the classical market of capital. But it also implies facing a major conceptual move: the classical conception of money and capital supporting such representations will have to be left behind. At stake are the foundations of the *classical theory*, from which Say's Law follows. Many of the tenets of orthodoxy rest on Say's Law, which Keynes considers the "axiom of parallels" of the orthodoxy (in an analogy to the abandoned Euclidean geometry) and one of the basis of its doctrine.

> It is, then, the assumption of equality between the demand price of output as a whole and its supply price which is to be regarded as the classical theory's 'axiom of parallels'. Granted this, all the rest follows – the social advantages of private and national thrift, the traditional attitude towards the rate of interest, the classical theory of unemployment, the quantity theory of money, the unqualified advantages of *laissez-faire* in respect of foreign trade and much else which we shall have to question.
>
> (Keynes 1939 [1936]: 21; I.2.VI)

Notes

1 There was also an appeal to the hypothesis of ignorance. Among the authorized opinions challenging Keynes competence in the field of theory, that of J.A. Schumpeter should be stressed: "I can, however, testify to the fact that Keynes, whose knowledge of economic literature and particularly of contemporaneous and non-English literature was not of the first order [. . .]" (Schumpeter 1986 [1954]: 1274).

2 Marshall's interest in Keynes's intellectual education was evident. When in 1905 Keynes still struggled to choose between mathematics and economics, Marshall wrote to his friend and colleague John Neville Keynes: "Your son is doing excellent work in economics. I have told him that I should be greatly delighted if he should decide on the career of a professional economist. But, naturally, I should not exert pressure on him". In 1908, he offered 100 pounds of his own to have Keynes deliver a series of lectures [. . .] Marshall's support was also crucial for his eventual appointment as director of the *Economic Journal* in the Autumn of 1911 when he was just 28 years old. He would remain at that post for 33 years (Harrod, 1951).

3 As money is considered to be a commodity, the *classical theory* uses the phrase "money value", which is equal to money purchasing power and the inverse of the general level of prices.

4 An additional terminological remark: the term *marginalism* is used instead of the more frequent *neoclassical* because the marginalist current came onto the scene with the explicit objective of challenging the classical political economics, in an episode known as "marginalist revolution". From now on, we will refer to *marginalists* and *Ricardians* to distinguish both groups, saving the term *classical,* which will be used in Keynes's sense. In brief, Keynes's *classical theory* includes *Ricardians* and *marginalists*.

5 In the marginalist tradition, the categories of value, exchange value and price are used as synonyms. Although significant differences may be observed as to the terminological choices of each author, for the purposes of the present discussion we will use the mentioned terms as synonyms.

6 The seventeenth century mercantilism already knew this "law" that, according to Barbon, means that: "Plenty, in respect of that occasion, makes things cheap; and scarcity, dear" (Barbon, 1690). The Ricardian school also explains thus market price: "The temporary or Market Value of a thing, depends on the demand and supply; rising as the demand rises, and falling as the supply rises" (Mill, 1909 [1848]: III.6.3).

7 As Walras affirms, Menger arrives at the same conclusion but in a peculiar way: in his explanation, there are first-order goods (those consumed and, therefore, having a direct utility) and higher order goods, whose utility is indirect because it originates in their being used to produce useful goods: "Among the most egregious of the fundamental errors that have had the most far-reaching consequences in the previous development of our science is the argument that goods attain value for us because goods were employed in their production that had value to us. [. . .] On the contrary, it is evident that the value of goods of higher order is always and without exception determined by the prospective value of the goods of lower order in whose production they serve" (Menger, 2007 [1871]: 150).

8 Schumpeter compares his success with that achieved by the *Wealth of Nations,* and concludes that Marshall's success has been as big as A. Smith's (Schumpeter, 1986 [1954]).

9 His eagerness to cover economic thinking (particularly, the British) with a varnish of unity led Marshall, in many cases, to treat deep conceptual differences as if they were merely terminological and definitional questions. His expository style consisted in introducing his own solutions to the different controversies, no matter how thorny, as if they were the natural result of common sense. To certain extent, his conciliatory style is evidence of his great tolerance and, in many occasions, of his modesty, as he thus almost always avoided direct controversies.

10 As for Ricardo's stylistic flaws as a source of confusion, he says: "His exposition is as confused as his thought is profound; he uses words in artificial senses which he does not explain, and to which he does not adhere; and he changes from one hypothesis to another without giving notice. If then we seek to understand him rightly, we must interpret him generously, more generously than he himself interpreted Adam Smith" (Marshall, 1920 [1890]: App.I.1).

11 In Marshall's view, Ricardo's careless writing led even those who faced Socialists to error: "And yet Rodbertus and Karl Marx claim Ricardo's authority for the statement that the natural value of things consists solely of the labour spent on them; and even those German economists who most strenuously combat the conclusions of these writers, are often found to admit that they have interpreted Ricardo rightly, and that their conclusions follow logically from his. This and other facts of a similar kind show that Ricardo's reticence was an error of judgment" (Marshall, 1920 [1890]: App.I.12).

12 Marshall justifies his replacement of the term usually employed to refer to what Mill and most economists called "capitalist's abstinence": "The sacrifice of present pleasure for the sake of future, has been called *abstinence* by economists. But this term has been misunderstood: for the greatest accumulators of wealth

are very rich persons, some of whom live in luxury, and certainly do not prac-
tise abstinence in that sense of the term in which it is convertible with abste-
miousness. What economists meant was that, when a person abstained from
consuming anything which he had the power of consuming, with the purpose
of increasing his resources in the future, his abstinence from that particular act
of consumption increased the accumulation of wealth. Since, however, the term
is liable to be misunderstood, we may with advantage avoid its use, and say
that the accumulation of wealth is generally the result of a postponement of
enjoyment, or of a *waiting* for it. Or, in other words again, it is dependent on
man's *prospectiveness;* that is, his faculty of realizing the future" (Marshall
1920 [1890]: IV.VII.31).

13 Most current microeconomics texts avoid all reference to Ricardo, even when
acknowledging their Marshallian inspiration. Historians of economic thought,
however, cannot ignore this determining aspect. Blaug, for example, seems to
admit the reconciliation between classicists and *marginalists:* "In 1891, Marshall provided a reconciliation between marginal utility economics and classical
economics which made the new ideas palatable by showing that they could be
fitted together into a wider context" (Blaug, 1990 [1962]: 308). Schumpeter,
on the other hand, completely rejects Marshall's attempt to reconcile both
schools in his *History of Economic Analysis* "So brilliant a light will attract
moths – there are a certain number of obscure Ricardian writers. [. . .] Finally,
economists of later generations – conspicuous instances were J. S. Mill and A.
Marshall – may pay homage to a great name of the past in such a way as to hide
from themselves and others the full extent of the gulf that separates them from
him (Schumpeter, 1986 [1954]: 450). And also: "Marshall's theoretical structure [. . .] is fundamentally the same as that of Jevons, Menger, and especially
Walras, but that the rooms in this new house are unnecessarily cluttered up with
Ricardian heirlooms, which receive emphasis quite out of proportion to their
operational importance" (Blaug, 1990 [1962]: 804).

14 Only when constant returns and constant marginal costs are assumed does an
increase in the normally produced quantity not change prices.

15 More precisely, Marshall holds that Ricardo never intended to posit that the
only source of value is labor. The argument, then, is not with Ricardo but with
Ricardo's interpreters, such as Rodbertus and Marx, who defended such position; they are accused of misreading or, rather, misrepresenting the *Principles of
Political Economy and Taxation.*

16 Jevons, for example, believed that value was a determination prevailing in Crusoe's island, where utility was its source: "Even Robinson Crusoe must have
looked upon each of his possessions with varying esteem and desire for more,
although he was incapable of exchanging with any other person" (Jevons, 1888
[1871]: IV.8). Marshall held, likewise, that sacrifice should be the source of
value in the economy of the hypothetical isolated individual: "Robinson Crusoe had to do only with real costs and real satisfactions: and an old-fashioned
peasant family, which bought little and sold little, arranged its investments of
present 'effort and waiting' for future benefits on nearly the same lines" (Marshall, 1920 [1890]: V.IV.6).

17 The current version of *marginalism* generally includes three factors of production, and not just two, as Marshall does: labor, capital, and land. In some text
books, a fourth "factor" is even added on: the "entrepreneurial" factor. In Marshall's theory of value, there is, however, no room for land or nature as a component of real cost. Employing nature in productive processes does not imply

any original "sacrifice". In fact, Marshall's theory of rent is aligned (by Marshall's own admission) with the Ricardian theory of differential rent, according to which the rent is a surplus appropriated by the owners of superior land. Even though for the farmer the rent is a part of costs, its magnitude is determined by the price of the produce, and not by the effort accumulated on the land. Land or, in general, nature is not a factor, comparable to labor and waiting, because it does not represent any sacrifice and, therefore, is not a source of value (Marshall, 1920 [1890]; VI.IX.5).

18 This is the same adjustment process described by Adam Smith in his well-known passage on the invisible hand; according to him, resources (capital) go to the most profitable activity, without the intervention of any non-economic force (Smith 1904 [1776])).

19 When Hicks, in his famous book *Value and Capital,* tries to make Marshall's partial approach to a certain extent compatible with Walras's general approach, he does so by introducing in the "theory of demand or of the consumer" a second commodity along with the one Marshall analyzed in isolation. He then proposes to analytically decompose price variation into a "substitution effect" and an "income effect". The hypothetical case of the Giffen-type goods is then introduced. Concerning the way how Marshall avoids studying the income effect through the introduction of a constant marginal utility money, Hicks says: "it is indeed one of those simplifications of genius, of which there are several instances in Marshall" (Hicks, 1978 [1937]: 32). However, although the reciprocal changes in the marginal utilities of the two commodities discussed together are acknowledged in his explanation, it is assumed that there is a constant purchasing power money in which prices are expressed: "the indifference diagram, measuring its two 'commodities' along its two axes, is only useful when the consumer can be thought of as spending his income upon two 'commodities' and two 'commodities' only: this usually means, in practice, that it must be applied to the case in which we are interested in problems of the demand for one physical commodity, and measure along the other axis all other commodities lumped together (Marshall's *money*). (Hicks, 1978 [1937]: 45). In this aspect, the modern version of the theory of demand still rests, ultimately, on the artificial money of the First Treatise, since, without mentioning it, it builds a world with one or two commodities *plus* money.

20 In *Value and Capital,* Hicks rejects the utilitarianism underlying Marshall's presentation: "If one is utilitarian in philosophy, one has the perfect right to be utilitarian in one's economics. But if one is not (and few people are utilitarians nowadays), one also has the right to an economics free of utilitarian assumptions" (Hicks, 1978 [1937]: 18). Instead of discussing one isolated good, he includes two goods. Thus, the marginal utility is only relevant in relative terms (marginal rate of substitution) and determines relative prices. Even so, as has been mentioned, the constant utility of money is implicit: "But the problem of related goods cannot be treated on a two-dimensional indifference diagram. It needs three dimensions to represent the two related goods and money (the necessary background)" (Hicks, 1978 [1937]: 45).In an extreme case, money is just one commodity more, and the only solution is that of general equilibrium, so that Hicks's solution is only partial, so to speak. However, as will be seen, Walras too has to adopt an arbitrary and highly unsound conception of money when studying general equilibrium.

21 One of the most ingenious ways of "integrating" a monetary explanation of interest with that associating interest and physical return of capital is the one

laid out by Wicksell. Marshall intends to solve such dualism by means of his distinction between the short and the long terms. Wicksell, instead, analytically divides the phenomenon of the rate of interest: he defines a "natural" rate of interest that corresponds to the laws of the First Treatise, and another rate determined by the state of the "loans" that depends, in turn, on the amount of money. He then makes a more refined attempt at unifying both Treatises. He asserts that the prices of commodities are modified when there is a discrepancy between these two rates, the "natural" rate and the "loan" rate, since the abundance of money drives the monetary rate of interest downwards, stimulating the demand of commodities in general, and therefore tends to inflate prices or, at least some of them. Later, the automatic adjustment will take place. Foreign trade and money scarcity will force banks to reduce once again the rate of interest to its natural level (Wicksell, 1947 [1911]). In the *Treatise*, Keynes draws on this solution, but in *The General Theory* he instead categorically rejects the distinction between a natural and a monetary rate of interest.

22 Ricardo puts forward a system of administration of note issuing to replace the gold standard, which he considers to be a waste of resources. The basic rule would be regulating emission so that the value of the notes reflects what the gold would have if it were in circulation.

23 In spite of his opposition to the theory of a general lack of demand, Ricardo held that, on account of its own laws, capitalism creates an internal obstacle that hinders the unlimited growth of production. He based this limitation on his theory of distribution. According to Ricardo, real wage is fixed and tied to the level of subsistence, but the increasing need of food will lead to the use of increasingly less fertile lands. His theory of value (specifically, of rent) leads him to posit that the price of agricultural products will consequently grow, leaving an increasing proportion of wealth in the hands of the landowner class.

   Thus, capital gains will be reduced but not as a result of a lack of profitable opportunities, but because of the accumulation of resources in the hands of landowners.

24 In his 1927 article "Wage Policy and Unemployment", Pigou, one of the most renowned *marginalists,* explained post-war unemployment by resorting to the only way of characterizing it according to the classical labor market: "The position is this. If wage-earners insist on maintaining a real rate of wages above the economic level in the sense defined above, and if no mitigating action is undertaken by the State, an abnormal volume of unemployment, with all the material and moral waste that this implies, is the inevitable concomitant [. . .]. I conclude, therefore, that insistence by wage-earners upon maintaining uneconomically high wage-rates must involve large unemployment and associated social evils, and that, in a democracy such as ours, these evils cannot be effectively cancelled. The inference is that it is against the interest of the community as a whole for wage earners to insist upon uneconomically high wages-rates. That interest requires the restoration, at not too distant a date, of an equilibrium between wage-rates and demand and supply conditions" (Pigou, 1927: 366). Keynes's criticisms were leveled at an utterly real rival: the orthodox theory of his times (and of the present age).

25 The trust in Say's Law in the long term does not require a similar reconstruction, as it was part of the explicit beliefs of the *classical theory*.

3 Keynes's critique of the classical theory

[T]he classical school ignored the problem, as a consequence of introducing into their premises conditions which involved its non-existence; with the result of creating a cleavage between the conclusions of economic theory and those of common sense. The extraordinary achievement of the classical theory was to overcome the beliefs of the 'natural man' and, at the same time, to be wrong. [. . .] One recurs to the analogy between the sway of the classical school of economic theory and that of certain religions. For it is far greater exercise of the potency of an idea to exorcise the obvious than to introduce into men's common notions the recondite and the remote

Keynes, The General Theory

Introduction

In this chapter, we will offer a summary that will help contrast in a more synthetic way the classical system against Keynes's system, which will be discussed in Chapter 4. On the basis of the previous overview of the *classical theory*, it is possible to distinguish the variables that are considered independent from the ones treated as dependent in the classical system. Dependent variables are those that the classicists consider to be determined by causal economic relationships, by laws or trends. Those phenomena that the classicists take as given, that is, those whose determination they do not intend to explain in their theory, become, instead, independent variables. See, first, the First Classical Treatise on value and distribution. Individuals' preferences and productive techniques are there considered to be exogenous. Also exogenous to the system is the amount available of each factor of production (capital, land, and labor). The main endogenous variables are prices, the traded amounts of commodities and the retributions of the factors of production. Nominal wage and employment volume are determined in the labor market. In the capital market, saving and investment volumes, and the rate of interest are set. The equality of demand and supply determines the revenue of the productive factors within the system.

Forcing slightly the argument of the First Treatise, a goods aggregate supply and demand curve may also be obtained.[1] It is enough to apply the usual classicists' method, that is, projecting the individual behavior of a firm or a consumer onto the society as a whole. Thus, the aggregate volume of output and the general level of prices also become endogenous variables. It was earlier shown that the classical system ensures that the level of output will always tend to coincide with the level corresponding to full employment.

In the Second Treatise, it is somehow more difficult to distinguish between determining and determined elements. Initially, money is any commodity and, as such, has its price set by the First Treatise's law of value. When the value of money is established according to the general laws of demand and supply, the amount of money is an endogenous variable that depends on circulation needs, determined by the general traffic of commodities. In this case, the general level of prices is also endogenous. But the laws of the system are completely transformed when the amount of inconvertible money becomes determined by the banking system and by government.

The quantitative equation determines, then, the level of prices according to the income velocity of money, which is an exogenous variable. At the same time, the rate of interest becomes a variable that is directly regulated by banks (bank rate) and, as such, exogenous. In the First Treatise, money does not make any difference or, rather, does not exist as such: it does not circulate nor can it be lent. The economy is non-monetary.

In Chapter 4, we will show that, as a result of his critique of the classical system, Keynes develops a system that differs from the classical one in its choice of endogenous and exogenous variables, in its analysis of the three main markets (goods, labor, and capital), in its conception of money, and in the role played by Say's Law.

The results obtained in this study – some of which have been synthetically presented – lay the groundwork to undertake the presentation of Keynes's system in itself, an undertaking that had to be postponed until a complete background, on one hand, and all the building blocks of the new theoretical construct, on the other, had been made available to the reader. Putting all the pieces in place is all that is left to be done now.

A terminological clarification should also be made. On one hand, Keynes uses the term "system" or "economic system" to refer to the economic processes that take place in real world. He states, for example, that

> it is an outstanding characteristic of the economic system in which we live that, whilst it is subject to severe fluctuations in respect to output and employment, it is not violently unstable. Indeed it seems capable of remaining in a chronic condition of sub-normal activity for a considerable period without any marked tendency either towards recovery or towards complete collapse. Moreover, the evidence indicates that

full, or even approximately full, employment is of rare and short-lived occurrence.

(Keynes, 1939 [1936]; 249-250; IV.18.III)

But, on the other hand, Keynes would use the same phrase ("economic system") to refer to the theoretical representation of major economic processes, considered as a whole. In the following exposition this term will be used instead of the more frequent "model", since the latter is indiscriminately employed to refer to any mathematical exercise where economic variables are used, although such exercise may be meant to depict exclusively a merely partial and isolated aspect of a highly complex phenomenon.

The term "model" is even used to denote any kind of "hypothesis" regarding the relationship existing among a few selected phenomena, fragmentary in nature.

The term "system", instead, refers to a more ambitious and, simultaneously, more accurate project, because it is designed to reproduce the way in which economy works as a whole: it is for this reason that one single term, "system", refers just as much to the real economy as to its theoretical representation. The construction of the theoretical system is a sensitive operation that requires the completion of three tasks: first, it is necessary to identify the more relevant economic phenomena (the variables involved); once this has been done, it has to be decided which of these phenomena will be considered non-modifiable data (given variables or parameters), which will be determining factors (exogenous or independent variables) and which will be the elements determined by the system (endogenous or dependent variables). In Keynes's words: it has to be made "clear which elements in the economic system we usually take as given, which are the independent variables of our system and which are the dependent variables" (op.cit.).

Finally, it is necessary to accurately identify the direct and indirect causal relationships that link these phenomena (which may be represented by means of functions): based on the parameters and the causal relations, certain values of the independent variables determine the values of some of the dependent variables, which in turn set the value of other dependent variables, and so on. The term "system", on the other hand, helps differentiate the *sequential* expository method chosen by Keynes from the *simultaneous* method usually employed by classical economics.

Chapter 3 is organized as follows: Initially, some general additional observations on the nature of the system that Keynes intends to build will be presented. First, the precise objectives and aims that the whole construction is meant to serve have to be explained, according to the previous exposition.

Next, as in the case of the classical system, the given factors, the dependent and independent variables of Keynes's system will be identified. Finally, some methodological aspects will be discussed.

In Chapter 4, the proposal developed by Keynes to replace the *classical theory*, that is to say, his system, will be explained.

I Keynes's system conditions and nature

Objective: to determine the level of employment

It may be said that the most significant rupture between the new system and the *classical* one is what Keynes's system defines as its main unknown: "The ultimate object of our analysis is to discover what determines the volume of employment" (Keynes, 1939 [1936]). This is, therefore, as Keynes calls it, the *quaesitum* of the system: the volume of employment of the available resources. The analysis is strictly restricted to the Marshallian short term:

> We take as given the existing skill and quantity of available labour, the existing quality and quantity of available equipment, the existing technique, the degree of competition, the tastes and habits of the consumer.
> (Keynes, 1939 [1936]: 245; IV.18.I)

The *classical theory* was built in the shelter of the assumption of the full employment of resources – all the supplied capital and labor *must* find an equivalent demand under equilibrium conditions.

Keynes's system, instead, intends to shed light on the conjunction of factors that result in a level of employment and output whose *equilibrium* volume is below that of full employment, without the system creating any incentive or trend towards recovery.[2]

The new "model" must admit the existence of idle capacity, and explain the determinants of its magnitude. Briefly, Keynes seeks to build a system capable of explaining unemployment as an equilibrium situation. The volume of employment is not already *given* – as was the case in the *classical theory* – so that its magnitude does not necessarily coincide with the total amount of resources ready to be employed. More precisely, he intends to explain the constellation of economic forces that, given a total stock of available capital and labor, set a determined level of equilibrium employment and output. Thus, the possible equilibriums for a level of output are many and not just the single possibility of full employment. The classical system simply cannot produce this result. Keynes attempts to offer a *general* theory of employment, that is, one able to encompass all possible equilibriums,

> [T]he fluctuations in real income under consideration in this book are those which result from applying different quantities of employment

(i.e. of labour – units) to a given capital equipment, so that real income increases and decreases with the number of labour – units employed.

(Keynes, 1936: 114; III.10.I)

To achieve this objective, Keynes considers it necessary to eliminate the split between the First and the Second Treatise that the classicists had turned into a dogma, that is, he intends to reconcile the theory of value and the theory of money since, in his view, this is "a false division" (*op. cit*). The mistake translates, firstly, in a double – contradictory – determination of prices. The *classical theory* offers two different explanations for the level of prices and, consequently, for also its opposite, the purchasing power of money. The theoretical dualism of the classicists must be replaced with a general theory of prices.

Such theoretical duplication repeats in the case of other crucial variable: the rate of interest, whose fluctuations are associated with certain causes when the *classical theory* develops its First Treatise, and to others when it faces the same phenomenon in the Second Treatise. In the framework of the theory of value and distribution, the rate of interest derives from the reciprocal action of supply and demand of "free" capital, but in the theory of money it becomes an effect of the movement of monetary variables and the state of credit. Keynes seeks to find a *general* theory of interest.

> Thus the classical school have had quite a different theory of the rate of interest in Volume I, dealing with the theory of value from what they have had in volume II, dealing with the theory of money. They have seemed undisturbed by the conflict and have made no attempt, so far as I know, to build a bridge between the two theories.
>
> (Keynes, 1939 [1936]: 183; IV.14.I)

The root of the problem lies in the First Treatise of the *classical theory*, where it is pretended that money does not exist and, taking that argument to an extreme, it is concluded that there are no fundamental differences (that is, in relative prices) between a money-less economy and a monetary economy as concerns the retributions of the factors and the level of employment. But prices and the rate of interest are monetary phenomena, as the *classical theory* itself later has to admit in its Second Treatise, replacing its previous explanations with new theories. Marshall's work, according to Keynes, is corrupted by such inconsistencies:

> The perplexity which I find in Marshall's account of the matter is fundamentally due, I think, to the incursion of the concept 'interest', which belongs to a monetary economy, into a treatise which takes no account

of money. 'Interest' has really no business to turn up at all in Marshall's *Principles of Economics*.

(Keynes, 1939 [1936]: 189; IV.14a.I)

Keynes's theoretical trajectory is plagued with partial experiments designed to escape this duality. In the *Tract*, he tried to explain variations in prices by resorting to the Second Treatise's monetary instrument par excellence: the classical quantitative theory. But he was soon forced to introduce various intricacies and subtle detours to the original argument to adapt that theory to the new economic problems.

Thus, he managed to avoid the conclusion to which the quantitative theory leads when applied directly – any increase in the quantity of money is proportionally transferred to prices. In the *Treatise*, Keynes was no longer content with the modified, qualified, more sophisticated versions of the quantitative theory, but felt forced to abandon it definitively in order to incorporate a series of "real" elements that intervene in price determination. His fundamental equations reflect the relationship between some "real" (saving, investment, and benefits) and some monetary (the new non-automatic movements of the rate of interest and the quantity of money) factors. In *The General Theory*, the most characteristic monetary tool of the *classical theory*, that which entails and forces a radical split from the theory of value, does not play any role in Keynes's explanation, as he himself emphatically states in the preface to the French edition: "The following analysis registers my final escape from the confusions of the Quantity Theory, which once entangled me" (Keynes, 1939 [1936]).

The sum of these elements points to the second trait that will characterize the Keynesian system, as opposed to the *classical theory:* Keynes seeks to represent the complete workings of what he calls a *monetary economy* – the First Classical Treatise, instead, referred to a *non-monetary economy*. Thus, the dichotomy of a theory split into two Treatises is solved, unifying the "monetary" and "real" aspects within a single consistent explanation. Keynes intends no less than to merge the theory of value and the theory of money. After putting forward most of his innovations, he states that "[o]ne of the objects of the foregoing chapters has been to escape from this double life and to bring the theory of prices as a whole back to close contact with the theory of value" (Keynes, 1939 [1936]: 293; V.21.I).

In contrast with the *classical theory*, which departed from a non-circulating commodity money with constant purchasing power in the theory of money put forward in the First Treatise, the new system will have, *from its inception*, to account for changes in money's purchasing power, monetary needs concerning circulation, effects of the decisions made by the banking system, and the existence of a monetary interest rate. Based on these elements, Keynes's system will determine the equilibrium level of employment, which may not necessarily coincide with the voluntary supply of labor. The system will thus become a representation of the workings of a monetary economy.

Synthetically, involving not only "real" but also some strictly monetary variables, Keynes's system will yield as its result a short-term equilibrium output and employment level. In short, this is the discovery that distinguishes *The General Theory* from the *Tract*, the *Treatise,* and the whole *classical theory:* "in certain conditions, the system could be in equilibrium with less than full employment" (Keynes, 1939 [1936]). It will also be, in turn, a *general theory* inasmuch as it will include the classical assumption of full employment as one of the possible equilibriums. The short-term equilibrium output level with variable employment will thus be obtained in the context of a *monetary economy*.

New elements in the Keynesian economic system

Keynes's system operates within the context of the short term, so that the existing resources are considered fixed. However, as was argued in the previous chapters, the selection of dependent and independent variables here does not coincide with that of the *classical theory*. A quick inventory reveals remarkable differences in judgment, all of them stemming from the historical transformations incurred in the different spheres stressed by Keynes: the labor market, the monetary arrangements, and the investment decisions.

For Keynes, wages are determined through bargaining between workers organized in trade unions and their employers.

In Keynes's system, the nominal wage (the wage-unit) becomes an independent variable, an input of the economic system.

The quantity of money is, in Keynes's system, an independent variable, and as such, it is not subject to the action of the economic forces depicted by the system but depends on an external factor: governmental decision. The monetary authority will be in charge of determining the volume of non-convertible paper money in circulation in the country.

Also, in Keynes's system, the return that capitalists expect to obtain is not based on objective information but rather becomes an independent variable of "psychological" character, which varies according to expectations concerning a basically uncertain future. And this enterprise expected return is compared to money's rate of interest: investment and saving become dependent variables: "Thus the traditional analysis is faulty because it has failed to isolate correctly the independent variables of the system. Saving and investment are the determinates of the system, not the determinants" (Keynes, 1939 [1936]).

Finally, Keynes begins to consider the proportion of cash that the public wishes to keep in hand as a variable.

In *The General Theory*, he calls "preference for liquidity" the desire to hold cash. He makes this new variable dependent on the public's "psychology", as, once again, it is not determined by the causal action of other variables in the system: it functions independently, and yet it is not fixed in the short term, but changes in accordance with other factors that will be later discussed.

When Keynes mentions the independent variables involved in his explanation, he only synthesizes the conclusions at which he arrived by observing the transformations of the capitalist society that have just been listed. From this point of view, his choice of independent variables implies a critique of the *classical system*, incapable of portraying the workings of a *modern* economy, after the changes that took place in the early twentieth century; independent and dependent variables are not the same now.

> Thus we can sometimes regard our ultimate independent variables as consisting of (i) the three fundamental psychological factors, namely, the psychological propensity to consume, the psychological attitude to liquidity and the psychological expectation of future yield from capital – assets, (2) the wage – unit as determined by the bargains reached between employers and employed, and (3) the quantity of money as determined by the action of the central bank; so that, if we take as given the factors specified above, these variables determine the national income (or dividend) and the quantity of employment. But these again would be capable of being subjected to further analysis, and are not, so to speak, our ultimate atomic independent elements.
>
> (Keynes, 1939 [1936]: 246–247; IV.18.I)

This enumeration lays the groundwork for the presentation of the "causal relationships" among variables, that is, the *system* proper. The main dependent variable is no longer, as it already was in the *Treatise* and the *Tract*, the level of prices, but the volume of aggregate production and, therefore, of employment, as set within the analytical Marshallian short term. The great novelty of *The General Theory* may lie here: in having chosen the level of employment as the characteristic dependent variable of its system: "Our dependent variables are the volume of employment and the national income (or national dividend) [. . .]" (Keynes, 1939 [1936]).

The reconstruction of the system's components, as well as of the role they play in the system, is not yet complete. All the variables involved in Keynes's explanation have yet to be collected; with that aim, it is necessary to identify the intermediate components of the mechanism, those variables situated between the independent variables and the main unknown that is meant to be solved: the *quaesitum* (question), that is, the level of employment. These dependent variables include, on one hand, the level of aggregate consumption and investment, and on the other, the general level of prices, the rate of interest, and the real wage. However, as may be observed, the dependent variables also exhibit a hierarchy or order as to its determination: they are involved in a causation train, a determinate dependence sequence. This way of representing economic processes will not be familiar to the reader used to the models of the contemporary *classical theory*, where a multi-causality typical of simultaneous determination is usually assumed. Some elements characteristic of Keynes's methodology need be explored.

Some methodological considerations

Before reconstructing Keynes's *system*, it is necessary to discuss an aspect of "methodological" nature regarding the particular manner adopted to *explain* economic phenomena in *The General Theory*. More than a new research method or a singular conception of the operation of economic processes, it might be said that the novelty lies in a particular form of presenting the results of the enquiry or, in Keynes's words, in a particular form of "thinking the economy": "an organised and orderly method of thinking out particular problems" (Keynes, 1939 [1936]). It is, all in all, a particular *expository method*. But this method is different from the prevailing *mathematic method* (thus is how Keynes calls it), so it is convenient to list the arguments wielded in *The General Theory* to choose this modality over the other.

It has been mentioned that Keynes calls *economic system* (and not *model*) his way or *representing* "the causal sequence of economic events" (Keynes, 1939 [1936]). The first step the researcher should take to erect this *system* consists in isolating the different elements of the problem he wishes to explain establishing certain causal relationships between them. In mathematical terms, such operation translates into the identification of the factors that are to be considered as given, those that will be taken as independent variables – determining elements, that is, elements whose causes are not explained by the system itself – and dependent variables – determinate elements, that is, "effects". Once the variables have been identified and catalogued, a new problem that, as will be seen, may have different solutions raises: the different modes of presenting these causal relationships.[3]

The first difficulty that has to be faced when building the *system*, therefore, relates to the options available when selecting the relevant economic elements and classifying them into given factors, independent and dependent variables. Keynes admits that the choice of variables and their typification is a largely arbitrary operation, as it stems from appreciations that are highly "subjective" in character, that is, from the researcher's capacity; that classification is exclusively based on observation and practice.[4]

> The division of the determinants of the economic system into the two
> groups of given factors and independent variables is, of course, quite

arbitrary from any absolute standpoint. The division must be made entirely on the basis of experience, so as to correspond on the one hand to the factors in which the changes seem to be so slow or so little relevant as to have only a small and comparatively negligible short – term influence on our *quaesitum*; and on the other hand, to those factor in which the changes are found in practice to exercise a dominant influence on our *quaesitum*.

(Keynes, 1939 [1936]: 247; IV.18.I)

The "arbitrary" aspect refers, precisely, to the researcher's capacity to perceive those elements of the economic process in their historical dimension. Besides, this is one of the reasons that led Keynes to discard the *classical system*, and his motives are made explicit. There still remains the task of establishing the "determination relationships" connecting the selected variables, that is, the "causal sequence" that links them. It is necessary to relate the variables distinguishing, first, causes from effects. For Keynes, the phenomena exert mutual influence upon themselves, in a determinate way and in a determinate direction. Once the causal relationships have been identified, the most adequate way of *presenting* them will have to be decided upon. It is in connection with this issue that *The General Theory* is significantly distanced from the expository mode prevailing in mainstream economic theory.

Keynes holds that the simultaneous, purely mathematical expository method is incapable of properly reflecting causal relationships by itself. Besides, by using only functions and equations to reflect the links between different phenomena, the possibility of evaluating the mutual and complex interaction between variables is restricted to those limited connections that the "models" explicit.

In his previous works, Keynes had already warned about the misunderstandings to which the mathematical expository method sometimes leads.[5] In the *Tract*, he criticized the quantitative theory from this point of view, challenging the suitability of a mere equation to express the complex causality of monetary phenomena. In fact, identities reflecting relationships between phenomena do not and cannot have the character of an explanation, since they are mere truisms, tautologies: "in fact, the [quantitative] theory, stated thus, is a truism, and as nearly as possible jejune" (Keynes, 1923). In the *Treatise*, he challenged again the explanatory power of the identity on which the quantitative theory is based: to explain the movement of prices, it is not enough to link some variables through an accounting equation, but an explicit and accurate "causal sequence" has to be established:

The Fundamental Problem of Monetary Theory is not merely to establish identities or statical equations relating (e.g.) the turnover of monetary instruments to the turnover of things traded for money. The real task of such a theory is to treat the problem dynamically, analysing the different elements involved, in such a manner as to exhibit the causal process by which the price-level is determined, and the method of transition from one position of equilibrium to another.

(Keynes, 1935 [1930]: 133)

It is for this reason that he abandons the quantitative equation – it is not monetary theory or even an explanation. It only reflects an identity that does not specify the causal process or distinguish between determining and determined variables.

A thorough analysis of the capacity of equation systems to adequately represent economic laws is beyond the scope of this study. We only present here Keynes's views concerning this subject, with the purpose of characterizing the particular traits of the way in which he presents his own *system*. According to Keynes, a static equation reflects a precise quantitative relation between the variables involved in its formulation; however, it does not express causality or, at least, not explicitly. It may be concluded that a function is capable of expressing an accurate relation of correspondence between variables, but not an univocal relation of causality, except when such relation is established independently of the function by explicitly identifying which variables are determining and which determined, that is, which are endogenous and which exogenous. However, this is not always the case; particularly, in a set of multiple functions, it is not possible to order the direction of causality between the endogenous variables.

In other words, the direction of the causal relation, that is, which is the cause and which the effect, is not made explicit.

This is a problem inherent in any strictly mathematical formulation of economic laws. But there is still another difficulty in purely mathematical representation that leads Keynes to reject it. It is true that functions and equations help establish a defined and accurate relation between variables, but such representation is not suitable when trying to explain highly complex economic problems, where multiple causal factors intervene, as the mutual interaction between determined factors is, by definition, not taken into account.

> It is a great fault of symbolic pseudo – mathematical methods of formalising a system of economic analysis [. . .] that they expressly assume strict independence between the factors involved and lose all their cogency and authority if this hypothesis is disallowed.
>
> (Keynes, 1939 [1936]: 297–298; V.21.III)

Keynes devoted scathing criticism to the abuse of mathematical expressions in economics (even though in those days the mainstream had not reached its present-day level of sophistication). Keynes resorts to a different method, which he considers adequate to avoid the overly strict and, for that reason, according to him, much more simplistic (contrary to the commonly held view that these are more complex) representations that are typical of the purely mathematical models.

The solution he finds consists in specifying the *main* causal relations, leaving the door open to think *afterwards* about all the secondary links between variables. He holds this to be the adequate expository method for economic theory because an initial working schematic explanation that at the same time is also powerful, defined, and clear is thus obtained: it has the virtue of shedding light on the main flows of causality, so that those provisional results may later be qualified through the intervention of new elements.

> The object of our analysis is, not to provide a machine, or method of blind manipulation, which will furnish an infallible answer, but to provide ourselves with an organised and orderly method of thinking out particular problems; and, after we have reached a provisional conclusion by isolating the complicated factors one by one, we then have to go back on ourselves and allow, as well as we can, for the probable interaction of the factors amongst themselves. This is the nature of economic thinking. Any other way of applying our formal principles of thought (without which, however, we shall be lost in the wood) will lead us into error.
>
> (Keynes, 1939 [1936]: 297; V.21.III)

An orderly "method of thinking" is, besides, thus offered. When comparing it to the systems of simultaneous equations of the mathematical system, some advantages may be noted.

No doubt, an equation system has the virtue of establishing *defined* links among all the variables involved in the problem. If the system is well built, and the number of unknowns equals that of equations, it is capable of providing a set of accurate values for all the dependent variables.[6] But this is not enough.

As has been said, the mathematical method erases causal relations among main factors and, at the same time, leaves out secondary links. All the factors appear to be mutually connected and seem to have the same hierarchy: the "logical" sequence of determination cannot be seen.

How to build a *system* that makes it possible, instead, to represent this kind of relation among phenomena? Keynes replaces the method of simultaneous resolution with one of sequential resolution. In the previous quotes, he mentioned the causal "sequence" or "process" linking phenomena. In *The General Theory* this sequence is represented by means of a "stepped" resolution. However, the intention is not to reflect an actual temporal sequence, as in practice phenomena do not occur sequentially. This is simply a resource aimed at representing the most relevant causal relations in an understandable way. An excerpt, among many, from *The General Theory* illustrates Keynes's procedure:

> Money, and the quantity of money, are not direct influences at this stage of the proceedings. They have done their work at an earlier stage of the analysis.
>
> (Keynes, 1939 [1936]: 164)

According to this expository method, analysis progresses in stages. The procedure is simple: based on a set of independent variables, the value of a determined factor is obtained. Then, that dependent variable becomes input for another explanation.

Thus, the "sequential sequence", which Keynes references, begins to take shape. In *The General Theory*, an expository method of this kind is in fact used, which only occasionally resorts to equations, as it uses "*everyday language*", contrary to the mathematical systems made up of simultaneous resolution equations. In this way, emphasis is placed on the causation train that strings the more relevant phenomena together, thus shaping a reasoning that is considered the main explanation. After unveiling the more significant mechanisms, the exposition must go on, since once this schematic – but understandable – exposition has been completed, Keynes begins to assess the possible secondary effects of each determining factor.

> Thus the position of equilibrium will be influenced by these repercussions; and there are other repercussions also. Moreover, there is not one of the above factors which is not liable to change without much warning, and sometimes substantially. Hence the extreme complexity of the actual course of events. Nevertheless, these seem to be the factors which it is useful and convenient to isolate. If we examine any actual problem along the lines of the above schematism, we shall find it more manageable; and our practical intuition (which can take account of a more detailed complex of facts than can be treated on general principles) will be offered a less intractable material upon which to work.
>
> (Keynes, 1939 [1936]: 249; IV.18.II)

For this reason, it is necessary to continue evaluating the interaction among phenomena, as the first result found after examining primary causal relations does not thoroughly describe the definitive resting position. It still remains that one take into account the remaining mutual relations among variables. In a system of simultaneous equations, all these interactions are present *since the beginning*, and the solution is definitive, but Keynes seems to believe that even though the mathematical form of expressing economic processes ensures, undoubtedly, consistency, it does so at the expense of blurring the understanding of the economic argument "in a maze of pretentious and unhelpful symbols".

In other words, it may be asserted that Keynes's system is amenable to mathematical formulation in the framework of a system of simultaneous determination equations, as this merely entails a difference as to the expository method that is, therefore, not related to the time sequence but to the causation train.[7] What is under discussion is the most suitable expository form. If all the relations are simultaneously expressed, as is always the case in an equation system, all the elements are mutually determined.

Keynes, instead, prefers to focus the attention on the backbone of his reasoning, stressing the interactions he deems to be the principal ones and separating them from the rest to provide "an organised and orderly method of thinking out particular problems".[8] In brief: Keynes prefers an exposition grounded on a hierarchically organized sequence of causes to the causal simultaneity of the systems of equations.[9]

As for the objectives that this economic system has to reach, Keynes recognizes that there is a further purpose that should also be mentioned on account of its practical and historical relevance. It is, besides, a factor that is key to understanding the influence that *The General Theory* came to have among economists. Once the causal relations between variables have been specified, it is possible to accurately identify those points in the chain of events where the government can have an impact through its actions. Thus, the *economic system* becomes a "scientific" base to ponder the different options of economic policy that have a bearing on the *quaesitum* – employment – as well as on any other variable: "Our final task might be to select those variables which can be deliberately controlled or managed by a central authority in the kind of system in which we actually live (Keynes, 1939 [1936]: 247; IV.18.I).

Keynes's *system* becomes thus a "user manual" – probably the first with such ambitious aims – for the new instruments in the field of economic policy available to the government. The historical development of capitalism laid in the hands of the authority the ability to decide over certain variables that were earlier subject to automatic mechanisms, such as the quantity of money, the rate of interest and, partially, nominal wages.

II Critique of the *classical theory:* general aspects

The congenital anachronism of the classical theory

The elements presented so far expose several flaws of the *classical theory*, associated with a change in the historical phase. As has been mentioned, according to Keynes, the orthodox doctrine was unable to account for the economic processes that characterized twentieth-century capitalism. In the final chapter of *The General Theory*, Keynes assesses his objections to the *classical theory* and concludes that,

> Our criticism of the accepted classical theory of economics has consisted not so much in finding logical flaws in its analysis as in pointing out that its tacit assumptions are seldom or never satisfied, with the result that it cannot solve the economic problems of the actual world.
>
> (Keynes, 1939 [1936]: 378; V.24.III)

Keynes identifies numerous transformations in the economic situation of his times that contradict certain aspects on which the *classical theory* was premised. However, the factual basis of such premises had already ceased to exist; the doctrine, therefore, became unsuitable to describe the world as it is, and so became an anachronistic theory. Once these differences stemming from historical change have been pointed out, it is possible to list a distinct class of issues that Keynes encountered in the classical system. We are talking about the strictly theoretical *flaws*, that is, flaws in the field of consistency, the reasoning, and the logic of the classical system.

For the time being, only the logical flaws of the classical *system* will be discussed. However, the content of the *classical theory* is not exclusively restricted to its system. The historical problems, as well as the logical flaws present in the construction of the theory itself lead to a series of even *deeper* disagreements that distance Keynes from the classicists. Any *system* – whether the classical or Keynes's – is designed to represent (causal) relations among economic phenomena, that is, it seeks to explain how the different variables are quantitatively determined, as well as their mutual interaction. However, the economic *categories* themselves, that is, the nature of those "objects" and "laws" (phenomena) that the system links causally or mathematically, still remain to be discussed. An economic *system* is nothing more than a network of determined relations among different categories and concepts. The categories are the elements in the system. But those relations do not exhaust all the items to be researched by the economic theory: the examination of those elements in themselves, categories and concepts, still remains to be carried out.

To shed light on the difference between a *system* and the economic concepts, and to point out the kind of problems we are talking about, let's take as an example any economic category, e.g. the rate of interest. On one hand, the theory explains how its level is determined, identifying the main causes of its quantitative fluctuations, that is, what other variables bear influence on its magnitude, and how. But on the other, there is also another issue altogether different from mere quantitative determination, to which the economic theory has devoted much effort since its inception: the enquiry into the nature of the rate of interest. In other words, the search of the adequate answers to the following questions: What is the rate of interest? Why, in a capitalist society, does the owner of capital receive after a given period a portion of wealth larger than what he initially committed when he puts this wealth to work as capital? And, in turn, what is capital, a seemingly material object that is at the same time capable of "creating" new wealth or, at least, of placing the social wealth created otherwise in the hands of its owner? It may well be seen that such questions refer to the deep foundations of economic theory, to its primary explanations. Let's now set this issue in the context of the debate held by Keynes and the classicists. We know that, in Keynes's view, the rate of interest is not determined like the *classical theory* would say that it is; the same is true in connection with prices, employment, wages etc. Well then, the discrepancies between systems regarding the choice of given factors, independent and dependent variables, and the way in which each is determined are mere manifestations on the quantitative surface of the phenomena that express different – sometimes opposing – conceptions of the nature of commodity's value, money and capital. This matter will be addressed in the conclusion to this work.

Before reviewing in detail the "logical" aspects of the classical reasoning that Keynes explicitly challenges in *The General Theory*, we should mention all the fundamental objections related to economic changes that force, by their own weight, a reframing of the old theories.

The more serious flaw in the *classical theory* is the assumption of full employment that permeates the whole architecture of the *classical system*. During the first thirty years of the twentieth century, the capitalist economy had offered compelling evidence that it could work with a high level of idle capacity and a significant proportion of the existing resources – particularly, workers – involuntarily unemployed; in practice, the economy did not seem to exhibit any automatic tendency to recovery. The *classical theory* appeared, in this field, incompetent and unarmed, as it had simply excluded that possibility from its system. It never asked explicitly about the factors determining the volume of employment of available resources, but rather assumed that they were in a permanent state of full employment.

From the early nineteenth century, Say's Law had helped economists reject that argument: the insufficient demand is not the real cause of the crises, the stagnation, or the difficulties to broaden capitalist production and commerce. Since Say's days, Ricardians, *marginalists*, that is, the currents that had in its own turn prevailed, had endorsed this explanation.

Say's Law was part of the classical system – Ricardian and Marshallian, although it was mainly used to discuss long-term problems. According to Keynes, that same law – slightly reframed – is the only viable theoretical foundation available to support the assumption of full employment. It becomes an argument capable of denying the possibility that involuntary unemployment might exist: whenever there are idle resources willing to be employed, production will grow, as the system automatically creates – by definition, inasmuch as the product equals income – the required purchasing power to increase production. Say's Law thus becomes the heart that, by its very beat, gives life to the assumption of full employment.

However, it will not be enough for Keynes to show that the assumption of full employment is inadequate since it does not reflect the reality of the period. His attack is also aimed at each and every classical mechanism that implicitly or explicitly supports this assumption. Below, we will discuss the theoretical criticisms that Keynes levels at these mechanisms: the classical system collapses when it is shown that there is nothing to guarantee that aggregate demand will always grow at the same pace as the increase in production, driven by the growth in income and in the "real" retributions of the factors.

Keynes compares the economists to Candide, Voltaire's character, whose unrelenting faith prevented him from perceiving the misery that surrounded him. Based on their theory, the classical economists could only adopt one of two attitudes: either categorically denying the theoretical status of unemployment or trusting the task of remediating it to the blind forces of the economy:

> The celebrated *optimism* of traditional economic theory, [. . .] has led to economists being looked upon as Candides, who, having left this world for the cultivation of their gardens, teach that all is for the best in the best of all possible worlds provided we will let well alone [. . .] For there would obviously be a natural tendency towards the optimum employment of resources in a society which was functioning after the manner of the classical postulates. It may well be that the classical theory represents the way in which we should like our economy to behave. But to assume that it actually does so is to assume our difficulties away
>
> (Keynes, 1939 [1936]: 33; I.3.III)

These theoretical mistakes had, in turn, dismal practical consequences, which inevitably damaged the disciplinary prestige of economics. For to a classical economist, there was no other option than that of considering that the trade unions' struggle for their wages was, ultimately, the most importance hindrance to these restorative forces. According to the classical system, the economy tends to its recovery unless certain "external forces" hinder its normal development:

> A classical economist may sympathise with labour in refusing to accept a cut in its money-wage, and he will admit that it may not be wise to make it to meet conditions which are temporary; but scientific integrity

forces him to declare that this refusal is, nevertheless, at the bottom of
the trouble.

(Keynes, 1939 [1936]: 16; I, 2, IV)

If nothing changed, Keynes warned, the theory would make its supporters
as naive as they were unpopular. Economics, as a science, would end up
completely losing its political influence as a result of insisting on its old
path: these "divergences of opinion between [Keynes, and] fellow economists [. . .] have for the time being almost destroyed the practical influence
of economic theory, and will, until they are resolved, continue to do so.
(Keynes, 1939 [1936]: vi; Preface).

In this chapter, we will examine the general theoretical aspects that
account for the weakness of the *classical theory*, before reviewing Keynes's
specific criticism of the classical market of labor, the classical market of
capital, and the classical quantity theory.

These general aspects, together with the questions relevant to the expository method, constitute the framework of Keynes's system.

First and Second Treatises' dualism: Say's Law

The system Keynes built is meant to break the link between the conception
of money and Say's Law, and therefore, to shatter the assumption of full
employment. In fact, the most immediate and effective defense of Say's
Law rests on the singular representation of money that characterizes the
classical theory both in its First as in its Second Treatises.

It has been pointed out that the *classical theory* cannot determine the
level of employment as a whole. This incapacity is fed by its conception of
money in the First Treatise, which entails endorsing Say's Law. The paradoxical contradiction from which it cannot free itself lies in that, in order to
contemplate unemployment, it has to abandon the First Treatise's conception of money as a *numeraire* or as a standard of prices.

But if the money of the Second Treatise is introduced, many of the
conclusions to which the theory had arrived at in its First Treatise collapse because there emerges a new determination of prices, of the rate
of interest, etc. As soon as money as such is introduced into the system,
the *classical theory of value* flounders – as long as the *classical theory*
of value is endorsed, there is no room for money. The assumption of full
employment and the workings of Say's Law uphold their rule based on
this conundrum.

To escape this trap, Keynes will have to devise a system capable of yielding as a result short-term equilibrium unemployment in an economy that
should from its inception include strictly monetary variables and phenomena. The development of a new theory of money becomes a condition to
escape subjection to Say's Law. At the same time, this implies formulating

a single theory of interest and another of prices. Seen in this light, the development of a system based on a monetary economy with equilibrium unemployment, as Keynes attempts to do, seems to be the only possible way of eliminating the theoretical dualism of the two classical treatises.

The fallacy of composition in the classical theory

When unifying both treatises, do the theories of value and distribution also collapse or is it only the classical theory of money that which succumbs? Does the First Treatise survive and the Second fail, or must both be replaced?[10]

The *classical theory* intends to build its arguments on the basis of the free will of individual demanders and suppliers – consumers and producers – where it expects to discover the ultimate source of determination of the prices.[11] Its main result is the price of each particular commodity or the system of relative prices for all individual commodities, which is the same. *However, the aggregate volume of production is not an unknown.* As to the factors of production, the case is different; there, what seems to be a theory of aggregate supply and demand is introduced.

This is so because capital and labor appear to be highly homogeneous elements, whose aggregate seems to be as simple as plausible. It is true that the *classical theory* does not contain the aggregate output, the general level of prices and the aggregate consumption as its objects of study. However, it cannot avoid taking part in the debates about inflation and deflation, cycles and crises, the volume of foreign trade, the establishment of wages, the decline of profits, economic growth and its consequences etc., as otherwise it would leave a host of key economic problems out of its sphere of concern. To do so, it is forced to deal with national output as a whole. These issues used to be treated as side aspects of the theory, separated from the main theoretical body, the theory of value and distribution.

Under such circumstances, but also when they have to consider the "whole" market of an item, the classicists have to devise a method to refer to the rational behavior of all the enterprises of the same branch, and not just of a particular enterprise – all the consumers of one commodity, not an isolated consumer. When dealing with issues linked to the growth of the system, they have to go even further and consider not a specific industry but the national output as a whole – not the consumers of one commodity, but the consumption of all commodities. How does the *classical theory* conduct aggregate analysis? The method it applies is simple. There are two possible ways of referring to the joint behavior of several economic units, which are essentially coincident: either a simple addition (aggregation) of individual behaviors or an addition followed by a division, that is, an average. The first option assumes that the behavior of all the producers (or consumers) of an industry as a whole cannot be different from the "addition" of the individual behavior of each enterprise (or agent). The second is the average that Marshall made popular with his "representative" agent approach.

There, the step of linear aggregation is omitted to reach the average behavior directly. Basically, both methods rest on the same principle: the behavior of the whole is immediately equitable to the behavior of an individual specimen.[12]

Keynes rejects this method that consists of referring to the economy as a whole through simple aggregation, employing the usual resource of explaining, first, individual behavior to infer from it the behavior of the whole through analogy, generalization, or more roughly, addition. Thus, all consumers become one. That consumer is the result either of a, so to speak, "fleshing out" process (by means of the addition of the behavior of all consumers) or else of a double movement, a "fleshing out" followed by a "slimming down" by means of an average calculation. In that way, the *classical theory* avoids the question of output as a whole by lightly assuming that the aggregate is ruled by the same laws than the individual, but besides, according to Keynes, this methodology reveals a deep shortcoming since it ultimately has no method of approaching the issue other than by analogy. This approach leads the *classical theory* to ignore all the restrictions that bear on the behavior of the economy when studied as a whole, and to the impossibility of discussing, for example, the effect of a general decline in wages, as it is assumed that labor will react and face the same options as an isolate worker. The classical school not only does not even present the problem, but also lacks the theoretical tools to do so:

> But if the classical theory is not allowed to extend by analogy its conclusions in respect of a particular industry to industry as a whole, it is wholly unable to answer the question what effect on employment a reduction in money-wages will have. For it has no method of analysis wherewith to tackle the problem.
>
> (Keynes, 1939 [1936]: 260; V.19.I)

In the Preface to the French edition of 1939, this criticism is even more openly stated. The *classical theory's* inability to depict the real world is compounded by this methodological shortcoming, which may be catalogued as a true fallacy of composition. Even worse: persuaded that no objections may be posed to its aggregation method, since, according to its conception, the whole cannot be but the sum of its parts, and the options and choices of the whole must in essence be the same as those of the individual, the *classical theory* became accustomed to the dubious practice of taking a part for the whole (*pars pro toto*).

> I have called my theory a *general* theory. I mean by this that I am chiefly concerned with the behaviour of the economic system as a

whole, – with aggregate incomes, aggregate profits, aggregate output, aggregate employment, aggregate investment, aggregate saving rather than with the incomes, profits, output, employment, investment and saving of particular industries, firms or individuals. And I argue that important mistakes have been made through extending to the system as a whole conclusion which have been correctly arrived at in respect of a part of it taken in isolation.

(Keynes, 1939)

This same claim made by Keynes reappears again and again in the exposition of his system. The key aspect in the criticism to this analytical resource lies in the fact that the same method (extending by analogy individual behavior to society) is also the resource on which the classical "test" of Say's Law rests. Therefore, the issue is also linked to the classical conception of money and the classical assumption of full employment. But what is, in Keynes's view, the serious difficulty that arises from these innocent additions?

First, when the *classical theory* represents individual decisions to consume with the purpose of obtaining the total demand of certain commodity, it always assumes that an individual's income is given. From here, it follows that the individual freely decides whether he will spend his income according to his will. When he decides not to consume in the present, it is always assumed that such consumption is postponed until a later date, and that his saving grows commensurately, but it is also asserted that this decision to not consume does not modify the individual's total amount of income. In other words, when representing individual decisions between consumption demand and saving level, the *classical theory* assumes that the income of the individual is fixed, that is to say that, for the purpose of this discussion, income is an independent variable not affected by the split between consumption and saving. Until here, Keynes agrees. However, he challenges the deduction that follows from this argument applying the classical method of moving from the part to the whole. Specifically, he questions the validity of applying this same reasoning to explain a similar problem but one that pertains to the economy as a whole. The analogy method leads the *classical theory* to the absurd conclusion that the increase or decrease in aggregate demand does not have any impact on the level of aggregate income that is, in turn, equal to aggregate production. Seen in this light, this mistaken method of aggregation becomes another pillar of Say's Law:

> Though an individual whose transactions are small in relation to the market can safely neglect the fact that demand is not a one – sided transaction, it makes nonsense to neglect it when we come to the aggregate demand. This is the vital difference between the theory of the economic behaviour of the aggregate and the theory of the behaviour of

the individual unit, in which we assume that changes in the individual's own demand do not affect his income.

(Keynes, 1939 [1936]: 85; II.7.V)

When exploring this question in more detail, the various consequences of the aggregation method are unveiled. The *classical theory* holds that, at social level, saving is necessarily equal to investment. This is due to the fact that on the "free" (available to be invested) capital market, equilibrium is reached when supply equals demand. Capital supply is nothing but the saving of individuals, and capital demand is nothing but capitalists' investment. The *classical theory*, therefore, posits that saving is identical to investment, as this is a corollary of its theory of market equilibrium. Now, when instead of focusing on an individual and his decisions the analysis is centered on the aggregate of all individuals, it is necessary to admit that the issue of the decisions of saving and investment cannot be restricted to the capital market, but that it has other consequences, since the investment demand is also one of the components of the aggregate demand of goods.

When the operation of Say's Law was discussed, it was shown that for the *classical theory*, the determination of investment and saving are always premised on a *given* level of income and output. When unveiling the hidden premises of the *classical theory* of investment, Keynes points out what is obvious: the assumption is plausible in the case of one individual, but not for the aggregate. When an individual does not devote a portion of his income to current consumption, he adds it to his accumulated wealth, that is, he saves. But if in a society, saving increases, says Keynes, demand does not necessarily also increase. Saving does not bring about an immediate or necessary increase in investment demand. We will discuss this question in detail when we present Keynes's system, together with its causation sequence, which allows for the resolution of this conundrum. For the time being, what has been said suffices to reinforce Keynes's claim: the procedure consisting of inferring the form of a social process from the description of an individual's behavior, that is, by simple analogy, entails fallacious reasoning:

> Thus the old–fashioned view that saving always involves investment, though incomplete and misleading, is formally sounder than the new–fangled view that there can be saving without investment or investment without 'genuine' saving. The error lies in proceeding to the plausible inference that, when an individual saves, he will increase aggregate investment by an equal amount. It is true, that, when an individual saves he increases his own wealth. But the conclusion that he also increases aggregate wealth fails to allow for the possibility that an act

of individual saving may react on someone else's savings and hence on someone else's wealth.

(Keynes, 1939 [1936]: 83; II.7.V)

Although at aggregate level saving is always equal to investment, this does not imply – as is obvious – that this bottom line is true for each individual: the addition of his own new savings is not necessarily equal to the value of his own new capital investments.

At a social level, instead, during a given period, the total of new real investments must equal the difference between income and consumption. But it does not follow from here that when an individual saves, investment will increase automatically, still less that when a society suddenly reduces its total consumption, by that same act, it will trigger an equal increase of the production of capital goods destined to satisfy future consumption. The false assumption that every individual act of saving is equal to the purchase of a new investment, compounded by the use of the mistaken method of projecting onto the aggregate what is assumed to be valid for the individual become two pillars that support Say's Law and the unshakable assumption of full employment, two of the aspects of the *classical theory* that Keynes seeks to eradicate from his own construction. Money gets also entangled in this same mechanism, as when an individual saves with the intent of preserving wealth, he can do so, in practice, by purchasing an equipment of new capital – thus increasing investment – or of old capital – a transference is thus effected without the need of increasing production; however, he can also keep, if he deems it convenient, cash in hand or buy a debt title that accrues interest. The first possibility, that is, that total saving would not become new investment goods, is not contemplated by the classical system, simply because it equates society to an individual. The classical conception of money as a standard of value and means of exchange does not admit, in turn, this last possibility, that is, that saving might not be embodied in capital goods purchases but in the acquisition of money or bonds. Classical money, now linked to the issue of aggregation, is but another pillar of Say's Law and the assumption of full employment.

Based on this objection, Keynes rejects Say's Law as a whole. While in the case of an individual the decision to invest does not modify his own income, it does so in the case of the society as a whole, since total investment is a component of aggregate demand, together with global consumption demand.

My contention that for the system as a whole the amount of income which is saved, in the sense that it is not spent on current consumption, is and must necessarily be exactly equal to the amount of net new investment has been considered a paradox and has been the occasion of widespread controversy. The explanation of this is undoubtedly to be found in the fact that this relationship of equality between saving and investment, which necessarily holds good for the system as a whole, does not hold good at all for a particular individual. There is no reason whatever why the new investment for which I am responsible should bear any relation whatever to the amount of my own savings.

(Keynes, 1939)

Keynes was highly concerned about this issue, as he saw there the key to rejecting Say's Law validity, independently of the examination of each of the mechanisms involved. The individual decision to modify the amount of consumption or saving does not provoke a variation of the individual's income under any circumstance. However, when the analysis is focused on the society as a whole, what appears as a way of spending (or not spending) aggregate income becomes, on the other hand, a source of aggregate demand. It is for this reason that Keynes holds that, through investment decisions, changes in aggregate demand impact on an income that can no longer be considered given, as was instead done in the case of the individual.

> Quite legitimately we regard an individual's income as independent of what he himself consumes and invests. But this, I have to point out, should not have led us to overlook the fact that the demand arising out of the consumption and investment of one individual is the source of the incomes of other individuals, so that incomes in general are not independent, quite the contrary, of the disposition of individuals to spend and invest; and since in turn the readiness of individuals to spend and invest depends on their incomes, a relationship is set up between aggregate savings and aggregate investment which can be very easily shown, beyond any possibility of reasonable dispute, to be one of exact and necessary equality. Rightly regarded this is a banale conclusion. But it sets in motion a train of thought from which more substantial matters follow.
>
> (Keynes, 1939)

Let's examine some of the most general consequences.

At the beginning of this section, it was pointed out that the *classical theory* has as its starting point individual behavior, deemed to be essentially free and voluntary. From that individual's liberty of action, immense social advantages are then inferred; the defense of *individual capitalism* and the policy of *laissez-faire* rest on the foundation of such reasoning. But Keynes's methodological objection leads, naturally, to the study of the restrictions faced by that apparently non-conditioned individual will, which the classicists consider the ultimate drive of the economic system: in fact,

the individual is taken as the only active "subject" as it is he who, ultimately, makes the decisions that are later reflected upon the behavior of the
aggregate. The issue may be framed in the terms of the previous problem:
according to the *classical theory*, the isolated individual decides according
to his preferences what portion of his income he will spend purchasing consumption goods and, by difference, what portion he will devote to saving.
He may also decide what his investment demand (new capital equipment)
will be. But according to the cited passages, Keynes's system establishes a
causal sequence according to which consumption and investment determine
the total volume of output and, therefore, of income. Once the total amount
of income has been thus established, saving appears as a residue – the portion of that income not destined to consumption. Therefore, any individual
attempt to increase saving is, in fact, subject to a social process that cannot
be considered to be given. What is, then, the real power of individual will?
Keynes says,

> A decision to consume or not to consume truly lies within the power
> of the individual; so does the decision to invest or not to invest. The
> amount of aggregate income and of aggregate saving are the *result* of the
> free choices of the individuals whether or not to consume and whether
> or not to invest; but they are neither of them capable of assuming an
> independent value resulting from a separate set of decisions taken irre-
> spective of the decisions concerning consumption and investment.
>
> (Keynes, 1939 [1936]: 65; II.6.II)

In the explanation offered by Keynes, the freedom of the individual is con-
strained, and it operates within the leeway determined by social laws that
transcend it. A single man can, if he so wishes, increase his savings. But if
all of them do so at the same time, consumption demand and, with it, the
income of all individuals will fall. If income decreases, saving will fall,
with the result that they will not be able to carry out their plans simultaneously, at least not in "real" terms, since they will not be capable of saving
in the form of investment goods that have not been produced. Such reasoning leads to considering other forms of saving other than capital goods (as
money). Although only some of the results of Keynes's system have been
anticipated, they will suffice to rebut the classical method, whether it be that
of simple aggregation or else of the representative agent: neither of them
provides a solid basis to conduct an analogy that will adequately represent
the laws ruling the movement of the whole.

The alleged "freedom" of the individual must now be subject to the
system's law equating saving and investment, which results in the need to
change the status generally conferred to individual decisions by the *classical
theory*. Instead of it being such decisions that which unconditionally drive

the system, it will have to be admitted that they are strictly subject to certain results that exceed their capacity to act. The absolute "free will" of the individual agent thus becomes mere appearance. Similarly, what is "good" for the individual may not be for society. The classical economists cannot distinguish one approach from another because, for them, the individual accurately represents the whole and, even, the government; therefrom, they infer their prescriptions: "We have to accept them as an inevitable result of applying to the conduct of the State the maxims which are best calculated to 'enrich' an individual" (Keynes, 1936: 131; III.10.VI).

The rejection of this mechanical link between the individual and the system bears significant consequences in other spheres, like that of money. The amount of inconvertible money in circulation is fixed and dependent on the state's decision. An individual is in a position to voluntarily decide the amount of cash in hand he wants to keep, but the total addition of those amounts, apparently as free and unconditional as the amount held by an individual, must necessarily match the total volume of available bills. If this is so, then it is not true that all the individuals can decide the *real amount* of their money holdings at the same time.

> The above is closely analogous with the proposition which harmonises the liberty, which every individual possesses, to change, whenever he chooses, the amount of money he holds, with the necessity for the total amount of money, which individual balances add up to, to be exactly equal to the amount of cash which the banking system has created. In this latter case the equality is brought about by the fact that the amount of money which people choose to hold is not independent of their incomes or of the prices of the things (primarily securities), the purchase of which is the natural alternative to holding money. Thus incomes and such prices necessarily change until the aggregate of the amounts of money which individuals choose to hold at the new level of incomes and prices thus brought about has come to equality with the amount of money created by the banking system. This, indeed, is the fundamental proposition of monetary theory.
>
> (Keynes, 1939 [1936]: 85; II.7.V)

Again, the explanation offered by Keynes is enigmatic at this point of our explanation. However, even without exploring the mechanism in detail, we wish to stress that the same conclusion appears again and again: the laws that explain the determinations of the system as a whole cannot be obtained by merely repeating at a larger scale that which is valid for an individual. Individuals, on the contrary, can only passively obey these general movements that take place behind their backs or, rather, over their heads and beyond their voluntary acts. Other illustration may be provided by the determination of real wages at social scale, which exceeds in Keynes's system the will of individual workers, or even of the collectively organized workers. The differences between what is expected to happen in a particular industry and the real processes that affect the economy as a whole are crucial, and it is a mistake to substitute one explanation for the other,

> In the case of a change peculiar to a particular industry one would expect the change in real wages to be in the same direction as the change in money – wages. But in the case of changes in the general level of wages, it will be found, I think, that the change in real wages associated with a change in money – wages, so far from being usually in the same direction, is almost always in the opposite direction.
>
> (Keynes, 1939 [1936]: 10; I.2.II)

This discussion shows the effort that Keynes has to exert, and the distance that separates him from the *classical theory* and its typical methods, when trying to consider how the laws of the economic system as a whole affect individual decisions. This path leads him to take the system as a whole, not individual will, as a departure point for his analysis, which implies just as much a rejection of the classical economics' resort to aggregation as of the representative agent. General laws cannot be deduced by analogy. On the contrary, their role consists in conditioning not only the decisions of the individual but also their effective results. We should then analyze from this perspective the legitimacy of the current split of economics into two spheres: one corresponding to microeconomics; the other, to macroeconomics. This fundamental issue will be discussed in the conclusions to this study.

Problems of measurement

The challenges do not end here. Because even if the relevant causal relations among the different social phenomena were identified, the problem of measuring them would still remain. In fact, the relations represented by means of mathematical functions refer to the (quantitative) magnitude of economic processes. The difficulty involved in "measuring" social processes, as opposed to their individual counterparts, may be illustrated with a simple example. When studying the determinations of the quantity produced and the price of a particular commodity, the assumption that the relevant product is perfectly homogeneous is absolutely justifiable. Analytically, it is admitted that all the units are exactly similar and that their price is the same. Now, the study of the economy as a whole renders untenable the assumption of commodity homogeneity. If the evolution of production as a whole is to be explained, as well as the causes of its growth or fall, or even its current level, it is crucial to find a way to accurately refer to its total volume. For Keynes, this issue is fundamental, since he intended to make the level of production (and employment) as a whole the main unknown (*quaesitum*) of his system.

Here, again, strong disagreements with the *classical theory* emerge. When economists such as Marshall and Pigou referred, as they frequently did, to the national dividend or income, they were talking precisely about the aggregate volume of current output and *real* income, not about the product value or the money income.

Furthermore, to calculate the genuine production of a period, they had to subtract the depreciation of the existing capital from the value of the new output, as a portion of the product is devoted to replacing the depletion of capital equipment. It is this *net* magnitude that counts, as that is the amount that can be used for consumption or to widen the existing equipment, as new investment. Whenever the *classical theory* referred to these aggregates, it did so ignoring any measurement problem in the calculation of the product or the real (in quantity of goods) and *net* (subtracting depletion) income. According to Keynes,

> On this basis an attempt is made to erect a quantitative science. But it is a grave objection to this definition for such a purpose that the community's output of goods and services is a non–homogeneous complex which cannot be measured, strictly speaking, except in certain special cases, as for example when all the items of one output are included in the same proportions in another output.
>
> (Keynes, 1939 [1936]: 38; II.4.II)

It is not surprising, however, that the classical school, accustomed to studying a "moneyless" economy, one that was analogue to a barter economy, and also accustomed to extending its analysis of the individual to the aggregate, should consider it natural to assume that aggregate output could be treated as if composed of only one commodity with different uses.

However, Keynes states that this procedure hides a serious conceptual problem, since there is no accurate way to measure the net product of a society in physical terms due to the fact that such product is made up of countless heterogeneous goods. Also untenable is the pretension (which he attributed then to Pigou, although with time it has become generalized) to calculate, as if it could be measured, the depreciation of the capital equipment in real terms, which would imply assuming that after one year, for example, two items of capital equipment had to be computed as if they were less than two physical units because they have depreciated:

> [S]ince this deduction is not a deduction in terms of money, he [Pigou, AK] is involved in assuming that there can be a change in physical

quantity, although there has been no physical change; i.e. he is covertly introducing changes in *value* [. . .] Moreover, he is unable to devise any satisfactory formula to evaluate new equipment against old when, owing to changes in technique, the two are not identical.

(Keynes, 1939 [1936]: 38; II.4.II)

That is, even though such considerations were theoretically correct, those units of measurement cannot be transferred to the real world with the purpose of building a quantitative science.

Keynes's judgment of the question of measuring aggregate output is definitive: there is not – and therefore it should not be searched for – any formula to measure product and capital in real or net terms. In other words, measuring new production by means of the physical quantity of goods, which implies adding different amounts of diverse physical objects that, on account of that reason, cannot be simply added up, is doomed to failure by its own nature. It is a theoretical chimera because it makes no sense to measure this "amount of net physical goods" in practice, least of all compare the amounts measured at two different moments. In fact, any purported measurement of physical output (real and net) introduces, somehow or other, value considerations, even though hiding them:

The problem of comparing one real output with another and of then calculating net output by setting off new items of equipment against the wastage of old items presents conundrums which permit, one can confidently say, of no solution.

(Keynes, 1939 [1936]: 39; II.4.II)

These same criticisms appear later in connection with prices when the economy is studied in aggregate terms. Even though Keynes himself had contributed to the controversy regarding price indexes in his *Treatise*, when he puts forth his new system, he states his dissatisfaction with all of them, as they do not allow for the accurate study of price evolution. In *The General Theory* he holds that all price indexes are equally arbitrary:

[T]he well – known, but unavoidable, element of vagueness which admittedly attends the concept of the general price – level makes this term very unsatisfactory for the purposes of a causal analysis, which ought to be exact.

(Keynes, 1939 [1936]: 39; II.4.II)

A contemporary reader will surely feel somehow uncomfortable with these remarks, as all macroeconomics of Keynesian origin seems to have overlooked them. In fact, standard models generally and quite naturally include these two aggregate variables: net product in real terms (the amount of new physical goods produced in different periods) and also the general level of prices. Keynes's claims seem to have fallen on deaf ears. However, we will see, his objections have serious consequences for the analysis of the economy considered as a whole.

The famous Marshallian cross diagram (supply and demand) meant for the study of certain product assumes a complete homogeneity of the relevant good: the price – just one – is shown on one axis, and the quantity – of a homogeneous product – on the other; both measures are accurate, not ambiguous, and are founded on admissible assumptions,

> In the case of an individual firm or industry producing a homogeneous product we can speak legitimately, if we wish, of increases or decreases of output. But when we are aggregating the activities of all firms, we cannot speak accurately except in terms of quantities of employment applied to a given equipment.
>
> (Keynes, 1939 [1936]: 40; II.4.III)

Therefore, it is not admissible that the diagram be applied to the analysis of the aggregate market of goods. To do so, on one hand, would require an accurate measure of the total physical production of heterogeneous commodities. To add up those quantities of different goods, their prices (values, according to Keynes) would necessarily have to be used as homogenizing factor. On the other axis, a measure of the general prices of goods would have to be introduced, with all the conflicts this involves, since some "representative" basket would have to be chosen. The effort is further complicated because by modifying the volume of output, prices are also modified and, therefore, the aggregation arrangement collapses before having even drawn the curves, so that in the case of aggregate production, prices are involved in both axes. The innocent comparison of the "real" aggregate output at two different points involves the same conceptual errors: "two incommensurable collections of miscellaneous objects cannot in themselves provide the material for a quantitative analysis" (Keynes, 1939 [1936]: 39; II.4.II).

The Keynesian and anti-Keynesian economists that followed him simply chose to ignore such objections and "project" the market of a particular good to the aggregate, even if it is not justified. However, it is not appropriate nor feasible to represent with the Marshallian cross the aggregate market of products. The alleged measures of the quantity (the net real output) and of the price (the general level of prices) do not furnish a base for the construction of a causal system as Keynes tried to devise. He assigns these alleged "measures" a limited role, that of exclusively historical or statistical description. Resorting to them may simplify the analysis, but at the expense of depriving it of any conceptual and quantitative accuracy. The scant interest that Keynes's conclusive – and ironic – observations attracted among his followers is remarkable and highly suspicious.

> To say that net output to – day is greater, but the price – level lower, than ten years ago or one year ago, is a proposition of a similar character to the statement that Queen Victoria was a better queen but not a happier woman than Queen Elizabeth, a proposition not without meaning and not without interest, but unsuitable as material for the differential calculus. Our precision will be a mock precision if we try to use such partly vague and non – quantitative concepts as the basis of a quantitative analysis.
>
> (Keynes, 1939 [1936]: 40; II.4.II)

How could the actual variations of "real" output in time be calculated in the absence of that measure? The units of measure suggested in *The General Theory* intend to overcome these difficulties. With a closer look, Keynes states, the problem is not so serious, since the criticized units are not, in fact, necessary for his purposes.

The measures used in Keynes's system are two. On one hand, the amount of employment measured in worked units; one hour of ordinary employment (labor-unit) is taken as a unit, and the relation between the basic hour wage and the wage of an hour of employment of special labor is used as a multiplying factor to compute an hour of special work. The wage corresponding to an hour of ordinary employment will be the wage-unit, while the volume of employment is measured in labor-units. The quotient of the product money-value and the wage-unit is the quantity of ordinary work hours the output can buy in each situation, that is, a measure of the output in labor-units. The other unit used by Keynes is money, employing money prices current in each occasion. All the problems stemming from heterogeneity and index numbers thus vanish.

> In dealing with the theory of employment I propose, therefore, to make use of only two fundamental units of quantity, namely, quantities of money – value and quantities of employment. The first of these is strictly homogeneous, and the second can be made so. For, in so far as different grades and kinds of labour and salaried assistance enjoy a more or less fixed relative remuneration, the quantity of employment can be sufficiently defined for our purpose by taking an hour's employment of ordinary labour as our unit and weighting an hour's employment of special labour in proportion to its remuneration; i.e. an hour of special labour remunerated at double ordinary rates will count as two units. We shall call the unit in which the quantity of employment is

measured the labour – unit; and the money – wage of a labour – unit we shall call the wage – unit.

(Keynes, 1939 [1936]: 41; II.4.III)

Output is thus measured not in physical or real terms, but relative to the amount of employment of labor paid to use the existing equipment. Qualified labor will be considered as ordinary labor multiplied proportionally to its retribution.

> It is my belief that much unnecessary perplexity can be avoided if we limit ourselves strictly to the two units, money and labour, when we are dealing with the behaviour of the economic system as a whole; reserving the use of units of particular outputs and equipments to the occasions when we are analysing the output of individual firms or industries in isolation; and the use of vague concepts, such as the quantity of output as a whole, the quantity of capital equipment as a whole and the general level of prices, to the occasions when we are attempting some historical comparison which is within certain (perhaps fairly wide) limits avowedly imprecise and approximate.
>
> (Keynes, 1939 [1936]: 43; II.4.III)

To describe the causal relation linking phenomena pertaining to the economy considered as a whole, Keynes suggests, therefore, two units of measure: labor and money. Aggregate income in wage-units – the quotient of money income and wage-unit – strictly measures the quantity of hours of "ordinary" (simple) labor that income can purchase. From now on, Keynes will not measure income, consumption, money demand etc., as the *classical theory* did, that is, by means of a vague reference to real or physical terms, but in labor hours. His choice of units, based on labor hours, obeys, according to the author of *The General Theory*, deep conceptual aspects that will be discussed in the last chapter of this book.

The preceding pages compiled the criticisms leveled at some general aspects of the *classical theory*: its method, its purposes, its field of application, the consequences of its prescriptions, its internal contradictions, and particularly its anachronistic character. We should now discuss in detail those particular aspects of the *classical theory* to which Keynes analytically objected in his *General Theory*. The main unknown of the new economic system is the level of employment and output. If the *classical theory* had taken the trouble to rigorously test the validity of Say's Law in the short term, on which it (tacitly) rests the whole weight of the assumption of full employment, it would have been forced to show that *there are economic mechanisms that act automatically* whose workings guarantee a causal sequence like the following: each increase in output taken as a whole necessarily triggers a commensurate increase in income – which is undeniable – which will be directed, also necessarily, to the effective purchase of the whole amount of new goods that have been produced: "The classical theory assumes, in other words, that the aggregate demand price (or proceeds) always accommodates itself to the aggregate supply price" (Keynes, 1939 [1936]: 22; I.2.VIII). It is implicitly assumed that any increase in current supply acts as a stimulus that provokes an exactly equivalent increase in current demand. In that case, and only in that case, entrepreneurs will always be ready to hire workers until the supply of hands willing to be employed is exhausted, that is, until reaching the level of absolute full employment. This implies that every weakness in consumption is compensated with an equivalent increase in investment. This is how Say's Law works in the short term.

Although Say's Law works through a series of mechanisms, the *classical theory* replaced detailed discussion of each of these with the axiom of full employment, which is premised on them. According to Keynes, blind faith in Say's Law and in its outcome, full employment, went even further, as no representative of the *classical theory* undertook the rigorous study of aggregate demand's determining factors. Such study was substituted by the trust in that the equivalence of the increase in global supply and global demand could be taken for granted. According to Keynes, aggregate demand was ignored for more than a century.

> The idea that we can safely neglect the aggregate demand function is fundamental to the Ricardian economics, which underlie what we have been taught for more than a century. Malthus, indeed, had vehemently opposed Ricardo's doctrine that it was impossible for effective demand to be deficient; but vainly. For, since Malthus was unable to explain clearly (apart from an appeal to the facts of common observation) how and why effective demand could be deficient or excessive, he failed to furnish an alternative construction; and Ricardo conquered England as completely as the Holy Inquisition conquered Spain. Not only was his theory accepted by the city, by statesmen and by the academic world. But controversy ceased; the other point of view completely disappeared; it ceased to be discussed. The great puzzle of effective demand with which Malthus had wrestled vanished from economic literature. You will not find it mentioned even once in the whole works of Marshall, Edgeworth and Professor Pigou, from whose hands the classical theory has received its most mature embodiment. It could only live on furtively, below the surface, in the underworlds of Karl Marx, Silvio Gesell or Major Douglas.
>
> (Keynes, 1939 [1936]: 32; I.3.III)

The absence of a thorough and rigorous scrutiny of the determinants of demand considered as a whole is a necessary consequence of the trust in that supply stimulates *per se* demand. In summary, studying the actual behavior of aggregate demand and its components will be one of the main objectives of Keynes's system: "If, however, this is not the true law relating the aggregate demand and supply functions, there is a vitally important chapter of economic theory which remains to be written and without which all discussions concerning the volume of aggregate employment are futile (Keynes, 1939 [1936]: 26; I.3.I)(*op. cit.*41 [26]; I.3.I).

Keynes developed a special critique meant to rebut each of the classical devices. It is naturally convenient to begin our review with the market where the services of the "factor" labor are bought and sold.

III Critique of the *classical theory:* the mechanisms of Say's Law

Critique of the classical labor market

Even though the classicists did not study how the level of output, and therefore of employment, is determined in the short term, the classical aggregate market of labor contains an explanation of employment in general and, of its flipside, unemployment. This is the reason why Keynes starts his critique by attacking the labor market. This is the classical theory of employment, at least, the only available one. A brief review of the classical explanation will allow us to introduce Keynes's objections.

Labor supply and demand curves establish a level of equilibrium for the level of employment and real wage (proportional to the nominal wage if prices are considered to be fixed).

The starting point for this construction is the analysis of individual agents' behavior: the firm and the worker considered in isolation.

According to *classical theory*, each entrepreneur is willing to increase his demand for labor until the value of the marginal product attributable to the last – marginal – hired unit equals real wage; under the assumption that in the short-term labor returns are diminishing, a negatively sloped labor demand curve is thus established for each firm. To get the labor demand of the economy as a whole, it is enough to resort to Pigou's method – the only one accepted by the classicists: addition.

The first postulate of the *classical theory* of employment is the equality of labor productivity as a whole and real wage. If they are striving to obtain maximum profits, each firm has obvious incentives to hire the number of workers that its demand curve indicates at each level of real wage. Only a non-economic power could force a firm to hire a higher or lower number of workers. However, if those forces existed, they would be external to the system, therefore the equality between real wage and productivity is a postulate that embodies an economic law: under normal conditions, its compliance is not in doubt.

Labor supply is deducted from the rational behavior of the individual worker. Each worker is willing to supply more hours of work until the point where the increasing disutility of the additional hour equals the current real wage (the utility of remuneration). This behavior accounts for the fact that the amount of work that each individual plans to supply increases as the level of real wage becomes higher. Throughout the supply curve – whether the individual curve, corresponding to a specific occupation, or the aggregate one – the disutility corresponding to each volume of employment equals real wage (its utility). This is the second postulate of the classical theory of employment.[13] Keynes also calls this condition a "postulate", because it is assumed that every individual will behave so that the hours of work supplied given the current wage will comply with this requirement, and also because if the postulate is not fulfilled, there is an incentive pushing the worker to modify his offer. If he is working the amount of hours he considers optimal, and his real wage decreases, he will desire to reduce the number of worked hours. If he is not working enough (disutility is less than wage), he will offer more work at the current wage, and he will be ready to reduce his wage. Only in the case when the second postulate is fulfilled for all the workers will none of them be willing to leave his job or reduce his wage. Market variables tend to move towards the resting point. This makes the conditions of equilibrium a suitable depiction of the labor market: at the point where supply intersects demand, the first and second postulates are simultaneously fulfilled. When the combination of real wage and level of employment falls outside the supply or the demand curves, it triggers an adjustment process. There will be incentives leading entrepreneurs, workers or both to modify their behavior regarding the amount and price of labor. Once the market is at equilibrium, instead, it will not be possible to find a single entrepreneur willing to hire more workers, nor a single worker willing to supply more hours than he currently works. Labor market equilibrium is, therefore, a description of full employment. But the condition upon which the inexistence of unemployment is premised is even less restrictive: it is enough to have the combination of real wage and volume of employment at any point of the labor supply curve, since every point on the supply curve represents an optimal plan for workers. In fact, all the points on the labor supply curve are also cases of full employment.

Classical theory assumes that the labor market is either in equilibrium or moving towards equilibrium, provided that no obstacle external to the system enters into action. In other words, it trusts in the presence of strong trends towards full employment based on purely economic forces. As in any other market, outside equilibrium, there is either excess supply or excess demand, and when this happens, it is expected that the processes aimed at restoring equilibrium will set in motion. For this reason, Keynes adequately calls this explanation based on the labor market *classical theory of employment*. The aforementioned mechanism is enough in itself to show that in classical economics there is a "natural", automatic tendency towards full employment.

Workers' psychological preferences determine supply; the physical conditions of production determine entrepreneurs' demand; the usual working of the market does the rest. Wage increases or decreases until it reaches the equality of the physical marginal productivity of labor and its marginal disutility for all workers. As long as this double equality is not reached, there will be forces pushing the variables that will not be at rest until such condition is fulfilled.

In synthesis, the meaning of the *classical theory* of employment represented by the labor market is that when equilibrium is reached and labor demand equals supply, all the individuals who desire to work can, and the real wage is at a level simultaneously compatible with both postulates.

Here is where Keynes's famous claim is situated: the *classical theory of employment* is directly incapable of representing the situation where a man or a group of men are involuntarily unemployed as a resting point in its system. In fact, if wage inexorably moves towards its resting point, sooner or later it will be equal to the marginal disutility of labor, that is, the maximum of hours that workers are willing to offer. Thus, if a person or a group of people do not work, this can only be coded in one way within the framework of *classical theory*: because they are unwilling; in technical terms, the reason is that the real wage is not enough to compensate for the marginal disutility brought about by working an additional hour; the current wage does not "pay for" the sacrifice of working. This is a particular type of unemployment that, on account of its nature, will be called *pure voluntary unemployment in equilibrium*, which stems from the impossibility of forcing a worker who does not wish to work to do so because, by definition, any worker who does not work judges the current wage insufficient to induce him to offer his labor. But this strictly voluntary situation cannot be seriously considered to account for real unemployment. It is true that, as Keynes admits, *classical theory* also considers the case of workers who are transitorily unemployed because they are changing from one employment to another, in what is known as "frictional" unemployment. Frictional unemployment does not qualify as true unemployment – as a problem – as, even though such a transition is to a certain extent inevitable, it is true that sooner or later those workers will find an occupation.

In brief, based on this explanation, it is easy to demonstrate the system's capacity to move to full employment by its own means. Workers are involuntarily unemployed when real wage is higher than marginal disutility. In that case, they are willing to work for less so that the adjustment proceeds through a decrease in the wage accepted by workers themselves. As the real wage decreases, the amount of labor that the entrepreneurs are willing to hire gradually increases (first postulate: negatively sloped supply curve). It is very important to bear in mind how this adjustment allegedly works: workers, in this case sellers, control the price of what they sell and accept its reduction; buyers *afterwards* increase the demand of labor at a reduced wage, compatible with the lower marginal productivity corresponding to a higher level of employment.

Unemployment is compatible with the *classical theory of employment;* this would be a case of involuntary unemployment typical of the adjustment process, that is, it would be, strictly speaking, *disequilibrium involuntary unemployment.* But herein lies the problem: Keynes does not admit this as an explanation of prolonged unemployment as it is, precisely and according to the classicists, a situation of disequilibrium. The only possibility of extending the situation within the classical analytical framework is introducing an *ad hoc* hypothesis, external to the economic explanations of the system, regarding the existence of some external factor hindering the adjustment of the wage. But even so it would still be a state of disequilibrium of the labor market brought about by the system's malfunctioning:

> For the Classical Theory has been accustomed to rest the supposedly self-adjustment character of the economic system on an assumed fluidity of money-wages; and, when there is rigidity, to lay on this rigidity the blame of maladjustment.
>
> (Keynes, 1939 [1936]: 257; V.19.I)

Now, for the situation of disequilibrium unemployment to persist in time there has to be some cause that provokes rigidity. The *classical theory* states that if the real wage does not descend to its equilibrium level, if it is "rigid downwards", it must surely be due to workers' behavior (or the laws that were passed to benefit them or their "institutions"). For a classical economist, the private portrait of unemployment and its causes is the following: unemployment prevails, there are workers individually willing to work at the current real wage, as it is higher than their marginal disutility. But this individual drive fails owing to the obstacles collectively posed since, as a group, workers refuse to accept a reduction of their nominal and real wage (whose movement is allegedly symmetrical).[14] In Keynes's words,

> Thus writers in the classical tradition, overlooking the special assumption underlying their theory, have been driven inevitably to the conclusion, perfectly logical on their assumption, that apparent unemployment (apart from the admitted exceptions) must be due at bottom to a refusal by the unemployed factors to accept a reward which corresponds to their marginal productivity. A classical economist may sympathise with

labour in refusing to accept a cut in its money – wage, and he will admit that it may not be wise to make it to meet conditions which are temporary; but scientific integrity forces him to declare that this refusal is, nevertheless, at the bottom of the trouble.

(Keynes, 1939 [1936]: 16; I.2.IV)

A new type of unemployment appears in the classical system. Now individual workers are ready to work for less, but there is opposition to wages being cut down to their efficient level. This would seem to be a case of *disequilibrium involuntary unemployment* compounded by the existence of an obstacle that hinders, delays or even prevents the movement of the wage towards its equilibrium magnitude, which would put an end to unemployment.

A terminological dilemma emerges here: when analyzing the causes of this kind of unemployment admitted by *classical theory*, it would seem to match the definition of involuntary unemployment – workers desire to work more but they cannot. However, the will of workers prevents wage reduction.

While individual workers are willing to work at the current wage and even ready to accept a wage cut, aggregate labor, voluntarily, supports with its collective action a real wage that is higher than the equilibrium wage. Keynes chooses to assign more weight to this latter reason, and he is right because, as a collective phenomenon, unemployment originates in this case in the conscious action of workers as agreed in the process of collective bargaining. Therefore, he prefers to call it *voluntary unemployment* as well. It is not a case of *individual voluntary unemployment but unemployment attributable to the collective, albeit voluntary, attitude of labor*. Even so, from an economic point of view, this is a disequilibrium situation because there are economic tendencies pushing wages downwards. It remains to be seen if those forces are more powerful than the extra-economic forces that hinder adjustment, that is, if the downward tendency of wages owing to an excess of supply overcome, sooner or later, the reluctance to accept a wage cut. After all, according to the classical explanation, this phenomenon is also voluntary: the will of individual workers (for whom the current wage surpasses work disutility) ready to work for less seems to oppose the will of unionized workers preventing a wage cut. The final level of wages is the result of both forces. In the classical explanation, the only aspect that should be evaluated is whether the nominal wage is absolutely rigid, relatively rigid, simply "sticky" or, finally, flexible. Following *classical theory*, it should be admitted that no sooner the conflict is "solved" and rigidity flexibilized, wages will descend until vacating the market. This kind of unemployment is, ultimately, voluntary as well.

For, admittedly, more labour would, as a rule, be forthcoming at the existing money – wage if it were demanded. The classical school reconcile this phenomenon with their second postulate by arguing that, while the demand for labour at the existing money – wage may be satisfied before everyone willing to work at this wage is employed, this situation is due to an open or tacit agreement amongst workers not to work for less, and that if labour as a whole would agree to a reduction of money – wages more employment would be forthcoming. If this is the case, such unemployment, though apparently involuntary, is not strictly so, and ought to be included under the above category of 'voluntary' unemployment due to the effects of collective bargaining, etc.

(Keynes, 1939 [1936]: 8; I.2.II)

Briefly, the *classical theory of employment* holds that the labor market moves towards equilibrium with full employment by itself. If a worker is unemployed, it is because he is changing from one occupation to another – frictional unemployment – because he finds the current wage insufficient – individual voluntary unemployment, or else because he refuses, together with the other unemployed workers, to work at a lower wage – collective voluntary unemployment. The latter possibility seems to be the most problematic, although the characterization of its causes implicitly points to the solution: it is enough for the workers to accept (or be forced to accept) a cut in their money wage, thus accepting a fall in their real wage, to "unlock" the market mechanism. So far, pure classical reasoning. In any case, it is interesting to focus our attention once again on the way in which the adjustment is assumed to proceed: to put an end to unemployment, labor must simply abandon its resistance or obstinacy and accept a cut in their nominal wage, therefore, in their real wage. Employment will grow until it reaches the point where no one else will be willing to work, according to the second postulate. Full employment will have been attained. Keynes does not only challenge the classical explanation of the cause of unemployment, but also the description of the adjustment, once the alleged hindrance – resistance to wage cut – has been removed:

> The traditional theory maintains, in short, *that the wage bargains between the entrepreneurs and the workers determine the real wage*; so that, assuming free competition amongst employers and no restrictive combination amongst workers, the latter can, if they wish, bring their real wages into conformity with the marginal disutility of the amount of employment offered by the employers at that wage. If this is not true, then there is no longer any reason to expect a tendency towards equality between the real wage and the marginal disutility of labour.
>
> (Keynes, 1939 [1936]: 11; I.2.II)

The whole reasoning concerning the causes of unemployment and its efficient remedy rests, therefore, on the capacity of the workers, as suppliers, to voluntarily reduce their real wage by agreeing to have their nominal wage cut. Let's take a closer look at the passage cited above: Keynes argues that if the workers are not in a position to voluntarily adjust their real wage downwards, the mechanism that makes the tendency to full employment effective vanishes, the second postulate is nullified, and the whole classical construct of the labor market collapses from a single blow. This possibility merits a detailed analysis.

The issue does not revolve around the workers' (taken individually or collectively) capacity to cut their nominal wage; that is out of the question. However, if workers are proved to be simply incapable of reducing the economy's average real wage, even if they are willing to do so, then a problem arises in the classicists' theoretical reasoning. Even though workers individually "suffered" on account of a difference between real wage and marginal disutility and were willing to solve the problem by accepting a money-wage cut, their will would not translate into an effective real wage reduction if they lacked the effective means to reduce real wages. But, on the other hand, in such a case, all the arguments implicit in the classical account of unemployment would collapse. Workers' attitude would have no effect on unemployment. The labor market could not be considered a real market where the usual mechanisms of adjustment operate towards equilibrium. And this is so simply because the real wage would not be determined on the labor market.

How could it then be possible to speak about a genuine market when the suppliers lack the means to modify the price of the item they are selling (in this case, their labor force)? Unemployment would become an equilibrium situation, but equilibrium, so to speak, on a different market, a market where the level of employment is determined, which would no longer be the labor market. Beyond their desires and practices, the power to grant reductions in the variable that must effect the adjustment would not be in the hands of the workers (neither individually nor collectively), because they do not control that variable, that is, they do not control real wages.

So, Keynes's critique of the labor market goes precisely along those lines. Workers are incapable of setting the level of their real wage or even of controlling the direction of its variations. The orthodoxy attributes to the workers the responsibility of fulfilling the second postulate, which allegedly reflects their optimal decisions, and assumes that they control the price of what they offer. But workers, individually or collectively, lack the power to "adjust" the labor market. Keynes "proves" such impossibility based on no more and no less than the classical theory of normal prices, as formulated by Marshall:

> The second postulate flows from the idea that the real wages of labour depend on the wage bargains which labour makes with the entrepreneurs. It is admitted, of course, that the bargains are actually made in

terms of money, and even that the real wages acceptable to labour are not altogether independent of what the corresponding money – wage happens to be. Nevertheless it is the money-wage thus arrived at which is held to determine the real wage. Thus the classical theory assumes that it is always open to labour to reduce its real wage by accepting a reduction in its money-wage. The postulate that there is a tendency for the real wage to come to equality with the marginal disutility of labour clearly presumes that labour itself is in a position to decide the real wage for which it works, though not the quantity of employment forthcoming at this wage.

(Keynes, 1939 [1936]: 10–11; I.2.II)

To show that the *classical theory of employment* hides a flagrant contradiction, it is enough to relate the aggregate labor market to the *classical theory* of value. Reductions in the nominal wage of the economy bring about a decrease in the marginal prime cost of all commodities and, therefore, according to *classical theory* itself, always provoke a fall in prices. Workers' control over real wage is limited or non-existent. Keynes demands consistency of the *classical theory:* when moving from an isolated market to the aggregate, it has to abandon the assumption of money's constant purchasing power. Prices in general move in the same sense that the average nominal wage.

Now the assumption that the general level of real wages depends on the money – wage bargains between the employers and the workers is not obviously true. Indeed it is strange that so little attempt should have been made to prove or to refute it. For it is far from being consistent with the general tenor of the classical theory, which has taught us to believe that prices are governed by marginal prime cost in terms of money and that money – wages largely govern marginal prime cost. Thus if money – wages change, one would have expected the classical school to argue that prices would change in almost the same proportion, leaving the real wage and the level of unemployment practically the same as before, any small gain or loss to labour being at the expense or profit of other elements of marginal cost which have been left unaltered.

(Keynes, 1939 [1936]: 11; I.2.II)

The forces that drive the second postulate *do not exist in practice*, which is inferred from the beliefs of *classical theory* itself. Labor only has the power to reduce its nominal wage. But the consequence of this fact is not only that the labor market is unable to reach a resting position, but a much more significant one: this "market" lacks the forces to push it to that position. It is not a market in effective terms, if by market one means a set of mechanisms determining the traded amount and price of a good. The *classical theory of employment* must be discarded. In its place, Keynes will have to put forward a new theory of the determination of real wages based on a set of completely different forces.

> There may exist no expedient by which labour as a whole can reduce its real wage to a given figure by making revised money bargains with the entrepreneurs. This will be our contention. We shall endeavour to show that primarily it is certain other forces which determine the general level of real wages. The attempt to elucidate this problem will be one of our main themes. We shall argue that there has been a fundamental misunderstanding of how in this respect the economy in which we live actually works.
>
> (Keynes, 1939 [1936]: 13; I.2.II)

When pondering the nature of this critique of the labor market, Keynes's objections concerning the method applied by classical economics to give the analytical step required to move from a particular market to an articulate valid representation of the economy as a whole come once again to the forefront. The methods of analogy, addition or representation lead to mistaken conclusions because, when studying the *aggregate* labor market, it is not possible to ignore that the changes introduced in the general level of nominal wage necessarily affect the marginal costs of commodities in general, which can well be ignored when studying each industry or occupation separately. It is the *classical theory of prices* that leads the classicists to contradiction. In fact, when looking at an occupation in isolation, it would seem reasonable to assert that nominal wages move in the same direction as real wages, however such a relation cannot be held as valid for the economy as a whole.

> In the case of a change peculiar to a particular industry one would expect the change in real wages to be in the same direction as the change in money – wages. But in the case of changes in the general level of wages, it will be found, I think, that the change in real wages associated with a change in money – wages, so far from being usually in the same direction, is almost always in the opposite direction. When money – wages are rising, that is to say, it will be found that real wages are falling; and when money – wages are falling, real wages are rising. This is because, in the short period, falling money – wages and rising real wages are each, for independent reasons, likely to accompany decreasing employment; labour being readier to accept wage – cuts when employment is falling off, yet real wages inevitably rising in the

same circumstances on account of the increasing marginal return to a given capital equipment when output is diminished.

(Keynes, 1939 [1936]: 10; I.2.II)

Now, the aggregate labor market was the only instrument that *classical theory* had in its toolbox when trying to explain unemployment. Theoretical criticism deprives it of that tool, which was no more than a careless projection of the individual curves of supply and demand onto employment as a whole. However, as may be seen, there are no effective forces reconciling the general level of real wages with employment marginal disutility.[15]

In fact, according to Keynes's criticism, it is completely unsuitable to talk about equilibrium or disequilibrium in this labor market, when the stimuli for adjustment cannot be in any way translated into effective action on the relevant variables for equilibrium. As may be seen, this is independent from the empirical fact that nominal wages tend to decrease when there is unemployment because of "labour being readier to accept wage – cuts when employment is falling off". For if each fall in nominal wage is followed by an equivalent cut in prices that leaves real wage relatively unchanged, a cut in wages will be pointless.[16]

To this "theoretical" criticism at which Keynes arrives when juxtaposing the labor market and the *classical theory* of value, he adds an empirical objection. If the second postulate were true, then the workers would be ready to abandon their jobs when the real wage decreases, as the labor supply curve is positively sloped.

But if this were the case, then it would be enough to raise the general level of prices to reduce employment. However, this is not the actual behavior of labor:

> A fall in real wages due to a rise in prices, with money – wages unaltered, does not, as a rule, cause the supply of available labour on offer at the current wage to fall below the amount actually employed prior to the rise of prices.
>
> (Keynes, 1939 [1936]: 12–13; I.2.II)

Facts do not support or, rather, refute the classical construct. For the attitude that the *classicists* attribute to labor would lead them to abandon their jobs every time employment increased and (in the short term, with diminishing returns) prices rose, without nominal wages increasing consequently. From the "political" point of view, Keynes's critique frees labor from the responsibility for unemployment that orthodoxy usually lays on it:

> Thus it is fortunate that the workers, though unconsciously, are instinctively more reasonable economists than the classical school, inasmuch

as they resist reductions of money – wages, which are seldom or never of an all – round character, even though the existing real equivalent of these wages exceeds the marginal disutility of the existing employment; whereas they do not resist reductions of real wages, which are associated with increases in aggregate employment and leave relative money – wages unchanged, unless the reduction proceeds so far as to threaten a reduction of the real wage below the marginal disutility of the existing volume of employment. Every trade union will put up some resistance to a cut in money – wages, however small. But since no trade union would dream of striking on every occasion of a rise in the cost of living, they do not raise the obstacle to any increase in aggregate employment which is attributed to them by the classical school.

(Keynes, 1939 [1936]: 14–15; I.2.III)

This critique has an extraordinarily destructive effect on the system based on the *classical theory*. At a single blow, the only mechanism to which the *classical theory* could resort to explain the determination of two key variables, the aggregate level of employment and the real wage of the economy, is destroyed. *Keynes's system* will have to put forward a new theory of employment. That explanation will have to take into account aggregate demand. A lack of global demand will be the main cause of *equilibrium involuntary unemployment*, and neither the reasons that led to such scenario nor the remedy can be found in labor behavior.

In fact, there is only one point where the marginal disutility of labor becomes somehow economically relevant: the point that sets the real wage at such a level that no one else is willing to work. It is a maximum limit to employment that is reached when the real wage has decreased to the point where no new available hands are found. Thus, labor can only stop an increase in employment when supply has been exhausted; this is absolute full employment:

> Thus the volume of employment is not determined by the marginal disutility of labour measured in terms of real wages, except in so far as the supply of labour available at a given real wage sets a maximum level to employment.

(Keynes, 1939 [1936]: 30; I.3.II)

Classical theory believed that the economy moved towards the level of employment corresponding to full employment by its own means. There, the elasticity of employment as a whole must be non-existent: it is not possible to increase supply any further. The problem is that, after Keynes's critique, it is no longer possible for the *classical theory* to rely on the aggregate labor market as a mechanism that guarantees the rule of Say's Law. The focus will therefore have to shift to the classical market of capital, where the volume of investment is set, to see if the classical school is able to find there support for its trust in the inexorable automatic movement towards full employment.[17]

Critique of the classical capital market

The *classical theory of the rate of interest* is contained in the aggregate "free" (free to be invested) capital market, which is the analytical locus where the classicists also place the determination of the levels of saving and investment. This is the explanation offered by the first *marginalists;* it was adopted by Marshall in the late nineteenth century, and is the theory of the rate of interest that orthodox microeconomics has endorsed up to the present. Keynes describes its fundamental traits in the preface to the first French edition of *The General Theory*.

> In recent times it has been held by many economists that the rate of current saving determined the supply of free capital, that the rate of current investment governed the demand for it, and that the rate of interest was, so to speak, the equilibrating price-factor determined by the point of intersection of the supply curve of savings and the demand curve of investment.
>
> (Keynes, 1939)

The free play of competition between those who offer and those who demand drives the market towards equilibrium. In equilibrium, the amount of free capital offered equals the amount demanded, a situation brought about by the movement of the rate of interest. Marshall held that the decision to save stemmed from the comparison of the rate of interest and "the sacrifice involved in the waiting for the enjoyment of material resources" (Marshall, 1923: 232; IV.VII.8). The saving curve is, therefore, positively sloped. The decision to demand capital is ruled by the fact that the entrepreneur, in turn, "will push the investment of capital in his business in each several direction until what appears in his judgment to be the margin of profitableness is reached" (Marshall, 1920 [1890]: V.IV.12).

The investment curve is negatively sloped. The *classical theory* of investment and of the rate of interest could also be represented by means of two postulates, as Keynes did with the *classical theory of employment*. After all, the *classical theory* believes to have found a single tenet to account for the reward corresponding to each factor of production: the equating of supply and demand. The first postulate provides the demand curve of free capital (investment), and the second, the supply curve (saving).

The two postulates of the *classical theory* of investment and the interest rate could be framed as follows: according to the first postulate, the rate of interest equals the marginal product of capital; the second postulate states that, when certain amount of capital is saved, the utility of the rate of interest equals the marginal disutility of the waiting corresponding to that capital volume.

Based on this explanation, the *classical theory* draws its conclusions concerning the magnitude of interest (price) and of investment (capital).

An example of the *modus operandi* is the following: assuming a fixed level of income, when consumption decreases, the saving corresponding to each level of the rate of interest is consequently increased. Such an increase in saving brings about a reduction of the rate of interest and an increase in investment demand – plausibly – equivalent to the original fall in consumption. If this is so, then the aggregate demand will remain constant and equal to the previous *given* volume of output and income. This mechanism ensures that the alleged cuts in consumption demand will not affect aggregate demand, since investment replaces consumption, but it may also be used to supplement the adjustment of the classical labor market (the theoretical and empirical bases of which have been challenged in the previous section). Joining the labor market and the capital market, it may be shown that if the labor market adjusted by means of a wage cut, and that cut triggered a fall in workers' consumption, investment would increase to compensate for the reduction in aggregate demand, the volume of which would therefore remain constant.

Based on the same mechanism, it is possible to argue that the increases in output will also not be limited by a dearth of demand. Let's now assume that there is an increase in output and income. The new income could be completely destined to consumption, so that demand would increase as much as output, and placing the new goods would pose no problem. But if, instead, a portion of the new income were not devoted to consumption, that additional income would, by definition, become saving. The classical capital market comes to the aid of effective demand, and allows for the fulfillment of Say's Law once again. The increase of capital supply pushes the rate of interest downwards, thus generating a stimulus to increase investment demand, which comes to complete the weak consumption demand. Thus, the complete additional output is always demanded, whether it is consumption or investment. In this way, the classical theory of investment and of the rate of interest becomes a fundamental element in the defense of Say's Law: the rate of interest, in turn, is the transmission belt that translates any reduction in current consumption demand into an equivalent increase in the current investment demand.

Keynes severely questions the assumptions underlying this explanation, that is, the way in which the *classical theory* represents the market of "free" capital. Next, we will present the set of criticisms Keynes now levels at the *classical theory* of investment and of interest. The starting point is a new attack on the consistency of the *classical theory*, which is weakened every time the method of simple aggregation is employed to project the behavior of the individual onto society as a whole without any further qualification.

Both the curve for *individual* capital supply and the curve for *individual* capital demand are constructed on the assumption that the *individual's income* remains constant. The curves for saving and investment are reciprocally "independent", because their shape and position originate in technical conditions of profitability and individuals' psychology; both are exogenous parameters and do not have any mutual relation. Though plausible when dealing with an isolated individual, this assumption collapses due to its absurdity when trying to study aggregate saving and investment. In this case, as in others, analogy introduces evident logical problems; like when considering society as a whole, the certainty is destroyed that an autonomous increase in saving brings about an increase in investment. Changes in the volume of investment of a society must necessarily affect aggregate income in some way. And, in turn, the level of saving surely depends on the level of income, which can no longer be considered a fixed amount. Besides, changes in aggregate investment entail changes in consumption and, therefore, in aggregate demand, so that income is affected also in this case. To sum up: at aggregate level, the determination of the rate of interest cannot be resolved on the capital market taken in isolation simply because an exogenous shift of the investment curve affects the level of income, thus modifying the savings curve. As may be observed, the *classical theory* becomes inconsistent once the assumption is removed that the levels of output and income are fixed and given; this problem originates, again, in a false analogy of the part and the whole.

The independent variables of the *classical theory* of the rate of interest are the capital demand curve and the influence of the rate of interest on the saved portion of a given income.

> the *classical theory* of the rate of interest seems to suppose that, if the demand curve for capital shifts or if the curve relating the rate of interest to the amount saved out of a given income shifts or if both these curves shift, the new rate of interest will be given by the point of intersection of the new position of the two curves. Buy this is a nonsense theory. For the assumption that income is constant is inconsistent with the assumption that these two curves can shift independently of one another. If either of the shift, then, in general, income will change, with the result that the whole schematism based on the assumption of a given income breaks down.
>
> (Keynes, 1939 [1936]: 179; IV.14.I)

But the evident failure of the assumption of a total fixed income that guarantees the autonomy of aggregate savings relative to aggregate investment shows, simply, that the classicists lack an adequate method to determine the volume of investment and the level of the rate of interest for the economy as a whole. Say's Law involvement is double, as on one hand it supports the axiom of full employment and, on the other, its relevance hinges on a capital market founded on this very same assumption:

> The *classical theory* not merely neglects the influence of changes in the level of income, but involves formal error.
>
> (Keynes, 1939 [1936]: 179; IV.14.I)

It is evident, however, that the aggregate capital market cannot assume a fixed income and

> [t]hus the functions used by the classical theory, namely, the response of investment and the response of the amount saved out of a given income to change in the rate of interest, do not furnish material for a theory of the rate of interest.
>
> (Keynes, 1939 [1936]: 181; IV.14.I)

The consequences of this criticism are also decisive: now the aggregate capital market collapses, which will force Keynes to offer in his system a new explanation of the determination of the rate of interest, since the one furnished by the *classical theory* is logically mistaken. It will also be necessary to abandon the assumption that the investment and the saving functions are mutually independent, that they do not affect nor depend on the volume of output, finally, that they are "determining", not determined factors – independent variables set by technology and individual preferences in the course of time – in the system.

> Thus the traditional analysis is faulty because it has failed to isolate correctly the independent variables of the system. Saving and investment are the determinates of the system, not the determinants [. . .]. The traditional analysis has been aware that saving depends on income but it has overlooked the fact that income depends on investment, in such fashion that, when investment changes, income must necessarily change in just that degree which is necessary to make the change in saving equal to the change in investment.
>
> (Keynes, 1939 [1936]: 183–184; IV.14.I)

Thus, Keynes proves the theoretical inconsistency of the *classical theory* of interest based on the aggregate capital market. However, the objections do not end here. There still remain to be pointed out other obscure points that have already been mentioned: the "empirical" problem of the saving curve, and the double determination of the rate of interest in the context of the *classical theory* of value and of money.

The *classical market of capital* construct involves a fundamental assumption: the positive slope of the savings curve. It is assumed that – *given* an income – an individual will increase his savings ratio every time the rate of interest rises. According to the *classical (marginalist)* explanation, this is due to the fact that a reward that is higher than waiting will induce the individual to replace a higher proportion of current consumption for future consumption. But at the same time, when the aggregate is considered, even the *classical theory* admits that total saving is a remainder, the difference between total income and total expenditure on consumption. If this is true, the classical hypothesis that the aggregate curve for savings is positively sloped relative to the rate of interest is another way of saying that aggregate consumption at a given income level exhibits the opposite behavior: when the rate of interest grows, an increase in saving and a reduction in consumption should occur.

> For the classical theory of the rate of interest, which was based on the idea that the rate of interest was the factor which brought the supply and demand for savings into equilibrium, it was convenient to suppose that expenditure on consumption is *cet. par.* negatively sensitive to changes in the rate of interest, so that any rise in the rate of interest would appreciably diminish consumption. It has long been recognised, however, that the total effect of changes in the rate of interest on the readiness to spend on present consumption is complex and uncertain, being dependent on conflicting tendencies, since some of the subjective motives towards saving will be more easily satisfied if the rate of interest rises, whilst others will be weakened. Over a long period substantial changes in the rate of interest probably tend to modify social habits considerably, thus affecting the subjective propensity to spend – though in which direction it would be hard to say, except in the light of actual experience. The usual type of short – period fluctuation in the rate of interest is not likely, however, to have much direct influence on spending either way.
>
> (Keynes, 1939 [1936]: 93; III.8.II)

This is a consistency test that the *classical theory* does not seem to be capable of passing. According to Keynes, at aggregate level the volume of consumption does not react negatively to changes in the rate of interest; therefore, neither can the opposite behavior be attributed to aggregate savings, as such relation does not actually seem to exist. The support the *classical theory* needs to shift from the representation of individual to that of aggregate behavior in the capital market is thus denied, since saving does not react clearly to changes in the rate of interest, neither in the short or the long term. Thus, based on observation, Keynes begins to rebut one of the strongest pillars of *classical theory*. Marshall called "waiting" the sacrifice for which the rate of interest should compensate in order to have an individual postpone his consumption. The propensity to save does not depend, therefore, on the rate at which the waiting is rewarded. Keynes goes even further: this relationship is false not only in connection with the aggregate, but also with the individual.

He points out that given a fixed income, an individual should not be expected to substantially reduce his consumption, even when the rate of interest rises significantly:

> There are not many people who will alter their way of living because the rate of interest has fallen from 5 to 4 percent, if their aggregate income is the same as before [. . .]. Apart from this, the main conclusion suggested by experience is, I think, that the short – period influence of the rate of interest on individual spending out of a given income is secondary and relatively unimportant, except, perhaps, where unusually large changes are in question.
>
> (Keynes, 1939 [1936]: 94; III.8.II)

Taking into account these observations, *The General Theory* will try to show that, once the product is no longer considered a given and becomes a dependent variable of the system, the aggregate volume of saving behaves contrary to the *classical system's* prediction: it will generally tend to diminish when the rate of interest rises. This is so because – anticipating results – an increase in the rate of interest will provoke, *ceteris paribus*, a fall in current investment and, therefore, in current saving, which is a fixed portion of income. If income is not, like the *classical system* does, assumed to be constant, the curve relating total saving and interest rate should be negatively sloped, as is the investment demand curve:

> Thus, even if it is the case that a rise in the rate of interest would cause the community to save more *out of a given income*, we can be quite sure that a rise in the rate of interest (assuming no favourable change in the demand – schedule for investment) will decrease the actual aggregate of savings.
>
> (Keynes, 1939 [1936]: 111; III.9.II)

The conclusion is categorical: if consumption does not depend directly on the ordinary fluctuations of the rate of interest, then saving will not either:

the function of free capital supply as conceived by the *classical theory* does not match experience. Keynes's theory will have to provide a new, different characterization of the causes of consumption and saving variations.

Second, a fundamental critique of theoretical nature still remains: the aforementioned classical determination of interest corresponds to the First Treatise. However, apart from that explanation, the classicists provide a different one when revisiting the issue in the Second Treatise. The contradiction between both explanations resurfaces then, as, according to Keynes, the *classical theory* of value is not consistent with its theory of money:

> [I]t has been usual to suppose that an increase in the quantity of money has a tendency to reduce the rate of interest, at any rate in the first instance and in the short period. Yet no reason has been given why a change in the quantity of money should affect either the investment demand – schedule or the readiness to save out of a given income. Thus the classical school have had quite a different theory of the rate of interest in volume I dealing with the theory of value from what they have had in volume II dealing with the theory of money.
>
> (Keynes, 1939 [1936]: 182–183; IV.14.I)

After criticizing the First Treatise (volume I)'s theory of the rate of interest, its inconsistency with the Second Treatise (volume II) is exposed.

The question is, essentially, the following: the *classical theory* employs a single category (rate of interest) to refer to a phenomenon associated to "capital" on one hand and to money on the other. The classical approach splits the phenomenon but uses a single category for it, thus falling into inconsistency. The bewilderment caused by this double explanation, according to which the rate of interest seems to be subject, on one hand, to a stream of flows linked to capital physical productivity and, on the other, to certain purely monetary effects, led some economists to suggest distinguishing a "natural" rate of interest from a "market" rate of interest. The first stems from capital supply and demand becoming equal, the second, from loan availability. The latter is linked to the amount of money, because an increase in the currency in circulation that goes to the banking system stimulates credit, thus reducing the market rate of interest. This explanation implies the endorsement of the quantitative theory, although it incorporates the rate of interest as a part of the mechanism driving price changes. It also assumes, like the *classical theory*, a given level of employment. And lastly, it relies on a relationship between both interest rates such that the "natural" rate works as a gravitational center for the "money" rate. In other words, contrary to classical theory, these theories – Keynes calls them neo-classical – use two categories to refer to a single phenomenon. Authors such as Böhm–Bawerk or Wicksell, but also Keynes himself in the *Treatise*, explored this path.

However, in *The General Theory*, the two-interest-rate solution is discarded (the issue will be discussed in detail later).

> [I]t is the attempt to build a bridge on the part of the neo – classical school which has led to the worst muddles of all. For the latter have inferred that there must be *two* sources of supply to meet the invest-ment demand – schedule; namely, savings proper, which are the sav-ings dealt with by the classical school, *plus* the sum made available by any increase in the quantity of money (this being balanced by some species of levy on the public, called 'forced saving' or the like). This leads on to the idea that there is a 'natural' or 'neutral' or 'equilibrium' rate of interest, namely, that rate of interest which equates investment to classical savings proper without any addition from 'forced savings'.
>
> (Keynes, 1939 [1936]: 183; IV.14.I)

In the classical framework, there is no solution for this problem: two different theories explain the rate of interest, a "real" rate in the First Treatise, and a "money" rate in the Second. By splitting the rate of interest, the confusion is not cleared up. For Keynes, as will be later seen, the rate of interest is a strictly monetary phenomenon. Besides, it is independent from the "real" capital return, which is measured by the marginal efficiency of capital. There are two different phenomena and two sets of factors that influence each variable: "I now read these discussions as an honest intellectual effort to keep sepa-rate what the *classical theory* has inextricably confused together, namely, the rate of interest and the marginal efficiency of capital" (Keynes, 1939 [1936]: 352; VI.23.V). The *classical theory* first muddles and then merges into one single category two phenomena that are different in nature and whose varia-tions have different causes and effects: the rate of interest and capital yield. Whatever it is, the new theory of interest that Keynes puts forth will have to distinguish both categories before looking for their determinants.

Some profound consequences of abandoning the classical capital market begin to take shape: How, then, is the "price" of capital set? Some explana-tions that Keynes rejects may be pointed out. The usual explanation that the price of a capital good is simply equal to its future yield capitalized at the current rate of interest, as Keynes states (and Marshall accepts in his *Principles*) cannot be turned into a theory of the rate of interest because in order to obtain that price it is necessary to know first the value for the rate of interest, which cannot stem from its own relationship to yield. The example devised by Marshall assumes that if a machine valued at $100 gives a net annual yield of $3 "in equilibrium", the implied rate of interest is 3 percent. But then he notes that as the rate of interest is precisely 3 percent, capital investments will only be directed to the machines that offer that yield.

As Keynes points out, "Marshall was well aware that we are involved in a circular argument if we try to determine along these lines what the rate of interest actually is" (Keynes, 1939 [1936]: 140; IV.11.II). A theory that attempts to figure out the interest rate based on the relation between the price of a capital equipment and its yields, on one hand, and intends, at the same time, to equate the price of the equipment to the yields discounted precisely at that same rate is logically untenable. In Keynes's view, two different explanations are required for interest and yields:

> I would, however, ask the reader to note at once that neither the knowledge of an asset's prospective yield nor the knowledge of the marginal efficiency of the asset enables us to deduce either the rate of interest or the present value of the asset. We must ascertain the rate of interest from some other source, and only then can we value the asset by 'capitalizing' its prospective yield.
>
> (Keynes, 1939 [1936]: 137; IV.11.I)

These criticisms will not only condition Keynes's choice of his system's endogenous and exogenous variables, as well as their form of determination, but they are also leveled at the core of two fundamental economic concepts such as capital and money.

Keynes's proposals will be discussed later.

The impact of this critique of Say's Law may now be examined. After his devastating criticism of the aggregate market of capital, Keynes exposes the "tacit assumption" that in this connection supports the permanent full employment on which the *classical theory* relies. What should be the behavior of the rate of interest to become a transmission belt for Say's Law, thus ensuring sufficient demand for any volume of output? The curve for the aggregate demand of capital defines one relationship between the rate of interest and the volume of investment. To ensure that aggregate demand keeps pace with aggregate supply, the rate of interest has to automatically and inexorably position itself at the adequate level to produce a variation in investment demand of the required magnitude. If this were the case, any fall in consumption would generate an increase in saving that would lower the interest rate to the point where investment compensates for the fall in consumption demand. Furthermore, on this basis, it is possible to define a level of interest rate that is compatible with the absolute full employment that Keynes calls a neutral or optimum interest rate. The *classical theory* implicitly assumes that the rate of interest is always pushed to its neutral level: in such a case, investment is enough to purchase the output in excess of consumption needs that correspond to full employment. This is a tacit assumption that is not accompanied by any specification of the actual mechanism that guarantees such a result.

> The above gives us, once again, the answer to the question as to what tacit assumption is required to make sense of the classical theory of the rate of interest. This theory assumes either that the actual rate of interest is always equal to the neutral rate of interest in the sense in which we have just defined the latter, or alternatively that the actual rate of interest is always equal to the rate of interest which will maintain employment at some specified constant level. If the traditional theory is thus interpreted, there is little or nothing in its practical conclusions to which we need take exception. The classical theory assumes that the banking authority or natural forces cause the market – rate of interest to satisfy one or other of the above conditions; and it investigates what laws will govern the application and rewards of the community's productive resources subject to this assumption. With this limitation in force, the volume of output depends solely on the assumed constant level of employment in conjunction with the current equipment and technique; and we are safely ensconced in a Ricardian world.
>
> (Keynes, 1939 [1936]: 243–244; IV.17.VI)

However, neither the "actual" forces of the First Treatise nor the "monetary" causes of the Second ensure the rate of interest that automatic and optimum position. According to Keynes, those forces, whose effect is implicitly assumed in the short-term of Say's Law, do not actually exist:

> If the rate of interest were so governed as to maintain continuous full employment, Virtue would resume her sway; the rate of capital accumulation would depend on the weakness of the propensity to consume. Thus, once again, the tribute that classical economists pay to her is due to their concealed assumption that the rate of interest always is so governed.
>
> (Keynes, 1939 [1936]: 112; III.9.II)

The last den where Say's Law could dwell, supporting the assumption of full employment, is the aggregate market of goods, which leads, in turn, to the study of those forces that have a bearing on the general level of prices. Keynes's critique covers, too, these mechanisms of *classical theory*.

Critique of the classical quantity theory of the Second Treatise

What is the amount of money required to support trade during certain period of time? How do changes in money quantity impact its value and, therefore, prices in general? The quantitative theory emerged to answer these questions.

In its simpler version, it is an identity that doesn't explain anything: the addition of the transactions conducted during an interval of time multiplied by the price of each, that is, the total value of transactions, must necessarily equal the value of the total amount of money in circulation times its rotation velocity. This simple equation, stemming from the mere observation of the exchange process, may be turned into an *explanation* of the level of prices or of the amount of currency in circulation, depending on the posited causation direction. Throughout the protracted ruling of the gold standard, the amount of currency in circulation was only considered to be an arbitrary magnitude for analytical speculation purposes (as in Locke and later, Hume), and economists strived, rather, to explain the different mechanisms through which the amount of gold in each national sphere of circulation tended to adjust to the requirements of domestic trade transactions. When there was an excessive amount of gold, prices would modify, and the trade balance would tilt so that gold would drain outwardly or enter into circulation until recovering a level suitable for local production. Fluctuations in money quantity and prices were considered to be a result of external, transitory "disturbances". The amount of gold, commodity money with value of its own, was set according to the requirements of commodity traffic, and, as a result of these movements, its market price tended to equate its normal price, determined, in turn, by production costs.

The collapse of the gold standard completely modifies this scenario. Thoroughly understanding the exact consequences of money emission becomes crucial when the state begins to be responsible for permanently regulating the amount of inconvertible bills, that is, bills with no "intrinsic" value, put into circulation. The quantitative equation thus turns into a theory of prices generally endorsed by classical theory. In fact, as the value of transactions and the value of money in circulation – multiplied by its velocity – must necessarily be equal, an increase in the quantity of money may, apparently, only result in a proportional increase in prices or a change in money velocity of circulation. If this is considered to be more or less fixed in the short term, then the classical theory of prices of the Second Treatise ensues: variations in the amount of money bring about proportional changes in prices. Here is the second theory of prices.

> So long as economists are concerned with what is called the Theory of Value, they have been accustomed to teach that prices are governed by the conditions of supply and demand; and, in particular, changes in marginal cost and the elasticity of short – period supply have played a prominent part. But when they pass in volume II, or more often in a separate treatise, to the Theory of Money and Prices, we hear no more

of these homely but intelligible concepts and move into a world where prices are governed by the quantity of money, by its income – velocity, by the velocity of circulation relatively to the volume of transactions, by hoarding, by forced saving, by inflation and deflation *et hoc genus omne;* and little or no attempt is made to relate these vaguer phrases to our former notion of the elasticity's of supply and demand.

(Keynes, 1939 [1936]: 292; V.21.I)

Strangely, the explanation of the Second Treatise also rests on the results of Say's Law, so that Keynes has more than enough reasons to reject it.

The *classical quantity theory* rests on two pillars. These are two assumptions, one concerning the workings of the system as a whole, the other regarding the particular characteristics of money. Both are inadequate and false:

for the purposes of the real world it is a great fault in the Quantity Theory that it does not distinguish between changes in prices which are function of changes in output, and those which are a function of changes in the wage – unit. The explanation of this omission is, perhaps, to be found in the assumptions that there is no propensity to hoard and that there is always full employment.

(Keynes, 1939 [1936]: 209; IV.15.IV)

First, whenever the quantity of money grows and, according to the quantitative theory, the value of transactions (i.e. price times quantity of traded goods) increases, the *classical theory* plainly rejects the possibility that such an increase may result from an increase in the volume of transactions, that is, of output.

How is this conclusion reached? The mechanism is twofold: first, as Keynes states, the quantitative equation usually considers income value without distinguishing price and quantity. But when it does, it assumes, once again, that outcome is constant (presumably at the level corresponding to full employment). In this case, the volume of the output cannot ever increase, with the result that it will always be prices that vary as a consequence of changes in money quantity.

It is for this reason that it can be said that also the quantity theory rests on the assumption of full employment and, therefore, on Say's Law. The critique of the labor market has shown that the second classical postulate of employment does not reflect reality, which implies that a cut in real wages does not entail a sufficiently powerful discouragement of workers to lead them to abandon their jobs. It is not true that in any situation real wage is equivalent to marginal disutility of labor. The economy is not always at its maximum level of voluntary employment.

This result gains new significance now, as only under such a circumstance would all emission of money provoke an inflationary increase in prices. When the second postulate of the *classical theory* of occupation collapses, it drags down with it the traditional version of the quantitative theory, which in its mechanical conception considers inflationary any increase in money quantity:

> The view that *any* increase in the quantity of money is *inflationary* (unless we mean by inflationary merely that prices are rising) is bound up with the underlying assumption of the classical theory that we are always in a condition where a reduction in the real rewards of the factors of production will lead to a curtailment in their supply.
>
> (Keynes, 1939 [1936]: 304; V.21.V)

The other weak point of the quantity theory is the assumption of a fixed velocity of circulation in the short term (as well as in the long term). In Cambridge, the term income-velocity was used to refer to the ratio of income that the public wished to keep as cash in hand, ratio associated to habits and customs; it was assumed that such ratio neared 1:15, and tended to remain constant no matter what the circumstances. In the cited passage, it is pointed out that the *classical quantitative theory* excludes in its description the propensity to hoard, that is, the will of the public to hold certain amount of money in cash in excess of their needs in terms of transactions. But no sooner does Keynes set out to analyze whether there does in fact exist a certain ratio between the level of income and the amount of cash that the public hold, he finds that such ratio is not constant, that its fluctuations do not stem from "habits and customs" or from long-term considerations relative to the banking system, but from actual variables that his system must accurately reflect, and he remarks that

> the 'income – velocity of money' is, in itself, merely a name which explains nothing. There is no reason to expect that it will be constant. For it depends, as the foregoing discussion has shown, on many complex and variable factors. The use of this term obscures, I think, the real character of the causation, and has led to nothing but confusion.
>
> (Keynes, 1939 [1936]: 299; V.21.IV)

The key factor, overlooked by classical theory, should be found in the fact that the public, under certain circumstances, wish to hoard bills in cash, and do so on account of precise and rational motives. There is no fixed ratio between money demand and income: the assumption of a constant velocity of circulation, therefore, does not reflect reality either, so that the quantitative theory is no longer an adequate explanation of price variations.

Keynes develops his explanation from that perspective, which will lead him to explore new paths when investigating the nature of money. Thus, he reaches the conclusion that "only in the event of money being used solely for transactions and never as a store of value, would a different theory [to that he himself puts forward] become appropriate", that is, the old quantitative theory (Keynes, 1939 [1936]: 182; IV.14.I).

The quantitative theory of the Second Treatise considers money's function only to be a means of exchange or of circulation. It does not allow for any reason inducing the public to hold money other than the purpose of carrying out certain purchases. But, for Keynes, money is also a "store" of purchasing power, of wealth: "in this connection we can usefully employ the ancient distinction between the use of money for the transaction of current business and its use as a store of wealth" (Keynes, 1939 [1936]: 168; IV.13 II). When taking into account this new function of money, the quantitative theory is incapable of representing money demand (which it reduces to a mere fixed ratio of income).

If money is also considered an adequate means to store wealth, changes in income will not be the only cause of modification in the desired holdings of money. This situation could be represented, albeit imperfectly, if the assumption of a constant income-velocity were dropped. But that modification is not enough; the quantitative theory disregards some variables that are key to understanding the problem.

The ratio between money and income varies because the demand of money obeys other causes linked to the incentive to hoard. The quantitative theory does not take into account the effects of the rate of interest on money demand and subsumes all other factors under changes in income-velocity. For this reason, it will have to be abandoned.

> [T]he term 'income – velocity of money' carries with it the misleading suggestion of the presumption in favour of the demand for money as a whole being proportional, or having some determinate relation, to income, whereas this presumption should apply, as we shall see, only to a *portion* of the public's cash holdings; with the result that it overlooks the part played by the rate of interest.
>
> (Keynes, 1939 [1936]: 194; IV.15.I)

In Keynes's view, the desire to hold money in cash in excess of the needs inherent to circulation originates in the possibility of obtaining gains and avoiding losses as a result of future changes in interest rate. Ignoring other complex considerations concerning this theory (that will be discussed later), this demand may be called "speculative" only because individuals take into account expected prospective values of the rate of interest when deciding to keep their money in cash. By completely excluding this possibility, the *classical theory* overlooks the additional demand of money stemming from these changes. For this reason, Keynes concludes that classical theory implicitly assumes that economy is unchanging and static, in the sense that there exists absolute certainty concerning the future values of the rate of interest; in such a situation, all individuals would prefer any alternative interest-accruing option to store their wealth, rather than keeping idle balances in cash as

> In a static society or in a society in which for any other reason no one feels any uncertainty about the future rates of interest [. . .] the propensity to hoard (as we might term it), will always be zero in equilibrium.
> (Keynes, 1939 [1936]: 208; IV.15.IV)

In short, the endorsement of the quantity theory rests on two assumptions: first, by turning output volume into a fixed value, the reason why an increase in the quantity of money is reflected as an increase in the total money income is that prices, never the "real" income, have risen. Keynes thus unveils the hidden presence of the classical assumption of a constant level of employment in the quantity theory. But the quantitative theory also assumes that all the existing bills are in circulation – save for the proportion that banks keep in cash out of their total deposits – because it does not take into account any incentive to store wealth as cash. Thus, by denying the existence of a propensity to hoard bills on account of "speculative" motives, the notion that the rate of interest has no connection with the demand of money is created. It is under these premises, and only under those circumstances, that quantitative theory could be held to be valid. And this could only happen in static conditions in which the future is equal to the present.

Enough charges have been presented to discard the *classical quantitative theory*. It is necessary, therefore, to develop a new *general theory of prices*, different from the one put forward in the classical *Second Treatise*.

Notes

1 The classicists, actually, referred to industrial output as a whole, but they did so only when undertaking the study of the long term. Marshall should also be credited for the metaphor, later also extended to the consumer, of "representative enterprise", which helps study the output of a set of enterprises (of a particular branch or of the whole economy).

2 In the preface to the *Treatise,* Keynes states, "My object has been to find a method which is useful in describing, not merely the characteristics of static equilibrium, but also those of disequilibrium, and to discover the dynamical laws governing the passage of a monetary system from one position of equilibrium to another" (Keynes, 1935 [1930]: v). A dramatic contrast with *The General Theory* emerges in the brief, albeit crucial, chapter 1, where Keynes states clearly that his purpose is to consider unemployment as a situation of stable

equilibrium. This is, in fact, one of the most significant points of breakup with *classical theory*.

3   As for the research method aimed at identifying cause-effect relationships, Marshall stated in his *Principles of Economics*: "It is the business of economics, as of almost every other science, to collect facts, to arrange and interpret them, and to draw inferences from them. [. . .] All the devices for the discovery of the relations between cause and effect, which are described in treatises on scientific method, have to be used in their turn by the economist: there is not any one method of investigation which can properly be called the method of economics; but every method must be made serviceable in its proper place, either singly or in combination with others" (Marshall, 1920 [1890]: 29; I.II.1).

4   Modern epistemology generally calls "context of discovery" an undoubtedly key part of the activity of the scientist: the moment when and the way in which the mechanisms or the laws of nature or society are deciphered. About this stage of scientific activity, however, the different methodological approaches do not have much to say. They do, instead, offer diverse descriptions and prescriptions concerning theories' "corroboration" or, rather, their "refutation" (canonical contributions to the prolific debate of modern epistemology may be found in Popper, 1967; Lakatos, 1978; Kuhn, 1971). In economics, there is not a single accurate method to definitively corroborate or refute a hypothesis, whether it be theoretical or empirical, which should make consensus among scientists the decisive factor for the acceptance of a new theory: "It is astonishing what foolish things one can temporarily believe if one thinks too long alone, particularly in economics (along with the other moral sciences), where it is often impossible to bring one's ideas to a conclusive test either formal or experimental" (Keynes, 1939 [1936]: vii; Preface). This parallel between Keynes's and Kuhn's conceptions concerning scientific development seems to be, however, inadequate. Keynes does not trace the origin of changes in prevailing (economic) theories to changes in researchers consensus but to the historical processes and the dominant social forces that represent them (Keynes 1939 [1936]).

5   The use of mathematics to express economic theories strongly attracted the first marginalists. Jevons, for example, considered it a distinguishing trait that differentiated the emerging line of thinking from its predecessor: "I do not write for mathematicians, nor as a mathematician, but as an economist wishing to convince other economists that their science can only be satisfactorily treated on an explicitly mathematical basis" (Jevons, 1888 [1871]: Preface). Concerning the criticism of mathematics applied to economic problems, Walras says in his Preface to *Elements*, "As for the economists who, without knowing mathematics, without even knowing what mathematics consists of, have decided that mathematics cannot possibly serve to clarify economic principles, they can go their way repeating that "*human liberty will never allow itself to be put into equations*" or that "mathematics abstracts from the frictions *that are everything in the moral sciences*", and other forcefully expressed niceties [. . .] they will always have to face the alternative either of avoiding this discipline and of developing applied economics without having developed theoretical economics, or of approaching it without the necessary intellectual resources, and, in that case, of producing at the same time very bad economic theory and very bad mathematics" (Walras, 2003 [1874]: Preface; xvi-xvii; emphasis in the original). Marginalism largely chose to apply a mathematical method.

6   Keynes's cautious attitude regarding the use of mathematical language when displaying economic relations completely coincides with the objections raised

by Marshall, who used to express economic relations in everyday language in the main body of his books, leaving the use of mathematic symbols to appendixes or footnotes. Without going any further, his famous cross diagram that represented supply and demand appeared in a footnote.

7 In his famous article subtitled "A suggested interpretation", Hicks tries for the first time to translate the sequential exposition of Keynes's system into the simultaneous method (1937), which proves that between both expository forms there are two-way paths. Walras, for example, was a fervent advocate of the mathematical expository method; however, he accepts the possibility that his own system be expressed using the other method. In his *Elements,* he says: "But this whole theory is mathematical; that is to say, although *the exposition can be made in ordinary language*, the demonstration of the theory must be made mathematically. The demonstration rests wholly on the theory of exchange [. . .]. And only mathematics can make clear to us how and why, current equilibrium prices not only in exchange but also in production, capital formation and circulation, are attained by raising the price of services, products, and new capital goods for which the demand exceeds the supply, and by lowering the price of those for which the supply exceeds the demand" (Walras, 2003 [1874]: Preface, xi). In the Walrasian system, the amount of factors involved is such that it would probably be impossible to link them using ordinary language. This is far from the case with Keynes's *system.*

8 As may be seen, this interpretation differs from that of many renowned readers of *The General Theory* who wish to read in Keynes's exposition some sort of hidden "dynamic", to which they tend to refer with the vague name of "historical time" (Asimakopulos, 1991). V. Chick, for example, states that "Keynes' method is something of a compromise, using the partial equilibrium method to analyze a market taken in isolation, then feeding the result back into the mainstream of economic events, which were themselves moving meanwhile. There is a distinct time-stream of events, in sharp contrast to general equilibrium, where everything happens at once, or partial equilibrium, where everything happens in the market being analyzed and nothing is allowed to happen in other markets, while the economist back is turned" (Chick, 1991 [1983]: 15). The first sentence seems to share the interpretation offered here, but coincidences cease when it is asserted that this is a method aimed at portraying the effect of time, and not merely an analytical method to represent causality. Keynes's particular trait is simply his expository style, not the treatment of time. To understand Keynes's conception of the effect of time, the distinctions handed down by Marshall have to be taken into account. As will be seen, dynamic and static in *The General Theory* have to do with other aspects. Past events are incorporated into the production equipment, and the future bears influence on the present through the expectations that affect the calculation of asset return, liquidity preference, and cost of equipment use. But all decisions are made, it could be said, instantly. It is the analysis, and only the analysis, which establishes priority relations.

9 The methodological question is a side -issue in this study. It has been discussed only to show the differences between Keynes's method and the more widespread mathematical simultaneous method. However, the nature of these causal relations and their explanatory power are in themselves subjects that may also be discussed.

10 These questions gain significance in light of the structure of mainstream modern economic theory. This is so because the First Treatise became a complete and unique branch of the orthodoxy's analytical corpus: microeconomics. In a more

current version, the question would be: can microeconomics resist Keynes's critique?

11 In the last analysis, the Marshallian source of value is also the result of the individual's psychological appreciation. The real costs of each commodity, both in the Robinsonian case of an isolated individual as in a primitive society or modern economy, are nothing but the "subjective costs" related to the effort of work and the sacrifice of waiting. Keynes's view regarding this explanation will be later discussed.

12 Marshall explains his method of the "representative firm", a subtle and innovative construct, as follows. As usual, his arguments are duly qualified, although once the device is introduced into the analysis, he seems to easily forget his initial qualms: "Thus a representative firm is in a sense an average firm. But there are many ways in which the term 'average' might be interpreted in connection with a business. And a Representative firm is that particular sort of average firm, at which we need to look in order to see how far the economies, internal and external, of production on a large scale have extended generally in the industry and country in question. We cannot see this by looking at one or two firms taken at random: but we can see it fairly well by selecting, after a broad survey, a firm, whether in private or joint-stock management (or better still, more than one), that represents, to the best of our judgment, this particular average" (Marshall 1920 [1890]: 318; IV.XII.2). Although introduced as a practical resource to choose one firm among many, it is in fact a merely analytical resource.

13 The modern marginalist explanation of the labor market is slightly different, since it has adopted the ordinal approach of utility, similarly to the theory of the consumer. In the case of the ordinal approach, the condition for maximization is that the quotient of marginal utilities, the marginal rate of substitution, be equal to the quotient of prices. Such formulation is only semantically different from the second postulate, since it does not require the law of diminishing marginal utility, allows for the evaluation of income effect, and does not assume a fixed money utility. In our exposition, however, we use the Marshallian expression to which Keynes refers since the criticisms still apply, in general terms. The treatment of the labor market has become more complex in modern approaches, but its essence remains unchanged.

14 Other explanations similar to wage rigidity, based on information, coordination or other problems have been attempted. However, when those are analytically considered, the situation on the labor market is identical to the one we have described.

15 If labor does not have a bearing on real wages, what is the origin of the obstinate resistance to any reduction in nominal wage, and reciprocally, the fierce struggle to obtain pay raises? Is it a prototypical case of the so-called monetary illusion on the part of labor? Keynes denies it. Although in aggregate terms an increase (or reduction) in nominal wage does not translate into an equivalent raise (or fall) in real wage, Keynes holds that the struggle for wage rises and the opposition to wage cuts is premised on valid reasons. Each particular group of workers has very good reasons to pursue a pay rise. If they obtain it, they will benefit in comparison with the rest of the workers, but if they don't, their particular purchasing power would be damaged if another group obtained a wage increase, as the nominal wage of the first group would remain fixed while prices would to a certain extent increase. In section II, chapter 2, *The General Theory*, it is shown that labor action is not based indeed on a naive "monetary illusion" but on the possible real loss (or gain) in the purchasing power of the different groups of

workers' wages: "*It is sometimes said that it would be illogical for labour to resist a reduction of money-wages but not to resist a reduction of real wages. For reasons given below [. . .], this might not be so illogical as it appears at first; and, as we shall see later, fortunately so.*" (Keynes, 1939 [1936]: 9; I.2.II). As will be understood, although the average real wage might remain fixed, if a group of workers obtains an increase in money-wage in excess of the average rise, they will obtain a higher real wage, even though the prices of the goods that they themselves produce are correspondingly raised.

16 As will later be seen, reductions in nominal wage may affect employment, but not because they are "directly" reflected on real wages, encouraging entrepreneurs to hire more workers. The labor market, as was pointed out, is not the "locus of determination" of real or nominal wage and employment.

17 Independently, M. Kalecki reaches the same conclusion: "the reduction of wages in a closed system does not lead to an increase in production; [. . .] The slogan 'rigid wages as a cause of unemployment 'proves in the light of the above analysis to be entirely unfounded. Equally despairing is the case of the supporters of such slogan who preach that collective bargaining bring unemployment and poverty to the working class by making wages rigid" (Kalecki, 1936, "El mecanismo de la recuperación" quoted in Feiwell, 1987 [1975]: 49; translation EO).

4 *The General Theory* by Keynes

> The orthodox answer is to blame it on the working men for working too little and getting too much.
>
> —*Keynes, The Economic Consequences of Mr. Churchill*

Introduction

Keynes's main objective is to build a system capable of reflecting the movements of a money economy essentially different from a barter economy.

There, the short term equilibrium level of production may differ – and frequently will – from that corresponding to full employment; therefore, in the short term it is necessary to contemplate the possibility that a part of the existing capital equipment be unemployed and that a part of the population willing to work be unable, thus ending involuntarily unemployed.

The following explanation will begin with what Keynes calls his *general theory of employment*. A system capable of explaining the determinants of the level of employment as a whole must also reflect the definitive abandonment of Say's Law. This implies discarding the idea that any possible volume of output necessarily matches the amount of aggregate demand, and that something drives the economic system to increase production until the available resources have been completely depleted.

However, as Keynes states "If, however, this is not the true law relating the aggregate demand and supply functions, there is a vitally important chapter of economic theory which remains to be written and without which all discussions concerning the volume of aggregate employment are futile" (Keynes, 1939 [1936]: 26; I.3.I).

This "new chapter" of economic theory is none other than the system put forward in *The General Theory*, which separately studies the function of aggregate supply and the function of aggregate demand, distinguishing and dealing separately with the set of determinants relevant to each. This is the end of the "axiom of the parallel lines" of the *classical theory*, which asserted that global demand always increased and decreased at the same rate and in the same ratio as supply, so that the examination both of the composition and of the causal factors that affected the different elements of aggregate demand could be dismissed without any loss to the analysis. In fact, the *classical theory* implicitly relied on Say's Law, which ensured that supply and demand coincide at any level of employment, so that the separate study of supply and demand became pointless.

But if aggregate supply and demand coincide only at one point, where the level of equilibrium employment is determined, it becomes necessary to study aggregate supply and aggregate demand independently. This is Keynes's war cry, and his system's pathos.

We will begin by discussing the determinants of aggregate supply.

I Beyond Say's Law

The determinants of aggregate supply

The representation of aggregate supply is one of the least original aspects of Keynes's theory, although it should not be neglected on that account. First, in contrast to the global supply of the *classical theory*, aggregate supply is not defined as the relation between the amount of total (real) production and the "price" of a "unit" of output, that is, the curve for aggregate supply is not approached as a generalization of the supply curve for a particular item, since aggregate supply is composed of incommensurate products. Keynes instead decides to refer to a function of aggregate supply that links the different levels of employment to *the price of aggregate supply*, which equals the addition of the factorial costs and the profit the entrepreneur should be able to obtain in order to be willing to hire that amount of labor.[1] For each level of employment, there is a corresponding supply price (that is, the amount of each article multiplied by its production costs), enough to cover costs and a "normal" entrepreneur's profit. Thus, the volume of aggregate supply is, first and foremost, a magnitude expressed in money terms, not in physical units.

As the price of aggregate supply is strongly dependent on costs, the form of the function will be conditioned by the hypothesis put forth concerning yields.

For Keynes, in the short run and for the industry as a whole, returns are undoubtedly diminishing, so that supply price will increase more than proportionally to increases in employment volume: the increase in the produced volume is strengthened as a result of the increase in unit costs due to the decrease in marginal productivity. This is the schedule that entrepreneurs have in mind when making their decisions concerning the volume of production and employment. They will always try to maximize their profit, that is, obtain a maximum difference between the sale price and the production cost. The aggregate supply function, therefore, indicates what value sales must reach to induce certain volume of employment.

The problem of the determination of the level of employment in the short term comes down to the following: given the cost structure that determines the form of the supply function, entrepreneurs will hire the amount of labor corresponding to the value of the sales that, according to their expectations, they can effectively place on the market. Independently of the form aggregate supply may take, entrepreneurs will decide a volume of employment according to the amount of sales expected. To approach some problems regarding the determination of the level of equilibrium employment, it is not necessary yet to discuss the determinants of the function of aggregate supply, although it is precisely in that field where Keynes's main contribution lies. We may provisionally make the extreme assumption that the price of aggregate demand – the expected value of sales revenue – is given and constant for any level of employment. If this is true, that arbitrary level fulfills the requirement of independence relative to aggregate supply. The level of employment is that which corresponds to the point of the function of aggregate supply where supply price matches demand price. With this simple change, the ties with *classical theory* are broken: the system now admits a solution of equilibrium unemployment.

Now the level of production and employment is no longer a datum, as in the classical system. Besides, there is no tendency towards full employment. In fact, the economy remains steady at that point; it is a situation of balance as entrepreneurs (who determine the level of output) are obtaining maximum profits, therefore, there is no incentive to increase or decrease production.

Keynes calls the resting point *effective demand*, and the curve that gathers the levels of expenditure corresponding to each level of employment *aggregate demand*. The name has to do with the fact that entrepreneurs must estimate in advance the demand corresponding to each level of employment. They need that information, individually and as a whole, to decide upon the volume of employment based on their cost structure, also corresponding to each level of employment. Only the point of aggregate demand where it intersects the supply function is a point where demand will become effective: only at that point does supply equal demand. The aggregate demand function relates hypothetical employment volumes with prospective sales. At the point where it becomes equal to costs, entrepreneurs' expected profits are maximized – that is the meaning of the term "effective demand".

This simple explanation – which assumes that aggregate demand is fixed at an arbitrary level – entails in itself a revolution in mainstream economic thinking. Even before examining the determinants of aggregate demand, with merely admitting that this function does not yield values equal to those of the supply function for each volume of employment, it is possible to obtain the explanation Keynes sought.

The distance that separates this explanation from that offered by classical thinking is remarkable: the system has thus got rid of the assumption of full employment. However, the explanation sounds familiar because it is practically identical to the one Marshall uses to determine equilibrium production in certain industry in the short term. Let's compare the following excerpt from Marshall's *Principles* with Keynes's quote:

> When therefore the amount produced (in a unit of time) is such that the demand price is greater than the supply price, then sellers receive more than is sufficient to make it worth their while to bring goods to market to that amount; and there is at work an active force tending to increase the amount brought forward for sale. On the other hand, when the amount produced is such that the demand price is less than the supply price, sellers receive less than is sufficient to make it worth their while to bring goods to market on that scale; so that those who were just on the margin of doubt as to whether to go on producing are decided not to do so, and there is an active force at work tending to diminish the amount brought forward for sale. When the demand price is equal to the supply price, the amount produced has no tendency either to be increased or to be diminished; it is in equilibrium.
>
> (Marshall, 1920 [1890]: V.III.18)

In both cases, there is an adjustment of the produced amount, which is modified until matching aggregate sales with the addition of the costs associated with bringing a good to market (including normal profits).[2] Given the technology that determines, together with nominal wages, the production costs corresponding to each level of employment, the level of employment adjusts until it reaches the point where the supply price is equal to the demand price.

A particular trait of Keynes's system is that it was conceived in such a way that everything occurs in the present because, ultimately, current employment cannot depend on anything but current decisions. Marshall's market reached its normal equilibrium in the course of time, through the entrance and exit, the birth and death, of enterprises within industry.

Both Marshall's normal equilibrium and Keynes's effective demand point at aggregate level presuppose an adjustment process, but they describe a current state of equilibrium where what was required to reach a resting point has already taken place. In *The General Theory*, the adjustment of the level of output takes place, so to speak, in entrepreneur's minds, as it follows the tradition of the Marshallian *normal equilibrium* and, therefore, is not a transitory market equilibrium. For that reason, the supply normal price matches production costs (including normal profits). This is a fundamental and, apparently, largely misunderstood trait of the explanation: Keynes's system is designed to describe equilibrium states, not to analyze a movement towards equilibrium.

Is this, then, a static or a dynamic system? Keynes asserts that it is dynamic, but his notion of dynamics differs from the one generally associated with that term.

For Keynes, a dynamic conception of the economy implies accepting that the future is different from the present. The future is inherently uncertain; however, it affects current decisions. The dynamic character of the *system* is thus introduced through two mechanisms: expectations incorporate the future into the analysis, as represented by decision-makers. Thus, the future has a bearing on the present.

The past is reflected, in turn, in the capital equipment – including stock – available in the analyzed period. The system does not move forward in time but, on the contrary, everything happens during a single period: the present; however, the present is not equal to the past or the future: agents are aware of this, and such differences influence the determination of the variables.[3]

Of course, if expectations failed to accurately anticipate the future, the system would have to undergo an adjustment. But even though the analysis focused on the adjustment process throughout time, the study of the adjustment process triggered by inaccurate predictions does not help to explain why at a certain moment – the present – employment happens to be at a certain level. In any case, it will be necessary to specify how employment will vary in the following period, based on the new data of the problem, where the past is involved as a present fact, as a new input for decisions. It is for this reason that Keynes generally assumes that variables are found exactly at the levels anticipated by expectations. However, Keynes briefly examines what would happen if those anticipated calculations were not to come true in reality. Such disquisitions are not, anyhow, the focus of his concerns. What really matters is how the current level of employment is determined, and to that end, it suffices to take into account that entrepreneurs have to predict what will happen in the future, and whether they do so right or wrong, it will be those hypotheses that will lead them to produce certain amount in the current period.

As has been mentioned, for the time being, the discussion of the most original aspect of Keynes's analysis – the determination of aggregate demand – will be postponed, to focus the attention on certain fundamental issues associated with the "supply side" or, more specifically, with the price of aggregate supply. First, we will study how expectations are treated in *The General Theory*, as well as their effect on the system's "dynamic"; second, we will investigate the role played by expected profits in the "adjustment" process and reflect upon the level of the equilibrium nominal wage and real wage.

Expectations and dynamics in Keynes's system

The decisions that lead to setting the current level of employment at a certain magnitude are the exclusive right of entrepreneurs. It is they who individually decide the amount of labor hours they are willing to associate to the capital equipment they have (which cannot be enlarged in the short term). Logically, an entrepreneur will never increase his production beyond the volume of product he can effectively place on the market (including the normal levels of stock he wishes to hold in his warehouse). This implies that at every moment he has to predict the volume of sales and create his own expectations concerning the level of demand he will have to meet. Current production and employment are decided on the basis of those expectations about the future. Time intervenes in the system through the representation entrepreneurs have of the future:

> Time usually elapses, however – and sometimes much time – between the incurring of costs by the producer (with the consumer in view) and the purchase of the output by the ultimate consumer. Meanwhile the entrepreneur (including both the producer and the investor in this description) has to form the best expectations he can as to what the consumers will be prepared to pay when he is ready to supply them.
>
> (Keynes, 1939 [1936]: 46; II.5.I)

For the purpose of determining the current level of employment, it does not matter whether the current expectations turn out to be accurate in the future or, on the contrary, if the real level of demand is different from that originally expected. The analysis erases, with representation purposes, the uncertainty that entrepreneurs may have had in practice. It is not a question of Keynes not admitting that the future is uncertain; much to the contrary, he stresses this fact again and again. However, at each moment, the decision concerning how much to produce must be made, so that somehow or other, entrepreneurs have to form an image of the future, no matter how imperfect or groundless. They make their decisions based on such speculation:

> An entrepreneur, who has to reach a practical decision as to his scale or production, does not, of course, entertain a single undoubting expectation of what the sales – proceeds of a given output will be, but several hypothetical expectations held with varying degrees of probability and definiteness. By his expectation of proceeds I mean, therefore, that expectation of profits which, if it were held with certainty, would lead to the same behavior as does the bundle of vague and more various possibilities which actually makes up his state of expectation when he reaches his decision.
>
> (Keynes, 1939 [1936]: 40n; I.3.I)

As has been pointed out earlier – and will be discussed in more detail later – entrepreneurs pursue their maximization of profits, and to achieve it, they have to work out the supply price and the demand price corresponding to each level of production and employment as accurately as they can. For the system, that imperfect knowledge of the future is simply just another datum.

In line with the Marshallian tradition concerning expectations, Keynes differentiates long-term expectations, where revenue is estimated by taking into account the impact of planned "additions" to capital equipment on costs, from short-term expectations, which exclude all changes to productive equipment. As has been said, whether expectations come true or not does not have any bearing on the problem itself.

Past expectations play, no doubt, a key role in the formation of present expectations. It could be argued that when forming current expectations, entrepreneurs take into account the success or failure of past expectations.

However, whether fulfilled or not, past expectations are reflected in the current state of capital equipment and in the current stock, since if calculations were wrong and production was excessive, then stocks must have grown. Therefore, to make a decision concerning the volume of production it is enough to take into account entrepreneurs' expectations regarding future sales and costs, together with the currently available capital equipment:

> Nevertheless past expectations, which have not yet worked themselves out, are embodied in the to – day's capital equipment with reference to which the entrepreneur has to make to – day's decisions, and only influence his decisions in so far as they are so embodied. It follows, therefore, that, in spite of the above, to – day's employment can be correctly described as being governed by to – day's expectations taken in conjunction with to – day's capital equipment.
>
> (Keynes, 1939 [1936]: 50; II.5.II)

What is the impact if expectations concerning either costs or sales are mistaken? These mistakes in predictions only matter inasmuch as they affect entrepreneurs' decisions regarding the current volume of employment. It is usually argued that flawed expectations will result in an involuntary accumulation or depletion of stocks.[4] Therefore, variation in the stock of unsold commodities would be an accurate indicator that could even replace expectations themselves; it would be like feeling the pulse of production. Keynes, however, rejects this resource because, even though simplifying the analysis, it does so at the expense of overlooking other relevant elements. Besides, as has already been said, his study does not focus on the adjustment process but on short-term equilibrium.

> Mr. Hawtrey regards the daily decisions of entrepreneurs concerning their scale of output as being varied from the scale of the previous day

by reference to the changes on their stock of unsold goods. Certainly, in the case of consumption goods, this plays an important part in their decisions. Buy I see no object in excluding the play of other factors on their decisions; and I prefer, therefore, to emphasize the total change of effective demand and not merely that part of the change in effective demand which reflects the increase or decrease of unsold stocks in the previous period. Moreover, in the case of fixed capital, the increase or decrease of unused capacity corresponds to the increase or decrease in unsold stocks in its effect on decisions to produce; and I do not see how Mr. Hawtrey's method can handle this at least equally important factor.

(Keynes, 1939 [1936]: 76; II.7.II)

To make their decisions concerning the volume of labor they will hire, entrepreneurs take into account their expectation regarding aggregate demand as a whole.

The results of a mistake will not only be reflected in stock variation. Let's assume, for example, that entrepreneurs expect sales to increase in the following period and increase, consequently, their current production, thus incurring higher costs. If demand *as a whole* is then below expectations, the entrepreneurs will suffer a loss, not only regarding consumption goods, but also on account of unused capacity. In brief, demand does not depend on supply. Later it will be seen that transitorily increased proceeds due to failed expectations may affect consumption, but not investment. Thus, finally, employment will recover its earlier level of equilibrium. This is what happens when expectations fail to be fulfilled.

Thus the proceeds realised from the increased output will disappoint the entrepreneurs and employment will fall back again to its previous figure [. . .] For if entrepreneurs offer employment on a scale which, if they could sell their output at the expected price, would provide the public with incomes out of which they would save more than the amount of current investment, entrepreneurs are bound to make a loss equal to the difference [. . .] At the best, the date of their disappointment can only be delayed for the interval during which their own investment in increased working capital is filling the gap.

(Keynes, 1939 [1936]: 261; V.19.II)

To understand the factors that determine the level of current employment, it is enough to take into consideration current expectations regarding the price of supply and the price of demand; the levels of expected profit for each employment volume are thus obtained. In fact, the key variable is not the level of stock but profit, which is the value that entrepreneurs wish to maximize and, therefore, the magnitude on which they base their production decisions. Next, we will briefly examine the problem of benefit determination.

General theory of wage and profit

The choice of the volume of production and employment is based on entrepreneurs' perceptions of their expected amount of profit. Actually, they hire in each period the volume of labor that maximizes their expected future profits. In this sense, *The General Theory* is similar to Marshall's explanation for one branch of production, but is also close to what Keynes had already explored in his *Treatise on Money*, where a higher than normal level of profit promoted production, while a profit below that level resulted in a decrease in production.[5]

The *Treatise's* explanation failed because, as was previously mentioned, all the construction rested on the assumption that the level of employment was given. In *The General Theory*, "disequilibriums" in profits – extraordinary profits – are not studied; all the analysis focuses on the maximization of current profit and on its equilibrium level, which results in a variable level of employment during each period. In spite of these differences (given and variable employment, profit equilibrium vs. disequilibrium), as in the *Treatise*, the key variable that entrepreneurs observe and estimate when setting the volume of production is also in this case expected profit.

The determination of profit in Keynes's system should therefore be studied, an aspect also neglected by the mainstream macroeconomics that came later.

To better understand the question of profits, it is helpful to study first the case of an individual firm. The benefit obtained by an entrepreneur is nothing but the difference between sales revenues and the total costs which he has to incur when hiring a certain volume of employment.[6] Although apparently obvious and indistinguishable from that put forth by classical economics, this definition differs from the latter in its analysis of costs. In the short term, the cost of equipment use has to be added to factors' cost. The latter encompasses the cost of inputs purchased from other entrepreneurs, but also the loss of value experienced by equipment, as a result of its use in the productive process.[7] An individual entrepreneur will define a volume of employment such that he may obtain a maximum difference between revenue and costs:

> The entrepreneur's profit thus defined is, as it should be, the quantity which he endeavours to maximise when he is deciding what amount of employment to offer.
>
> (Keynes, 1939 [1936]: 23; I.3.I)

If this is the behavior of an individual entrepreneur, when production as a whole is considered, the same conclusion is arrived at: the equilibrium level of employment is reached at the position where entrepreneurs as a whole expect to obtain maximum profit

> [I]n a given situation of technique, resources and factor cost per unit of employment, the amount of employment, both in each individual firm and industry and in the aggregate, depends on the amount of the proceeds which the entrepreneurs expect to receive from the corresponding output. For entrepreneurs will endeavour to fix the amount of employment at the level which they expect to maximise the excess of the proceeds over the factor cost.
>
> (Keynes 1939 [1936]: 24–25; I.3.I)

At that point, and only at that point, entrepreneurs will not be ready to hire more labor than what their expectations concerning profits prescribe. When the demand price – their expected sales revenue – is lower than the supply price, that is, than the costs of the factors, they will be encouraged to reduce output, because that level of employment does not correspond to maximum profit. If, on the contrary, expected sales exceed the supply price, they will decide to produce a higher amount. Keynes states that entrepreneurs will increase employment and production until they hit the limit set by demand, and that this will also be the point where maximum profit will be obtained.

Upon closer inspection, this statement reveals the tacit hypothesis on which it rests. Production "stops" at the point where supply price reaches the level of effective demand, because at a higher level, sales fall beneath supply price, and profits decrease. The inverse of such a proposition implies that entrepreneurs are willing to increase employment as long as there is greater demand. However, to hold that the economic process works in this way, it is necessary to show that profits increase whenever the level of employment increases.

Only in such a circumstance will entrepreneurs increase the level of employment and production until demand is exhausted. If it were not so, then the effective demand would set a maximum level of employment, but entrepreneurs might prefer a lower volume of employment, both assuming that profits remained constant or that benefits decreased at some point before that limit. This is why Keynes has to demonstrate that "real" profit grows concomitantly with an increase in production, acting as a spur for entrepreneurs, who will increase employment, provided that expected sales cover aggregate costs.

Keynes's construct, actually, rests on this hypothesis: profits increase *pari pasu* with employment. This is the reason why entrepreneurs are ready to increase production and employment as long as there is enough demand.

For if they cannot sell output, profits are affected. In fact, profits are the real engine of production. For this reason, in Keynes's system, the results promised by Say's Law can also be obtained by merely matching the function of aggregate supply and the function of aggregate demand at all their points. Under these unreal circumstances, goods would always be sold on the market; the price of global supply is equal to the price of global demand for any level of employment. Now, even though supply would equal demand at all points, entrepreneurs would only have incentives to keep raising employment when profits increase in the short term. The limit is reached only when the real wage – equal to productivity – is so low that nobody wishes to work. When aggregate supply matches aggregate demand, the only genuine equilibrium is at full employment, because profits reach their maximum level at that point.

> That is to say, effective demand, instead of having a unique equilibrium value, is an infinite range of values all equally admissible; and the amount of employment is indeterminate except in so far as the marginal disutility of labour sets an upper limit.
>
> (Keynes, 1939 [1936]: 26; I.3.I)

When, as Keynes holds, aggregate demand *intersects* aggregate supply at a single point, employment has a unique equilibrium value. But if, as the classicists assumed, Say's Law is fulfilled, supply and demand hit equilibrium at multiple points. Furthermore, the only stable equilibrium is conditioned by the depletion of resources, for if profit always increases, the behavior of producers will drive occupation until full employment is attained. In the classical system,

> competition between entrepreneurs would always lead to an expansion of employment up to the point at which the supply of output as a whole ceases to be elastic, i.e. where a further increase in the value of the effective demand will no longer be accompanied by any increase in output [. . .] Thus Say's law, that the aggregate demand price of output as a whole is equal to its aggregate supply price for all volumes of output, is equivalent to the proposition that there is no obstacle to full employment.
>
> (Keynes, 1939 [1936]: 26; I.3.I)

Keynes's system dismantles this mechanism: it is not always possible to sell all output so that the point of maximum profit does not coincide with that of full employment.

As employment increases, so does profit. How do wages behave? A new clue is now added to the movement of factors' income.

Sooner or later, the maximum limit to output and employment, wherein labor is no longer willing to work because real wage decreases as employment grows, is reached. Keynes's theory posits the opposite movement of real wage and real profit: when employment increases, real wage necessarily falls while real profit increases. In Keynes's system, variables in monetary terms, that is, nominal wage, nominal profit and the level of prices will adjust to fulfill this rule. If entrepreneurs are always willing to increase the level of employment until demand is depleted, real profit must grow along with employment. Real wage must diminish when output grows to reach a point where laborers are no longer willing to offer their hands. Keynes reaches these conclusions by applying classical theory. The assertion that real wages necessarily decrease as employment grows is based on the assumption of diminishing returns in the short term. The critique of the second postulate showed that labor does not have the power to set its real wage. The labor market is not, actually, a real market because supply and demand do not set "prices" as a result of their reciprocal action. Workers have no way of affecting real wage, which is inexorably linked with output's physical determinations: entrepreneurs as a whole will only hire laborers as long as their marginal retribution is lower than their marginal contribution. For each level of employment, there is only one determinate level of real wage: that where it equals the marginal product of labor. If in the short term, labor returns diminish with regards to output, in the short term the real wage will decrease as employment increases, and a relation ensuring these results will necessarily have to be established between nominal wages and prices.[8] This is the fundamental theory of real wage that Keynes's system puts forth.

> [W]ith a given organisation, equipment and technique, real wages and the volume of output (and hence of employment) are uniquely correlated, so that, in general, an increase in employment can only occur to the accompaniment of a decline in the rate of real wages. Thus I am not disputing this vital fact which the classical economists have (rightly) asserted as indefeasible. In a given state of organisation, equipment and technique, the real wage earned by a unit of labour has a unique (inverse) correlation with the volume of employment.
>
> (Keynes, 1939 [1936]: 17; I.2.VI)

Keynes remains strictly in the classical lane: for each level of employment, the marginal productivity of labor and the real wage are equal; both are decreasing relative to the volume of output:

> This is simply the obverse of the familiar proposition that industry is normally working subject to decreasing returns in the short period during which equipment etc. is assumed to be constant.
>
> (Keynes, 1939 [1936]: 17–18; I.2.V)

The difference from the classical view lies in the fact that for Keynes the level of employment is determined at the point where aggregate supply becomes equal to aggregate demand. With the level of employment set, real wage also becomes established. As returns in the short term are diminishing, real wage is doomed to fall. Nothing can be done in this connection by either laborers or capitalists. But this necessarily implies that as employment rises, the purchasing power of wages falls, and this movement is also inexorably accompanied by an increase in profits: "Thus if employment increases, then, in the short period, the reward per unit of labour in terms of wage – goods must, in general, decline and profits increase" (Keynes, 1939 [1936]: 17; I.2.V).

In the second chapter of *The General Theory*, Keynes states that there is an inverse relation between the real retribution of labor and entrepreneurs and provides a simple illustration. When output increases in a mono-product economy, if the real wage accompanies the diminishing evolution of productivity, the portion of the total output that goes to labor is reduced. Real wage falls for all workers, not just for the marginal worker, and profits rise. Therefore, entrepreneurs enjoy an increase in the proportion of wealth they receive in terms of goods.

Thus, a great leap is taken from the *classical theory* of profit.

Throughout his argument, Keynes calculates profit as a residual, and only a residual: the difference between sales price and production cost. For the *classical theory*, this explanation no doubt corresponds to the "enterprise", "trade-derived", "short-term" profit. For the classicists, capital is a production factor with diminishing returns, like labor, and the benefits of the "capitalist" class stem from there. Here, instead, any fall in real wage is reflected as a reduction in the amount of goods that workers as a group can purchase, which frees a portion of the product which is then appropriated by capitalists; this explanation is repeated throughout *The General Theory:*

> For, in the first place, the increase of employment will tend, owing to the effect of diminishing returns in the short period, to increase the proportion of aggregate income which accrues to the entrepreneurs.
> (Keynes, 1939 [1936]: 120–121; III.10.III)

The absence of capital as a factor of production finds its explanation in Keynes's fundamental conception of capital, which will be studied later in Chapter 5.

For the time being, the inverse relation between profits and wages allows us to infer the main characteristics of Keynes's theory of wage and prices measured in money. In a money economy (as opposed to the previous example), real wage is nothing but the quotient of money wage and the general level of prices. The evolution of nominal wage and prices has to jointly validate the first postulate of the *classical theory* of employment, which Keynes takes as his own.[9]

If not the level, at least the necessary relation that there must be between prices and wages can already be predicted, because, whenever employment rises, there has to occur a larger increase in prices than in money wages to have real wages reduced in consonance with entrepreneurs' decisions. Next we will study, therefore, the movement of nominal wages and the *general theory of prices*.

General theory of prices

Keynes's position regarding the determination of nominal wages differs from that of the classicists in that it introduces the effects of historical transformations upon variables. Negotiations between labor and entrepreneurs are embodied in "bargains" or general agreements that set the value of nominal wages by mutual consent. This is one of the system's independent variables. Its being "exogenous" does not imply, of course, that it cannot be modified or that its variations will not affect the economic system, but rather that its value does not result from the action of the economic causes depicted by the theory; its value, instead, seems to depend exclusively on the relative force of entrepreneurs and capitalists "*as determined by the bargains reached between employers and employed*" (Keynes, 1939 [1936]: 247; IV.18.I). Its value is given.[10]

In *The General Theory*, the nominal wage is an exogenous variable, so that there is no obstacle that may hinder the assessment of the behavior of the system's other variables assuming the nominal wage to be fixed independently of the level of employment. In fact, Keynes uses this resource to simplify the remainder of the exposition.

Something else may be said regarding the reasons why Keynes considers the nominal wage to be constant, an assumption that has, on the other hand, been responsible for countless misrepresentations by later literature. In direct opposition to the beliefs embodied in the *classical theory*, Keynes intends to prove the thesis that the nominal wage does not directly impact aggregate demand or, rather, that the movements of the nominal wage do not strengthen or weaken aggregate demand (one of the mechanisms of Say's Law). The classicists had considered wage rigidity primarily responsible for unemployment. Keynes is in a position to assume that wages do not move because their fluctuations do not *directly* impact aggregate demand and, through it, on employment, like the classicists tacitly assumed. The interpretations that make the fixed nominal wage the core of *The General Theory* are nothing but a veiled restoration of the *classical theory*, of its assumptions and its main conclusions:

> The argument [that Keynes refutes] simply is that a reduction in money–wages will *cet. par.* stimulate demand by diminishing the price of the

finished product, and will therefore increase output and employment up to the point where the reduction which labour has agreed to accept in its money – wages is just offset by the diminishing marginal efficiency of labour as output (from a given equipment) is increased.

(Keynes, 1939 [1936]: 257; V.19.I)

Assuming it to be fixed is Keynes's clever way of shifting the focus towards the real causes of unemployment. It is also because of the absence of a direct impact of the nominal wage on demand that the study of the consequences of a change in money wage (exogenous) can be postponed to the end of the exposition (specifically, Chapter 19 of *The General Theory*).

The adoption of a constant nominal wage in most of the exposition, however, does not stem from an intention to reflect the actual behavior of money wages.

The system may also be solved assuming any other nominal wage level or behavior. The assumption of a "rigid" nominal wage is not a necessary condition of Keynes's theory, and at the same time, neither does the fact that it be, for example, downwardly flexible disturb its fundamental result: equilibrium unemployment, which is clearly stated at the very beginning of *The General Theory*'s presentation, much to the doubtless surprise of those who have believed the statement that wage rigidity is the paradigmatic Keynesian cause of unemployment:

> [W]e shall assume that the money – wage and other factor costs are constant per unit of labour employed. But this simplification, with which we shall dispense later, is introduced solely to facilitate the exposition. The essential character of the argument is precisely the same whether or not money – wages, etc., are liable to change.
>
> (Keynes, 1939 [1936]: 27; I.3.II)

As Keynes argues, the assumption of fixed wages for any level of employment is fruitful for expository purposes, as it allows one to emphasize a key point in the theory. As employment rises, nearing the level of full employment, real wages must diminish to fulfill the first classical postulate endorsed by Keynes, that is, the equality between real wage and the diminishing productivity of labor. Money-wages do not exhibit any economic tendency to decrease (it will be seen that, in practice, the opposite is true) as output and employment increase, so that prices must increase to reconcile real wage with decreasing labor productivity. The *general theory of prices* has to discover the causes that bring about an increase in prices when employment rises and real wage falls, without resorting to the descending movement of money-wages.

The *classical theory* of employment assumed that the remedy for unemployment, conceived as an excess of supply in the labor market, entailed a fall in real wages that were directly determined by workers on the labor market, according to the second classical postulate. To this end, the second classical postulate tacitly assumed that labor had a power (which it in fact lacks) to fix its real wage.

> The second postulate flows from the idea that the real wages of labour depend on the wage bargains which labour makes with the entrepreneurs. It is admitted, of course, that the bargains are actually made in terms of money, and even that the real wages acceptable to labour are not altogether independent of what the corresponding money – wage happens to be. Nevertheless it is the money – wage thus arrived at which is held to determine the real wage. Thus the classical theory assumes that it is always open to labour to reduce its real wage by accepting a reduction in its money – wage.
>
> (Keynes, 1939 [1936]: 10–11; I.2.II)

But the second classical postulate has already been discarded. Labor can only influence the money-wage. Therefore, it is completely possible to make the extreme assumption that nominal wages remain unchanged or even rise when employment grows: thus, a representation is formed that is the exact opposite to that which the *classical theory* had devised, where real wages moved always in the same direction as nominal wages, as Keynes states.

The difference is that while for the classicists the value of the real wage is set by labor, for Keynes, the variable subject to bargaining is the money-wage, since the real wage is always subject to the marginal productivity rule: only one real wage corresponds to each level of employment. This is one of the issues on which Keynes's critique of Pigou's *Theory of Unemployment* focuses[11]:

> Thus Professor Pigou believes that in the long run unemployment can be cured by wage adjustments; whereas I maintain that the real wage (subject only to a minimum set by the marginal disutility of employment) is not primarily determined by 'wage adjustments' (though these may have repercussions) but by the other forces of the system.
>
> (Keynes, 1939 [1936]: 278; V.19a)

Those "other forces of the system" include, on one hand, the law that guarantees the equality between the real wage and the marginal productivity of labor, both under unemployment and the less frequent case of full employment. On the other hand, the price movements that keep such a relation at any (exogenous) level of money-wage.

The assumption that money-wages are constant, however, is at odds with the aim of developing a general theory, that is, a theory allowing for all possible equilibriums. In fact, as employment increases, real wage decreases;

in the end, a position will be reached where nobody will be willing to work at a wage equivalent to labor productivity, which will have reached a very low value. That is the level of occupation corresponding to full employment. What happens from then on in connection with money-wages? If demand keeps pushing entrepreneurs to produce more, labor will be in a position to demand higher wages. The assumption that nominal wages are fixed for all levels of employment cannot be held in the case of full employment, as once it is reached, money-wages will be modified, although real wage will not.

Assessing the reaction of wages in a full employment scenario, within the general framework, does not entail any difficulty whatsoever since, as has been mentioned, even though assuming the nominal wage to be constant renders the exposition simpler, the system will also be able to explain its changes, both under conditions of full employment (where the invariability of wages cannot continue to be held even as an assumption) and of unemployment. Although the system considers the wage-unit as a variable stemming from the "extra-economic" struggle between salaried workers and entrepreneurs, Keynes is aware that, in general, as employment increases, labor's bargaining leverage should be expected to increase, and the nominal wage to rise. Reciprocally, labor will be ready to more smoothly accept wage cuts – in money – when employment is falling. This trend, however, is not enough to define the level of nominal wage resulting from those negotiations.

What can be asserted, instead, by virtue of the technical law linking real wages to productivity, is that real wage will evolve inversely.

> It would be interesting to see the results of a statistical enquiry into the actual relationship between changes in money–wages and changes in real wages. In the case of a change peculiar to a particular industry one would expect the change in real wages to be in the same direction as the change in money–wages. But in the case of changes in the general level of wages, it will be found, I think, that the change in real wages associated with a change in money–wages, so far from being usually in the same direction, is almost always in the opposite direction. When money–wages are rising, that is to say, it will be found that real wages are falling; and when money–wages are falling, real wages are rising. This is because, in the short period, falling money–wages and rising real wages are each, for independent reasons, likely to accompany decreasing employment; labour being readier to accept wage–cuts when employment is falling off, yet real wages inevitably rising in the same circumstances on account of the increasing marginal return to a given capital equipment when output is diminished.
>
> (Keynes, 1939 [1936]: 10; I.2.II)

Although, for the sake of simplicity, Keynes assumes nominal wages to be fixed, he admits that there are tendencies that push it upwards as the level of employment rises: "When there is a change in employment, money-wages tend to change in the same direction as, but not in great disproportion to, the change in employment" (Keynes, 1939 [1936]: 251; IV.18.III).

However, not much can be said regarding the magnitude of these variations; ultimately, it is an exogenous variable. Anyway, in practice, these movements are not highly pronounced. Although the struggles of labor intensify when employment grows, their demands, according to Keynes, move within relatively strict limits. Otherwise, the system would become highly unstable:

> struggle for money–wages [. . .] is likely, as employment increases, to be intensified in each individual case both because the bargaining position of the worker is improved and because the diminished marginal utility of his wage and his improved financial margin make him readier to run risks. Yet, all the same, these motives will operate within limits, and workers will not seek a much greater money–wage when employment improves or allow a very great reduction rather than suffer any unemployment at all.
>
> (Keynes, 1939 [1936]: 252–253; IV.18.III)

Although frequently mentioned in a descriptive way in *The General Theory*, these "tendencies" are not turned into "laws" ruling the behavior of wage-units simply because the system has to be capable of studying the possibility that money-wages be also reduced in times of unemployment or at any time.

An authoritarian regime, says Keynes, could impose a brutal wage cut, "flexibilizing" labor claims, and *The General Theory* has to be capable of accounting also for the effects of such a policy. However, again, it is not a rule:

> To suppose that a flexible wage policy is a right and proper adjunct of a system which on the whole is one of *laissez – faire*, is the opposite of the truth. It is only in a highly authoritarian society, where sudden, substantial, all–round changes could be decreed that a flexible wage policy could function with success.
>
> (Keynes, 1939 [1936]: 269; V.19.III)

It is clear, therefore, that money-wages can rise, fall or remain constant as employment grows. Even Keynes examines the historical experience, which seems to support his hypothesis regarding the reverse behavior of real and nominal wages.

> Yet it might be a provisional assumption of a rigidity of money–wages, rather than of real wages, which would bring our theory nearest to the

facts. For example, money–wages in Great Britain during the turmoil and uncertainty and wide price fluctuations of the decade 1924–1934 were stable within a range of 6 per cent, whereas real wages fluctuated by more than 20 per cent. A theory cannot claim to be a *general* theory, unless it is applicable to the case where (or the range within which) money–wages are fixed, just as much as to any other case. Politicians are entitled to complain that money–wages *ought* to be highly flexible; but a theorist must be prepared to deal indifferently with either state of affairs. A scientific theory cannot require the facts to conform to its own assumptions.

(Keynes, 1939 [1936]: 276; IV.19a.III)

Let's now look at the most important question, that is, the theory of prices: if the system does not furnish elements to determine the exact value of money-wages but, at the same time, states that real wages should fall when output rises, this is simply because it is capable of explaining how prices move in accordance with that requirement. In short, nominal wage is an exogenous variable, but the level of prices is determined by the system, which has a *general theory of prices*.

Keynes undertakes to free the theory of prices from the double life to which the classicists sentenced it. To that end, he abandons the quantity theory, and offers an explanation of prices in line with the "general theory of value".

The following analysis registers my final escape from the confusions of the Quantity Theory, which once entangled me. I regard the price level as a whole as being determined in precisely the same way as individual prices; that is to say, under the influence of supply and demand. Technical conditions, the level of wages, the extent of unused capacity of plant and labour, and the state of markets and competition determine the supply conditions of individual products and of products as a whole. The decisions of entrepreneurs, which provide the incomes of individual producers and the decisions of those individuals as to the disposition of such incomes determine the demand conditions. And prices – both individual prices and the price-level – emerge as the resultant of these two factors. Money, and the quantity of money, are not direct influences at this stage of the proceedings. They have done their work at an earlier stage of the analysis.

(Keynes, 1939)

The innovation is evident: prices do not directly and proportionally vary with the quantity of money, but rather, as in the case of the nominal wage, their variations influence prices through their impact on aggregate demand.

This is the reason why the *general theory of prices* can be exposed regardless of changes in the quantity of money. Later we will explore how currency emission, considered a (exogenous) decision of the monetary authority, influences demand.

For the time being, it is necessary to figure out how the level of prices is determined at the resting point when aggregate supply equals aggregate demand. Prices result from the action of a set of factors, which can be perfectly understood in terms of the First Treatise's laws. The *general theory of prices* is a key part in the integration of the First and the Second Treatises to a system that describes a money economy subject to singular laws.

> In a single industry its particular price–level depends partly on the rate of remuneration of the factors of production which enter into its marginal cost, and partly on the scale of output. There is no reason to modify this conclusion when we pass to industry as a whole. The general price–level depends partly on the rate of remuneration of the factors of production which enter into marginal cost and partly on the scale of output as a whole, i.e. (taking equipment and technique as given) on the volume of employment.
>
> (Keynes, 1939 [1936]: 294; V.21.II)

This is the essence of the *general theory of prices:* they depend on the retribution of the factors and on the volume of employment. To ensure that labor productivity and real wages are equal, assuming a fixed nominal wage, Keynes has to demonstrate that prices increase as the level of employment increases.

Let's take a closer look at this explanation.

Nominal wages are a component of the marginal cost, so that an increase in the wage-unit translates directly into an increase in prices. Until this point, the reasoning is simple, but it does not solve the problem, since if this were the only factor affecting prices, and the relation between prices and nominal wages strictly proportional, it would not be possible to find the mechanism that guarantees that real wages will fall as employment grows. And, on the other hand, the assumption of a fixed nominal wage – extending it to include the nominal reward of the other factors of production – would damage the system's consistency. These problems are solved by including the second factor mentioned by Keynes: employment growth as a cause of price increase. This relation is supported by Keynes's hypothesis about short-term diminishing returns, because, therefore, regardless of the level of money-wages, the marginal unit cost will always tend to grow. Keynes lists a series of reasons why returns are effectively diminishing.

When there is equilibrium with unemployment, the level of occupation is such that there is a surplus of the capital equipment installed capacity.

That is, a part of the facilities, machines etc. are idle. If employment is then increased and labor does not demand a rise in wages, why do entrepreneurs' costs increase? Keynes answers: because resources are not homogeneous, swappable and identically efficient. If they were so, returns would be constant, and costs and prices should not rise.[12]

Labor's lack of homogeneity, in turn, results in workers' remuneration not being strictly proportional to their efficiency. As more workers are hired at the same nominal wage, the efficiency of the productive equipment diminishes (and this variation is not subsumed in the differences in wage scale).

The need to hire less efficient workers at the same wage results in an increase in the product unit laborcost, in spite of the fact that the wage-unit in general may not grow, that is "if the wage of a given grade of labourers is uniform irrespective of the efficiency of the individuals, we shall have rising labour-costs, irrespective of the efficiency of the equipment" (Keynes, 1939 [1936]: 299; V.21.IV). This is the first factor that accounts for diminishing productivity. But the non-homogeneity of the productive equipment should also be considered. If it were the case that, as employment grew, less efficient equipment was being used, unit costs would also tend to increase due to that circumstance: "if equipment is non-homogeneous and some part of it involves a greater prime cost per unit of output, we shall have increasing marginal prime costs over and above any increase due to increasing labour-costs" (loc. cit.).

The desired result is thus obtained. Given the previous clarifications, it may be said that the diminishing productivity drives unit costs upwards as employment increases, and that with them, normal prices of goods in general rise and, hence "in general, supply price will increase as output from a given equipment is increased. Thus increasing output will be associated with rising prices" (Keynes, 1939 [1936]: 300; V.21.IV).

The sources of increase in the general level of prices do not end there. The non-homogeneity of labor and capital considered so far assumed that entrepreneurs would find the necessary and required resources to increase output notwithstanding.

The difficulty in finding equally qualified workers made for an imperfectly elastic supply. But an even more extreme case may be considered: it could happen that a certain grade of worker or machine be completely depleted when a certain degree of progress in output growth is reached. Until this point, it seemed that the full employment of all resources was simultaneously reached, which does not seem to be plausible.

> [I]n general, the demand for some services and commodities will reach a level beyond which their supply is, for the time being, perfectly inelastic, whilst in other directions there is still a substantial surplus of resources without employment. Thus as output increases, a series of

'bottle–necks' will be successively reached, where the supply of particular commodities ceases to be elastic and their prices have to rise to whatever level is necessary to divert demand into other directions.

(Keynes, 1939 [1936]: 300; V.21.IV)

The bottlenecks that emerge in certain sectors as employment grows become another cause of rises in price, regardless of the money-wage level. The supply of certain factors is imperfectly elastic, but the supply of others becomes inelastic once certain level is reached, while in the case of others still, it is completely inelastic. Obviously, if enough time passes, any particular dearth may be supplied, particularly when equipment is concerned. This is why time plays a key role: a sudden considerable leap in aggregate demand may trigger many of these short-term bottlenecks.

These are the factors that trigger increases in costs and, therefore, in prices, regardless of changes in the wage-unit. This being said, the effects of the movement of the nominal wage may now be reconsidered. The money-wage is treated as an exogenous variable, defined as a result of the struggle between entrepreneurs and capitalists. Anyway, there is a "tendency" for nominal wages to rise when employment grows. Labor always seeks to raise wages, and, entrepreneurs, to reduce them. As employment grows, workers enjoy a greater bargaining power and are, furthermore, willing to raise the stakes. Entrepreneurs, in turn, get higher profits, are "doing better businesses" and, therefore, are more prone to grant pay increases.

However, the rate of increase may not be expected to be constant as employment grows.

To sum up: when employment rises, prices tend to increase more than the money-wage on account of diminishing returns. The fact that the other factors included in the marginal cost, that also receive a money reward, exhibit different supply rigidities and inelasticities could be considered as well. Keynes mentions the use marginal cost as the more relevant aspect to be taken into account.

It is thus demonstrated that the real wage tends to fall when employment and output grow. The *general theory of prices* explains the level of prices for any level of aggregate demand.

This implies that "we have in fact a condition of prices rising gradually as employment increases" (Keynes, 1939 [1936]: 296; V.21.III).

Only the behavior of prices with full employment remains to be examined. When a bottleneck emerged in a particular industry, the price of its product tended to rise, as the quantity could not be increased. At full employment, there is no surplus of labor at the current real wage. From that moment, if aggregate demand rises in terms of money, the nominal wage will have to be increased exactly in the same proportion to maintain the real wage at the level of the marginal productivity that corresponds to full employment. If wages would grow more rapidly than the level of prices, employment equilibrium would be found at a lower output point.

This is the only circumstance under which the phenomenon of "true inflation" or absolute inflation takes place. With full employment, any increase in effective demand results in the proportional increase of retribution of the factors, which in turn raises prices commensurately, until thus depleting the total amount of added aggregate demand. Therefore, in Keynes's view, true inflation only occurs with full employment, where employment cannot increase any further, even though the price of global demand may rise:

> When a further increase in the quantity of effective demand produces no further increase in output and entirely spends itself on an increase in the cost–unit fully proportionate to the increase in effective demand, we have reached a condition which might be appropriately designated as one of true inflation.
>
> (Keynes, 1939 [1936]: 303; V.21.V)

Apart from that extreme case, prices will grow whenever aggregate demand rises along with the level of employment. As long as there is idle capacity, sudden increases in prices may in fact occur due to the non-linear nature of money-wage increase; Keynes refers to these as positions of "semi-inflation".

In brief, assuming fixed nominal wages, price movement is subject to changes in demand. When the economy is in a situation of full employment, any increase in aggregate demand translates into an increase in factors' costs and an equal rise in prices. While there is unemployment, it could be said that an increase in aggregate demand in monetary terms will be "split" into three parts: "between the rise of prices, the rise of wages, and the volume of output and employment" (Keynes, 1939 [1936]: 298; V.21.IV).

Nominal wages are, therefore, exogenous proper, non-rigid, and in principle, their changes are supposed to impact directly on prices, since they modify money prime cost. From here follow some conclusions that are directly opposite to those of the classical system.

First, it may be seen that if the movements of nominal wages were violent, prices would generally experience strong fluctuations. However,

> workers will not seek a much greater money–wage when employment improves or allow a very great reduction rather than suffer any unemployment at all. But here again, whether or not this conclusion is plausible *a priori*, experience shows that some such psychological law must actually hold.
>
> (Keynes, 1939 [1936]: 253; IV.18.III)

Based on the connection between variables put forth by Keynes, it may be seen that the apparent "solution" to unemployment on which the classical system relied would not remedy the situation, but rather would worsen the difficulties:

> [I]f labour were to respond to conditions of gradually diminishing employment by offering its services at a gradually diminishing money–wage, this would not, as a rule, have the effect of reducing real wages and might even have the effect of increasing them, through its adverse influence on the volume of output. The chief result of this policy would be to cause a great instability of prices, so violent perhaps as to make business calculations futile in an economic society functioning after the manner of that in which we live.
>
> (Keynes, 1939 [1936]: 269; V.19.III)[13]

The classicists used to warn workers about the bleak consequences of their resistance to wage cuts; they even emphatically urged the government to intervene in order to make them see reason. If Keynes's explanation is considered valid, then it may be said that they were absolutely wrong. Not only is unemployment not reduced (at least directly through the adjustment of the labor market) thus, but prices will tend to massively fall, which apart from being a source of instability, will also disturb income distribution in various ways.

First, it cannot be assured that the fall of all wages will be harmonic, so that some groups of workers will be unfairly more damaged than others (op. cit.). Furthermore, by reducing prices the portion of real income appropriated by other factors whose remuneration has not been cut will increase. There will be a redistribution of income from capitalists and workers to rentiers, who have guaranteed fixed incomes in terms of money.

Deflation, at the same time, can arouse an unwarranted optimism among entrepreneurs; this positive effect for production may be offset by the resistance that workers would oppose when feeling the impact of impoverishment. But at the same time, deflation will have an impact on indebted entrepreneurs, raising the real burden of their obligations.

Through this expedient, the fall in wages will aggravate depression rather than alleviate it.[14]

> [T]he depressing influence on entrepreneurs of their greater burden of debt may partly offset any cheerful reactions from the reduction of wages. Indeed if the fall of wages and prices goes far, the embarrassment of those entrepreneurs who are heavily indebted may soon reach the point of insolvency, with severely adverse effects on investment. Moreover the effect of the lower price–level on the real burden of the

national debt and hence on taxation is likely to prove very adverse to business confidence.

(Keynes, 1939 [1936]: 264; V.19.II)

Keynes's system turns the fall of nominal wages that the *classical theory* universally prescribed as the best remedy to the problem of unemployment into a way of aggravating, not curing, the disease. Anyway, we will have to wait for the exposition on the factors that impact on aggregate demand to be able to evaluate all the effects of changes in money-wages.

From micro to macro

The previous exposition began with the discussion of how the volume of equilibrium employment is decided in the economy as a whole. From the very beginning, Keynes refuses to split the laws ruling the decision concerning employment in the individual firm from those governing the decision pertaining to the aggregate of firms: in both cases, the level of output and employment corresponds to the objective of maximizing benefits.

However, from a methodological point of view, there is no resort to aggregation. Once the amount of labor hours that will be used in the industry in general is known, how employment is distributed among individual firms has to be explained. To use current terms, this analytic step might be described as the pursuit of a "microeconomics" corresponding to "macroeconomics".

The supply function that the *classical theory* generally used – and uses – to study the behavior of individual firms represents the *amount of product measured in physical units* that an enterprise is willing to offer at each possible value of the unit price, obtaining maximum profit. Keynes points that a problem arises in connection with units of "*dubious quantitative character*". But the objection raised against the supply curve in the context of a money economy considered as a whole is more conclusive. The functions of ordinary supply of an individual firm or a particular good are built assuming that the output of the whole industry is fixed, because income is assumed to be constant when, in fact, the functions of individual supply are subject to change when the aggregate output is modified.

The same may be said about the demand functions employed by *classical theory* for each good, which assume a determinate level of aggregate income. If aggregate income changes, all demand curves will have to change.

The rejection of the traditional curves for supply and demand rests on the fact that they assume a given level of output and income, which renders them useless when trying to fit them within the framework of a system like the one put forth by Keynes, a system that, precisely, has managed to free itself from the assumption of a fixed level of employment.

> When, therefore, we are examining the response of individual industries to changes in *aggregate* employment, we are necessarily concerned, not with a single demand curve for each industry, in conjunction with a single supply curve, but with two families of such curves corresponding to different assumptions as to the aggregate employment. In the case of the employment function, however, the task of arriving at a function for industry as a whole which will reflect changes in employment as a whole is more practicable.
>
> (Keynes, 1939 [1936]: 281; V.20.I)

If the aggregate level of employment and output changes at a global level, something similar must surely be happening in each industry. A two-way street is thus created between the individual firm and output as a whole. So far, the function of aggregate supply, which univocally related product supply price to each possible level of employment, was used to describe the conditions of production. The inverse of that function linked the different levels of employment corresponding to each *product* value, measured in wage-units. That is the function of aggregate employment.

In equilibrium, the level of employment is such that the function of aggregate supply equals aggregate demand: that is the point of effective demand.

Assuming that the composition of output and demand remains constant across industries, it may be asserted that for each level of aggregate effective demand, there is a single proportion by which it is distributed – in the short term – among different industries.

To that aggregate level of demand corresponds a total volume of employment. The same may be said regarding each particular industry, where the function of employment for the individual industry determines the corresponding level of employment according to the portion of aggregate demand in wage-units distributed to the specific good produced by that industry. Thus, the function of employment for each industry determines the portion of total employment corresponding to each branch.

Adopting the assumption that there is a given distribution, the employment in each industry is uniquely determined at each level of aggregate demand.

In contrast to the functions of physical supply (in goods) generally used, the functions of employment for individual industries thus defined may be aggregated to obtain the function of employment for the industry as a whole. All of them rely on aggregate demand measured in wage-units, and are expressed as homogeneous labor hours.

These functions were developed assuming that any increase in aggregate demand would be distributed among different goods in the same proportion as it was originally distributed. Each industry would receive a fixed ratio, which would always be the same, of the wage-units devoted to expenditure. This assumption is very restrictive since, in the first place, when aggregate demand increases, purchases are not distributed among goods in the original proportion and secondly because the prices of the different goods will answer differently to the increase in demand. Demand employment elasticity varies by industry. Thus, if the increase in aggregate demand takes place in the least elastic branches, the total increase in employment will be less than if it had centered on those branches with higher employment elasticity.

The employment function exclusively considered demand size, but for a thorough treatment, the direction in which demand is channeled should also be taken into account. If demand aims at goods from industries with low employment elasticity, prices will rise and, with them, entrepreneurs' profits. Elasticity also depends on the size of the available stocks, as they make it possible to answer to an unexpected increase in demand.

It is evident that an analysis of this kind is not possible within the matrix of classical thinking for two reasons. First, the second postulate of the classical labor market rejects the possibility of an increase in expenditure measured in wage-units. If expenditure, and, with it, employment were to rise, a diminished labor productivity would drive real wages downwards. Workers should abandon their jobs to reconcile marginal disutility with the diminished real wage. Thus, following the *classical theory*, employment should decrease with each increase in expenditure.

But this is not all. With a fixed level of employment, any increase in money expenditure will translate into a proportional rise in nominal wages, so that the mere hypothesis that expenditure increases in terms of wage-units becomes nonsensical.

The clue discovered by Keynes regarding a connection between the employment generated by individual firms and output as a whole was abandoned, partly, because this approach sets aside the traditional tools of analysis employed by the classical school, that is, of what is known today as microeconomics.

II The determinants of aggregate demand

Introduction

As we have seen, with the purpose of provisionally exploring first some of the theoretical consequences that followed Keynes's breakup with Say's Law, it was assumed that the amount of aggregate demand was fixed and did not vary when employment changed. This "constant" demand function for all levels of employment made it possible to emphasize the main distinguishing trait of *The General Theory* as regards its practical outcomes:

if aggregate demand is insufficient, the system positions itself in an equilibrium situation with a level of employment lower than full employment, a situation in which there is a mass of workers willing to work, given that the real wage is higher than the marginal disutility of labor. The state of equilibrium with unemployment, as was proved, is attained by merely disassociating variations in aggregate demand and movements in aggregate supply, that is, disabling the mechanism of Say's Law.

Both when studying entrepreneurs' individual and joint actions, it was also pointed out that they decide the volume of employment they will hire with a sole objective in mind: obtaining the maximum expected profit. "Expected" because current decisions about employment volume have to take into account the likelihood of fulfillment of certain future events that are not known currently.

Now we have to turn to expectations referring to the different levels of aggregate demand that correspond to each level of employment, which had so far been considered to be of a fixed and arbitrary magnitude. For the purposes of the study of aggregate demand determinants, Keynes differentiates the portion of expenditure directed to *consumption* from that destined for *investment*. The roots of such division may be found in classical thinking; in fact, separating aggregate consumption expenditure from investment expenditure is not in the least original.

The expenditure in goods purchased by entrepreneurs to support the *productive* process are generally called "investment"; "consumption" is the expenditure in finished goods, that is, those which will not undergo any further commercial or manufacturing process. The use to which the goods are put is what turns them into consumption or investment goods, but different uses are also associated with two different groups of purchasers.

> Expenditure on consumption during any period must mean the value of goods sold to consumers during that period, which throws us back to the question of what is meant by a consumer–purchaser. Any reasonable definition of the line between consumer–purchasers and investor–purchasers will serve us equally well, provided that it is consistently applied. Such problem as there is, e.g. whether it is right to regard the purchase of a motor–car as a consumer–purchase and the purchase of a house as an investor–purchase, has been frequently discussed and I have nothing material to add to the discussion. [. . .] The criterion must obviously correspond to where we draw the line between the consumer and the entrepreneur.
>
> (Keynes, 1939 [1936]: 61–62; II.6.II)

Current investment is therefore defined as the total of mutual purchases made by entrepreneurs, although the "depletion" of capital equipment used during the corresponding period (which we have termed "use cost") should be discounted from that amount. The amount of expenditure not devoted to consumption, that is, investment is reflected on an equivalent increase in the value of capital equipment.[15] In *The General Theory*, the mandatory equality of the increase in the value of the productive equipment (investment) and savings is simply inferred from the accounting definition of both magnitudes: in a given period, the value of the product – the price of aggregate supply – is equal to expenditure – the price of demand – and the income of the community. Saving is the difference between total expenditure and consumption; investment is the difference between output total value and consumption goods value. Current saving must be equal to current investment, regardless of the fact that the decisions determining each of these magnitudes may be made by different groups of individuals whose actions are not jointly coordinated. This equality is imposed, so to speak, with the fierce need of an accounting identity, regardless of the will of individuals, so that, as Keynes states

> [T]he amount of saving is an outcome of the collective behaviour of individual consumers and the amount of investment of the collective behaviour of individual entrepreneurs, these two amounts are necessarily equal, since each of them is equal to the excess of income over consumption.
>
> (Keynes, 1939 [1936]: 63; II.6.II)

The now familiar split of aggregate expenditure into consumption and investment is one of the essential qualities of Keynes's system.[16] The function of aggregate demand has to depict the relation between changes in the level of employment and these two components of demand, so that to estimate the future expenditure associated with each level of employment it is necessary to calculate, on one hand, consumption and, on the other, investment. The convenience and the need to study independently the determination of each component of expenditure stems from the fact that the principles that rule them are essentially different, as the subjects who make the relevant decisions and the aims they pursue are also different.

The following exposition should, therefore, be split into two sections: the investigation of the determinants of consumption and of those of investment. The first matter may be briefly dealt with; it is a part of any economist's *conventional knowledge*, and there is not much to be added in this field. With the development of the controversy that followed the publication of *The General Theory*, the debate took other paths. When Keynes initiates the examination of the determinants of aggregate demand in *The General Theory's* Chapter 8, he states that his reflections on the characteristics of aggregate supply are not novel; it is demand that requires a more thorough enquiry as it concentrates most of the controversial aspects. In the current context, it might be appropriate to reverse the terms.

Keynesian macroeconomics has largely discarded the discussion of the supply function as has just been presented. At the same time, a part – although, it is true, only a part – of Keynes's explanation about consumption determinants has become part of the heritage that is ingrained in any present-day economist's common sense. However, much material pertaining to Keynes's analysis of the causes that determine the level of investment that was later discarded remains hidden. Important clues regarding the nature of capital and money are included there.

Aggregate consumption: Say's Law at 80 percent

From a strictly formal perspective, the evidence that the variations in the volume of employment that entail changes in the price of supply and income *do not produce by themselves*, necessarily, equivalent increases in aggregate demand is enough to rebut Say's Law. What cannot be denied, however, is that if the economy is experiencing a situation of unemployment, increases in income will bring about *some* increase in the demand considered as a whole. If both variations, in output and demand, were equal, Say's Law would recover its rule. Keynes, in turn, accepts that demand must increase when income rises, but first he restricts the direct relation between output and demand exclusively to consumption and, second, he states that only a portion of income increase is devoted to expanding consumption. In other words: briefly, the refutation of Say's Law rests on the fact that only one of the two components that together constitute total expenditure depends on the level of income, while the other, investment, does not bear any direct dependent relation with the expected level of output and employment. The order of determination, therefore, becomes the exact opposite of that put forth by the classicists: for them, demand adjusted always to the volume of output, which thus tended to increase with no other limit than full employment. In Keynes's system, once the amount of investment has been determined based on entrepreneur's expectations, the level of aggregate demand is obtained; together with aggregate supply, such level sets the level of equilibrium employment. Thus, the central conclusion of a theory of employment that has freed itself from Say's Law is reached:

> Since consumers will spend less than the increase in aggregate supply price when employment is increased, the increased employment will prove unprofitable unless there is an increase in investment to fill the gap.
> (Keynes, 1939 [1936]: 98; II.8.III)

Consumption depends on the level of employment, in contrast to investment, the other constituent of expenditure with which it makes up the expected aggregate demand. But, as will be seen, consumption absorbs only a portion of income, so that investment always has to absorb the unsold balance of the total amount produced. To hold this argument valid, it is crucial to demonstrate that there is always an unspent balance of income in excess of what the community decides to consume. Consumption increases and decreases when employment rises and falls. But consumption is never enough to place all output. If this point is proved, then the employment level of equilibrium and, therefore, the system's level of production come to rest on the investment decisions that entrepreneurs make based on their expectations.

Keynes intends to prove that aggregate consumption in terms of wage-units depends mainly of one variable in the short term: the level of income measured in wage units.[17] To a certain extent, this approach entails some risks for the argument deployed, since if it could be shown that all income is spent on consumption, the system would always be positioned at the level of full employment. This is why Keynes also has to prove that, due to a set of (at least in the short term) unalterable causes such as psychology, habit, customs, human nature, institutions, social practices – or whatever it might be – only a portion of current income is destined to the purchase of consumption goods, and not all of it.[18] Ultimately, the fact that aggregate present consumption absorbs only a – relatively stable – portion of current income can, according to Keynes, be empirically confirmed.[19]

Keynes argues that the main cause of variation in the volume of consumption is income variation, as he considers the subjective factors to be given. The functional relation among those variables is called propensity to consume (currently, consumption function). However, this is not the only variable that affects consumption decisions. It is important to mention the reasons put forward by Keynes to dismiss other sources of potential variation.

First, consumption seems to depend on real income rather than on money income. In the system, an individual's real income movements, in the short term, are approximately equal to those of income.

When the nominal wage is modified, consumption increases by the same proportion, provided that the other money-wages increase equally. This circumstance is also contemplated in the consumption function, which relates consumption and income as measured in wage units. However, this is just an approximation, as, first, on account of the diminishing returns, the income purchasing power in terms of goods will actually grow less than the purchasing power of labor units. This is the same as saying that real wage decreases when employment increases because prices grow higher than nominal wages.

Second, as has been pointed out, an increase in employment tends to modify income distribution: on one hand, the share of wage earners decreases while profits increase. But additionally, those profits undergo a redistribution: the proportion taken by entrepreneurs rises relative to what rentiers, who receive a fixed money income, get due to the increase in prices. With the qualifications just made, Keynes's marginal propensity to consume adequately reflects the influence of changes in wage-unit. It is not expressed in "real" (quantity of goods) terms due to the impossibility of aggregating the non-homogeneous goods already mentioned.

As the determining factor lies in changes in real rather than money income, it is also true that the decisions to consume are strongly dependent on income considered in net terms. However, this factor should be considered separately only when changes in net income are not concomitant to changes in gross income. As this is a particular case, it is not advisable to include it as part of the propensity to consume determining factors. However, that is not the case with unexpected losses in capital goods' money value (windfall losses), which impact wealth owners' propensity to consume. If Keynes does not include this argument in the consumption function either, it is because its relevance is minor, and because the system cannot contribute any information concerning this question. This category includes, for example, sudden obsolescence due to technical change. The weight of changes introduced in government's tax policy should also be considered, although, again, it is not sufficiently relevant to be included among the factors that determine the function. Apart from these three variables, Keynes studies another two that could be potential factors in the propensity to consume. Although Keynes mentions his motives to dismiss them, turning consumption into a function that depends exclusively on the level of income, the controversies that arose after the publication of *The General Theory* render the discussion of the influence of the rate of interests and future income on consumption particularly important.

Keynes admits that changes in the rate of discount through time, that is, the exchange ratio between present and future goods, affects the propensity to consume. Although this ratio should also include expected changes in future prices, as well as different kinds of risks that may modify the future purchasing power, this factor may be identified, *grosso modo*, with the rate of interest. The question is the following – do changes in the rate of interest decisively affect decisions concerning the amount of present consumption? An affirmative answer would imply the need to include the rate of interest among the factors of the propensity to consume. This is, no doubt, a sensitive issue as it is critical for most of the refutation of the *classical theory*. It should be remembered that in the classical market of capital there existed a savings function that was inversely dependent on the rate of interest, so that

for the classical theory of the rate of interest, which was based on the idea that the rate of interest was the factor which brought the supply and demand for savings into equilibrium, it was convenient to suppose that expenditure on consumption is *cet. par.* negatively sensitive to changes in the rate of interest, so that any rise in the rate of interest would appreciably diminish consumption.

(Keynes, 1939 [1936]: 98; II.8.III)

In fact, the classicists hold that savings depend on the rate of interest so that, necessarily, the level of consumption must also be tied to it. The relevance of this discussion cannot be exaggerated, as variations in the rate of interest and their effect on investment become a mechanism to keep Say's Law alive. The classical theory's argument is as follows: when the consumption demand with a given income decreases, saving then increases, triggering a fall in the rate of interest. When the rate of interest decreases, in turn, investment demand necessarily grows, according to the classical explanation. Therefore, any fall in consumption automatically tends to be offset by an increase in investment, and vice versa. Thus, the possibility that aggregate demand may weaken is excluded: consumption and investment behave as two plates on a balance scale – when one of them goes down, the other necessarily goes up, while the height of the axis remains fixed.

But does that relation actually exist? Is present consumption actually modified whenever the rate of interest changes? Keynes answer is negative. It is evident that marked fluctuations could lead to a change in consumption, but if the rate of interest decreases (or increases) by, say, a percentage point, there will not be a high number of people changing their living habits in the short term.[20]

It has long been recognised, however, that the total effect of changes in the rate of interest on the readiness to spend on present consumption is complex and uncertain, being dependent on conflicting tendencies, since some of the subjective motives towards saving will be more easily satisfied if the rate of interest rises, whilst others will be weakened. Over a long period substantial changes in the rate of interest probably tend to modify social habits considerably, thus affecting the subjective propensity to spend – though in which direction it would be hard to say, except in the light of actual experience. The usual type of short – period fluctuation in the rate of interest is not likely, however, to have much direct influence on spending either way.

(Keynes, 1939 [1936]: 93; III.8.II)

Therefore, the definition of the propensity to consume may disregard the rate of interest, at least as a direct determinant. Thus neglecting secondary influences (such as sudden changes in the value of assets caused by changes in the rate of interest), Keynes states:

the main conclusion suggested by experience is, I think, that the short – period influence of the rate of interest on individual spending out of a given income is secondary and relatively unimportant, except, perhaps, where unusually large changes are in question.

(Keynes, 1939 [1936]: 94; III.8.II)

The attack on the propensity to consume as defined by *The General Theory*, as has just been exposed, became one of the most treaded paths in the successive attempts to restore the *classical theory*. The first attempt is that which has just been mentioned – asserting that consumption depends negatively on the rate of interest, as in that way the classical explanation of the market of capital is restored in a single blow. The rate of interest comes to be once again the price that balances savings supply and capital demand, contrary to Keynes's objections.

Keynes brings attention to another variable that may also be considered relevant to the decision regarding the amount of present consumption: expectations concerning future income or, rather, the relation between present and future income. Accepting such a dependent relation would also be fatal for the explanation, since in that case it could not be asserted that when present income rises, consumption also grows, but by a smaller proportion.[21] Again, Keynes ponders and rejects this variable because he considers it insignificant, since while some individuals think that their incomes will grow, others will believe that their situation will head in the opposite direction, thus canceling the effect on average, that is

> whilst it may affect considerably a particular individual's propensity to consume, it is likely to average out for the community as a whole. Moreover, it is a matter about which there is, as a rule, too much uncertainty for it to exert much influence.
>
> (Keynes, 1939 [1936]: 95; III.8.II)

The effort made by Keynes to show that the volume of consumption depends almost exclusively on the level of present income is amply justified, since any explanation that considers consumption to be dependent on the rate of interest, on variables that are vague or alien to the system, or that reinforces the propensity to consume as employment falls, threatens Keynes's theory and thus restores Say's Law.[22] Keynes holds, then, that

> whilst the other factors are capable of varying (and this must not be forgotten), the aggregate income measured in terms of the wage – unit is, as a rule, the principal variable upon which the consumption – constituent of the aggregate demand function will depend.
>
> (Keynes, 1939 [1936]: 96; III.8.II)

Briefly, for Keynes, the propensity to consume is a function that exclusively depends on income (both measured in wage-units); this is the only relevant "objective factor". Now, it is necessary to quantitatively study the effect of income variations on consumption, that is, the *slope* of the propensity to consume (or consumption function), which can be called *marginal* propensity to consume. The subjective motives that lead people to consume only a part of their income are, according to Keynes, "Precaution, Foresight, Calculation, Improvement, Independence, Enterprise, Pride and Avarice" (Keynes, 1939 [1936]: 96; III.8.II). If people are willing to save on account of such motives, there are causes that drive governments, institutions, and business corporations to do the same: enterprise, liquidity, improvement, financial prudence (Keynes, 1939 [1936]: 96; III.8.II). The force of these psychological motives is considered to be given in the short term, so that the marginal propensity to consume is higher than 0 but lower than 1, and remains stable.

> [W]e take it as a fundamental psychological rule of any modern community that, when its real income is increased, it will not increase its consumption by an equal *absolute* amount, so that a greater absolute amount must be saved, unless a large and unusual change is occurring at the same time in other factors [. . .] This means that, if employment and hence aggregate income increase, *not all* the additional employment will be required to satisfy the needs of additional consumption.
>
> (Keynes, 1939 [1936]: 97; III.8.III)

Based on this material, it is possible to develop an account of the evolution of employment different from that stemming from *classical theory*. Entrepreneurs know that any increase in output and employment triggers an increase in consumption demand whose magnitude differs from that of the increase in output, so that investment demand must always fill the gap. The entire system therefore depends on current investment demand for employment to increase,

> given what we shall call the community's propensity to consume, the equilibrium level of employment, i.e. the level at which there is no inducement to employers as a whole either to expand or to contract employment, will depend on the amount of current investment.
>
> (Keynes, 1939 [1936]: 27; I.3.II)

Thus, the customary exposition of Keynesian theory in terms of the *investment multiplier* may be easily avoided: if the value of the marginal propensity to consume is known, it is possible to establish a definite relation between income expansion and investment increase. To complete the exposition of Keynes's system, the last step, that will be taken next, leads us to the study of the factors that influence investment volume.

Investment determination: marginal efficiency of capital

In Keynes's system, the order of causality chooses current investment as *causae causantes* of the level of employment, and equilibrium output as its *quaesitum*. Entrepreneurs define the volume of investment according to a set of motives that will be discussed next. Once the value of investment has been determined, it is possible to obtain the amount of aggregate demand based on the marginal propensity to consume – considered to be fixed in the short term; with this information, the level of equilibrium employment, which, according to the amount of demand, will be more or less distant from full employment, may be found.

Starting from a situation of equilibrium with unemployment, a variation in current investment causes an increase or decrease in employment, which has a multiplied effect on income. The system does not offer any practical means to substantially modify the marginal propensity to consume; therefore, economic fluctuations must mainly originate in the factors that affect investment. This is, then, the *causal sequence* of Keynes's system.

> An increase (or decrease) in the rate of investment will have to carry with it an increase (or decrease) in the rate of consumption; because the behaviour of the public is, in general, of such a character that they are only willing to widen (or narrow) the gap between their income and their consumption if their income is being increased (or diminished). That is to say, changes in the rate of consumption are, in general, in the same direction (though smaller in amount) as changes in the rate of income. The relation between the increment of consumption which has to accompany a given increment of saving is given by the marginal propensity to consume. The ratio, thus determined, between an increment of investment and the corresponding increment of aggregate income, both measured in wage-units, is given by the investment multiplier.
>
> (Keynes, 1939 [1936]: 248; IV.18.II)

Macroeconomics adopted – *grosso modo* – Keynes's explanation. However, as regards to investment determinants, the usual notion differs widely from that put forth by *The General Theory*. The more radical difference lies in the fact that contemporary macroeconomics discarded the concept of marginal efficiency of capital coined by Keynes to refer to the expected return on investment.

The concept of marginal efficiency represents Keynes's attempt to avoid the characterization of return on capital typical of the *classical theory;* on account of various reasons, it is crucial to the system laid out by *The General Theory*. However, it was completely absent during the subsequent debate. The *classical theory* holds that capital is a factor of production comparable to labor and that, therefore, it is always possible to calculate its marginal return in physical terms (equivalent to the partial derivative of the function of aggregate output).

According to the law of diminishing marginal productivity, the additional product decreases when the volume of capital in use increases. The rate of interest, in turn, is a component of this theory of capital, as it is nothing but the reward received by that productive factor for its services. It is inferred from there that, to maximize profits, enterprises incorporate new capital to production according to the curve for investment demand, negatively sloped relative to the rate of interest.[23]

But in *The General Theory*, marginal efficiency has nothing to do with the *physical* marginal product of capital goods. Neither is it equal to the benefit obtained by a firm corresponding to the employment of different volumes of capital. The marginal efficiency of capital is the expected return in money, stemming from the employment of a determinate capital asset. Capital goods are not homogeneous; consequently, Keynes never refers to capital volume as a whole, not even in the case of one enterprise. Nor does he believe it possible to quantify the marginal product of capital in terms of goods. Keynes distances himself so much from the classical conception of capital that he feels forced to devote an entire chapter of *The General Theory* to the study of the nature of capital. The conceptual debate about Keynes's understanding of capital will be part of our Chapter 5. For the time being, it is enough to recover Keynes's definition, altogether different from the classic one. Let's see.

When the entrepreneur decides to purchase a *certain* capital asset, he has to estimate the future monetary revenue he will obtain when selling the product in the production of which the relevant capital asset is involved, as well as the expenses associated with the same production process.

Such a calculation must consider the entire lifespan of the investment (like Keynes, we use the term "investment" in singular as a synonym for "capital equipment"). The difference between revenue and expenditure for each period are the annuities that the investment entitles to the holder. On the other hand, the capital equipment has a certain replacement cost, that is, a supply price that will enable the producer of the equipment to manufacture an additional unit, a price that depends on its cost of production that is also expressed in money. The marginal efficiency of the equipment is the discount rate that equals the present value of the expected benefits corresponding to an additional unit of equipment with its supply price. Each *particular type of equipment* – and not capital in general or aggregate capital – has its own marginal efficiency: an expected return rate linked to the commissioning of an additional unit of equipment.

Usually, the *classical theory* draws the curve for investment demand with a negative slope, as it assumes that capital has diminishing returns in physical terms. But Keynes may also draw a curve that links the marginal efficiency of each item of equipment with the total investment on that same item.

The so-called marginal efficiency curve is negatively sloped relative to the investment volume for two converging circumstances, linked to the influence of changes in investment on the market price of equipment, on one hand, and on the sale price of the product, on the other. But in contrast to the classical explanation, the inverse relation between the amount of investment and its return does not stem here from the physical productivity of capital itself, nor does this explanation link units of product with units of capital. The reasoning is as follows: when investment in a particular capital equipment increases, its supply price (the replacement cost) will rise due to the pressure exerted by demand on the producers of that equipment and, on the other hand, as the product obtained with its aid reaches the market in larger volumes, future revenue will fall on account of the pressure exerted by the growth of that product's supply on its price. Both factors contribute to reducing the return on new capital equipment when investment increases: the replacement cost rises, annuities decrease. The marginal efficiency curves for all capital equipment may be drawn. Each of them links a rate of marginal efficiency with the amount of investment on that equipment, but it is also possible to draw a new aggregate curve of capital marginal efficiency linking the investment volume to the general marginal efficiency rate (the highest of all). This will be the investment demand curve for the economy as a whole.

Entrepreneurs decide how much to invest at each moment by comparing capital marginal efficiency to the current market rate of interest. There is, therefore, an incentive to increase the amount of investment until there is no capital equipment whose marginal efficiency exceeds the rate of interest: in equilibrium, the marginal efficiency of capital becomes equal to the rate of interest. It should be noted that once the curve for the marginal efficiency of capital equipment is obtained, it is necessary to know the magnitude of the rate of interest (which must come from another source) to estimate the amount of investment. And even though in equilibrium the rate of interest always tends to equal capital marginal efficiency, the former is not linked to, or rather, does not result from, capital return. Another difference from the traditional approach resides in that the rate of interest is not used to estimate the future return on capital. In equilibrium, *ex definitione*, the supply price of each capital asset is equal to its demand price calculated as the current value of annuities discounted at the current rate of interest. The reason is that, in equilibrium, investment situates itself at the point where the marginal (diminishing) efficiency equals the rate of interest. Thus, Keynes managed to conceptually separate the return on capital from the interest rate, which comes from a different source. If they are treated as two different concepts, it is, naturally, because their form of determination is also different, so that

> neither the knowledge of an asset's prospective yield nor the knowledge of the marginal efficiency of the asset enables us to deduce either the rate of interest or the present value of the asset. We must ascertain the rate of interest from some other source, and only then can we value the asset by 'capitalising' its prospective yield.
>
> (Keynes, 1939 [1936]: 137; IV.11.I)

The concept of capital marginal efficiency is, no doubt, one of the most fundamental innovations of Keynes's system. Capital yield thus defined includes in its calculation not only the annuities obtained in the current period, but also expectations concerning the complete series of annuities that the equipment will yield throughout its lifespan. All the future economic conditions that may impact expected annuities thus become determinants of present investment.

At the end of Chapter 4, we will apply the causal sequence of Keynes's system to assess the effects of changes in exogenous variables on unknowns; it will then be seen that most of the consequences of the scenarios imagined by entrepreneurs when trying to foresee future events affect mainly the marginal efficiency of capital, and it is *only* through its changes that they modify the volume of current investment. The marginal efficiency of capital is the most sensitive factor in Keynes's entire system:

> It is important to understand the dependence of the marginal efficiency of a given stock of capital on changes in expectation, because it is chiefly this dependence which renders the marginal efficiency of capital subject to the somewhat violent fluctuations which are the explanation of the trade cycle.
>
> (Keynes, 1939 [1936]: 143; IV.11.III)

Contrary to the static character of the classical system, Keynes intends his system to be dynamic. Dynamics, for Keynes, is a conceptual question, not a simple procedure associated with more advanced mathematical instruments suitable for studying the progress of an economy in time. The system's dynamic, instead, lies in its ability to show how past and future effectively influence variable values in the present. Keynes seeks to make his system dynamic precisely by means of this resource: in the present decisions setting the level of investment, future yields, as expressed by the marginal efficiency of capital, are involved. Obviously, however, they can only be portrayed as expectations concerning the future level of the variables (in this case, annuities):

> It is by reason of the existence of durable equipment that the economic future is linked to the present. It is, therefore, consonant with, and agreeable to, our broad principles of thought, that the expectation of the future should affect the present through the demand price for durable equipment.
>
> (Keynes, 1939 [1936]: 146; IV.11.V)

On the other hand, by differentiating the rate of interest from the marginal efficiency of capital, it is possible to reflect how investment amount decisions are actually made in the new historical situation, which, as discussed *in extenso* in Chapter 3, depends on investors', and not on active entrepreneurs', perceptions. Investment becomes the result of the comparison between alternative uses of wealth, rather than being considered as the only channel through which savings flow. This new theory of investment differs from the classical one, where entrepreneurs increased their stock of capital by incorporating new equipment whose physical yield they knew with certainty. According to Keynes's explanation, when purchasing a capital asset (new or existing), it is necessary to factor in certain estimations regarding the evolution of the economy as a whole during a period that is as long as the expected lifespan of the investment. As investment is the cornerstone in employment determination: these calculations play a crucial role in determining the level of output. However, under the "individualistic capitalism of our times" (Keynes's times) no dedicated resources are devoted to the careful study of such a yield: the investors' class cannot undertake such a study because it is distanced from the production process, and it can only focus on prospective yields derived from the purchase and sale of titles to assets it does not manage, of whose actual yield it is unaware. Thus, the organized investment markets (where securities are traded) guide society's resources towards speculative short-term opportunities; the marginal efficiency is disassociated from the actual prospective yield of each investment.

> As the organisation of investment markets improves, the risk of the predominance of speculation does, however, increase. In one of the greatest investment markets in the world, namely, New York, the influence of speculation (in the above sense) is enormous. [. . .] This is only another way of saying that, when he purchases an investment, the American is attaching his hopes, not so much to its prospective yield, as to a favourable change in the conventional basis of valuation, i.e. that he is, in the above sense, a speculator. Speculators may do no harm as bubbles on a steady stream of enterprise. But the position is

serious when enterprise becomes the bubble on a whirlpool of speculation. When the capital development of a country becomes a by-product of the activities of a casino, the job is likely to be ill-done.

(Keynes, 1939 [1936]: 158–159; IV.12.VI)

Under such conditions, exaggerated fluctuations may be expected, which may be not grounded on the variation of the capital marginal efficiency and which instead measure prospective yields based on business estimations that are continuously being revaluated. As may be seen, according to Keynes, speculation in twentieth-century capitalism does not stem from the proliferation of certain "financial institutions", but from the fact that by concentrating, capital comes to be of such a magnitude that its ownership cannot be limited to just one individual and is, therefore, traded on the stock exchange: the source of instability is deeply rooted. On the other hand, investment lies in the hand of large masses of inexperienced and unknowledgeable investors, whose opinions on the future are as uncertain as they are capricious and unstable. An investor has no more elements to form his expectations than the market mood: far is the nature of the classical capital market assumed to be capable of equaling time preference and the physical yield of capital assets (Keynes will also base his distancing from this representation on conceptual grounds). At least, the marginal efficiency will have to be sensitive to these market mood changes, completely divorced from the actual business returns.

> This means, unfortunately, not only that slumps and depressions are exaggerated in degree, but that economic prosperity is excessively dependent on a political and social atmosphere which is congenial to the average business man. If the fear of a Labour Government or a New Deal depresses enterprise, this need not be the result either of a reasonable calculation or of a plot with political intent; it is the mere consequence of upsetting the delicate balance of spontaneous optimism. In estimating the prospects of investment, we must have regard, therefore, to the nerves and hysteria and even the digestions and reactions to the weather of those upon whose spontaneous activity it largely depends.
>
> (Keynes, 1939 [1936]: 162; IV.12.VII)

To complete the presentation of Keynes's system, the way in which the current rate of interest is set is the only topic that remains to be discussed.

General theory of the rate of interest

Another of Keynes's fundamental breaks with the *classical theory* takes place in the field of the explanation regarding the determinants of the rate of interest. The classical market of aggregate capital, where the rate of interest appeared as the "price" balancing supply and demand, rested on the assumption of a fixed income. By removing this assumption, evidently unsuitable for the analysis of the economy as a whole, the rate of interest became a variable that could not be determined by market parameters. But besides, the deeper theoretical problem of the double explanation of the rate of interest remained unresolved: the classical theory considered it a "real" phenomenon in the context of its theory of value and distribution, First Treatise, and a "monetary" phenomenon in the Second Treatise. The concept of marginal efficiency of capital that has just been introduced constitutes a crucial step in the reconciliation of the two treatises sought by Keynes with the purpose of composing a single system able to portray a money economy. The notion of marginal efficiency shows clearly that capital yield is altogether different from the rate of interest. Two substantial differences stand out. On one hand, the rate of interest may become a strictly monetary phenomenon. But additionally, while expectations concerning future revenues are factored in the calculation of the marginal efficiency, the rate of interest appears as an eminently current phenomenon, in the sense that at any moment, a current observable level of the rate of interest is established, even though the perception of the future that money holders have influences its determination, as will be later shown. The rate of interest depends on the present conditions of the money market, but the marginal efficiency of capital, on the other hand, incorporates a crucial estimation of prospective yields:

> Even the rate of interest is, virtually, a *current* phenomenon; and if we reduce the marginal efficiency of capital to the same status, we cut ourselves off from taking any direct account of the influence of the future in our analysis of the existing equilibrium.
>
> (Keynes, 1939 [1936]: 145–146; IV.11.V)

The *general theory of the rate of interest* definitively breaks away from classical tradition. In Keynes's 1939 preface for the French readers of *The General Theory*, this rupture is emphasized, a rupture that also entails a distancing from the theories put forward in the *Treatise*, still in line with Wicksell's ideas. The gist of the new argument is that the rate of interest must be considered to be the factor balancing the supply and demand of money, not of "free" (real) capital or of the credit market.

> Another feature, especially characteristic of this book, is the theory of the rate of interest. In recent times it has been held by many economists that the rate of current saving determined the supply of free capital, that the rate of current investment governed the demand for it, and that the rate of interest was, so to speak, the equilibrating price-factor

determined by the point of intersection of the supply curve of savings and the demand curve of investment. But if aggregate saving is necessarily and in all circumstances exactly equal to aggregate investment, it is evident that this explanation collapses. We have to search elsewhere for the solution. I find it in the idea that it is the function of the rate of interest to preserve equilibrium, not between the demand and the supply of new capital goods, but between the demand and the supply of money, that is to say between the demand for liquidity and the means of satisfying this demand. I am here returning to the doctrine of the older, pre-nineteenth century economists.

(Keynes, 1939)

The classical authors did not get along well with this split of the theory of the rate of interest into two, one associated with capital (First Treatise), the other linked to monetary factors (Second Treatise); they could not choose either one or the other, and again and again they encountered their inability to reconcile them, even dividing the same category into two, but unable to solve the real problem: the natural and market interest rate. Keynes frees himself and solves the problem through the conceptual separation of the marginal efficiency of capital and the purely monetary rate of interest.

The explanation of the rate of interest of monetary lineage has as its starting point the study of the options faced by an individual when willing to hoard his wealth instead of spending it. First, he has to determine the ratio of monetary income he will devote to consumption and, therefore, by subtraction, the proportion of savings. The marginal propensity to consume rules this first decision where, as has already been discussed, the rate of interest is not decisively involved. Let's take a closer look at what is implied in a decision to save: an individual saves today in order to consume in the future. He currently has an amount of wealth available, but he wants to defer his purchasing power to a future date. He therefore now has to make a new and different decision, independently of the previous one, not linked to the amount of his saving (which stems from the marginal propensity to consume and save out of a given income) but rather with the way how he wishes to store his purchasing power. The magnitude and the determination of the rate of interest have to do with this latter decision, not with the former.

The sequence is the following. The individual receives his income as money. Generally speaking, two different possible ways of keeping his wealth to spend it later are available to him. He can, on one hand, keep his money as cash in hand, that is, in a liquid form, immediately realizable; or he can, on the other, relinquish that immediate purchasing power to other individual against the promise of recovering it later with an increase with respect to the original amount. If he chooses the latter, he will receive a title recognizing his ownership of a "debt". Keynes generically refers to this kind of operation as the purchase of a debt – or a bond – to encompass the various existing options.[24] If in the future he needs that purchasing power to make it immediately effective, he will have to sell that debt title, and will receive in exchange its current price, which is ruled in turn by the current conditions of the debt (or bonds) market. If he keeps his money in cash, he will receive no additional amount as interest.

For now, based on this explanation, the rate of interest is no longer the amount an individual receives simply as a reward for deferring his consumption through an act of saving, and becomes instead an additional amount obtained, more specifically, for transitorily relinquishing immediate purchasing power, for parting with his money in cash. Interest is the reward obtained in exchange for transferring liquidity.

> It should be obvious that the rate of interest cannot be a return to saving or waiting as such. For if a man hoards his savings in cash, he earns no interest, though he saves just as much as before. On the contrary, the mere definition of the rate of interest tells us in so many words that the rate of interest is the reward for parting with liquidity for a specified period. For the rate of interest is, in itself; nothing more than the inverse proportion between a sum of money and what can be obtained for parting with control over the money in exchange for a debt for a stated period of time.
>
> (Keynes, 1939 [1936]: 167; IV.13.II)

Keynes's argument against the classicists is compelling: in fact, nobody would be willing to part with his money in cash with the purpose of hoarding his wealth if he did not receive a reward in exchange. It is not a mere reward but rather a payment for not consuming, more precisely, for not keeping that wealth as money and thereby relinquishing liquidity. The interest rate is defined as a percentage relation between the original price of the debt and the price at which that debt may be sold in a specified term. Once the future price of the debt has been established, the increase in its current market price is proportional to the reduction of the interest rate, so that

> the interest rate interest is, in itself, nothing more than the inverse proportion between a sum of money and what can be obtained for parting with control over the money in exchange for a debt for a stated period of time.
>
> (Keynes, 1939 [1936]: 167; IV.13.II)

Now, a nominal rate of interest can never be negative, as then all money owners would hoard it rather than part with it in exchange for less, so that whenever a debt is bought, an additional amount is received as interest after some time. However, seen in this light, the original question is modified: why would anyone wish to hoard his wealth as money in cash when he thus earns no interests – assuming that the risk of non-payment is equal in both cases – instead of lending it at an interest? And this being so, where does the desire originate to hoard money in cash? Keynes calls "speculation" the motive that leads individuals to hoard part of their wealth as money in cash, instead of turning it entirely into interest-accruing debt titles. He does so because the rational behavior of a saver compels him to always take into account the expected evolution of the value of the relevant titles, that is to say, to speculate. When an individual purchases a debt with the intention of preserving his wealth he must necessarily take into account his estimation of the future market price of that title. He must do this because if the market price of the debt decreased, his original purpose (preserving his wealth) would be frustrated: he would be purchasing a debt title at a certain price to sell it afterwards at a lower value. Furthermore, if the individual finds that the market price of the debt is currently higher than its future price, he will be better off keeping his money in cash to buy the title later once its price has fallen. But besides, it may be said that it is necessary to have differing perceptions concerning the future across individuals, since to have one sell a title and other purchase it, their views regarding the prospective price of the title must be opposite. Uncertainty concerning future values of the rate of interest (and therefore, of the future prices of debts) is a necessary condition to have some individuals keep the portion of wealth they want to hoard and not spend in liquid form. If the future prices of debt titles could be known beforehand, and they could not change without notice, there would be no reason to hoard wealth as money in cash.

> This necessary condition is the existence of *uncertainty* as to the future of the rate of interest, i.e. as to the complex of rates of interest for varying maturities which will rule at future dates. For if the rates of interest ruling at all future times could be foreseen with certainty, all future rates of interest could be inferred from the *present* rates of interest for debts of different maturities, which would be adjusted to the knowledge of the future rates.
>
> (Keynes, 1939 [1936]: 167; IV.13.II)

Although debt titles appear at first sight as the natural and most profitable way of keeping wealth, the fact that there is uncertainty regarding the future value of the rates of interest (and its inverse, the price of bonds) turns the money in cash into a suitable means to hoard. The money thus comes to play a role that the *classical theory* had denied it: storing purchasing power.

It should be remembered that the strongest argument in support of Say's Law and the "analogy" of the actual economy and a barter economy was precisely associated with the categorical rejection of that idea: in *classical theory*, money is merely a vehicle, a means, as according to that theory, commodities are actually purchased with commodities; no other source of money demand was therefore recognized except that entailed by money's role as a means of exchange.

For Keynes, instead, money is a form of "treasure". The connection between this conception and the fundamental theory of money will be discussed in Chapter 5.

Keynes calls "liquidity-preference" the desire to keep money in cash. So far, we have only discussed the role of the *speculative-motive* as a source of preference for liquidity. Whenever individuals' opinions regarding the current level of interest rates differs, a number of them will keep their money with the purpose of purchasing bonds at a later date. Obviously, it is not a question of speculating only in the sense of obtaining extraordinary profits; individuals keep their money as a rational way of saving when they expect the price of bonds to fall; this is the only way they can avert losses.

The "market" where the rate of interest is set works in the following way. At each particular moment, the individuals who expect a fall in debt prices (a rise in rates of interest) have reasons to keep their money in cash and to sell their debts. This group behaves with a "bearishness" attitude. Those who believe, instead, that debt prices will rise have an incentive to offer their money on loan today or to buy long-term debt. They exhibit an attitude of "bullishness". Bears, who want money in cash and are willing to sell bonds in the expectation that their price will later fall, negotiate with bulls, who are willing to purchase bonds parting with their money in cash in the belief that their prices will rise, ones pushing downwards, the others upwards, thus setting the price of bonds and their "reverse", the rate of interest. What is the form of the function of demand for money that serves as treasure? When the rate of interest increases, debt titles become cheaper, some bears become bulls and do not longer wish to hold cash, so that the liquidity-preference brought about by the speculative motive diminishes.

A function representing money holding with speculation purposes, dependent on the rate of interest, may be established. This curve will be negatively sloped: "there is a continuous curve relating changes in the demand for money to satisfy the speculative motive and changes in the rate of interest as given by changes in the prices of bonds and debts of various maturities" (Keynes, 1939 [1936]: 197; IV.15.I).

Expectations play, therefore, a leading role in the speculative demand for money. Keynes notes that there is no completely stable quantitative relation between the demand aimed at satisfying the speculative motive and the rate of interest, because, in any case, what drives the speculative demand is not the absolute level of the rate of interest but the difference between the market rate of interest and a level of the rate of interest deemed to be *safe*. Given a certain state of expectation, the public will consider a certain value safe and, every time the market rate falls under that level, there will be more bears and less bulls, so that speculative demand will tend to increase. When there is an organized market for the purchase and sale of debt titles (bonds) – as there is today – what is the safe value is defined on the basis of countless individuals' perceptions.

Therefore, according to Keynes, the demand for money is a highly psychological phenomenon. The amount of money required to satisfy the speculative motive thus depends on the relation between the current rate of interest and the state of expectations,

> Just as we found that the marginal efficiency of capital is fixed, not by the 'best' opinion, but by the market valuation as determined by mass psychology, so also expectations as to the future of the rate of interest as fixed by mass psychology have their reactions on liquidity-preference.
> (Keynes, 1939 [1936]: 170; IV.13.III)

Other motives leading the public to keep money in cash must be added to the preference for liquidity caused by the speculative motive. Here finally, the traditional sources of the demand for money emerge. Although the individual demand for money translates into a single amount, other reasons motivating it may be identified apart from "speculation". First, there is the *"transactions-motive"*.

A period elapses between the moment when income is collected and the moment when payments are made; it is necessary to hold cash in hand to bridge that interval. Something similar occurs in the case of enterprises, which need sufficient cash available to pay for their expenses until the moment when they sell their products. In both cases (individual or institutional transactions), the mass of money that should be held in cash depends largely on the level of income. The other cause that leads the public to keep money in cash is the *"precautionary-motive"*. A certain amount of cash is held to provide for contingencies, to take advantage of opportunities, and to meet future liabilities fixed in terms of money without running the risk of losing value. It is also true that the demand for money to satisfy these motives depends also on the cost of transitorily obtaining money when needed, a cost that may be assimilated to the rate of interest.

Modern "Keynesian" macroeconomics usually explains the relationship between the demand for money and the rate of interest through the so-called "opportunity cost" of money. Keynes himself admits that the need to hold money in cash also depends on the cost of bank deposits, and on the cost of entering and exiting the market, although he states that "it may be, however, that this is likely to be a minor factor except where large changes in the cost of holding cash are in question" (op. cit.). In all cases, the problem of the "cost of opportunity" of money is associated with the transaction and precautionary-motives. Thus, the modern explanation accepts the relationship between the holding of money and the rate of interest, overrating the problem of the "cost of money" that Keynes dismissed and neglecting, at the same time, the speculative-motive; thus, one of the main ways through which expectations (that is, dynamics) are included in the discussion is discarded. The struggle between "bears" and "bulls" that worried Keynes since the *Treatise* stops being the determinant of the rate of interest (Fischer et al, 1989). This is one of the points in connection with which the misrepresentation of Keynes's theory by his followers becomes more shameless, as this distinction motivated one of a few instances of the author's explicit complaint regarding the first interpretations of his contribution. The theory of interest, Keynes states, is not associated with the market of "loanable funds" but with the supply and demand of money for speculation, which is not the same. One is a case of hoarding wealth without a definite purpose; the other, instead, an instance of applying wealth to a productive end.[25]

However, in general, it is accurate to say that the demand for money to satisfy these two motives depends mainly on the general activity of the economic system, as expressed by the level of income, so that a function establishing that relation may be built.

Having exclusively examined the demand for (and not the supply of) money, some substantial differences from the classicists may already be pointed out. In the First Treatise, the *classical theory* conceived of money as a mere *numéraire* or price standard. Then, in the Second Treatise, it assigned money a new role – that of serving as a means of exchange or a means of circulation. When Keynes recognizes the role played by the interest rate in the demand for money he is recovering the role played by money as value deposit, as treasure, which the classicists had discarded. The classical concept of velocity of circulation or income velocity was meant to jointly represent all the elements that impacted the ratio of income held in cash, but excluded from that determination the current rate of interest. The opposition between such an explanation and Keynes's is decisive, since the income velocity may well portray the demand for money for transactions but never the speculative demand:

> the term 'income-velocity of money' carries with it the misleading suggestion of a presumption in favour of the demand for money as a whole being proportional, or having some determinate relation, to income, whereas this presumption should apply, as we shall see, only to a *portion* of the public's cash holdings; with the result that it overlooks the part played by the rate of interest.
>
> (Keynes, 1939 [1936]: 194; IV.15.I)

The omission is not minor. On one hand, the demand for money is always a fixed ratio of income in the *classical theory*. On the other, as has been mentioned, adding to this the assumption of a fixed output, the quantitative theory cannot conceive of a result of the increase in the quantity of money other than a proportional increase in prices.

So far, we have only reached halfway through the presentation of the general theory of the rate of interest. The variables intervening in the determination of the total demand for money are the level of income, which determines the demand for money on account of the transactions and speculation-motives, and the rate of interest, which reflects a balance in the struggle between bears and bulls. As may be seen, it is the presence of the speculation-motive that will not only open the door for the monetary determination of the rate of interest, but that will also, through its effects, make a tool available to the monetary authority to indirectly influence the level of employment.

> In normal circumstances the amount of money required to satisfy the transactions-motive and the precautionary-motive is mainly a resultant of the general activity of the economic system and of the level of money-income. But it is by playing on the speculative-motive that monetary management (or, in the absence of management, chance changes in the quantity of money) is brought to bear on the economic system.
> (Keynes, 1939 [1936]: 196–197; IV.15.I)

The other aspect that must be taken into account in connection with the determination of the interest rate is, therefore, the supply of money. One of the characteristic traits of Keynes's system is the fact that he includes in his causal sequence a fundamental aspect derived from the historical transformations that took place during the twentieth century: the abandonment of the gold standard, which enabled the government to unconditionally regulate the quantity of money. Money supply thus becomes an "exogenous" variable that depends on the government's will and whose volume cannot be explained as a result of the action of any economic force in the system.

The total amount of money that the government emits, M, must necessarily be divided between the two motives that push individuals to have a wish for money, that it, the total amount of M is distributed between $M1$ and $M2$, corresponding to the demand to satisfy the transactions and precautionary motives, and to the speculative demand to use money as a value deposit. The consequences of money emission on the rate of interest may now be studied. For each interest rate level, there is a $L2$ demanded amount of money stemming from the speculative-motive. Let's assume that the government decides to increase the quantity of money and that, initially, the level of income remains equal, so that transactions and precautionary demand do not change; and let's also assume that neither do expectations concerning future rates of interest. These assumptions that help us study changes in the rate of interest stemming from an increase in the quantity of money will later be eliminated. The money in excess of that required to satisfy the needs derived from these two motives cannot exit circulation, so that if an individual does not wish to hold money, he will have to keep it anyway or that money will have to be absorbed by the speculative-motive, which is exactly the same, until the increase in speculative demand is enough to equal the increase in supply. However, as nobody wishes to keep that new and larger amount of money in cash, a portion of it will be devoted to the purchase of bonds, so that the price of bonds will tend to rise. Some of the "bulls" that held their bonds awaiting for their price to rise will judge that their value has already increased too much, and will settle their positions in exchange of cash, thereby swelling the ranks of bears.

Thus, additional money is absorbed by the speculative demand, but bond prices change, so that the interest rate moves in the opposite direction. The new rate of interest is thus determined, being the "price" that balances bears' sales and bulls' purchases.[26] So the rate of interest reconciles the fixed supply of money and the differences in views concerning the future value of the rate of interest, given that such differences are the source of the speculative demand for money. To break from *classical theory*, the assumptions regarding the fixed level of income and unchanging expectations still have to be discarded.

The fact that the speculative demand for money has at its base the uncertainty concerning the future price of bonds turns the rate of interest into a "highly psychological" phenomenon, as has been mentioned. The curve for liquidity-preference to satisfy the speculative-motive is defined at each level of the rate of interest, if expectations are considered as given. A change in expectations – for example, due to changing perceptions regarding the future policy of the Central Bank or the government – may trigger violent modifications in the position and slope of the curve. For this reason, Keynes attributes liquidity-preference stability to the diversity in views. In fact, if there were a unanimous opinion on the adequacy of the monetary policy, the rate of interest and the price of bonds would change even though no transactions were performed on the market. Individual holdings of money would be identically distributed, but the rate would change, simply because the curve for liquidity-preference shifts when opinions change. If everybody had the same expectations, then bonds would not change hands.

> Thus, in the simplest case, where everyone is similar and similarly placed, a change in circumstances or expectations will not be capable of causing any displacement of money whatever; it will simply change the rate of interest in whatever degree is necessary to offset the desire of each individual, felt at the previous rate, to change his holding of

cash in response to the new circumstances or expectations; and, since everyone will change his ideas as to the rate which would induce him to alter his holdings of cash in the same degree, no transactions will result. To each set of circumstances and expectations there will correspond an appropriate rate of interest, and there will never be any question of anyone changing his usual holdings of cash.

(Keynes, 1939 [1936]: 198; IV.15.I)

Emission, however, does not affect exclusively the speculative-motive *L2*, although this is its direct effect. The increase in the supply of money implies a reduction of the interest rate. But, as has been shown, the interest rate was the missing element to complete the causation train that explains investment determination. A decrease in interest rate will generally bring about an increase in investment and, therefore, in aggregate demand and income (how this increase is split, in turn, into an increase in output and employment, and an increase in prices has already been discussed). When analyzing the indirect effects of changes in the quantity of money *M*, it is possible to conceive of a situation where money demand might inversely react to changes in the rate of interest, whereas investment and income grow, and transaction needs increase. To this, the fact that the "cost" of holding money, expressed as a loss of interest, will decrease along with the rate of interest must also be taken into account.

Thus, the curve that represents the total demand for money must be negatively sloped relative to the rate of interest. The supply of money, in turn, is defined by the monetary authority. Changes in the amount of money affect the rate of interest; the latter, in turn, is involved in the determination of investment and, therefore, of employment. By including the rate of interest in the system, a complete picture of the workings of a monetary economy is formed; in such an economy the emission of money impacts the level of equilibrium employment through a definite causal sequence that is missing in the *classical theory:* "We have now introduced money into our causal nexus for the first time, and we are able to catch a first glimpse of the way in which changes in the quantity of money work their way into the economic system" (Keynes, 1939 [1936]: 173; IV.13.III).

The general theory of the rate of interest is the last station in the complete presentation of Keynes's system. In the next section, we will briefly consider some of the effects brought about by changes in the independent variables on the system's unknowns. Before leaving this field, however, we should mention the significant changes this causal sequence introduces in the classical conception of money.

Keynes's theory of the rate of interest focuses on money supply and demand movements. Return on capital is subsumed in the marginal efficiency of capital. Marshall and the classicists in general failed to offer a single explanation for interest, lost as they were in an ocean of various and vague contradictory definitions. Keynes believes to have unraveled the secret, but the new explanation leads him to singular reflections: the confusion between the phenomena of "return" and "interest" must be hiding a deeper confusion between the categories of "capital" and "money". When Keynes analyzes Marshall's passages, he is forced to distinguish between concepts that are in fact different but that in the classical tradition are synthesized as single categories.

> It is to be noticed that Marshall uses the word "capital" and not "money" and the word "stock" and not "loans"; yet interest is a payable for borrowing *money*, and "demand for capital" in this context should mean "demand for loans and money for the purpose of buying a stock of capital-goods". But the equality between the stock of capital-goods offered and the stock demanded will be brought about by the *prices* of capital-goods, not by the rate of interest. It is equality between the demand and supply of loans of money *i.e.* of debts, which is brought about by the rate of interest.
>
> (Keynes, 1939 [1936]: 186; IV.14a.I)

From this perspective, the new question posed by Keynes may be stated simply. Money can create interest; capital, in turn, yields a profit for his owner. Well then, if the factors governing return on capital and money's rate of interest are different, their sources must also be different. In other words, capital and money are two different things. What is the nature of money, on one hand, and of capital, on the other, if both have the capacity to produce more than their original value? Why is the future price of a debt higher than its current price, and why does the sum of the annuities of a capital good exceed its replacement cost? In Chapter 5, the answers Keynes offers to these questions will be examined.

III Keynes's complete system

Brief presentation of Keynes's system: why does Keynes prefer changes in the quantity of money over wage cuts?

Finally, all the elements composing Keynes's *system* may be gathered, establishing the causal order that links the relevant phenomena to obtain the always determined value of the main dependent variable, his *quaesitum*: the equilibrium level of employment, a level of employment that will be stable, but that, notwithstanding, will not necessarily coincide with full employment.

Keynes is aware that apart from the relations that he stresses as being primary, there is another series of complex links among relevant phenomena.

However, he postpones the study of the multiple secondary mutual repercussions among factors for an analytical "second round". The method he argues for is characterized by its capacity to represent a clear cause-effect sequence.

First, a set of determining elements is isolated, and a determinate causation relationship is established among them. An equilibrium point is thus obtained that includes in its determination the most significant relations. This first simple arrangement allows the economist to picture a "structure" that threads the different relevant factors. But the equilibrium thus obtained needs further review, on account of the changes brought about by the modifications in the value of the dependent variables. The sequential method must consider the results of these different and successive iterations.

Let's remember that the process is purely analytical, a way of reasoning that does not pretend to reflect the evolution of the system in time.

> Thus the position of equilibrium will be influenced by these repercussions; and there are other repercussions also. Moreover, there is not one of the above factors which is not liable to change without much warning, and sometimes substantially. Hence the extreme complexity of the actual course of events. Nevertheless, these seem to be the factors which it is useful and convenient to isolate. If we examine any actual problem along the lines of the above schematism, we shall find it more manageable; and our practical intuition (which can take account of a more detailed complex of facts than can be treated on general principles) will be offered a less intractable material upon which to work.
>
> (Keynes, 1939 [1936]: 249; IV.18.II)

The method used to represent the system differs substantially from the mathematical method of general equilibrium. It is true that a sequential iterative method may result in the exclusion of certain repercussions, while the method of the general equilibrium guarantees, through algebraic expression, that all the direct and indirect relations be factored in the result. However, this method of simultaneous resolution hides to a certain extent the economic reasoning underlying the "beauty" of its mathematic consistency. No cross-influence can be overlooked when the system is articulated by means of a system of equations with the same number of equations and unknowns. The system may be solved thoroughly and completely, but at the expense of dissolving the more relevant causal relations by assuming that all connections have equal hierarchy, that is, the hierarchy of an equation that must be verified in equilibrium.

Keynes's criticism of previous attempts, such as Pigou's, at providing a mathematical explanation for complex economic problems is largely methodological: he denounces that method as "pseudo-mathematical" and "non-causal":

> The object of our analysis is, not to provide a machine, or method of blind manipulation, which will furnish an infallible answer, but to provide ourselves with an organised and orderly method of thinking out particular problems; and, after we have reached a provisional conclusion by isolating the complicating factors one by one, we then have to go back on ourselves and allow, as well as we can, for the probable interactions of the factors amongst themselves.
>
> (Keynes, 1939 [1936]: 297; V.21.III)

Next we will summarize what might be considered the backbone of Keynes's system.

The most relevant factors have already been identified; among them, it is necessary to specify those that are considered fixed in the short term. Obviously, this does not mean that they are immutable, but rather that for the analytical period considered it is convenient to take them as given. The method is, ultimately, the same suggested by Marshall to analytically differentiate the short and the long term. The system is meant to investigate the causes of unemployment in the context of given equipments of capital and labor, that is, in the short term.

> We take as given the existing skill and quantity of available labour, the existing quality and quantity of available equipment, the existing technique, the degree of competition, the tastes and habits of the consumer, the disutility of different intensities of labour and of the activities of supervision and organisation, as well as the social structure including the forces, other than our variables set forth below, which determine the distribution of the national income.
>
> (Keynes, 1939 [1936]: 245; IV.18.I)

With these elements, it is possible to establish the curve for aggregate supply in terms of wage-units, which depends on the physical conditions of production since a single volume of income measured in terms of the wage-unit corresponds to each level of employment. The employment function corresponding to each industry may also be defined, which will show how total employment is distributed among different branches once the equilibrium employment level has been established.

An equivalent to the labor supply curve linking the desire to work and the real wage may also be known – the only relevant point is that where no worker is willing to work because the wage is excessively low. That is the level of employment that corresponds to full employment, where the employment function as a whole is no longer elastic.

This is what is known about the function of supply and of employment as a whole, considered virtually fixed in the short term. The point where the function of aggregate supply intersects the function of aggregate demand will set the equilibrium level of employment. With the objective of maximizing profit, entrepreneurs offer a certain amount of employment, bearing in mind their expectations concerning the level of aggregate demand that corresponds to each level of employment. It is in the determination of aggregate demand where the independent variables of the system are largely involved.

> [W]e can sometimes regard our ultimate independent variables as consisting of (i) the three fundamental psychological factors, namely, the psychological propensity to consume, the psychological attitude to liquidity and the psychological expectation of future yield from capital-assets, (2) the wage-unit as determined by the bargains reached between employers and employed, and (3) the quantity of money as determined by the action of the central bank; so that, if we take as given the factors specified above, these variables determine the national income (or dividend) and the quantity of employment. But these again would be capable of being subjected to further analysis, and are not, so to speak, our ultimate atomic independent elements.
>
> (Keynes, 1939 [1936]: 246–247; IV.18.I)

Keynes calls the variables grouped under (1) above "psychological" because they depend on individuals' will or habits.

A further classification derived from the previous explanation may be also offered. The first of these variables, the marginal propensity to consume, is not subject to strong fluctuations in the short term. However, the other two, the marginal efficiency of capital and the liquidity-preference, strongly rely on the state of expectations, as has been seen, thus becoming a link between present and future, thereby granting a dynamic (in Keynes's sense) character to the system.

The other two independent variables included should be considered "extra-economic", given that their value comes from decisions and processes that the system cannot reflect by means of "laws". They could also be called "political" variables, which would be accurate only to a certain extent, as the wage-unit results from the struggle between labor and entrepreneurs, and the quantity of money is determined by the economic authority. Both are considered exogenous on account of the essentially historical reasons discussed in Chapter 2.

We have so far introduced all the independent variables and the given factors. Finally, the dependent variables, whose values result from the cause-effect relations in the system, are investment and consumption, the two building blocks of aggregate demand.

Once aggregate demand is known, the level of income and, therefore, the equilibrium supply price will also be known, which leads us via a direct path to the level of employment, Keynes's *quaesitum*.

> [T]he given factors allow us to infer what level of national income measured in terms of the wage-unit will correspond to any given level of employment; so that, within the economic framework which we take as given, the national income depends on the volume of employment, i.e. on the quantity of effort currently devoted to production, in the sense that there is a unique correlation between the two.
>
> (Keynes, 1939 [1936]: 246; IV.18.I)

The system's equilibrium is reached at the point where the functions of aggregate supply and aggregate demand measured in terms of the wage-unit become equal. Thus, by knowing the value of the wage-unit, determined by the struggle between labor and capitalists, the corresponding level of prices is obtained.

Next, the logical steps that reflect the causal relations embodied in the argument are listed, thus establishing the "analytical" order in which variables are determined. The factors determining the value of each variable are shown between brackets, both those originating outside the causal sequence (exogenous variables) and those that result from a previous or later step in the causal sequence (endogenous variables).

Step 1: The rate of interest is set at the level where the *current supply of money* [exogenous: defined by government] equals the *liquidity-preference* [psychological: expectations concerning future rates and level of employment (step 5)].

Step 2: The amount of new *investment* is defined at the point where the *marginal efficiency of capital* [psychological: expectations concerning future yields] equals the *rate of interest* (step 1).

Step 3: Income will increase or decrease according to the magnitude of the *marginal propensity to consume* [psychological: society's habits; fixed in the short term] that determines the investment *multiplier* (step 2).

Step 4: A level of *aggregate demand* is thus determined, equal to the addition of *investment* (step 2) and *consumption* (step 3).

Step 5: The *level of employment* is set so that *aggregate supply* (dependent on the physical conditions of production, which are fixed in the short term) equals *aggregate demand* (step 4).

Step 6: Changes in the *level of employment* (step 5) will be accompanied by an analogous variation in *prices* due to a rise in costs attributable to diminishing returns in the short term plus variations in the *wage-unit* [exogenous: set by collective bargains].

Step 7: Variation in *employment* (step 5), as translated into changes in *prices* (step 6) and in *wage-unit* (step 6) prompts a similar variation in *liquidity-preference*, which forces a return to step 1.

Step 8: Variation in prices (step 6) may also impact on the *marginal efficiency of capital* and the *marginal propensity to consume*, which forces a return to steps 2 and 3.

The advantages and disadvantages associated with the causal sequence method can now be specifically appreciated. The successive iterations modify the value of the variables, the final magnitude of which may remain relatively undetermined. That is precisely the problem avoided by a simultaneous resolution system (of equations). However, the truth is that a sequential method is effective when what is sought is to reveal the exact direction of causal links, and not just a mere functional relation, and to stress the distinction between main and secondary causes.

As may be seen, any change in independent variables affects the employment equilibrium level. But, no doubt, it is the "psychological" variables, that is to say, those subject to the whims of future expectations and to the malleable state of businesses' trust, that which decisively contribute to render the system unstable. And it is precisely future expectations that establish the singular *dynamic* of the system – as opposed to a static system: "The schedule of the marginal efficiency of capital is of fundamental importance because it is mainly through this factor (much more than through the rate of interest) that the expectation of the future influences the present" (Keynes, 1939 [1936]: 145; IV.11.V).

The meaning of a static theory in Keynes's view may now be understood: it is one where the future is identical to the present (specifically, a "stationary state"). The difficulty does not so much lie in assessing different hypotheses regarding the accuracy of individuals' expectations, but in reflecting in individuals' behavior the fact that their estimation of variables future values affects their current decisions. In a static economy, there is no need to predict the evolution of parameters that never change. But there is a deeper difference between a system that does not contemplate the future and the reality of facts. In a static economy, money is useless as a means of treasuring wealth. And it is precisely through that function that money influences the rate of interest. This is, furthermore, the fact that enables the government to have an impact on investment determinants and, through them, on the level of employment. The result is compelling: an economy that is static in this sense is also a non-monetary economy. Therefore, it is not only a question of how decisions are made when considering the future, but also of the elements that make up the real world in a monetary economy, that is, an economy where future circumstances that men cannot predict with any certainty, and differences of opinion among individuals are factored in. Such is the significance of this aspect that this trait of Keynes's system is anticipated, prematurely and, for the same reason, cryptically, in the preface to *The General Theory*.

> A monetary economy, we shall find, is essentially one in which changing views about the future are capable of influencing the quantity of employment and not merely its direction. But our method of analysing the economic behaviour of the present under the influence of changing ideas about the future is one which depends on the interaction of supply and demand, and is in this way linked up with our fundamental theory of value.
>
> (Keynes, 1939 [1936]: vii; Preface)

In the following pages, Keynes's system will be applied to the study of the effects of changes in the exogenous variables that depend on "extra-economic" factors, that is, money supply determined by the monetary authority and money-wages (the wage-unit), a result of the struggle between entrepreneurs and labor. Thanks to the preceding causal sequence, the consequences derived from changes in each of them may be easily analyzed.

Consequences of changes in the amount of money

An increase in the amount of money has a direct effect that stimulates, in principle, the level of employment. Keynes argues that the consequences of an increase in the stock of money are the same, regardless of the particular form in which the government injects the money into circulation. If it chooses to cover its deficit emitting money, the increased expenditure will immediately result in an increase in income, which will tend to increase the needs of money for transactions and precautionary ends. So far the interest rate is not affected. However, the increase in the level of income is transitory, and cannot be held at a level that is sufficiently high to have the transaction-motive absorb all the additional existing money.

Part of the excess cash goes to the debt market, pushing down the rate of interest, which in turn causes the speculative demand for money to grow in such a magnitude as to hoard the excess balance. But the consequences do not end there: the fall of the rate of interest encourages (further still) employment, strengthening the demand for transactions. Initially, income grows and, therefore, the demand of money for transactions, but the money in circulation is poured then into the debt market until $M2$ equals the speculative demand at a lower rate, provoking a genuine rise in income that increases, again, the demand of money for transactions. At all times, the increase in M has to be somehow distributed between $M1$ and $M2$, according to how the transactions and the speculative demand vary.

The alternative way of emitting money is through the so-called open market operations that impact directly on the interest rate level, so that the outcome is the same as in the previous case:

> Thus at one remove this case comes to the same thing as the alternative case, where the new money can only be issued in the first instance by a relaxation of the conditions of credit by the banking system, so as to induce someone to sell the banks a debt or a bond in exchange for the new cash.
>
> (Keynes, 1939 [1936]: 200; IV.15.II)

As regards the effect of emission on the level of employment, the complete reasoning goes as follows: when the amount of money is increased, the rate of interest tends to decrease, which in turn encourages investment and, through the investment multiplier, contributes to increasing total income. However, this sequence may encounter setbacks due to the presence of secondary links among variables.

In this chapter, we have shown that even when the increase in the amount of money impacts effective demand, the latter will be, in turn, subject to a new split into an increase in prices and an increase in employment (and output). As aggregate demand grows, the physical conditions of production, together with the wage-unit "tendency" to increase, provoke a rise in prices that absorbs a proportion of the money destined to demand. A series of mechanisms is an obstacle, therefore, in the path that leads from changes in the quantity of money to changes in employment, mechanisms that can interfere in the magnitude and even in the direction of the outcome suggested by a simpler analysis. In fact, it might well be that the expansive movement be offset. Certain hypotheses regarding changes in "psychological" variables break, one by one, the links that make up the simple causal chain. However, if liquidity preference increase equals money supply increase, the rate of interest will not fall. If, instead, the rate of interest effectively decreases but the marginal efficiency of capital does so at a quicker pace, investment will not be stimulated. An even if investment grows but, at the same time, the propensity to consume weakens, employment will not increase.

Last, if employment in fact grows, the increase in income will raise liquidity-preference thereby prompting a rise in interest rate, with its negative consequences on investment and aggregate demand (step 7 in the causal sequence).

The "missing link" in the classicists' analysis, whose absence lead them to endorse the quantitative theory, may thus be identified through this reasoning: the role played by the rate of interest. The classicists assumed that a direct modification of prices would occur as a necessary answer to fluctuation in the amount of money, neglecting that the first step in the chain is, precisely, the variation in the rate of interest; thus, they could do nothing but overlook the effects of monetary expansion on investment and employment. The differences with respect to the quantity theory are drastic: according to *Keynes's system*, increases in the quantity of money are not directly transferred to prices. On the contrary, an increase in the amount of money affects the level of prices exclusively through its influence on aggregate demand. Going backwards, the causal sequence we have just introduced and its successive offsetting factors emerge. The truth is that if changes in money supply cannot modify the rate of interest, they will never impact prices or employment. When the rate of interest is in fact modified, a process is triggered that is similar to that typical of any change in interest rate, except for the case when governmental action affects specially and unfavorably – which in fact may very well happen – the expectations that determine the marginal efficiency of capital, liquidity preference or the marginal propensity to consume.

> The primary effect of a change in the quantity of money on the quantity of effective demand is through its influence on the rate of interest. If this were the only reaction, the quantitative effect could be derived from the three elements – (*a*) the schedule of liquidity-preference which tells us by how much the rate of interest will have to fall in order that the new money may be absorbed by willing holders, (*b*) the schedule of marginal efficiencies which tells us by how much a given fall in the rate of interest will increase investment, and (*c*) the investment multiplier which tells us by how much a given increase in investment will increase effective demand as a whole.
>
> (Keynes, 1939 [1936]: 298; IV.21.IV)

Due to their distance from the traditional analysis, the offsetting factors preventing the increase in the quantity of money from having a favorable impact on the level of employment merit a closer study. The first step in the causal sequence assumed that liquidity-preference did not vary. But the attempts to reduce the rate of interest through money emission may be thwarted due to their repercussions on expectations.

In an extreme case, liquidity preference grows proportionally to the supply of money, while the rate of interest remains constant. Two different factors converge to bring about this hypothetical result. First, the demand for money motivated by precaution may increase, which will directly lead to an additional portion of the money emitted being absorbed without leaving the new money vacant for speculation. On the other hand, if the public unanimously believes that the rate of interest has fallen below a safe level, they will massively adopt a bearish attitude, ready to absorb increasing amounts of money leaving the rate of interest unchanged. This situation is now widely known as a "liquidity trap"; in the usual explanation, however, the two abovementioned processes have been confused.

> Nevertheless, circumstances can develop in which even a large increase in the quantity of money may exert a comparatively small influence on the rate of interest. For a large increase in the quantity of money may cause so much uncertainty about the future that liquidity-preferences due to the precautionary-motive may be strengthened; whilst opinion about the future of the rate of interest may be so unanimous that a small change in present rates may cause a mass movement into cash.
>
> (Keynes, 1939 [1936]: 172; IV.13.II)

There are several other reasons that may cause the rate of interest to exhibit a resistance to falling. The feeling that the rate of interest is at a high or low level depends on what the public conventionally understands to be its "safe" level. The government, on the other hand, can relatively easily control the short-term rate of interest, forcing reductions by means of open market operations, but its power over the long-term rate is considerably less. Under certain conditions regarding expectations, speculative demand may be modified to offset any increase in the quantity of money.

> [T]he long-term rate may be more recalcitrant when once it has fallen to a level which, on the basis of past experience and present expectations of *future* monetary policy, is considered 'unsafe' by representative opinion [. . .]. Thus a monetary policy which strikes public opinion as being experimental in character or easily liable to change may fail in its objective of greatly reducing the long-term rate of interest, because $M2$ may tend to increase almost without limit in response to a reduction of r below a certain figure. The same policy, on the other hand, may prove easily successful if it appeals to public opinion as being reasonable and practicable and in the public interest, rooted in strong conviction, and promoted by an authority unlikely to be superseded.
>
> (Keynes, 1939 [1936]: 203; IV.15.II)

The movements of the liquidity-preference curve may be drastic, hindering the full effect of changes in monetary supply. Ultimately, just as the marginal efficiency rests on estimates that are partially arbitrary but that take hold merely because the majority is convinced that they are valid, the rate of interest may be fixed at any level, provided that the public believes that this is the correct level. In Keynes's words:

> It might be more accurate, perhaps, to say that the rate of interest is a highly conventional, rather than a highly psychological, phenomenon. For its actual value is largely governed by the prevailing view as to what its value is expected to be. *Any* level of interest which is accepted with sufficient conviction as *likely* to be durable *will* be durable; subject, of course, in a changing society to fluctuations for all kinds of reasons round the expected normal.
>
> (Keynes, 1939 [1936]: 203; IV.15.II)

But, notwithstanding the much discussed possibility that the rate of interest might stubbornly stay at certain minimum value beyond which it refuses to fall in spite of the monetary authority's initiatives, the result of equilibrium with unemployment does not rest, as has been seen, on this exceptional circumstance. The problem is a different one: in the system, there is no "automatic", "mechanical" or "natural" economic trend that pushes the rate of interest downwards.[27] It is one thing to consider the rate of interest "rigid", and a different one to argue that its equilibrium level does not guarantee full employment. Moreover, Keynes does not believe that the rigidity of the rate might entail a threat to full employment. In fact, the famous "liquidity trap", that hypothetical situation where the economy becomes a world of bears, is highly unlikely. Unlikely and also not very reasonable because in a state of "liquidity trap", the financing options open to the government would be practically innumerable at the current rate, which shows, by *reductio ad absurdum*, that such a hypothesis is far from reality.

> There is the possibility, for the reasons discussed above, that, after the rate of interest has fallen to a certain level, liquidity-preference may become virtually absolute in the sense that almost everyone prefers cash to holding a debt which yields so low a rate of interest. In this event the monetary authority would have lost effective control over the rate of interest. But whilst this limiting case might become practically important in future, I know of no example of it hitherto [. . .] Moreover, if such a situation were to arise, it would mean that the public authority itself could borrow through the banking system on an unlimited scale at a nominal rate of interest.
>
> (Keynes, 1939 [1936]: 207; IV.15.III)

Historical experience showed Keynes that, until that moment, there had been only two cases of extreme fluctuation in the rate of interest due to sudden movements, in either direction, of the liquidity-preference curve.

At one extreme, there is what he called "currency crisis" or "flight from the currency", a phenomena that affected Russia and Central Europe in the immediate post-war period. Liquidity-preference collapsed, and the public would not accept money in cash or debts in money. The rate of interest rose, but at the same time the marginal efficiency would increase due to an expected even greater increase in the level of prices. The other extreme case is its opposite. Keynes calls "crisis of liquidation" or "financial crisis" the episodes that transpired in the United States in 1932, when nobody was ready to part with their cash under any circumstance. These are two exceptional cases that should not mislead the analyst who seeks to explain chronic unemployment.

According to *The General Theory*, changes in the quantity of money have to deal with variations in liquidity-preference if they are to have any effect on the rate of interest.

The effect of emission on the other two psychological variables of the system, the marginal efficiency of capital and the propensity to consume, still remains to be examined. When changes in the quantity of money result in changes in current prices and, particularly, when there are expectations that the monetary policy will also affect future prices, it should be expected that the capital marginal efficiency and the marginal propensity to consume also react to such expectations. An outlook of increasing prices stimulates the marginal efficiency of capital, while increasing the weight of debts and modifying income distribution to the detriment of laborers and rentiers, and the benefit of entrepreneurs. Real income redistribution impacts in turn on the propensity to consume and the multiplier (see the next section).

In brief, nothing guarantees (a) that variations in the amount of money will have a real effect on the rate of interest; and (b) that a change in the rate of interest will effectively influence the level of employment. Monetary policy is not – always – an efficient weapon to fight unemployment.

Consequences of the fall in money wages

The classicists used to trust that employment would recover as a result of the system's alleged automatic trend to reduce nominal and real wages when there was unemployment. Keynes showed that the second classical postulate is not valid, which means that labor does not have any means to reduce its real wage and that there are no forces that may push them to accept significant money wage cuts. Further, a fall in employment brings about – like the first postulate states – an increase in wages' purchasing power and, besides, the increase in unemployment generally drives nominal wages in the opposite direction. Having gathered all the system's building blocks and mechanisms, we are in a position to study the effect of an exogenous fall in nominal wages on the level of employment. Again, the consequences of such a change in employment must be found in the analysis of the reaction of aggregate demand.

> [W]e have shown that the volume of employment is uniquely corre-
> lated with the volume of effective demand measured in wage-units,
> and that the effective demand, being the sum of the expected consump-
> tion and the expected investment, cannot change, if the propensity to
> consume, the schedule of marginal efficiency of capital and the rate of
> interest are all unchanged. If, without any change in these factors, the
> entrepreneurs were to increase employment as a whole, their proceeds
> will necessarily fall short of their supply-price.
>
> (Keynes, 1939 [1936]: 260–261; V.19.II)

Keynes rejects the classicists' simple and "intuitive" explanation that aggregate supply tends to increase as a mere result of the reduction of wage costs. The results of a wage cut cannot be correctly analyzed if the study of aggregate demand is neglected. If, when there is a reduction in money wages, entrepreneurs simply decide to increase employment because costs have decreased, they will suffer losses, unless effective demand has increased by exactly the same proportion. And it has been shown that there are no automatic trends that may invariably push aggregate demand to the same level as that of supply, so it is necessary to examine how changes in money wages impact on demand.[28]

A reduction in nominal wages produces a fall in marginal cost and, therefore, in prices. This variation may modify the marginal propensity to consume, given that income is redistributed from wage earners to capitalists in general, and from entrepreneurs to rentiers. But such change in income composition will have dubious effects on the propensity to consume, and further, those effects will probably be negative in the case of the level of employment, since it is the poorer classes of society (labor) who devote the largest portion of their income to consumption. A fall in wages does not necessarily stimulate the consumption component of aggregate demand.

Neither will the marginal efficiency of capital be univocally affected by a fall in current prices or by expectations concerning their future evolution. For a wage cut to favor investment, it has to be only transitory, so that prices later return to their initial level; the marginal efficiency will then react favorably, since the current cost of equipment decreases, and future revenues on sales performed when prices rise again increase. But if, on the contrary, new wage cuts are expected, the marginal efficiency will adjust downwards, and current investment will be thus damaged. According to this analysis, a sustained reduction in wages will tend to reduce, at the same time, prices and employment. Besides, the fall in prices will negatively affect indebted entrepreneurs by increasing the real weight of their debts (Keynes takes into account the so-called "Fisher effect").

There remains, therefore, only one analytical resource, based on Keynes's system, supporting the notion that a fall in nominal wages brings about an improvement in employment: its effect on liquidity-preference. A cut in wages increases the "real" quantity of money, assuming the nominal amount of money fixed.

In both cases (fixed wage and increase in the quantity of money or a fixed amount of money and a reduction in wages), the stock of currency in circulation as measured in wage-units increases (a "speculative real balances" effect). If this is so, the more favorable effects on employment stemming from a wage cut must equal those achieved with an increase in the quantity of money, since a fall in wages may stimulate employment through a fall in the rate of interest. However, the efficacy in increasing employment will be subject to the same aspects that qualify the stimulant effects of an expansive monetary policy.

> We can, therefore, theoretically at least, produce precisely the same effects on the rate of interest by reducing wages, whilst leaving the quantity of money unchanged, that we can produce by increasing the quantity of money whilst leaving the level of wages unchanged. It follows that wage reductions, as a method of securing full employment, are also subject to the same limitations as the method of increasing the quantity of money. The same reasons as those mentioned above, which limit the efficacy of increases in the quantity of money as a means of increasing investment to the optimum figure, apply *mutatis mutandis* to wage reductions. Just as a moderate increase in the quantity of money may exert an inadequate influence over the long-term rate of interest, whilst an immoderate increase may offset its other advantages by its disturbing effect on confidence; so a moderate reduction in money-wages may prove inadequate, whilst an immoderate reduction might shatter confidence even if it were practicable.
>
> (Keynes, 1939 [1936]: 267–268; V.19.II)

Based on this analysis, Keynes advices the supporters of wage cut to abandon that misguided path, which is partially similar to an increase in the quantity of money, but only achieves the same effects *at best*. For, at a closer look, for that initiative to exert a favorable effect it is necessary to assume that the wage cut will be uniform, which cannot be guaranteed in a *laissez-faire* society; and if it were, it will arouse social conflicts that could depress entrepreneurs' expectations. By prescribing a wage cut, the inadequacy of the income redistribution in favor of those who receive a fixed rent in money is also overlooked; the damaging effects of the increase in debts' real weight are ignored; and finally, it is not noticed that sudden changes in wages could reduce through that via the rate of interest, but they could also diminish the marginal efficiency of capital and, together with it, the volume of investment, and aggregate demand as a whole.

In short, according to Keynes, it is always preferable to resort to changes in the amount of money rather than to wage cuts that, according to his system, are associated with all the dangers that have just been listed. But all in all, the effectiveness of a wage-cut is subject to the same doubts than monetary policy (plus the ones we have added).

The other point that Keynes makes to rebut the premises on which the ruinous prescriptions of the classicists are based, and thus discredit such recommendations, is that, even in the hypothetical case that wages fell without stop whenever there is labor supply excess, full employment would not be guaranteed. Such a trend, on the other hand, does not exist:

> There is, therefore, no ground for the belief that a flexible wage policy is capable of maintaining a state of continuous full employment; – any more than for the belief that an open-market monetary policy is capable, unaided, of achieving this result. The economic system cannot be made self-adjusting along these lines.
>
> (Keynes, 1939 [1936]: 267; V.19.II)

The analysis that has just been presented based on Keynes's system and supported by excerpts from *The General Theory* leaves no room for doubt: the system remains in equilibrium with unemployment even if money-wages are reduced, as the classicists expect and prescribe. What is therefore remarkable is the fact that the view, first, and the dogma, later, that Keynes's system rests on a special assumption decreeing, according to some authors, wage rigidity, and, according to others, rate of interest rigidity, may have become widespread.[29]

Notes

1 The price of aggregate supply is calculated by subtracting the use cost, a concept Keynes uses to reflect the physical and moral depletion of the elements involved in production.

2 Always present in this explanation is an assumption concerning the form of returns. In the short term, both Marshall and Keynes suppose them to be diminishing. This is the reason why, for Keynes, the price of global supply is an increasing function of the level of employment, both taken as a whole. And also for this reason, the adjustment does not affect only the amount produced (as is generally believed) but also the normal price.

3 This conception of dynamics is reflected in certain analytical method. Under certain circumstances, Keynes wonders, as in the case of the multiplier, what the adjustment velocity will be. However, he generally assumes that equilibrium has already been reached.

4 For an illustration of this explanation of the adjustment, see the traditional textbook *Economy* (Fischer et al., 1989: 583) or Blanchard's *Macroeconomía*, where stock movement is the main indicator relied on to guide changes in production, because it is considered to be equivalent to an investment change: "If, on the contrary, sales are smaller than production, firms accumulate stocks: investment in stocks is positive" (Blanchard and Pérez Enrri, 2000: 70; translation EO).

5 These "extraordinary" gains or losses triggered variation in the volume of production and gave rise to a "profit disequilibrium". These special categories are discarded because, first, they cannot be measured or precisely defined (what is, after all, a "normal" level of profit for the system as a whole, when the normal level is generally defined as an average). In *The General Theory,* unlike the *Treatise,* current savings is always equal to investment, as a result of the mechanisms that will be explained next.

6 In the Marshallian short term, enterprises may obtain benefits resulting from the difference between revenue and costs. Marshall terms such benefits "quasi-rents". In the Walrasian general equilibrium, there is no place for these benefits. Keynes extends Marshall's analysis to the economy as a whole, in a state of normal short-term equilibrium.

7 Classical economists did not take this component of cost into account; in the short term, they generally exclusively matched the supply price of a unit of product to its factorial marginal cost. For Keynes, the supply unit price equals the addition of the marginal cost of the factors and the marginal cost of use. The *classical theory* erred in overlooking the cost of equipment use because, even assuming a full integration of industry, the marginal "disinvestment" in equipment cannot be dismissed (see Keynes, 1939 [1936]: 71 and ff.). Use cost is for Keynes a factor that has a bearing on entrepreneurs' decision, and is relevant because it incorporates expectations over the future into their estimations.

8 In his long discussion on the nature of return, Marshall considers an industry operating under conditions of increasing, constant, or decreasing productivity. In *Principles,* he held that if returns are increasing, the determination of prices through the forces of supply and demand is logically challenged. However, in the short term, this difficulty could be overcome, as Marshall always seemed to prefer the more plausible hypothesis of diminishing returns.

9 In 1939, two years after publishing *The General Theory,* Keynes wrote an article defending these conclusions from attacks based on new statistical studies by J. L. Dunlop and L. Tarshis, since his conclusions in this field had aroused controversy: "In any case, these facts do not support the recently prevailing assumptions as to the relative movements of real wages and output, and are inconsistent with the idea of there being any marked tendency to increasing unit-profit with increasing output" (Keynes, 1939: 48–49).

10 It has to be admitted, however, that the *classical theory,* through Marshall, contemplated the possibility that wages became the result of the struggles between laborers and capitalists: "If the employers in any trade act together and so do the employed, the solution of the problem of wages becomes indeterminate; and there is nothing but bargaining to decide the exact shares in which the excess of its incomings over its outgoings for the time should be divided between employers and employed" (Marshall, 1920 [1890]: VI.VIII.38). However, Marshall concludes that this does not affect the classical explanation: "And though they are on a larger and more imposing scale in this modern age than before; yet now, as ever, the main body of movement depends on the deep silent strong stream of the tendencies of normal distribution and exchange; which 'are not seen'"

(ibid.). Seen thus, Keynes only generalizes that "possibility" so that wages become "indeterminate".

11 Pigou agrees that what is bargained is the money-wage, but he holds that this bargaining is reflected on real wages.

12 In some passages, Keynes refers to certain prices that are not determined by the abovementioned laws: these are the "managed" or monopoly prices, where additional considerations other than marginal cost are involved (Keynes, 1939 [1936]). However, he does not specify what these additional aspects to be considered are or how important such prices unaffected by the general laws are. In other words, he remains within the tradition that assumes perfect competition.

13 Patinkin used this quotation to argue that Keynes *in fact stated that* nominal wages tend to fall when there is unemployment. Such an interpretation is untenable and completely alien to Keynes's system. Furthermore, it was used to assert that in unemployment conditions, Keynes himself admitted that the system was not in a state of equilibrium. If that was the case, Keynes's explanation would focus on unemployment *considered as a state of disequilibrium* (Patinkin, 1959 [1956]: 220–221; 493–494). As a result of this interpretation, which we challenge, Keynes becomes a classicist once again. Anyway, Patinkin's proposal was the first in an extended saga of interpretations that read *The General Theory* as an enquiry into disequilibrium.

14 The influence of price fall during a period of depression is known as "Fisher effect", in honor of the explanation Fisher offers in this article *"The Debt Deflation Theory of Great Depressions"* (Fisher, 1933: 345 and ff.).

15 To obtain the amount of net investment, it is also necessary to subtract equipment depreciation and unexpected losses (or profits) brought about by sudden obsolescence, destruction, catastrophe, or by also unexpected variations in market value (windfall losses).

16 The most original contributions of the period started looking for the cause of price adjustment in the inequality of savings and investment (Böhm-Bawerk, Wicksell, Keynes himself in the *Treatise*). When Keynes writes *The General Theory,* he rejects these explanations and returns to the classical stance that saving equals investment in all cases. His innovation will consist in showing that it is not the rate of interest that which reconciles both magnitudes, but rather the level of employment and production.

17 Chapter 8 of *The General Theory* studies the different "objective factors" that influence consumption decisions, dismissing the relevance of the rest.

18 He calls "subjective factors" the aspects that limit expenditure in consumption to a determined fraction of the income. He will also assume that these subjective factors are not modified in the short term "except in abnormal or revolutionary circumstances" (Keynes, 1939 [1936]: III.8.I). Therefore, they may be considered given, "in general, we shall in what follows take the subjective factors as given; and we shall assume that the propensity to consume depends only on changes in the objective factors" (loc. cit.).

19 Many attacks on Keynes's argument have focused on this explanation, appealing to the actual form of the consumption function.

20 The current of macroeconomics called "new classicists" still relies on the old mechanism of the *classical theory*, without qualifications and ignoring both the subtleties of the debate and the unlikely correspondence of such a mechanism to facts. A widely used textbook asserts, for example, with total impunity that "economists call this result *intertemporal substitution effect*. That is, the increase in the rate of interest induces us to postpone current expenditure to the

future. Similarly, a higher rate of interest makes it worthwhile saving a larger portion of our income to consume more goods later" (Barro, 1983: 76). Consumption thus depends on the rate of interest and full employment becomes a dogma, contrary to Keynes's view.

21 Milton Friedman's A *Theory of Consumption Function* was the first attempt to attack Keynes's consumption theory based on this resource and gave way to what would later be called "Theory of the permanent income" (Friedman, 1957).

22 The so-called "Pigou effect" of real balance effect belongs to the same family of objections to Keynes's theory and leads to the vindication of Say's Law. If consumption depends not only on current income but also on the holding of real balances (the purchasing power of money in the hands of the public), then the fall in prices accompanying the reduction of employment will entail a strengthening of the propensity to consume, This "solution" to the dilemma raised by *The General Theory* was originally suggested by Pigou (1943), and generalized by Patinkin (1959 [1956]), who turns the real balance effect into the cornerstone of the full employment economy.

23 Walras and Marshall also coincided on this question. Contemporary treatises of microeconomics offer exactly the same characterization. They take as a starting point a function of production in physical terms to obtain the marginal return on capital and the demand curve as a function of the rate of interest. The "new classicists" follow suit (see, for example, Barro, 1983). Macroeconomics textbooks of Keynesian descent build, in general, an investment curve that is negatively sloped relative to the rate of interest, and state, for example, that "the curve for investment demand corresponds to a given level of investment expected benefits. If firms are more optimistic regarding future levels of benefits [. . .] they will desire to invest more" (Fischer et al., 1989: 689; tran. EO). No clear definition of what is meant by "level of benefits" is offered; it is also assumed that investment is always financed with a bank credit on which an expected rate of interest, allegedly somehow related to the physical productivity of capital, will be paid.

24 The frontier between money and debts is conventional, and depends on the maximum term considered to be compatible with the term "liquidity" or "immediate" purchasing power. Keynes includes within the term "money" bank's debts to depositors (bank term deposits). Once the term is fixed, whatever is not "money" may generically be easily called "debt". Different forms of credit may also be treated likewise without any objection, since Keynes admits that there exist at any moment a "complex" of interest rates for debts of differing nature and maturity, although theoretically it may be more convenient, in order to simplify the analysis, to refer to such a set of different conditions with the single term "rate of interest".

25 In his article *Alternative Theories of the Rate of Interest* (1937), Keynes states: "The alternative theory held, I gather, by Prof. Ohlin and his group of Swedish economists, by Mr. Robertson and Mr. Hicks, and probably by many others, makes it to depend, put briefly, on the demand and supply of *credit* or, alternatively (meaning the same thing), of *loans*, at different rates of interest. Some of the writers (as will be seen from the quotations given below) believe that my theory is on the whole the same as theirs and mainly amounts to expressing it in a somewhat different way. Nevertheless the theories are, I believe, radically opposed to one another" (Keynes, 1937: 241). The anti-Keynesian theory of the loanable funds, however, prevailed.

26 In the *Treatise,* a similar mechanism was mentioned, but it referred to a different issue: bears and bulls set the relation between assets and debts purchases,

rather than the rate of interest given a quantity of money. This was a theory of investment and its return: "The price level of investments as a whole, and hence of new investments, is that price level at which the desire of the public to hold savings-deposits is equal to the amount of savings-deposits which the banking system is willing and able to create" (Keynes, 1935 [1930]:143). The explanation is similar to that of "loanable funds" that was dismissed in *The General Theory*.

27 In "Mr. Keynes and the Classics", the article by Hicks that inspired the Neo-classical synthesis, it is stated that the most original contribution of Keynes's system lies precisely in this "rigidity" of the interest rate: "from many points of view, is the most important thing in Mr. Keynes' book" (Hicks, 1937).

28 Here we are discussing exclusively the case of a closed economy. In an open economy, a wage cut will certainly improve the trade balance, lowering the price of domestic products, but it may surely have a negative impact on consumption on account of its disfavorable effect over the terms of exchange.

29 The seminal articles by J. Hicks (1937) and F. Modigliani (1944) called the attention on the rigidity of the rate of interest and wages, respectively. Modigliani states that "It is usually considered as one of the most important achievements of the Keynesian theory that it explains the consistency of economic equilibrium with the presence of involuntary unemployment. It is, however, not sufficiently recognized that [. . .] this result is due entirely to the assumption of 'rigid wages' and not to the Keynesian liquidity preference" (Modigliani, 1944: 65).

5 Keynes's system

Fundamental concepts

> For if orthodox economics is at fault, the error is to be found not in the superstructure, which has been erected with great care for logical consistence, but in a lack of clearness and of generality in the premises.
>
> —*Keynes, Preface to The General Theory*

I A foray into money and capital

Some conclusions: the theoretical contributions of Keynes's system

In this section, as a kind of preliminary conclusion, we will offer an initial assessment of Keynes's contributions to economic theory. A clarification, therefore, must first be made. When examining the background of *The General Theory*, as has been done earlier, two circumstances stand out which have been frequently ignored. First, in his own words, Keynes seeks to "escape from habitual modes of thought and expression [. . .] which ramify, for those brought up as most of us have been, into every corner of our minds" (Keynes, 1939 [1936]: Preface). In other words, one of his main and explicit purposes is to break from the *classical theory*. Keynes presents himself as a critic of orthodoxy. However, and this is the second point that should be made, his ideas were rapidly absorbed by the *classical theory*, albeit in a very peculiar fashion. This assimilation process entailed, on one hand, the complete discarding of his critique of the inherited theory and, on the other, the careful selection of the aspects of his construction that were either "worthwhile", convenient or possible to rescue. In short, Keynes's thought, initially conceived as a break with the mainstream, was finally integrated to orthodoxy itself after a process of smoothing out its "rough spots".

It is important, therefore, to remember the procedure used to incorporate a portion – and only a portion – of Keynes's positions. The orthodoxy, on one hand, pretended to ignore all challenges and, on the other, had to adopt some of the new ideas. To be able to do both simultaneously, however, it had to split its theoretical corpus into two: in microeconomics, the old *marginalist* ideas took refuge, unchanged and impervious to criticisms; while macroeconomics, an *ad hoc* theoretical branch introduced to include Keynes's ideas, took over the system outlined in *The General Theory* and adapted it to the orthodoxy's expository method and its preconceived notions.

In this book we seek to draw attention once again to Keynes's break with *classical theory* with the purpose of examining how far it reached.

In the exposition of *The General Theory*, three different levels or depths of analysis coexist. On one hand, Keynes puts forth a new *economic system* to study the determination of the level of equilibrium employment, that is, the first level, the *system;* at the same time, he deploys a critique leveled at the main aspects of the *classical theory* that clash with his system, that is, the second level, a *critique*. But there is a third expository level, generally ignored by subsequent economists belonging to all schools of thought. Keynes devotes a significant portion of his work to a thorough analysis of the nature of capital and money. In those chapters, some modifications are suggested that also affect, and very clearly, the *classical theory of value*.

The hypothesis we will try to prove is that the *General Theory* is an indivisible unit, that is, that the foundations of Keynes's system, as well as his critique of traditional thought, feed and rest on his particular conceptions of capital, money, and value. If Keynes undertook to discuss the fundamental concepts, introducing certain apparently "metaphysical" considerations, it is simply and plainly because his *economic system meant to determine observable variables* is not consistent with the definitions of capital and money put forth by the *classical theory*, but rather rejects them as alien bodies. The system and the classical definitions are incompatible. In other words, the classical assertions of what capital and money are do not fit into the description of the observable variables' behavior that the system posits. This is, no doubt, the reason that pushes Keynes to venture a foray into such a sensitive territory. Keynes could have stopped at the representation of the variables' movements, at the exposition of his system (or "model"), as macroeconomics would do later. However, he did not. Keynes followers entirely discarded Keynes's foundations, even reproaching him for including such inconvenient digressions in his most relevant work, as if by so doing he would taint it and render it unnecessarily vulnerable to criticism. However, if the analysis of the elemental economic forms – commodity, money, capital – that Keynes undertakes was explained in terms of the inadequacy of the classical categories, his contribution would undoubtedly gain a new place in the history of economic analysis, a place that the usual interpretations, restricted to macroeconomics and unable to reach a greater conceptual depth in their analyses, have refused it.

Since the emergence of political economy as a discipline independent from the moral sciences, the main currents of economic thought have differentiated themselves from one another, first and foremost, by the differences in the basic concepts of their foundations. The major controversies among the different schools have centered on their diverse explanations of the nature of commodities, money and capital; of the origin of value and of profit. Most specialists in the history of economic thought, for example, admit that the fundamental differences among marginalists, Ricardians and Marxists – to mention just the main schools, all of them created during the nineteenth century, belong to the field of basic categories. If the concepts put forth in the *General Theory* were substantially different from those introduced by previous schools, Keynes's contribution would rise to a higher category, as thus it would no longer be considered as just a system with some original traits that essentially draws, anyway, on classical theory, to become a real current of thinking capable of debating with earlier schools in the field of primary categories. And if so it were, Keynes's distancing from the classical theory could be considered to be definitive.

The latter is the main hypothesis of this book: the most transcendental contribution of Keynes's consists, precisely, in his attempt to move forward, an attempt that resulted from following the trace of his own representation of economic laws which led him to formulating, at a higher level of abstraction, questions concerning the origin of those observable phenomena. Therefore, it has to be shown that the shift from the system to the elementary categories is not some whim or crazy notion of Keynes, but rather a theoretical need emanating from his own proposal. It has to be shown that there is a connection that links the different levels of analysis that exist in the *General Theory*, a necessary link between the system and those fundamental categories.

When considering Keynes's contribution to economic theory it is necessary to distinguish, however, the objectives pursued, on one hand, and the results obtained, on the other. Disregarding the advice of Keynes's followers and paying attention, instead, to the original argument of the *General Theory*, something that should be obvious is discovered: underlying every "model", there is always, whether it is explicit or not, a certain conception of the ultimate nature of economic phenomena.

It is in this field of debate that the major currents of economic thinking, including the *marginalist*, engage. Keynes's main merit lies in his effort to ground not only empirically but also conceptually his choice of variables, of function forms, of expository method. However, rescuing and weighting this aspect of his contribution is not the same, obviously, as stating that his theories of money, capital and value are correct. On the contrary: in this way, his explanations stand much more exposed, bare, and only then does it become possible to undertake a critique beyond the mere assessment of his contribution's practical and empirical content, to enter the field of the discussion of its deep theoretical foundations, those that inescapably distance it from the *marginalist* school.

It will be later shown that Keynes was unavoidably forced to discuss the fundamental concepts of the *General Theory* by showing, first, that the *classical theory's* conceptions of the nature of money and capital necessarily lead to a description of the behavior of certain observable phenomena, and that the behavior of variables derived from the *classical foundations* openly contradicts the performance of variables as reflected by Keynes's *economic system*. This first step makes it possible to understand why the classical foundations themselves have to be replaced. Then, Keynes's reflections on capital, money and value will be discussed. Finally, a concise critique of those theories will be offered.

Brief note on the relevance of this discussion

It has to be admitted that the interest in the discussion of the fundamental concepts of economic theory is out of fashion. It would seem that economics is exclusively devoted to collecting the quantitative reflections of empirical phenomena by means of mathematical functions. This impression, however, is completely false. Such perception hides, always and in every case – even though the economist that argues for it might be unaware of this – a definite conception of the basic categories. What happens is, in fact, that the orthodoxy – any orthodoxy, indeed – tends to transform, in practice, its own explanations into a dogma that, as such, is no longer open to discussion. Now then, the *General Theory*, which tried to challenge that dogma at its deeper level, led to a split of the theory that left the foundations, once again, unchallenged. But both that revolution and its apparent resolution reveal, in fact, a crisis that has not yet come to an end: even today, mainstream economics tries to re-unite microeconomics and macroeconomics, and battles between a current that demands the restoration of the classical school and another that seeks to move forward to its definitive abandonment. How important, if at all, are, then, the fundamental categories for contemporary economic theory, given that the theory usually acts as if such categories did not even exist?

Present day macroeconomics represents the movements of aggregate variables – that is, the purely quantitative aspect of economic phenomena – by means of mathematical relations that establish causal links among them.

A typical question is, for example, "On what factors does consumption depend?" The answer adopts the form of a relationship between the magnitude of current consumption and the magnitude of other variables, for example, current income – the well-known Keynesian function of consumption.

By establishing this relationship, the analytical operation is, in fact, three-fold. On one hand, implicitly or explicitly, some factors that are assumed to have no bearing on consumption are discarded; at the same time, other elements that influence consumption, albeit indirectly, through their impact on income, are identified; and last, a description of the particular way in which changes in the variable taken here as independent affect the other, that is, the function form and, therefore, the sign and slope of its derivatives at each point, is provided. How does the researcher come to establish such relation? He does so by resorting to his ability to identify in experience empirical regularities, that is, certain mutually associated phenomena that generally occur simultaneously.[1]

Complex phenomena are observed as they occur in reality, that is, in their immediate chaotic appearance, and an attempt is made to establish the internal connections linking those phenomena. Theory takes it upon itself the task of presenting regularities as "economic laws" or trends.

The *economic system* outlined in *The General Theory*, for example, follows suit. At this level, macroeconomic theories only depict reality, that is, establish a series of functional relations among observable variables to "explain" or "predict" phenomena. The relevance in practice of such explanations cannot be denied. They offer an understanding of what the effect of economic phenomena will be but besides, inasmuch as individuals or governments are capable of deliberately controlling or exerting influence on such factors, they become a guide for factual decisions. Keynes's system – and macroeconomics – focuses particularly on those factors under the rule of government, thereby providing a sort of "user's manual" to economic policy.

Many of these instruments are new – they are a historical novelty that emerged during the first decades of the twentieth century. This explains, in part, the emergence of macroeconomics. But, at least in Keynes's version, the theoretical enquiry does not stop here.

When economic theory is exclusively devoted to raising questions concerning changes in variables' values, neglecting a deeper discussion on the nature of phenomena, that is, when it stops at the description of such quantitative relations without asking what is it that it measures, it leaves out of the field of science a set of highly relevant questions. *Classical theory*, in its early-twentieth-century version, provided answers for those questions. Today, many of those *classical* elements still survive in the terrain of micro-economics, but they seem to be alien to macroeconomics.

Specifically, Keynes seeks to explain the source of capital yield, and why money is capable of "producing" interest. As will be later shown, the *classical theory* offers its own answers to these questions, but they do not satisfy the needs of Keynes's system. Faced with this situation, the author of *The General Theory* was forced to put forth a new set of answers to those questions in order to be consistent with his own innovations. The conflict thus emerges, precisely, because the definitions and explanations furnished by the *classical theory* on the nature of capital and money are not compatible with Keynes's system. If this is the case, it is difficult to explain the indifference with which Keynes's followers dismissed the problem without even discussing it. However, an objection could be raised to that claim: if the problem is as vitally important as we are asserting here, how was it possible for macroeconomics to have ignored it? Or rather, what are the consequences of such neglect? Some answers to both questions may be attempted. If macroeconomics managed to survive without venturing into such debates, it is because it borrowed from common sense the definitions of its categories. In fact, it is thus possible to talk about money and capital without resorting to a theoretical or conceptual explanation but, simply, to a descriptively rigorous definition that allows for a clear distinction of the relevant elements to the exclusive effect of measuring them. Thus, the notions of money and capital typical of macroeconomic theory differ from those of common sense only in the more accurate nature of their specification of the items that have to be taken into account when measuring (i.e. bank fixed-term deposits, financial instruments, money in circulation; capital goods, ownership securities). But when trying to elucidate what capital is and why it yields a profit that remains in the hands of its owner, the economist has to trust completely in his intuition, in immediate, non-scientific knowledge. The same goes for money. Macroeconomics limits itself exclusively to conventionally distinguishing what will be considered "money" when the variables intervening in the mathematical functions are quantified. Thus, it dodges the questions that have worried economists since Adam Smith – and many more long before him – to trust, instead, in "what everybody knows". But, again, what is capital? What is the source of the profits that remain in the hands of its owner? What is money? Why, when given in loan, does it accrue interest? What is the source of goods' value? Macroeconomics thus became an a-conceptual discipline that measures things, objects (variables) whose nature it does not bother to research, supposedly leaving that task to microeconomics.

Microeconomics is, instead, the sphere of economic theory that did not exclude those old questions from its concerns. However, the explanations it offers today coincide almost completely – at least, with respect to their contents – with those furnished by what Keynes calls *classical theory*. Like *classical theory*, microeconomics looks for answers in the behavior of the individual, which it considers "rational". But beyond its "microfoundations", it also includes a fundamental theory that, as will be seen, assigns certain particular properties and qualities to capital and money – there is a concept of money, capital and good in microeconomics. Even though the rational individual with his "maximizing" behavior is the subject of its explanations, it is precisely because of capital and money's specific attributes, their singular nature, that they are desired by that individual.

According to the foundations of marginalism, the desire to purchase a commodity stems from the commodity's utility in its capacity to satisfy certain needs. Commodities have a price because they are useful, but besides they are available in limited quantities, they are scarce. This *general* explanation has to contemplate the *particular* cases of money and capital, which are commodities, but, at the same time, are more than that. The non-convertible bill does not seem to have a utility of its own and yet, it is desired. Capital is not devoted to immediate consumption and yet, it is also desired. Asserting that they are coveted because of their yields leads to a logical contradiction if it is then held that the yield originates precisely in the fact that capital and money are objects of desire: they are desired because they yield a return, but they yield a return because they are desired. The classical theory (in Keynes's sense, that is, Ricardians and marginalists) – like Smith, Ricardo, Marx etc. – puts forth its own theories to answer these questions. The debate in this terms appeared in the works of the first marginalists, and although it is "outmoded" today, the aspects of these problems that remain valid for marginalism are the concern of microeconomics. It is those explanations that have to be contrasted against those offered by Keynes in the least read pages of *The General Theory*.

The picture of current orthodoxy is thus completed. Macroeconomics, as has been mentioned, disregards such complex discussions and limits itself to the description of the behavior of the variables through its systems of equations. However, it comes across an obstacle. Whenever it tries to resort to microeconomics to look for its foundations, it encounters contradiction. Keynes, in turn, sought to escape from this new double life to which the theory was condemned because of its inability to solve the problem of its foundations, laying a unique groundwork for explanations that refer both to isolated industries and the economy as a whole. Furthermore, he meant, precisely, to unify the theory of value and the theory of money, thus overcoming the inconsistencies of the classicists.[2]

When the *marginalist* theory emerged as a new current of thinking that distinguished its ideas from those of its predecessors through a process considered to be "revolutionary" by its founders (late nineteenth century), such a consideration was not only based on the new description provided concerning the observable movements of economic phenomena and their reciprocal relations, or on the "mathematical" method it used, but rather, precisely, on its attempt to offer new arguments regarding the internal nature of such phenomena. Walras, Menger, Jevons, and Marshall himself shared the objective of reshaping the foundations of economics, partially or completely toppling the Ricardian school. The harshest struggles between marginalists and Ricardians revolved around a new proposal meant to replace the theory of value. The new explanation of value originally rested, on one hand, on the marginal utility, and on the new theory of distribution, on the other.[3] Briefly, the distance between the schools of economic thinking does not stem from the diverse understandings of the apparent movement of prices, but from the origin of price or value itself, not only from the causes of variations in the magnitude of interest and profit, but from their origin and nature.

Last, the most noticeable dearth that affects an economic theory that does not enquire into the foundations of its own categories should be mentioned. There is a remarkable difference between the approaches that do and those that do not undertake this "rough" task, spurning it on account of its high degree of abstraction. By leaving aside the conceptual aspects, a theory lacks the adequate elements to frame its contribution in one of the main interest areas of economics, a field that has attracted the attention of its representatives since its emergence as a science. We are talking about the capacity that economics originally had – or, at least, believed to have – as a branch of knowledge to unveil the nature itself of the return on capital, of the money interest, and of the source of value of goods, which, together, are the theoretical elements that ground the contributions of this science to the understanding of the historical conditions that led to the emergence of capital, money and commodity, and, for the same reason, the research on the future of the capitalist society. If economics relinquishes this task, not only the transformations that separate one social form from the other – Antiquity, Feudalism, Capitalism – are left out of its field of study, but also the different stages which capitalism underwent become unintelligible. Thus, economics can only describe – but not understand – the way quantitative relations change through time, modifying or replacing equations in its systems every time economic conditions experience a mutation. However, it can say nothing about the origin or the direction of such transformations.

Present day economics usually disregards these problems, recurring to the argument of *disciplinary specialization:* these are, it asserts, "political", "institutional", and "historical" questions, not strictly economic ones. However, again and again, it violates its self-imposed restriction by applying its "laws" to explain the economy of a distant past, as if such laws were as valid then as in present-day societies: the argument of the split into different subjects thus turns out to be a mere trap. It is stated, on one hand, that the specificity of capitalism is not a problem to be solved by economics; on the other, it is pretended that these economic laws are universal, eternal and immutable, as they originate, allegedly, in human nature, in the unchanging "psychology" of the individual. It would thus seem that capitalist society has no specific traits that distinguish it from previous societies: man is, essentially, always the same, so that there must have existed commodities, money, and capital always, although, it is true, under primitive forms.

First, economics refrains from taking part in the debate on the historical character of its categories by appealing to the pretext that this issue does not belong to its field of study. But then, it applies its laws indiscriminately. The ultimate image – although this is not always explicitly argued – is that capitalist society is the "natural" way of life for men, and that those "political", "institutional" aspects are merely secondary.

As will be seen, Keynes does not belong to this tradition since he ventures into the difficult questions about the foundations of economic theory.

II In the opposite direction: from Keynes's system to the fundamental economic forms

The need of a new analysis of capital and money

Chapter 16 of *The General Theory* delves into the problems linked with the analysis of the nature of capital. In Chapter 17, the traits that make money a source of interest are studied. What has been stated so far will help show that Keynes's enquiries into money and capital cannot be taken as mere secondary reflections, independent from the rest of the *General Theory*, as if they were incidental notes, brightening up the exposition, meant to be taken into account or disregarded according to the disposition of the reader towards the interesting albeit inconsequential questions of abstract theory. It is neither petulance nor whim that drives Keynes's foray into such complex considerations, but rather the push to venture into this hard theoretical terrain comes from the questions opened by his own *economic system* of causal relations, with its given factors, its dependent and independent variables. Furthermore, without the analysis of money and capital, his theory would remain unfinished, incomplete.

There is, therefore, a pressing *need*, not of a personal order but rather *theoretical*, that leads Keynes to undertake the analysis of money and capital, and forces him, besides, to include his conclusions in *The General Theory*. His analysis tours novel routes, distanced from the traditional course traced by his *classical* teachers and is, for the very same reason, extremely polemical. His conclusions are controversial and more vulnerable to criticism than other portions of his argument. It is for this reason that their inclusion in *The General Theory* pose an enigma that is worth considering: why would Keynes add to his contributions these new pieces of theory if they were not essential for guaranteeing the consistency of his argument? Keynes is generally credited with a dazzling persuasive power; many of his interpreters usually see in him a true discourse strategist.

If this were the case, those same authors should be in a position to explain why he did not exclude those exceedingly abstract and highly sensitive debates if his explicit objective was persuading his peers.[4] What motives led him to include those supposedly weak points? There must have been, at least for Keynes, powerful reasons to do so.

There is no need to investigate too hard to find them. In fact, Keynes stresses the close link between these theoretical questions and the other elements in his argument once and again, as if to persuade the reader that they are important; however, in light of the debate that followed the publication of his book, it should be said that his performance in this terrain was far from successful.

To prevent the discussion from drifting toward the barren field of personal motivations, the argument has to be strictly restricted to the rational sphere: what are, then, the strong links that connect Keynes's *economic system* to his novel theory of capital and money?

The first factor – and surely the most visible – that makes a review of the classical concepts of money and capital essential lies at the core of Keynes's original explanation of the determination of investment volume.

The *classical theory* systematically mixed up return on capital and money interest, merging them into one single category. *The General Theory*, instead, outlines two different causal sequences: one of them involves the variables that impact on the rate of interest, and the other includes the elements that affect the marginal efficiency of capital. Thus, Keynes manages to portray how the amount of investment is actually determined, an amount that tends to increase until it reaches the point where the marginal efficiency of capital equals the rate of interest. If the elements involved in the quantitative determination of each of these two phenomena differ, it is because the interest and the marginal efficiency of capital are *essentially* two different things, which means that they also originate in different sources.

The *classical theory* accounted for a single phenomenon that entailed a single causal sequence when, in fact, there are two different phenomena and two different sources. Therefore, even if Keynes admitted without any objection the explanation offered by the classical theory of interest, he would be forced to specify which of his two categories – interest or marginal efficiency – the theory applies to, and in that hypothetical case, he would still have to deal with the analysis of the other phenomenon. Keynes, indeed, had to discard the only classical explanation available. But beyond the split into rate of interest and capital yield, there are other major reasons that force Keynes to venture into the analysis of capital and money, which originate in remarkable contradictions between his system and the classical theory regarding the causal relations linking the observable variables.

The merging of the rate of interest and capital yield is, therefore, one of Keynes's reasons for making a foray into the field of theoretical foundations. But, second, *classical theory* held that savings is causally linked to the rate of interest; Keynes believes the opposite. An increase in savings in the *classical market of capital* – due to changes in savers' psychology, in expectations or in exogenously determined incomes – necessarily brings about an increase in investment.

In the classical sequence, the heightening of the desire to save is the cause, and the increase in investment is its consequence. In fact, if in the classical market of capital the supply curve is moved outwards, savings will increase for every possible level of the rate of interest, so that, *ceteris paribus*, the rate of interest will have to decrease, thus inducing an increase in capital demand, that is, in the volume of investment. From this picture, the conclusion may be drawn that frugality, that is, increases in savings, is beneficial to the economic activity, since it cheapens the retribution that the owner of wealth demands in exchange for his capital – it reduces the retribution demanded in exchange for the waiting. If the desire to save increases endlessly, investment grows more and more, and capital accumulates relentlessly. Marshall states that

> speaking generally, an increase in the power and the willingness to save will cause the services of waiting to be pushed constantly further; and will prevent it from obtaining employment at as high a rate of interest as before. That is, the rate of interest will constantly fall.
>
> (Marshall, 1920 [1890]: VI.II.37)

This passage talks about the growth of capital in the long term, but may also be applied to the problem of the short-term. The increase in the "propensity to save" is valued by classical theory as an incentive for employment, since it promotes the productive use of "free" capital and makes national income grow.

In Keynes's system, instead, saving is considered to be a mere residual of income, once the decision concerning the portion that will be devoted to consumption has been made. For the propensity to save of the community as a whole is always a relatively stable proportion of income. When the volume of aggregate income is modified, it is not the propensity to save but the magnitude of saving that changes. From this point of view, it is not saving but decisions concerning the level of expenditure (consumption and investment), as reflected in aggregate demand, which drive the increase in employment. Saving is passive and its effect on employment is, in any case, negative: on one hand, it is a residual, but also, if the propensity to save increases, the multiplier decreases and with it, employment falls:

> Saving, in fact, is a mere residual. The decisions to consume and the decisions to invest between them determine incomes. Assuming that the decisions to invest become effective, they must in doing so either curtail consumption or expand income. Thus the act of investment in

itself cannot help causing the residual or margin, which we call saving, to increase by a corresponding amount.

(Keynes, 1939 [1936]: 64; I.6.II)

The classical causal train may be compared to that derived from Keynes's system. While the *classical theory* argued that an increase in the desire to save is expansive, in Keynes's system the propensity to save is the other side of the propensity to consume. What is at stake is the proportion of aggregate income that is devoted to consumption and that which is earmarked for saving: they are, so to say, supplementary. When in Keynes's system the propensity to save increases, *ceteris paribus*, the portion of income devoted to current demand as consumption expenditure decreases, which results in a fall in employment. As may be seen, this is an image of the world opposite to that built by the classicists. Orthodox recommendations of austerity, based on *classical theory*, turn out to be fateful when its consequences are assessed applying Keynes's *system*. Against common sense and the *classical theory*, saving should not be considered "to build wealth", but rather, its increase triggers a curtailment of current demand, so that, for Keynes, "the growth of capital depends not at all on a low propensity to consume but is, on the contrary, held back by it" (Keynes, 1939 [1936]: 373; VI.24.I). An increase in the will to save, according to *classical theory*, will help lower the cost of capital and, therefore, promote the growth of product; in the *General Theory*, on the contrary, the same circumstance results in a reduction of employment:

> an individual decision to save does not, in actual fact, involve the placing of any specific forward order for consumption, but merely the cancellation of a present order. Thus, since the expectation of consumption is the only *raison d'être* of employment, there should be nothing paradoxical in the conclusion that a diminished propensity to consume has *cet. par.* a depressing effect on employment.
>
> (Keynes, 1939 [1936]: 211; IV.16.I)

This is, therefore, another of the reasons that account for Keynes's inquiry into fundamental categories: according to his system, an increase in the propensity to consume does not promote improvements in employment, but rather does the opposite. The difference in understandings is due to the fact that, in blatant opposition to the classical doctrine, the propensity to save does not rule here the movements of the rate of interest or the marginal efficiency of capital. Savings is not the source of accumulation because it does not necessarily translate into investment expenditure. Therefore, capital does not simply grow with an increase in savings. What is, then, capital?

If *Keynes's system* is seriously taken, then it becomes crucial to subject that question to discussion once again, as is argued in *The General Theory* when it states that

> The obstacle to a clear understanding is, in these examples, much the same as in many academic discussions of capital, namely, an inadequate appreciation of the fact that capital is not a self-subsistent entity existing apart from consumption. On the contrary, every weakening in the propensity to consume regarded as a permanent habit must weaken the demand for capital as well as the demand for consumption.
>
> (Keynes, 1939 [1936]: 106; III.8.IV)

The enquiry into the foundations cannot be avoided: underlying the *classical theory* and the *General Theory* there are different conceptions of capital.

There is still a third difference between capital as conceived of in Keynes's system and as in the *classical theory*, derived from the previous one. The *classical theory* posits that, *ceteris paribus*, a higher rate of interest incentives savings by compensating largely the sacrifice of waiting. From this explanation, the prescription to hold a high rate of interest with the purpose of promoting saving is inferred. Keynes recognizes here a suggestion that is typical of orthodox economists in times of crisis:

> The justification for a moderately high rate of interest has been found hitherto in the necessity of providing a sufficient inducement to save. But we have shown that the extent of effective saving is necessarily determined by the scale of investment and that the scale of investment is promoted by a *low* rate of interest.
>
> (Keynes, 1939 [1936]: 375; VI.24.II)

The direct link that the classicists establish between rate of interest and desire to save leads to the fateful advice of keeping a high rate of interest to encourage capital accumulation. In *The General Theory*, the effect of the increase in the rate of interest is the opposite to that anticipated by the *classical theory* through its positively sloped capital supply curve. For the classicists, if the curve for savings does not change, an increase in the rate of interest is necessarily associated to an increase in savings. For Keynes's system, instead, if there are no variations in the propensity to save, the fall of the rate of interest will result in an increase in the level of saving:

> aggregate saving is governed by aggregate investment; a rise in the rate of interest (unless it is offset by a corresponding change in the demand-schedule for investment) will diminish investment; hence a rise in the

rate of interest must have the effect of reducing incomes to a level at which saving is decreased in the same measure as investment.

(Keynes, 1939 [1936]: 110–111; III.9.II)

In these last two observations, not only are two opposite behaviors of the variables posited, but also a complete reversal in the direction of causality is introduced: according to the first quotation from Marshall, an increase in savings – considered here as an independent function, that is, a function that can change its form and position – causes an increase in investment; in Keynes's argument, saving is "passive" and adjusts until it equals the volume of investment that arises from the equaling of the marginal efficiency of capital and the rate of interest. Thus, in Keynes's system, the rate of interest does not impact the propensity to consume and, consequently, does not influence either the propensity to save. New questions then arise: where does the desire to save originate if a fall in the rate of interest does not weaken it? What is money? Why does it yield interest?

A simple comparison of variables' behavior makes it possible to identify a last difference between Keynes's system and the classical theory that, as will be seen, is also linked to the conceptual foundations, that is, to the explanation of the very nature of the rate of interest. For the classicists, the supply of capital increases when the rate of interest rises, because individuals are willing to sacrifice a larger portion of their present consumption in exchange for an increase of their future consumption when the retribution they receive for so doing is higher, that is, when, as was assumed, the rate of interest grows. On account of this same reason, the increase in the interest rate should induce them to delay consumption reducing their present expenditure. In Keynes's economic system, instead, the propensity to consume and, therefore, the propensity to save a portion of income, does not depend decisively or in a definite form on the rate of interest.

For the classical theory of the rate of interest [. . .] it was convenient to suppose that expenditure on consumption is *cet. par.* negatively sensitive to changes in the rate of interest, so that any rise in the rate of interest would appreciably diminish consumption. It has long been recognised, however, that the total effect of changes in the rate of interest on the readiness to spend on present consumption is complex and uncertain, being dependent on conflicting tendencies, since some of the subjective motives towards saving will be more easily satisfied if the rate of interest rises, whilst others will be weakened. [. . .] The usual type of short-period fluctuation in the rate of interest is not likely, however, to have much direct influence on spending either way.

(Keynes, 1939 [1936]: 93; III.8.II)

Both the behavior of the variables and the relations established among them are substantially different for the classicists and Keynes, which leads us once again to the question concerning the underlying explanation of the phenomenon of interest. For the classicists, an adequate depiction of human nature should contemplate an unquestionable psychological fact: human beings are "impatient" and they always prefer present consumption to future consumption. For the *classical theory*, this is a decisive factor when giving an account of the nature of capital and of interest. But the *General Theory* dares challenge that postulate concerning human nature. Thus, the *classical theory of capital* stands deprived of its fundamental axiom. Why is a rate of interest paid if individuals do not deem saving to be a sacrifice, but rather refrain from consuming on account of other motives, as the *General Theory* argues?

However, for Keynes, changing the functional relations that link economic phenomena, that is, changing "models" is not enough: he has to plainly reject the classical explanation of the fundamental categories. The rate of interest is no longer the factor that balances supply and demand of "free" capital. But neither is thus obtained the value of the marginal efficiency of capital. As Keynes points out, such "perplexities" force one to dig deeper, venturing into the dark regions of the fundamental concepts, so that "certain deeper perplexities, which may arise when we try to probe still further into the whys and wherefores" (Keynes, 1939 [1936]: 213; IV.16.I).

The theoretical incompatibility that arises in connection with the phenomena associated to capital also affects the sphere of money. The behavior that the *classical theory* attributes to money is completely different from that described by Keynes's system.

In the First Treatise, individuals demanded money on account of its utility, as it was considered to be similar to any other commodity. In the Second Treatise, money was demanded in order to be used as a means of exchange: now it lacks a utility of its own; thus, the total need of money that the system has depends on the amount of transactions. For Keynes, instead, apart from the need derived from transactions and precaution, the demand for money stems from the most significant trait that money as such has, at least the most significant as regards the determination of the level of employment: money can also be used as treasure. Thus, in Keynes's explanation, the rate of interest results from the relation between the supply of money in excess of circulation needs and the demand for money as "store" of value, which depends, in turn, on uncertain expectations concerning the future value of the rate of interest. A monetary theory of the rate of interest cannot be based on a limited concept of money as that posited by the *classical theory*, where the only role assigned to money is in the performance of purchases and sales.

In the Second Treatise, the *classical theory* admitted, to a certain extent, that changes in the quantity of money impacted the rate of interest, and tried – to no avail – to reconcile this new explanation with the one offered in the First Treatise. However, changes in the rate of interest due to "monetary" phenomena were deemed transitory disturbances that displaced the rate of interest from its "natural" level, determined by equilibrium on the capital market. In this case, the rate of interest would act as a transmission mechanism of the quantitative theory. Finally, the market rate of interest would return to the level dictated by the intersection of capital supply and demand.[5] This explanation was also rejected in all by the *General Theory*. Rather than admitting – implicitly or explicitly – the existence of two different rates of interest, Keynes's system definitively breaks with this explanation, and with the quantitative theory in all its forms by clearly distinguishing money's rate of interest and the marginal efficiency of capital. In the General Theory, the rate of interest is the "price" that equals the supply of money determined by government and liquidity preference.

As may be seen, neither the *classical theory* of money in the First Treatise nor that of the Second Treatise is able to support these causal sequences. In fact, the *classical theory* tried to prove by every means possible that money is just a "means", and that purely monetary phenomena are unable to modify relative prices, the volume of output or the retribution of labor and capital in real terms, either immediately or after a period of time. Clearly, this is not the role played by money, as depicted in *The General Theory*.

It is for this reason that, unfortunately for Keynes, the classical question concerning the origin of the rate of interest is now twofold: he will have to unveil the source of capital yield and, therefore, he will also have to study the nature of capital as such. But he will be forced as well to perform a similar analytical operation in connection with money and the rate of interest.

In brief, the elements provided by the *classical theory* of the rate of interest as determined on the capital market, and those furnished by the *classical theory* of money, based on the quantity theory that regulates either the quantity of intrinsic-value money or the price of non-intrinsic value money, translate into a set of dependent and independent variables, and some causal sequences leading to conclusions that contradict what *Keynes's system* asserts regarding the behavior of the economy.

The consequences of an increase in the quantity of money, an increase in savings, changes in the rate of interest, etcetera, are all different. And the ensuing practical recommendations are also diametrically opposed.

The crucial significance that these problems have for Keynes cannot be exaggerated. In fact, in his system, the main cause of disequilibrium is linked to a dearth in investment brought about, precisely, by the volatility of capital marginal efficiency, on one hand, and by the difficulties that prevent the rate of interest from reaching the position that guarantees full employment. Next we will show that the *classical theory*, which defines the rate of interest as a reflection of psychological preferences through time, on one hand, and as a result of the physical productivity of capital, on the other, imposes a definite limit – psychological and technical-material – to the movements of the rate of interest, which is evidently incompatible with Keynes's system and with the recommendations derived from it. How could it be shown that the marginal efficiency is highly changing and the rate of interest persistent on the basis of the *classical theory?* There is not anyone or anything that, from the classical point of view, could significantly modify – least of all "permanently" – production techniques or human psychology: in this terrain the classical system is forced then to trust in the blind economic forces. Keynes's system demands different foundations.

From the classical market of capital to the concept of capital in classical theory

For the *classical theory*, the rate of interest is determined by the "real" forces that operate on the capital market, and just as wages are the retribution of the "labor factor", the rate of interest is the retribution of the "capital factor". Now, this determination of the retribution received by capital is closely linked with some intrinsic traits attributed to capital itself. The *classical theory* had, no doubt, its own "concept" of capital, that is, its own explanation concerning the characteristics that differentiate capital from the rest of the commodities and from anything else.

What is, ultimately, for the classicists, capital? In the classical market of capital, the rate of interest is the "price" that reconciles capital demand (investment) and capital supply (saving). This notion leads to some precise and necessary conclusions concerning what capital itself is. Marshall devotes an appendix of his *Principles* to the discussion of the "definitions of capital" and concludes, in his typical style, that the explanation set forth in his book (undoubtedly marginalist in origin) is, in fact, a synthesis of all previous definitions: "The connection of the productiveness of capital with the demand for it, and of its prospectiveness with the supply of it has long been latent in men's minds" (Marshall, 1920 [1890]: 62n; Appendix E).[6]

If this definition is analyzed, its conceptual consequences will be immediately understood. Capital is, first of all, a commodity, which means, in marginalist terms, that it is both useful and scarce. However, it is not an ordinary good, any good; in order to be capital, it must necessarily and concurrently have two attributes: *prospectiveness* and *productiveness*. Not all goods are *prospective;* to be so, they have to be capable of being used as a means to postpone consumption, that is, as a good that is apt for materializing the will to save. It might be thought, therefore that all durable goods provided by nature or labor must be considered a capital good. This is not so. For the classicists (represented here by Marshall), capital is also *pro-ductive*. A durable good will only be considered capital if it is productive, that is, if it contributes to the process of manufacturing other goods so that through its employment, the physical volume of output is increased.

What is the relation between these definitions and the classical market of capital and the rate of interest? The classical school holds that human nature is such that individuals always prefer to consume their wealth (or income) in the present rather than in the future; in Marshall's words: "the postpone-ment of gratifications involves in general a sacrifice on the part of him who postpones" (Marshall, 1920 [1890]: VI.VI.3). Capital goods offer the pos-sibility to defer consumption, but, according to the classical school, human psychology turns saving into a sacrifice, originally called "abstinence", to represent thus the suffering implied in not consuming for someone who has certain wealth; Marshall, instead, prefers to call that same sacrifice "wait-ing".[7] This definition of the nature of capital is related to the classical theory of interest rates as follows. Man always prefers to consume in the present rather than in the future, so that to induce him to save, relinquishing his wealth to turn it into a capital good, he has to receive in exchange a retribu-tion that compensates the sacrifice of waiting. In contrast to the motivations that lead men to purchase a good destined to be immediately enjoyed, the holding of a prospective capital good under the form of saving must ensure an additional reward; such retribution or additional payment associated to capital goods is, precisely, the rate of interest. Marshall says: "human nature being what it is, we are justified in speaking of the interest on capital as the reward of the sacrifice involved in the waiting for the enjoyment of material resources" (Marshall, 1920 [1890]: IV.VII.30).[8]

The higher the rate of interest, the larger the supply of wealth to be turned into *prospective* goods (given the "disutility" of the waiting) will be. The rate of interest is, in fact, the measure of "impatience": "The unwillingness to postpone enjoyment, and thus to save for future use, is measured by the interest on accumulated wealth which just affords a sufficient incentive to save for the future" (Marshall, 1920 [1890]: I.II.20). This is the reason why the savings curve that links the amount of capital supplied and the rate of interest is positively sloped. But this is not enough.

The rate of interest exists, according to the marginalist explanation, because men are only willing to turn their resources into a *prospective* good, postponing consumption, if they receive in exchange a compensa-tion for the sacrifice involved in waiting: that is why there would not exist saving if there were no rate of interest, if the individual who saved did not receive more than what he originally gave. But to reward those who "wait" purchasing capital goods, these goods should have a second property – they have to be *productive*, since, as Marshall reminds us "Everyone is aware that no payment would be offered for the use of capital unless some gain were expected from that use" (Marshall, 1920 [1890]: VI.VI.3). If people were to save in *prospective, non-productive* goods, there would be no additional wealth to pay to he who waits. For this reason, the rate of interest becomes necessary due to the disutility of the waiting, but it becomes possible on account of capital productivity that "creates" the means to compensate the individual who saves, given that when capital is employed in production, it contributes to creating more wealth, which may be used to pay the saver.[9] Demand for capital goods is associated with this second attribute, and the rate of interest originates, on the other hand, in "the services which capital renders in production, and for which interest is the payment" (Marshall, 1920 [1890]: VI.VI.10). The higher the rate of interest, the smaller the capital demanded by producers: this is a negatively-sloped capital demand curve.

For the classicists, the phenomenon of interest rests on two "natural" conditions: a psychological one, stemming from human nature – the "disutility" of the waiting – and a technical one originating in the physical nature of productive processes – the capacity to "produce". Both of them meet and converge in capital goods, that are both productive and prospective at the same time, that is, that "produce" and work as a means to "postpone" consumption. If a good were not productive, no interest would be paid for it; if it were not prospective, a means to defer consumption – deferring enjoyment to the future, nothing would be demanded in exchange for its use. This is how the rate of interest arises from the specific traits of capital goods. The classical market of capital is nothing but the embodiment of this conception since, as Marshall argues, "the supply of capital is held back by the *prospectiveness* of its uses, men's unreadiness to look forward, while the demand for it comes from its *productiveness*, in the broadest sense of the term" (Marshall, 1920 [1890], 57n; VI.VI.I).

The theoretical consequences of this conception of capital are as numerous as they are important.[10] Only two of them will be mentioned: the first makes evident one of the fundamental motives that force Keynes to reject this theory of capital; the second makes it possible to ponder the deep theoretical effect derived from this change of front. First, the *classical theory* holds that capital is a particular kind of good (capital, it should be remembered, is a "real" good) that may be used *at the same time, necessarily*, to save, to defer consumption, and to produce. This theory of capital has as its inevitable result a blind trust in Say's Law and, therefore, it also results in the *classical* assumption of full employment, assumption from which Keynes means to free economics. According to the *classical theory* of capital, that disregards, besides, the existence of money, when an individual (or the society) receives its income, he can do only one of two things with it:

either he devotes it to present consumption, turning his wealth into a means of enjoyment, or he defers consumption, that is, saves.

But according to this theory of capital, savings are necessarily embodied in capital goods (prospective), and those capital goods are, in turn, productive, so that savings always become (or more precisely, are always) investment. Every act of saving is at the same time an act of investment. No other form of saving, of preserving wealth, is conceived of, so that the old proverb is true once again: supply creates always its own demand, because if income is not spent on consumption goods, it is spent on investment goods. Thus, the reason why Keynes has to replace this theory of capital with a new, different theory, one compatible with his own system becomes clear.

Second, this theory of capital and of the rate of interest should be in no way taken as a secondary aspect of the classical theory, particularly of the marginalist wing of the theory; rather, it constitutes one of its specific traits. Particularly, this conception of capital plays a leading role in Marshall's theory of value. It should be remembered that for Marshall the normal price is determined by each item's cost of production. Those production costs are made up, ultimately, of two "real costs", associated with two natural and inevitable sacrifices linked with production itself:

> The exertions of all the different kinds of labour that are directly or indirectly involved in making it; together with the abstinences or rather the waitings required for saving the capital used in making it: all these efforts and sacrifices together will be called the *real cost of production* of the commodity.
>
> (Marshall, 1920 [1890]: V.III.5)

On this basis, it is posited that capital and labor are two comparable efforts or sacrifices.

Through this explanation, capital becomes a "factor" of production; this is one of the main traits that distinguish *marginalism* from earlier and subsequent schools of economic thinking. In fact, the theory that makes capital a source of value was wielded as the main argument against the theory of value based exclusively on labor; and Marshall did not refrain from using it to rebut his antagonists:

> If we admit that [a commodity] is the product of labour alone, and not of labour and waiting, we can no doubt be compelled by inexorable logic to admit that there is no justification for Interest, the reward of waiting; for the conclusion is implied in the premise.
>
> (Marshall, 1920 [1890]: VI.VI.15)

He accuses, therefore, those who claimed Ricardo to be the author of such a theory as having misrepresented his ideas:

> Rodbertus and Marx do indeed boldly claim the authority of Ricardo for their premiss; but it is really as opposed to his explicit statement and the general tenor of his theory of value, as it is to common sense.
> (Marshall, 1920 [1890]: VI.VI.15)

Essentially, Marshall's theory holds that the sources of value are two: labor, but also the waiting associated with the acquisition of capital goods, as "the postponement of gratifications involves in general a sacrifice on the part of him who postpones, just as additional effort does on the part of him who labours" (Marshall, 1920 [1890]: VI.VI.16).

This conception of the origin of value also applies, naturally, to the origin of surplus. The authors who held that, for Ricardo, only labor was the origin of value would arrive at the conclusion that workers are subjected to exploitation:

> They argued that labour always produces a "Surplus" above its wages and the wear-and-tear of capital used in aiding it: and that the wrong done to labour lies in the exploitation of this surplus by others. But [. . .] it is the product of their labour, together with that of the employer and subordinate managers, and of the capital employed; and that capital itself is the product of labour and waiting: and therefore the spinning is the product of labour of many kinds, and of waiting.
> (Marshall, 1920 [1890]: VI.VI.15)

For Marshall, instead, as the aforementioned paragraph shows, the interest gained by the owner of capital should be considered a reward for the genuine sacrifice of the waiting and is, therefore, as legitimate as the wage with which the exertions of the worker are rewarded. Besides, due to the fact that the disutility of the waiting is a trait inherent in human nature, capital and interest are part of productive processes in any historical period and in any conceivable social form; even "Robinson Crusoe had to do only with real costs and real satisfactions: and an old-fashioned peasant family, which bought little and sold little, arranged its investments of present 'effort and waiting' for future benefits on nearly the same lines" (Marshall, 1920 [1890]; V.IV.26).[11]

To sum up, the *classical theory of capital* does not only provide an explanation of the movements of the rate of interest based on supply and demand, but it is also one of the pillars of the classical theory of value. The exertion of labor and the sacrifice of the waiting are the two real costs and, therefore, the two original sources of value of commodities. In the following pages, we will see how Keynes rejects and then replaces this explanation of the nature of capital and the origin of the rate of interest. Thus, it will become clear that Keynes's system has no connection to the classical (marginalist) theory of capital, which, indifferent to all criticism, provides its foundations to present-day microeconomics.

III Keynes's rebellion against the classicists

1 Capital and its yield

First step: the end of the waiting

Next, we will see that Keynes's theoretical construct will face new, eminently conceptual challenges. The *classical theory* holds that the "natural" level of the rate of interest, independent of any monetary transitory disturbance, is determined by a technical factor – productivity – and a psychological factor – time preference. Capital itself, therefore, is characterized by *productivity* and *prospectiveness*. Thus, the rate of interest is only modified as a result of changes in the technical origin of productivity or the time preferences of the public. Here, besides, one of the two "natural" sources of value has to be found: it is this "natural propensity" of man (his innate *impatience* and his aversion to frugality) that makes it necessary to add the sacrifice of the waiting to the exertion of labor when computing the real costs that determine the value of products; such real costs have existed throughout the history of man. On the other hand, the innate resistance to accumulating wealth, correlative to the greater enjoyment associated to immediate consumption, becomes an immovable hindrance to the decrease of the rate of interest: given certain "impatience rate", when the interest rate diminishes, savings decrease and accumulation together with it.[12] In equilibrium, the rate of interest must equal the rate of substitution of present consumption for future consumption; if the capital volume does not change, nothing can move the rate of interest from the position to which it inevitably returns: in the classical theory, human nature sets a precise limit to the reduction of the rate of interest.

Keynes's *system* cannot admit a theory of capital of this sort, full of practical consequences. Against traditional thinking, *the General Theory* posits that interest is a purely monetary phenomenon, determined by the relation between money supply and the liquidity-preference curve. It is true that in its determination certain psychological factors, linked to the uncertainty concerning the future values of the rate of interest, intervene; these are speculative motives. As may be seen, the rate of interest pertaining to money does not coincide with the classical rate of interest, which is the "fair" and necessary reward for the sacrifice of waiting. Keynes's ideas on this question cannot be clearer.

In contrast, the *classical theory* considered the rate of interest as an eminently "real" phenomenon, rather than a monetary one – at best, the monetary and credit context could be transitory disturbances, and the *classical theory of capital* considered that the act of saving was, essentially, an act of deprivation, which implied a certain degree of "suffering".

The break with the explanation that the rate of interest is a reward for the suffering of the waiting is as crucial as it is definitive for Keynes. The reasons that lead a man not to consume a certain portion of his income in order to save it stem also from certain traits inherent in human psychology, but such motives bear little relation to the saver's abnegation or sacrifice. According to the *General Theory*,

> There are, in general, eight main motives or objects of a subjective character which lead individuals to refrain from spending out of their incomes. These eight motives might be called the motives of Precaution, Foresight, Calculation, Improvement, Independence, Enterprise, Pride and Avarice.
>
> (Keynes, 1939 [1936]: 107–108; III.9.I)[13]

According to Keynes, men keep a portion of their material wealth to consume it in the future on account of these motives, and they need no compensation to reward their waiting. The notion of "human nature" is completely different in Keynes. Firms, institutions, and governments also devote a part of their income to saving. The institutions' reasons to act in this way are not similar either to those posited by the classical school, as they include the motives enterprise (make new investments), liquidity, improvement, and financial precaution.

Based on this conception of the causes that motivate saving, the conclusions arrived at are radically opposed to those emanating from the classical ideas: human psychology is such that saving would occur even if the well-known "retribution for the waiting" did not exist at all. It is possible to conceive of a society that saves a portion of its income independently of the level of the rate of interest, because the motives listed by Keynes always lead the society to put aside a part of its wealth for the future. There are, so to say, "positive values" that lead societies to save – saving is not a sacrifice. In fact, in Keynes's system, the propensity to save is considered to be relatively stable in the short term; its variations, specifically, do not obey the changes in the rate of interest in a definite fashion. Keynes states that

> the strength of all these motives will vary enormously according to the institutions and organisation of the economic society which we

presume, according to habits formed by race, education, convention, religion and current morals, according to present hopes and past experience, according to the scale and technique of capital equipment, and according to the prevailing distribution of wealth and the established standards of life. [. . .] We shall, that is to say, take as given the main background of subjective motives to saving and to consumption respectively.

(Keynes, 1939 [1936]: 108–109; III.9.I)

In other words, it is convenient to consider all of these factors as fixed in the short term, the period to which the analysis of the *General Theory* is restricted; remarkably, none of them is affected by the rate of interest.

The differences, however, do not end here. The changes introduced in the theory of capital also challenge the contents and the outcomes associated with the acts of saving performed both by the individual and the society. For the *classical theory*, an act of saving was equal to deferring consumption, which was achieved by *purchasing a good that would be part of the productive capital*. This was "real" saving, as reflected on the "real" capital market. In Keynes's system, instead, the decision to save does not necessarily translate into the purchasing of certain capital good. This is the reason why an increase in saving does not result automatically in an increase in investment. Keynes's theory of capital succeeds in breaking one of the primary mechanisms of Say's Law. It is neither true that when a society decides to save more, that very same act triggers a *productive* process (an act of investment) aimed at satisfying a future demand implicit in saving itself. Say's Law would still be valid if that were so, because every time consumption decreases today, an equivalent future demand is guaranteed, which supports the present level of production. In Keynes's system, saving is a different thing, its aims are different and its embodiment is different.

The absurd, though almost universal, idea that an act of individual saving is just as good for effective demand as an act of individual consumption, has been fostered by the fallacy, much more specious than the conclusion derived from it, that an increased desire to hold wealth, being much the same thing as an increased desire to hold investments, must, by increasing the demand for investments, provide a stimulus to their production; so that current investment is promoted by individual saving to the same extent as present consumption is diminished.

(Keynes, 1939 [1936]: 211; IV.16.I)

Keynes's rejection of the explanation of the rate of interest based on abstinence may be translated as follows. The classical theory of the waiting assumes that man is naturally endowed with a basic push towards present enjoyment derived from consumption, and states that if man or the society as a whole decides not to devote all its wealth to present consumption or not to devote all its labor to present enjoyment, it is making a sacrifice for which it ought to be compensated. With his "subjective factors", Keynes means to show that there are many reasons, also attributed to human nature, to not consume all the available wealth today, even if in the future no additional enjoyment is obtained. If, apart from the desire to enjoy in the present, human instincts include components such as precaution, foresight, calculation, improvement, independence, enterprise, pride and avarice, men will naturally tend to put aside a part of their resources to consume them in the future, independently of the level of the rate of interest. Saving (deferring present enjoyment) is not, therefore, an act associated with suffering, disutility or displeasure, but rather a product of a set of genuine human needs that drive men to "store" a portion of their wealth. That abstract and isolated individual who suffers when he works as much as when he does not consume, that is the leading character in a theory of value based on "effort" and "abstinence" is replaced with a man who, in society, has legitimate motives to save. Apart from needs satisfied with present consumption, other genuine new needs emerge that are only satisfied with future consumption, and this requires "happily" abstaining from consuming the whole income.

The demand for consumption goods does not only involve the present but also the future; the future is not equal to the present (but worse, because it is further on), but rather there are certain present desires involving a future satisfaction. It is, so to speak, a dated demand. However, in capitalist society, such desired future consumption, whose materialization date has not been set yet, forces the individual to preserve in some way a portion of his wealth, of his purchasing power over goods, leaving it aside for the future, that is, saving it.[14]

Now, once an individual decides to store wealth to consume it at some future date, he has to also decide how. According to the *classical theory*, there is, essentially, one single way: saving is always materialized through a new "free" capital good. If the money is given to a bank, the situation will change very little: the bank will loan it, and it will adopt the shape of productive capital. For Keynes, the desire to store wealth may be satisfied by purchasing a title of ownership representing rights over the revenue generated by a new investment, or by buying, alternatively, an old, already existing, investment. This first observation is enough to contradict the idea that every act of individual saving always and necessarily results in a new investment: in fact, it may exclusively involve the transfer of an already existing investment. But besides, according to Keynes's theory, wealth may be kept in a novel way, not contemplated by the classical theory: purchasing a debt title (bond) or directly storing money in cash. An individual's saving may increase without society's investment consequently increasing, and without a rise in the rate of interest, which depends on other forces.

What are, then, Keynes's objections to the old theory of abstinence? First, saving is not an individual sacrifice demanding an additional payment as a rate of interest. Second, physical capital is not the only object through which saving may be realized; when earlier on we mentioned the new role assigned by Keynes to money as a value deposit, it was not possible to elaborate on the deep consequences of this perspective, consequences that now become evident. Saving is not a synonym for supplying wealth for the purchase of a new capital good; for Keynes, saving is not embodied in new *prospective* goods: it may also be realized in the purchase of existing capital equipment, in money in cash or in debt titles bearing interest. Saving is no longer a positively sloped curve relative to the rate of interest, as used to be drawn in the classical market of capital.

The effects of this deep break with the *classical theory* cannot go unnoticed. Nothing seems to suggest that for the society as a whole, the decision to save may have the negative connotation on which the doctrine of interest rests in the *classical theory*. One of the two links of the theory of capital built on *productiveness* and *prospectiveness* is thus broken. Interest does not stem from the *prospectiveness* of capital simply because the waiting is not a sacrifice.

The consequences are, however, more far reaching: they affect, also, the classical theory of value. For Marshall, the *sacrifice of the waiting* was a real cost associated with every production and, as such, a distinctive aspect of his theory of value: will the waiting still be for Keynes a necessary real cost in every productive process? What are the consequences of his distancing from the classical doctrine in the field of the theory of value? Marshall had made the "exertion" and the "waiting", labor and capital, the foundation of every price and the cornerstone supporting his distancing away from other currents of economic thinking.

How far does the *General Theory's* distancing go? Keynes got rid of the theory of capital and the rate of interest based on the waiting, but this does not mean that in his system the rate of interest and the return on capital be absent. No doubt, capital bears a yield, as much as money bears an interest.

What is the nature of these phenomena? Capital is no longer considered as a *prospective* good or, at least, the rate of interest does not stem from that quality. The other quality that the classicists used to attribute to capital, *productiveness*, still has to be assessed.

Second step: the end of capital productiveness

Although Keynes managed to free himself from the definition of interest as a necessary retribution for the waiting, the classical theory of capital still has one of its two pillars: the source of interest could still be capital productiveness.[15] The possibility still remains that the capital rate of interest may originate in the "natural" or "technical" capacity of capital to increase the volume of output. The classical theory held that, in equilibrium, the rate of interest should be equated with capital productivity. In the Chapter 11 of the *General Theory*, it is first of all remarked that the classical definition of productivity is ambiguous in itself:

> [t]he *Marginal Productivity* or *Yield* or *Efficiency* or *Utility* of Capital are familiar terms which we have all frequently used. But it is not easy by searching the literature of economics to find a clear statement of what economists have usually intended by these terms.
>
> (Keynes, 1939 [1936]: 137–138; IV.11.II)

The claim made by Keynes is powerful. It is generally assumed that the productivity of capital may be calculated as the variation in physical productivity that results from the infinitesimal increase in the amount of capital used, with the other factors being held constant. More precisely, the productivity – marginal product – is defined as the quotient between the variation in the physical quantities of output and the variation in the volume of capital employed. However, ahead of the so-called "capital controversy", Keynes points out the obvious measurement, but also conceptual, difficulties entailed in this definition.[16] To measure the "physical" magnitude of capital as a whole – social, but also of a firm's – it is necessary to add non-homogeneous quantities of goods, which requires including in the calculation the value of each of them, thus transforming them in magnitudes of equal nature expressed in units of value. An aggregation (the summation of the value of capital components) may thus be performed, but at the expense of rendering the result invalid, because it is precisely the value of capital goods that is meant to be obtained by calculating productivity.[17] To calculate productivity, the rate of interest should be known, but the determination of the rate of interest requires, in turn, knowing the value of productivity. Doubts are also raised when trying to specify what is exactly understood by "a unit of capital" when, as happens in the case of social capital, what is referred to is a heterogeneous collection of goods.

> There are at least three ambiguities to clear up. There is, to begin with, the ambiguity whether we are concerned with the increment of physical product per unit of time due to the employment of one more physical unit of capital, or with the increment of value due to the employment of one more value unit of capital. The former involves difficulties as to the definition of the physical unit of capital, which I believe to be both insoluble and unnecessary. It is, of course, possible to say that

ten labourers will raise more wheat from a given area when they are in a position to make use of certain additional machines; but I know no means of reducing this to an intelligible arithmetical ratio which does not bring in values. Nevertheless many discussions of this subject seem to be mainly concerned with the physical productivity of capital in some sense, though the writers fail to make themselves clear.

(Keynes, 1939 [1936]: 138; IV.11.II)

The procedure suggested by Keynes to estimate capital yield separates itself completely from the classical definition. The concept of *marginal efficiency of capital* makes no reference to capital productivity in physical terms. When, in the reconstruction of Keynes's system, this novel definition was put forth, it was not still the right moment to deduce its deeper theoretical consequences, which will be discussed now. The prospective yield in money of capital equipment throughout its lifespan (the revenue from the sales of the products attributed to its employment, minus the production costs, are called annuities *A1, A2, . . . An* by Keynes) is compared to its present supply price (*P*), that is, how much it would cost to produce a new unit of equipment (its replacement cost).

Marginal efficiency is always associated to particular capital equipment, and it is calculated as the discount rate that equals the current value of the annuities that would result from the employment of an additional unit of equipment and its supply price. For the marginal efficiency of a capital equipment to be positive – to attract investors it should be positive and higher than the current rate of interest – the addition of the annuities it bears should surpass its replacement cost.

It would seem right to state, therefore, that also capital equipment is for Keynes, in a certain sense, "productive", as the total value of its output through time exceeds the initial value of the investment. It should be noted, however, that the definition excludes from its inception the idea that productivity in physical terms exists and can be measured, because all the sums are computed in expected purchase and sale prices rather than in physical quantities of heterogeneous and, therefore, incomparable goods. Even so, capital equipment, apparently, has to produce through its lifespan more "value" than what production actually costs, which involves a notion of "productivity" in terms of value.

The *classical theory* assumed that capital goods were "productive" goods. To understand Keynes's view on this question, the precise meaning of such an assertion has to be taken into account. Marshall and Böhm-Bawerk, for example, disagreed on their appreciation of the nature of capital productivity. For Böhm-Bawerk all lengthy production methods yielded a higher productivity *in physical terms*. The lengthier (*or more indirect*), the more efficient. The high productivity of lengthy or *roundabout* methods became the core of his explanation of interest; capital was simply made up of the intermediate goods involved in these *roundabout* more fruitful methods. Marshall, in turn, agreed that the employment of capital should always reward the loss of enjoyment through a higher productivity, although that increase in product was not necessarily explained by a lengthier production method. For this reason, in the case of Marshall, the fundamental core of his explanation is in the need to give always a reward for the waiting, and this is what forces men to choose more productive methods that allow them to pay a rate of interest to the saver. What does exactly mean that capital is productive?

Keynes has his own position in this debate. He favors, first, Marshall's idea of productivity, opposite from Böhm-Bawerk's: not every *productive* process is more efficient only because it is lengthier. The consequences of this choice are crucial, as has been seen, because, unlike Marshall, Keynes does not accept the explanation of the rate of interest based on impatience. Keynes says:

> It is true that some lengthy or roundabout processes are physically effi-
> cient. But so are some short processes. Lengthy processes are not phys-
> ically efficient because they are long. Some, probably most, lengthy
> processes would be physically very inefficient, for there are such things
> as spoiling or wasting with time.
>
> (Keynes, 1939 [1936]: 214; IV.16.II)

Thus, laconically, Keynes moves away from the *classical theory of capital*, which assumes that capital has two inherent qualities at the same time: *productivity* and *prospectiveness*. This means that if the goods employed in lengthy productive processes are purported to be capital, there is no physical or technical determination guaranteeing that the results derived from their employment will be greater in physical or value terms. As has been mentioned, capital productivity played a key role in the *classical theory:* Marshall found the foundation of capital interest in the sacrifice of the waiting that forced men to choose only those *lengthy* production methods that were productive to obtain, thus, a difference in product or value that would pay for the interest; Böhm-Bawerk's theory held that *roundabout* productive processes were, necessarily, more efficient, and that it was enough to value future goods less for the difference in value to become a profit, in the shape of an interest rate. The first argument had to be abandoned when the link between the rate of interest and the sacrifice of the waiting was broken. The second pillar of the *classical theory of capital* is now rejected: it cannot in any way be asserted that lengthy processes are more productive in any sense.

But then, if *lengthy* methods are not necessarily more productive, how does Keynes explain the general adoption of methods that take longer when their efficiency is not necessarily higher? The key lies – once again – in demand: the "positive" desires of men are not limited just to present consumption, but they involve, rather, also future needs. As has been said above, men's needs are distributed throughout time: some have to be met in the present, but others can exclusively be satisfied in the future. Among present desires involving future needs, there are some that have a precise date of realization; others, instead, are subject to uncertainty, and this is the reason why saving does not necessarily translate into an investment that sets in motion a new particular *productive* process.[18] But the truth is that there are certain future needs known today that entail the adoption of some lengthy processes, independently of their being more productive or not.

In a few words, it is production that will have to adapt itself to the schedule set by those dated future desires. Also in this field, it is demand that rules. The length of methods, that is, the length in time of productive processes does not mean in itself more efficiency, but rather that time is conditioned by a delivery date set by demand requirements. Even though there might exist processes that effectively become more productive on account of their length, it would be pointless to adopt them when it is not possible to expect an adequate volume of demand for the date when the finished product will be available.

> Given the optimum amount of roundaboutness, we shall, of course, select the most efficient roundabout processes which we can find up to the required aggregate. But the optimum amount itself should be such as to provide at the appropriate dates for that part of consumers' demand which it is desired to defer. In optimum conditions, that is to say, production should be so organised as to produce in the most efficient manner compatible with delivery at the dates at which consumers' demand is expected to become effective. It is no use to produce for delivery at a different date from this, even though the physical output could be increased by changing the date of delivery.
>
> (Keynes, 1939 [1936]: 215; IV.16.II)

All these elements lead to the same conclusion, upon which it is necessary to insist. Capital "interest" does not spring from the need to reward the waiting, but neither from the higher intrinsic productivity of lengthy processes. Capital, as opposed to what the *classical theory* posits, cannot be considered *productive and prospective* by nature. Keynes thus abandons the theory that traces the origin of capital interest rate to the psychological qualities inherent in human nature, and to the techno-physical qualities of certain lengthy productive methods. What is then the origin of the return yielded by capital equipment?

Two results are derived from the previous reasoning, results that contradict the very essence of the *classical theory*. First, capital, made up of the equipment involved in lengthy production processes, cannot be considered a "production factor" comparable to labor in any way. This is so because the reasons wielded to raise it to that condition, which are generally two, do not exist in Keynes's scheme. The first reason to turn capital into a productive factor is based on the assumption that the waiting is one of the necessary sacrifices of production, one of the costs that men, in any historical period, have to pay to obtain a product. Thus, capital goods, similarly to labor, are turned into "productive factors" because labor and waiting thus become two equivalent sacrifices or efforts; men, to produce, have to overcome his natural inclination to immediately consume and to devote all his time to leisure: the effort of work and the sacrifice of the waiting are, therefore, the two real costs of every product.

But besides, the other argument put forth to support the treatment of capital as a "productive factor" assumes that the material goods that make up capital have productive powers of their own; capital is thus placed, also from this perspective, on the same level as labor. Capital is a factor of production because it contributes to it physically, materially, and because both labor and capital produce equally.

In the *General Theory*, instead, capital is not a result of abstinence, and neither does it have productivity. Capital, according to Keynes, is not capable of producing by itself; besides, by earmarking certain goods for future consumption, men are not forced to experience a sacrifice equivalent to that of work; if men save, it is on account of other radically different motives, and they do not need to receive a reward for so doing: they do so in exchange for pleasure, and do not experience any suffering.

The theoretical consequences of these divergences are extraordinary. If capital is not productive, it is not, therefore, a factor of production. Capital is thus "debased". For Marshall, the factors of production were two: capital and labor. For Keynes, labor, aided by the state of the technique and operating in a certain natural environment, is the only source of value. Abstinence is not a "real" cost and interest is not the price of a service paid in exchange for the physical contribution of the addition of value performed by equipment. The *theory of capital* implicit in Keynes's *system*, and explicitly expounded in Chapter 16 of the *General Theory* does not coincide with that of the *classical theory* but is not, either, totally novel; rather, it follows the line of some earlier traditions. In fact, before the marginalist revolution, some theoretical schools considered labor and only labor as the source of social wealth, and as the only "real" cost of the product. By rejecting the notion that capital creates value, that it is productive, and by denying that saving is a sacrifice, Keynes is left with only one factor of production and only one source of value: labor.

In a passage that his "interpreters" consider, at best, enigmatic, Keynes acknowledges the consequences of his distancing himself from the *classical theory*, which, in Marshall's version, considered two factors of production: capital and labor. Keynes's distancing is not in the least enigmatic: it is the necessary result of his theory, which negates capital productivity. Due to his particular terminological choices, Keynes calls the Ricardians who endorsed the theory of value founded on labor "pre-classicists".

> I sympathise, therefore, with the pre-classical doctrine that every-
> thing is *produced by labour*, aided by what used to be called art and
> is now called technique, by natural resources which are free or cost a
> rent according to their scarcity or abundance, and by the results of past
> labour, embodied in assets, which also command a price according to
> their scarcity or abundance. It is preferable to regard labour, including,
> of course, the personal services of the entrepreneur and his assistants,
> as the sole factor of production, operating in a given environment of
> technique, natural resources, capital equipment and effective demand.
> (Keynes, 1939 [1936]: 213–214; IV.16.II)

This paragraph, together with others that follow it in Chapter 16 of *The General Theory* lead our analysis of Keynes's ideas in unexpected directions.

2 Keynes's theory of value

The expository order in which Keynes puts forth his new explanation, different from the traditional one, of the problem of unemployment in *The General Theory* is, certainly, singular and may be responsible to a certain extent for the indifference with which his successors approached the purely conceptual stretches of this work. In fact, most of the most renowned economists of all time (among them, Keynes) would begin the presentation of their system by introducing the primary categories – commodity, money, capital – to undertake later on, when the terrain had already been duly prepared, the discussion of the connections among those concepts and observable phenomena. Keynes reverses the usual order: after introducing, at the very beginning of the book, his system for the determination of observable variables, he devotes the final chapters to expose its foundations. We have already shown that, in spite of this peculiar expository order, there is a direct and necessary link between the system (or "model") put forth in the *General Theory* and the particular conceptions of money, capital and value posited by Keynes.

According to the First Treatise of the *classical theory*, real production costs were "labor and waiting", the two sacrifices that man has to make to obtain any useful product that nature does not provide him for free, with the objective of meeting his needs and securing the enjoyments he obtains through consumption. Marshall held that in every human society – even the solitary "society" of Crusoe on his island – the economic problem is always one and the same: how to assign the waiting and labor to obtain present and future satisfaction. Goods are valuable because men have to sacrifice their leisure (working) and their present consumption (saving and investing) to obtain them. In a market society, price becomes a reflection, a manifestation of such exertions and sacrifices, since the normal price of goods adjusts, ultimately, to real costs, inevitable and attributable to capital and labor expenses.

In the *General Theory*, Keynes uses the word "sympathize" to refer to his endorsement of the so-called theory of labor value, a word chosen, it is true, with certain meanness, given the magnitude of the assertion that follows it, emphasized in the original: "everything is *produced by labour*". But is Keynes actually persuaded that labor and only labor is the source of value and wealth? In fact, this fundamental theory of the origin of price allows us to reframe his argument on a new basis. Three reasons lead us to hold that it is possible to reconstruct Keynes's argument on the basis of a theory that founds value exclusively on labor. The first argument has already been discussed: the empirical results of his system, the quantitative and causal relation it establishes among variables, contradict an explanation based on the waiting as an inevitable cost, and on productivity as the physical source of profitability. That is, the classical theory of capital (and of value) is not compatible with Keynes's explanation of the empirical rate of interest and the marginal efficiency of capital or with their empirical manifestations.

Second, the hypothesis that only labor generates value is implicit even in the choice of measurement units employed in the system. That is, to build his system, Keynes used labor time, measured in hours of "ordinary" labor, as the only genuine measure of the volume of output. Keynes himself connects both choices explicitly. After stating that only labor is productive, he adds: "This partly explains why we have been able to take the unit of labour as the sole physical unit which we require in our economic system, apart from units of money and of time" (Keynes, 1939 [1936]: 214; IV.16.II).

Last, as will be seen, this explanation not only sheds new light on some fragments of the book, otherwise obscure and even incomprehensible, but also, without it, many of Keynes's assertions would be directly absurd. To prove the consistency of these theories of capital and value, it is enough to show that Keynes's entire system does not clash with them, as it in fact does with the traditional explanations offered by the *classical theory*.

Thus, Keynes comes closer to the theory commonly attributed to Ricardo (for Keynes, "pre-classical"), which shouldn't be too surprising: in fact, Marshall himself considers Ricardo his true inspiration and founder of the classical school. But at this crucial point, Keynes moves away from his teacher, Marshall. The theory of value that states that the price of any commodity exclusively reflects the expenditure corresponding to the labor required to produce the good had received harsh criticisms, as in the production of almost every product, other inputs resulting from past labor are used, which also make up the monetary immediate cost of the corresponding good. What is found, however, if the analysis goes back to the primary, genuine, irreducible costs? At the end of the road to the original sources of commodity value, Marshall would find two "real" costs, labor and capital, exertion and waiting; Keynes finds, instead, only labor.

For Keynes, the normal price of any commodity equals its labor cost, which measured in wage-units makes it possible to estimate the quantity of labor-units, that is, the amount of "simple" labor required to produce each commodity. The normal price must, therefore, be the money expression of the quantity of simple labor units employed, that is, the quantity of labor multiplied by the wage-unit.

Although this conclusion follows from the previous reasoning, the question concerning the origin of capital yield still remains unanswered. For, even though the explanation of the disutility of the waiting and that of the physical productivity of the productive equipment may be rejected, the existence of a return in excess of the amount invested in each capital equipment, that is, of a "profitability" that ends in the hands of the owner of such equipment, is a factual, unquestionable truth. However, as the source of that payment cannot be traced to the natural psychology of men, neither to the equally natural physical productivity of machinery, the need that the marginal efficiency of capital (what the classicists used to call rate of interest) be positive disappears. Still, Keynes will have to develop a new theory of capital capable of unveiling the origin of that difference, admitting that it can be positive, negative, or null. In *The General Theory*, an alternative to the classical theory of profit is offered: the theory of capital and yield based on scarcity, which replaces the theory of productivity and prospectiveness:

> It is much preferable to speak of capital as having a yield over the course of its life in excess of its original cost, than as being *productive*. For the only reason why an asset offers a prospect of yielding during its life services having an aggregate value greater than its initial supply price is because it is *scarce*.
> (Keynes, 1939 [1936]: 213; IV.16.II; emphasis in the original)

The return on capital is simply defined: it is the difference between the net money income that capital renders over its life and its replacement cost, also measured in money. According to Keynes, such a difference emerges because of a single reason: because capital is *scarce*, rather than because it is productive, as the *classical theory* stated (both in Marshall's as in his detractor, Böhm-Bawerk's versions). The *theory of the scarcity* of capital as the source of its yield is one of Keynes's original contributions. But what is the meaning of capital scarcity? To simplify the explanation, the consequences of the scarcity of any given good should be studied first. The argument goes as follows: the only real cost of production is labor. More or less labor is required to produce a commodity according to the state of technology, the stock of past labor products that are used as productive equipment, natural resources, and demand. The normal price of all goods is, ultimately and when production is not restricted in any way, a reflection of the real costs of production that are, in turn, proportional to the quantity of labor required to produce them. Any commodity will have a normal price that is proportional to the quantity of labor involved. But if for any reason the quantity produced is not enough to satisfy demand needs, then a situation of scarcity emerges, and the price of the product is set above that determined by the amount of labor.

The same may happen in connection with any service, as "there are all sorts of reasons why various kinds of services and facilities are scarce and therefore expensive relatively to the quantity of labour involved" (Keynes, 1939 [1936]: 215; IV.16.II). That is, when on account of any circumstance an amount of product or service smaller than that demanded is produced, due to the existence of a limit upon the volume of output, the sale price will be higher that the quantity of labor required in its production (its "normal supply price").

Now let's examine the case of capital equipment.

Here, scarcity is reflected in the relation between the production cost of equipments and the sale price of their services over time. In terms of Keynesian categories, there is scarcity when the replacement cost of the equipment is lower than the summation of all the annuities (without applying any discount yet).

Thus, the positive yield, that is, that difference, stems from scarcity, which may be shown with a simple hypothetical experiment: if the produced volume of that capital equipment were increased, the yield would decrease to the extreme where it would become null. Marginal efficiency "measures" the (discounted percentage) difference between annuities and cost, and decreases when output grows on two accounts: first, a larger demand of the same capital equipment leads to the supply price of the equipment rising (due to diminishing returns); at the same time, however, the larger future supply of its "services" will tend to reduce its price and, therefore, the expected annuities. When scarcity decreases, then, yield diminishes.

These are all the elements required to frame a true *Keynesian theory of value*, different in its essential characters from the *classical theory*. This theory explains the determinants of the prices of all commodities, including capital equipments and their services. The real cost of the products is exclusively made up of labor requirements. Commodities' prices, therefore, according to this explanation, should recognize as their sole source the amount of labor. However, it is also necessary to explain how the other three elements that determine market prices intervene in the setting of prices: natural resources, capital equipments that are, in turn, a product of past labor, and demand.

It is convenient to discuss first the simplest case: the determination of the price of a good manufactured through a *productive* process that takes practically no time, does not entail the use of goods whose production, in turn, takes time, and does not involve the use of natural resources. Such products will obviously be sold at a price that is proportional to the time of labor involved, which in this case is, besides, their only direct money cost. That will naturally be their normal price. It is worth stressing that here this theory and the "pre-classical doctrine" coincide. This example is similar to the famous "early and rude state of society" imagined by Smith in Chapter 6 of his *Wealth of Nations:*

> In that early and rude state of society which precedes both the accumulation of stock and the appropriation of land, the proportion between the quantities of labour necessary for acquiring different objects seems to be the only circumstance which can afford any rule for exchanging them for one another. If among a nation of hunters, for example, it usually costs twice the labour to kill a beaver which it does to kill a deer, one beaver should naturally exchange for or be worth two deer. (Smith, 1904 [1776]: 47)

That is the same explanation that Ricardo tried to broaden in order to encompass the processes where labor instruments were also used: the price of the product will then tend to equate the total labor time required to produce them over time. As may be seen, in this "pre-classical" theory of value, the involvement of "capital goods" in production can be smoothly integrated. Ricardo's revision is as follows:

> Even in that early state to which Adam Smith refers, some capital, though possibly made and accumulated by the hunter himself, would be necessary to enable him to kill his game. Without some weapon, neither the beaver nor the deer could be destroyed, and therefore the value of these animals would be regulated, not solely by the time and labour necessary to their destruction, but also by the time and labour necessary for providing the hunter's capital, the weapon, by the aid of which their destruction was effected.
>
> (Ricardo, 1821 [1817]: 1.30)

The same principle may be thus applied to determine the value of the products that use instruments in their production; the value is then equivalent to the labor applied not only directly "but the labour also which is bestowed on the implements, tools, and buildings, with which much labour is assisted" (Ricardo, 1821 [1817]: 1.29). All the goods produced by present labor, "assisted" by the products of past labor: value reflects both types of labor. This is the same that Keynes states.

With this in mind, Keynes's theory of capital may be examined again. How does scarcity intervene in this explanation? When certain special circumstances arise in a particular product's market, raising demand over supply and preventing the normal redressing of the situation by means of an increase in output, the "market" price of the commodity will increase, deviating until exceeding the normal price, that is, a value that is proportional to the time of labor required to produce the good. Keynes calls *scarcity* any situation that keeps the price of a product on a level higher than its real labor costs. For commodities in general, under pure competence conditions, *scarcity* price is merely accidental.

This analysis of the apparent movement of prices is shared by many authors belonging to different traditions. Ricardo, for example, establishes thus the difference between the "natural" and the "market" prices, keeping the distinction introduced by Smith in Chapter 7 of his *Wealth of Nations:*

> in making labour the foundation of the value of commodities, and the comparative quantity of labour which is necessary to their production, the rule which determines the respective quantities of goods which shall be given in exchange for each other, we must not be supposed to deny the accidental and temporary deviations of the actual or market price of commodities from this, their primary and natural price.
>
> (Ricardo, 1821 [1817]: 4.1)

This is also the distinction Marshall endorsed when separating the market and the normal prices. When, for some reason, supply is lower than demand, a situation of scarcity emerges that raises the market price over the normal price.

For Keynes, *scarcity* is a shortage, stemming from a limitation in production, in the amount produced relative to needs, a shortage that translates into an increase in the price of the product or of its services above their requirements in terms of labor. As the *Ricardian school* held, scarcity thus understood is a merely transitory phenomenon, because whenever the price of a commodity is above its "natural" value of price, an adjustment process is triggered:[19] the amount produced will tend to increase, and the price to decrease, until returning to its "natural" or "normal" level, proportional to the amount of labor applied to the production of the relevant good. This is the reason why in the definition of the "normal" price of a commodity, transitory scarcity cannot be taken into account. Scarcity dominates the price only when it is not possible to increase production; in that case, price rises beyond the real costs of production – made up, in Keynes's account, only of labor – proportionally to the strength demand might have relative to the limited supply. The extreme case has to do with the useful resources provided by nature in limited amounts. Marshall himself calls "scarcity price" the price over the costs of production that has to be paid when supply is limited. He explains this resorting to a fictitious example:

> Let us suppose that a meteoric shower of a few thousand large stones harder than diamonds fell all in one place; so that they were all picked up at once, and no amount of search could find any more. These stones, able to cut every material, would revolutionize many branches of industry; and the owners of them would have a differential advantage in production, that would afford a large producer's surplus [. . .] Then *the price of the services rendered by the stones would have been governed by the natural scarcity* of the aggregate output of their services in relation to the demand for those services; and the aggregate surplus or rent would most easily be reckoned as the excess of this *scarcity price* over the aggregate expenses of working the stones.
>
> (Marshall, 1920 [1890]: V.IX.8; emphasis added)

The price of the services that may be obtained by the use of a good whose production is limited by nature, but that is useful for production or consumption, and is therefore demanded, is a scarcity price.

Marshall calls *rent* the difference between the normal price (if there were no obstacles to increasing the produced amount of the good) and the scarcity price. Apart from the "meteoric shower", this is the case of limited natural resources, for example, workable land: as demand grows, given that the amount of available land cannot keep pace, the price is permanently modified, increasing over costs, and thus a rent for the owner of the land is generated. As Marshall states:

> Land, houses, and live stock are the three forms of wealth which have been in the first rank of importance always and everywhere. But land differs from other things in this, that an increase in its value is often chiefly due to an increase in its scarcity; and is therefore a measure rather of growing wants, than of growing means of meeting wants.
>
> (Marshall, 1920 [1890]: IV.VII.44)

It may thus be seen that through his notion of the scarcity price, Keynes comes closer to the "old" distinction, also present in Ricardo, between reproducible and non-reproducible products. The price of the products that can be multiplied is ruled by labor-time, whereas the price of the latter is *a scarcity price*, which stems exclusively from the conditions governing demand. The well-known quotation of chapter I of Ricardo's *Principles* describes this double source of value:

> Possessing utility, commodities derive their exchangeable value from two sources: from their scarcity, and from the quantity of labour required to obtain them. There are some commodities, the value of which is determined by their scarcity alone. No labour can increase the quantity of such goods, and therefore their value cannot be lowered by an increased supply. [. . .] Their value is wholly independent of the quantity of labour originally necessary to produce them, and varies with the varying wealth and inclinations of those who are desirous to possess them. These commodities, however, form a very small part of the mass of commodities daily exchanged in the market. By far the greatest part of those goods which are the objects of desire, are procured by labour; and they may be multiplied.
>
> (Ricardo, 1821 [1817]; 1.4–6)

Taking into account the above-mentioned theoretical elements, it is possible to reconsider Keynes's stance on value and the role played by capital goods. In the first example we studied, the output of a commodity where only labor was involved was discussed. Now, we are in a position to examine what happens in the case of a good whose production involves the "services" of a natural resource whose quantity is absolutely limited and is, for that reason, "absolutely scarce". In the price of that good, it is not only the labor-time directly required to produce that has to be factored in, but also the rent corresponding to the natural resources that are traded at a scarcity price. The scarcity price of the services of a non-reducible object provided by nature will move away from the production cost according to the pressure exerted by demand.

There is still one last element among those intervening in price determination that remains to be examined, an element that made us take this detour in our exposition: capital goods, which Keynes considers a result of past labor, but have, besides, a scarcity price, and are the base on which he supports his particular *theory of capital scarcity*. There has to be some particular circumstance that holds the condition of *scarcity* valid in the production of capital goods. And such scarcity is not founded, as in the case of natural resources, on the fact that these goods are products offered by nature and cannot, therefore, have their amount increased in any way. If any limit to the amount of capital goods produced could be found, an explanation of capital yield would be obtained; capital yield would then be equivalent to the difference between the production cost of the equipment in labor and the (higher) aggregation of the price of the services that equipment renders over its lifespan. The return obtained would be a scarcity product if it could be proved that such difference stems from a hindrance that prevents the produced quantity to grow until the aggregation of annuities decreases equaling the value of the capital good replacement cost, and that, therefore, it adopts the form of a positive marginal efficiency.[20] The scarcity price associated with the services of capital equipment has to be involved, besides, in the prices of all the goods in whose production capital is employed, prices that are not only determined by the quantity of labor directly or indirectly required to produce them, but that must also pay tribute on account of the scarcity of the capital involved in the production of the relevant goods.

Keynes reasons as follows: if the circumstances that cause the scarcity of capital equipments limiting their production volume did not exist, the quantity of such equipments would tend to increase, thus reducing the sum of the annuities until the point when the summation of the expected annuities equals the replacement cost. The marginal efficiency of capital would in that case equal zero, which for Keynes's theory is perfectly conceivable because capital is not productive "in itself", nor is saving conditioned upon the existence of interest. The impact on the value of the products that employ capital, in the hypothetical case that capital equipments were no longer scarce (unlimited as to its quantity) is obvious: in such a world, the price of goods that involve capital in their production would exclusively depend on the amount of labor (and on natural resources' rents), just as the goods that do not require capital, as was earlier argued:

> the products of capital selling at a price proportioned to the labour, etc., embodied in them on just the same principles as govern the prices of consumption-goods into which capital-charges enter in an insignificant degree.
>
> (Keynes, 1939 [1936]: 221; IV.16.IV)

To complete Keynes's explanation of capital yield, the *cause* of the mentioned *scarcity* of capital equipment still remains to be identified. And this cause lies in the fact that capital goods are purchased at a certain moment (the current period) but may also be employed in later periods: they may be used to "preserve" wealth, that is, "It is by reason of the existence of durable equipment that the economic future is linked to the present" (Keynes, 1939 [1936]: 146; IV.11.V). Capital goods cannot be sold immediately, but rather their services must be applied over time: they become a deposit of value but, also, they compete against other forms of accumulating wealth. In Keynes's economic system, there is an alternative way of doing this. In the *General Theory*, money also serves to store value, thus becoming an alternative option to the ownership of capital goods. Therefore, the purchase and the production of productive equipment compete with money accumulation, since both have the quality of linking present and future; like capital (durable) goods, "the importance of money essentially flows from its being a link between the present and the future" (Keynes, 1939 [1936]: 293; V.21.I). Men have desires, on account of the mentioned motives, that can only be satisfied through the accumulation of wealth that will be employed in the future. Money and durable goods are the two available ways of doing this, and this alternative bears consequences that impact on the determination of value of capital good services; such "competence" with money is reflected on the very scarcity of capital goods.

The supply of capital goods does not increase until marginal efficiency is reduced to zero because nobody would be willing to invest his present wealth in the purchase of a capital good if its yield was not higher than the current rate of interest.

The rate of interest thus becomes a barrier that limits the production of capital goods, and supports their scarcity relative to demand, becoming the ultimate source of their yield. This is the cornerstone of the Keynesian theory of capital yield since

> For the only reason why an asset offers a prospect of yielding during its life services having an aggregate value greater than its initial supply price is because it is *scarce*; and it is kept scarce because of the competition of the rate of interest on money. If capital becomes less scarce, the excess yield will diminish, without its having become less productive – at least in the physical sense.
>
> (Keynes, 1939 [1936]: 213; IV.16.II)

One of the two questions that Keynes had to answer is thus resolved: the question of the origin of the surplus value that the owner of the capital obtains in excess of the original cost of his purchase. But another still remains to be answered, no doubt, concerning the origin of money interest. The importance of the rate of interest is intensified in light of the *theory of capital scarcity*, because capital is scarce on account of the existence of the interest rate on money. It is the rate of interest that which sets a limit to the increase in the production of capital goods, thereby making services more costly, raising the price of such goods over the labor time required for their production.

The rate of interest is, according to Keynes, the factor that sets a limit to production and makes capital goods *scarce*. On one hand, their production is limited, since if the price of their services were further reduced, it would always be more profitable to purchase an interest-yielding debt, and on the other, demand exerts pressure to raise their price: scarcity stems from the difference between demand and a limited supply, and from scarcity derives, in turn, the return obtained by selling the services of an equipment at a price that exceeds the value set by the volume of labor required to produce it.

The source of an interest yielded by a money with no intrinsic value

Keynes's fundamental theory of money and the rate of interest is the last stop in this study. The relevance of money in the *General Theory* cannot be overrated. Consumption is established as a fixed ratio of income, so that the weight of the determination of the volume of employment rests on the size of investment demand. Entrepreneurs' decisions concerning how much to invest depends, on one hand, on their estimations concerning prospective yield, measured by capital marginal efficiency. It has been shown that capital yield originates in the condition of relative scarcity in which capital goods are kept. But such scarcity is brought about, precisely, by the "competition" between the yields on capital equipment and the rate of interest, given that these are the two alternative options to store wealth.[21] The nature and origin of money's rate of interest thus becomes a scientific puzzle of utmost importance for Keynes since, somehow, the system's level of employment is conditioned by the level of the rate of interest, capable of "stopping" the process of investment. What is money and why, by lending it, does its owner obtain a rate of interest?

The *classical theory of money* identified two functions in money: its role as a measure of value, in the First Treatise, and as a means of circulation, in the Second Treatise. Keynes criticizes the *classical theory* of money not only because of its contradictory nature, but also because it omits a third role played in practice by money: a store of value. In fact, the conclusions of the *classical theory* are arrived at "[o]nly in the event of money being used solely for transactions and never as a store of value" (Keynes, 1939 [1936]: 182; IV.14.I). This function, neglected and dismissed by the classicists, was recognized, however, by earlier theories of money: it is an "old" distinction that has to be reinstated to adequately characterize money, "we can usefully employ the ancient distinction between the use of money for the transaction of current business and its use as a store of wealth" (Keynes, 1939 [1936]: 168; IV.13.II).

Keynes introduces money as a store for value in his theory, and he does so because if he did not, he could not represent analytically the real way how investment expenditures are made: the purchase of a capital equipment is decided by comparing its yield against the current monetary rate of interest; but this, in turn, forces him to admit that wealth can be accumulated either as capital equipment or as money deposits. Money works as a "treasure". To make this possible, it is necessary to acknowledge that role that the *classical theory* would deny money when asserting that it should be considered a "means" or a "vehicle" of purchasing power, and that it is never "desirable" in itself since its utility stems from the commodities that can be currently purchased with it.

Such functional difference leads us to the heart of the matter. The relationship of the *classical theory* with money had always revolved around the determinants of money "value". The dilemma of the quantity theory lies in this replacement, for when commodity-money circulates, it is the prices of the other goods (and its own value) that seems to determine the quantity of money required, whereas when what circulates is paper money, the quantity of money seems to determine commodities' prices (and the "value" of money). The *classical theory* of money thus remained bogged down in these paradoxes without being able to order or conceptually understand them.

It could be said that the economic transformations of the early twentieth century spared Keynes some of the problems that troubled the classicists. The definitive abandonment of the gold standard is the historical basis upon which the *General Theory* rests to postulate, *ex definitione* and without the need of resorting to further explanations, that the amount of bills in circulation is fixed by government. It is not necessary to even mention gold, the commodity-money, in the argument. As to the motives that lead individuals to wish to hold certain amount of money, not only the role of money as a means of circulation is taken into account, a role that prompts the demand for money on account of the transaction-motive, but also the role of money as store of value or treasure – linked to the precautionary motive and, particularly, to the speculative motive – is added.

This is the first singularity of money in the *General Theory*, as opposed to the classical conception: bills have the capacity to store value, and from that capacity an additional demand for money springs.

Supply is given, and the demand for transactions depends largely on the volume of output and income, so that the excess resulting from the difference between available money and the amount required for business transactions is absorbed by the storing function. Individuals will have to distribute among them that quantity of money that works as treasure: if somebody does not wish to keep money in cash, he may lend it as a "debt", and thus, as a result of such change of hands, the rate of interest is determined. According to this explanation, the rate of interest bears no relation whatsoever to capital yield or time consumption preferences. The rate of interest is, simply, the reward for parting with the liquidity embodied in money. However it may be, money is capable of returning to its owner pregnant with interest. Keynes's "valueless money" keeps and creates value. Why?

The essential properties required to be money

The chapter devoted to studying "The Essential Properties of Interest and Money" is the longest in the *General Theory*. Its content, however, was almost unanimously discarded by subsequent economists, even by those who accepted – more or less faithfully – Keynes's *system* as their own. The reasons to ignore the fundamental theory of money, if explicitly stated at all, are largely as inadequate as insufficient.[22]

The chapters devoted to the enquiry into the fundamental categories contain, however, Keynes's explicit search for the adequate answers to the questions that his own *system* implicitly raises, questions that the *classical* tradition cannot answer with its theories of capital, money and value. Keynes is aware that, without this conceptual elaboration, his approach would be incomplete, because the *system* refers to the behavior of certain phenomena described employing economic categories such as capital, money, interest, yield and value, and the author finds that such categories do not fit into the inherited explanations. If Keynes did not attempt to find his own answers, the system would work in a vacuum, as it would refer to unknown concepts, which cannot be understood based on the *classical theory*. This need to go deeper into the concept of money itself is, for Keynes, the "natural" course for his research, in spite of it not being in the least so for contemporary macroeconomics.

> It seems, then, that the *rate of interest on money* plays a peculiar part in setting a limit to the level of employment, since it sets a standard to which the marginal efficiency of a capital-asset must attain if it is to be newly produced. That this should be so, is, at first sight, most perplexing. It is natural to enquire wherein the peculiarity of money lies as distinct from other assets, whether it is only money which has a rate of interest, and what would happen in a non-monetary economy. Until we have answered these questions, the full significance of our theory will not be clear.
>
> (Keynes, 1939 [1936]: 222; IV.17.I)

It is helpful to first take a closer look at the classical concept of money, so that when later dealing with Keynes's explanation, the contrast between both may be easily established. What is money ultimately for the classicists? As has already been pointed out, the classical departure point consisted in taking any commodity, the value of which was determined by the general laws that rule all relative values, to turn it then into a *numéraire* – Walras – or leave its value fixed – Marshall – turning it thus into a *value* measure or standard for all the system. Actually, any commodity qualified to become commodity-money, for money stemmed from an analytical need. To this conception, an additional explanation is afterwards added: given the intricacy that would characterize a generalized process of exchange in a barter economy, money, independently of the requirements imposed by the system, must exist as it would be practically impossible to do without it. Seen as a fundamental "explanation" of money's origin and nature, it should be said that this characterization is quite peculiar: it states that given that money actually exists, then it must exist. Then, it is descriptively argued that, as money must work as a measure standard, and given that some commodities are, on account of their physical traits, more appropriate than others to perform this task, the responsibility of being money falls "naturally" on them. Specifically, precious metals perfectly meet the requirements of being meltable, divisible, and of embodying a high value in little material substance. This being said, gold becomes the money of the First Treatise: it is an ordinary commodity with variable relative value, ruled by the general laws, but with a fixed intrinsic value, thanks to an analytical assumption. So much for the classical theory of value in the First Treatise; as for the Second Treatise, the conception of money has a different root. Initially, a new function, also "evident", is added. As commodity-money has value on account of it being a commodity itself, but expressing concurrently the value of all the other goods due to it being money as well, all commodities must, first, be exchanged for gold, as in fact they are. Gold is thus put into circulation, playing the role of a means of exchange.

It is then observed, in passing, that in the real world, gold can be replaced in its circulatory role by many other representatives *with no intrinsic value*. In the First Treatise, no definition of money was offered as it was assumed that it could be any commodity; in the Second Treatise, a conceptual definition of money is not provided either, which is compounded by the fact that, through a sleight of hand, money is replaced by valueless papers, without furnishing an adequate theoretical justification. Money with intrinsic value that does not circulate, whose quantity is determined according to the system's "needs", is replaced with circulating money that does not have intrinsic value and that, besides, seems to be exclusively a "means" to trade commodities.

Herein lies, precisely, the conceptual challenge that Keynes has to face: his *general theory of money* has to deal from its inception with a valueless money rather than with commodity-money. The definition of the nature of money, therefore, does not seem to be as natural and simple. What Keynes first notices in this fiat money is not these two basic functions, but rather the fact that it is an adequate means to preserve or "store" value; thus, what distinguishes money as such is that it can be used as a store of wealth, as treasure, and that the struggle to keep it is solved through the emergence of a rate of interest on debts; the rate of interest itself must be understood as a reward for parting with money in cash. Thus, Keynes's theory of money dovetails with his explanation of capital. It is not a question of spotting money's particular traits contrasting it against commodities in general, but against capital, as both capital assets and money share the property of yielding a return. Instead of beginning, like the classicists, with a list of the "observable" functions played by money, his question refers directly to the origin of money's "yield", the rate of interest. If the explanation begins with valueless fiat money, the first thing that becomes blatantly obvious is that those stamped papers become very similar to physical assets, and that such a similarity cannot stem from their useful qualities, as they simply have not got any. On the other hand, nothing is achieved by asserting that money is an instrument designed to simplify exchange: this explanation does not help find the origin of money's rate of interest but, rather, turns money into a passive vehicle of exchange. Therefore, Keynes has no other option than to approach the core of the problem: both money and capital goods yield a return, but those returns must surely come from different sources. Capital goods yield a return because they are scarce.

What is the source of money yield? The comparison between money "yield" and the return on physical assets entails a complication: as in practice both are expressed in terms of money, money's "pure" yield is always combined with the "pure" yield that different assets bear. To identify the differences between money and all the other assets, Keynes first needs to express the yield provided by each asset, including money, in a pure form. With this purpose, he resorts to a clever procedure devised by P. Sraffa.[23] The idea consists in calculating the rate of interest on each good in terms of itself as the percentage difference between the present and future quantities of the relevant good that currently have equal "exchange value".

In his example, if 100 quarters of wheat are worth today the same as 105 quarters of wheat to be delivered in a year's time, then the annual interest rate of wheat as measured in wheat terms is 5 percent. The own-rate of interest is the difference between two quantities of wheat with equal value but contracted to be delivered at different moments. The same operation may be carried out with each durable asset, and even with money: its rate of interest is nothing but the percentage difference between a spot quantity of money and the quantity of money that the market will supply in a years' time in exchange for that same sum. The rate of interest of money will be 5 percent if $100 have to be paid today to obtain $105 in a year, "[t]hus for every durable commodity we have a rate of interest in terms of itself; – a wheat-rate of interest, a copper-rate of interest, a house-rate of interest, even a steel-plant-rate of interest" (Keynes, 1939 [1936]: 224; IV.17.I).

The definition of the own-rates of interest has an actual embodiment in the case of goods for which there is a market where, in practice, future contracts are traded; in that case, the own-rate of interest may be estimated effectively as the relation between the spot price and the "future" price in money of the contracts traded (the calculation should be such that the result should not involve the rate of interest on the money in which both prices are expressed). Keynes resorts to this tool to equal the yields of all durable assets, thus placing on the same level and rendering mutually comparable the marginal efficiency of different capital equipment and the money-rate of interest: "So far, therefore, the money-rate of interest has no uniqueness compared with other rates of interest, but is on precisely the same footing" (Keynes, 1939 [1936]: 225; IV.17.I). From here on, Keynes seeks to distinguish the return on capital (on durable goods) from those on money, to analytically isolate the essential qualities of money. And here is where novelties begin.

Keynes posits that the own-rate of interest of each good is constituted by three "attributes" that all assets and durable goods – including money – have in different degrees: the capacity to contribute to production or to supply services to a consumer in a period of time, q *(yield)*; the wastage or storage costs required to keep the asset, c (carrying cost); and, lastly, its liquidity premium, l.[24] The rate of interest for each good in terms of itself is calculated as $q - c + l$. The first two elements were – tacitly – present in the definition of the marginal efficiency of capital, but a new quality that becomes a new source of "rate of interest" of all assets now emerges: liquidity. Any asset, in principle, possesses a certain "yield" stemming from its liquidity.

> [T]he power of disposal over an asset during a period may offer a potential convenience or security, which is not equal for assets of different kinds, though the assets themselves are of equal initial value. There is, so to speak, nothing to show for this at the end of the period in the shape of output; yet it is something for which people are ready to pay something. The amount (measured in terms of itself) which they are willing to pay for the potential convenience or security given by this power of disposal (exclusive of yield or carrying cost attaching to the asset), we shall call its liquidity-premium l.
>
> (Keynes, 1939 [1936]: 226; IV.17.II)

Thus, the rate of interest of the different assets stems from the combination of the three factors: its *output* minus its *carrying cost* and its liquidity, due to the "convenience or security" it offers. The *classical theory*, in turn, also held that the rate of interest was associated with certain immanent attributes of capital goods: their prospectiveness and their productivity. Both qualities are, so to speak, natural. Human nature is such that men prefer present enjoyments to future ones, and that is why an interest is claimed in exchange for parting with wealth and postponing consumption. Capital is prospective because it is a suitable means to defer enjoyment. On the other hand, the technical nature of certain lengthy processes is such that by employing capital equipment, the volume of output grows. The surplus that capital is able to yield on account of it being productive is what then becomes the necessary rate of interest for equipment to be used in roundabout processes. Based on this classical explanation, it is not possible to conceive of any form of society where man would not be accompanied by capital, and where an interest should not be paid (explicitly or implicitly) in exchange for its use.

Keynes's theory of capital scarcity accepts that, under current circumstances, capital offers a yield to its owner. The exclusive reason for such a situation is that the quantity of capital goods produced is *scarce* relative to the demand for their services.

Capital yield is the price that has to be paid for capital *scarcity*. It does not stem from the sacrifice made by the man who has to wait instead of consuming, or from the higher productivity of lengthy or roundabout processes. If the conditions that cause scarcity were to disappear, capital yield would disappear with them, because by increasing output and, therefore, the quantity of an asset supplied, its marginal efficiency would tend to decrease. This explanation of capital yield is, so to speak, subsumed under the above-mentioned theory of the yield of durable goods. It is possible to establish a general law for the stock of assets as a whole according to which the yield of each of them (their own-rate of interest) would tend to become equal to the rest, since if the rate of interest of a capital good were higher than the other rates of interest, investment would flow in that direction and, therefore, the supply of that good would increase until its yield reached the level of the other own-rates of interest: "As output increases, own-rates of interest decline to levels at which one asset after another falls below the standard of profitable production" (Keynes, 1939 [1936]; 229; IV.17.II). There are, thus, "automatic economic forces" that push, first, the own-rates of each asset until they all become equal, and then exert pressure until they are equivalent to zero; for the cancellation of the yield to occur, obviously, the output of all assets should be capable of growing without limits. It may also be the case that the economy reaches full employment before the rate of interest of all goods equals zero. In any case, output increases and all the own-rates of interest decrease simultaneously:

> Thus with other commodities left to themselves, 'natural forces,' i.e. the ordinary forces of the market, would tend to bring their rate of interest down until the emergence of full employment had brought about for commodities generally the inelasticity of supply.
>
> (Keynes, 1939 [1936]: 235; IV.17.III)

This is another way of framing Keynes's general conception of the obstacles posed to attaining full employment. The inexorable decline of yield would come to a halt if the own-rate of interest of any asset would decrease at a slower pace than the others or if it would directly stop diminishing, and if that good were furthermore capable of absorbing resources limitlessly. For, under such circumstances, the increase in the output of all the other goods would also come to a halt. That asset whose rate refuses to decrease would play the same role that money plays in the system of the General Theory, since, as Keynes asserts,

> It is now apparent that our previous statement to the effect that it is the money-rate of interest which sets a limit to the rate of output, is not strictly correct. We should have said that it is that asset's rate of interest which declines most slowly as the stock of assets in general increases, which eventually knocks out the profitable production of each of the others.
>
> (Keynes, 1939 [1936]: 229; IV.17.II)

If there were an asset in the economic system that, on account of its special qualities, had an own-rate of interest that was reluctant to fall or an own-rate of interest that would fall more slowly than the others, that asset would be the *money* in the system, and this is precisely what Keynes needed to prove; however, the reason of this reluctance has not yet been explained.

> In attributing, therefore, a peculiar significance to the money-rate of interest, we have been tacitly assuming that the kind of money to which we are used to has some special characteristics which lead to its own-rate of interest in terms of itself as standard being more reluctant to fall as the stock of assets in general increases than the own-rates of interest of any other assets in terms of themselves.
>
> (Keynes, 1939 [1936]: 229; IV.17.III)

The strategy that Keynes employs to find the essential properties of money is thus outlined. All the assets that yield a return (including money) have been put on an equal footing. The rate of interest of all of them tends to decrease "naturally" when output increases, on one hand, and when their demand falls, on the other. The asset whose rate of interest falls more slowly than the others is, from this point of view, the money of the system. Therefore, the particular properties of the asset whose own-rate of interest is reluctant to decrease should be identified, based on the theory of capital yield, because these qualities would ultimately be the essential properties of money. Once this enigma is solved, it will be possible to answer new questions. First, the existence of an active with such properties is the cause of insufficiency in investment and employment. Can money, therefore, be "abolished"? Because if it could, the output of all assets would grow, and their yield would fall until full employment were attained. The very definition of money, and of its relation with the yield and the output of the other assets leads Keynes to assert that "in the absence of money and in the absence – we must, of course, also suppose – of any other commodity with the assumed characteristics of money, the rates of interest would only reach equilibrium when there is full employment" (Keynes, 1939 [1936]: 235; IV.17.III).

What characteristics must an asset have for its own-rate of interest not to reduce "naturally", as all the others do? The behavior of the rate of interest of an asset other than money may be described as follows: first, when its yield is higher than that of the other assets, there is an incentive to increase its output. Second, such an increase in its output contributes to choke off the demand of its services and, thereby, to reduce its scarcity price, thus diminishing its yield q (stemming from scarcity). But besides, the increased output of an asset tends to raise its carrying cost c. Output increase, the ensuing decrease of q and the increase in c reduce together an asset's yield (its own rate of interest) that thus tends to become equal to the general level. Therefore, the conditions for an asset's yield to decrease when it is higher than the rest are, to summarize, three, namely:

1   When the yield of an asset rises above the other rates of interest, its output must tend to increase: supply has to be elastic.
2   When output increases, demand has to fall or at least be stable because the services of the other goods become cheaper: substitution elasticity has to be different from zero.
3   The carrying cost of the asset has to increase together with the increase in the holding of the asset.

If all these conditions are met, the own-rate of interest of a good tends to become equal to the others and, in general, tends to decrease when the volume of output of the relevant good increases. Then, all the rates tend to decrease until full employment is attained, a situation that is reached when the supply of all assets stops being elastic. Consequently, if the three above-mentioned conditions were met for all assets, the situation of scarcity that prevails when there is an asset whose rate does not decrease would be eliminated. Ordinary durable commodities meet these three requirements. But, following what has been said, it is possible to analytically infer the special characteristics of the asset that works as money in the system, that is, the asset whose rate of interest does not react to the stimuli that bring about the decrease of its yield. It has to be an asset whose quantity is always scarce relative to demand, so that its yield is always high. For this to be so, it supply should not "naturally" increase when its yield grows. Thus, one of the mechanisms that lower the own-rate of interest of each asset stops working:

> money has, both in the long and in the short period, a zero, or at any rate a very small, elasticity of production, so far as the power of private enterprise is concerned, as distinct from the monetary authority; – elasticity

of production meaning, in this context, the response of the quantity of labour applied to producing it to a rise in the quantity of labour which a unit of it will command.

(Keynes, 1939 [1936]: 230; IV.17.III)

In fact, the "output" of fiat money, which is in the hands of the authority, is inelastic. This attribute behaves as described, since the high yield of money does not automatically stimulate production and, therefore, does not to automatically reduce the rate of interest. However, this is not an exclusive quality of money, but rather it is shared with natural resources, whose production is absolutely inelastic. There is, therefore, another quality that also contributes to the same result: the demand for the asset "money" does not decrease when its "price" rises. That is, in contrast to what happens in connection with the demand of any other commodity, even if the scarcity value of the asset is high, its demand does not decrease. And this quality is inferred from the fact that it cannot be replaced in its functions with any other asset:

> it has an elasticity of substitution equal, or nearly equal, to zero which means that as the exchange value of money rises there is no tendency to substitute some other factor for it; – except, perhaps, to some trifling extent, where the money-commodity is also used in manufacture or the arts.
>
> (Keynes, 1939 [1936]: 231; IV.17.III)

Thus, a low elasticity of substitution is the other factor that contributes to its yield not decreasing easily. Now, where can this unending desire for money originate?

> This follows from the peculiarity of money that its utility is solely derived from its exchange-value, so that the two rise and fall *pari passu*, with the result that as the exchange value of money rises there is no motive or tendency, as in the case of rent-factors, to substitute some other factor for it.
>
> (Keynes, 1939 [1936]: 231; IV.17.III)

Money is the asset whose rate of interest is not "automatically" reduced. This is due, as has been seen, to the fact that its production elasticity is equal to zero (or low), as is the case with its substitution elasticity. The last characteristic mentioned by Keynes, which contributes to the same outcome, is that its carrying cost is also low. "In this connection the low (or negligible) carrying-costs of money play an essential part. For if its carrying costs were material, they would offset the effect of expectations as to the prospective value of money at future dates" (Keynes, 1939 [1936]: 233–234; IV.17.III).

This attribute is also fundamental, since otherwise the yield would tend to decrease when the holding of money increases on account of the rise in c. In general terms, it may be asserted that "an essential difference between money and all (or most) other assets that in the case of money its liquidity-premium much exceeds its carrying cost, whereas in the case of other assets their carrying cost much exceeds their liquidity-premium" (Keynes, 1939 [1936]: 227; IV.17.II).

This is, then, Keynes's theory on money's singularities and their effects. In short, the asset that has these three qualities to the highest degree will be that whose own-rate of interest will decline more slowly as its output increases and, therefore, that will be the asset that will work as money.

> The significance of the money-rate of interest arises, therefore, out of the combination of the characteristics that, through the working of the liquidity-motive, this rate of interest may be somewhat unresponsive to a change in the proportion which the quantity of money bears to other forms of wealth measured in money, and that money has (or may have) zero (or negligible) elasticities both of production and of substitution. The first condition means that demand may be predominantly directed to money, the second that when this occurs labour cannot be employed in producing more money, and the third that there is no mitigation at any point through some other factor being capable, if it is sufficiently cheap, of doing money's duty equally well.
>
> (Keynes, 1939 [1936]: 234; IV.17.III)

In a modern economy, non-convertible money satisfies the requirement of having low production elasticity perfectly. However, such a requirement is not strictly met, not even when money is paper. The available quantity of the asset that works as money does not exclusively depend on the units in stock, but has to be computed in terms of its purchasing power: the "real" supply of money. The real supply of money may be increased even if there is no emission, by means of a fall in prices. But also, a fall in wages reduces the demand of money for transactions, increasing the volume available for speculation, without increasing the volume of emitted money either, so that "even though the quantity of money cannot be increased by diverting labour into producing it, nevertheless an assumption that its effective supply is rigidly fixed would be inaccurate" (Keynes, 1939 [1936]: 232; IV.17.III).

Therefore, if it were necessary to identify which of the two qualities is the most important for an asset to be money, the difficulty to extinguish demand, and not the inelasticity of "real" supply, should be chosen. In such a case, there will not be natural tendencies to reduce the rate of interest of the asset working as money, if its carrying cost is low, but mainly if its "liquidity premium" is high, since, in that case, the demand for money is never diverted towards other forms of wealth. This seems to be the key to the entire question, so that, ultimately "Unemployment develops, that is to say, because people want the moon; – men cannot be employed when the object of desire (i.e. money) is something which cannot be produced and the demand for which cannot be readily choked off" (Keynes, 1939 [1936]: 236; IV.17.III).

A reverse trip: from money that yields interest to money as a price standard

This fundamental explanation of the traits that characterize money still has to be tested against the other functions that money plays in practice. As will be seen, Keynes does not take it for granted that money has to "naturally" play all the roles that are assigned to it in practice. On the contrary, he tries to establish a conceptual link between functions. For the time being, money is "liquid" and, therefore, has a particularly high yield, which is difficult to reduce. However, this quality does not turn it into a "measure of values" or the standard for contracts.

All durable goods have their own-rate of interest, therefore, all of them can equally work as a standard to measure the marginal efficiency of the other goods. Like in the First Treatise, it would seem that any (durable) commodity could play the role of *measure of values*. Now then, a commodity becomes a standard when debts and wages are expressed in units of it. But there is no reason why the asset that functions as money in Keynes's terms should also play this second role and, conversely, the fact of being a *measure of value* does not turn that asset in one with a reluctant-to-fall rate of interest. However, both functions feed off of each other. First, *Keynesian* money (with a reduction-resistant rate of interest) is prone to be selected also as a standard, because the fact that the rate of interest should not change easily when the quantity of money increases, and, for the same reason, the tendency of its future price to bear a more or less fixed ratio to its *spot* price, bestows it a stability that makes it suitable to work as the standard in which wages are expressed. Furthermore, as Keynes's money entails, by definition, low carrying costs, it has some conditions that may lead to it being selected as standard.

> [T]he commodity, in terms of which wages are expected to be most sticky, cannot be one whose elasticity of production is not least, and for which the excess of carrying-costs over liquidity-premium is not least. In other words, the expectation of a relative stickiness of wages in terms of money is a corollary of the excess of liquidity-premium over carrying-costs being greater for money than for any other asset.
>
> (Keynes, 1939 [1936]: 238; IV.17.IV)

But, secondly, the fact that wages and contracts may be stable in terms of money makes that asset even more liquid and, therefore, a further motive to select it to play the role of money. The effect is "cumulative": a function attracts the other and feeds off of it.

> Thus we see that the various characteristics, which combine to make the money-rate of interest significant, interact with one another in a cumulative fashion. The fact that money has low elasticities of production and substitution and low carrying-costs tends to raise the expectation that money-wages will be relatively stable; and this expectation enhances money's liquidity-premium and prevents the exceptional correlation between the money-rate of interest and the marginal efficiencies of other assets which might, if it could exist, rob the money-rate of interest of its sting.
>
> (Keynes, 1939 [1936]: 238; IV.17.IV)

Thus concludes Keynes's explanation of the essential properties of money. Keynes does not start from observable money to "describe" its functions, but rather tries to show that the system *must* have an asset that behaves in a certain way on account of its particular traits. After presenting his fundamental theory of money, he wonders what assets are prone to become money on account of their characteristics. He states that gold, silver and bank notes all have the fundamental characteristics typical of money (high liquidity premium and low carrying cost). Besides, bank notes, fundamentally, but also gold and silver – in a non-producing country – meet the requirement of having a null elasticity of production. This is the reason why metals finally play the role of money. Thus, both the functions of money as the "material" it is made of are analytically inferred from its essential qualities, and not the reverse (as was the case in *classical theory*).

The (analytical) possibility that none of the existing assets may have such main properties remains to be examined. If such asset did not exist, the economy would be, according to Keynes, a genuinely non-monetary economy. "Consider, for example, an economy in which there is no asset for which the liquidity-premium is always in excess of the carrying-costs; which is the best definition I can give of a so-called 'non-monetary' economy" (Keynes, 1939 [1936]: 239; IV.17.V). In such a case, land – with a low production and substitution elasticity – would probably become the asset whose rate of interest would have the same characteristics as those of money's.

As such, it will be the real "money" in the system, independently of which asset is selected as a measure of value. But once land becomes money, its liquidity will increase, joining the other properties, so that probably land would finally play also the role of standard.

It is this theory of money which leads Keynes to offer a singular point of view regarding the internal limitations of the economic system. The obstacle to the decline of the interest rate does not lie, as Marshall held, in man's psychological preference for present over future enjoyment – "impatient" time preferences. The reason for the high level that usually characterizes the rate of interest resides, instead, in the equally high liquidity premium of the asset that plays the role of money.

> That the world after several millennia of steady individual saving, is so poor as it is in accumulated capital-assets, is to be explained, in my opinion, neither by the improvident propensities of mankind, nor even by the destruction of war, but by the high liquidity-premiums formerly attaching to the ownership of land and now attaching to money.
>
> (Keynes, 1939 [1936]: 242; IV.17.V)

Keynes's theories of money and capital lead to highly original conclusions regarding the past and the future of human history.

The social reform suggested in the General Theory

Keynes's theory of capital and his theory of money not only are key to understanding his entire economic system, as they make intelligible some aspects of the determination of variables that do not agree with classical theory, but also confer meaning to many otherwise enigmatic assertions that populate the book, which become meaningful when analyzed in the light of these theories.

In fact, it could be said that Keynes's explanation contains two types of proposals regarding government action. First, he provides elements for a "scientific management" (as he called it in the *Treatise*) of the new policy tools that capitalism historical transformation has laid on the hands of the authority. The criticism he levels at the *classical theory's* traditional prescriptions is conclusive. Specifically, the abandonment of the gold standard turned, according to Keynes, the determination of the nominal quantity of money into an exclusive decision of government. The *classical quantitative theory* held that changes in the amount of non-convertible money always resulted in proportional changes in prices. It was also asserted – more clearly in Wicksell's version – that variations in money quantity transferred to prices through changes in credit conditions and, therefore, through variations in the rate of interest. Sooner or later, however, the rate of interest returned to its "natural" level.

The General Theory arrives at completely different conclusions. It shows that changes in the quantity of money impact, first, on the rate of interest (an eminently "current" and monetary phenomenon that has nothing to do with capital productivity and the disutility of the waiting). Variations in the rate of interest, in turn, work as a transmission belt that impacts wage level, through its relation with investment demand. Here, one of the most original aspects of Keynes's explanation emerges. By discarding the assumption that output is always fixed at the level corresponding to full employment, demand movements result in a combination of variations in prices and in output volume. Thus, monetary policy does not exclusively affect prices, but rather, through the rate of interest and investment, it becomes an instrument to influence output and employment. Government cannot be content with exclusively pursuing the classical objective, which consisted in keeping money's purchasing power stable; now, it also has a method to intervene in the economic system that allows it to regulate the level of employment – even though its instruments might not be completely reliable.

The General Theory provides compelling arguments for abandoning the old prescription, inspired in *classical theory*, that the government could only contribute to job creation through wage policy. The classical theory of employment stated that unemployment was caused by wages' downward rigidity, since there was no full employment when workers refused to accept a wage compatible with labor marginal productivity, which was mainly a consequence of collective bargaining. The classical theory thus suggests the government should exert influence on the level of nominal (and real) wages or, at least, favor the conditions to have wages freely adjust towards their equilibrium level: the government has to flexibilize wage movement. In open opposition to the classical theory, Keynes argues that this alleged control over wages that government has is only effective in an authoritarian society, therefore, one contrary to the spirit of *laissez-faire*. Only in such a case could a generalized wage cut be achieved. He also says that even if such a reduction of nominal wages were to take place, the results achieved would not be those expected.

According to *The General Theory*, the consequences of an average nominal wage cut should not be analyzed in the context of the *classical labor market* (which was challenged and dismissed), but rather, its repercussions on the volume of aggregate demand have to be studied. Keynes shows that, ultimately, a wage cut has similar effects (at best) to those obtained increasing the amount of money, because the fall in prices that accompanies wage cuts increases the quantity of money in terms of its purchasing power, freeing a portion of the cash that was previously employed for transactions, and leaving it available for the speculative-motive. He thus shows that the governmental policy of wage deflation, based on *classical theory's* precepts, is either powerless or similar in its effects to an expansive monetary policy. Once shown that both instruments have similar effects on demand, Keynes argues that if the real amount of money is to be increased, it is always more convenient to do so by means of a monetary policy rather than through wage cuts; the latter option has undesirable "side-effects". The conclusion is categorical. There is no automatic force in the system that makes nominal wages fall when there is unemployment, and if there should be such force, it would not be capable of directly modifying real wages. Second, even if wages did fall, their effect on employment would be ambiguous and, at best, comparable to an increase in the quantity of money, an option that is always preferable. To end, apart from the fact that its effectiveness is not guaranteed, the policy of reducing nominal wages by decree is an intervention suitable for an authoritarian government, that is, a government capable of affecting all wages at a time. To conclude, wage rigidity is not the cause of unemployment, nor flexibility its solution. All the remedies, both monetary and wage-oriented, prescribed by the classical school to cure unemployment are thus dismantled: "There is, therefore, no ground for the belief that flexible wages policy is capable of maintaining a state of continues full employment" (Keynes, 1939 [1936]: 267; V.19.II).

There remains, therefore, the possibility of resorting to monetary policy as an instrument to increase employment. However, Keynes shows in his *system* that the gears linking the quantity of money and the level of employment may be in some cases unconnected. According to Keynes, this is due to the fact that the demand for money – the liquidity preference, the investment demand – the capital marginal efficiency curve, and the consumption demand – the propensity to consume – all depend on certain factors in the determination of which the changing (and ungrounded) expectations of men regarding an uncertain future are involved. Of these three elements, there is one that is particularly fluctuating and that becomes the main cause of output and employment oscillations. The weight of Keynes's argument rests decisively on the immense instability that is typical of investment decisions in a society such as the contemporary, where the ownership of capital is divorced from enterprises' management; the volume of investment is determined, therefore, in the whimsical market of securities (the stock exchange). To sum up, although changes in the quantity of money do not result in a proportional variation of prices – as the classical quantitative theory posited – and can, eventually, promote employment, this governmental policy instrument is not always completely effective. The rate of interest refuses, in certain cases, to be subject to this control but, basically, capital marginal efficiency is ruled by the whims of speculative investment. And speculation is not exclusively driven by the greed of speculators, but by the new way in which investments are made in a system like the one that emerged in the early twentieth century. In such conditions, monetary policy turns out to be an inadequate mechanism to fight unemployment: "for my own part I am now somewhat skeptical of the success of a merely monetary policy directed towards influencing the rate of interest" (Keynes, 1939 [1936]: 164; IV.12.VIII). In other words,

> [i]n existing conditions – or, at least, in the condition which existed until lately – where the volume of investment is unplanned and uncontrolled, subject to the vagaries of the marginal efficiency of capital as determined by the private judgment of individuals ignorant or speculative, and to a long-term rate of interest which seldom or never falls below a conventional level.
>
> (Keynes, 1939 [1936]: 325; VI.23.IV)

Chronic unemployment seems to be inevitable. In short, it is not possible to postulate that monetary policy is effective in creating employment. For although it may eventually be possible to make the rate of interest reach a level consistent with full employment (optimal or "neutral" rate) by controlling emission, nothing can be done to forestall the fluctuations associated with the instability inherent in private decisions determining the volume of investment. And herein lies the deeper root of the problems. In fact, nothing guarantees that the capital marginal efficiency curve will be stable, as well as situated at the appropriate level. Therefore, even assuming that the government would manage to reduce the rate of interest to the desired level, the volatility of expectations on the prospective yields of equipment goods may hinder the adequate growth of private investment: aggregate demand will continue to be insufficient, in spite of the achievements reached in the monetary sphere. For Keynes's system, the most serious problems do not seem to lie in "wage rigidity" or in the "liquidity trap". Even without resorting to them, the uncertain nature of the future permeates investment decisions, thus controlling aggregate demand and the level of employment,

> [i]n conditions of *laissez-faire* the avoidance of wide fluctuations in employment may, therefore, prove impossible without a far-reaching change in the psychology of investment markets such as is no reason to expect. I conclude that the duty of ordering the current volume of investment cannot safely be left in private hands.
>
> (Keynes, 1939 [1936]: 320; VI.22.II)

This is a brief synthesis of the outcomes and recommendations that stem from Keynes's *economic system*, whose final words are that, given the new historical conditions, only exempting the private sector of the responsibility of determining the investment volume could guarantee the avoidance of unemployment. The state is in a condition to undertake a more complex task and one which is, furthermore, impossible to delegate – assuming the mission of organizing investments directly. This is a kind and a scope of intervention much more ambitious than the mere implementation of monetary or tax policies, supported by what Keynes considers to be the "spontaneous" changes underwent by society during the early twentieth century: the "socialization" of investments is a result of history, at least partially.

> I expect to see the State, which is in a position to calculate the marginal efficiency of capital-goods on long views and on the basis of the general social advantage, taking an ever greater responsibility for directly organising investment; since it seems likely that the fluctuations in the market estimation of the marginal efficiency of different types of capital, calculated on the principles I have described above, will be too great to be offset by any practicable changes in the rate of interest.
>
> (Keynes, 1939 [1936]: 164; IV.12.VIII)

Keynes's advice contrasts with what is generally known as Keynesian policies. But his proposals do not end here. In fact, his foray into the basic categories of political economics – commodity, money, capital – lays the groundwork for a much more resolute proposal, aimed at transforming society more radically. In other words, Keynes wonders: what are the limits of the capitalist system? What outcome can be expected from a "massive" state intervention? To answer these questions, it is necessary to leave the *economic system* – that would stop working – to enter the field of the foundations put forth by Keynes.

In "present day individualistic capitalism", capital marginal efficiency, that is, capital yield, is, according to Keynes, an outcome of the scarcity price of equipment goods, whose production is limited on account of the competition with money's rate of interest. If government would undertake to substantially and steadily increase the volume of investment, the scarcity that characterizes the production of capital equipment could be overcome. Keynes imagines a situation – that could be reached within a generation, in his view – where government would manage to reduce capital marginal efficiency to almost zero. How? Through the "social organization of investments", that is, creating a situation where capital equipment would be plentiful.

> I should guess that a properly run community equipped with modern technical resources, of which the population is not increasing rapidly, ought to be able to bring down the marginal efficiency of capital in equilibrium approximately to zero within a single generation; so that we should attain the conditions of a quasi-stationary community where change and progress would result only form changes in technique, taste, population and institutions, with the products of capital selling at a price proportionate to the labour, etc., embodied in them on just

the same principles that govern the prices of consumption-goods into which capital-charges enter in an insignificant degree.

(Keynes, 1939 [1936]: 221; IV.16.IV)

Only on the basis of the analysis undertaken in the previous chapters, which probed into the foundations of *The General Theory*, is it possible to understand the meaning of this paragraph, which would otherwise seem to be simply meaningless: in the world imagined by Keynes, all the goods will have their price set by the amount of labor embodied in them – and the scarcity of natural resources; the labor time will rule the price both of the products that employ capital in their production as of those that do not. This would be the absolute rule of the "Ricardian" law of value. Government would then become a true leading character not just in monetary policy but in a reform that would overturn the roots of capitalism.

> If I am right in supposing it to be comparatively easy to make capital-goods so abundant that the marginal efficiency of capital is zero, this may be the most sensible way of gradually getting rid of many of the objectionable features of capitalism. For a little reflection will show what enormous social changes would result from gradual disappearance of a rate of return on accumulated wealth. A man would still be free to accumulate his earned income with a view to spending it in a later date. But this accumulation would not grow.
>
> (Keynes, 1939 [1936]: 221; IV.16.IV)

The objective would be, therefore, to get rid of the reprehensible – in Keynes's view – qualities of capitalism: the question is not putting an end to private property, not even extinguishing the "healthy" entrepreneurial spirit or the possibility of saving.[25] He imagines a world where wealth accumulated under the form of capital equipment or money would be an adequate means to store value, which would not, however, yield an additional return to its owner.

This world that Keynes believes possible, based on his studies of the nature of commodity, money and capital, entails the end of yield as we know it, since it stems from the scarcity of capital equipment. The sale of capital services would just be enough, according to Keynes, to pay for its labor cost (including the entrepreneur's), the only inescapable real cost, plus an additional amount to cover risk (which in aggregate terms becomes zero). This implies that all goods, durable and non-durable, would be sold at a price equivalent to the amount of labor:

> I feel sure that the demand for capital is strictly limited in the sense that it would not be difficult to increase the stock of capital up to the point

where its marginal efficiency had fallen to a very low figure [. . .] the aggregate return from durable goods in the course of their life would, as in the case of short-lived goods, just cover their labour-cost of production *plus* an allowance for risk and the cost of skill and supervision.

(Keynes, 1939 [1936]: 375; VI.24.II)

Thus, the more reprehensible character produced by capitalism in its, according to Keynes, last stage would disappear: the rentier, that is, the investor that knows nothing about investments – it could not possibly be otherwise, as he does not have direct control over enterprises – but that, in spite of his ignorance, has in his power the critical determination of the level of investment and, through it, of demand, without having objective bases to make such decisions nor taking into account the interests of society as a whole. Keynes thus imagines a kind of capitalism where no positive return could be obtained from capital investments. This would in turn imply that the rate of interest would not set a limit to the production of equipment, since the latter would fundamentally be in the hands of the state.

Now, though this state of affairs would be quite compatible with some measure of individualism, yet it would mean the euthanasia of the rentier, and, consequently, the euthanasia of the cumulative oppressive power of the capitalist to exploit the scarcity-value of capital. Interest to-day rewards no genuine sacrifice, any more than does the rent of land. The owner of capital can obtain interest because capital is scarce, just as the owner of land can obtain rent because land is scarce. But whilst there may be intrinsic reasons for the scarcity of land, there are no intrinsic reasons for the scarcity of capital [. . .] it will be possible for communal saving through the agency of the State to be maintained at a level which will allow the growth of capital up to the point where it ceases to be scarce.

(Keynes, 1939 [1936]: 375–376; VI.24.II)

As was pointed out in the Introduction, the review of the *foundations of economic theory* undertaken by Keynes showed the way to an inquiry into capitalism's future transformation, its historical limits, and its new possibilities. On the other hand, according to his prognosis, the social system is in a situation of extreme danger, faced with which economists do not only remain indifferent but by imposing their traditional prescriptions, inspired in the *classical theory*, do nothing but hasten the fall to the bottom, since as Keynes states

[t]he world will not much longer tolerate the unemployment which, apart from brief intervals of excitement, is associated – and, in my

opinion, inevitably associated – with present-day capitalistic individualism. But it may be possible by a right analysis of the problem to cure the disease whilst preserving efficiency and freedom.

(Keynes, 1939 [1936]: 381; VI.24.III)

Keynes's theory promises a possible way of overcoming the miseries typical of the current stage of individualistic capitalism. If the state would wisely intervene putting an end to capital marginal efficiency, changes, also inevitable, would not need be violent. It is in this possibility that Keynes trusts, and he believes his trust to be firmly grounded: it is based on his *General Theory* considered as a *unit*, that is, in his *theory of history*, his *economic system*, and the theoretical *foundations* on which it rests. Changes will take place in any case, but Keynes thinks there are two possible ways how such transformations can occur: gradually, based on his advice, or otherwise and as a result of the implementation of unsuitable prescriptions through revolution.

> I see, therefore, the rentier aspect of capitalism as a transitional phase which will disappear when it has done its work. And with the disappearance of its rentier aspect much else in it besides will suffer a sea-change. It will be, moreover, a great advantage of the order of events which I am advocating, that the euthanasia of the rentier, of the functionless investor, will be nothing sudden, merely a gradual but prolonged continuance of what we have seen recently in Great Britain, and will need no revolution.
>
> (Keynes, 1939 [1936]: 376; VI.24.II)

Critique of Keynes: collapse of his theory of interest

Next, we have to examine the outcomes Keynes arrives at when he is forced to dismiss the classical theories of capital, money and value. The reasons that lead him away from Marshall's legacy are firmly grounded, but what could be said regarding the theoretical proposals he offers instead? As regards capital yield, the *marginalist* theory provides a dual explanation.

Keynes answers by challenging the two pillars on which the *classical theory* of capital rests: capital is not *productive*, he states, and also, savings does not entail any sacrifice for men. Thus, together with the source of classical interest, its need also vanishes.[26] What is the origin, then, of the reward that the owner of a capital good receives? Keynes's answer is simple (and, as will be seen, quite old in its origin): if the capitalist obtains a profit, it is because capital equipment is scarce and, for that very reason, its services are sold through time at a higher price than the cost of production of the equipment. Profit stems, therefore, from a *sale* that, on account of certain circumstances (*scarcity*), makes it possible to obtain a value higher than cost, that is, than the normal price. This theory of profit is far from the *classical* explanation, and could be considered of mercantilist descent. In fact, some authors that are generally considered to belong to the mercantilist current would explain the emergence of a surplus as the difference between the cost price and the sale price; this surplus was called *profit upon alienation*.[27]

The main objection that may be raised to an explanation of this kind is the following: even though the source of a circumstantial profit, linked to the selling of a commodity or a particular group of commodities, may well be understood thus, it is not possible to account for the net total profits obtained by society as a whole with this argument, since if the prices of the products whose manufacturing involves the use of capital raise over the production cost (in labor terms), the other products must, necessarily, sell below their production cost. In other words, if the first commodities are sold for more labor than they actually embody, for more than they are actually worth, then although the seller might reap a benefit, the buyer loses an equal one: there is no way how the origin of global net "profits" stemming from such nominal rise in prices may be understood. Society cannot get wealthier in this way, not at all. What is a profit for some always entails a loss for others. The theory of scarcity capital yield is apt to represent a redistribution of "surplus", but it cannot identify its source.

Although this critique challenges the foundations of Keynes's scarcity theory of profit, two aspects typical of his explanation should be recognized. First, in this context, the profits of capital equipment owners become contingent, as they are subject to the condition of scarcity that affects capital production. That is, if capital services derive their high price (a surplus over cost) from scarcity, such a return on capital is not eternal, but rather will vanish as soon as the obstacle preventing equipment production growth vanishes. This latter reasoning leads to the "proposals" to reform capitalism put forth by Keynes, completely alien to the *classical* system. No sooner do we agree that capital "interest" does not pay for the capitalist's sacrifice (the waiting) nor does it originate in the physical productivity of capital, then we have to admit that commodities' prices exclusively represent labor time, since, of the two sources of value mentioned by Marshall, one will have already disappeared. In Keynes's view, the ideal society is one where products are traded based on their labor content. In that imaginary world, the rentier disappears, but not private property or salaried labor. Later, we will elaborate on this theory of value exclusively founded on labor.

Second, the scarcity theory implies admitting that capital yield is, in essence, different from the rate of interest that gains the holder of money, thus bestowing upon money a leading role in the theoretical structure built by Keynes. What may be objected to in this original theory of money? On one hand, money is "nominalized": it is transformed into a money that is desirable in itself, which provides an argument against the classical link that inexorably binds every act of buying with a reciprocal act of selling. Keynes can thus see that in a monetary economy, money separates sales and purchases. Selling a commodity does not necessarily translate into an immediate purchase of another commodity. But this conception of money must also be accompanied by an explanation of the motive why an individual may desire to withhold the produce of his sales (money), a description of the particular way in which purchases are postponed, and the consequences of such postponement. When an individual (or a society) saves in money in cash, consumption is postponed *sine die*, without there being any clear signal that may trigger any act of production.[28] This may be so because an act of saving is not equivalent to an explicit "order" to manufacture a specific product that will be consumed on certain future date; but it is possible also because money may be used to accumulate purchasing power without buying any new commodity or new capital equipment. Thus, increases in monetary income (and in the quantity of money) do not always result in equivalent increases in demand, since saving may take the shape of storing money in cash. Money is an outlet for the system, and this is the reason why it should provide a justification for those individuals who wish to store wealth as money in cash, instead of purchasing a capital good.[29] There should exist, therefore, a motive that prompts individuals to keep money as such. That is, on the other hand, Keynes introduces a notion of money different from the classical one, but he is also forced to explain the origin of the purely monetary rate of interest.[30]

These are the reasons that make the rate of interest the cornerstone of Keynes's theoretical construct. Keynes, so to speak, shifts the question about the origin of profit from capital to money. If capital gain is not *necessary*, as it stems from scarcity, the rate of interest (of purely monetary origin) becomes, instead, an autonomous self-supporting element, and likewise becomes responsible for capital scarcity. The particular way in which Keynes tries to explain the phenomenon of interest, closely connected with his fundamental theory of money, should thus be examined.

A faithful and rigorous exposition of Keynes's theory on the essential properties of money contained in *The General Theory* reveals its indubitable originality, both as regards its contents and the procedure adopted to present it. Instead of descriptively listing the functions of money or of identifying money with the traits typical of the commodities that actually play the role of money, Keynes follows the opposite road, and tries to infer the essential properties of money from the ability to yield a return that characterizes it. The initiative is, in itself, relevant, particularly when contrasted with the discussion of money in the *classical theory*.

It is not difficult, however, to identify the weak points in his argument. Keynes promised to give an answer to the question concerning the origin of the interest. In a first approach, he resorts to the same explanation he had given in connection with capital marginal efficiency. The point he seeks to make is that, in a sense, money is just like capital goods, but has, in contrast, certain qualities that prevent the scarcity that raises its value from disappearing; this is why its own-rate of interest refuses to fall more than that of any other durable good. After dismissing other hypotheses, Keynes concludes that the main attribute of the asset that works as money is its liquidity, since money does not have a significant carrying cost nor does it bear yield. Thus, the rate of interest on money becomes, essentially, a pure liquidity premium.

This argument entails, however, a vicious circle: an asset becomes money because it is liquid, but its liquidity rests precisely on the fact that it is money. Liquidity and money become thus synonymous. Identifying one as cause and the other as effect is, therefore, an arbitrary decision. The same kind of circular reasoning may be found at other segments of the fundamental theory of money when Keynes's argument is closely examined. Liquidity appears first "postulated" as an attribute of all durable assets that yield an interest. Further on, employing a very singular language, money is attributed the "peculiarity" that its *utility* stems exclusively from its *exchange value*. For this reason, when its price rises, its demand does not fall, which seems to be a different definition of liquidity. But then liquidity becomes the special quality that turns the asset money into a "store of wealth of stable value", a trait associated, in turn, to wage stability and debts expressed in money. However, later on, this relationship is reverted once again: it would then seem that wage contracts are stable, precisely, because they are expressed in money. Liquidity now explains the standard and the standard explains liquidity.

Finally, when Keynes tries to shed light on his explanation referring to a non-monetary economy,[31] liquidity is associated to a collection of the assets' "physical" characteristics, which does nothing but show that the concept of liquidity lacks clarity:

> In such an economy capital equipments will differ from one another (*a*) in the variety of the consumables in the production of which they are capable of assisting, (*b*) in the stability of value of their output (in the sense in which the value of bread is more stable through time than the value of fashionable novelties), and (*c*) in the rapidity with which the wealth embodied in them can become 'liquid', in the sense of producing output, the proceeds of which can be re-embodied if desired in quite a different form.
>
> (Keynes, 1939 [1936]: 240; IV.17.V)

Therefore, in an economy where there is no "purely" liquid asset, decisions regarding the method of storing wealth should be highly changing.

However, as Keynes immediately states, it is enough that an active be considered the most liquid at each given moment to render his theory of money valid also in a moneyless economy. In other words, according to his definition, every asset is, to a certain extent, "liquid" and, therefore, curiously enough, the presence of money is obligatory even in a non-monetary economy.

> The conception of what contributes to 'liquidity' is a partly vague one, changing from time to time and depending on social practices and institutions. The order of preference in the minds of owners of wealth in which at any given time they express their feelings about liquidity is, however, definite and is all we require for our analysis of the behaviour of the economic system.
>
> (Keynes, 1939 [1936]: 240; IV.17.V)

The same kind of circularity that was previously pointed out emerges again when examining the other two attributes of the asset that becomes money: the null elasticity of production and the null elasticity of substitution. In a footnote, it is asserted that these characteristics that are capable, for example, of turning land into a money asset, can also endow this asset with liquidity, that is to say that, Keynes argues,

> The attribute of 'liquidity' is by no means independent of the presence of these two characteristics. For it is unlikely that an asset, of which the supply can be easily increased or the desire of which can be easily diverted by a change in relative prices, will possess the attribute of 'liquidity' in the minds of owners of wealth. Money itself rapidly loses the attribute of 'liquidity' if its future supply is expected to undergo sharp changes.
>
> (Keynes, 1939 [1936]: 241n; IV.17.V)

To sum up, Keynes seeks to explain the nature of the return yielded in practice by capital equipment in terms of the rate of interest, and the rate of interest as a result of the liquidity of certain assets. Nobody doubts that, in practice, money is "liquid". But Keynes fails to explain the very foundation of that liquidity that he pretends to associate to the return yielded by money, rather than to money's capacity to serve as a means of circulation. Thus, his theory of the rate of interest collapses, since the rate of interest turns out to be, essentially, a synonym for the liquidity premium that individuals are willing to pay due to the fact, precisely, that money is liquid.

The path Keynes follows to try and solve the problem of money specificity leads him, therefore, to a dead end. Clearly, there is no doubt that money "stores" value. Nor can it be denied that money can be loaned in exchange for a rate of interest. However, resting all the weight of the explanation on the attribute of liquidity is the same as stating, ultimately, that money is demanded because it stores value, and it stores value because it has a liquidity premium, and that, finally, it bears interest inasmuch as it has its own liquidity premium.

Although Keynes rightly distinguishes an entrepreneur's profit from the rate of interest associated to money, and discards the *classical theory*, he does not succeed, on account of the aforementioned reason, in putting forth a satisfactory alternative theory of the origin of the "surplus" over costs. While he concludes that capital yield may be nullified as a result of equipment abundance, he also holds that the rate of interest, instead, stems from liquidity premium, which he considers eternal, and whose precise nature he is not able to clearly disentangle.

This is, besides, the basis for his theory of value, remarkably different from that of Marshall's: the price of non-durable goods in the production of which no capital is employed reflects the amount of labor required for its production. Durable capital equipments, instead, render services throughout their lifespan, and the addition of their annuities surpass production costs because the amount of capital goods is not enough; and scarcity is due to the fact that their profitability "competes" with a monetary rate of interest that refuses to fall. The price of the goods that require the services of capital assets in their production rises over labor costs for the same reason. Capital is not a "factor" of production, so that Keynes argues that if capital yield could be reduced to zero, all prices would be proportional to the labor time employed directly and indirectly in their production.

As it is probably impossible to reduce the rate of interest below a certain value on account of the fact that money is, according to Keynes, naturally "liquid", to reach that objective, capital equipment output can be, instead, increased through a "socially controlled" (Keynes, 1939 [1936]: VI.22.IV) rate of investment, which leads Keynes to argue for "the great social advantages of increasing the stock of capital until it ceases to be scarce" (Keynes, 1939 [1936]: VI.22.IV). It has to be admitted that the connection between his reform proposals for capitalism and his theoretical foundations is indisputable, independently of the lack of soundness of the latter.

In this last chapter, some conclusions will be drawn based on these results. As anticipated in the Introduction, the fundamental purpose of this book is to show that *The General Theory* is a complete theoretical unit. Most interpretations completely reject this point of view, claiming that it is not possible to unite the different pieces of the argument: the book would be, rather, plagued with inconsistencies, exaggeration, inaccuracies, mistakes and insurmountable logical mistakes. It could be said, therefore, that very few interpreters have approached the ideas put forth in *The General Theory*, seriously considered as a whole. Although unaccompanied by a rigorous study, the charges were accepted as a dogma, and allowed Keynes-ians to move swiftly away from the complex legacy Keynes left. Once this verdict became established as an undeniable truth, the way was paved to select some isolated fragments of Keynes's argument, according to the interpreter's bias, and to have them endorsed by many economists who unanimously claimed that these were the few original ideas put forth by the author that were worth keeping. This is the reason why the other widespread "interpretive" strategy, once the whole argument had been dismissed, con-sisted in finding some "hidden truth" in the text, ideas not explicitly men-tioned that would allegedly synthesize the essential elements of Keynes's contribution, the "hidden spirit" of the *General Theory*.[32] Each author felt authorized to select the portions of the book that coincided with his own beliefs. *The General Theory* was no longer a respectable and respected text of economic theory and became a mere "source of inspiration", as if it were a work of art filled with more or less valid insights instead of the finished exposition of a theoretical system; and all this without the orthodoxy taking the trouble of developing a critique of the entire conceptual development that it put forth.

IV Final remarks: the bankruptcy of the "Keynesian consensus"

It should not be understood, however, that this objection seeks to discourage the interpretive work that successive generations may undertake on a major text; nor does it encourage some other extreme attitude, somehow opposed to the aforementioned one – turning some texts into little less than "sacred scriptures", to which new theories must appeal in a search for legitimacy. What is denounced here is that *The General Theory* underwent a process of "selective appropriation": only some isolated segments of the argument were kept, without a rigorous critique of the theory taken as a whole. To illustrate this attitude, it is worth quoting the telling obituary published by P. Samuelson in *Econometrics*:

> Here is the secret of The General Theory. It is a badly written book, poorly organized; any layman who, beguiled by the author's previous reputation, bought the book was cheated of his 5 shillings. It is not well suited for classroom use. It is arrogant, bad-tempered, polemical, and not overly generous in its acknowledgements. It abounds with mares' nests and confusions [. . .]. In it the Keynesian system stands out indis-tinctly, as if the author were hardly aware of its existence or cognizant of its properties; and certainly he is at his worst when expounding its relations to its predecessors. Flashes of insight and intuition intersperse tedious algebra. An awkward definition suddenly gives way to an

unforgettable cadenza. When it finally is mastered, we find its analysis to be obvious and at the same time new. In short, it is a work of genius.
(Samuelson, 1967 [1946]; 400–401)

According to the quoted paragraphs, feelings ranging from whim to igno-rance guided the author of *The General Theory*, who, notwithstanding or, rather, for this reason, is considered a *genius*. Evidently, such serious accusations must be thoroughly grounded, but such grounds were never ever offered. Seventy-five years after the publication of the text, the main reproach to Keynes's critics but also to his followers is this: they never took the trouble of reconstructing the whole argument put forth in *The General Theory*, a task that should logically precede any critical intention. Such a reconstruction is not a part of Keynes's legacy in the context of the official theory; what was instead preserved was his economic system of causal relations, his "model", which was, besides, "reframed" so that it could smoothly fit the traditional analytical framework in the department of macroeconomics.[33]

An unprejudiced analysis, however, shows that the *economic system* put forth by Keynes is not compatible with the foundations that the *classical theory* offers. This is the reason why *The General Theory* not only rejects the neo-classicists' full employment "model", but also abandons the set of elemental categories posited by the traditional theory: capital, money, commodity. When it becomes possible to connect the *system* with the fun-damental concepts that support it, a new perspective to assess the contribu-tions of *The General Theory* opens up.

In the Preface, Keynes states that the main objective of his book is a conceptual one: it consists in reconciling the *theory of value* and the *theory of money*, thus obtaining a picture of a *monetary economy*. When a worried mainstream faced *The General Theory*, it chose, almost unanimously, to dismiss the chapters and the sections of the book that dealt with the fun-damental categories. However, such dismissal forced orthodox economics to pay a high price. It endorsed the "model" that Keynes put forth, but dis-missed its foundations. However, it could neither rely on the old founda-tions of the *classical theory*, which were incompatible with the new *system*.

The orthodoxy, thus, faced a dilemma: it could, on one hand, reject any reference to the theory of value, of money, and of capital, thus falling into a conceptual vacuum, or it could, instead, endorse Keynes's foundations, which forced it to acknowledge the inconsistency of classical foundations. This quandary was not solved in either of these ways, but rather an inter-mediate possibility was chosen: the division of economic theory into two unconnected branches, microeconomics and macroeconomics.

In the field of microeconomics, the old foundations of the *classical theory*, contributed mainly by Marshall and Walras, were maintained.

Macroeconomics, instead, became accustomed to building its models without discussing the concepts of money, capital, and value. It devoted itself to the description of the relations among the different observable phenomena, without enquiring into their conceptual content. The separation into microeconomics and macroeconomics was, so to speak, a defensive strategy implemented in the face of Keynes's critique. But contradictions would soon emerge.

For a while, mainstream economics candidly indulged in this double life, during the period that was called "Keynesian consensus". But a new global economic crisis, triggered in the early 1970s, smashed such fragile agreement. A period of confusion, fragmentation, and polarization then began. While some economists disowned the whole Keynesian episode, and demanded the restoration of the *classical theory*, others took the opposite road, and decided to revisit *The General Theory*. The mainstream has not yet generally accepted any of the numerous solutions proposed to reestablish unity.

Our investigation, however, showed that, with *The General Theory*, Keynes did not mean to establish a new branch within the context of the inherited economic theory (macroeconomics), but rather sought to expose the historical, logical, and empirical flaws of the *classical theory; The General Theory* is nothing but a raw and lucid expression of the crisis that the *classical theory* experienced in the early twentieth century. Keynes held that the old theories of value, money and capital should be abandoned, and he put forth other foundations, essentially different from the classical foundations, to replace them.

We have explained those new foundations and we have, besides, offered a critique of Keynes's proposals. The conclusions that may be drawn from this work seem to be contradictory: while Keynes's attempt to criticize the weak classical foundations, and to find the theoretical foundations of his own system are positively assessed, it is subsequently claimed that such foundations are unable to stand by themselves. The questions that Keynes meant to answer do not find there a suitable reply: what is the nature of money, of capital, of the rate of interest, of profit?

This book does not offer a positive presentation of those theoretical issues. But the enquiry that here comes to its end, allows us to stress some conclusions associated with the results obtained.

As has been shown, by rejecting the theory of capital as a factor of production, and of the waiting as a real (subjective) cost of production, Keynes reunites with the theory of value based on labor. If capital were not in any way "scarce", the prices of all commodities would be proportional to the labor time required to produce the relevant goods. A direct connection between the ideas of Keynes's and of the Ricardians' is thus exposed. From this point of view, the reason that led most post-war Marxists and Ricardians to show some affinity with the ideas put forth in *The General Theory* may be easily understood.[34] This is not the place to discuss this question, but some of the points where the coincidence is obvious may be pointed out: modern Ricardians assert that wages are set through "class struggle", and in Keynes's view, wages are exogenous; the view that an increase in public expenditure may lead, through a peaceful via, to a planned economy is present both in *The General Theory* as in the works of some of the most renowned Marxists of that period. Also the perception that capitalist crisis stems from demand's weakness, and that it is exacerbated, particularly, by the monopolistic nature of capitalism helps bring closer Ricardians' and Keynes's positions.[35] Finally, modern theories that draw on Ricardo exhibit a common weak point with Keynes's: they do not succeed in explaining the origin of profit in a compelling way.

Finally, a general assessment of the study we have carried out may be attempted. First, contrary to most current interpretations, it was shown that Keynes's contributions must be framed within the context of his own conception of the economic changes experienced by society, since, from his first works, he maintained an almost unchanged vision of the major stages of capitalism. His hypothesis was that the world was undergoing a transition period. On this hypothesis he based his interpretation of the violent changes that came one after the other during the first third of the twentieth century: the First World War, the violent post-war inflationary episodes, the Great Depression. From his point of view, all these episodes should be considered necessary symptoms of that historical transition. His deepest criticisms of the classical school did not denounce the theory from a formal perspective, but rather claimed that its premises, probably well suited to a previous stage, had become anachronistic due to those deep economic changes. This conception drove Keynes to start a revolution in thought: economic theory should be capable of reflecting the economic situation prevailing in this new stage, accompanying the inevitable changes instead of opposing them, appealing to the old dogma.

Unlike the orthodox economists, Keynes must be credited with trying to understand the nature of such transformations, and to associate them with changes in the official economic thinking. However, his characterization of the stages in human economy cannot be taken as anything more than conjecture. His strongest thesis stresses the progress of capital concentration, and examines its effects on the capitalist class and the working class, but it cannot (and does not try to) explain, instead, the very origin of that concentration. On the other hand, the Malthusian spirit of his ideas – the so-called "humanity economic problem" – should also be questioned, both theoretically and empirically. His hypotheses as to the major stages of human history should no doubt be closely and systematically studied, in the context of the numerous existing studies on the matter. Keynes never tried to carry out a deep enquiry in this field.

However, he was convinced that there was a strong link between history and economic theory. Modern macroeconomics did not inherit this concern. Some of the more fertile and current ideas put forth in *The General Theory* are contained in his critique of the *classical theory*. Keynes is the first to point out the problematic split of the classical theoretical corpus into two unconnected treatises; his conclusions may be applied to the current condition of the mainstream. And as Keynes holds, this is a key that leads to revisiting the theories of capital and money.

We do not find appropriate, instead, his characterization of the *classical theory* as a merger of *Ricardians* and *marginalists*. It is not just a terminological issue, but rather this association hides certain theoretical positions. Indeed, the alleged coincidence of marginalism and Ricardo is not an invention of Keynes's – as we have seen, it stems from the particular interpretation of Ricardo's work carried out by Marshall. According to this reading, Ricardo should be considered an early marginalist. It is true that Keynes takes advantage of this marginalists-Ricardo merger built by Marshall to point out some of the weak points shared by both schools. Both Ricardians and marginalists had stumbled upon serious troubles when seeking to undertake the discussion of money, and held that, ultimately, capitalist economy could be represented as a barter system, introducing money in the final stage of analysis. This notion of money is, besides, the source of other mistake, since from here follows the unconditional endorsement of Say's Law. Here, Ricardo and Marshall effectively become one, and are jointly responsible for the assumption of the full employment of resources. Both Ricardians and marginalists had dismissed the study of the causes of unemployment. Although these elements bring Ricardo close to the marginalists, there are also remarkable differences between them.

It may be easily noted that, to ground his interpretation, Marshall is forced to stretch and misrepresent Ricardo's arguments to turn him, to his own advantage, into an early adherent of the theory of value based on "exertion" and "waiting". Ricardo's exegesis by Marshall was widely rejected, even by the first *marginalists* who, like Jevons, Walras, and Menger, chose to build their system in opposition to that of Ricardo and J. S. Mill's, instead of incorporating them to their own project.

With his version of the *theory of value*, Ricardo meant to show that the only source of commodity value is labor (and not "capital"). Actually, the issue is more complex (and out of the scope of the present study). It could be said that Marshall succeeded in appropriating Ricardo's ideas to a certain extent, since the explanation of value of the latter was tainted by flaws and unsolved issues. Ricardo himself was incapable, precisely, of introducing "capital" in the determination of prices. Thus, he fell into a theoretical dualism: on one hand, he asserted that only the time of labor required to produce each commodity determined its relative price, but he acknowledged, at the same time, that the duration and composition of production processes bore an influence on relative prices. Ricardo's theory of value was inconsistent with the law of the equal rates of profit. Ricardo's flaws led even many self-proclaimed Ricardians to abandon the original formulation.

John Stuart Mill, for example, tried to address the flaws posed by Ricardo's theory by substituting his theory of value based on labor with a theory based on production costs. This ambiguity paved the way for the appropriation of Ricardo attempted at by Marshall. This brief discussion illustrates how Keynes's merger of Marshall and Ricardo under the label of classical theory only contributes to obscuring important theoretical debates.

However, Keynes's characterization of the *classical theory* gains particular relevance in light of the *theory of money* and the *theory of capital* put forth in *The General Theory*. When the incompatibility of his *system* and the *marginalist* foundations provided by Marshall becomes obvious, Keynes claims that he "sympathizes" with the "pre-classical" doctrine that capital is a factor of production, so that, as *The General Theory* posits, labor is the only source of value.

Surprisingly, it may be observed that when Keynes discards the marginalist foundations – being useless as a basis for his new explanations – he is forced to endorse, instead, the foundations corresponding to the other pillar of the classical theory: the Ricardian school and, more particularly, Ricardo.

Marshall tried to make Ricardo a *forerunner* of marginalism; as regards the origin of value, Keynes becomes a *Ricardian*. The theories of *capital scarcity* and *money liquidity*, examined from the point of view of the history of economic analysis, may be considered singular efforts aimed at including in the Ricardian explanation two theoretical issues that are, no doubt, poorly solved (if not absent) in Ricardo's work. In fact, Ricardo had not been able to consistently explain the influence of "capital" – he calls "capital" all the instruments of production in general – on value, and he had neither given account of the origin of money, which he approaches, first, as any commodity acting as a price standard, and then, separately, as a means of circulation. Thus, Keynes puts forth his own theories of capital, money, and value that could be incorporated to Ricardo's system through an analytical exercise.

However, the *theory of money liquidity* as source of the rate of interest is not free from inconsistencies. The same happens with the *theory of capital scarcity*, incapable of accounting for the origin of surplus. The main deficit of the whole analysis lies in its ineffectiveness at establishing an internal connection among value, money and capital, which it tries to explain, instead, through their mutual differences. To sum up: although the line of work inaugurated by Keynes regarding the fundamental categories of economic theory is worth rescuing – particularly when contrasted to the classical theory – and credited on account of the objectives it pursues, the outcomes achieved are rather disappointing.

This, obviously, does not diminish the merit of his critique of the *classical theory*, which in spite of having been dismissed by *marginalists* themselves, has not lost even a speck of its profundity and current validity. On the contrary, this critique offers a significant lesson: any "model", no matter how empirical or abstract it may look in its formulation and conclusions, is always supported by a given set of theoretical foundations. The most powerful and productive critical work takes place, precisely, in this forgotten field.

In this book, we have meant to show that *The General Theory* is no exception; on the contrary, our main objective has been to shed light on Keynes's foundations.

Notes

1 When a habitually repeated relation between two phenomena, a regular joint variation, is observed in practice, the mere verification of such repetition in the past does not authorize, however, the establishment of a causal relation between both phenomena. First, there is the problem of identification: if there does exist an obstinate direct or inverse relation between both variables, which is the cause and which, the effect? But then there is another, more serious, problem: both phenomena may be, in turn, consequences of a different phenomenon, a third term ignored in the explanation. Against the empiricist *"post hoc ergo propter hoc"*, Hume's famous objection is raised: "how often must we repeat to ourselves, that the simple view of any two objects or actions, however related, can never give us any idea, of power, or of a connexion betwixt them: that this idea arises from the repetition of their union: that the repetition neither discovers nor causes any thing in the objects, but has an influence only on the mind [. . .]?" (Hume, 2014 [1739]). Thus enters the well-known "induction problem". Most econometric tradition that has become widespread ignores these old dilemmas: it arrives at causal conclusions based on the mere observation of repetitions and the joint variation of two or more magnitudes.

2 In Chapter 21, *The General Theory,* Keynes suggests to the classical economists a sort of compromise that would enable them to preserve their theories. His proposal is similar to the current split into microeconomics and macroeconomics, but Keynes demanded that they admitted from the beginning that their explanations were based on unreal assumptions: "So long as we limit ourselves to the study of the individual industry or firm on the assumption that the aggregate quantity of employed resources is constant, and, provisionally, that the conditions of other industries or firms are unchanged, it is true that we are not concerned with the significant characteristics of money. But as soon as we pass to the problem of what determines output and employment as a whole, we require the complete theory of a monetary economy" (Keynes, 1939 [1936]: 293; V.21.I). It could be said that his suggestion was accepted, but without publicly acknowledging either the causes of such division or the conceptual limitations of the theory of the individual firm.

3 In the first *marginalists,* this explanation of value is in its pure state. For Marshall, instead, as we saw in Chapter 2, the marginalist theory of value is as partial as the Ricardian, based only on supply conditions. There is much more to be said concerning the exact elements that made *marginalism* a new theoretical current. Here we are stressing exclusively the conceptual aspect, following, for

example, the renowned historian of economic thinking Mark Blaug who states that "it is ordinarily assumed that the term 'marginal revolution' refers to the almost simultaneous, but completely independent, discovery of the principle of diminishing marginal utility as the cornerstone of the new static microeconomics, carried out by Jevons, Menger and Walras during the early 1870's" (Blaug, 1985 [1962]: 374).

4 H. Minsky, among many others, understands that Keynes used to implement any type of rhetorical resources and that he was even capable of misrepresenting his own views only to convince his interlocutor: "Thus in interpreting *The General Theory* to determine what is vital and what is not essential to the radical revision Keynes believed he was formulating, it is necessary both to prune away concessions made to the old – concessions which were either inadvertent [. . .] or consciously opportunistic, due to Keynes's desire to speed the adoption of correct policy [. . .]." (Minsky 1987 [1975]: 24)

5 The most earnest attempts to unify the two-fold *classical theory* of interest, such as Wicksell's or even Keynes's in the *Treatise,* chose then to split at least the category "rate of interest" if not the phenomenon itself. Thus, a "natural" rate of interest was posited as opposed to the "market" rate of interest. These are all attempts at articulating what will then become expressed in the split into two different categories put forth in *The General Theory:* money rate of interest and capital marginal efficiency.

6 Nos parece adecuado traducir de esta manera los términos que emplea Marshall: *"prospectiveness"* y *"productiveness"*. En la traducción española de los Principios se emplea la palabra "perspectivas" en lugar de "prospectividad", de manera que en los pasajes citados textualmente se utilizará esta última

7 Senior was the first economist who based the theory of interest on abstinence; it was Macvane who suggested replacing the term with a less controversial one, "waiting", even though the content of the explanation is exactly the same. Marshall states his reasons for this choice: "Karl Marx and his followers have found much amusement in contemplating the accumulations of wealth which result from the abstinence of Baron Rothschild, which they contrast with the extravagance of a labourer who feeds a family of seven on seven shillings a week; and who, living up to his full income, practises no economic abstinence at all. The argument that it is Waiting rather than Abstinence, which is rewarded by Interest and is a factor of production, was given by Macvane in the Harvard *Journal of Economics* for July, 1887" (Marshall, 1920 [1890], 99n; IV.VII). It is Proudhon, a non-Marxist, however, one of the authors who most exploit the doubtful moral connotations of the term "abstinence".

8 In his influential *Capital and Interest,* Böhm-Bawerk argued that the "waiting" was the distinctive trait of Marshallian theory: "I do not think I am wrong in designating the view held by Marshall as in essentials a cautiously formulated abstinence theory with an improved terminology. In its fundamentals his doctrine is in complete agreement with that of Senior. The formation of capital demands on the part of capitalists a real sacrifice which consists in the postponement of enjoyment and forms an independent element in the cost of production side by side with labour. For this an independent payment must be found in the price of goods after the manner and according to the laws (to be sure, more carefully formulated by Marshall) by which in general costs influence the price of goods" (Böhm-Bawerk, 1947 [1884]: 556)

9 Marshall maintained an intense argument with the Austrian school, represented by Böhm-Bawerk, regarding the nature of capital and the origin of interest.

Böhm-Bawerk stated that interest stemmed from capital productivity, which in turn originated from the fact that lengthy or roundabout processes were always more productive. In Marshall's view, capital goods needed to have the two mentioned attributes. In fact, "There are however innumerable processes which take a long time and are roundabout; but are not productive and therefore are not used; and in fact he [Böhm-Bawerk, AK] seems to have inverted cause and effect"(Marshall, 1920 [1890]: 583n; VI.VI.1). According to Marshall, it is not true that every roundabout process is more productive, but rather that the disutility of the waiting turns into capital productive goods that, therefore, bear an additional product that makes it possible to pay interest as compensation.

10 Schumpeter's view should be compared to the disdain with which these theoretical issues are now approached: "it is not recognized sufficiently that Böhm-Bawerk's criticisms of existing explanations of interest awoke a new awareness of the problem involved in that view of the matter. It is true, more or less, that all the theories of interest survived that had been inherited from the preceding period. Even a theorist of Pareto's rank felt no compunction in declaring that the fact that (physical) capital bears interest was not more of a problem than is the fact that the cherry tree bears cherries. But the standing of some of the simple theories that used to satisfy a majority of economists rapidly declined. Few writers cared to go on holding that because one can produce more wheat with the help of a harrow than without it, a net return must result from using it" (Schumpeter, 1986 [1954]: 892).

11 In this connection, beyond the different emphasis that some authors place on capital productivity and by others on its prospectiveness, there is complete agreement among all the currents of *marginalism,* even between two rivals such as Marshal and Böhm-Bawerk, who argues: "Interest is not an accidental 'historico-legal' category, which makes its appearance only in our individualist and capitalist society, and will vanish with it; but an *economic* category, which springs from elementary economic causes, and therefore, without distinction of social organizations and legislations, makes its appearance wherever there is an exchange between present and future goods. Indeed, even the lonely economy of a Crusoe would not be without the basis of the interest phenomenon, the increasing value of goods and services preparing for the services of the future" (Böhm-Bawerk, 1891 [1884]: 371). Capital and its rate of interest are for *marginalism* eternal and unchanging phenomena, typical of human nature and of productive processes.

12 In Marshall's words: "Everyone is aware that the accumulation of wealth is held in check, and the rate of interest so far sustained, by the preference which the great mass of humanity have for present over deferred gratifications, or, in other words, by their unwillingness to 'wait'" (Marshall, 1920 [1890]: VI.VI.5). Already in his 1930 *Treatise,* Keynes had begun to move away from this explanation stressing, instead, the insufficiency of expenditure and, more precisely, the weakness of investment as obstacles to accumulation (and employment): "It has been usual to think of the accumulated wealth of the world as having been painfully built up out of that voluntary abstinence of individuals from the immediate enjoyment of consumption which we call Thrift. But it should be obvious that mere abstinence is not enough by itself to build cities or drain fens. [. . .] It is enterprise which builds and improves the world's possessions. [. . .] For enterprise is connected with thrift not directly but at one remove; and the link which should join them is frequently missing" (Keynes, 1935 [1930]: 148–149; II). If, as the classical theory holds, savings and investment are two sides of the same

kind of good (capital), it could never be suggested, as Keynes did in 1930, that an increase in savings does not always translate into an increase in investment.

13 Individuals consider it convenient to set aside a portion of their current income as saving to satisfy certain needs that cannot be satisfied with their current income. Among such desires, Keynes mentions the need to address unforeseen contingencies (precaution); to save for old age and family education (foresight); to be better off in the future (improvement); to feel independent; to have a capital available to undertake projects (enterprise); to bequeath a fortune (pride); and, last, an innate and irrational tendency to not consume (avarice).

14 If this argument is extended just a little, man's social life, his history, suddenly becomes, we could say, more feasible; the accumulation of material wealth, the use of work instruments, the development of powerful tools to appropriate nature, in short, essential aspects that distinguish human beings from other animal species appear as *needs in themselves* and not just as the product of the painful deferment of the only need that is otherwise recognized in men: the immediate and voracious pleasure of present consumption. Because, on such a basis, if there were no reward for the waiting through interest, the human species would find its activity reduced, according to this view, as a sort of tribute paid to its own "genetic" determinations, to the immediate consumption of the products offered by nature that men can obtain without employing tools: under this interpretation, the specifically human nature turns man into a beast, a condition from which only the emergence of the capital rate of interest rescues him.

15 As was previously pointed out, a controversy about the problem of capital "productivity" as the source of interest rate existed among the members of the marginalist school. The theory of Böhm-Bawerk focused on the higher productivity of lengthy processes. This higher productivity drives men to devote a portion of their wealth to productive investment. Productivity is at the core of this theory, as was the abstinence in the case of Marshall's. However, both of them are supplementary, as Marshall needs capital to be *productive* to make it possible to pay an additional sum for the sacrifice of the waiting, and Böhm-Bawerk needs man to be impatient for saving to have a limit.

16 A. Monza sets at this point the beginning of the capital controversy of the 1960's: "It was the problem of capital measurement that which led to the controversy" (Monza, 1972: 19). Few have mentioned Keynes as a forerunner of such debate between marginalists and modern Ricardians.

17 The other implicit ambiguities in this definition mentioned by Keynes refer, first, to the problem of the unit of measurement of productivity, that is, to the absence of a definition on the question whether physical productivity should be considered an absolute amount or a rate comparable to the interest rate: is it a number of capital units or a percentage? The second additional problem mentioned is linked with time. Capital equipment is used during more than one period, but productivity is usually measured only in one period, the first. The classical theory does not say anything about how the yields obtained in distant periods should be treated, as they cannot be "discounted" applying the rate of interest without getting caught in a circular reasoning.

18 Man saves a portion of his wealth in the form he considers best to preserve his purchasing power through time. Saving does not always imply, as has been said, an actual desire to consume something at a precise date and, least of all, the mere act of saving is capable of articulating that precisely dated need. This is the reason why the mere act of individual or social savings cannot trigger a *lengthy productive process* that will result in the desired product at the desired

date. Keynes evaluates what would happen in the hypothetical case that men, whenever they save, would "announce" beforehand – in the Walrasian style – what and how much they will wish to consume. Even in that case, if men would explicitly state – if there were an economic mechanism that would allow for such an act – both the character as the precise future date of their consumption need, even in that case, the act of saving would not necessarily trigger *in the present* an investment equivalent to the decrease in consumption. A case may exist where – as Keynes notes – there is no required production method whose "length" is precisely the adequate one. Let's assume that today there were announced a desire to consume a particular good in three years' time, and the corresponding act of saving was performed. The adequate means of producing such good may not necessarily imply that its production begins today devoting such resources to investment.

19 Adam Smith uses the famous metaphor of the invisible hand to describe the workings of this mechanism. It is an automatic mechanism that guides private investment to increase output in those branches where price is higher than the "natural" price: "As every individual, therefore, endeavours as much as he can both to employ his capital in the support of domestic industry, and so to direct that industry that its produce may be of the greatest value; every individual necessarily labours to render the annual revenue of the society as great as he can. He generally, indeed, neither intends to promote the public interest, nor knows how much he is promoting it. By preferring the support of domestic to that of foreign industry, he intends only his own security; and by directing that industry in such a manner as its produce may be of the greatest value, he intends only his own gain, and he is in this, as in many other cases, led by an invisible hand to promote an end which was no part of his intention" (Smith, 1904 [1776]; IV.2.9).

20 If capital equipment were scarce, their yield would be similar to land rent. Marshall himself was aware of this similarity, which led to him to naming "quasi-rent" the return yielded by capital equipment: "the term *Quasi-rent* will be used in the present volume for the income derived from machines and other appliances for production made by man [. . .] we cannot properly speak of the interest yielded by a machine. If we use the term "interest" at all, it must be in relation not to the machine itself, but to its money *value*" (Marshall, 1920 [1890]; II.IV.12). It is very likely that Keynes's choice of letter "Q" to refer to the annuities yielded by equipment may have been based on the similarity of rent and capital return. Capital renders a scarcity quasi-rent on account of several reasons that will be mentioned next. For Marshall, quasi-rents were a short-term phenomenon.

21 The prospective yield is a variable that depends on future expectations of sales, that is, on the future strength of demand: annuities, based on which capital marginal efficiency is calculated, are thus established. The marginal efficiency of capital based on entrepreneurs' expectations is the variable subject to the most violent fluctuations in Keynes's system.

22 With respect to chapter 17, Joan Robinson holds that "[W]hen Keynes was writing [. . .] the chapter, he admitted that he was groping for ideas that were new to him, and I do not think that he ever quite succeeded in seizing them" *(*Robinson, 1956, p. 138, quoted in Asimakopulos, 1991, p. 103*)*. A. P. Lerner, one of the few authors that study this subject, begins his article by admitting that "Almost every tribute to the originality, brilliance, and importance of Keynes's General Theory of Employment, Interest and Money during the fifteen years since its publications, has admitted that it is a badly written book. Of no part of the book is this more true than of Chapter 17" (Lerner, 1952; 172). I. Kregel is also one

of the few economists that took Keynes's theory of money seriously, to share, criticize or at least explain it. See his interesting article "Markets and Institutions as Features of a Capitalistic Production System" (Kregel, 1988).

23 In the lengthy Chapter 17, a single reference to the work of other authors is included, an article written by Sraffa (1932) where he harshly criticizes *Price and Production,* published by F.A. Hayek in 1931. Sraffa challenged Hayek's entire reasoning aimed at showing that in a moneyless economy, there would never be any disturbance in relative prices, interest rates, and employment. He would then try to prove that in a monetary economy, through a banking policy aimed at keeping the product of money quantity and the velocity of money constant, money could be made to be "neutral", that is, as in the case of a moneyless economy, there would be no disturbances in real variables. Specifically, the rate of interest would always remain on its "natural" level. Sraffa's clever refutation consists in showing that in a moneyless economy, there would not be just one, but many rates of interest. The "real" natural rate mentioned by Hayek does not exist and cannot be analytically defined. In fact, there would be as many interest rates as there are goods. Thus, Hayek's entire case for his "banking system" collapses, since it is impossible to find a single natural rate of interest equivalent to that of a moneyless economy. In line with Keynes, Sraffa also points out that the problem lies, precisely, in the (classical) conception of money, which dismisses its role as value deposit: "The money which he contemplates is in effect used purely and simply as a medium of exchange. There are not debts, no money contracts, no wage agreements, no sticky prices in his suppositions" (Sraffa, 1932: 44). Keynes borrows from here the Sraffian idea of the own-rate of interest pertaining to each good.

24 Los términos que emplea Keynes en el original en inglés son *"carrying cost"* para el factor *c* y *"liquidity premium"* para el factor *l*.

25 Keynes says that under such circumstances there would be room for private property, although not for the gains derived from the mere ownership of capital goods: "Though the rentier would disappear, there would still be room, nevertheless, for enterprise and skill in the estimation of prospective yields about which opinions could differ [. . .]. But it is not unlikely that, in such circumstances, the eagerness to obtain a yield from doubtful investments might be such that they would show in the aggregate a negative net yield" (Keynes, 1939 [1936]: 220; IV.16.IV).

26 Referring to this mutual relation of productivity and prospectiveness, Schumpeter argues: "Marshall had no difficulty in formulating an explanation of interest that took account of abstinence4 without being open to logical objection. In fact, he succeeded in reviving the productivity theory as well by linking it to the element of abstinence. If physical capital is to yield not only returns but also net returns, something must prevent it from being produced up to the point at which its earnings would no more than repay its cost. Abstinence qualifies – logically – for the role of this something" (Schumpeter, 1986 [1954]: 893).

27 James Stuart was, among the last mercantilists, one of the most outstanding proponents of this theory, which split the price of a commodity into two different parts: the "real value of the commodity" and the "profit upon alienation"; the latter varies according to the state of demand (quoted in Rubin, 1989 [1929]: 68). The explanation of the profit originated by trade was adopted, to a certain extent, by the marginalist theory, although it was considered to be a "market" phenomenon, that is eliminated when the price reaches its normal value. The modern version of *marginalism* agrees that there are profits like these in the

short term but both in the long term as in the general equilibrium with perfect competition, the purely commercial profit must be null, as Walras admits when he asserts that the entrepreneur *"ne faisant ni bénéfice ni perte"*.

28　In the notes taken in class by Keynes's students before the publication of *The General Theory* (1933), published in subsequent years, his use of the circulation formula conceived by Marx (Commodity – Money – Commodity) is mentioned. Keynes "credits Marx with having pointed out that in a capitalist economy money transactions cannot be reduced to barter transactions Businessmen pay out money in order to make more money; they don't pay out commodities to make more commodities." (Skidelsky, 1994: 497n). Even so, his theory of money has to offer a special motive driving individuals to store money in cash. Furthermore, it should explain the origin of the monetary rate of interest.

29　It should be noted that Keynes does not seek to account for capitalist crises but, rather, he tries to unveil the causes of a more or less protracted stagnation in production, whose main cause he finds to be the weakness of investment.

30　In equilibrium, the quantity of money and the liquidity preference determine a rate of interest that, in turn, given capital marginal efficiency, defines the volume of investment. In equilibrium, also, investment equals saving, and a portion of the money is stored, and the rest is used for transactions. Given the exogenous variables, a single equilibrium level is "immediately" determined for the endogenous variables.

31　The term "non-monetary" is used in the previously specified sense, that is, meaning that there is no asset with a liquidity premium higher than its carrying cost.

32　This is the case of the "disequilibriumist", "institutionalist", "financial fragility" etc. readings, where most of the ideas Keynes effectively argued for in *The General Theory* are first discarded, appealing to barely elaborated upon motives, to claim, then, that the most substantial contribution of his work is hidden in what Keynes actually thought but never stated clearly. These authors devote themselves to "complete", so to speak, his argument in certain direction.

33　The more resolutely and unjustifiably discarded chapters of *The General Theory* were the strictly theoretical ones. Alvin Hansen, one of the architects of the neoclassical synthesis, who also undertook the task of spreading Keynes's ideas in the United States, says in his well-known *A Guide to Keynes,* for example: "These chapters [16 and 17] are indeed another detour which could be omitted without sacrificing the main argument" (Hansen, 1966 [1953]: 140).

34　The figure of Piero Sraffa, the most important of modern Ricardians, a "protegé" of Keynes's in Cambridge, seems to synthesize both approaches. It is possible to attempt an "integration" of Sraffa's system and Keynes's ideas concerning money for the short term (see Kicillof, 2005: 462).

35　The obvious affinity of Paul Sweezy (1967) with Keynes's ideas, for example, was one of the most telling expressions of these coincidences.

Bibliography

Akerlof, G. and Yellen, J. (1985) A Near-Rational Model of the Business Cycle, With Wages and Prices Inertia. *Quarterly Journal of Economics*, 100, Supplement, 823–838.

Arestis, P. (1992) *The Post-Keynesian Approach to Economics*, Aldershot, Edward Elgar.

—— (1996) La economía postkeynesiana: hacia la coherencia. *Buenos Aires Pensamiento Económico*, 2.

Argandoña, A. and Al, E. (1996) *Macroeconomía avanzada I y II*, Madrid, McGraw-Hill.

Asimakopulos, A. (1991) *Keynes's General Theory and Accumulation*, Cambridge: Cambridge University Press.

Bagehot, W. (1968 [1873]) *Lombard Street*, México DF, Fondo de Cultura Económica.

Barbon, N. (2005 [1690]) *A Discourse of Trade*. The Lord Baltimore Press. 1905. Ed. Jacob H. Hollander. Library of Economics and Liberty. 12 October 2006, IN www.econlib.org/library/YPDBooks/Barbon/brbnDT1.html.

Barro, R. J. (1985 [1979]) Money and the Price Level Under the Gold Standard. In Eichengreen, B. (Ed.) *The Gold Standard in Theory and History*. New York and London, Methuen.

—— (1983) *Macroeconomía*, México DF, McGraw-Hill.

Blanchard, O. (1997) *Macroeconomía*, Madrid, Prentice Hall.

—— (2000) *Macroeconomía*, Madrid, Prentice Hall.

Blanchard, O. and Pérez enrri, D. (2000) *Macroeconomía*, Buenos Aires, Prentice Hall.

Blaug, M. (1990 [1962]) *Economic Theory in Retrospect*, London, Cambridge University Press.

Bleaney, M. (1985) *The Rise and Fall of Keynesian Economics*, Hampshire and London, Macmillan.

Böhm-Bawerk, E. V. (1891 [1884]) *The Positive Theory of Capital*, London, Macmillan.

—— (1947 [1884]) *Capital e interés*, México DF, Fondo de Cultura Económica.

—— (1895) The Origin of Interest. *Quarterly Journal of Economics*, 9, 380–387.

Bonefeld, W. (1996) Monetarism and Crisis. In Bonefeld, W. and Holloway, J. (Eds.) *Global Capital, National State and the Politics of Money*. Houndmills, Macmillan Press.

Bourges, E. (1990) Sindicatos por industria. *Historia del Movimiento Obrero, Centro Editor de América Latina*, 23.

Boyer, R. (1985) Formes d'organisation implicites à la Théorie Générale. In Barrère, A. (Ed.) *Keynes aujourd'hui: Théories et politiques*. Paris, Economica.

Branson, W. H. (1990 [1972]) *Macroeconomía y política económica*, México DF, Fondo de Cultura Económica.

Braun, O. (1975) Introducción. In Braun, O. (Ed.) *Teoría del capital y la distribución*. Buenos Aires, Tiempo contemporáneo.

Carabelli, A. M. (1988) *On Keynes Method*, New York, St. Martin´s Press.

Chick, V. (1990 [1983]) *La macroeconomía según Keynes: Una revisión de la teoría general*, Madrid, Alianza Editorial.

——— (1991 [1983]) *Macroeconomics After Keynes*, Cambridge, MIT Press.

Clarke, S. (1988) *Keynesianism, Monetarism and the Crisis of the State*, Vermont, Edward Elgar.

——— (1994) *Marx´s Theory of Crisis*, New York, St. Martin's Press.

Cleaver, H. (1985 [1979]) *Una lectura política de El Capital*, México DF, Fondo de Cultura Económica.

Clower, R. (1965) The Keynesian Counter Revolution: A Theorical Appriasal. In Hahn, F. H. and Brechling, F. P. R. (Eds.) *The Theory of Interest Rates*. London, Macmillan.

Clower, R. and Leijonhufvud, A. (1975) The Coordination of Economic Activities: A Keynesian Perspective. *American Economic Review*, 65, Papers and Proc., 182–188.

Cunliffe-Committee (1985 [1918]) Cunliffe Committee on Currency and Foreign Exchanges After the War. In Eichengreen, B. (Ed.) *The Gold Standard in Theory and History*. New York and London, Methuen.

Davidson, P. (1978) *Money and the Real World*, London, Macmillan.

——— (1978) "Por qué es importante el dinero: lecciones recibidas en medio siglo de teoría monetaria." In C. F. Obregón Díaz (Ed.) *Keynes: la macroeconomía del desequilibrio*. Trillas, México.

——— (1991) Is Probability Theory Relevant for Uncertainty: A Post Keynesian Perspective. *Journal of Economic perspectives*, 5, 29–43.

De Angelis, M. (1997) Class Struggle and Economics: The Case of Keynesianism. *Research in Political Economy*, 16, 3–53.

——— (1997) *Social Relations and the Keynesian Multiplier*, London, University of East London.

De Brunhoff, S. (1985) La critique keynesienne du "laissez faire". In Barrère, A. (Ed.) *Keynes aujourd'hui: Théories et politiques*. Paris, Economica.

De Gortari, E. (1964) *Dialéctica de la física*, México DF, UNAM.

De Vroey, M. (2004) The History of Macroeconomics Viewed Against the Background of the Marshall-Walras Divide. In M. De Vroey, & K. D. Hoover (Eds.) *The IS-LM Model: Its Rise, Fall, and Strange Persistence*. HOPE, 36, 57–91.

Dillard, D. (1942) Keynes and Proudhon. *The Journal of Economic History*, 2(1), 63–76.

——— (1981 [1948]) *La teoría económica de John Maynard Keynes: Teoría de una economía monetaria*, Madrid, Aguilar.

———— (1954) The Theory of a Monetary Economy. In Kurihara, K. K. (Ed.) *Post Keynesian Economics*. New Brunswick, Rutgers University Press.

Dobb, M. (1973 [1927]) *Salarios*, México DF, Fondo de Cultura Económica.

Dow, S. (2001) Post Keynesian Methodology. In Holt, R. and Pressman, S. (Eds.) *A New Guide to Post Keynesian Economics*. London, Routledge.

Dumenil, G. and Levy, D. (2002) *From Prosperity to Neoliberalism: Europe Before and After the Structural Crisis of the 1970s*, MODEM-CNRS and CEPREMAP-CNRS, IN www.cepremap.s.fr/levy

Duval, N. (1992) Hombres y luchas obreras; las primeras décadas del siglo XX. *Historia del Movimiento Obrero, Centro Editor de América Latina*, Vol. 108.

Eichengreen, B. (1985) Editor's Introduction. In Eichengreen, B. (Ed.) *The Gold Standard in Theory and History*. New York and London, Methuen.

Engles, F. (1983) *Anti – Dühring: La subversión de la ciencia por el señor Eugen Dühring*, México DF, Grijalbo.

Eshag, E. (1965) *From Marshall to Keynes: An Essay on the Monetary Theory of the Cambridge School*, New York, Kelley.

Estay, J. R. and Manchón, F. C. (1997) *Keynes . . . hoy*, México DF, Benemérita Universidad de Autónoma de Puebla y Universidad Autónoma Metropolitana – Xochimilco.

Feiwell, G. R. (1987 [1975]) *Michal Kalecki: Contribuciones a la teoría de la política económica*, México DF, Fondo de Cultura Económica.

Ferguson, C. E. and Gould, J. P. (1979) *Teoría Microeconómica*, México DF, Fondo de Cultura Económica.

Fischer, S., Dornbusch, R. and Schmalensee, R. (1989) *Economía*, Madrid, McGraw Hill.

Fisher, I. (1933) The Debt-Deflation Theory of Great Depressions. *Econometrica*, 1, 337–357.

Fohl, C. B. and Darida, F. (1965) Las era de las revoluciones. In Parias, L.-H. (Ed.) *Historia General del Trabajo*, México DF y Barcelona, Grijalbo.

Ford, A. G. (1960/1985) Notes on the Working of the Gold Standard Before 1914. In Eichengreen, B. (Ed.) *The Gold Standard in Theory and History*. New York and London, Methuen.

———— (1962) *The Gold Standard 1880–1914 Britain and Argentina*, Oxford, Clarendon Press.

Friedman, M. (1985 [1956]) Nueva formulación de la teoría cuantitativa del dinero. In Mueller, M. G. (Ed.) *Lecturas de Macroeconomía*, México DF, Compañía Editorial Continental.

———— (1957) *A Theory of Consumption Function*, Princeton, Princeton University Press.

———— (1964) How Has the General Theory Stimulated Economic Research? In Leckachman, R. (Ed.) *Keynes and the Classics*. Boston, D. C. Heath and Company.

Friedman, M. and Friedman, R. (1997 [1980]) *La libertad de elegir*, Barcelona, Grijalbo.

Friedman, M. and Schwartz, A. J. (1963) *A Monetary History of the United States, 1961–1960*, Princeton, Princeton University Press.

Frisch, R. (1933) Propagation Problems and Impulse Problems in Dynamic Economics. In *Economic Essays in Honour of Gustav Cassel*. London, Allen & Unwin Ltd.

Galbraith, J. K. (1993 [1954]) *El crac del 29*, Barcelona, Ariel.

——— (1983 [1975]) *El dinero: De dónde vino. Adónde fue*, Buenos Aires, Hyspamerica.

Garegnani, P. (1985) Capital et demande effective. In Barrère, A. (Ed.) *Keynes aujourd'hui: Théories et politiques*. Paris, Economica.

Goldner, L. (1999) *The Remaking of the American Working Class. Restructuring of Global Capital*, IN http://home.earthlink.net/~lrgoldner/

Gralbraith, J. K. (1983) *El dinero De dónde vino a dónde fue*, Madrid, Ediciones Orbis.

Guerrero, D. (1995) *Competitividad: teoría y política*, Barcelona, Ariel.

——— (2000) *Macroeconomía y crisis mundial*, Madrid, Trotta.

Haberler, G. (1967 [1964]) La Teoría General después de diez años. In Lekachman, R. (Ed.) *Teoría General de Keynes Informe de tres décadas*. México DF, Fondo de Cultura Económica.

Hansen, A. (1966 [1953]) *Guía de Keynes*, México DF, Fondo de Cultura Económica.

Harcourt, G. C. (2006) *The Structure of Post Keynesian Economics*, Cambridge, Cambridge University Press.

Harris, S. (1966 [1953]) Introducción. In Hansen, A. (Ed.) *Guía de Keynes*. México DF, Fondo de Cultura Económica.

——— (1965) *The New Economics Keynes' Influence on Theory and Public Policy*, New York, Kelley.

Harrod, R. F. (1951) *La vida de John Maynard Keynes*, México DF, Fondo de Cultura Económica.

Hayek, F. A. (1932) Money and Capital: A Reply. *The Economic Journal*, 42, 237–249.

——— (2004 [1976]) Introduction. In Menger, C. (Ed.) *Principles of Economics Ludwig von Mises Institute*. Electronic online edition.

Heckscher, E. F. (1936) Mercantilism. *The Economic History Review*, 7, 11.

Hegel, G. W. F. (1968 [1812]) *Ciencia de la lógica*, Buenos Aires, Solar.

Henderson, J. M. and Quandt, R. E. (1980) *Microeconomic Theory: A Mathematical Approach*, New York, McGraw-Hill.

Heymann, D. and Leijonhufvud, A. (1995) *High Inflation*, Oxford, Clarendon.

Hicks, J. R. (1936) Review of the General Theory. *Economic Journal*, 46, 182, 238–253.

——— (1937) Mr. Keynes and the Classics: A Suggested Interpretation. *Econometrica*, 5, 147–159.

——— (1985 [1937]) Keynes y los "Clásicos": una posible interpretación. In Mueller, M. G. (Ed.) *Lecturas de Macroeconomía*. México DF, Editorial Continental.

Hicks, J.R. (1978 [1937]) Value and Capital: An enquiry into some fundamental principles of economic theory, Oxford, Clarendon Press.

——— (1967 [1965]) *Capital y crecimiento*, Barcelona, Bosch.

——— (1984 [1969]) *Una teoría de la historia económica*, Barcelona, Orbis.

——— (1974) *The Crisis in Keynesian Economics*, New York, Basic Books.

Hilferdin, R. (1910/1985) *O capital financiero*, San Pablo, Nova Cultura.

Hobsbawm, E. (1998 [1987]) *Historia del siglo XX*, Buenos Aires, Critica.

Hobson, J. A. (1902) *Imperialism*, London.

Holloway, J. (1996) The Abyss Opens: The Rise and Fall of Keynesianism. In Bonefeld, W. and Holloway, J. (Eds.) *Global Capital, National State and the Politics of Money*. Houndmills, Macmillan Press.

Hume, D. (1985 [1756]) On Money. In Eichengreen, B. (Ed.) *The Gold Standard in Theory and History*. New York and London, Methuen.

———(2014 [1739]) *A Treatise of Human Nature*, The University of Adelaide, IN https://ebooks.adelaide.edu.au/h/hume/david/h92t/index.html.

Iñigo Carrera, J. (1993) *El capital: razón histórica, sujeto revolucionario y conciencia*, Buenos Aires, Ediciones Cooperativas.

Itoh, M. (1980) *Value and Crisis: Essays of Marxian Economics in Japan*, New York, Monthly Review Press.

Itoh, M. and Lapavitsas, C. (1999) *Political Economy of Money and Finance*, HoundMills, Macmillan.

Jevons, W. S. (1888 [1871]) *The Theory of Political Economy*, London, Macmillan and Co., IN www.econlib.org/library/YPDBooks/Jevons/jvnPE.html; accessed 17 February 2015.

Kalecki, M. (1995) *Teoría de la dinámica económica: Ensayo sobre los movimientos cíclicos a largo plazo de la economía capitalista*, México DF, Fondo de Cultura Económica.

Keynes, J. M. (1997 [1919]) *Las consecuencias económicas de la paz*, Barcelona, Folio

——— (1920) *The Economic Consequences of the Peace*, New York, Harcourt, Brace, and Howe, Inc., IN www.econlib.org/library/YPDBooks/Keynes/kynsCP.html, accessed September 2011.

——— (1923) *A Tract on Monetary Reform*, London, MacMillan & CO.

——— (1924) Alfred Marshall. 1842-1924, *The Economic Journal*, 34, 135, 311–372.

——— (1925) *Am I a Liberal?*, IN www.hetwebsite.net/het/texts/keynes/keynes 1925liberal.htm, accessed September 2011.

——— (1997b [1925]) Las consecuencias económicas del Sr. Churchill. In Keynes, J. M. (Ed.) *Ensayos de persuasión*. Barcelona, Folio.

——— (1997c [1925]) Breve panorama de Rusia. In Keynes, J. M. (Ed.) *Ensayos de persuasión*. Barcelona, Folio.

——— (1926) *The End of Laissez-Faire*, IN http://mx.nthu.edu.tw/~cshwang/cs-economics/econ5005/04-Keynesian/Keynes-JM=The%20End%20of%20Lais sez%20Faire.pdf.

——— (1935 [1930]) *A Treatise on Money*, Brace and Company, Harcourt.

——— (1963 [1930]) Economic Possibilities for our Grandchildren. In *Essays in Persuassion*. New York, W.W.Norton & Co., 358–373.

——— (1997b [1930]) La gran depresión de 1930. In Keynes, J. M. (Ed.) *Ensayos de persuasión*. Barcelona, Folio.

——— (1931) *Essays in Persuassion*, IN www.gutenberg.ca/ebooks/keynes-essay sinpersuasion/keynes-essaysinpersuasion-00-h.html, accessed September 2011.

——— (1997a [1931]) *Ensayos de persuasión*, Barcelona, Folio.

——— (1997b [1931]) Mitigación por medio del arancel. In Keynes, J. M. (Ed.) *Ensayos de persuasión*. Barcelona, Folio.

——— (1933) *The Means to Prosperity*, IN www.gutenberg.ca/ebooks/keynes-means/keynes-means-00-h.html.

——— (1939 [1936]) *The General Theory of Employment, Interest and Money*, London, Macmillan.

——— (1973 [1936]) Preface to German edition of the general theory. In Donald, M. (Ed.) *The collected writings of John Maynard Keynes. Vol. 7*. London, Macmillan for The Royal Economic Society.

——— (2005 [1936]) *Teoría general de la ocupación, el interés y el dinero*, Buenos Aires, Fondo de Cultura Económica.

——— (1937a) Alternative Theories of the Rate of Interest. *The Economic Journal*, 47, 186, 241–252.

——— (1937b) The General Theory of Employment. *The Quarterly Journal of Economics*, 51, 2, 209–223.

——— (1937c) Prof. Pigou on Money Wages in Relation to Unemployment. *The Economic Journal*, 47, 188, 743–753.

——— (1939) *Preface to First French edition of the General Theory*, IN http://gutenberg.net.au/ebooks03/0300071h/frapref.html, accessed March 2017.

——— (1939b) Relative Movements of Real Wages and Output. *The Economic Journal*, 49, 193, 34–51.

——— (1973 [1939]) Preface to French Edition of the General Theory. In Donald, M. (Ed.) *The Collected Writings of John Maynard Keynes. Vol. 7*. London, Macmillan for The Royal Economic Society.

Kicillof, A. (2000a) La controversia de la especificidad. *I Congreso Electrónico sobre la Actualización de Das Kapital*, IN www.econ.uba.ar/ceplad.

——— (2000b) Ensayo sobre los Principios de Economía Política y Tributación de David Ricardo. *Documento CEPLAD*.

——— (2001) Causalidad estocástica: reino del fenómeno, miseria de la teoría. *VII Jornadas de Epistemología de las Ciencias Económicas*, Buenos Aires.

——— (2002) *Tres Keynes en la Teoría General*, Buenos Aires, Instituto de Investigaciones Económicas CEPLAD.

——— (2004a) *La macroeconomía después de Lord Keynes*, Buenos Aires, Instituto de Investigaciones Económicas FCE – CEPLAD.

——— (2004b) El capital según Lord Keynes. *Nueva Economía*, XIII.

——— (2004c) Las concepciones de Kuhn y Lakatos aplicadas al desarrollo de la economía: ¿reconstrucción histórica u operación ideológica? *IX Jornadas de Epistemología de las Ciencias Económicas, FCE, UBA*, Buenos Aires.

——— (2005) Génesis y estructura de la Teoría General de Lord Keynes. *Programa de Doctorado área Economía*. Buenos Aires, Universidad de Buenos Aires.

Kindleberger, C. P. (1997) *La crisis económica 1929–1939*, Barcelona, Folio.

Klein, L. R. (1954) The Empirical Foundations of Keynesian Economics. In Kurihara, K. K. (Ed.) *Post Keynesian Economics*. New Brunswick, Rutgers University Press.

——— (1961) *The Keynesian Revolution*, New York, Macmillan.

Kregel, J. (1985) Le multiplicateur et la preference pour la liquidite: deux aspects de la theory de la demande effective. In Barrère, A. (Ed.) *Keynes aujourd'hui : Théories et politiques*. Paris, Economica.

———— (1988) Mercados e instituciones como aspectos de un sistema de producción capitalista. In Ocampo, J. A. (Ed.) *Lecturas de economía postkeynesiana*. México DF, Fondo de Cultura económica.

Krugman, P. (1994) *Economía Internacional: Teoría y Política*, Madrid, McGraw – Hill.

Kuhn, T. (1971) *La estructura de las revoluciones científicas*, México DF, Fondo de Cultura Económica.

———— (1980) Lógica del descubrimiento o psicología de la investigación. *MIMEO cátedra Scarano, FCE, UBA*.

Kurihara, K. K. (1954) *Post Keynesian Economics*, New Brunswick, Rutgers University Press.

Laidler, D. (1999) *Fabricating the Keynesian Revolution: Studies of the Inter-War Literature on Money, the Cycle, and Unemployment*, Cambridge, Cambridge University Press.

Lakatos, I. (1978) *La metodología de los programas de investigación científica*, Buenos Aires, Alianza Universidad.

Lawson, T. (1988) Probability and Uncertainty in Economic Analysis. *Journal of Post Keynesian Economics*, 11, 38–65.

Leijonhufvud, A. (1976a) *Análisis de Keynes y de la economía keynesiana Un estudio de teoría monetaria*, Barcelona, Vicens – Vives.

———— (1976b) Keynes y los clásicos. In Clower, R.and Leijonhufvud, A. (Eds.) *La nueva teoría monetaria*. Madrid, Saltés.

Leijonhufvud, A. T. (1979) Deficiencias de la demanda efectiva. *The Swedish Journal of Economics*, 75, 1, Trad.: FUJANA, A. M., 27–48.

Lekachman, R. (1964a) Introduction. In Lekachman, R. (Ed.) *Keynes and the Classics*. Boston, D. C. Heath and Company.

———— (1964b) *Keynes and the Classics*, Boston, D. C. Heath and Company.

———— (1967 [1964]) *Teoría General de Keynes: Informe de tres décadas*, México DF, Fondo de Cultura Económica.

———— (1966) *The Age of Keynes*, New York, Vintage Books.

Lenin, V. I. (1975 [1917]) *El imperialismo: Fase superior del capitalismo*, Pekín, Ediciones en lenguas extranjeras.

Lerner, A. P. (1967 [1936]) La Teoría General. In Lekachman, R. (Ed.) *Teoría general de Keynes: Informe de tres décadas*. México DF, Fondo de Cultura Económica.

———— (1952) The Essential Properties of Interest and Money. *The Quarterly Journal of Economics*, 66, 172–193.

Levín, P. (1995) *El capital tecnológico*, Buenos Aires, Catálogos.

Lipsey, R. G. (1977 [1963]) *Introducción a la economía positiva*, Barcelona, Vicens Universidad.

Macmillan-Committee (1985 [1931]) Macmillan Committee on Finance and Industry. In Eichengreen, B. (Ed.) *The Gold Standard in Theory and History*. New York and London, Methuen.

Maddison, A. (1995) *La economía mundial 1820–1992: Análisis y estadística*, OCDE.

Malinvaud, E. (1977) *The Theory of Unemployment Reconsidered*, London, Basil Blackwell.

Malthus, R. (1890) *An Essay on the Principle of Population*, London, Ward Lock and Co.

Mankiw, G. (1985) Small Menu Cost and Large Business Cycles: A Macroeconomic Model of Monopoly. *Quarterly Journal of Economics*, 100, 529–537.

——— (1990) A Quick Refresher Course in Macroeconomics. *Journal of Economic Literature*, XXVIII, 4, 1645–1660,.

——— (2000) *Macroeconomics*, New York, Worth Publishers.

Mankiw, G. and Romer, D. (1991) Introduction. In Mankiw, R. and Romer, D. (Eds.) *New Keynesian Economics*. Cambridge, MIT Press.

Marglin, S. A. (1991) Lessons of the Gold Age. In Marglin, S. A. and Schor, J. B. (Eds.) *The Golden Age of Capitalism*. Oxford, Clarendon Press.

Marshall, A. (1920 [1890]) *Principles of Economics*, London, Macmillan and Co., Ltd., IN www.econlib.org/library/Marshall/marP.html.

——— (1923) *Money, Credit & Commerce*, London, Macmillan.

——— (1926) *Oficial Papers by Alfred Marshall*, London, Macmillan.

——— (1948) *Principles of Economics. An introductory volume*, London, Macmillan.

Marx, C. (1986 [1871]) *El capital: Crítica de la economía política*, México DF, Fondo de Cultura Económica.

——— (1987 [1959]) *Teorías sobre la plusvalía*, México DF, Fondo de Cultura Económica.

——— (1976) *Glosas marginales al "Tratado de economía política" de Adolph Wagner*, México DF, Siglo XXI.

Mattick, P. (1969) *Marx and Keynes: The Limits of the Mixed Economy*, Boston, Extending Horizons Books.

Mccloskey, D. N. and Zecher, J. R. (1985 [1976]) How the Gold Standard Worked, 1880–1913. In Eichengreen, B. (Ed.) *The Gold Standard in Theory and History*. New York and London, Methuen.

Menger, C. (2007 [1871]) *Principles of Economics*, Auburn, Alabama, Ludwig von Mises Institute, IN http://mises.org/sites/default/files/Principles%20of%20Economics_5.pdf.

Mill, J. S. (1874 [1844]) *Essays on Some Unsettled Questions of Political Economy*, London, Longmans, Green, Reader, and Dyer, IN www.econlib.org/library/Mill/mlUQP2.html; accessed 2 March 2015.

——— (1909 [1848]) Principles of Political Economy with some of their Applications to Social Philosophy, William J. Ashley, ed. London, Longmans, Green and Co., IN www.econlib.org/library/Mill/mlP33.html; accessed 29 May 2017.

Minsky, H. (1987 [1975]) *Las razones de Keynes*, México DF, Fondo de Cultura Económica.

——— (1985) Endettement, crédit et taux d'interet. In Barrere, A. (Ed.) *Keynes aujourd'hui: Théories et politiques*. Paris, Economica.

Minsky, H. P. (1982) *Can "It" Happen Again? Essays on Instability and Finance*, Armonk, Sharpe.

Modigliani, F. (1944) Liquidity Preference and the Theory of Interest and Money. *Econometrica*, 12, 45–88.

Monza, A. (1972) Nota introductoria a la reciente controversia en la teoría del capital. In Braun, O. (Ed.) *Teoría del capital y la distribución*. Buenos Aires, Tiempo Contemporáneo.

Negri, A. (1988 [1967]) Keynes and the Capitalist Theory of the State Post-1929. In Negri, A. (Ed.) *Revolution Retrieved: Selected Writings on Marx, Keynes, Capitalist Crisis and New Social Subjects*. London, Red Notes.

Patinkin, D. (1959 [1956]) *Dinero, Interés y Precio*, Madrid, Aguilar.

———— (s/f) Friedman ante la teoría cuantitativa y la economía keynesiana.

Pigou, A. C. (1917a) The Value of Money. *Quarterly Journal of Economics*, 32, 1, 38–65.

———— (1917b) The Value of Money. *The Quarterly Journal of Economics*, 32, 38–65.

———— (1927) Wage Policy and Unemployment. *The Economic Journal*, 37, 147, 355–368.

———— (1933) *The Theory of Unemployment*, London, Macmillan.

———— (1937) Real and Money Wages in Relation to Unemployment. *The Economic Journal*, 47, 405–422.

———— (1943) The Classical Stationary State. *The Economic Journal*, 53, 343–351.

Popper, K. (1967) La ciencia: conjeturas y refutaciones. In Popper, K. (Ed.) *El desarrollo del conocimiento científico: Conjeturas y refutaciones*. Buenos Aires, Paidos.

Prebisch, R. (1971) *Introducción a Keynes*, México DF, Fondo de Cultura Económica.

Puyana Ferreira, J. (1997) De Keynes a la síntesis neoclásica: surgimiento y desintegración del keynesianismo bastardo. In Estay, J. and Manchón, F. (Eds.) *Keynes . . . hoy*. Puebla, Benemérita Universidad Autónoma de Puebla.

Rey Pastor, J. (1963 [1952]) *Análisis matemático*, Buenos Aires, Kapelusz.

Ricardo, D. (1821 [1817]) *On the Principles of Political Economy and Taxation*, London, John Murray, IN www.econlib.org/library/Ricardo/ricP1.html; accessed 25 February 2015.

———— (1993 [1817]) *Principios de economía política y tributación*, México DF, Fondo de Cultura Económica.

Robinson, J. (1960 [1956]) *La acumulación de capital*, México DF, Fondo de Cultura Económica.

———— (1959) *Ensayos de economía postkeynesiana*, México DF, Fondo de Cultura Económica.

Román, H. (1990) 1926: huelga general en gran bretaña. *Historia del Movimiento Obrero, Centro Editor de América Latina*, 48.

———— (1991) Los límites del trade-unionismo Inglaterra. *Historia del Movimiento Obrero, Centro Editor de América Latina*, 54.

Rubin, I. I. (1989 [1929]) *A History of Economic Thought*, London, Pluto Press.

———— (1987 [1930]) *Ensayos sobre la teoría marxista del valor*, México DF, Cuadernos de Pasado y Presente.

———— (1990) *Essays on Marx's Theory of Value*, Montreal – New York, Black Rose Books.

Samuelson, P. (1967 [1946]) La Teoría General. In Leckachman, R. (Ed.) *Teoría General de Keynes. Informe de tres décadas*. México DF, Fondo de Cultura Económica.

———— (1983) *Economía*, Madrid, McGraw-Hill.

Sawyer, M. C. (1985) *The Economics of Michal Kalecki*, Houndmills, Macmillan.

Say, J-B. (1855 [1803]) *A Treatise on Political Economy*, C. R. Prinsep, trans. and Clement C. Biddle. (Ed.) Philadelphia, Lippincott, Grambo & Co., IN www.econ lib.org/library/Say/sayT15.html; accessed 1 March 2015.

———— (2002 [1803]) *Traité d'économie politique ou simple exposition de la manière dont se forment, se distribuent ou se consomment les richesses*, Edition électronique.

Schumpeter, J. A. (1936) Review of the General Theory. *Journal of American Statistical Association*, 31, 196, 791–795.

———— (1939) *Business Cycles*, New York, McGraw-Hill.

———— (1986 [1954]) *History of Economic Analysis*, London, Routledge.

———— (1983) *Diez grandes economistas: de Marx a Keynes*, Madrid, Alianza.

Screpanti, E. and Zamagni, S. (1997 [1993]) *Panorama de historia del pensamiento económico*, Barcelona, Ariel.

Shaick, A. M. (1990) *Valor, acumulación y crisis*, Bogotá, Tercer mundo editores.

Shaick, A. M. and Tonak, E. A. (1994) *Measuring the Wealth of Nations: The Political Economy of National Accounts*, Cambridge, Cambridge University Press.

Sheffrin, S. M. (s/f) *Expectativas racionales*, Alianza Universidad.

Skidelsky, R. (1994) *John Maynard Keynes: The Economist as Saviour 1920–1937*, London, Macmillan.

Skidelsky, R. (1996) *Keynes*, Oxford, Oxford University Press.

Smith, A. (1904 [1776]) *An Inquiry into the Nature and Causes of the Wealth of Nations*, Edwin Cannan (Ed.) London, Methuen & Co., Ltd. IN www.econlib.org/library/Smith/smWN2.html; accessed 24 February 2015.

Sraffa, P. (1932) Dr. Hayek on Money and Capital. *The Economic Journal*, 42, 165, 42–53.

———— (1996 [1951]) Introduction. In Ricardo, D. (Ed.) *On Principles of Political Economy and Taxation*. Cambridge, Cambridge University Press.

———— (1963 [1952]) *David Ricardo: Cartas 1816–1818*, México DF, Fondo de Cultura Económica.

———— (1983 [1960]) *Producción de mercancías por medio de mercancías*, Barcelona, Oikos-Tau.

Sweezy, P. (1974 [1942]) *Teoría del desarrollo capitalista*, México DF, Fondo de Cultura Económica.

———— (1967) John Maynard Keynes. In Lekachman, R. (Ed.) *Teoría General de Keynes, informe de tres décadas*. México DF, Fondo de Cultura Económica.

Sweezy, P. and Baran, P. (1966) *El capital monopolista*, México DF, Fondo de Cultura Económica.

Temin, P. (1990) *Lessons From Great Depression*, Cambridge, MIT Press.

Tobin, J. (s/f) *Acumulación de activos y actividad económica*, Buenos Aires, Alianza.

Triffin, R. (1985 [1968]) The Myth and Realities of the So-Called Gold Standard. In Eichengreen, B. (Ed.) *The Gold Standard in Theory and History*. New York and London, Methuen.

Varian, H. (1994) *Microeconomía Intermedia*, Barcelona, Antoni Bosch Editor.

Viner, J. (1967 [1936]) Keynes y las causas de la desocupación. In Leckachman, R. (Ed.) *Teoría General de Keynes: Informe de tres décadas*. México DF, Fondo de Cultura Económica.

Walras, L. (2003 [1874]) *Elements of Pure Economics*, London, Routledge.

Weeks, J. (1989) *A Critique of Neoclassical Macroeconomics*, London, Macmillan.

Whale, P. B. (1985 [1937]) The Working of Prewar Gold Standard. In Eichengreen, B. (Ed.) *The Standard in Theory and History*. New York and London, Methuen.

Wicksell, K. (1947 [1911]) *Lecciones de economía política*, Madrid, Aguilar.

Woodford, M. (1999) Revolution and Evolution in Twentieth-Century Macroeconomics. In Gifford, P. (Ed.) *Frontiers of the Mind in the Twenty-First Century*. Cambridge, MA, Harvard University Press.

Index

For Product Safety Concerns and Information please contact our EU
representative GPSR@taylorandfrancis.com Taylor & Francis Verlag GmbH,
Kaufingerstraße 24, 80331 München, Germany

Printed and bound by CPI Group (UK) Ltd, Croydon, CR0 4YY
01/05/2025
01858422-0012